T0189116

Communications
in Computer and Information Science   1687

More information about this series at https://link.springer.com/bookseries/7899

Ambika Prasad Shah · Sudeb Dasgupta ·
Anand Darji · Jaynarayan Tudu (Eds.)

VLSI Design and Test

26th International Symposium, VDAT 2022
Jammu, India, July 17–19, 2022
Revised Selected Papers

 Springer

Editors
Ambika Prasad Shah (iD)
Department of Electrical Engineering
Indian Institute of Technology Jammu
Jammu, India

Anand Darji
Department of Electronics Engineering
Sardar Vallabhbhai National Institute
of Technology Surat
Surat, India

Sudeb Dasgupta (iD)
Department of Electronics
and Communication Engineering
Indian Institute of Technology Roorkee
Roorkee, India

Jaynarayan Tudu
Department of Computer Science
and Engineering
Indian Institute of Technology Tirupati
Tirupati, India

ISSN 1865-0929   ISSN 1865-0937 (electronic)
Communications in Computer and Information Science
ISBN 978-3-031-21513-1   ISBN 978-3-031-21514-8 (eBook)
https://doi.org/10.1007/978-3-031-21514-8

This Springer imprint is published by the registered company Springer Nature Switzerland AG
The registered company address is: Gewerbestrasse 11, 6330 Cham, Switzerland

Preface

VLSI Design and Test (VDAT) is a leading event of the VLSI Society of India. The 26th VLSI Design and Test Symposium (VDAT 2022) was held during July 17–19 2022, at the Indian Institute of Technology Jammu, India. The theme of VDAT–2022 was "Chips to Startup for Sustainable Development". The objective of the symposium was to bring together professional engineers, academics, and researchers from India and abroad to discuss emerging topics of VLSI and related fields on a common platform and to share new ideas, experiences, and knowledge. The scientific program consisted of peer-reviewed paper presentations in parallel technical sessions. In addition, keynote lectures, presentations by industry professionals, panel discussions, tutorials, and a poster presentation were conducted during the conference. Each of the accepted conference papers has been lucidly presented as a book chapter in these proceedings, and these important contributions are grouped into six categories:

1. Devices and Technology
2. Sensors
3. Analog/Mixed Signal
4. Digital Design
5. Emerging Technologies and Memory
6. System Design

This year we received 220 papers from authors around the world. After a rigorous double-blind review process, the Program Committee selected 32 regular papers and 16 short papers for the proceedings with an acceptance rate of 21.8%. In all, 108 expert reviewers were involved in rating the papers and on average each paper received at least three independent reviews. The program of the symposium spanned over three days; the main conference program was preceded by a day of tutorial presentations that had eight tutorials delivered by eminent researchers and practitioners in the field. The symposium hosted the following tutorials:

1. Jai Gopal Pandey and Manabala Santosh, "SoC for Microsystem Development"
2. Saravana Kumar M, "Design of Continuous Time Analog to Digital Converters for Wireless Applications"
3. Preet Yadav, "The New Era of Mobility"
4. Yagya Dutt Mishra, "Analog Reliability Analysis for Mission-Critical Applications"
5. Shailesh Singh Chouhan, "Mixed-Signal Circuits in Deep Networks"
6. Kishan Mayani, Krushnakant Kori, and Saumya Shah, "Reduce test escape by adapting advanced fault models"
7. Vishal Sharma, "Compute-in Memory: An opportunity and its design challenges for AI Edge Devices"
8. Shivam Soni, Nairuti Shah, and Saurin Shah, "Testability Analysis and DFT Readiness at RTL stage"

Several invited talks and keynote speeches were delivered by experts from India and abroad enlightening the participants on various aspects of emerging issues in VLSI research. These talks were delivered by Sunita Verma (MeitY), Adit Singh (Auburn University, USA), Yogesh Singh Chauhan (IIT Kanpur), Sri Parameswaran (University of New South Wales, Australia), P. Chakrabarti (IIEST Sibpur), Satya Gupta (VLSI Society of India), and Chitra Hariharan (Intel). VDAT 2022 was a focused research event encompassing themes related to various disciplines of VLSI.

We sincerely thank all the officials and sponsors for their support in recognizing the value of this conference. We would like to express our thanks to the keynote speakers and the tutorial speakers for kindly agreeing to deliver their lectures. Thanks to the authors and reviewers of all the papers for their quality research work. We heartily thank every member of the conference committee for their unyielding support in making this event a success.

We hope that you enjoy the contributions in this book and that it will serve as a great reading for experts, students, practitioners, designers, researchers, and academics. We, the editors, would like to thank all the contributing authors, reviewers, and other supporting members for their help.

December 2022

Ambika Prasad Shah
Sudeb Dasgupta
Anand Darji
Jaynarayan Tudu

Organization

VDAT 2022 was organized by the Department of Electrical Engineering, Indian Institute of Technology Jammu, India.

Advisory Committee

Vishwani Agarwal	Auburn University, USA
Jaswinder Ahuja	Cadence, India
Satya Gupta	VLSI Society of India, India
Virendra Singh	IIT Bombay, India
Devesh Dwivedi	Global Foundaries, India
Chitra Hariharan	Intel Technology India Pvt. Ltd., India

Organizing Committee

General Co-chairs

Manoj Singh Gaur	IIT Jammu, India
Rajendra Patrikar	VNIT Nagpur, India

Conference Organizing Chair

Ambika Prasad Shah	IIT Jammu, India

Program Co-chairs

Sudeb Dasgupta	IIT Roorkee, India
Anand Darji	SVNIT Surat, India

Vice Program Chair

Jaynarayan Tudu	IIT Tirupati, India

Tutorial Co-chairs

Anand Bulusu	IIT Roorkee, India
Satyadev Ahlawat	IIT Jammu, India

Publication Co-chairs

Ambika Prasad Shah	IIT Jammu, India
Sonal Yadav	NIT Raipur, India

Finance Co-chairs

Sudhakar Modem	IIT Jammu, India
Biswanath Chakraborty	IIT Jammu, India

Local Organization Chair

Anup Shukla	IIT Jammu, India

Registration Chairs

Kushmanda Saurav	IIT Jammu, India
Ravi Kumar Arun	IIT Jammu, India

Publicity Co-chairs

Santosh Vishvakarma	IIT Indore, India
Usha Mehta	Nirma University, India
Bhupendra Vishwakarma	Cadence, India

Student Research Forum Chair

Amit Joshi	MNIT Jaipur, India

Exhibition and Design Contest Co-chairs

Kankat Ghosh	IIT Jammu, India
Bhupendra Reniwal	IIITDM Kancheepuram, India

Sponsorship Co-chairs

Preet Yadav	NXP Semiconductors, India
Navin Bishnoi	Marvell Semiconductors, India

Fellowship Chair

Shree Prakash Tiwari	IIT Jodhpur, India

Woman in Engineering Co-chairs

Dhanapathy Krishnamoorthy	Intel Technology India Pvt. Ltd., India
Joycee Mekie	IIT Gandhinagar, India

Technical Program Committee

Abhijit Asati	BITS Pilani, India
Abhijit Karmakar	CSIR-CEERI Pilani, India
Abhinav Kranti	IIT Indore, India
Abhishek Acharya	SVNIT Surat, India
Adit Singh	Auburn University, USA
Ajay Agarwal	IIT Jodhpur, India
Ambika Prasad Shah	IIT Jammu, India
Amit Degada	University of Kentucky, USA
Amit Joshi	MNIT Jaipur, India
Amit Singh	GGSI University, India
Anand Bulusu	IIT Roorkee, India
Anand Darji	SVNIT Surat, India
Ankur Beohar	VIT Bhopal, India
Ankush Srivastava	Qualcomm Inc, India
Ashok Kumar Suhag	BML Munjal University Gurgaon, India
Ashwani Rana	NIT Hamirpur, India
Avirup Dasgupta	IIT Roorkee, India
Baljit Kaur	NIT Delhi, India
Balwinder Raj	NITTTR Chandigarh, India
Behera Amit	IIT Roorkee, India
Bhupendra Reniwal	IIITDM Kancheepuram, India
Binod Kumar	IIT Jodhpur, India
Bishnu Prasad Das	IIT Roorkee, India
Brajesh Kumar Kaushik	IIT Roorkee, India
Chandan Giri	IIEST Shibpur, India
Chandan Karfa	IIT Guwahati, India
Darshak Bhatt	IIT Roorkee, India
Deepak Joshi	SVNIT Surat, India
Deepika Gupta	IIIT Naya Raipur, India
Devarshi Mrinal Das	IIT Ropar, India
Dhruva Ghai	Oriental University, India
Fabrizio Bonani	Politecnico di Torino, Italy
Gaurav Trivedi	IIT Guwahati, India
Gracia Rani	TCE Madurai, India
Hafizur Rahaman	IIEST Shibpur, India
Hailong Yao	Tsinghua University, China

Hemangee Kapoor	IIT Guwahati, India
Hitesh Shrimali	IIT Mandi, India
Jai Gopal Pandey	CEERI Pilani, India
Jai Narayan Tripathi	IIT Jodhpur, India
Jawar Singh	IIT Patna, India
Jaya Dofe	UNH, USA
Jaynarayan Tudu	IIT Tirupati, India
Jimson Mathew	IIT Patna, India
Karun Rawat	IIT Roorkee, India
Kunal Banerjee	Intel, India
Kusum Lata	LNMIIT Jaipur, India
Linga Reddy Cenkeramaddi	University of Agder, Norway
Manoj Kumar Majumder	IIIT Naya Raipur, India
Manoj Saxena	University of Delhi, India
Manu Bansal	Thapar University, India
Masahiro Fujita	University of Tokyo, Japan
Meetha Shenoy	BITS Pilani, India
Nandakumar Nambath	IIT Bombay, India
Naveen Kadayinti	IIT Dharwad, India
Neeraj Goel	IIT Ropar, India
Neha Karanjkar	IIT Goa, India
Newton Singh	IIT Bombay, India
Nihar Hage	IIT Bombay, India
Nihar Mohapatra	IIT Gandhinagar, India
Nirmal Kumar Boran	IIT Bombay, India
Nithin Chatterji	SVNIT Surat, India
Pallavi Paliwal	Ericsson, India
Pankaj Kumar Pal	NIT Uttarakhand, India
Pinalkumar Engineer	SVNIT Surat, India
Pooran Singh	Mahindra University, India
Preeti Panda	IIT Delhi, India
Rajaram Sivasubramanian	TCE Madurai, India
Rajat Subhra Chakraborty	IIT Kharagpur, India
Rajeevan Chandel	NIT Hamirpur, India
Rajesh Kedia	IIT Hyderabad, India
Rajesh Zele	IIT Bombay, India
Ramrakesh Jangir	Government Polytechnic Narwana, India
Rasika Dhavse	SVNIT Surat, India
Sandeep Goyal	Intel Technology India Pvt. Ltd., India
Sanjay Kumar Jana	NIT Sikkim, India
Santosh Vishvakarma	IIT Indore, India
Satyadev Ahlawat	IIT Jammu, India

Shigeru Yamashita	Ritsumeikan University, Japan
Shivam Verma	IIT BHU Varanasi, India
Shivendra Yadav	NIT Surat, India
Shouri Chatterjee	IIT Delhi, India
Shubhankar Majumdar	NIT Meghalaya, India
Simona Donati Guerrieri	Politecnico di Torino, Italy
Sitangshu Bhattacharya	IIIT Allahabad, India
Sivaramakrishna R.	IIT Bombay, India
Sk Subidh Ali	New York University, USA
Sourabh Jain	University of Texas at Austin, USA
Srinivas Boppu	IIT Bhubaneswar, India
Subhankar Mukherjee	Cadence Design Systems Inc., India
Subhasis Bhattacharjee	Synopsys Pvt. Ltd., India
Sudeb Dasgupta	IIT Roorkee, India
Sudip Roy	IIT Roorkee, India
Suhaib Ahmed Batt	SMVDU Katra, India
Sujay Deb	IIIT Delhi, India
Sujit Biswas	University of Surrey, UK
Surendra Rathod	IIT Roorkee, India
Tanmoy Pramanik	IIT Roorkee, India
Toral Shah	NMIMS University, India
Trupti Ranjan Lenka	NIT Silchar, India
Tuhin Subhra Das	IIEST Shibpur, India
Usha Mehta	Nirma University, India
Vineet Sahula	MANIT Jaipur, India
Virendra Singh	IIT Bombay, India
Vishal Sharma	NIT Hamirpur, India
Vishvendra Singh Poonia	IIT Roorkee, India
Vivek Garg	SVNIT Surat, India
Zuber Patel	SVNIT Surat, India

Sponsors

VLSI Society of India

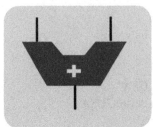

Ministry of Electronics and Information Technology, Government of India

Science Engineering and Research Board

eInfochips

Contents

Sensors

Analog/Mixed Signal

Digital Design

Emerging Technologies and Memory

System Design

Devices and Technology

FEM Modeling of Thermal Aspect of Dielectric Inserted Under Source & Drain of 5 nm Nanosheet

Vivek Kumar[1,2(✉)] ⓘ, Jyoti Patel[1], Arnab Datta[1], and Sudeb Dasgupta[1]

[1] Indian Institute of Technology Roorkee (IITR), Roorkee 247667, India
vivek.kumar@nituk.ac.in
[2] National Institute of Technology Uttarakhand, Srinagar (Garhwal) 246174, India

Abstract. Nanoscale device design beyond 20 nm technology nodes constrain material thermal conductivity and exacerbates the self-heating phenomenon in Multigate MOSFETs such as FinFET and Nanosheet. The presence of dielectric under the source and drain in stacked Nanoheet Transistors (SNT) exacerbates the Self Heating Effect because it breaks the heat flow path due to low thermal conductivity. From a performance and reliability standpoint, this research focuses on the thermal aspect of the SNT after insertion of the dielectric under the source and drain. The effect of dielectric insertion under the source and drain on lattice temperature was investigated using electrothermal simulation of single and double stack nanosheet transistors. The effects of dielectric insertion thickness under the source and drain on the substrate, as well as SNT channel temperature analyzed and its variation with width and extension length of SNT are explained.

Keywords: Nanosheet · Source drain dielectric · Self-heating effect

1 Introduction

Multi-gate (MG) geometry such as FinFET and SNT are potential strategies to improve traditional MOSFETs for nodes beyond 20 nm, minimizing leakage, handling short channel effect, and increasing drive-current/speed [1–3]. Unfortunately, these improvements are achieved by increasing the thermal resistance of device due to its confined structure which blockage heat flow of the device and leads to self-heating (SH). The performance (On current degradation) and reliability (Bias Temperature Stability & Hot Carrier Injection) are all affected by the considerable SH in nanoscale device [4, 5].

Various research groups have explored device SH in SNT. To investigate device, SHE coupled to Back End of Line (BEOL)/printed circuit board (PCB) joule heating [6], developed a physics-based thermal compact model. From their perspective, in comparison to other advanced devices (FinFET & Nanowires), SNT offer the best agreement between reliability and performance [7, 8]. Used a finite element modeling (FEM) simulator to investigate device SHE, considering the effect of device geometry and layout optimization of the stacked NSHFET in the sub-7 nm node. The SNT width was considered to be a crucial parameter in the tradeoff between thermal and electrical performance

© The Author(s), under exclusive license to Springer Nature Switzerland AG 2022
A. P. Shah et al. (Eds.): VDAT 2022, CCIS 1687, pp. 3–11, 2022.
https://doi.org/10.1007/978-3-031-21514-8_1

of the Nanosheet. In [9] the transient temperature response of the SNT was studied to develop a physics-based thermal compact model [10]. Explored the effect of thermal conductivity of interlayer dielectrics (ILD) and the number of nanosheet channels in vertical stacking on device SH. In [11] effect of interface thermal resistance (ITR) is discussed on thermal characteristics of the SNT, and with and without ITR thermal characteristics of SNT for different device dimension studied. Effect of vertical combo spacer to optimize electrothermal characteristics ofSNT discussed in [12]. Effect of SH on inter channel threshold voltage of SNT discussed in [13].

The SNT's vertical and gate-all-around nature causes parasitic capacitance between the substrate and the source and drain, which can be reduced by putting a dielectric under the source and drain as discussed in [14]. The effect of dielectric insertion on electrical characteristics is thoroughly discussed [15], demonstrating that sub sheet leakage and parasitic decreases. All the above literature discusses only electrical characteristics improvement; moreover, effect on thermal characteristics is still unexplored. Furthermore, since the experimental analysis of the thermal behavior of nanoscale devices beyond 20 nm technology via thermal imaging and direct measurement is still not possible, FEM electrothermal simulation is the preferred method of analysis.

In this work, best of the author's knowledge, first time we discussed the effect of dielectric insertion under source and drain on thermal characteristics of the SNT. Effect of SNT width and extension length on lattice temperature discussed and analyzed. Effect of Source drain dielectric on multi stack nanosheet thermal characteristics is also discussed and studied.This work has been ordered as follows, Sect. 2 explains about simulation setup and detail calibration process, Sect. 3 discusses results obtained with and without dielectric insertion under source and drain, and Sect. 4 summarizes the work.

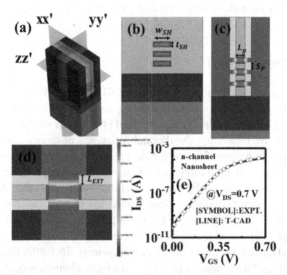

Fig. 1. (a) 3-DTCAD structure of gate all around Nanosheet, (b) 2D cut of SNT along XX' plane showing width and thickness of the sheet, (c) 2D cut of SNT along YY' plane, (d) 2D cut of SNT along ZZ' plane, and (e) Transfer characteristics (I_{DS}-V_{GS}) calibration of Nanosheet with experimental value given in [14].

2 Simulation Setup Calibration

Synopsys TCAD [16] commercial software is used to perform 3-D electrothermal simulations of Gate all around SNT 5 nm technology node. Table 1 lists the physical and electrical parameters, and Table 2 provides detail thermal parameters of the device used in this simulation. For simulation accuracy, the modeling setup is well calibrated with experimental data of three sheets SNT reported in [14]. Figure 1 describes the simulation setup and device calibration results. Figure 1(a) shows 3D SNT and its 2D cut plane along x, y, and z direction in Fig. 1(b)–(d) respectively.

Table 1. Physical & Electrical parameters of n-type Nanosheet

Parameters	Value
Gatelength (Lg)	12 nm
Sheet thickness (t_{SH})	8 nm
Sheet width (w_{SH})	25 nm
EOT (Effective Oxide Thickness)	0.9 nm
Sheet Pitch (S_P)	15 nm
S/D Extension length (L_{EXT})	8 nm
Work function of Gate Metal	4.4 eV
Saturation Velocity	4.5×10^7 cm/s
Channel Doping	1×10^{16}/cm^3
Source/Drain doping	1×10^{21}/cm^3

Device dimensions are in sub nanometer, so quantum correction models are used with drift diffusion models. To account for electron-hole scattering, bulk phonon scattering, and remote Coulomb scattering, the Philips unified mobility model, the thin-layer mobility model, the enhanced Lombardi model, and the remote Coulomb scattering are used. To include lattice temperature, thermodynamic model is used with proper thermal contact and interface thermal resistance. Electrical calibration was done through tuning of work function of gate metal and saturation velocity.

Thermal calibration was done through contact thermal resistance and thermal conductivity variation. All these parameters variation for calibration was under a reported limit of parameters only. Different region of the SNT have different thickness, temperature and doping so thermal conductivity varies accordingly. Which can be calculated using the Eq. (1) [12], under the assumption that z-axis is along the thickness of the silicon sheet, with the surfaces of

$$k(z) = k_0(T) \int_0^{\pi/2} \sin^3 \theta \left\{ 1 - \exp\left(-\frac{a}{2\lambda(T)\cos\theta} \right) \cosh\left(\frac{a-2z}{2\lambda(T)\cos\theta} \right) \right\} d\theta \quad (1)$$

The sheet being at $z = 0$ and $z = a$. Where $\lambda(T) = \lambda_0(300/T)$ nm is the temperature dependent MFP (Mean Free Path) of phonons and $\lambda_0 = 290$ nm is the MFP of phonons at

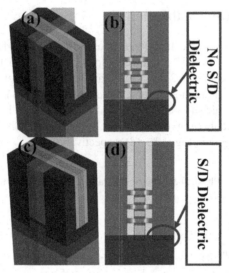

Fig. 2. (a) 3-D T-CAD structure of SNT without DISD, (b) 2D cut plane of 3D structure across the plane showing clear no DISD, (c) 3-D T-CAD structure of SNT with DISD, (d) 2D cut plane of 3D structure across the plane showing clearly DISD.

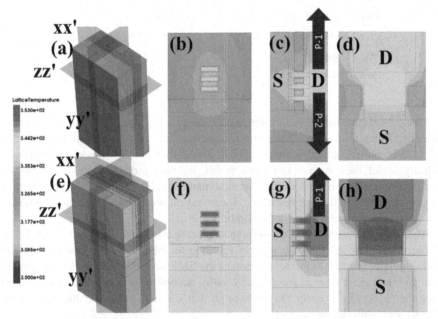

Fig. 3. (a) 3-D thermal contour of SNT without DSD, (b) 2D cut plane along XX', (c) 2D cut plane along YY', (d) 2D cut plane along ZZ'.

room temperature. $k_0(T)$ incorporates temperature dependence of thermal conductivity and can be expressed as-$k_0(T) = \frac{135}{a+bT+cT^2}$, where $a = 0.03, b = 1.56 \times 10^{-3}$ $1/K$, and $c = 1.65 \times 10^{-6}$ $1/K^2$. All electrical and thermal simulation is calibrated for single stack three sheet Nanosheet and extended the same setup for two stack Nanosheet simulation, and IV characteristics is verified.

Table 2. Thermal parameters used in simulation

Device thermal parameters	Value
Thermal Conductivity of sheet	0.25 W/K-cm
Thermal Conductivity of Source/Drain	0.62 W/K-cm
Thermal Conductivity of HfO$_2$	0.014 W/K-cm
Thermal Conductivity of Gate Metal	1.62 W/K-cm
Thermal Conductivity of Nitride	0.185 W/K-cm
Interface Thermal Resistance between interface oxide and HiK	8.3×10^{-8} m^2-K/W
Interface Thermal Resistance between interface oxide and Silicon Channel	1×10^{-8} m^2-K/W

3   Result and Discussion

In this section effects of dielectric insertion under source and drain are discussed and analyzed. As shown in Fig. 2, a dielectric is inserted under the source and drain epitaxy to reduce sub sheet leakage. In Fig. 2(a) 3 D structure and Fig. 2(b) 2D y-cut of single SNT without Dielectric Insertion under Source and Drain (DISD) is shown. Figure 2(c) and (d) is 3D and its 2D cut with DISD. Figure 3 shows the 3D & 2D thermal contours of SNT with and without DISD. Figure 3(b), (c), and (d) are the 2D cut planes of the 3D thermal contour of SNT without DISD shown in Fig. 3(a). Figure 3(f), (g), and (h) are the 2D cut plane of the thermal contour of the SNT with DISD shown in Fig. 3(e). There are mainly two heat flow paths in classical Nanosheet first one is through Contacts (P1) & second one is through the substrate (P2), as shown in Fig. 3(c). After dielectric insertion under source and drain heat flow path through the substrate is blocked due to lower thermal conductivity of dielectric, as shown in Fig. 3(g). In Fig. 3, we can compare that due to heat path blockage by DISD, the thermal resistance of the Nanosheet increased, so lattice temperature increased. Another observation from Fig. 3, by comparing all the 2D cut planes, we can comment that after the dielectric insertion, substrate temperature of Nanosheet reduces and simultaneously channel temperature increases due to heat path blockage. An increase in channel temperature is crucial from a device reliability perspective. Since channel temperature decides the hot carrier degradation and mobility degradation of the device.

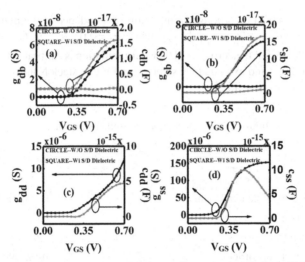

Fig. 4. (a) Drain to body conductance (g_{db}) and capacitance (c_{db}) variation with V_{GS}, (b) Source to body conductance (g_{sb}) and capacitance (c_{sb}) variation with V_{GS}, (c) Self Conductance(g_{dd}) and capacitance (c_{dd}) variation of drain with V_{GS}, (d) Self Conductance(g_{ss}) and capacitance (c_{ss}) variation of source with V_{GS}.

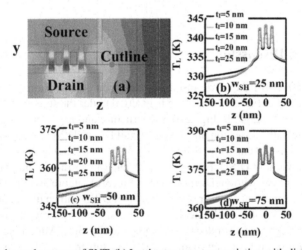

Fig. 5. (a) 2-D thermal contour of SNT, (b) Lattice temperature variation with dielectric thickness at 25 nm width, (c) Lattice temperature variation with dielectric thickness at 50 nm width, (d) Lattice temperature variation with dielectric thickness at 75 nm width.

Further, Fig. 4 shows the small-signal ac simulation, which shows the improvement in electrical characteristics of SNT. Figure 4(a) and (b) shows the conductance and capacitance plot between drain/source and substrate of the SNT with and without DISD. It can be concluded that after DISD, the capacitance between substrate and source/drain reduces, which is an improvement from the leakage and delay prospective. Moreover, the self-conductance of the drain and source are not affected, as shown in Fig. 4(c) and (d). For a single SNT device, thermal properties degrade & electrical properties improve. So, minimizing the thermal variation due to DISD, essential parameters from Nanosheet design which are width and extension length varied and its effect on lattice temperature (TL) discussed.

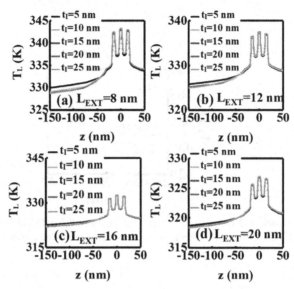

Fig. 6. (a) Lattice temperature variation with dielectric thickness at $L_{EXT} = 8$ nm, (b) Lattice temperature variation with dielectric thickness at $L_{EXT} = 12$ nm, (c) Lattice temperature variation with dielectric thickness at $L_{EXT} = 16$ nm, (d) Lattice temperature variation with dielectric thickness at $L_{EXT} = 20$ nm.

Figure 5(b), (c), and (d) show a 1D temperature profile along the cutline shown in Fig. 5(a) for 25 nm, 50 nm and 75 nm width, respectively. In Fig. 5, different width thickness of dielectric inserted under source and drain are varied to understand the effect extensively. Since an increase in device width leads to higher drive current and Fig. 5 explains that lattice temperature increases with nanosheet width, we can observe that at higher device width, substrate & channel temperature variation is higher than at lower width. Figure 6 explains the variation of lattice temperature along the cutline shown in Fig. 5(a) at different source/drain extension lengths and dielectric thickness under source and drain. Figure 6(a)–(d) explains that the variation of lattice temperature reduces with higher extension length since higher extension length leads to high ON resistance, leading to the lower current drive. Figure 7 shows the thermal characteristics of 2 stack Nanosheet transistor with and without DISD, and it can be concluded that there is a minute variation in channel temperature, but a significant difference is there in substrate temperature, which is due to more significant drain and source dimension.

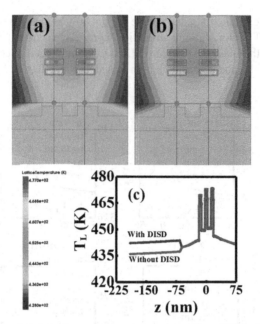

Fig. 7. (a) Double stack 2-D lattice temperature contour without DISD, (b) Double stack 2-D lattice contour with DISD, and (c) 1D variation of lattice temperature along the cutline shown in Fig. 1(a) and (b).

4 Conclusion

Self-heating effect after dielectric insertion under source and drain epitaxy was studied using electrothermal simulation of stacked Nanosheet transistors. Dielectric thickness inserted under the source/drain affects the substrate, and channel temperature is explored in detail through FEM simulation. Device width and extension length effects on modified structure studied. The device's small-signal ac performance was simulated and compared with and without DISD. Finally, the thermal and electrical characteristics of the SNT were analyzed and compared in detail.

References

1. Pan, C., et al.: Technology/system codesign and benchmarking for lateral and vertical GAA nanowire FETs at 5-nm technology node. IEEE Trans. Electron Device **62**(10), 3125–3132 (2015)
2. Zheng, P., Connelly, D., Ding, F., Liu, T.-J.K.: FinFET evolution toward stacked-nanowire FET for CMOS technology scaling. IEEE Trans. Electron Device **62**(12), 3945–3950 (2015)
3. Jang, D., et al.: Device exploration of nanosheet transistors for sub-7-nm technology node. IEEE Trans. Electron Devices **64**(6), 2707–2713 (2017)
4. Chhabria, V.A., Sapatnekar, S.S.: Impact of self-heating on performance and reliability in FinFET and GAAFET designs. In: IEEE 20th International Symposium on Quality Electronic Design, pp. 235–240. IEEE USA (2019)

5. Xu, C., Kolluri, S.K., Endo, K., Banerjee, K.: Analytical thermal model for self-heating in advanced FinFET devices with implications for design and reliability. IEEE Trans. Comput.-Aided Des. Integr. Circuits Syst. **32**(7), 1045–1058 (2013)
6. Ahn, W., Jiang, C., Xu, J., Alam, M.A.: A new framework of physics-based compact model predicts reliability of self-heated modern ICs: FinFET, NWFET, NSHFET comparison. In: IEDM Tech. Dig., pp. 1–4. IEEE, USA (2017)
7. Chen, W., Cai, L., Wang, K., Zhang, X., Liu, X., Du, G.: Self-heating induced variability and reliability in nanosheet-FETs based SRAM. In: International Symposium on the Physical and Failure Analysis of Integrated Circuits (IPFA), pp. 1–4. IEEE, Singapore (2018)
8. Cai, L., Chen, W., Du, G., Kang, J., Zhang, X., Liu, X.: Investigation of self-heating effect on stacked nanosheet GAA transistors. In: Proceedings International Symposium on VLSI Technology, Systems and Applications (VLSI-TSA), pp. 1–2. IEEE, Taiwan (2018)
9. Cai, L., et al.: A physics-based thermal model of nanosheet MOSFETs for device-circuit co-design. In: IEDM Tech. Dig., pp. 1–4. IEEE, San Francisco (2018)
10. Kang, M.J., Myeong, I., Kang, M., Shin, H.: Analysis of DC self-heating effect in stacked nanosheet gate-all-around transistor. In: Proceeding 2nd Electron Devices Technology and Manufacturing Conference (EDTM), pp. 343–345. IEEE, Japan (2018)
11. Venkateswarlu, S., Nayak, K.: Hetero-interfacial thermal resistance effects on device performance of stacked gate-all-around nanosheet FET. IEEE Trans. Electron Devices **67**(10), 4493–4499 (2020)
12. Liu, R., Li, X., Sun, Y., Shi, Y.: A vertical combo spacer to optimize electrothermal characteristics of 7-nm nanosheet gate-all-around transistor. IEEE Trans. Electron Devices **67**(6), 2249–2254 (2020)
13. Chung, C.-C., Ye, H.-Y., Lin, H.H., Wan, W.K., Yang, M.-T., Liu, C.W.: Self-heating induced interchannel Vt difference of vertically stacked Si nanosheet gate-all-around MOSFETs. IEEE Electron Device Lett. **40**(12), 1913–1916 (2019)
14. Loubet, N., et al.: Stacked nanosheet gate-all-around transistor to enable scaling beyond FinFET. In: 2017 Symposium on VLSI Technology, pp. T230–T231. IEEE, Japan (2017)
15. Jegadheesan, V., Sivasankaran, K.A.: Source/drain-on-insulator structure to improve the performance of stacked nanosheet field-effect transistors. J. Comput. Electron. **19**, 1136–1143 (2020)
16. *TCAD Sentaurus Suite*, Version O-2018.06, Synopsys, Mountain View, CA, USA (2012)

Differential Multi-bit Through Glass Vias for Three-Dimensional Integrated Circuits

Ajay Kumar$^{(\boxtimes)}$ and Rohit Dhiman

National Institute of Technology Hamirpur, Hamirpur, India
{ajayk,rohitdhiman}@nith.ac.in

Abstract. The paper presents glass as a potential material to advanced interposers for high-density three-dimensional (3-D) integration. Based on multi-bit through glass via (TGV) which comprises of vias filled with mixed carbon nanotube bundle (mCNTB) and separate metallic pads, the performance of differential multi-bit through glass vias (DM-TGCVs) is studied and analyzed. The effective complex conductivity of mCNTB is derived for computation of the high frequency behavior of DM-TGCVs. An equivalent circuit model of DM-TGCVs is then presented, with the effects of mean free path considered appropriately. The frequency dependent differential- and common-mode impedances are extracted up to 100 GHz through the partial-element-equivalent circuit technique. It is analyzed that DM-TGCVs exhibit superior performance than through silicon via counterparts in terms of improved insertion loss and reduced crosstalk. Using the proposed circuit model, characteristic impedance, and S-parameters of DM-TGCVs are exhaustively investigated for the various set of design parameters and verified by comparison with the full-wave electromagnetic simulations.

Keywords: Carbon nanotubes (CNTs) · Effective complex conductivity · Signal transmission · Through glass via (TGV) · Partial-element equivalent-circuit

1 Introduction

Three-dimensional integrated circuits (3-D ICs) have aroused intense research interest for the technology realm of "More-than-Moore" in the past decades [1]. High-aspect-ratio vertical interconnects also known as through silicon vias (TSVs) can mitigate the limitations of conventional planar ICs and enable the implementation of heterogeneous 3-D integration. TSVs provide an exciting alternative for the realization of high-performance electrical systems with higher speed, high-density packaging, wider bandwidth, and reduced power consumption [2, 3]. Despite of these advantages, however, several challenging issues exist with TSVs: (1) high fabrication cost due to inadequate wafer size (<30 cm) of interposer; (2) complex manufacturing processes required for electric isolation; (3) hysteresis problem due to the metal-oxide semiconductor structure of TSV; (4) reduced signal integrity at high frequencies, due to the finite conductivity of silicon, thereby limiting its applications in RF and mixed-signal systems [4–6]. In order to overcome these issues, glass has been proposed as a convincing substitute to silicon substrate in achieving cost-effective and high-performance 3-D integrated systems [7]. Due to excellent electrical resistivity of glass (1012–1016 Ω–cm), the glass interposer alleviates the use of dielectric and contributes to ultra-low signal loss in the frequency range over GHz. Other mechanical advantages of glass include the following– its comparable coefficient of thermal expansion with silicon, exceptional dimensional stability with a smooth surface, readiness of ultra-thin glass substrates in large panel sizes, availability of embedded substrate processes, roll-to-roll processes which enables significantly reduced fabrication cost [8]. Recently, a number of research studies are devoted to the design techniques of 3-D glass interposer which have been fabricated, measured, and adopted efficaciously. For example, Sukumaran et al. [9] developed a double-sided ultra-thin 3-D glass interposer with through packaging vias (TPVs) in silicon. The simulation study on 3-D glass interposer showed an improved magnitude of forward transmission coefficient and crosstalk to TSVs. The design, measurement, and fabrication study on glass interposer electromagnetic bandgap structure with defected ground plane achieved noise suppression below –40 dB and lower and upper cut-off frequencies of 5.82 and 9.67 GHz, respectively [10]. The electrical characteristics of TPVs in glass interposer were also modeled by deriving semi-analytic expressions of resistance-inductance-capacitance-conductance [11].

As vertical interconnect passing through glass interposer however, through glass vias (TGVs) suffer from the signal integrity issue which stems due to the low-loss characteristics of glass substrate [12–14]. Thus, when a signal TGV to other signal TGV is generated, glass substrate cannot impede the propagation of coupling noise, which imposes limitations on the quality of data transmission and thus degrades the overall IC performance. In order to circumvent these issues, transmission through differential signaling has been proposed in TGVs to ensure better signal integrity. One of the forms of differential signaling in TGV based 3-D ICs is the signal-ground-signal (SGS) architecture, which has been modeled and validated up to 20 GHz [15, 16]. The impacts of diverse design parameters on the signal characteristics of SGS differential TGVs (D-TGVs) have been studied in the frequency domain. It is demonstrated that D-TGVs comprising of carbon nanotubes (CNTs) are proficient in maintaining reduced coupling noise and better thermal characteristics than copper (Cu) counterparts. However, with the incessant scaling of technology, the highest frequency of concern in modern-day ICs is of the order of several tens of GHz. The frequency domain circuit model for TGVs valid upto 100 GHz is one of the strategic research pursuits, whereas the simulation studies reported in [9] and [14] are valid up to 40 GHz and 20 GHz, respectively. The concept of signal transmission utilizing differential multi-bit (DM) approach for TSVs has been delineated in [17–19], while little is known about mixed CNT bundle (mCNTB) TGVs. Consequently, this paper presents a wideband model of differential multi-bit TGVs filled with the mCNTB and term it as DM-TGCVs. The model so derived is valid from DC up to 100 GHz frequency range which enables circuit design, modeling, and optimization.

The remainder of this paper is organized as follows: In Section II, the structure of DM-TGCVs and equivalent circuit representation based on partial-element equivalent-circuit (PEEC) technique is presented. The effective complex conductivity of DM-TGCVs is formulated in Section III. Based on the proposed model, high frequency analysis of coupled DM-TGVs for the various set of design parameters is studied in section IV along with the suggestive process flow of fabricating DM-TGCVs. Finally, conclusions of the paper are drawn in section V.

2   Equivalent Circuit and Parameter Extraction

The schematic view of a pair of DM-TGCVs is presented in Fig. 1 and related physical dimensions and glass properties are in accordance with Table 1 [20]. Depending on the chirality of atoms, single-walled CNTs (SWCNTs) show both semiconducting and metallic characteristics while multi-walled CNTs (MWCNTs) are metallic only. Thus, in the schematic of multi-bit TGVs, CNTs in the central row are filled with semiconducting SWCNTs to enable the reduction of horizontal leakage. The either two sides of central row in TGVs are packed with mCNTs which are randomly distributed as to improve the overall performance. Previously, Subramaniam et al. reported Cu-SWCNT composite [21] that exhibits current density of 6.3×10^8 A·cm^{-2}, about 100× higher than Cu. Similar investigation has also been demonstrated in [22], where the experimental results showed that Cu-CNT is capable of achieving high electromigration resistance with only ~13% reduced electrical conductivity.

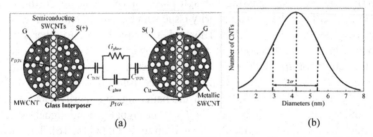

Fig. 1. (a) Top view of coupled mCNTB DM-TGVs. (b) The Gaussian distribution of outer diameter of CNTs in the mCNTB.

Table 1. TGV design parameters and respective symbols.

Symbol	Design parameters	Value
r_{TGV}	TGV radius	0.50 μm
h_{TGV}	TGV height	20 μm
p_{TGV}	Pitch between adjacent TGVs	5 μm
ε_{glass}	Permittivity	5 at 2.4 GHz
σ_{glass}	Electrical conductivity	1×10^{-14} S/m

The diameter (D) of CNTs in multi-bit composite TGVs follows Gaussian distribution, which is expressed as [23]

$$N(D) = \frac{A.n}{\sigma \sqrt{2\pi}} \cdot \exp\left[-\frac{1}{2}\left(\frac{D - D_{mean}}{\sigma}\right)^2 \right] \qquad (1)$$

where n, D_{mean}, σ represent tube density, mean diameter, and standard deviation respectively. In this paper, the cross-sectional area A is considered as $\pi \times (r_{TGV})^2$ with D_{mean} and σ as 4.2 nm and 1.25 nm, respectively. The paper takes into account 11 types of SWCNTs and MWCNTs with diameter values varying from 1 to 7.8 nm. The number of CNTs having a specific diameter D_i in the range of 1–7.8 nm are shown in Table 2. The number of CNTs at a fixed diameter for different tube densities varying from 10^{10} to 10^{13} cm^{-2} are presented in Table 3.

Table 2. Distribution of CNTs in multi-bit TGV and their corresponding diameters

Diameter (nm)	Number of SWCNTs	Number of MWCNTs
1.00	719	58914
1.68	2495	57138
2.36	6443	53190
3.04	12376	47257
3.72	17684	41949
4.40	18795	40838
5.08	14859	44774
5.76	8738	50895
6.44	3822	55811
7.12	1244	58389
7.8	301	59332

The equivalent π-model circuit representation of coupled DM-TGCVs and its simplified version are shown in Fig. 2(a) and (b). The impedance parameters of multi-bit TGVs are extracted by employing the PEEC method wherein TGVs are meshed into N filaments which are dependent on the operating frequency, f [24]. The elements in the impedance matrix are obtained as

$$Z_{ij} = \begin{cases} R_f + j\omega L_f, & i = j \\ j\omega M_{ij}, & i \neq j \end{cases} \tag{2}$$

with parameters in (2) described as [14].

$$R_f = \sqrt{\left(\frac{h_{TGV}}{\sigma_f \cdot \pi \cdot r_{TGV}^2}\right)^2 + \left[\left(\frac{p}{2r_{TGV} \cdot \sigma_f}\right)\left(\frac{h_{TGV}}{2\pi \cdot r_{TGV} \cdot \delta_s - \pi \cdot \delta_s^2}\right)^2\right]} \tag{3}$$

$$L_f = \frac{\mu h_{TGV}}{2\pi}\left[\ln\left(\frac{h_{TGV}}{r_{TGV}} + \sqrt{\left(\frac{h_{TGV}}{r_{TGV}}\right)^2 + 1}\right) + \frac{r_{TGV}}{h_{TGV}} - \sqrt{\left(\frac{r_{TGV}}{h_{TGV}}\right)^2 + 1}\right] \tag{4}$$

$$M_{ij} = \frac{\mu}{2\pi}\left[\ln\left(\frac{h_{TGV}}{p_{ij}} + \sqrt{\left(\frac{h_{TGV}}{p_{ij}}\right)^2 + 1}\right) + \frac{p_{ij}}{h_{TGV}} - \sqrt{\left(\frac{p_{ij}}{h_{TGV}}\right)^2 + 1}\right] \tag{5}$$

Table 3. Number of CNTs in multi-bit TGV for varying tube densities

Diameter (nm)	Number of CNTs for varying tube densities			
	$n = 10^{10}$ tubes/cm^2	$n = 10^{11}$ tubes/cm^2	$n = 10^{12}$ tubes/cm^2	$n = 10^{13}$ tubes/cm^2
1.00	1	10	101	1011
1.68	4	35	351	3509
2.36	9	91	906	9061
3.04	17	174	1741	17406
3.72	25	249	2487	24870
4.40	26	264	2643	26432
5.08	21	209	2090	20896
5.76	12	123	1229	12288
6.44	6	54	538	5375
7.12	2	17	175	1749
7.8	0	4	42	423

where R_f and L_f represent the resistance and self-inductance of the $i^{(th)}$–filament in TGV, M_{ij} is the mutual inductance between the $i^{(th)}$– and $j^{(th)}$–filaments, p_{ij} is the pitch between adjacent $i^{(th)}$– and $j^{(th)}$– filaments, σ_f is the conductivity of filament, δ_s models the skin depth, and ω is the signal angular frequency.

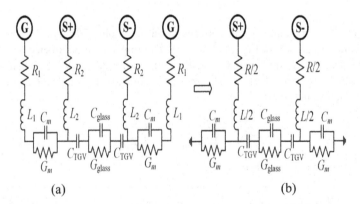

Fig. 2. (a) Equivalent circuit model and (b) simplified model of DM-TGCVs.

Furthermore, since isolation dielectric is not used in TGVs, the self-capacitance (C) mainly depends on the quantum element C_q and is calculated by

$$C = h_{TGV} \cdot C_q \cdot N_{ch} \cdot N(D) \tag{6}$$

where $C_q = 96.8$ aF/μm for a spin-less single conduction channel [25, 26], N_{ch} is the total number of conducting channels per shell of MWCNT. The glass capacitance, C_{glass} and glass conductance, G_{glass} are functions of TGV height as

$$C_{glass} = \pi \cdot \varepsilon_{glass} \cdot h_{TGV}/\cosh^{-1}(p_{TGV}/2r_{TGV}) \tag{7}$$

$$G_{glass} = 2\pi \cdot f \cdot h_{TGV} \cdot \tan\delta_{glass} \cdot C_{glass} \tag{8}$$

where, $\tan(\delta_{glass})$ specifies the loss tangent and equals 0.005 at $f = 2.4$ GHz. The mutual capacitance, C_m and mutual conductance, G_m between signal and ground part of each multi-bit TGV are determined as [27]

$$C_m = 2\varepsilon_{glass} \cdot h_{TGV} \cdot r_{TGV}/W_s \tag{9}$$

$$G_m = \sigma_{glass} \cdot C_m/\varepsilon_0 \cdot \varepsilon_{glass} \tag{10}$$

Based on the equivalent circuit model shown in Fig. 2(a), the magnitude of forward transmission coefficient in differential- ($S_{21|d}$) and common-mode ($S_{21|c}$) are calculated as [28]

$$S_{21|d} = \frac{2}{A_d + B_d/Z_1 + C_dZ_1 + D_d}; S_{21|c} = \frac{2}{A_C + B_c/Z_1 + C_cZ_1 + D_c} \tag{11}$$

with $Z_1 = 50$ Ω and ABCD parameters calculated as

$$\begin{bmatrix} A & B \\ C & D \end{bmatrix} = \begin{bmatrix} \cosh(\gamma_0 \cdot h_{TGV}) & Z_0\sinh(\gamma_0 \cdot h_{TGV}) \\ \sinh(\gamma_0 \cdot h_{TGV})/Z_0 & \cosh(\gamma_0 \cdot h_{TGV}) \end{bmatrix} \tag{12}$$

The characteristic impedance and propagation constant are calculated as [24, 27]

$$Z_o = \sqrt{\frac{R + j\omega L}{[G_o + (1-k)G_m + j\omega(C_o + (1-k)C_m)]}} \tag{13}$$

$$\gamma_o = \sqrt{(R + j\omega L)[G_o + (1-k)G_m + j\omega(C_o + (1-k)C_m)]} \tag{14}$$

where, k is the switching factor which is equal to either -1 or $+1$ for differential- and common-mode signal transmissions, respectively and G_o and C_o determined

$$G_o = \mathrm{Re}\left(\frac{j\omega C(G_{glass} + j\omega C_{glass})}{2G_{glass} + j\omega(2C_{glass} + C)}\right) \tag{15}$$

$$C_o = \mathrm{Im}\left(\frac{j\omega C(G_{glass} + j\omega C_{glass})}{2G_{glass} + j\omega(2C_{glass} + C)}\right)/\omega \tag{16}$$

In order to validate the efficacy of proposed model realized through PEEC, the electromagnetic HFSS simulations are performed for a pair of Cu DM-TGVs. The comparison of differential- and common-mode S-parameters obtained through the proposed model with HFSS simulations are illustrated in Fig. 3(a) and (b). As can be seen in Fig. 3(a), the magnitude of the forward transmission coefficient of insertion loss in differential-mode, $S_{21|d}$ (dB) is smaller than that in common-mode, $S_{21|c}$ (dB) i.e., $S_{21|d}$ (dB) < $S_{21|c}$ (dB). This is owing to the impact of mutual inductance which causes inductance in differential-mode to be smaller than the common-mode inductance. The model corroborates with HFSS simulations quite well upto 100 GHz.

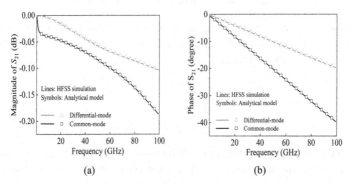

(a)   (b)

Fig. 3. (a) Magnitude and (b) phase of the S_{21}-parameters in differential- and common-mode configurations of coupled DM-TGVs.

3   Effective Complex Conductivity of Composite Cu-mCNTB TGVs

By the virtue of multi-bit TGVs, σ_{eff} is formulated for SWCNT bundle can be expressed as

$$\sigma_{cnt} = h_{TGV} \left[\frac{\sqrt{3}}{2} (D+s)^2 \cdot Z_{cnt,self} \right]^{-1} \tag{17}$$

For MWCNT bundle having m shells,

$$\sigma_{cnt} = h_{TGV} \cdot \frac{2}{\sqrt{3}(D+s)^2 \cdot f_{cnt}} \cdot \sum_{i=1}^{m} Z_{CNT}^{-1} \tag{18}$$

The inherent self-impedance of an isolated SWCNT or an individual shell of a MWCNT ($Z_{cnt,self}$) [28]

$$Z_{cnt,self} = \frac{h}{2q^2 N_{ch}} \left(1 + \frac{h_{TGV}}{\lambda_{eff}} + j\omega \frac{h_{TGV}}{2v_F} \right) + \frac{R_{mc}}{N_{ch}} \tag{19}$$

In (19), h is Planck's constant, q is electronic charge, v_F is the Fermi velocity whose value is equal to 8×10^5 m/s, R_{mc} is the imperfect contact resistance and is dependent on the fabrication process, N_{ch} is the number of conducting channels, and mean free path, $\lambda_{eff} = 1000\,D$.

For MWCNTs, the number of conducting channels of a given shell are calculated as [29]

$$N_{ch}(D, T) = \begin{cases} k_1 \cdot T \cdot D + k_2, & D \geq D_T/T \\ 2/3, & D < D_T/T \end{cases} \tag{20}$$

where $k_1 = 2.04 \times 10^{-4}$ nm^{-1} K^{-1}, $k_2 = 0.425$, and $D_T = 1300$ nm•K. Assuming closely-packed CNTs i.e., van der Waal's gap, $s = 0.34$ nm,

Based on the (17)–(20), the resistance (R_{mCNTB}) and inductance (L_{mCNTB}) of mCNTB are computed as

$$R_{mCNTB} = \left[\int N(D)/R(D)dD \right]^{-1} \tag{21}$$

$$L_{mCNTB} = \left[\int N(D)/L_k(D)dD \right]^{-1} \tag{22}$$

where and indicate the resistance and kinetic inductance of an isolated CNT. Then the conductivity of mixed CNT forest is defined as

$$\sigma_{cnt} = h_{TGV}/A \cdot (R_{mCNTB} + j\omega L_{mCNTB}) \tag{23}$$

with mCNTB on both sides of the central row of multi-bit TGVs, for different D_{mean} is computed. For an in-depth analysis, D_{mean} is varied as 2–, 4–, and 6 nm. At higher signal frequencies, Re (σ_{eff}) decreases since the term ωL_{mCNTB} from (23) dominates over RmCNTB. At $f = 1$ GHz, Re (σ_{eff}) is improved by nearly 78% when D_{mean} is increased from 2 to 6 nm. In Fig. 4(b), Im (σ_{eff}) varies in direct proportion to $\omega L_{mCNTB}/R_{mCNTB}^2$, thus drops with frequency and after $f > R_{mCNTB}/2\pi L_{mCNTB}$, it rises. The resonant frequency $R_{mCNTB}/2\pi L_{mCNTB}$ is equal to 157, 112, and 107 GHz with $D_{mean} = 2$–, 4–, and 6 nm, respectively.

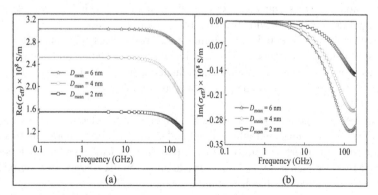

Fig. 4. (a) Real and (b) imaginary conductivities of mCNTB versus frequency with different D_{mean}.

Next, the frequency dependent resistance and inductance parameters of single TGV made of mCNTB as obtained using the PEEC method are illustrated in Fig. 5. With increasing D_{mean}, the resistance of TGV decreases, which means that it can provide superior electrical performance. Moreover, for a larger D_{mean} TGV shows reduced high frequency resistance, which means that the skin effect is suppressed. The reason for this behaviour is owing to the presence of considerably large L_k in MWCNTs which is about two orders of magnitude larger than the magnetic inductance. Meanwhile, in Fig. 5(b), inductance of TGV increases with increasing D_{mean}.

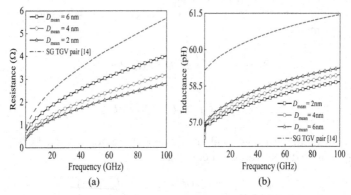

Fig. 5. Variation of (a) resistance and (b) inductance of single DM-TGCV versus frequency for different D_{mean}

4 Results and Discussion

The frequency dependent parameters of coupled DM-TGCVs such as R, L, insertion loss, and characteristic impedance are examined and analyzed in this section. The proposed analytical model utilizes equivalent circuit of coupled DM-TGCVs realized through PEEC technique combined with the effective complex conductivity of mCNTB. In Fig. 6(a) and (c), the differential- and common-mode resistances of coupled DM-TGCVs are shown. It can be observed that as D_{mean} increases, differential- and common-mode resistances show the same behaviour while inductance in the common-mode [Fig. 6(d)] is increased than differential-mode [Fig. 6(b)] due to the impact of mutual inductance between TGVs.

The influence of geometric and physical attributes on the electrical performance of DM-TGCVs are presented in Table 4. Practically, study of TGV characteristics in the differential-mode is more preferred. Thus, impact of various design parameters of the coupled DM-TGVs such as D_{mean}, r_{TGV}, p_{TGV}, and T on the characteristic impedance, insertion loss, and attenuation constant are investigated.

4.1 Characteristic Impedance

The effect of D_{mean} and r_{TGV} on the characteristic impedance is shown in Fig. 8. From (20), at lower frequencies, Z_o is seen to be dependent on R and $(G_o + 2G_m)$ while

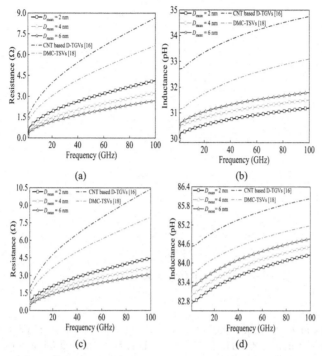

Fig. 6. Frequency dependence of (a), (b) differential-mode and (c), (d) common-mode impedance parameters for coupled DM-TGCVs. Variation of (a) resistance and (b) inductance of single DM-TGCV versus frequency for different D_{mean}

at higher frequencies, the effect of L and $(C_o + 2C_m)$ is dominant. Also in Table 4, with increasing D_{mean}, R decreases, L shows only a marginal increase, while all other circuit parameters in (20) remain unchanged. Therefore, as shown in Fig. 7(a), with Z_0 decreases in the entire frequency range increasing D_{mean}. At very high frequencies, the effect of D_{mean} on Z_0 is seen to be negligible as L remains almost unaffected. When r_{TGV} increases, R and L decrease significantly while all other parameters in (20) remain unchanged. Therefore, Z_0 in Fig. 7(b) continues to decrease in the whole frequency range.

4.2 Insertion Loss

When the mean diameter is increased from $D_{mean} = 2$ nm to $D_{mean} = 6$ nm, the resistance of DM-TGVs decreases while L shows only a marginal increase. Therefore, $S_{21|d}$ (dB) is increased in the low and middle frequency ranges. At high frequencies, since skin effect is much suppressed and $R \ll \omega L$, $S_{21|d}$ (dB) is thus determined by the conductor loss in the entire frequency range as seen in Fig. 8(a). At $f = 20$ GHz, $S_{21|d}$ (dB) is improved by 44% when D_{mean} is increased from 2 nm to 6 nm. The effect of increasing p_{TGV} replicates at high frequencies where L becomes the most dominant factor and is attributed to the reduction in mutual inductance between signal TGVs. Thus, with increasing p_{TGV}, $S_{21|d}$

Table 4. Impact of geometric and physical parameters on the electrical elements of composite DM-TGCVs

Parameter	R	L	C_m	G_m	C	G_o	C_o	$G_o + 2G_m$	$C_o + 2C_m$
$D_{mean}\uparrow$	↓	↗	→	→	↓	→	→	→	→
$r_{TGV}\uparrow$	↓	↓	↗	↗	↗	→	→	→	→
$f_{cnt}\uparrow$	↓	↓	→	→	→	→	→	→	→
$w_d\uparrow$	→	→	↓	↘	→	→	→	↓	↓
$p_{TGV}\uparrow$	↑	↑	→	↑	→	↓	↓	↘	↘
$h_{TGV}\uparrow$	↑	↑	↑	↑	↑	↑	↑	↑	↑
$A\uparrow$	↓	↓	↑	↑	↑	↑	↑	↑	↑
$\sigma_{eff}\uparrow$	↓	↓	→	→	→	→	→	→	→
$T\uparrow$	↗	→	→	→	↗	→	→	→	→
$tan\delta\uparrow$	→	→	→	→	→	↑	→	↑	→

The signs ↑, ↓, ↗, ↘, and → represent increase, decrease, slight increase, slight decrease, and remains constant.

(dB) increases at high frequencies, as seen in Fig. 8(b). With increasing r_{TGV}, S_{21ld} (dB) is decreased upto 100 GHz in Fig. 8(c). This is because a larger r_{TGV} decreases R and L. With increasing T, R and C increase slightly while $(C_o + 2C_m)$ and $(G_o + 2G_m)$ are unchanged since $C \ll C_{glass}$. This results in marginally increasing S_{21ld} (dB) with T at high frequencies and is presented in Fig. 8(d). The various analyses performed here determine that the proposed model leads to a good prediction of the characteristic impedance, insertion loss, and the results are in good agreement with HFSS.

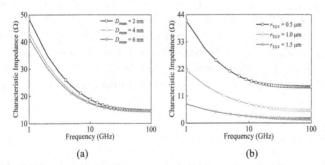

Fig. 7. Variation of the differential-mode characteristic impedance with different (a) D_{mean}, (b) p_{TGV}.

The signal integrity of proposed DM-TGCVs is determined by performing the transient analysis for DM-TGCVs. The input signal source is considered as a time-domain pseudo-random bit sequence (PRBS) with 20-Gbps data rate, 20-ps rising/fall edge, and the voltage swing varying from −0.5 to 0.5 V. The simulated eye diagram of DM-TGCVs

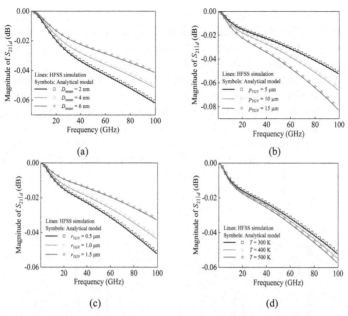

Fig. 8. Magnitude of insertion loss $S_{21|d}$ (dB) of DM-TGCVs with different (a) D_{mean}, (b) p_{TGV}, (c) r_{TGV}, and (d) T.

is shown in Fig. 9. It is apparent that quality of the eye diagram is good, i.e., peak to peak jitter is almost zero, eye-opening height is 0.992 V and eye width is 49.2 ps [18].

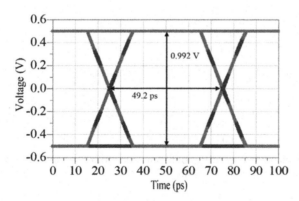

Fig. 9. Eye diagram of the proposed DM-TGCVs.

4.3 Extensions and Validation

The magnitudes of near-end [$S_{13|d}$ (dB)] and far-end [$S_{14|d}$ (dB)] crosstalk in coupled DM-TGCVs are compared with the experimental results [14] and TSV counterparts [18] for different λ_{eff} and are shown in Fig. 10. It is seen that $S_{13|d}$ (dB) and $S_{14|d}$ (dB) are reduced in DM-TGCVs. As an instance, for $h_{TGV} = 20\,\mu m$ and $\lambda_{eff} = 1000 \times D_{mean}$ at $f = 50\,GHz$, $S_{13|d}$ (dB) using the proposed DM-TGCVs and conventional TSVs utilizing multi-bit approach are found to be ~–85 dB and ~–75 dB, respectively. Thus, $S_{13|d}$ (dB) in DM-TGCVs is ~ one order of magnitude smaller in comparison to the similar TSVs. It is also seen that results of the proposed model confirm well with the experimental results for varying heights. The analyses here illustrate that the proposed model results in good estimation of near-end crosstalk and far-end crosstalk. Finally, in Fig. 11, comparison of insertion loss in differential- and common-mode signaling shows that $S_{21|d}$ (dB) and $S_{21|c}$ (dB) in DM-TGCVs show improved characteristics than similar TSVs. Thus, it is concluded that proposed model based on mCNTB is well suited for the electrical characterization of coupled DM-TGCVs.

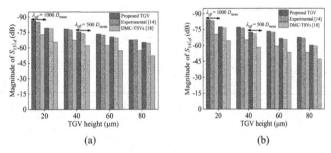

Fig. 10. Comparison of (a) $S_{13|d}$ (dB) and (b) $S_{14|d}$ (dB) with TSVs utilizing multi-bit approach and validation with the experimental results.

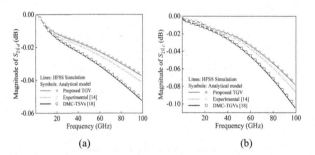

Fig. 11. Comparison of (a) $S_{21|d}$ (dB) and (b) $S_{21|c}$ (dB) with TSVs utilizing multi-bit approach and validation with the experimental results.

5   Conclusion

In this paper, an equivalent circuit model of mCNTB TGVs in differential multi-bit configuration valid up to 100 GHz is presented. The DM-TGCVs exhibit much reduced high frequency resistance extracted through the PEEC technique. The real and imaginary effective conductivities of DM-TGCVs are computed over a wideband range of frequencies. Utilizing the proposed model consisting of PEEC method and effective complex conductivity, differential- and common-mode impedances of the coupled DM-TGCVs have been computed numerically. It is analyzed that CNTs with larger D_{mean} in mCNTB bundle exhibit superior performance than CNTs having a smaller D_{mean}. In particular, D_{mean} and r_{TGV} are crucial parameters in the design of DM-TGCVs and at $f = 20$ GHz, $S_{21|d}$ (dB) improves by ~44 and ~78% as D_{mean} increases from 2 to 6 nm and r_{TGV} from 0.5 to 1.5 μm respectively. Based on the proposed model, the electrical performance of DM-TGCVs including characteristic impedance is extracted. The performance investigations in the present research work reveal that DM-TGCVs outperform TSV counterparts in terms of improved insertion loss and reduced crosstalk effects. From the present results, it is worth to eloquent that DM-TGCVs with larger D_{mean} and r_{TGV} are superior and potential replacement to TSVs for prospective 3-D IC applications.

References

1. Banerjee, K., Souri, S.J., Kapur, P., Saraswat, K.C.: 3-D ICs: a novel chip design for improving deep-submicrometer interconnect performance and systems-on-chip integration. Proc. IEEE **89**(5), 602–633 (2001)
2. Pei-Siang, S.L., et al.: Heterogeneous three-layer TSV chip stacking assembly with moldable underfill. IEEE Trans. Compon. Packag. Manuf. Technol. **3**(11), 1960–1970 (2013)
3. Zhao, W.-S., Yin, W.-Y., Wang, X.-P., Xu, X.-L.: Frequency and temperature-dependent modeling of coaxial through-silicon vias for 3-D ICs. IEEE Trans. Electron Devices **58**(10), 3358–3368 (2011)
4. Kim, H., Lee, H., Cho, J., Kim, Y., Kim, J.: Electrical design of silicon glass and organic interposer channels. In: Proceedings of the 2014 Pan Pacific Microelectronics Symposium, Kauai, HI, USA (March 2014)
5. Lim, J., et al.: Modeling and analysis of TSV noise coupling effects on RF LC-VCO and shielding structures in 3D IC. IEEE Trans. Electromagn. Compat. **60**(6), 1939–1947 (2018)
6. Piersanti, S., de Paulis, F., Orlandi, A., Fan, J.: Impact of frequency- dependent and nonlinear parameters on transient analysis of through silicon vias equivalent circuit. IEEE Trans. Electromagn. Compat. **57**(3), 538–545 (2015)
7. Sukumaran, V., Bandyopadhyay, T., Sundaram, V., Tummala, R.: Low-cost thin glass interposers as a superior alternative to silicon and organic interposers for packaging of 3D ICs. IEEE Trans. Compon. Packag. Manuf. Technol. **2**(9), 1426–1433 (2012)
8. Lu, H., et al.: Design, modeling, fabrication and characterization of 2–5-μm redistribution layer traces by advanced semiadditive processes on low-cost panel-based glass interposers. IEEE Trans. Compon. Packag. Manuf. Technol. **6**(6), 959–967 (2016)
9. Sukumaran, V., et al.: Design, fabrication and characterization of ultrathin 3-D glass interposers with through package vias at same pitch as TSVs in silicon. IEEE Trans. Compon. Packag. Manuf. Technol. **4**(5), 786–795 (2014)
10. Kim, Y., et al.: Glass interposer electromagnetic bandgap structure for efficient suppression of power/ground noise coupling. IEEE Trans. Electromagn. Compat. **59**(3), 940–951 (2017)
11. Tong, J., Sato, Y., Panayappan, K., Sundaram, V., Peterson, A.F., Tummala, R.R.: Electrical modeling and analysis of tapered through-package via in glass interposers. IEEE Trans. Compon. Packag. Manuf. Technol. **6**(5), 775–783 (2016)
12. Hu, D.-C., Hung, Y.-P., Chen, Y. H., Tain, R.-M., Lo, W.-C.: Embedded glass interposer for heterogeneous multi-chip integration. In Preceeding 65th Electronic Components and Technology Conference (ECTC), pp. 314–317 (May 2015)

13. Kumar, G., Bandyopadhyay, T., Sukumaran, V., Sundaram, V., Sung-Kyu, L., Tummala, R.: Ultra-high I/O density glass/silicon interposers for high bandwidth smart mobile applications. In: Proceedings IEEE 61st Electronic Components and Technology Conference (ECTC), pp. 217–223 (June 2011)
14. Park, G., et al.: Measurement and analysis of through glass via noise coupling and shielding structures in a glass interposer. IEEE Trans. Electromagn. Compat. **63**(5), 1562–1573 (2021)
15. Qian, L., Xia, Y., Shi, G., Wang, J., Ye, Y., Du, S.: Electrical–thermal characterization of through packaging vias in glass interposer. IEEE Trans. Nanotechnol. **16**(6), 901–908 (2017)
16. Qian, L., Shi, G., Ye, Y.: Electrical-thermal characterization of carbon nanotube based through glass vias for 3-D integration. In: IEEE 16th International Conference on Nanotechnology, pp. 663–666 (August 2016)
17. Vaisband, B., Maurice, A., Tan, C.W., Tay, B.K., Friedman, E.G.: Multi-bit CNT TSV for 3-D ICs. In: , pp. 1–5 (October 2020)
18. Hu, Q.-H., Zhao, W.-S., Fu, K., Wang, G.: Modeling and characterization of differential multi-bit carbon-nanotube through-silicon vias. IEEE Trans. Compon. Packag. Manuf. Technol. **10**(3), 534–537 (2020)
19. Guan, W., Lu, H., Zhang, Y., Zhang, Y.: A novel differential multi-bit carbon nanotube through silicon vias. In: Proceeding 4th International Conference on Advanced Electronic Materials, Computers and Software Engineering, pp. 1–5 (August 2021)
20. Kim, Y., et al.: "Measurement and analysis of glass interposer power distribution network resonance effects on a high-speed through glass via channel. IEEE Trans. Electromagn. Compat. **58**(6), 1747–1759 (2016)
21. Subramaniam, C., Yamada, T., Kobashi, K., Sekiguchi, A., Futaba, D.N., Yumura, M., Hata, K.: One hundred fold increase in current carrying capacity in a carbon nanotube-copper composite. Nat. Commun. **4**, Art. no. 2202 (July 2013)
22. Chai, Y., Chan, P.C.H., Fu, Y., Chuang, Y.C., Liu, C.Y.: Electromigration studies of Cu/carbon nanotube composite interconnects using Blech structure. IEEE Electron Device Lett. **29**(9), 1001–1003 (2008)
23. Haruehanroengra, S., Wang, W.: Analyzing conductance of mixed carbon nanotube bundles for interconnect applications. IEEE Electron Device Lett. **28**(8), 756–759 (2007)
24. Zhao, W.-S., Zheng, J., Liang, F., Xu, K., Chen, X., Wang, G.: Wideband modeling and characterization of differential through-silicon vias for 3-D ICs. IEEE Trans. Electron Devices **63**(3), 1168–1175 (2016)
25. Sarto, M.S., Tamburrano, A.: Single conductor transmission line model of multiwall carbon nanotube. IEEE Trans. Nanotechnol. **9**(1), 82–92 (May 2010)
26. Burke, P.J.: Luttinger liquid theory as a model of the gigahertz electrical properties of carbon nanotubes. IEEE Trans. Nanotechnol. **1**(1), 129–144 (March 2001)
27. Zhao, W.-S., et al.: Modeling of carbon nanotube-based differential through-silicon vias in 3-D ICs. IEEE Trans. Nanotechnol. **19**, 492–499 (2020)
28. Xu, C., Li, H., Suaya, R., Banerjee, K.: Compact AC modeling and performance analysis of through-silicon vias in 3-D ICs. IEEE Trans. Electron Device **57**(12), 3405–3417 (2010)
29. Zhao, W.-S., et al.: High-frequency modeling of on-chip coupled carbon nanotube interconnects for millimeter-wave applications. IEEE Trans. Compon. Packag. Manuf. Technol. **6**(8), 1226–1232 (2016)

Design of a Low-Voltage Charge-Sensitive Preamplifier Interfaced with Piezoelectric Tactile Sensor for Tumour Detection

Kingsuk Bag, Kislay Deep, Sharad Verma, Shashi Prabha Yadav, Manish Goswami, and Kavindra Kandpal$^{(\boxtimes)}$

Department of Electronics and Communication, IIIT Allahabad, Prayagraj, India
kavindra@iiita.ac.in

Abstract. Charge sensitive preamplifiers are indispensable components of transducer-interfacing systems as they are responsible for amplifying the signals detected by the sensor. The rapid scaling of MOSFETs in the modern era has made it quite difficult to design a charge-sensitive preamplifier that has high effective resistance, consumes low power, generates very little noise, and can operate at low frequencies. This work will target to design a charge sensitive preamplifier at a supply voltage of 1.1 V using the 65 nm technology node that is supposed to operate at low levels of frequency in the range of 10–100 Hz with a high gain and high net resistance. The proposed design was found to produce a maximum gain of 235 dB and a maximum effective resistance of 270 GΩ and having a very low value of noise spectral density (<0.7 mV/$\sqrt{\text{Hz}}$). The power consumed by the proposed design was also in the range of nW. The working of the amplifier is illustrated in a practical scenario by interfacing it with a tactile sensor which would be used in detection of submucosal tumours by adjudging their stiffness. The sensor is designed as a layered shell with piezoelectric material sandwiched between two layers of electric conductors. The modelled sensor is then interpreted in terms of a current source with a resistance and capacitance in parallel to interface it with the designed charge sensitive preamplifier. The output of the sensor is difference in potential in the range of a few mV which is proportional to the pressure acting upon it. The mentioned sensor is simulated in COMSOL, and the charge amplifier is designed in Cadence.

Keywords: Charge-sensitive preamplifier · Tactile sensor · Effective resistance · Piezoelectric · COMSOL

1 Introduction

The fundamental working of a preamplifier involves the extraction of a signal from the detector without affecting the inherent properties that the signal has. The SNR of the signal should remain preserved as it passes out of the preamplifier [1]. This implies that the preamplifier has to amplify the weak signals that it receives from the detector and then drive it through the interconnection between the preamplifier and the rest of the circuitry. The detected signal can often be very weak in nature and to preserve

© The Author(s), under exclusive license to Springer Nature Switzerland AG 2022
A. P. Shah et al. (Eds.): VDAT 2022, CCIS 1687, pp. 27–38, 2022.
https://doi.org/10.1007/978-3-031-21514-8_3

the qualities of the detected signal, the preamplifier, as well as the adjoining circuitry between the preamplifier and the detector, should not contribute to any addition of noise to the already weak signal [2]. To achieve this, the preamplifier is ideally located as close as possible to the detector. This approach also reduces the effect of parasitic capacitances [3]. The circuits which are responsible for the transmission of the detected signal are designed in such a way that they are in sync with the detector characteristics.

Preamplifiers are designed in various ways. The design depends on the parameter that they are supposed to sense and amplify [2]. It could be an input current, input voltage or an input charge that is being fed to the preamplifier.

1.1 Charge-Sensitive Preamplifiers

Charge-sensitive preamplifiers are known due to their properties of sensitivity towards charge or providing a gain in charge. They are mainly used in creating an interface between a sensor and the remaining circuitry [3]. The greatest challenge while designing a charge-sensitive preamplifier is to simultaneously reduce the power consumption as well as increase its sensitivity towards the input charge [5]. If the device is to be operated at a low frequency, then there comes a trade-off between the bandwidth at which the device can operate and the sensitivity of the device.

The basic configuration for a charge sensitive preamplifier can be illustrated as shown below:

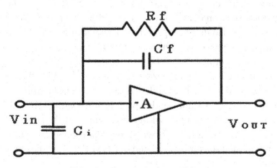

Fig. 1. Pre-charge amplifier

In Fig. 1, C_i represents the summation of the capacitance that emerges from the detector and also the stray capacitances of the interconnects. The feedback capacitance is represented by C_f and the open loop gain to be provided by the amplifier is given by A. Applying Miller's theorem, we can bring the feedback capacitance to the input side with a value of $(A + 1)*C_f$ and it is in parallel with the input capacitance C_i [6]. So the total value of the capacitance that is present in the input side has a value of $C_i + (A + 1)*C_f$. The amplifier is designed in such a way so that the gain that is calculated in the unfastened loop configuration is given by A, which has a very high value, and this results in the term $A*C_f$ gaining much priority and drowning out the C_i term.

From Fig. 1,

$$V_{\text{out}} = -A.V_{\text{in}} \tag{1}$$

But,

$$V_{in} = Q/[C_i + (A + 1)C_f] \tag{2}$$

In above equations Q represents the charge that has been provided as an output signal from the sensor or detector and is being fed to the preamplifier. As A is very large and $A * C_f \gg C_i$, we can write $Vin = Q/AC_f$.

Therefore,

$$V_{out} = -A.Q/AC_f = -Q/C_f \tag{3}$$

These observations have led to the conclusion that the output voltage is independent of the isolated capacitances that are present on the input side, hence it does not vary arbitrarily and can be considered as an accurate representation of the input signal [5].

The Charge-sensitive preamplifiers are widely used in various fields like medical imaging, amplifying signals from tactile sensors, photodiodes, etc. They also find application in radiation measurement instrumentation where the energy surge has to be detected for each pulse [9]. The goal of this paper is to design a charge-sensitive preamplifier operating at a very low voltage, having high gain, and generating minimal noise [9]. The basic hindrance to achieving this is that it requires a large value of feedback resistance(in range of GΩ) to operate at such low frequencies.

The pole frequency is given by

$$f = 1/(2 * \Pi * R_f * C_f) \tag{4}$$

There may be two ways to reduce the pole frequency to ensure a low bandwidth operation. Firstly, we may increase the value of C_f. But since the gain is inversely proportional to C_f, an increase in C_f implies a decrease in the gain which is not desirable. So the other viable option is implemented, that is the value of R_f is increased in order to decrease the corner frequency. The increment in the value of R_f also carries a catch along with it. We can't just put an arbitrarily large resistance as feedback as it will lead to other difficulties [8].

If off-chip resistances are used in the design, then there will be an unnecessary increase in the chip area as well as increased noise in the circuit which is highly undesirable. So, to resolve this dilemma we will try to increase the effective output resistance of our designed operational amplifier. In this way, we can increase the required feedback resistance without increasing neither the noise contribution nor the area required by the chip.

2 Application

The proposed preamplifier is to be interfaced with a tactile sensor which could be used in the detection of hardness of submucosal tumours. The entire setup could be mounted on top of an endoscope which would provide us critical information about the nature of oral tumours. The bigger aim of this endeavour is to predict whether a submucosal tumour is malignant or not based on its stiffness. The existing method [5, 6] of detection of submucosal tumours involves the use of ultrasound but this method is not accurate and often leads to falsified results. When dangerous lesions are found during standard endoscopy, we attempted to develop an alternate method for detecting submucosal cancers based on direct contact with a hardness sensor.

2.1 Sensor Mechanism

The sensing method employs a tactile sensor with structural electrodes. On the surface of a piezoelectric film two conducting layers are placed. They are usually metals and act like electrodes for the dielectric that is the piezoelectric material.

The outer contact forces exerted on the tactile sensor can be passed to the piezoelectric film through the interior and exterior structure when elastomers make contact with the tactile sensor by normal force. The piezoelectric film can produce two voltage outputs, one for the hard internal structure and one for the soft external structure, denoted V_1 and V_2, accordingly.

As a result, the ratio of output voltages from the interior structure and exterior packaging material can be used to determine the object's hardness level.

2.2 Modelling of Sensor

The modelling of the sensor has been done in COMSOL software. It is modelled as a layered shell with piezoelectric material sandwiched between two layers of electric conductors. The materials chosen for the simulation are Aluminium for the conducting layers and Lead Zirconate Titanate as the piezoelectric layer. The basic configuration of the sensor is shown in Fig. 2.

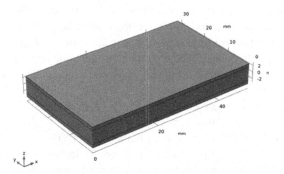

Fig. 2. 3D representation of piezoelectric sensor

The modelled sensor is subjected to two kinds of studies. One for determining the variation in the electric potential along the layers of the sensors and the other one for displacement that occurs upon application of stress.

The distribution of electric potential of the afore-mentioned sensor is represented in the following figure. The maximum voltage difference between the upper and lower plates has been found to be 20 mV (Fig. 3).

The displacement of the sensor with respect to the Z axis when acted upon by stress is represented in Fig. 4.

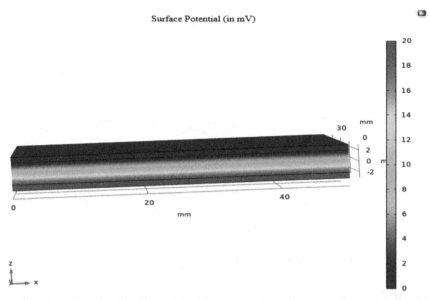

Fig. 3. Change in electric potential with applied pressure

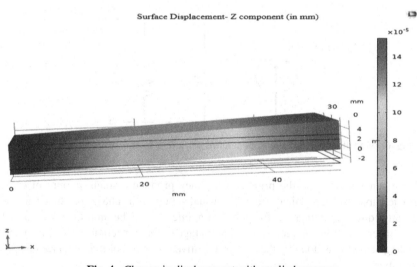

Fig. 4. Change in displacement with applied pressure

The voltage generated by the sensor as a function of applied pressure is illustrated in Fig. 5.

In order to interface the proposed sensor with the designed charge sensitive preamplifier, we have to model the sensor into its equivalent form. Here we have modelled it as a current source which also has a parallel resistor and a parallel capacitor. These

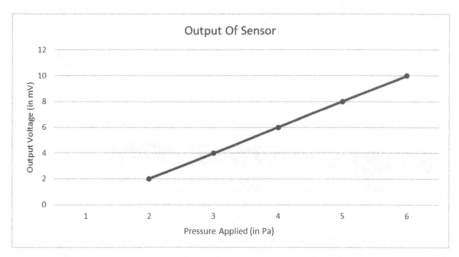

Fig. 5. Relation of output voltage with applied pressure

additional components are present to compensate for the diminishing charge from the piezo sensor.

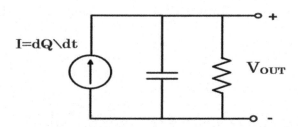

Fig. 6. Modelling the piezo sensors in terms of current source, resistor and capacitor

Piezo sensors work on the principle that they produce a small amount of charge when acted upon by mechanical stress. The usual values of the charge produced are very small and require amplification for practical applications. The amplifier must also be able to convert the input charge to an output voltage so that it becomes usable for further processing. This job is done by the charge sensitive preamplifier that we have designed in this paper.

The resistance in the above shown Fig. 6 is implemented by active devices instead of using a passive resistance. The combined model for the sensor coupled with the charge sensitive preamplifier is as shown below (Fig. 7):

3   Proposed Design

In the proposed work a pre-amplifier in 65 nm CMOS technology has been designed which is shown in Fig. 8. This op-amp configuration was constructed by a two-stage

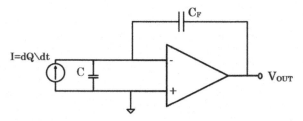

Fig. 7. Interfacing the sensor with the charge sensitive preamplifier

folded cascode structure [14]. Since the preamplifier is to be operated in a low frequency range, we will be requiring an extremely high value of resistor R_f (typically in range of a few hundred G Ω).

To address this issue, biased active devices have been used to generate this large value of R_f. The circuit consists of a two stage op-amp where a differential amplifier is being used in the first stage and a common gate amplifier is being used in the second stage.which is also a gain stage which provides a single ended output, which then passes through the voltage buffer because having a large value of R_{out} voltage loss at the preamplifier's output is minimized by this buffer [15].

The circuit operates with a supply voltage of 1.1 V and aspect ratios of each transistor of the design have been calculated. Furthermore, a 100 nA constant current source is being used to bias the circuit which in turn acts as a Wilson's current mirror. This Wilson's current mirror is used to control the net conversion gain and avoid saturation of voltage. Using Wilson's current mirror at the gain stage, also results in an increase in the value of $1/g_m$. This increment in the value of $1/g_m$ ultimately leads to the required increase in the value of the net output resistance.

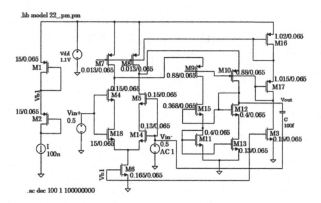

Fig. 8. Schematic for proposed design of the preamplifier

4   Simulation Results

The transfer function of the charge amplifier is plotted against frequency in Fig. 9(a). It is observed that the maximum value of the achieved gain is 235 dB in the frequency range of 10–100 Hz.

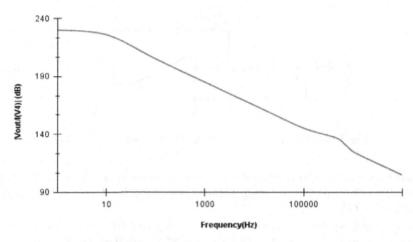

(a).- Transfer function vs frequency of the preamplifier in dB

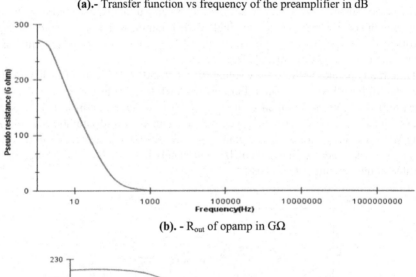

(b). - R_{out} of opamp in GΩ

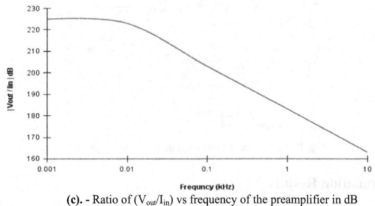

(c). - Ratio of (V_{out}/I_{in}) vs frequency of the preamplifier in dB

Fig. 9. (a) Transfer function vs frequency of the preamplifier in dB. (b) R_{out} of opamp in G Ω. (c) Ratio of (V_{out}/I_{in}) vs frequency of the preamplifier in dB. (d) Noise spectrum of op-amp

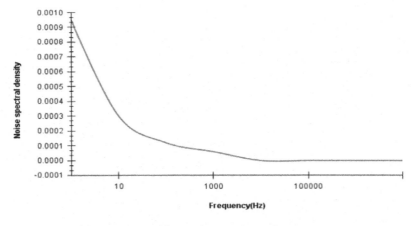

(d). - Noise spectrum of op-amp

Fig. 9. (*continued*)

The AC analysis of the circuit is done to plot the value of the feedback resistance (R_f). It is observed to have attained a maximum value of 270 GΩ in the intended range of operation.

The trans-impedance of the preamplifier (Ratio of V_{out} and I_{in}) is plotted vs frequency in Fig. 9(c) and this value comes out to be approximately 225 dB for the desired frequency range of 10–100 Hz.

The noise analysis of the proposed design has also been simulated (as shown in Fig. 9(d)) in the given range of frequency where the circuit is implemented. Lesser noise is observed for this design as compared to other similar papers [6, 7]. This noise occurs in the preamplifier as a result of feedback resistance. However, increasing the feedback resistance is one of the primary goals of the design resulting in a trade-off between the expected noise levels and the achievable charge sensitivity of the proposed preamplifier.

The designed preamplifier is finally interfaced with the tactile sensor and the graph of the final output voltage is plotted for different frequencies as the input pressure varies (Fig. 10).

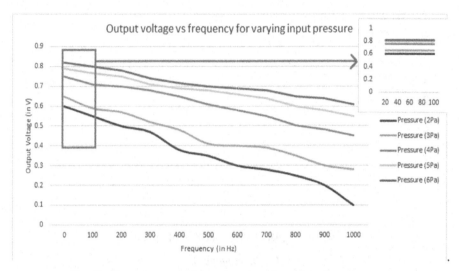

Fig. 10. V_{out} of preamplifier vs frequency for various input pressures

4.1 PVT Analysis of Simulation Results

To visualize the stability of our proposed design, a PVT analysis has been done where parameters like supply voltage temperature, and width of the MOSFETs in the preamplifier are varied from their reference values, and the 3-dB cut-off frequency and charge sensitivity of the preamplifier is measured [1]. Figure 11 shows the PVT analysis of our proposed preamplifier. From the result it is clear that on varying Vdd by ±10% from 1.1 V, there is a significant difference in the cut-off frequency but no change in sensitivity. Also, there have been no major changes in cut-off frequency, f_c and charge sensitivity with change in temperature or transistor width.

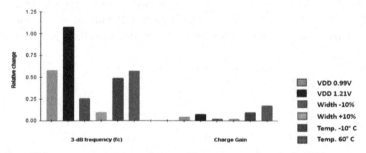

Fig. 11. Cut-off frequency and gain variation with respect to changes in Vdd, temperature and width

5   Comparison with Other Works

See Table 1.

Table 1. Comparison of this work with other existing research works

Parameters	Tech node	Supply voltage	Targeted frequency	Feedback capacitance	Sensitivity	Power analysis	Noise produced
Our work	65 nm	1.1 V	10 Hz	100 fF	9.5 mV/fF	728.79 nW	70 mV/$\sqrt{Hz}$
Ref. [2]	90 nm	1.2 V	14.5 Hz	1 pF	4.2 mv/fF	90.46 μW	195.25 mV/$\sqrt{Hz}$
Ref. [3]	180 nm	1.8 V	30 Hz	100 pF	8 mV/fF	2.1 μW	221.4 mV/$\sqrt{Hz}$
Ref. [4]	0.7 μm	2 V	200 Hz	1 pF	7.85 mV/fF	210.8 μW	95.25 mV/$\sqrt{Hz}$

6 Conclusion

The charge-sensitive preamplifier that has been designed in this work was targeted to possess low power consumption, operate even for low frequencies, have a low operating voltage, and contribute to very little noise. Ideally it should also realize a large pseudo feedback resistance so that we do not require additional passive devices in the circuitry and the output of the circuit should also not vary with varying parameters such as temperature. This charge amplifier is interfaced with the designed tactile sensor for submucosal tumour detection. The relationship between the pressure applied on the sensor and the voltage generated by it is found to be linear in nature.

The proposed design of the charge amplifier provides a large feedback resistance of around 270 GΩ. The gain of the system was also found to be very high in the range of 200 dB and the power consumption of the device is also very low (in the range of nW) 728.79 nW. The charge sensitivity of the preamplifier was calculated to be 9.5 mV/pF which is high in comparison to other existing designs. The noise spectral density of our proposed design is also quite low, <0.7 mV/Hz. The design was also found to be resilient to PVT variations.

The designed sensor is interfaced with the proposed charge amplifier. It was observed that the maximum output voltage after using the pre-amplifier is 0.82 V when the sensor is acted upon by a pressure of 3 Pa. This is a significant improvement to the original output of the sensor which was in the range of a few mV.

Acknowledgement. The authors of this paper would like to thank **IIITA seed grant no. IIITA/RO/323/2021**—for providing the software infrastructure used in the simulations.

References

1. Bhattacharjee, A., Kandpal, K.: A low power, charge-sensitive preamplifier integrated with a silicon nanowire biosensor. In: 2021 IEEE Latin America Electron Devices Conference (LAEDC), pp. 1–4 (2021)
2. Gupta, N., Kandpal, K.: Device-to-circuit integrated design of DMFET biosensor and its readout using CMOS pre-charge amplifier. In: 2020 IEEE 17th India Council International Conference (INDICON), pp. 1–7 (2020)
3. Wang, H., et al.: A charge sensitive pre-amplifier for smart point-of-care devices employing polymer-based lab-on-a-chip. IEEE Trans. Circuits Syst. II Express Briefs **65**(8), 984–988 (2018)

4. Binnie, T.D., et al.: An integrated 16×16 PVDF pyroelectric sensor array. IEEE Trans. Ultrason. Ferroelectr. Freq. Control **47**(6), 1413–1420 (2018)
5. Capra, S., Pullia, A.: Design and experimental validation of an integrated multichannel charge amplifier for solid-state detectors with innovative spectroscopic range booster. IEEE Trans. Nucl. Sci. **67**(8), 1877–1884 (2020)
6. Kandpal, K., et al.: A high speed-low power comparator with composite cascode pre-amplification for oversampled ADCs. J. Autom. Control Eng. **1**(4), 301–305 (2013)
7. Jalil, J., Ruan, Y., Li, H., Zhu, Y.: Comprehensive design considerations and noise modeling of preamplifier for MEMS electrometry. IEEE Trans. Instrum. Meas. **69**(6), 3223–3231 (2020)
8. Pinna, L., et al.: Charge amplifier design methodology for PVDF-based tactile sensors. Artic. J. Circuits Syst. Comput. (2019)
9. Jeong, M., Kim, G.: Development of charge sensitive amplifiers based on various circuit board substrates and evaluation of radiation hardness characteristics. Nucl. Eng. Technol. **52**(7), 1503–1510 (2020)
10. Choudhary, S., Bhat, S., Selvakumar, J.: High gain and low power design of preamplifier for CMOS comparator. In: 2016 3rd International Conference on Signal Processing and Integrated Networks (SPIN), pp. 63–66 (2016)
11. Hao, J., Deng, Z., He, L., Xue, T., Li, Y., Yue, Q.: A cryogenic CMOS preamplifier with very large dynamic range for HPGe detectors. In: 2020 IEEE Nuclear Science Symposium and Medical Imaging Conference (NSS/MIC) (2020)
12. Su, Y., Liu, X.: Design of a low noise low power preamplifier used for portable biomedical signal acquisition. In: 2016 9th International Congress on Image and Signal Processing, BioMedical Engineering and Informatics (CISP-BMEI), pp. 1742–1745 (2016)
13. Cabrera, C., Caballero, R., Costa-Rauschert, M.C., Rossi-Aicardi, C., Oreggioni, J.: Low-voltage low-noise high-CMRR biopotential integrated preamplifier. IEEE Trans. Circuits Syst. I Regul. Pap. **68**(8), 3232–3241 (2021)
14. Pezzotta, A., et al.: A low-power CMOS 0.13 μm charge-sensitive preamplifier for GEM detectors. In: Proceedings of 2013 International Conference on IC Design & Technology (ICICDT) (2013)
15. Al Jehani, N., Abbas, M.: Low power preamplifier for biomedical signal digitization. In: 2020 27th International Conference on Mixed Design of Integrated Circuits and System (MIXDES), pp. 107–111 (2020)

Design, Simulation and Optimization of Aluminum Nitride Based Accelerometer

Rahul Kumar Gupta[ID] and Sanjeev Kumar Manhas[(✉)][ID]

Indian Institute of Technology, Roorkee, India
{rahul_kg,sanjeev.manhas}@ece.iitr.ac.in

Abstract. In this paper, aluminum nitride based Z-axis vibration sensor with optimized structure is reported. The main objective of this work is to miniaturize of the device with special specification. The optimization of the accelerometer structure is done using finite element analysis (FEA) in COMSOL in order to get maximum sensitivity. The sensors with different geometries, namely circular annular structure and trampoline structure, are designed and simulated. Specifically, the sensor consists of a proof mass suspended with the continuous diaphragm in circular annular structure and four guided beams in the trampoline structure. Continuous diaphragm and guided beams behave as springs. The miniaturization of the device is done by choosing the proper value of size of proof mass and springs. Sensitivity mainly depends on the proof mass weight M and spring constant k. In this study to get maximum sensitivity the size of proof mass and springs is selected at which the sensitivity is maximum. Aluminum nitride piezoelectric layer with piezoelectric coefficient $d_{33} = 12$ pC/N is used to sense the displacement of the proof mass. The first eigen mode of the structures are found at 14.54 kHz and 13.50 kHz respectively for circular annular structure and trampoline structure. The sensitivity of the structure without the amplifier is found 3.22 mV/g in circular annular structure and 4.39 mV/g in trampoline structure at 100 Hz.

Keywords: Aluminum nitride · Second keyword · COMSOL · Vibrations · Diaphragm · Piezoelectric

1 Introduction

It is necessary to monitor the condition of a machine and structure. The most significance parameter is vibration to determine the dynamic characteristics and machine health. The miniaturized piezoelectric sensors are vastly used in the field of automotive, space, defense, medicine, and many other industrial applications There are various detection techniques to measure the vibration like capacitive, piezoresistive, piezoelectric, optical, resonant technique [1]. The main issues with the reported works on accelerometer are the low sensitivity and low resonance

© The Author(s), under exclusive license to Springer Nature Switzerland AG 2022
A. P. Shah et al. (Eds.): VDAT 2022, CCIS 1687, pp. 39–52, 2022.
https://doi.org/10.1007/978-3-031-21514-8_4

frequencies. In [3] the resonance frequency was reported 7.2 kHz 1 Hz–5 kHz frequency range which require a high precise low pass filter in read out circuit. This paper presents an optimized design of MEMs accelerometer for vibration measurement purpose which is based on the piezoelectric detection technique (PEDT). PEDT offers better linearity and temperature stability compared to piezoresistive and capacitive devices [2].

2   Piezoelectricity

The phenomenon of piezoelectricity was discovered in the late nineteenth century. It was observed that certain materials generate an electric charge or in general words voltage, when it goes under a mechanical stress. This is known as the direct effect of piezoelectricity [1]. Alternately, the same material would be able to produce a mechanical deformation (or force) when an electric field is applied to it. This is called the inverse effect of piezoelectricity [1]. It was first discovered in quartz by Jacques and Pierre Curie in 1880. The physical origin of piezoelectricity arises because of charge asymmetry within the crystal structure [6]. In piezoelectricity the important parameter is charge coefficient d_{ij} (C/N) which shows the amount of charge generated on the surfaces of the material on the i-axis to the force applied on the j-axis. In the Fig. 1 the force is applied in direction-3 and the charge is generated across the thickness of the material, and hence, this charge coefficient is denoted as d_{33}. If a force, F_3, is applied to the piezoelectric sample, then the charge generated is given by [6]

$$Q_3 = d_{33}F_3 \tag{1}$$

and so, the voltage produced from a rectangular block of area A, thickness t, and relative permittivity ϵ_r is [6]

$$V_3 = \frac{(d_{33}F_3t)}{(\epsilon_r\epsilon_0 A)} = \frac{(d_{33}t\sigma)}{(\epsilon_r\epsilon_0)} \tag{2}$$

where $\sigma = stress(N/m^2)$.

The reported values of d_{33} of AlN film in different literature is given in the Table 1.

Table 1. Reported values of d_{33} of AlN Film

Value (pC/N)	References
5.92	[3]
4.46	[4]
12	[5]

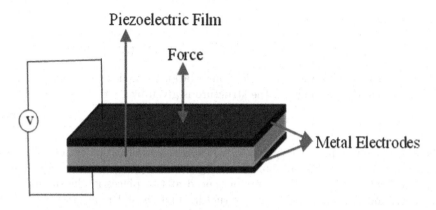

Fig. 1. Illustration of the piezoelectric effect

3   Simulation of Accelerometer

The simulation of the accelerometer is done using finite element analysis (FEM) in COMSOL. In this paper two designs are reported. The mathematical and FEM analysis has been done for both structures.

3.1   Circular Annular Structure

Mechanical Model. Figure 2 shows the 3-d structure of the circular annular structure. In this structure a circular proof mass is suspended by a continuous diaphragm which act as spring.

(a)   (b)

Fig. 2. 3-d Schematic of Circular Annular Structure a) Top view b) Bottom view

The spring constant of the diaphragm is given by [7]

$$k = 4\pi c(\lambda)D/b^2 \tag{3}$$

where b is the inner radius or proof mass radius, λ is the ratio of outer radius to the inner radius and D is given by

$$D = (Eh^3)/(12(1 - \nu^2)) \tag{4}$$

The value of $c(\lambda)$ is given by [7]

$$c(\lambda) = [4(\lambda^2 - 1)]/[(\lambda^2 - 1)^2 - (2\lambda ln(\lambda))^2] \tag{5}$$

where $E=$ Young's Modulus, $\nu =$ Poisson's Ratio, $h=$ Thickness of Diaphragm.
    The resonance frequency of the structure is given by

$$\omega_0 = \sqrt{(k/M)} \tag{6}$$

where M is the weight of accelerometer which is the combination of mass of proof mass and mass of the diaphragm. When 1g load is applied in Z-direction, it is observed that maximum stress is experienced at two places in the diaphragm, one is around the outer portion of structure and second is around the proof mass as shown in the Fig. 3. The piezoelectric patch is placed at the maximum stress area. It is also observed tensile stress is produced at outer electrode and compressive stress is produced at inner electrodes before the resonance frequency and vice versa after the resonance frequency as shown in Fig. 4(a,b). Because of the opposite stress produced at electrodes the voltage generated at outer and inner electrodes will be of opposite sign. To increase the output voltage or in general words to improve the sensitivity of the accelerometer, differential voltage concept is used.

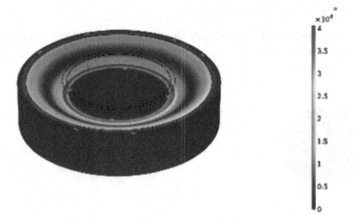

Fig. 3. Normal Stress after applying 1 g load

Optimization of Resonance Frequency and Output Voltage of Circular Annular Structure. The resonance frequency of the structure is vital important parameter to analyse the frequency range of the accelerometer. Since the targeted frequency range of the accelerometer 10 Hz to 2 kHz thus the first resonance frequency should be at least 6–7 times of the upper limit of frequency

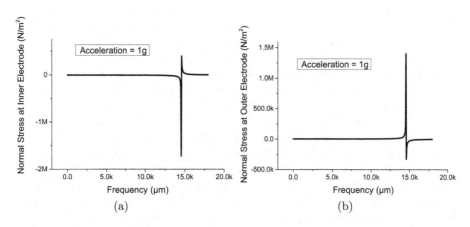

Fig. 4. Normal Stress by applying 1 g load a) At Outer Electrode b) At Inner Electrodes

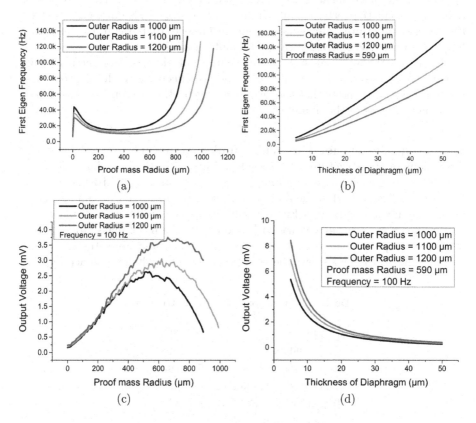

Fig. 5. Variation of first eigen frequency and voltage with proof mass and thickness of diaphragm for different outer radius and proof mass radius of 590 μm

range to get a linear output within the range. The optimization of the structure is done using COMSOL 5.6. In this structure there are some parameters, such as proof mass radius, total radius of the structure and thickness of the diaphragm, by which the resonance frequency of the structure can be varied.

Figure 5(a,b) shows the variation of resonance (eigen) frequency of the structure w.r.t the proof mass radius and thickness of diaphragm for different value of outer radius. It is observed that initially the resonance frequency decreases and goes to it's minimum value and then increases rapidly with respect to proof mass radius. The reason behind this type of pattern is the dependency of frequency with the values of k and M and the values of k and M depends on the proof mass radius and outer radius. For initial value of proof mass radius the value of k increases very slowly compare to the value of M but for larger value of proof mass radius k increases rapidly but the value of M increases gradually. It is also observed that resonance frequency achieves its minimum value at the value of proof mass radius which is 30–40% of the outer radius. Figure 5(b) shows that the resonance frequency also increases with the thickness of the diaphragm. But because of the mechanical strength, the thickness of the diaphragm can not be reduced beyond the certain limit. From Fig. 5(a,b) it is also observed that for the given value of proof mass radius and thickness of diaphragm, the resonance frequency is increasing by decreasing the outer radius.

Figure 5(c) shows that the output voltage of the accelerometer initially increases and goes to its maximum value and then decreases with the proof mass radius. Figure 5(d) shows that the output voltage of the accelerometer decreases with the thickness of the diaphragm.

Simulation Results for Circular Annular Structure. Table 2 shows the dimensions of the structure after the optimization. With these dimensions the first and second eigen modes are found at 14.54 kHz and 21.42 kHz respectively. When 1g load is applied in the Z-direction, the proof mass vibrates and generate the stress on the diaphragm. Figure 6(a,b) shows the variation of displacement of proof mass and output voltage with frequency. The proof mass vibrates with maximum displacement at first resonance frequency and gives the maximum output voltage. Figure 7 shows the variation of output voltage with acceleration

Table 2. Dimensions of circular structure

Parameter	Dimensions
Outer radius	1100 μm
Proof mass radius	590 μm
Thickness of diaphragm	10 μm
Height of the proof mass	500 μm
Thickness of AlN film	3.6 μm

for the different frequencies which proves the linearity of the accelerometer within the frequency range. The sensitivity of the accelerometer is found to be 3.22 mV/g.

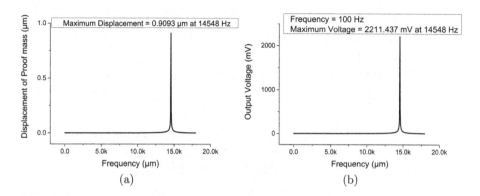

Fig. 6. Frequency Response of the accelerometer a) Frequency vs Displacement of Proof mass b) Frequency vs Output Voltage

3.2   Trampoline Structure

Mechanical Model. Figure 8 shows the 3-d schematic of trampoline structure accelerometer. In this structure proof mass is suspended by four fixed guided beam which act as spring.
The spring constant of the beam is given by [1]

$$k = \frac{12EI}{l^3} \tag{7}$$

where E is the young's modulus, l is the length of the beam and I is the moment of inertia of beam and it is given by,

$$I = \frac{(wt^3)}{12} \tag{8}$$

where t is the thickness of the beam and w is the width of the beam. The resonance frequency of the structure is given by

$$f = \frac{1}{2\pi}\sqrt{\frac{k}{M}} \tag{9}$$

where M is the weight of accelerometer which is the combination of mass of proof mass and mass of the beams. When 1g load is applied in the Z-direction the maximum stress is generated on the beam like circular annular structure as shown in Fig. 9 so the piezoelectric patch is placed at two places on the

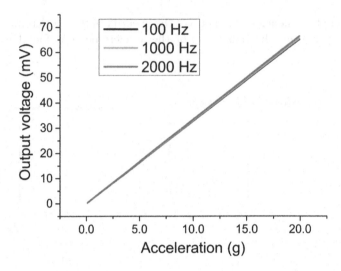

Fig. 7. Variation of output voltage with acceleration

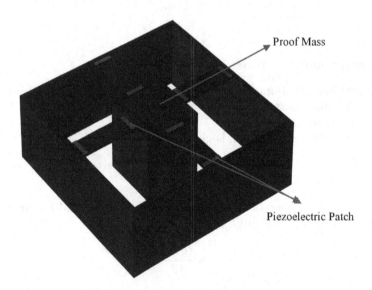

Fig. 8. 3-d Schematic of Trampoline structure

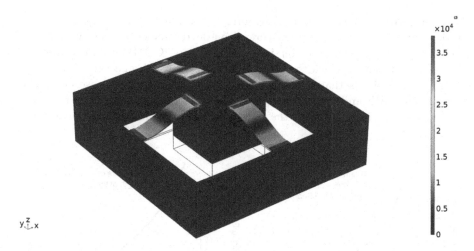

Fig. 9. Normal Stress after applying 1 g load

beam as shown in the Fig. 8. In this structure also, tensile stress is generated at outer electrode and compressive stress is generated at inner electrodes before the resonance frequency and vice versa after the resonance frequency as shown in Fig. 10(a,b) There are eight piezoelectric patches are placed in the structure, two patches on each beam as shown in the Fig. 8. In this structure also differential voltage concept is used in order to increase the sensitivity of the accelerometer.

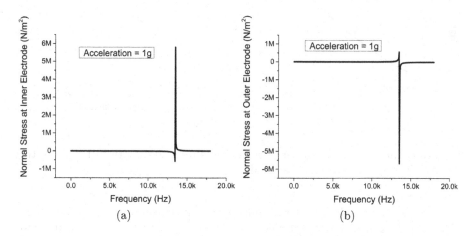

Fig. 10. Normal Stress by applying 1 g load a) At Outer Electrode b) At Inner Electrodes

Optimization of Resonance Frequency and Output Voltage of Trampoline Structure. In this structure also the resonance frequency and output voltage of the accelerometer is optimized using COMSOL 5.6 by varying the value of proof mass width, beam length, beam width and beam thickness. Figure 11(a,b) shows that the resonance (eigen) frequency decreases with the proof mass width and length of the beam. Figure 11(c,d) shows that the resonance frequency increases with the beam width and thickness of the beam.

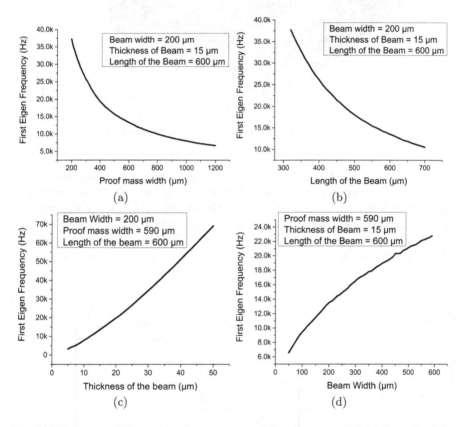

Fig. 11. Variation of First eigen frequency vs a) Proof mass width b) Length of the beam c) Thickness of Beam d) Beam width

It is also observed that the output voltage increases with the proof mass width and length of the beam whereas it deceases with the beam width and thickness of the beam as shown in the Fig. 12.

From the above optimization it is clear that there is a trade off between resonance frequency and the output voltage or in general words the sensitivity. So to increase the sensitivity of the accelerometer we can increase the proof mass width and length of the beam. But again because of mechanical strength, we can not increase the length of the beam beyond the certain limit.

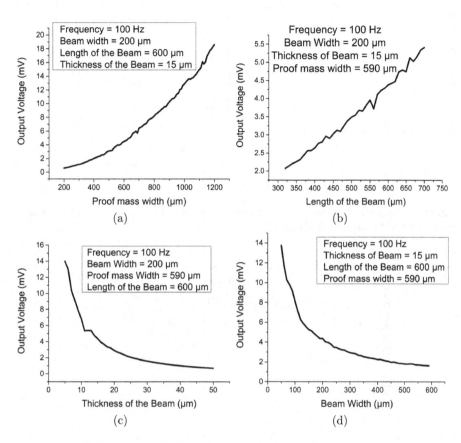

Fig. 12. Variation of Output Voltage versus a) Thickness of the Beam b) Beam Width c) Thickness of the Beam d) Beam Width

Table 3. Dimensions of trampoline structure

Parameter	Dimensions
Length of the beam	600 μm
Thickness of the beam	15 μm
Width of the beam	200 μm
Proof mass width	590 μm
Height of the proof mass	500 μm
Thickness of AlN film	3.6 μm

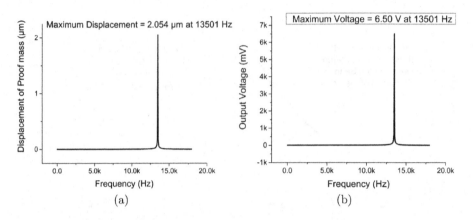

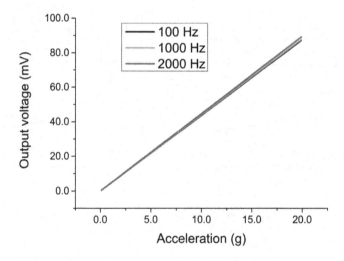

Fig. 13. Frequency Response of the Accelerometer a) Frequency vs Displacement of Proof mass b) Frequency vs Output Voltage

Fig. 14. Plot between Acceleration and output voltage

Simulation Results for Trampoline Structure. Table 3 shows that dimensions of the structure after the optimization. With these dimensions the first and second eigen modes are found at 13.50 kHz and 18.76 kHz respectively. When 1g load is applied in the Z-direction, the proof mass vibrates and generate the stress on the beams. Figure 13(a,b) shows the variation of the displacement of proof mass and output voltage with frequency. The proof mass vibrates with maximum displacement and generate the maximum output voltage at resonance frequency. Figure 14 shows the variation of output voltage with acceleration for different frequencies which shows the linearity of the accelerometer. The sensitivity of the accelerometer is found to be 4.39 mV/g.

Table 4. Comparison of reported data

Reference	Resonance frequency (kHz)	Sensitivity (mV/g)
[3]	7.2	1.49 at resonance
[4]	6	299.2 at resonance
[8]	6.26	1.2
[9]	23.50	0.24
This work (Circular Annular Structure)	14.54	3.22 100 Hz and 676.14 at resonance
This work (Trampoline Structure)	13.50	4.39 100 Hz and 3200.1 at resonance

4   Conclusions

Optimization of the piezoelectric accelerometer is vital important to obtain the maximum output voltage. In this paper design and optimization of the accelerometer structure are discussed. AlN film with thickness 3.6 μm is used for piezoelectric transduction. Both structures are symmetrical to reduce the cross sensitivity. The sensitivity is found to be 3.22 mV/g and 4.39 mV/g for circular annular structure and trampoline structure respectively. The comparison between this work and reported data is shown in Table 4

References

1. Liu, C.: Foundations of MEMS. Pearson Education India (2012)
2. Yaghootkar, B., Azimi, S., Bahreyni, B.: A high-performance piezoelectric vibration sensor. IEEE Sens. J. **17**(13), 4005–4012 (2017). https://doi.org/10.1109/JSEN. 2017.2707063
3. Chen, Z.H., et al.: The design of aluminum nitride-based lead-free piezoelectric MEMS accelerometer system. IEEE Trans. Electr. Devices **67**(10), 4399–4404 (2020). https://doi.org/10.1109/TED.2020.3019230
4. Zhang, L., Lu, J., Kuwashiro, S., Mitsue, M., Maeda, R.: Fabrication and evaluation of aluminum nitride based MEMS piezoelectric vibration sensors for large-amplitude vibration applications. Microsyst. Technol. **27**(1), 235–242 (2020). https://doi.org/ 10.1007/s00542-020-04941-3
5. Chauhan, S.S., Joglekar, M.M., Manhas, S.K.: High power density CMOS compatible micro-machined MEMs energy harvester. IEEE Sens. J. **19**(20), 9122–9130 (2019). https://doi.org/10.1109/JSEN.2019.2923972
6. Stephen, B., Graham, E., Michael, K., Neil, W.: MEMS Mechanical Sensors - Stephen Beeby
7. Wang, L.-P., Deng, K., Zou, L., Wolf, R., Davis, R.J., Trolier-Mckinstry, S.: Microelectromechanical Systems (MEMS) Accelerometers Using Lead Zirconate Titanate Thick Films (2002)

8. Trivedi, S., et al.: Piezoelectric MEMS vibration sensor module for machining quality prediction. In: 2020 IEEE Sensors. IEEE (2020)
9. Hindrichsen, C.C., et al.: Circular piezoelectric accelerometer for high band width application. In: SENSORS 2009 IEEE. IEEE (2009)

Low Loss Enabled Semi-superjunction 4H-SiC IGBT for High Voltage and Current Application

Mahesh Vaidya[1]($\boxtimes$) (ID), Alok Naugarhiya[2] (ID), Shrish Verma[2] (ID), and Guru Prasad Mishra[2] (ID)

[1] Department of ECE, Koneru Lakshmaiah Education Foundation, Vaddeswaram, AP, India
dr.maheshvaidya@gmail.com

[2] Department of ECE, National Institute of Technology Raipur, Raipur, Chhattisgarh, India
{anaugarhiya.etc,shrishverma,gpscmishra.etc}@nitrr.ac.in

Abstract. In this article, the new collector side Semi-Superjunction (Semi-SJ) concept has been explored for the first time in 4H-SiC insulated gate bipolar transistors (IGBT). The additional x-directional electric field component, which was not present in the conventional structure has been incorporated at the collector side of the proposed structure by formation of Semi-SJ region. The stacking of n and p-pillar creates the Semi-SJ region at the bottom side of the 4H-SiC IGBT. The two dimensional electric field component, i.e E_X and E_Y increases the overall electric field component in the proposed structure, and offers high breakdown voltage (BV) as compared to the conventional 4H-SiC IGBT. The proposed design offers 11% improvement in BV as compared to conventional one with supporting ability of about more than 15kV. The Semi-SJ section also supports the high doping concentration resulting huge rise in current handling ability. Furthermore, the Semi-SJ region also provides the charge coupling effect, which pulls down the mobile charge carriers from the drift region. This effect reduces the tail current by minimizing turn-off time and reduces the turn-off loss significantly. The proposed device offers 25% reduction in turn-off time in comparison with conventional design.

Keywords: IGBT · 4H-SiC · Energy loss · Breakdown voltage · On-state voltage

1 Introduction

The Silicon (Si) based power devices have reached to its saturation limit and experiencing difficulties to fulfill the requirement of the power electronics industry. The basic limitation of these Si-power devices are frequency and operating temperature. The excellent physical and electrical properties of Silicon Carbide

Supported by organization National Institute of Technology Raipur.

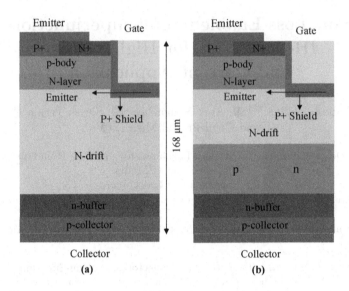

Fig. 1. Device structure (a) Conventional Trench 4H-SiC IGBT (b) Semi-SJ Trench 4H-SiC IGBT.

(SiC) such as high critical electric field, high carrier saturation velocity, high thermal conductivity makes it very effective material for future power devices [1]. The first SiC power diode has been commercialized in 2014 [2]. Furthermore, the planer and trench gate SiC-MOSFET came in to the market in 2011 and 2015, respectively [3,4]. But, due to the fabrication complexity, the SiC IGBT has not been commercialized yet. The p-channel IGBT was first time fabricated in 1996 due to the easily availability of low resistance n^+-substrate [5]. The p-channel IGBT has been studied extensively till 2010 due to immature n-channel SiC IGBT fabrication technology. In 2010, the free-standing technology provides the impressive option to fabricate n-channel SiC-IGBT [6]. After this development, an enormous research is being going on to improve the performance parameters of the 4H-SiC IGBT. The SiC IGBT shows excellent electrical characteristic of high blocking voltage, operating temperature range along with impressive current handling ability as compared to the Si-IGBT. The Si-IGBT is able to block the maximum voltage of about 8.4 kV [7], which has been increased to 27 kV in case of SiC IGBT [8]. The another key parameter other than the BV is turn-off loss. The IGBT suffers from the poor turn-off capability due to large tail current, which increases the turn-off loss [9]. To address this issue lots of development has also been done in Si-IGBT [10–16]. The same efforts have also been given for the improvement of 4H-SiC IGBT.

The numerous research has been going on for the development of the 4H-SiC IGBT [1,17–26]. The 15 kV symmetric and asymmetric 4H-SiC IGBT's performance have been observed to optimize the trade-off between E_{off} and V_{on} [18]. The CEL layer has been used to reduce the V_{on}. On the other hand authors stated that the buffer region specifications are the key parameters for better frequency

Table 1. Material properties considered for the simulation [17]

Parameters	Value	Discription
E_{G300} (eV)	3.24	Energy gap at 300k
$E_{G(ALPHA)}$ (eV/k)	4.15×10^{-4}	Bandgap model
$E_{G(BETA)}$ (eV/k)	-131	Bandgap model
Permittivity	9.7	Permittivity
Affinity	4.2	Affinity
AUGN (cm^6/s)	5×10^{-32}	Electrons' auger recombination rate
AUGN (cm^6/s)	2×10^{-32}	Holes' auger recombination rate
E_{ab} (eV)	0.2	Acceptor energy level
E_{ab} (eV)	0.1	Donor energy level
G_{vb} (eV)	4	Valance band degeneracy factor
G_{cb} (eV)	2	Conduction band degeneracy factor
LT.TAUN	5	Model for electrons lifetime
LT.TAUP	5	Model for holes lifetime
N_{srhn} (cm^{-3})	3×10^{17}	Concentration dependent SRH lifetime model for electrons
N_{srhp} (cm^{-3})	3×10^{17}	Concentration dependent SRH lifetime model for holes
ARICHN ($A/K^2 cm^2$)	110	Effective Richardson constant for electrons
ARICHP ($A/K^2 cm^2$)	30	Effective Richardson constant for holes

response in case of asymmetric IGBT, while p-substrate doping and drift region lifetime are the key factors for maximum frequency response in symmetric IGBT. The another article published by Sung et al. used the p-buried layer to reduce the saturation current of the 4H-SiC IGBT, which is essential for better short circuit capability. The strong short circuit ability has been obtained at the cost of large value of V_{on} [19]. Furthermore, in 2014, the detailed analysis of 4H-SiC n-IGBT has been carried out to obtained optimized results. The performance of the device has been observed with drift doping thickness and the carrier lifetime. At last Usman et al. stated that to block the 20 kV voltage, 175 μm thick drift region is needed with the doping concentration of about 2×10^{15} cm^{-3} with 1 μs minority carrier lifetime. In 2014, the 4H-SiC n-IGBT first time fabricated with the blocking capability of the 22 kV. To enhance the carrier lifetime, thermal oxidation process has been used, which offers the low V_{on} by enhancing the conductivity modulation [21]. Furthermore, to reduce the turn-off loss, Liu et al. proposed a new IGBT with backside n-p-n collector. The author shows almost 83% improvement in E_{off} with small degradation in V_{on} [22]. However, the another structure proposed by Liu et al. used a Schottky contact at the collector side which offer 84% turn-off loss at same value of V_{on} by provide fast electron extractor path to turn-off the device quickly [17]. The diode clamped p-shield region has been provided to protect the oxide region in 4H-SiC IGBT. This technique provide the conductivity modulation in order to reduce the V_{on} with fast switching ability [23]. In 2019, a new depletion controlled structure (DCS) 6.5 kV class 4H-SiC IGBT has been fabricated to achieve better switching ability. The fabricated device offers 17.6 mJ turn-off loss [24]. The trench collector heterojunction structure has been proposed by Wang et al. in 2020 [25]. The effective path to discharge the charge carrier has been used by the 4H-SiC IGBT in order to reduce the E_{off} by 76.4%. Moreover, in 2020 the on-state limitation of the 4H-SiC IGBT has been shown first time by Luo et al. with the help of TCAD simulation. The device with the conductivity modulation effect, authors stated that the Si-IGBT shows the superior performance as compared to the 4H-SiC IGBT [26]. The latest article published in 2021 shows the extensive review of SiC IGBT devices by Han et al. over the period of 30 years. The authors stated that due to the immature fabrication technology and intrinsic defects the SiC IGBT is not yet commercialized [1].

The very small contribution have been made till now in Superjunction (SJ) concept due to its complex simulation and fabrication technology. So, it can be a tremendous approach to emphasise on Semi-SJ concept to improve power rating of the 4H-SiC IGBT, which has not been explored yet. In this article, the simulation based detailed analysis about the Semi-SJ 4H-SiC IGBT is being investigated and its characteristics is also been compared with the conventional structure.

2   Structure and Mechanism

The Fig. 1 shows the conventional and proposed 4H-SiC IGBT. The half cell-pitch length and epitaxial length of both the structures are same, i.e., 2.1 µm and 168 µm, respectively. The proposed structure consists of the collector side Semi-SJ region in the drift region. The concentration of the simple drift portion of the proposed and the conventional SiC IGBT drift region is taken same of about 4.5×10^{14} cm^{-3}. Furthermore, to protect the device with immature breakdown even due to oxide and SiC interface charges, the P^+ shielding layer has been included below the gate terminal in both conventional and proposed 4H-SiC IGBT. Apart from the Semi-SJ portion, the other physical dimensions and doping of the proposed structures have been taken same as that of the conventional one in order to maintain the comparability. For the comparison and validation of the simulation environment the conventional structure presented in [17] have been simulated with the material and mobility based properties mentioned in the article. These properties are also mentioned in the table.

Figure 1(a-b) shows the conventional and proposed Semi-SJ 4H-SiC IGBT. The length and the doping of collector side Semi-SJ region selected such that the device offers at least 11% improvement in the breakdown voltage. The Semi-SJ region introduce the x-directional electric field which was absent in the normal drift arrangement. The presence of x and y-directional electric field increases the overall electric field profile and provides the higher BV in comparison with conventional IGBT. Furthermore, the Semi-SJ region supports higher doping

Table 2. Anisotropic mobility model for the simulation [17]

Parameters	Unit	Values
mu1n.caug	cm^2/V s	40
mu2n.caug	cm^2/V s	950
Ncritn.caug	cm^{-3}	2×10^{17}
deltan.caug	arbitrary	0.73
gamman.caug	arbitrary	-0.76
alphan.caug	arbitrary	0
betan.caug	arbitrary	-2.4
mu1p.caug	cm^2/V s	53.3
mu2p.caug	cm^2/V s	105.4
Ncritp.caug	cm^{-3}	2.2×10^{18}
deltap.caug	arbitrary	0.7
gammap.caug	arbitrary	0
alphap.caug	arbitrary	0
betap.caug	arbitrary	-2.1
vsatn	cm^2/s	2×10^7
vsatp	cm^2/s	2×10^7
betan	—	2
betap	—	1

concentration in the epitaxial region and reduces resistivity of the device result-ing enable the device to sustain high saturation current flows through the drift region. The presence of Semi-SJ portion on the collector side also yield the charge coupling effect and enable the fast charge extraction path to the device in order to turn-off early. This effect may also reduces the turn-off loss. The concept explained here is also validated with the simulation result discussed in next section.

3   Results and Analysis

In this section we have performed the simulation and the comparison analysis between the conventional and proposed Semi-SJ 4H-SiC IGBT. The simulation is performed with the help of SILVACO's ATLAS tool calibrated with the vari-ous physics based models like; AUGER, SRH, CONMOB, FLDMOB BGN etc. along with the material and mobility based property mentioned in the Tables 1-2. To evaluate the breakdown effect the anisotropic impact ionization effect has also been considered for the simulation. However, setting the simulation envi-ronment for the of SiC device is more critical than the Silicon based device due to numerical solution difficulties. The normal Silicon based device can run on

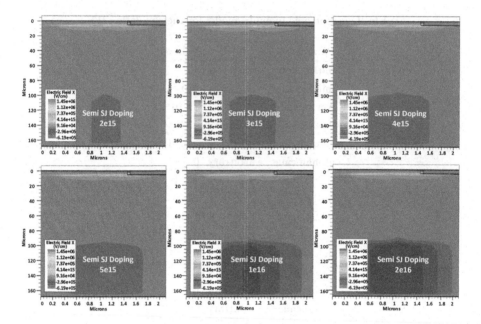

Fig. 2. Impact of the variation of Semi-SJ doping concentration on x-directional electric field.

the Silvaco's ATLAS on normal 64-bit precision environment. But, in this mode, the simulation for SiC device shows the convergence issue. So, atleast 128-bit precision is required to set the simulation environment of SiC IGBT [17].

The effect of variation of the Semi-SJ doping profile and Semi-SJ length with respect to the breakdown voltage and collector current characteristics is discussed here. The doping concentration of the drift region has been varied from 2×10^{15} to 2×10^{16}. The electric field inside the drift region rises as we increase the doping concentration of the Semi-SJ region, which is shown in Fig. 3(a). This behavior has been seen in the drift region because of the impression of depletion effectiveness, which is shown in Fig. 2. This effect of electric field increases the breakdown voltage of the device the same has been observed in Fig. 4. Similarly, the effect of increase in the concentration with respect to collector current density is also been shown in Fig. 3(b) with fixed Semi-SJ length, which does not show significant influence on it. The reason behind this is unable to significantly reduce the area specific on-resistance (R_{on}) due to the fixed length of the Semi-SJ region as well as low intrinsic concentration profile of 4H-SiC. The depletion region of p-n pillar increases in on-state mode with increase in collector potential as the 4H-SiC material is having low intrinsic profile. This results in negligible variation in the current density.

However, the effect of variation in Semi-SJ length shows the noteworthy influence on both the parameter; BV and collector current density, which is shown in Fig. 5(a-b). The increase in the length of the Semi-SJ increases the depletion effect and provide smooth potential distribution through out the drift

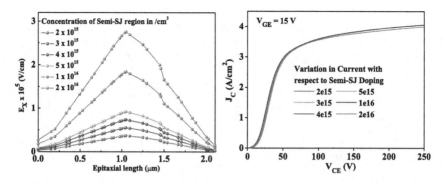

Fig. 3. Impact of the variation of Semi-SJ doping concentration on (a) x-directional electric field (b) Collector current.

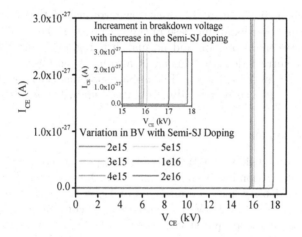

Fig. 4. Impact of the variation of Semi-SJ doping concentration with fixed Semi-SJ length on Breakdown Voltage

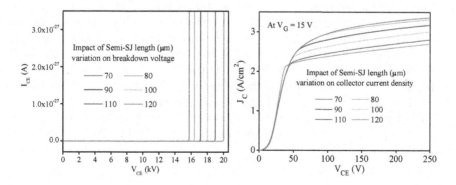

Fig. 5. Impact of the variation of Semi-SJ length on (a) Breakdown Voltage (b) Collector Current.

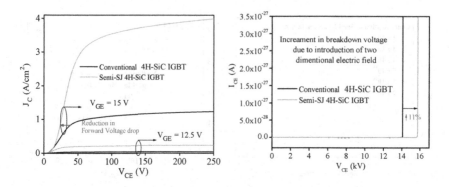

Fig. 6. Static performance comparison (a) Collector current Density (b) Breakdown voltage.

region resulting in increase in the breakdown voltage of the device shown in Fig. 5(a). On the other hand, increase in the thickness of the Semi-SJ affect the aspect ratio between SJ portion and normal drift region resulting in reduction of the collector current density. This effect also has been observed in Fig. 5(b). So, for the further analysis, the small Semi-SJ region has been considered which can provide the better current handling ability along with increased BV.

3.1   Static Analysis

To observe the static behavior of the IGBT the output current density and breakdown voltage comparison has been performed, which is shown in Fig. 6(a-b). The collector current density has been analyzed at $V_G = 12.5$ V and $V_G = 15$ V and plotted for the $V_{CE} = 0 - 250$ V. In comparison to conventional structure, the Semi-SJ portion of the proposed device supports higher concentration which reduces the R_{on}. This effect results in conductivity modulation by crowding of the charges in to the drift region and enhances the current density of the proposed device, which has also been clearly observed from Fig. 6(a). Moreover, the improvement in breakdown voltage is observed from Fig. 6(b). To observed the breakdown voltage characteristics, the avalanche multiplication effect has been observed in off-state, i.e., $V_G = 0$ V. Furthermore, the collector voltage increase linearly till the BV. Because of the involvement of two dimensional electric field, the overall electric field inside the drift region has been increased in the proposed device caused by the presence of Semi-SJ region. This impact of the electric field the equally distributed the potential profile inside the drift region and allows the proposed device to sustain large voltage along the epitaxial length. The proposed structure is able to improve the BV by 11% in comparison with conventional IGBT.

3.2   Transient Analysis

In this section, the transient performance of conventional and Semi-SJ 4H-SiC design have been examined, which is shown in Fig. 7. The device has been tested

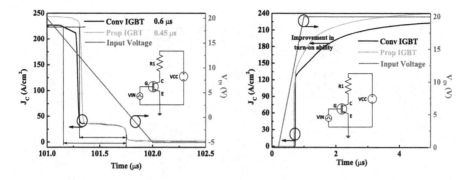

Fig. 7. Transient behavior comparison at resistive load (a) Turn-off comparison (b) Turn-on comparison.

with the help of resistive load circuit shown in inset of Fig. 7. The conventional SiC-IGBT suffer with the poor turn-off ability due to the large tail current during the transition from on-to-off state. The presence of Semi-SJ section in the proposed device offers the charge coupling effect with high electric field. The presence of high electric field extract the mobile charges quickly and all the mobile charges swept out early in on-to-off transition. This effect reduces the tail current and minimized the turn-off time by 25% in comparison with the conventional 4H-SiC IGBT. This reduction in the turn-off time may also reduces the turn-off energy loss during this transition and provide the alternative option with improved performance for low loss application. Furthermore, the turn-on ability has also been investigated and compared with the conventional 4H-SiC IGBT shown in Fig. 7(b). The presence of Sem-SJ section in the drift region provides the electric field and attract the charges in the channel leads to quickly turn-on behavior. So, the better turn-on and turn-off ability makes the proposed device to prefer in switching application where high voltage handling ability is being required.

4   Possible Fabrication Steps

The complications of the n-channel 4H-SiC IGBT has been overcome by the introduction of the free-standing technology proposed by Cooper in 2010 [6]. Figure shows the possible fabrication steps for the proposed SiC IGBT. The inverted growth process has been used for the fabrication process, which allows to grow all the critical layers. The process starts with the n-type substrate, over which low-basal-plane-defect (LBPD) template layer and a standard $1\,\mu$m n^{+} buffer layer is to be grown on the Si-face. Furthermore, the n-drift region is to be grown epitaxially. Over this n-drift region, the high doped n pillar is to be grown with the help of multi-epitaxial growth technique. In this n-pillars the Al implantation done at multiple time in order with suitable concentration to get charge balancing [27]. After formation of n-p pillars, the $1\,\mu$m n-buffer region

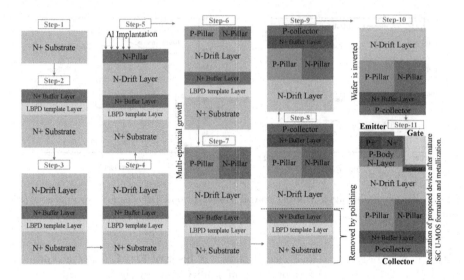

Fig. 8. Possible fabrication steps for Proposed Semi-SJ 4H-SiC IGBT.

and p-collector is to be grown epitaxially. Furthermore, the n^+ substrate, LBPD layer, and n^+ buffer layer then have to be removed by polishing at NovaSiC, and the wafer is inverted, with the p^+ collector at the bottom and the n-drift layer at the top. Above the n-drift region, finally the MOS portion can be created by the mature SiC UMOSFET process followed by the metallization process. These process steps have been shown in figure below (Fig. 8).

5   Conclusion

The Semi-SJ 4H-SiC IGBT has been investigated and compared with conventional 4H-SiC IGBT. The introduction of Semi-SJ region by arranging n-p pillars in stacking manner has been done at the collector side. This Semi-SJ region provides additional x-directional electric field component and increases the overall electric field, i.e. $E = \sqrt{E_X^2 + E_Y^2}$. This E_X component was not present in conventional drift structure. This rise in electric field increases the breakdown voltage of the proposed device by 11% in comparison with conventional structure. The Semi-SJ region also supports the high concentration profile in it and reduces the resistivity of the proposed design. This reduction in the resistivity dynamically increases the current handling capacity of the proposed device. The proposed Semi-SJ technique also enables the charge coupling effect at the bottom side of the devices resulting in high electric field in the interface of the pillars. The charges present in the drift region experiences these field and easily swept out from the region resulting reduction in tail current. This reduction in tail current minimizes the turn-off time and make the device to turn-off quickly in comparison with conventional structure. The proposed device offers 25% improvement in the turn-off time, which may also leads to reduce the turn-off loss. With the above advantages the proposed Semi-SJ 4H-SiC IGBT shows its expediency for the high voltage and current application.

Acknowledgements. I want to express my sincere thanks to National Institute of technology Raipur for providing the support to this research.

References

1. Han, L., Liang, L., Kang, Y., Qiu, Y.: A review of SiC IGBT: models, fabrications, characteristics, and applications. IEEE Trans. Power Electron. **36**(2), 2080–2093 (2021)
2. Kimoto, T., Cooper, J.A.: Fundamentals of silicon carbide technology: growth, characterization, devices and applications. John Wiley Sons, (2014)
3. She, X., Huang, A.Q., Lucia, O., Ozpineci, B.: Review of silicon carbide power devices and their applications. IEEE Trans. Industr. Electron. **64**(10), 8193–8205 (2017)
4. R. Semiconductor, 1200 V/180 a full SiC powermodule with integrated SiC trench mosfet,(2015). https://www.rohm.com/documents/11421/3508791/58F6889E_SiCTrenchMOSFET_ss(EN).pdf
5. Ramungul, N., Chow, T., Ghezzo, M., Kretchmer, J., Hennessy, W.: A fully planarized, 6H-SiC UMOS insulated-gate bipolar transistor. In: 54th Annual Device Research Conference Digest. IEEE Vol. 1996, pp. 56–57 (1996)
6. Wang, X., Cooper, J.A.: High-voltage n-channel IGBTs on free-standing 4H-SiC epilayers. IEEE Trans. Electron Devices **57**(2), 511–515 (2010)
7. Rahimo, M., et al.: Extending the boundary limits of high voltage IGBTs and diodes to above 8 kV. In: Proceedings of the 14th International Symposium on Power Semiconductor Devices and ICs. IEEE, pp. 41–44 (2002)
8. Van Brunt, E.: 27 kV, 20 a 4H-SiC n-IGBTs. In: Mater. Sci. Forum. Trans. Tech. Publ. **821–823**, 847–850 (2015)
9. Baliga, B.J.: The IGBT device: physics, design and applications of the insulated gate bipolar transistor. William Andrew (2015)
10. Chen, W., Cheng, J., Huang, H., Zhang, B., Chen, X.B.: The oppositely doped islands IGBT achieving ultralow turn off loss. IEEE Trans. Electr. Devices **66**(8), 3690–3693 (2019)
11. Vaidya, M., Naugarhiya, A., Verma, S.: Trench IGBT with stepped doped collector for low energy loss. Semicond. Sci. Technol. **35**(2), 025015 (2020)
12. Chen, W., Cheng, J., Chen, X.B.: A novel IGBT with high-k dielectric modulation achieving ultralow turn-off loss. IEEE Trans. Electron Devices **67**(3), 1066–1070 (2020)
13. Vaidya, M., Naugarhiya, A., Verma, S., Mishra, G.P.: Lateral variation-doped insulated gate bipolar transistor for low on-state voltage with low loss. IEEE Electr. Device Lett. **41**(6), 888–891 (2020)
14. Vaidya, M., Naugarhiya, A., Verma, S., Mishra, G.P.: A low-loss variable-doped trench-insulated gate bipolar transistor with reduced on-state voltage. Semicond. Sci. Technol. **36**(7), 075002 (2021)
15. Wei, J., Zhang, S., Luo, X., Fan, D., Zhang, B.: Low switching loss and EMI noise IGBT with self-adaptive hole-extracting path. IEEE Trans. Electron Devices **68**(5), 2572–2576 (2021)

16. Vaidya, M., Naugarhiya, A., Verma, S., Mishra, G.P.: Collector engineered bidirectional insulated gate bipolar transistor with low loss. IEEE Trans. Electr. Devices **69**(3), 1604–1607 (2022)

17. Liu, Y.-J., Wang, Y., Hao, Y., Fang, J.-P., Shan, C., Cao, F.: A low turn-off loss 4H-SiC trench IGBT with schottky contact in the collector side. IEEE Trans. Electr. Devices **64**(11), 4575–4580 (2017)

18. Sung, W., Wang, J., Huang, A.Q., Baliga, B.J.: Design and investigation of frequency capability of 15kV 4H-SiC IGBT. In: 21st International Symposium on Power Semiconductor Devices IC's, vol. 2009, pp. 271–274. IEEE (2009)

19. Sung, W., Huang, A.Q., Baliga, B.J.: A novel 4H-SiC IGBT structure with improved trade-off between short circuit capability and on-state voltage drop. In: 22nd International Symposium on Power Semiconductor Devices IC's (ISPSD), vol. 2010, pp. 217–220. IEEE (2010)

20. Usman, M., Nawaz, M.: Device design assessment of 4H-SiC n-IGBT a simulation study. Solid-State Electron. **92**, 5–11 (2014)

21. Brunt, E., et al.: 22 kV, 1 cm 2, 4H-SiC n-IGBTs with improved conductivity modulation. In: IEEE 26th International Symposium on Power Semiconductor Devices IC's (ISPSD), vol. 2014, pp. 358–361. IEEE (2014)

22. Liu, Y.-J., Wang, Y., Hao, Y., Yu, C.-H., Cao, F.: 4H-SiC trench IGBT with backside n-p-n collector for low turn-off loss. IEEE Trans. Electron Devices **64**(2), 488–493 (2016)

23. Wei, J., et al.: SiC trench IGBT with diode-clamped p-shield for oxide protection and enhanced conductivity modulation. In: IEEE 30th International Symposium on Power Semiconductor Devices and ICs (ISPSD), vol. 2018, pp. 411–414. IEEE (2018)

24. Watanabe, N., Yoshimoto, H., Mori, Y., Shima, A.: Improvement of switching characteristics in 6.5-kv SiC IGBT with novel drift layer structure. Mater. Sci. Forum Trans. Tech. Publ. **963**, 660–665 (2019)

25. Wang, Y., et al.: Low turn-off loss 4H-SiC insulated gate bipolar transistor with a trench heterojunction collector. IEEE J. Electron Devices Soc. **8**, 1010–1015 (2020)

26. Luo, P., Madathil, S.N.E.: Theoretical analysis of on-state performance limit of 4H-SiC IGBT in field-stop technology. IEEE Trans. Electron Devices **67**(12), 5621–5627 (2020)

27. Kosugi, R., et al.: Development of SiC super-junction (SJ) devices by multi-epitaxial growth. In: Materials Science Forum, vol. 778, pp. 845–850 (2014). https://doi.org/10.4028/www.scientific.net/MSF.778-780.845

Implications of Field Plate HEMT Towards Power Performance at Microwave X - Band

Khushwant Sehra[1] ⓘ, Jeffin Shibu[2] ⓘ, Meena Mishra[3], Mridula Gupta[1] ⓘ,
D. S. Rawal[3] ⓘ, and Manoj Saxena[4(✉)] ⓘ

[1] Department of Electronic Science, University of Delhi South Campus, New Delhi, India
`ksehra@electronics.du.ac.in`, `mridula@south.du.ac.in`
[2] Department of Electrical Engineering, Indian Institute of Technology Palakkad, Palakkad,
India
`121801055@smail.iitpkd.ac.in`
[3] Solid State Physics Laboratory, Defence Research and Development Organization,
New Delhi, India
`{mishra.meena.sspl,ds-rawal.sspl}@gov.in`
[4] Department of Electronics, Deen Dayal Upadhyaya College, University of Delhi,
New Delhi, India
`msaxena@ddu.du.ac.in`

Abstract. This work investigates the implications of field plate architectures on the power performance of AlGaN/GaN HEMTs at Microwave X – Band. The spread of the output power across the unwanted harmonics is investigated for different field plate lengths and physical insights are drawn on the basis of GaN HEMT's intrinsic and extrinsic parameters. The analysis is based on DC and RF calibrated simulation decks realized in Silvaco's Atlas Tool. The comparisons drawn on the basis of P_{OUT} at fundamental, second, and third order harmonics reveal the trade – offs between the device breakdown and its linearity and distortion at the RF band.

Keywords: HEMT · Field plate · Breakdown · Intrinsic · Extrinsic

1 Introduction

GaN HEMTs on SiC have been a focus of primary research for various defence and space agencies due to their capability of achieving high – power for mm – Wave radar and satellite applications [1–4]. The commercialization of GaN HEMTs has observed tremendous progress in terms of various modifications to both the epi – layer stack [5–8] and gate geometries [5, 9, 10] for targeting specific applications. For applications concerning high voltage operation, field plate technology has been accepted as the most viable solution for addressing several reliability issues in GaN HEMTs including the premature breakdown of the device due to localized peak electric fields [11–13]. Accordingly, different types of field plate architectures have been proposed over the years in an attempt to redistribute the peak electric fields localized at the gate edge [14–16]. These architectures not only improve the device breakdown characteristics but are

© The Author(s), under exclusive license to Springer Nature Switzerland AG 2022
A. P. Shah et al. (Eds.): VDAT 2022, CCIS 1687, pp. 65–75, 2022.
https://doi.org/10.1007/978-3-031-21514-8_6

also proved to suppress the trap – related dispersive effects by suppression of the virtual gate formation [17]. This consequently improves the RF performance of the device as the trap related gate – lag and drain – lag phenomenon is significantly suppressed [17–20]. Apart from these advantages, the feedback capacitances associated with the field plate structures deteriorate the ON – state resistance (R_{ON}), device gain and also limit the frequency response [21–23].

Several field plate architectures have also been reported to terminate at the source electrode [19, 22–24] which limits the R_{ON} degradation while improving the breakdown characteristics. Further, in such architectures, the parasitic capacitance is translated into an increased drain – source capacitance (C_{DS}) which can be absorbed while designing the output matching networks. This methodology prevents an increase in gate – drain (C_{GD}) feedback capacitance and can be optimized to achieve a higher gain [25, 26] with modest trade – offs to R_{ON} [26]. In several other literature, drain side electric – field has also been manipulated by means of drain field plates or Schottky extensions for improved device performance [27–29]. Apart from these, combinations of both the gate and source terminated field plates, i.e., the dual field plates [22, 23, 29] have also been used extensively for a variety of applications including high power density and radiation hardened operation.

Apart from the architectures discussed above, several novel field plate architectures have been proposed and demonstrated experimentally. Bothe et al. [3] demonstrate an improved X – band performance using a variation of source connected field plate, where the field plate does not overlap the gate electrode. The authors report a significant improvement in the suppression of the parasitic capacitances (C_{GS} and C_{GD}), along with an improvement in P_{OUT} (10W/mm) and PAE (60% at $V_{DS} = 50$ V) over the conventional source connected field plates. In yet another work, Soni et al. [4] have put forward design guidelines for a vertical field plate connected to the drain electrode for a noteworthy improvement in device breakdown, power performance, and linearity over the conventional HEMT architectures.

The above discussions bring forth the fact that the field plate architectures are an essential part of GaN HEMT development for high power applications, and that there is an ever – increasing need for optimizing the device architectures for minimizing the design trade – offs. In this regard, the work done in this manuscript is focused towards providing a different perspective of analyzing the field plate HEMT architectures by correlating them with their intrinsic and extrinsic elements.

In this work, the small-signal parameters of a Field Plate AlGaN/GaN HEMT are investigated for different field plate (FP) lengths. An attempt is made to provide a correlation between the intrinsic parameters and the power dissipated across the unwanted harmonics. This paper is structured as follows. Section 2 gives details regarding the device architecture and its modeling framework using Silvaco's TCAD Tools. Section 3 gives an optimization flow of the field plate length with regards to the impact on the DC characteristics whilst investigating the power spread across the unwanted harmonics. Finally, Sect. 4 summarizes the findings of this work.

2 Device Architecture and TCAD Methodology

This section gives details about the device architecture and the simulation framework adopted to model the experimental device through TCAD simulations.

2.1 Device Architecture

The device architecture analyzed in this work is a 1×200 μm Conventional AlGaN/GaN HEMT having a gate length (L_G) of 0.25 μm. The epi layer stack over the SiC substrate consists of a 1.7 μm Fe – doped GaN buffer with a 5 nm GaN channel layer. This is followed by a 22 nm AlGaN barrier layer with $\chi_{Al} = 0.25$. This is supported by a 3 nm GaN cap layer and surface passivation by 50 nm Silicon Nitride (SiN_x). The access regions between gate – source (L_{GS}) and gate – drain (L_{GD}) is 0.8 μm and 2.7 μm, respectively. The device dimensions are adapted from Raja et al. [30]. The device schematic is shown in Fig. 1(a) for reference. Also embedded is the Small Signal Equivalent Circuit (SSEC) representation of the AlGaN/GaN HEMT adapted from Dambrine et al. [31].

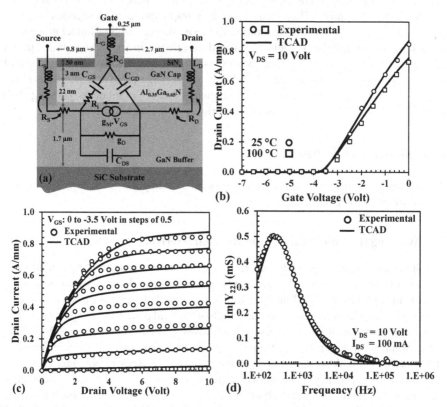

Fig. 1. (a) Schematic of the AlGaN/GaN HEMT along with its SSEC representation, Calibration of (b) transfer characteristics at 25 °C and 100 °C (c) output characteristics for V_{GS} −3.5 to 0 V (d) Im(Y_{22}) parameter. Experimental data were taken from Raja et al. [30].

2.2 TCAD Simulation Methodology

This work relies on Silvaco's 2D Device Simulator Tool, Atlas [32] for carrying out all the numerical simulations. The simulation deck has been calibrated to ensure the device simulations follow experimental behavior. In this regard, validation is performed with regard to the experimental data obtained from Raja et al. [30]. To capture the interactions between the carriers and trapping states in and between the different epilayers, Shockley-Reed-Hall (SRH) recombination model was invoked along with fermi to model the carrier statistics. The Fe – doped buffer was realized with the help of acceptor type traps with a trap density of 5×10^{16} cm^{-3} and an energy level of 0.462 eV. The energy level was tuned from the standard value of 0.5 eV [30] to tune the output admittance parameters and the OFF – state current [30, 33, 34]. The capture cross sections were set as 7×10^{-17} cm^2 and 1×10^{-20} cm^2 for electrons and holes, respectively in accordance with several experimental reports [30, 33, 34]. Further, Ibbetson et al. [35] theorize and experimentally demonstrate the existence of surface states to support the 2DEG at the AlGaN/GaN heterointerface. Accordingly, donor like surface states, characterized by an energy level of 0.5 eV and density of 2×10^{13} cm^{-2} were defined at the interface of SiN$_x$/GaN – cap layer. The electron and hole trap capture cross sections were set to 1×10^{-15} cm^2 [30, 33, 34]. In addition to these, the polarization model along with low and high field mobility models were tuned to calibrate the maximum drain current (I_{DS}), pinch – off voltage (V_{TH}), and the ON – state resistance (R_{ON}). A comparison of the resulting transfer characteristics (I_{DS}–V_{GS}) in Fig. 1(b), output characteristics (I_{DS}–V_{DS}) in Fig. 1(c), and output admittance parameters (Im(Y_{22}) - Frequency) in Fig. 1(d) with the experimental data [30] confirm the validity of the approach.

3   Results and Discussions

This section gives insights into the various aspects of field plate technology on both the DC and RF power performance.

3.1   Assessing the Impact on DC and RF Characteristics

A preliminary investigation of the device is carried out by incorporating a field plate connected to the Gate electrode. The calibrated simulation deck acts as a primer for realizing the Field Plate HEMT architecture. In this regard, the gate electrode is extended by a length L$_{FP}$, which characterizes the length of the field plate from the gate edge. The impact of L$_{FP}$ on the OFF – State device breakdown recorded at a $V_{GS} = -6$ V and $I_{DS} = 1$ mA/mm is shown in Fig. 2. Here, L$_{FP} = 0$ μm corresponds to the Conventional HEMT architecture. Also shown is the deterioration in the device operating frequency, i.e., the cut – off frequency (f$_T$) measured at the V_{GS} where maximum transconductance (g$_{m,max}$) is recorded. The trend observed in Fig. 2 is fundamental to the field plate architecture already reported in the literature [14–16, 22, 23]. The increase in field plate length results in a redistribution of peak electric fields, which otherwise are localized at the gate edge towards the drain electrode. This results in an improvement in the OFF – state breakdown voltage at the cost of an increased gate – drain capacitance which consequently deteriorates the device gain [25, 26]. This methodology is often used in order to optimize the field plate lengths to maximize the OFF – state breakdown voltage whilst inflicting modest trade – offs to the device gain.

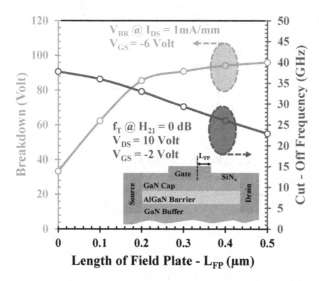

Fig. 2. Impact of field plate architecture on the DC and RF Characteristics of the DUT.

3.2 Correlation with Intrinsic and Extrinsic Parameters

In order to gain astute observations in the RF regime with field plate technology, intrinsic parameters of GaN HEMTs are investigated. The S - parameters are recorded in a frequency range of 500 MHz to 50 GHz for 35 different bias combinations (V_{GS}: -1 to -7 V and V_{DS}: 2–10 V) at 5 different Gate FP lengths (L_{FP}: 0.1–0.5 μm).

The bias dependent intrinsic parameters are extracted after stripping off the extrinsic parameters (bias - independent) from the admittance matrix following the methodology proposed by Dambrine et al. [31]. In order to better suit the theme of this work, the extrinsic parameters (or extrinsic resistances) are depicted in Fig. 3. Since the only modification in the device architecture is an increase in the field plate length (L_{FP}), it translates into an increased gate resistance (R_G) as shown in Fig. 3. The resistance associated with the remaining terminals, however, remains unaffected to a large extent with L_{FP}.

The intrinsic gate – drain capacitance (C_{GD}), gate – source capacitance (C_{GS}), gate – source charging resistance (R_i), and transit delay time (τ) as a function of field plate length (L_{FP}) under ON - state ($V_{DS} = 10$ V and $V_{GS} = -1$ V) and OFF - state ($V_{DS} = 10$ V and $V_{GS} = -7$ V) conditions are shown in Fig. 4(a–d), respectively. The increase in intrinsic capacitances (Fig. 4(a, b)) can be attributed to the increased coupling and fringing fields with the L_{FP} between the involved terminals. This is consequently responsible for the roll – off in the device cut off frequency (f_T) with increasing L_{FP}. Further, since R_i models

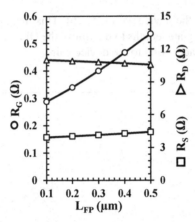

Fig. 3. Extrinsic parameters: R_G, R_D, and R_S for different field plate lengths (L_{FP}).

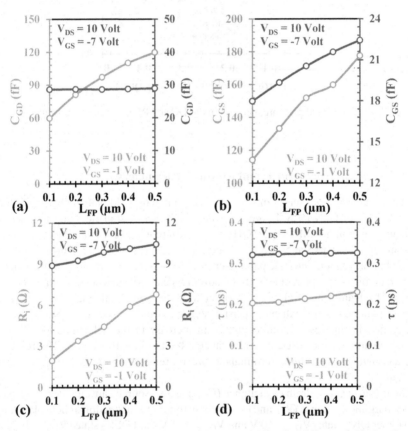

Fig. 4. Intrinsic parameters: (a) C_{GD} (b) C_{GS} (c) R_i and (d) τ for different field plate lengths (L_{FP}).

the undepleted gate channel, the increase in R_i with L_{FP} points towards an improved gate action by virtue of the passivation layer. This improvement has a direct consequence on the delay time (τ) which increases marginally with increasing L_{FP}. The investigation into the intrinsic elements of an FP HEMT gives insights into the optimization of the device architecture for high – power applications.

3.3 Impact on RF Power Performance

The device architectures investigated above are further analyzed for RF power performance. The investigation is carried out using Silvaco [32], and the output and input terminals are matched to 50 Ω Impedance. The field plate technology is widely accepted for high power applications since it gives room for operating the devices at higher voltages. This is best utilized when the devices are biased for Class AB operation. The Class AB operation is more appropriate for higher efficiencies at the cost of signal linearity. Nonetheless, this work gives a correlation towards the power spread across the unwanted harmonics across different field plate lengths (L_{FP}). The analysis is carried out at X – band ($f_0 = 8$ GHz) and the devices are deliberately biased at a $V_{DS} = 10$ V in order to maintain uniformity across the analyzed devices. The choice for $V_{DS} = 10$ V is as per the industry standard which limits the voltage rails at about $1/3^{rd}$ of the OFF – state breakdown for power analysis [36, 37]. The gate bias is configured for $I_{DS} = 100$ mA/mm to support Class AB operation.

The power metrics associated with the DUTs are summarized in Fig. 5. The shaded region in Fig. 5(a–e) represents the roll – off of the associated metrics when the field plate length (L_{FP}) is increased from 0.1 to 0.5 μm. The decrease in P_{OUT} at f_0 (Fig. 5(a)) can be attributed to the reduced $I_{D(Max)}$ as the L_{FP} is increased. This can be countered by increasing the voltage rails for drain bias within the industry specified limit, which for $L_{FP} = 0.5$ μm is identified to be 32 V (Fig. 2). This however limits the conversion efficiency of the Power Amplifier (PA), as the input DC power supply is increased. The fall in P_{OUT} at f_0 can be linked to the increase in both R_G (Fig. 3), and R_i (Fig. 4(c)) with L_{FP}. The decrease in Gain depicted in Fig. 5(b) can be correlated to the capacitance that stems due to the interaction between the field plate extension and the 2DEG at the AlGaN/GaN heterointerface. This capacitance translates to an increased gate – drain capacitance (C_{GD}) as visualized from the intrinsic plots of C_{GD} as a function of L_{FP} in Fig. 4(a). Since, PAE is dependent upon the P_{OUT} at f_0, the roll – off in PAE is indirectly dependent upon the R_G and R_i as discussed above.

A superficial look into the spread of P_{OUT} at second [$2f_0$] and third harmonic [$3f_0$] observed in Fig. 5(d–e) points toward the improvement in both the linearity performance as well as lower intermodulation distortion. This also seems to be the case when the 1dB compression point (P_{1dB}) and Third Order Intercept (OIP_3) are analyzed in Fig. 5(f) for the different cases. However, it is to be noted, that the field plate device in essence sports a lower current compared to its conventional counterpart. When the device architecture is analyzed at a similar output power level by raising the supply voltage in field plate architectures, a higher amount of distortion and degradation in linearity can be inferred for the field plated devices. Thus, the power performance in field plate architectures comes at the cost of linearity and high distortion as depicted in Fig. 5. The correlation provided between the power metrics presented in Fig. 5 and the discussion with regard to the intrinsic and extrinsic parameters (Figs. 3 and 4) is useful for device engineers to optimize the field plate lengths whilst inflicting modest trade – offs to the power performance.

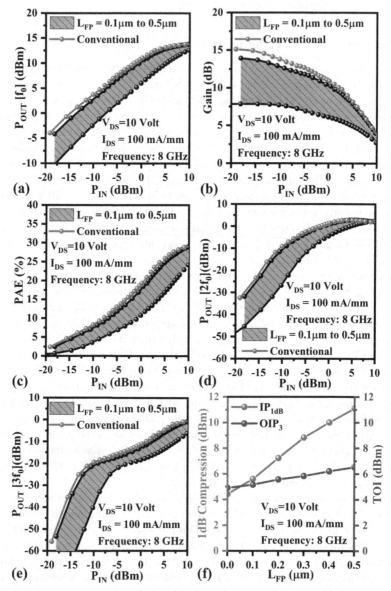

Fig. 5. Spread of (a) P_{OUT} [f_0], (b) Gain, (c) PAE, (d) P_{OUT} [$2f_0$], (e) P_{OUT} [$3f_0$] with L_{FP}, and (f) Impact of L_{FP} on IP_{1dB} and OIP_3 parameters.

4   Conclusions

The intrinsic and extrinsic parameters of a Conventional and Field Plate HEMT architecture have been investigated in this work for understanding the power performance of field plate devices at X – band. The comparisons demonstrate the increase in both the parasitic capacitances (C_{GS} and C_{GD}) as well as the parasitic resistances (R_i and R_G) to be the dominant cause for the roll – off observed in the power metrics. There is a clear trade – off between the length of the field plate which enables high power operation at the cost of linearity and distortion. The results presented gives a new insight into the operation of field plate HEMT architectures. The analysis presented can be extended to the novel field plate architectures for optimization not only using the breakdown – frequency or breakdown – R_{ON} trade – offs, but also from the perspective of the power spread across the unwanted harmonics.

Acknowledgement. The authors would like to acknowledge the Star Scheme Program funded by the Department of Biotechnology, Ministry of Science and Technology, Government of India at DDUC, DU; IASc – NASI SRFP 2021 Reg. No.: ENGS972; and DU IoE Grant Ref. No.: IoE/2021/12/FRP for providing the financial assistance. This work was also supported by Delhi University IoE Grant Ref. No. (IoE-DU/MRP/2022/056); Solid State Physics Laboratory (SSPL) CARS Project No.: 1115/TS/SPL/CARS-95/2022 funded by Defence Research & Development Organization (DRDO); and DST-SERB Project Ref. No.: SPG/2021/00306.

References

1. Trew, R. J., Shin, M. W., Gatto, V.: Wide bandgap semiconductor electronic devices for high frequency applications. In: IEEE Gallium Arsenide Integrated Circuit Symposium, pp. 6–9 (1996). https://doi.org/10.1109/GAAS.1996.567625
2. Nguyen, C., et al.: GaN HFET technology for RF applications. In: IEEE Gallium Arsenide Integrated Circuits Symposium, cat. no. 00CH37084, pp. 11–14 (2000). https://doi.org/10.1109/GAAS.2000.906263
3. Bother, K.M., et al.: Improved X-Band performance and reliability of a GaN HEMT with sunken source connected field plate design. IEEE Electron Device Lett. **43**(3), 354–357 (2022). https://doi.org/10.1109/LED.2022.3146194
4. Soni, A., Ajay, Shrivastava, M.: Novel drain-connected field plate GaN HEMT designs for improved V_{BD}–R_{ON} tradeoff and RF PA performance. IEEE Trans. Electron Devices. **67**(4), 1718–1725 (2020). https://doi.org/10.1109/TED.2020.2976636
5. Sehra, K., Kumari, V., Gupta, M., Mishra, M., Rawal, D.S., Saxena, M.: A Π-shaped p-GaN HEMT for reliable enhancement mode operation. Microelectron. Reliab. **133**(114544), 1–14 (2022). https://doi.org/10.1016/j.microrel.2022.114544
6. Chen, J., et al.: Decoupling of forward and reverse turn-on threshold voltages in Schottky-type p-GaN gate HEMTs. IEEE Electron Device Lett. **42**(7), 986–989 (2021). https://doi.org/10.1109/LED.2021.3077081
7. Wang, Y., Hu, S., Guo, J., Wu, H., Liu, T., Jiang, J.: Enhancement of breakdown voltage in p-GaN gate AlGaN/GaN HEMTs with a stepped hybrid GaN/AlN buffer layer. IEEE J. Electron Devices Soc. **10**, 197–202 (2022). https://doi.org/10.1109/JEDS.2022.3145797
8. Chen, D., et al.: Microwave performance of 'buffer-free' GaN-on-SiC high electron mobility transistors. IEEE Electron Device Lett. **41**(6), 828–831 (2020). https://doi.org/10.1109/LED.2020.2988074

9. Verma, M., Nandi, A.: GaN based trigate HEMT with AlGaN back—barrier layer: proposal and investigation. Semicond. Sci. Technol. **37**(6), 1–7 (2022). https://doi.org/10.1088/1361-6641/ac6970

10. Rey, A.D.L., Albrecht, J.D., Saraniti, M.: A Π-shaped gate design for reducing hot-electron generation in GaN HEMTs. IEEE Trans. Electron Devices **65**(10), 4263–4270 (2018). https://doi.org/10.1109/TED.2018.2863746

11. Wang, M., Chen, K.J.: Off-state breakdown characterization in AlGaN/GaN HEMT using drain injection technique. IEEE Trans. Electron Devices **57**(7), 1492–1496 (2010). https://doi.org/10.1109/TED.2010.2048960

12. Meneghesso, G., Meneghini, M., Zanoni, E.: Breakdown mechanism in AlGaN/GaN HEMTs: an overview. Jpn. J. Appl. Phys. **53**(10), 1–8 (2014). https://doi.org/10.7567/JJAP.53.100211

13. Yang, F., et al.: Study of drain injected breakdown mechanisms in AlGaN/GaN-on-SiC HEMTs. IEEE Trans. Electron Devices **69**(2), 525–530 (2022). https://doi.org/10.1109/TED.2021.3138841

14. Wong, J., et al.: Novel asymmetric slant field plate technology for high-speed low-dynamic Ron E/D-mode GaN HEMTs. IEEE Electron Device Lett. **38**(1), 95–98 (2017). https://doi.org/10.1109/LED.2016.2634528

15. Hasan, M.T., Asano, T., Tokuda, H., Kuzuhara, M.: Current collapse suppression by gate field-plate in AlGaN/GaN HEMTs. IEEE Electron Device Lett. **34**(11), 1379–1381 (2013). https://doi.org/10.1109/LED.2013.2280712

16. Wu, Y.-F., et al.: 30-W/mm GaN HEMTs by field plate optimization. IEEE Electron Device Lett. **25**(3), 117–119 (2004). https://doi.org/10.1109/LED.2003.822667

17. Brannick, A., Zakhleniuk, N.A., Ridley, B.K., Shealy, J.R., Schaff, W.J., Eastman, L.F.: Influence of field plate on the transient operation of the AlGaN/GaN HEMT. IEEE Electron Device Lett. **30**(5), 436–438 (2009). https://doi.org/10.1109/LED.2009.2016680

18. Saito, Y., Tsurumaki, R., Noda, N., Horio, K.: Analysis of reduction in lag phenomena and current collapse in field-plate AlGaN/GaN HEMTs with high acceptor density in a buffer layer. IEEE Trans. Device Mater. Reliab. **18**(1), 46–53 (2018). https://doi.org/10.1109/TDMR.2017.2779429

19. Saito, W., et al.: Field-plate structure dependence of current collapse phenomena in high-voltage GaN-HEMTs. IEEE Electron Device Lett. **31**(7), 659–661 (2010). https://doi.org/10.1109/LED.2010.2048741

20. Komoto, J., Saito, Y., Tsurumaki, R., Horio, K.: Analysis of slow – current transients or current collapse in AlGaN/GaN HEMTs with field plate and high – k passivation layer. Microelectron. Reliab. **134**(114552), 1–9 (2022). https://doi.org/10.1016/j.microrel.2022.114552

21. Karmalkar, S., Mishra, U.K.: Enhancement of breakdown voltage in AlGaN/GaN high electron mobility transistors using a field plate. IEEE Trans. Electron Devices **48**(8), 1515–1521 (2001). https://doi.org/10.1109/16.936500

22. Neha, Kumari, V., Gupta, M., Saxena, M.: TCAD – based optimization of field plate length & passivation layer of AlGaN/GaN HEMT for higher cut – off frequency & breakdown voltage. IETE Tech. Rev. **39**(1), 63–71 (2020). https://doi.org/10.1080/02564602.2020.1824624

23. Neha, Kumari, V., Gupta, M., Saxena, M.: Investigation of proton irradiated dual field plate AlGaN/GaN HEMTs: TCAD based assessment. Microelectron. J. **122**(105405), 1–8 (2022). https://doi.org/10.1016/j.mejo.2022.105405

24. Saito, W., et al.: Suppression of dynamic on-resistance increase and gate charge measurements in high-voltage GaN-HEMTs with optimized field-plate structure. IEEE Trans. Electron Devices **54**(8), 1825–1830 (2007). https://doi.org/10.1109/TED.2007.901150

25. Wu, Y.-F., More, M., Wisleder, T., Chavarkar, P.M., Misha, U.K., Parikh, P.: High-gain microwave GaN HEMTs with source-terminated field-plates. In: IEEE International Electron Devices Meeting, pp. 1078–1079 (2004). https://doi.org/10.1109/IEDM.2004.1419386

26. Saito, W., et al.: High breakdown voltage AlGaN-GaN power-HEMT design and high current density switching behavior. IEEE Trans. Electron Devices **50**(12), 2528–2531 (2003). https://doi.org/10.1109/TED.2003.819248

27. Lian, Y.-W., Lin, Y.-S., Lu, H.-C., Huang, Y.-C., Hsu, S.S.H.: AlGaN/GaN HEMTs on silicon with hybrid Schottky-ohmic drain for high breakdown voltage and low leakage current. IEEE Electron Device Lett. **33**(7), 973–975 (2012). https://doi.org/10.1109/LED.2012.2197171

28. Lian, Y.-W., Lin, Y.-S., Lu, H.-C., Huang, Y.-C., Hsu, S.S.H.: Drain E-field manipulation in AlGaN/GaN HEMTs by Schottky extension technology. IEEE Trans. Electron Devices **62**(2), 519–524 (2015). https://doi.org/10.1109/TED.2014.2382558

29. Saito, W., Kuraguchi, M., Takada, Y., Tsuda, K., Omura, I., Ogura, T.: Design optimization of high breakdown voltage AlGaN-GaN power HEMT on an insulating substrate for $R_{ON}A$ – V_B tradeoff characteristics. IEEE Trans. Electron Devices **52**(1), 106–111 (2005). https://doi.org/10.1109/TED.2004.841338

30. Raja, P.V., Nallatamby, J.-C., Dasgupta, N., Dasgupta, A.: Trapping effects on AlGaN/GaN HEMT characteristics. Solid – State Electron. **176**(107929), 1–11 (2021). https://doi.org/10.1016/j.sse.2020.107929

31. Dambrine, G., Cappy, A., Heliodore, F., Playez, E.: A new method for determining the FET small-signal equivalent circuit. IEEE Trans. Microw. Theory Tech. **36**(7), 1151–1159 (1988). https://doi.org/10.1109/22.3650

32. Silvaco Inc.: ATLAS TCAD tool version 5.30.0.R, Santa Clara, CA, USA. www.silvaco.com. Accessed 15 May 2022

33. Sehra, K., Kumari, V., Gupta, M., Mishra, M., Rawal, D.S., Saxena, M.: Impact of heavy ion particle strike induced single event transients on conventional and π–Gate AlGaN/GaN HEMTs. Semicond. Sci. Technol. **36**(3), (035009)1–11 (2021). https://doi.org/10.1088/1361-6641/abdba3

34. Subramani, N.K., et al.: Low-frequency noise characterization in GaN HEMTs: investigation of deep levels and their physical properties. IEEE Electron Device Lett. **38**(8), 1109–1112 (2017). https://doi.org/10.1109/LED.2017.2717539

35. Ibbetson, J.P., et al.: Polarization effects, surface states, and the source of electrons in AlGaN/GaN heterostructure field effect transistors. Appl. Phys. Lett. **70**(2), 250–252 (2000). https://doi.org/10.1063/1.126940

36. Wolfspeed: G28V5 Process Fact Sheet. https://assets.wolfspeed.com/uploads/2020/12/Wolfspeed_G28V5.pdf. Accessed 15 May 2022

37. Wolfspeed: G50V3 Process Fact Sheet. https://assets.wolfspeed.com/uploads/2020/12/G50V3.pdf. Accessed 15 May 2022

Investigation of Traps in AlGaN/GaN HEMT Epitaxial Structure Using Conductance Method

Chanchal[1,2(✉)], Ajay Kumar Visvkarma[1,2], Hardhyan Sheoran[3], Amit Malik[2], Robert Laishram[2], Dipendra Singh Rawal[2], and Manoj Saxena[4]

[1] Department of Electronic Science, University of Delhi, New Delhi 110021, India
chanchal0210saraswat@gmail.com
[2] Solid State Physics Laboratory, New Delhi 110054, India
[3] Department of Physics, Indian Institute of Technology, New Delhi 110016, India
[4] Department of Electronics, Deen Dayal Upadhyaya College, University of Delhi, New Delhi 110078, India

Abstract. In this article, an investigation has been carried out to determine the trap density and trap energy level using parallel conductance method for AlGaN/GaN HEMT epitaxial structure. Capacitance-Voltage (C–V) and Conductance-Voltage (G–V) measurements with frequency (1 kHz – 10 MHz) and temperature (25 and 250 °C) variations have been performed on large area Schottky pad having area $150\ \mu m^2 \times 150\ \mu m^2$. Two different types of traps have been observed with different time constants and densities. In the low frequency range between 1 and 10 kHz slow traps with density (2.79×10^{12}–$1.79 \times 10^{13}\ cm^{-2}$) and time constant (~0.159 ms) at an energy level of 0.39 eV from E_C have been observed whereas in the high frequency range greater than 1 MHz a continuum of ultra-fast traps has been observed with density between 1.94×10^{12} and $6.25 \times 10^{12}\ cm^{-2}$ with time constant of 19.9 ns at 0.18 eV from E_C is observed. It is also identified that at high temperature the time constant and trap density for ultra-fast traps has reduced whereas the density of slow traps has a significant increment with similar time constant.

Keywords: Capacitance – voltage – frequency measurement ·
Conductance – voltage – frequency measurement · AlGaN/GaN HEMTs · Slow traps · Fast traps · Parallel conductance method

1 Introduction

The demand of Gallium Nitride (GaN) based solid state devices and electronics has risen significantly in the past decade due to their exceptionally well material properties. The wide band-gap (3.4 eV) and critical breakdown electrical field makes them suitable for high temperature applications (>3 MV/cm), and due to its high saturation velocity (2.6×10^7 cm/s) and high mobility (2DEG mobility ~2000 $cm^2V^{-1}s^{-1}$) enables its usage for high power RF electronics. GaN has ability to form hetero-structure with its alloy ternary compounds (AlGaN or InGaN) giving rise to the formation of an ultra-thin conduction

A. P. Shah et al. (Eds.): VDAT 2022, CCIS 1687, pp. 76–84, 2022.
https://doi.org/10.1007/978-3-031-21514-8_7

channel at the hetero-interface commonly referred as a two-dimensional channel that too without any external doping. This is possible because of its inherit spontaneous polarization which is assisted by piezoelectric polarization developed between the epitaxially grown hetero-structure (such as AlGaN/GaN system) [1–5].

Unlike other semiconductor materials, the performance of GaN based devices is also affected by the presence of various types of traps in the material system used for the fabrication of these devices. To characterize these traps, different techniques and analytical models have been developed which are applicable at material as well as fabricated device level [6–9]. As these traps interact with frequency and voltage bias, techniques based on frequency dependent C–V and G–V measurements turns to be very effective and efficient. Especially, the parallel conductance method is a more sensitive technique for trap characterization than capacitance-based techniques. This is because the conductance of the equivalent circuit varies with the interference of the traps. The response of traps with frequency and voltage bias adds on the conductance of the circuit giving rise to a peak generation in the conductance – voltage curve plot. This makes it a popular technique to extract the density of interface traps (D_{it}) in a dielectric-semiconductor system [10–12].

In this article, the above-mentioned frequency dependent parallel conductance technique is employed to determine the traps densities and energy level in the AlGaN/GaN hetero-structure. Two different types of traps have been identified using G-V-f data set. One has a higher time constant that is slow traps (0.159 ms) with density ranging between 2.78×10^{12} and 1.79×10^{13} cm^{-2} and the other with a smaller time constant (19.89 ns) i.e., fast traps with D_{it} varying between 1.9×10^{12} and 6.25×10^{13} cm^{-2}. At high temperature the interaction of these traps gets affected resulting a fall in the decrease of the respective time constants along with variation in the D_{it} concentration.

2   Experimental Details

The AlGaN/GaN HEMT epitaxial wafer used in this study was grown in-house using metal organic chemical vapor deposition (MOCVD) technique in the Aixtron close coupled showerhead (CCS) reactor [13]. Figure 1 shows AFM image of step flow surface morphology of the sample with rms roughness 0.28 nm. The layer structure consists of AlGaN barrier layer of 27 nm with Al mole fraction of 24 percent in AlGaN. Unintentionally doped GaN buffer of 2.5 μm separated by an atomistic thin layer of 1–2 nm AlN between the barrier and buffer layers. SiC template is used as a substrate to grow this barrier and buffer layer with a nucleation of AlN layer ~100 nm to minimize the dislocation density in GaN buffer [14]. The 2DEG carrier concentration (n_s) and 2DEG electron mobility (μ_{2DEG}) were determined using contactless Hall measurements and were found to be around 9.12×10^{12} cm^{-2} and 1950 cm^{2}V^{-1}S^{-1} respectively.

Before fabrication of devices on this Al$_{0.24}$Ga$_{0.76}$N/GaN HEMT epi-wafer a standard organic cleaning is carried out with trichloroethylene (TCE), acetone and iso-propyl-alcohol (IPA) one by one for 10–15 minutes each.

The fabrication involves definition and deposition of ohmic metal stack Ti/Al/Ni/Au (320 nm) using electron beam evaporation system at room temperature which is annealed further using a rapid thermal annealing system at 820 °C for 90 s to achieve a low resistance ohmic contact. Mesa isolation is carried out using Oxford RIE etching system under

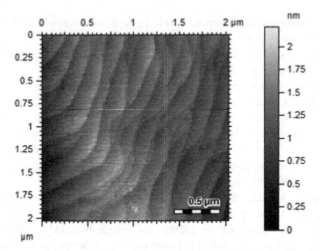

Fig. 1. AFM images of the step flow surface morphology of the sample. The RMS roughness value on scan area 2 μm × 2 μm is 0.28 nm.

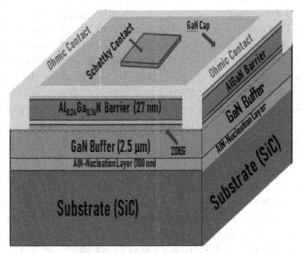

Fig. 2. Cross-sectional view of fabricated diode with Schottky area 150 μm^2 × 150 μm^2 on $Al_{0.24}Ga_{0.76}N$ /GaN HEMT epitaxial wafer.

BCl_3/Cl_2 gas chemistry. Finally, Schottky contact metal Ni/Au (240 nm) is deposited after photo-lithography patterning using same electron beam evaporation system [9].

The fabricated diode of area 150 μm^2 × 150 μm^2 is shown in Fig. 2 and process flow chart in Fig. 3. Frequency-dependent C–V and G–V measurements have been performed on this diode at temperatures 25 and 250 °C using Keithley's Agilent semiconductor parametric analyzer 4200-SCS having a frequency range of 1 kHz to maximum up-to 10 MHz.

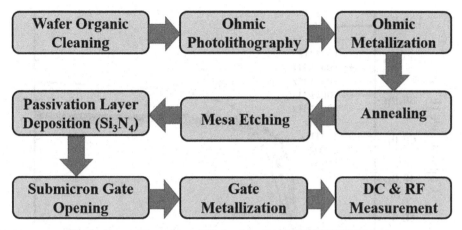

Fig. 3. Process flow chart of fabrication of AlGaN/GaN HEMT device

3 Results and Discussion

The measured frequency-dependent C-V-T at room temperature of 25 °C is shown in Fig. 4. The dispersion in C–V characteristics curves with frequency is due to the presence of traps at the AlGaN/GaN interface. These traps change the flat-band voltage and on state capacitance. To get more insight of this interaction between traps, frequency and applied voltage bias the frequency-dependent parallel conductance versus voltage (G_P–V) variation have been also recorded along with the C–V which is shown in Fig. 4. We have observed an increase in capacitance with the frequency (Fig. 4) which shows that slow traps may not be able to follow the high-frequency signal due to higher time constant and so they are not able to contribute to Schottky Capacitance at higher frequency [14].

It is evident from the above two graphs that the traps are being present at the AlGaN/GaN interface and are participating in the frequency dependent measurements. Hence to extract the quantitative information about these traps, conventional parallel conductance method is applied with these measurements.

$$\frac{G_P}{\omega} = \frac{qD_{it}}{2\omega}\left(\frac{\ln(1+\omega^2\tau_s^2)}{\tau_s}\right) + \frac{qD_{it}}{2\omega}\left(\frac{\ln(1+\omega^2\tau_f^2)}{\tau_f}\right) \tag{1}$$

$$D_{it} \approx \frac{2.5}{Aq}\left(\frac{G_P}{\omega}\right)\text{max} \tag{2}$$

A normalized value of G_P/ω is plotted against the logarithmic of frequency as show in Fig. 5. And assuming a continuous trap levels the parallel conductance can be expressed as Eq. 1 [12, 15]. Where ω is measurement frequency in radians, q is elementary charge τ_s and τ_f are the time constants for the slow and ultra-fast traps respectively. The D_{it} can be extracted from the peak of G_P/ω using Eq. 2

Figure 6 shows the two peaks that corresponds to two distinct kinds of traps one having a high time constant occurring at low frequency nearly 1 kHz or below (measurement system lower limit) and the other peak at high frequencies >1 MHz.

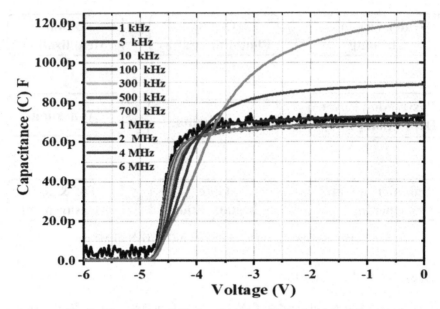

Fig. 4. Dispersion in C–V characteristics with frequency variation.

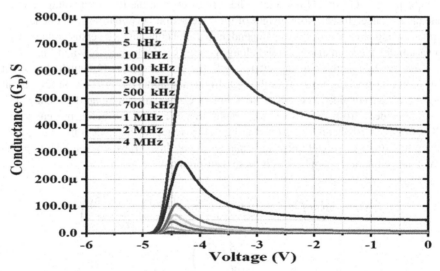

Fig. 5. Frequency dependent G_P–V characteristics curves of the same Schottky pad of area $150\,\mu m^2 \times 150\,\mu m^2$.

In the high frequency the peaks are found to be near about 6–8 MHz in this region the time constant is quite extremely low owing to ultra-fast trapping levels. τ can simply be determined using the radial frequency as $1/2\pi f$. Using the values of extracted values

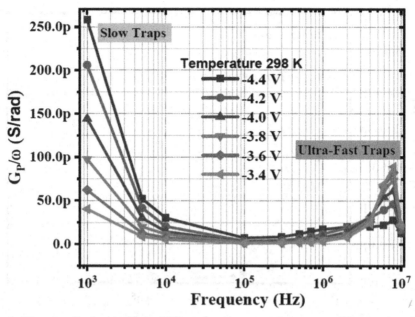

Fig. 6. The normalized equivalent parallel conductance versus frequency at different voltage bias.

Table 1. Extracted parameters from frequency-dependent parallel conductance technique

Bias voltage (V)	D_{it} (cm^{-2}eV^{-1})		Time constant		Trap energy level (eV)	
	Slow traps ($\times 10^{12}$)	Ultra-fast traps ($\times 10^{12}$)	Slow traps (10^{-4})	Ultra-fast traps (10^{-9} s)	Slow traps	Ultra-fast traps
−4.4	17.9	1.94	1.59	19.9	0.39	0.19
−4.2	14.3	3.19	1.59	19.9	0.39	0.19
−4.0	9.99	4.25	1.59	19.9	0.39	0.19
−3.8	6.79	5.10	1.59	19.4	0.39	0.19
−3.6	4.30	5.76	1.59	18.9	0.39	0.19
−3.4	2.79	6.25	1.59	18.7	0.39	0.18

of τ the trap energy level can be estimated using Eq. 3 [12, 14].

$$E_T = kT\ln(\tau_T \sigma_T V_T N_C) \tag{3}$$

where E_T is the trap energy level with respect to the conduction band, k is the Boltzmann's constant, T is temperature, σ_T is the capture cross section taken as 3.4×10^{-15} cm^2, V_T is the average thermal velocity (2.6×10^7 cm/s), and N_C is the effective density of states in GaN ($4.3 \times 10^{14} \times T^{3/2}$ cm^{-3}) [12, 13]. The extracted parameters are shown in Table 1 which is in well agreement with the available literature.

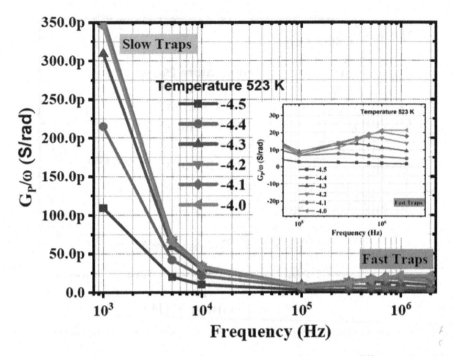

Fig. 7. The normalized equivalent parallel conductance versus frequency at different voltage bias of AlGaN/GaN HEMT at 250 °C.

Table 2. Extracted parameters from frequency dependent parallel conductance technique at 250 °C

Bias voltage (V)	D_{it} (cm^{-2}eV^{-1})		Time constant		Trap energy level (eV)	
	Slow traps ($\times 10^{13}$)	Ultra-fast traps ($\times 10^{12}$)	Slow traps (10^{-4})	Ultra-fast traps (10^{-7}s)	Slow traps	Ultra-fast traps
−4.3	2.14	0.90	1.59	0.79	0.72	0.42
−4.2	2.42	1.21	1.59	1.59	0.72	0.49
−4.1	2.47	1.40	1.59	2.27	0.72	0.46
−4.0	2.39	1.49	1.59	5.3	0.72	0.50

This procedure of traps extraction is repeated at 250 °C and the obtained results are tableted in Table 2 along with Fig. 7 which shows the normalized parallel conductance vs frequency diagram. From Fig. 7 and Table 2, it can be clearly inferred that the time constants have reduction with increase in temperature. Secondly the trap energy level has changed to a deeper level with respect to conduction band. This is because of as the temperature increases the trap activity occurs a much faster rate and traps near conduction band appears to be less interactive with the applied frequency range.

The traps in the deep becomes dominating at this stage as their activity is well visible with applied bias and frequency range. Also, the rise in temperature a diverse effect on trap density as the density of the slow is observed to be higher at high temperature in comparison to room temperature condition. Whereas, the fast traps shows a reduction in trap density which is due the higher activity of trapping states.

4 Conclusion

Parallel conductance method is employed in order to examine the activity of different traps at room temperature and at high temperature. Two types of distinct traps have been observed with different time constants and energy level with a ranging trap density. A continuum of ultra-fast trap is observed near 8 MHz frequency at room temperature at an energy level of 0.19 eV. This trap level is not observed at when the measurements have been repeated at 250 °C, rather a different trap energy level is observed near 1 MHz frequency with trap energy level of 0.45 eV and has a lesser trap density in comparison to room temperature extracted D_{it}. Slow traps were also observed and are affected in a different manner, a rise in trap density is observed at high temperature. The slow traps trap energy level shifted deep with temperature rise. These observations are important in determining the operation of HEMT devices at high temperature ranges.

Acknowledgment. Authors are thankful to the GaN MMIC team, Solid State Physics Laboratory, DRDO, New Delhi, India for providing the opportunity to carry out this work, and the Indian Institute of Technology, New Delhi, India for their experimental support.

References

1. Mishra, U.K., Shen L., Kazior, T.E., Wu, Y.-F.: GaN-based RF power devices and amplifiers. Proc. IEEE. **96**(2), 287–305 (February 2008). https://doi.org/10.1109/JPROC.2007.911060
2. Pengelly, R.S., Wood, S.M., Milligan, J.W., Sheppard, S.T., Pribble, W.L.: A review of GaN on SiC high electron-mobility power transistor and MMICs. IEEE Trans. Microw. Theory Tech. **60**(6), 1764–1783 (2012). https://doi.org/10.1109/TMTT.2012.2187535
3. Ambacher, O., et al.: Two-dimensional electron gases induced by spontaneous and piezo-electric polarization charges in n- and Ga-face AlGaN/GaN heterostructures. J. Appl. Phys. **85**(6), 3222–3233 (1999). https://doi.org/10.1063/1.369664
4. Ibbetson, J.P., Fini, P.T., Ness, K.D., Den Baars, S.P., Speck, J.S., Mishra, U.K.: Polarization effects, surface states, and the source of electrons in AlGaN/GaN heterostructure field effect transistor. Appl. Phys. Lett. **77**(2), 250–252 (2000). https://doi.org/10.1063/1.126940
5. Su, M., Chen, C., Rajan, S.: Prospects for the application of GaN power devices in hybrid electric vehicle drive systems. Semicond. Sci. Technol. **28**, 074012 (2013). https://doi.org/10.1088/0268-1242/28/7/074012
6. Sharma, C., Visvkarma, A.K., Laishram, R., Malik, A., Narang, K., Vinayak, S., Singh, R.: Cumulative dose γ-irradiation effects on material properties of AlGaN/GaN hetero-structures and electrical properties of HEMT devices. Semicond. Sci. Technol. **34**, 065024 (2019). Author, F., Author, S.: Title of a proceedings paper. In: Editor, F., Editor, S. (eds.) Conference 2016, LNCS, vol. 9999, pp. 1–13. Springer, Heidelberg (2016)

7. Raja, P.V., Nallatamby, J.-C, DasGupta, N., DasGupta, A.: Trapping effects on AlGaN/GaN HEMT characteristics. Solid State Electron. **176**, art. no. 107929, 1–15 (February 2021). https://doi.org/10.1016/j.sse.2020.107929

8. Gassoumi, M.: Characterization of deep levels in AlGaN/GaN HEMT by FT-DLTS and current DLTS. Semiconductors **54**, 1296–1303 (2020). https://doi.org/10.1134/S1063782620100127

9. Visvkarma, A.K., Sehra, K., Chanchal, Laishram, R., Malik, A., Sharma, S., Kumar, S., Rawal, D.S., Vinayak, S., Saxena, M.: Impact of gamma radiation on static, pulsed I-V and RF performance parameters of AlGaN/GaN HEMT. IEEE Transac. Electron Device. **69**(5), 2299–2306 (2022). https://doi.org/10.1109/TED.2022.3161402

10. Simons, A.J., Tayarani-Najaran, M.H., Thomas, C.B.: Conductance technique measurements of the density of interface ststes between ZnS:Mn and p-silicon. J. Appl. Phys. **70**(9) (1991). https://doi.org/10.1063/1.349042

11. Zhu, J., Ma, X., Hou, B., Chen, W., Hao, Y.: Investigation of trap states in high Al content AlGaN/GaN high electron. AIP Adv. **4**(037108) (2014). https://doi.org/10.1063/1.4869020

12. Amir, W., Shin, J., Shin, K., Kin, J., Cho, C., Park, K., Tsutsumi, T., Sugiyama, H., Matsuzaki, H., Kim, T.: A qualitative approach for trap analysis between Al0.25Ga0.75N and GaN in high electron mobility transistors. Sci. Rep. **11** (2021). https://doi.org/10.1038/s41598-021-0176-4

13. Keller, S., Parish, G., Fini, P.T., Heikman, S., Chen, C.H., Zhang, N., DenBaars, S.P., Mishra, U.K., Wu, Y.F.: Metalorganic chemical vapor deposition of high mobility AlGaN/GaN heterostructures. J. Appl. Phys. **86**, 5850–5857 (1999). https://doi.org/10.1063/1.371602

14. Khan, R., et al.: Effect of fully strained AlN nucleation layer on the AlN/SiC interface and subsequent GaN growth on 4H-SiC by MOVPE. J. Mater. Sci. Electron. **30**, 18910–18918 (2019). https://doi.org/10.1007/s10854-019

15. Osvald, J.: Interface traps contribution to capacitance of Al_2O_3/(GaN)AlGaN/GaN heterostructures at low frequencies. Phys. E. **93**, 238–242 (2017). https://doi.org/10.1016/j.physe.2017.06.022

16. Whiteside, M., Arulkumaran, S., Dikme, Y., Sandupatla, A., Ng, G.I.: Improved interfaced state density by low temperature epitaxy grown AlN for AlGaN/GaN metal-insulator –semiconductor diodes. Mater. Sci. Eng. B **267**, 114707 (2020). https://doi.org/10.1016/j.mseb.2020.114707

Unveiling the Impact of Interface Traps Induced on Negative Capacitance Nanosheet FET: A Reliability Perspective

Aniket Gupta[1], Govind Bajpai[1], Navjeet Bagga[2], Shashank Banchhor[3], Sudeb Dasgupta[3], Anand Bulusu[3], and Nitanshu Chauhan[1,3(✉)]

[1] National Institute of Technology Uttarakhand, Uttarakhand, India
[2] PDPM IIIT Jabalpur, Jabalpur, India
[3] Indian Institute of Technology Roorkee, Roorkee, India
nitanshu.chauhan@nituk.ac.in

Abstract. Reliability and yield are major concerns of nano-scaled devices. Bias temperature instability (BTI) has always been one of the major reliability issue for the semiconductor transistors. BTI induced interface traps play a vital role in defining important figures of merits such as threshold voltage (V_{TH}), ON current, and I_{ON}/I_{OFF} in terms of the reliability of the transistor, especially in p-type devices. In this paper, for the first time, we investigate the impact of the Si-SiO2 interface traps (N_{it}) on the performance of the p-type Negative Capacitance Nanosheet (NC-NS) FET. Using well-calibrated TCAD models our results demonstrate that: 1) the end of life (EOL) concentration (i.e., shift of threshold voltage ($\Delta V_{TH} = 50\,\mathrm{mV}$) in threshold voltage degradation is improved in NC NSFET as compared to baseline NSFET; 2) the smaller degradation in I_{ON}/I_{OFF} and subthreshold slope (SS) is achieved in NC-NSFET. We investigate and evaluate the performance metrics of NC-NS FET in comparison to the baseline NSFET. Our result reveals that NC-NSFET exhibit 2.5 times less degradation in V_{TH}, and 11.76x less degradation in I_{ON}/I_{OFF} ratio.

Keywords: Negative capacitance · Interface traps · Polarization switching · Nanosheet · Reliability

1 Introduction

IN the nano-scaled below sub10nm technology nodes, the prime focus of research is to achieve fast switching with minimal power dissipation. Ferroelectric (FE) based Field Effect Transistors (FETs) receive immense research due to their excellent behavior of providing steep subthreshold slope (SS) [1–4]. FE material has an inherent property of negative capacitance when stabilized with proper FE thicknesses and other relevant FE parameters [5,6]. A conventional FET can be turned into an NC-FET by replacing the high-K oxide with an FE layer at the gate stack of the transistor even without changing the fabrication mask and process steps [7]. NCFETs are promising candidates to provide SS below

A. P. Shah et al. (Eds.): VDAT 2022, CCIS 1687, pp. 85–96, 2022.
https://doi.org/10.1007/978-3-031-21514-8_8

the Boltzmann limit (i.e., 60mV/decade) due to an internal voltage amplification based on capacitance matching with the underlying transistor [8]. Besides the operating mechanism and other performance metrics, the transistor reliability would always be a prime concern of the research. In general, Negative Bias Temperature Instability (NBTI) is one of the major reliability perspectives [9–11]. High electric field at the $Si - SiO_2$ interface results in an increase in trap concentration [9–11] and, in turn, degrades the performance of the transistor. The presence of trap charges varies the threshold voltage and results in aging of the devices. In this work, we analyze the impact of interface trap concentration on the performance of NC-Nanosheet FET in comparison with the baseline Nanosheet FET (see Fig. 1).

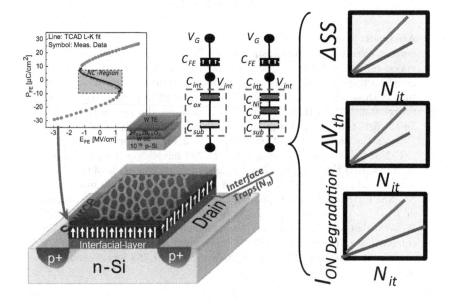

Fig. 1. Objective illustration: showing the pictorial representation in NC based device having PBTI. The degradation due to PBTI is extracted in Device's Figures of Merits such as Threshold Voltage, ON current, Subthreshold Slope. Here the reference devices are Nanosheet FET and Negative Capacitance Nanosheet FET.

Our Key Contribution: 1) Our results demonstrate that due to internal voltage amplification resulting in enhanced gate control in NC-NSFET, reduces the impact of trap charges; 2) Through pre-aging and post-aging device analysis, we investigate the worst-case impact of traps on the performance metrices such

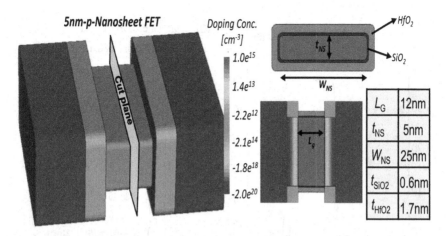

Fig. 2. Schematic of baseline Nanosheet FET along with a cross section and the geometric parameters for the baseline Nanosheet FET.

as V_{TH} shift, I_{ON}/I_{OFF} and SS degradation. The analysis predicts the end of lifetime for low-power (when NC-NSFET operating at equivalent voltage resulting in same Ion as in baseline NSFET) and high-performance scenarios (when NC-NSFET operating at same voltage as in baseline NSFET) respectively.

2   TCAD Setup and Calibration for Device Simulation

5nm baseline p-Nanosheet FET is shown in Fig. 2 along with 2D cross-section, showing the doping profile and device dimensions (Fig. 2b). The device has been simulated through commercial *Sentaurus TCAD tool* [13] with proper tuning of gate work function, doping of S/D extension, and high field parameters. In our simulation framework, the quantum confinement models has also been included to account for the short dimension effects. The model parameter were carefully tuned to well-calibrate the transfer characteristics of the baseline device (Fig. 3a) against the reported experimental data [12]. The NC-NSFET had been realized by replacing the high-k oxide layer with FE layer of same thickness. To account for NC effect in FE layer the L-K model is additionally deployed in TCAD, which is described by the bulk L-K parameters (α, β and γ) and these are calibrated

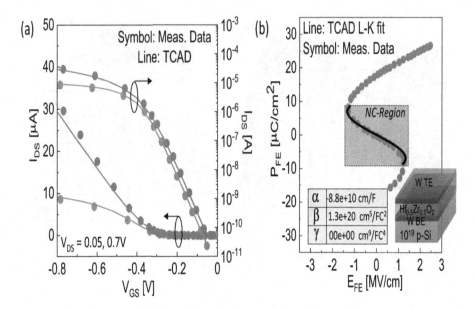

Fig. 3. (a) show the baseline Nanosheet FET calibration with transfer characteristics and demonstrating the good match between TCAD results and measurement data [12]; (b) shows the calibration of L-K parameter with the experimental data [5].

with the experimentally reported polarization - electric field curve [5] as shown in Fig. 3b. For the amplification in the surface potential, the Electric field inside the FE layer can be defined as:

$$E_{FE} = 2\alpha P_{FE} + 4\beta P_{FE}^3 + 4\gamma P_{FE}^5 - 2g\Delta P_{FE} + \rho\left(\frac{dP_{FE}}{dt}\right) \tag{1}$$

where α, β and γ are the Landau coefficients. The domain interaction coefficient g and the viscosity coefficient ρ in L-K equation are $1e^{-4}$ cm$^3/F$, $2.25e^4$ Ωcm, respectively, taken from [13]. Other FE parameters: α, β and γ are extracted by fitting the Landau model to an experimentally-measured polarization-electric field curve [5] (Fig. 3 (b)). Including a FE layer improves the drivability as compared to the baseline NSFET result in higher I_{ON}, lower I_{OFF} and reduced SS as shown in Fig. 4. The impact of trap charges on the performance metrices has been unveiled by considering the donor type Si-SiO$_2$ interface trap charges of different concentration in simulation set-up.

3   Results and Discussion

In NCFET, presence of ferroelectric (FE) layer in the gate stack results in an internal voltage amplification that in turn allows higher gate controllability, thus ameliorate the performance in presence of higher trap concentration, as

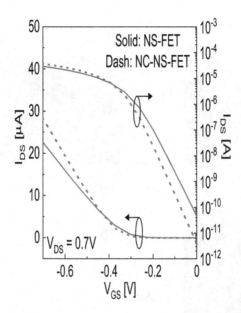

Fig. 4. Impact of replacing the high-k HfO_2 in the baseline Nanosheet (NSFET) FET with an FE layer to realize NC effect demonstrating the improvements in the drain current (I_{DS}) as compared to baseline NSFET.

compared to baseline NSFET. However, the enhanced interface field in case of NC-NSFET also result in higher N_{it} concentration which presents a tradeoff scenario between the reliability and the performance of the transistor. In this work, the pre-aging and post aging device characteristic is analysed both for baseline NSFET and NC NSFET and worst case performance degradation in baseline NSFET and NC NSFET is predicted.

3.1   Impact of Trap Concentration (N_{it}):

Figure 5 shows and compares the vertical electric field distribution in p-type baseline (Fig. 5a) and NC (Fig. 5b-c) nanosheet FET operating under different scenarios (i.e., low power and high performance) respectively. It is evident from Fig. 5d that an increase in E-field across the interface results in increased the trap concentration (N_{it}) at the $Si - SiO_2$ interface [10,14]. Figure 6(a-d) and Fig. 7 shows the impact of N_{it} on the linear transfer and saturation transfer characteristics for both the baseline and NC-Nanosheet FETs. We can conclude

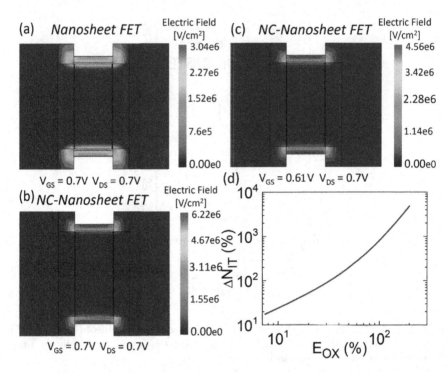

Fig. 5. (a) The vertical E-Field distribution in the baseline p-Nanosheet (b) shows the vertical E-Field distribution in p-NC-Nanosheet operating at high performance scenario (i.e., NC-effect in HfO_2 layer results in 105% higher interface field); (c) shows the vertical E-Field distribution p-NC-Nanosheet operating at equivalent voltage (Low power scenario) (i.e. still NC-FET exhibit 50% higher interface field); (d) shows how an increase in the field across the SiO_2 layer results in higher interface trap concentration [14].

that the impact of the increase in trap concentration at the $Si - SiO_2$ interface is more pronounced in the baseline NSFET as compared to NC-NSFET due to better electrostatic integrity in case of NC-NSFET. The electrostatic integrity can also be verified by the threshold voltage shift vs N_{it} (Fig. 8a). Figure 8a shows that the simulated end of lifetime (EOL) N_{it} conc. for both baseline nanosheet FET and NC-NSFET. However, In case of baseline NSFET the end of lifetime N_{it} (EOL N_{it}) is 2.5 times less than the EOL N_{it} conc. of the NC-NSFET.

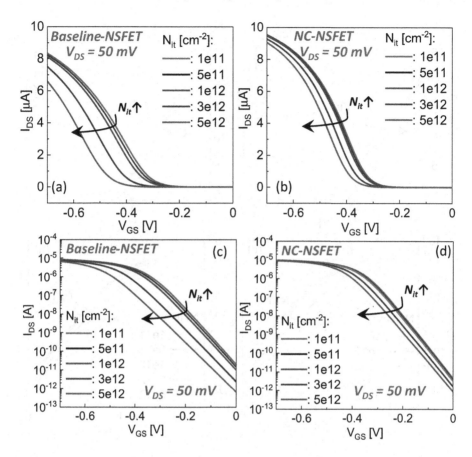

Fig. 6. (a-d) Transfer characteristic at different N_{it} of the baseline nanosheet and NC Nanosheet for the linear region. NC-NS shows lesser degradation in performance of I_{ON}

However, the higher interface E-Field reduces the EOL N_{it} for NC-NSFET. The predicted EOL conc. $(11.2e^{12})$ from Fig. 5d is quite high as compared to the simulated EOL conc. $(4.2e^{12})$ in case of NC-NSFET which is attributed by the modulation of polarization of the FE layer (Fig. 8(b-c)) and in turn changes the drivability of the device.

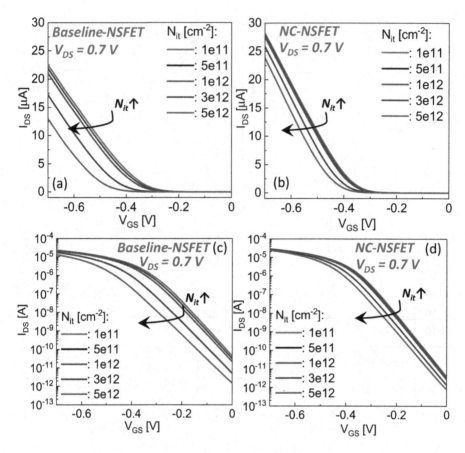

Fig. 7. (a-d) Transfer characteristic at different N_{it} of the baseline nanosheet and NC Nanosheet for the saturation region. NC-NS shows lesser degradation in performance of I_{ON}

3.2   Performance Evaluation with EOL in Low Power and High Performance Scenarios:

(Figure 9) compares the performance degradation between the baseline NSFET and the NC-NSFET for the two scenarios i.e., low power and high performance scenarios. In the low power scenario, we decrease the gate voltage in NC-NSFET such that the current in the NC-NSFET is equivalent to the baseline NSFET (required $V_{GS} = 0.61V$). The extracted degradation in %I_{ON} the case of NC-NSFET is smaller than the baseline NSFET (Fig. 9(a)). This is because the equivalent gate voltage is responsible for small trap concentration. The I_{ON}/I_{OFF} is

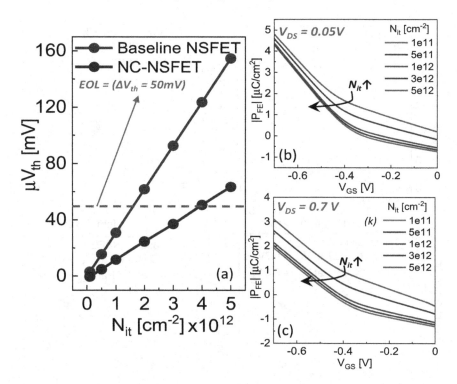

Fig. 8. (a) The change in threshold voltage (ΔV_{th}) at different N_{it} (b) and (c) show the FE polarization in linear and saturation condition respectively.

also higher in the NC-NSFET ((Fig. 9(b)). For the high performance case even with the increased trap conc., In NC-NSFET, the higher gate controllability overcomes the impact of trap charges and therefore the percentage degradation in I_{ON} (Fig. 9c) and I_{ON}/I_{OFF} ((Fig. 9(b,d)) is higher as compared to baseline NS FET. The cumulative degradation for the baseline NSFET and the NC NSFET can also be seen in Fig. 10(a-c). It clearly shows that although higher gate electric field in NC NSFET shows higher trap concentration but the gate control is still higher and the device shows lesser performance degradation in transistor Figure of Merits (FOMs).

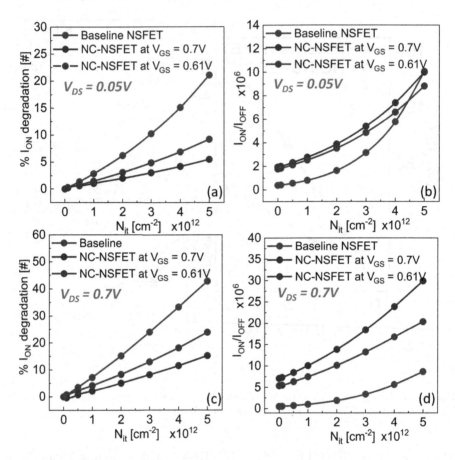

Fig. 9. (a) and (c) show the percentage I_{on} degradation in linear and saturation regime respectively. (b) and (d) show the I_{on}/I_{off} for linear and saturation regime respectively for NC and baseline nanosheet.

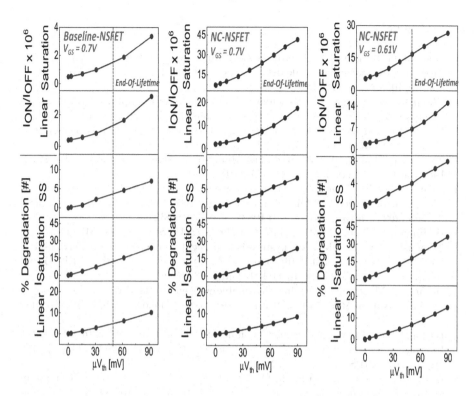

Fig. 10. (a-c) Cumulative degradation in transistor FOMs for baseline NSFET and NC NSFET both for low power and high performance scenario.

4 Conclusion

Presence of trap charges play a crucial role to describe the aging, i.e., reliability of a transistor. Using well-calibrated TCAD models, we have investigated the impact of $Si - SiO_2$ traps on the performance of p-type NC-NSFET in comparison to baseline NSFET. We found that an enhanced gate control in the NC-NSFET due to FE polarization, overcomes the impact of trap charges present at the interface. This reduces the percentage performance degradation and improves the aging of the devices Thus, ensuring the immunity of NC-NSFET against NBTI as compared to baseline NSFET.

References

1. Salahuddin, S., Datta, S.: Use of negative capacitance to provide voltage amplification for low power nanoscale devices. Nano Lett. **8**(2), 405–410, (2008). https://doi.org/10.1021/nl071804g.
2. Chauhan, N., Bagga, N., Banchhor, S., Datta, A., Dasgupta, S., Bulusu, A.: Negative-to-positive differential resistance transition in ferroelectric FET: physical insight and utilization in analog circuits. IEEE Trans. Ultrason. Ferroelectr. Freq. Control **69**(1), 430–437 (2022)
3. Zhou, J., et al.: Negative differential resistance in negative capacitance FETs. IEEE Electron Device Lett. **39**(4), 622–625 (2018)
4. Chauhan, N.: BOX engineering to mitigate negative differential resistance in MFIS negative capacitance FDSOI FET: an analog perspective. Nanotechnology **33**(8), 085203 (2021). https://doi.org/10.1088/1361-6528/ac328a
5. Hoffmann, M., Max, B., Mittmann, T., Schroeder, U., Slesazeck, S., Mikolajick, T.: Demonstration of high-speed hysteresis-free negative capacitance in ferroelectric hf0.5zr0.5o2. In: 2018 IEEE International Electron Devices Meeting (IEDM), pp. 1–4 (2018). https://doi.org/10.1109/IEDM.2018.8614677
6. Hoffmann, M., et al.: Unveiling the double-well energy landscape in a ferroelectric layer. Nature **565**(7740) 464–467 (2019). https://doi.org/10.1038/s41586-018-0854-z
7. Bajpai, G., et al.: Impact of radiation on negative capacitance finfet. In: 2020 IEEE International Reliability Physics Symposium (IRPS), pp. 1–5 (2020). https://doi.org/10.1109/IRPS45951.2020.9129165
8. Bajpai, G., Gupta, A., Prakash, O., Chauhan, Y.S., Amrouch, H.: Soft errors in negative capacitance fdsoi srams. In: 2021 5th IEEE Electron Devices Technology Manufacturing Conference (EDTM), pp. 1–3 (2021). https://doi.org/10.1109/EDTM50988.2021.9421043
9. Prakash, O., Gupta, A., Pahwa, G., Henkel, J., Chauhan, Y.S., Amrouch, H.: Impact of interface traps on negative capacitance transistor: device and circuit reliability. IEEE J. Electron Devices Soc. **8**, 1193–1201 (2020). https://doi.org/10.1109/JEDS.2020.3022180
10. Gupta, A., et al: Traps based reliability barrier on performance and revealing early ageing in negative capacitance FET. In: 2021 IEEE International Reliability Physics Symposium (IRPS), pp. 1–6 (2021). https://doi.org/10.1109/IRPS46558.2021.9405185
11. Garg, C., et al.: Investigation of trap-induced performance degradation and restriction on higher ferroelectric thickness in negative capacitance FDSOI FET. IEEE Trans. Electron Devices **68**(10), 5298–5304 (2021)
12. Loubet, N., et al.: Stacked nanosheet gate-all-around transistor to enable scaling beyond FINFET. In: Symposium on VLSI Technology, vol. 2017, pp. 230–231 (2017)
13. Sentaurus device user guide, version p-2019.03-sp1, synopsys, inc. mountain view, CA, USA. https://www.synopsys.com/. Accessed Apr 2020
14. Mahapatra, S. (ed.): Fundamentals of Bias Temperature Instability in MOS Transistors. SSAM, vol. 52. Springer, New Delhi (2016). https://doi.org/10.1007/978-81-322-2508-9

Impact of Temperature on NDR Characteristics of a Negative Capacitance FinFET: Role of Landau Parameter (α)

Rajeewa Kumar Jaisawal[1] (ID), Sunil Rathore[1] (ID), P. N. Kondekar[1],
and Navjeet Bagga[2]([✉])

[1] Electronics and Communication Engineering Department, VLSI Design and Nano-Scale
Computational Lab, PDPM-IIITDM Jabalpur, Jabalpur 482005, India
[2] IIT Bhubaneswar, Bhubaneswar, India
navjeet.bagga9@gmail.com

Abstract. Negative Differential Resistance (NDR) is an inherent property of Negative Capacitance (NC) based devices, i.e., a decrease in the drain current (I_D) with increasing drain voltage (V_{DS}). The analysis of NC-based devices in TCAD is strongly dependent on the reliable choice of the Landau parameters (α, β, γ, ρ, g). In this paper, using well-calibrated TCAD models, we investigated: (i) the influence of the temperature on the Landau parameters (primarily on α); (ii) the dependency of NDR on 'α' using a semi-empirical model; (iii) how does the change in temperature modulates the NDR region of the NC-FinFET; (iv) the electrical characteristics of NDR-free NC-FinFET. In the proposed study, we have taken the silicon (Si) doped HfO_2 as a ferroelectric (FE) layer in the gate stack of the baseline FinFET to realize NC-FinFET. The impact of varying FE layer thickness and temperature on the NC regime is thoroughly investigated.

Keywords: Negative Capacitance · Landau parameters · Negative differential resistance · FinFET · Si-doped

1 Introduction

In the recent semiconductor chip manufacturing industries, the FinFETs are considered front-runner transistors due to their enhanced electrostatic gate control and better scalability for low-power and high-performance applications [1–4]. However, the physical insight into the FinFET still faces the hindrance of Boltzmann tyranny of the 60 mV/decade on the subthreshold slope (SS). By keeping the same underlying physics of the carrier transport, the concept of negative capacitance (NC) could be realized in the baseline FinFET to achieve steeper SS, which is obtained by placing an FE-layer in the gate stack of the baseline transistor [5, 6]. The FE polarization results in an internal voltage amplification, which enhances the applied vertical electric field integrity; thus, the device exhibits the steep slope characteristics, higher ON current, and improved switching speed compared to the baseline device [7–9]. The literature is abounding with the circuit-level investigations of the improved performances of the NC-based circuits by utilizing the capacitance matching of the FE and dielectric (DE) layers [10, 11]. In general, the FE polarization is not only altered by the gate voltage (V_{GS}) but is significantly affected by the drain voltage (V_{DS}). Thus, the NC-based devices show a notable trend in the output characteristics, i.e., a decrease in drain current with an increase in V_{DS} (for specific V_{GS}), resulting in a negative differential resistance (NDR). The NDR is an inherent property of NC devices that is strongly dependent on the Landau parameters, biasing, and thickness of the FE layer [12, 13]. The conventional perovskite materials show the ferroelectricity at higher thicknesses, whereas, in recent technological nodes, the ferroelectricity can be achieved in a very thin HfO_2 layer using specific dopants. The dopants like Silicon (Si), Zirconium (Zr), Yttrium (Y), etc., offers ferroelectricity in the HfO_2 layer with having different Landau parameters [14, 15].

The dopant-specific Landau parameters (α, β, γ, ρ, g) play a vital role in reliable TCAD analysis of NC-based devices. The change in Landau parameters changes the span of the NC region explained by the S-curve (in the polarization-field loop of the FE layer) [16]. Therefore, the characteristics of the NC-based devices will be altered based on the Landau parameter. One of the critical factors affecting the Landau parameters is the temperature which significantly modulates the 'α'. To the best of our knowledge, the impact of temperature on 'α' and, in turn, on NDR has not been explored. Therefore, in this work, we have investigated the effect of varying the ambient temperature from 250K to 350K on NDR characteristics of the NC-FinFET using the well-calibrated TCAD model. *Our Key Contributions*:

(i)   The impact of temperature on Landau parameters and thus on the capacitance matching is explained using a semi-empirical model.
(ii) Investigation of temperature-induced NDR mitigation.
(iii) The impact of temperature variation on the electrical characteristics of the NC-FinFET has been discussed.

The rest of the paper is organized as follows: Sect. 2 explains the device structure and calibration framework. The acquired results and semi-empirical model are mentioned in Sect. 3, followed by the conclusion in Sect. 4.

2   Device Structure and Simulation Setup

A 14 nm industry-standard FinFET is employed in our study as a baseline device, as shown in Fig. 2(a). The channel and source/drain (S/D) regions are uniformly doped. In contrast, the Gaussian doping profile (GP) is used in the extension regions to minimize the random dopant fluctuations (RDF) and mimic the realistic scenario. TiN is used as a metal gate, and Si_3N_4 is used as a spacer to mitigate the gate-S/D fringing capacitance. The effective oxide thickness (EOT) comprises the stack of high-k (HfO_2) and low-k (SiO_2) gate dielectrics. The drain current of FinFET has been normalized by effective channel width (W_{eff}), which is given as $W_{eff} = 2F_h + F_w$ (where F_h & F_w are fin height and width, respectively). The Sentaurus TCAD [17] is used in our study, and the models governing the carrier transport phenomenon are well-calibrated with experimental data [3] of the baseline FinFET, as shown in Fig. 2(b).

TCAD framework includes a drift-diffusion model for carrier transport and the SRH model to account for carrier generation and recombination. The Caughey-Thomas model

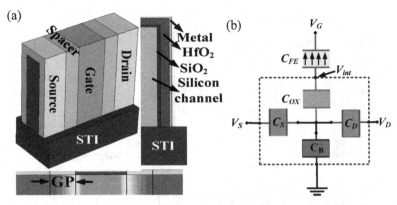

Fig. 1. (a) 3D schematic of the Negative Capacitance FinFET structure, realized by replacing the high-k layer of the baseline FinFET (Fig. 2a) with a Si-doped HfO_2 layer, which acts as a ferroelectric (FE) layer; (b) the equivalent capacitive network of an NC-FinFET shows all the capacitances. Here, V_G, V_S, V_D, and V_{int} show the gate, source, drain, and internal voltages.

for high field saturation, the Lombardi model to alleviate mobility degradation due to high-k dielectric, the ballistic mobility model to capture short channel effects, and the doping dependent (UniBo) mobility model to account for lattice scattering and electron-hole scattering are used [18]. We have also employed a quantum potential model to capture the small geometric effects. All the relevant parameters are tuned to the pre-scribed limit to achieve a good match in simulation and experimental data (Fig. 2b). In our simulation study, the Si-doped HfO_2 layer is used as a FE layer, with a remanent polarization (P_r) and coercive field (E_c) of 10 μC/cm^2 and 1 MV/cm, respectively. The static Landau coefficients: $\alpha = \frac{-3\sqrt{3}}{4}\frac{E_c}{P_r}$, $\beta = \frac{3\sqrt{3}}{8}\frac{E_c}{P_r^3}$, and $\gamma = 0$ are extracted by fitting the experimental P-E (polarization-electric field) curve, as shown in Fig. 2(c, d). The FEPolarization model is incorporated into the TCAD setup to obtain the requisite nega-tive capacitance characteristics. Finally, the NC-FinFET (Fig. 1a) is realized by replacing the high-k dielectric layer with a Si-doped HfO_2-based FE-layer with appropriate Lan-dau parameters (α, β, γ, ρ, g). In our simulation, we have considered quasi-static analysis for the uniform domain FE layer; thus, the values of ρ (2.25 $\times$ 10^4 Ω-cm) and g (1 $\times$ 10^{-4} cm^3/F) are kept constant, as mentioned in the TCAD manual. However, the other Landau parameters, i.e., α, β, γ, are dopant specific and need attention while simulating NC-based devices. For the Si-doped HfO_2 FE layer, the default values of $\alpha = -1.3 \times 10^{11}$ cm/F, $\beta = 6.49 \times 10^{20}$ cm^5/F/C^2, $\gamma = 0$. Figure 2(e) shows the transfer character-istics of NC-FinFET and baseline FinFET, which reveal that ~30% enhancement in I_{ON} and ~11.8% improvement in SS is achieved using NC-FinFET.

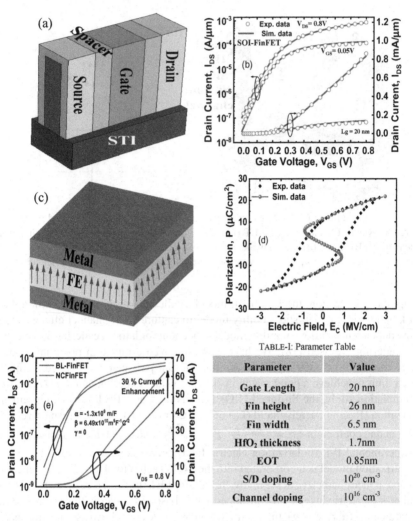

Fig. 2. (a) 3D schematic view of the baseline FinFET; (b) TCAD Calibration showing a good fit in the simulation and experimental data of the transfer characteristics (I_{DS}–V_{GS}) of baseline FinFET [3]; (c) schematic of metal-ferroelectric-metal (MFM) capacitor; (d) fitted polarization-electric field (P-E) hysteresis characteristics with the S-curve Landau-Khalatnikov equation [15]; (e) demonstration of current amplification in I_{DS}-V_{GS} characteristics by incorporating the FE layer of thickness 1.7 nm in the gate stack and realized an NC-FinFET. Table-I mentioned all the parameters used in the simulation unless stated otherwise.

3 Results and Discussion

In an NC-FinFET, the FE-layer polarization (P) strongly depends on V_{GS} and V_{DS}. In FE material, the ferroelectricity arises due to the unique intrinsic relation of the critical electric field (E_{fe}) and its polarization (P), which can be modeled by using the Landau-Khalatnikov (LK) expression [11] given as follows:

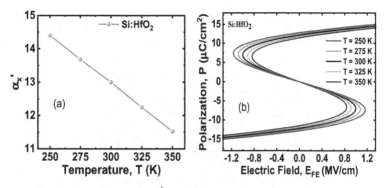

Fig. 3. (a) Shows that the coefficient (α_x') varies linearly with temperature, thus, changing the value of α. This results in the change in the NC region; (b) S-curve for the Si-doped HfO$_2$ FE layer for different values of α, changes due to temperature.

$$E_{fe} = \frac{V_{fe}}{T_{fe}} = 2\alpha P + 4\beta P^3 + 6\gamma P^5 + \rho \frac{dP}{dt} - 2g\Delta P \qquad (1)$$

where α, β, and γ are the static Landau parameters, whereas ρ and g are dynamic Landau parameters. In the general TCAD study, we employed the Landau parameter (α, β, γ, ρ, g) in the physics file to incorporate the NC phenomenon, explained using S-curve. In our analysis, we have assumed the uniform polarization due to the homogeneous monodomain of thin layer FE material. So, the minimum possible permissible value of domain interaction coefficients (g) provided in TCAD has been selected to resemble our assumptions. The parameter 'α' is susceptible to the temperature. However, the impact of temperature on β and γ is insignificant [20]. Therefore,

$$\alpha = \alpha_x' \times 10^{10}(T - T_C) \qquad (2)$$

where T$_C$ is the Curie temperature and taken as 650K for the Si-doped FE material. α_x' is a coefficient that varies linearly with temperature, as shown in Fig. 3(a). As the temperature increases the α_x' decreases due to decreases in the values of coercive electric field (E$_c$) and span of the negative capacitance region, which ultimately alter the S-curve (Fig. 3b).

The NC can be stabilized by placing a FE layer in series with a DE layer. The resultant capacitive network of the gate stack in NC-FinFET is shown in Fig. 1(b). The internal voltage can be coupled with V$_{GS}$ and V$_{DS}$ as follows:

$$dV_G = dV_{int} + dV_D \qquad (3)$$

$$dV_{int} = \frac{dV_{GS}}{\frac{|C_{fe}| - C_{ox}}{|C_{fe}|}} - \frac{dV_{DS}}{\frac{|C_{fe}| - C_{ox}}{C_D}} \qquad (4)$$

$$dV_{int} = AdV_{GS} - BdV_{DS} \qquad (5)$$

where, $C_{fe} = \frac{1}{2\alpha'_x \times 10^{10}(T-T_c)T_{fe}}\left(\mu\frac{F}{cm^2}\right)$. and $C_{ox} = \frac{3.4}{EOT(nm)}(\mu F/cm^2)$. C_D is the parasitic drain capacitance.

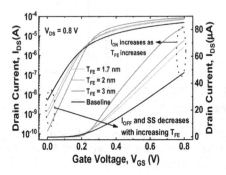

Fig. 4. The transfer characteristics of NC-FinFET show the impact of varying FE-layer thickness.

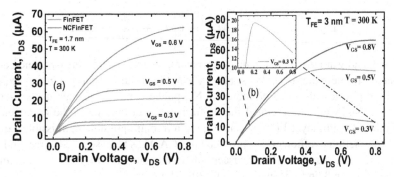

Fig. 5. (a) Shows the output characteristics (I_{DS}-V_{DS}) showing that NDR does not occur at the lower value of T_{fe}, due to the dominance of amplification factor (A); (b) shows that NDR occurs at higher T_{fe} at lower V_{GS} due to the dominance of BdV_{DS} in Eq. (3).

The internal voltage amplification modulates the surface potential based on the capacitance matching [12] and thus results in improved I_{ON} and SS, as shown in Fig. 4 for different T_{fe} values. It can be seen from Eq. (3) that the internal node potential (V_{int}) is a function of the amplification factor (A) and drain coupling factor (B) [19]. It is clear that the FE capacitance is inversely proportional to FE thickness (T_{fe}). Therefore, for higher T_{fe}, the amplification factor 'A' weakens the capacitance matching, which implies the dominance of BdV_{DS} on V_{int}, resulting in an NDR. In contrast, NDR is not found for lower T_{fe} (Fig. 5a). Further, an increase in V_{GS} leads to the dominance of AdV_{GS}, resulting in diminishing the NDR, as shown in Fig. 5(b). The increase in V_{GS} enhances the vertical electric field and results in higher I_{ON} even though the factor 'A' decreases with higher T_{fe} (Fig. 4). As per Eq. (3), the factor 'A' is a function of FE-layer capacitance, which is dependent on α'_x. Therefore, as α'_x is a function of the temperature (Fig. 3a), 'A' also varies with temperature. Therefore, the NDR region in the output characteristics would vary with the temperature, as shown in Fig. 6(a). As we increase the temperature, α'_x would decrease, resulting in an enhancement in C_{fe}. Thus, factor 'A' increases in Eq. (5), which results in decreases in NDR, as shown in Fig. 6(a). However, when the V_{GS} increases, AdV_{GS} dominate in Eq. (3), mitigating the NDR at $V_{GS} = 0.6V$ (Fig. 6b). Therefore, the increase in temperature decreases the span of the negative capacitance regime in the S-curve, which shrinks due to the impact of temperature on the Landau coefficient (α).

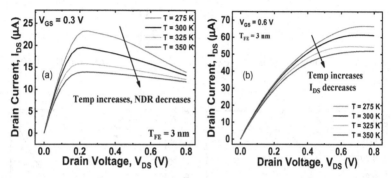

Fig. 6. The output characteristics of NC-FinFET showing the impact of temperature on NDR at $V_{GS} = 0.3$ V; (b) I_{DS}-V_{DS} of NC-FinFET showing the effect of temperature on NDR at $V_{GS} = 0.6$ V. At high gate voltage the NDR is not present due to dominance of AdV_{GS} amplification factor.

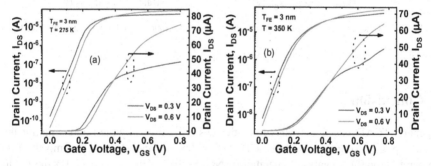

Fig. 7. (a, b) shows the transfer characteristics of NC-FinFET at T = 275 K and T = 350 K for both lower and higher V_{GS}. The characteristics reveal that the SS and threshold voltage deteriorates with an increase in temperature due to the overall impact of mobility, bandgap narrowing, and Landau parameter (α).

The cumulative effect of temperature and V_{GS} on NDR is shown in Fig. 7. I_{DS}-V_{GS} characteristics show that the NDR is more pronounced at lower V_{GS} and lower temperatures. Further, the increase in temperature deteriorates the overall electrical characteristics of the NC-FinFET such as subthreshold swing (Fig. 7), threshold voltage (Fig. 7), transconductance (Fig. 8a), and gate capacitance (Fig. 8b), which can be explained using conventional Eqs. (6) and (7). The increase in temperature reduces mobility and causes the bandgap narrowing, resulting in reduced I_{ON} and enhanced leakage current [21].

$$\mu_{eff} = \mu_{eff0}\left(\frac{T}{T_0}\right)^{-2} \qquad (6)$$

where T_0 is the room temperature, and T is the lattice temperature. μ_{eff0} and μ_{eff} are obtained at room temperature and lattice temperature, respectively.

$$E_{BG}(T) = E_{BG}(T_0) - \frac{AT^2}{T+B} \qquad (7)$$

where, $E_{BG}(T_0)$ is considered as 1.16 eV, A = 4.73 × 10^{-7} eV/K, and B = 636 K for Si material.

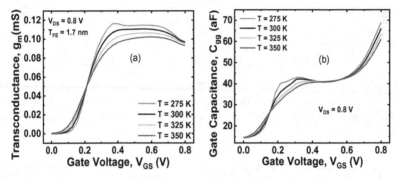

Fig. 8. Shows the impact of temperature on (a) transconductance; (b) the gate capacitance (C_{gg}).

4   Conclusion

A general TCAD-based analysis of NC devices is governed by the Landau parameters (α, β, γ, ρ, g). Using well-calibrated TCAD models, we investigated the impact of the temperature on the Negative Capacitance (NC) FinFET. This work explores the modulation of negative differential resistance (NDR) with varying temperatures. The NDR is dependent on biasing (i.e., V_{GS}, V_{DS}), ferroelectric thickness, and Landau parameters. The semi-empirical model suggests that the Landau parameter α is a vital function of temperature. Therefore, the change in temperature alters the Landau parameter (α), thus modulating the span of the NC region, i.e., the S-curve. This, in turn, affects the NDR characteristics. Therefore, the impact of temperature is worth exploring to achieve a reliable NDR-free operation.

Acknowledgment. N. Bagga greatly acknowledged the support received from the PDPM IIITDM Jabalpur, project title "Design and Performance Investigation of Negative Capacitance Tunnel FET for Digital/Analog Applications," project no. IIITDMJ/ODRSPC/2022/88.

References

1. Jin, M., et al.: Reliability characterization of 10nm FinFET technology with multi-VT gate stack for low power and high performance. In: IEEE International Electron Devices Meeting (IEDM), pp. 15.1.1–15.1.4 (December 2016). https://doi.org/10.1109/IEDM.2016.7838420
2. Jaisawal, R.K., et al.: Assessing the analog/RF and linearity performances of FinFET using high threshold voltage techniques. Semicond. Sci. Technol. **37**(05), 055010 (April 2022). https://doi.org/10.1088/1361-6641/ac6128
3. Lin, C.-H., et al.: High performance 14nm SOI FinFET CMOS technology with 0.0174μm2 embedded DRAM and 15 levels of Cu metallization. In: IEEE International Electron Devices Meeting, pp. 3.8.1–3.8.3 (December 2014). https://doi.org/10.1109/IEDM.2014.7046977
4. Rathore, S., Jaisawal, R.K., Suryavanshi, P., Kondekar, P.N.: Investigation of ambient temperature and thermal contact resistance induced self-heating effects in nanosheet FET. Semicond. Sci. Technol. **37**(5), 055019 (April 2022). https://doi.org/10.1088/1361-6641/ac62fb
5. Bagga, N., Ni, K., Chauhan, N., Prakash, O., Hu, X.S., Amrouch, H.: Cleaved-gate ferroelectric FET for reliable multi-level cell storage. In: IEEE International Reliability Physics Symposium (IRPS), pp. P5-1–P5-5 (March 2022). https://doi.org/10.1109/IRPS48227.2022.9764553
6. Lin, Y.-K., et al.: Analysis and modeling of inner fringing field effect on negative capacitance FinFETs. IEEE Trans. Electron Devices. **66**(4), 2023–2027 (April 2019). https://doi.org/10.1109/TED.2019.2899810
7. Salahuddin, S., Datta, S.: Use of negative capacitance to provide voltage amplification for low power nanoscale devices. Nano Lett. **8**, 405–410 (2008). https://doi.org/10.1021/nl071804g
8. Chauhan, N., et al.: BOX engineering to mitigate negative differential resistance in MFIS negative capacitance FDSOI FET: an analog perspective. Nanotechnology **33**, 085203 (2022). https://doi.org/10.1088/1361-6528/ac328a
9. Jaisawal, R.K., Kondekar, P., Yadav, S., Upadhyay, P., Awadhiya, B., Rathore, S.: Insights into the operation of negative capacitance FinFET for low power logic applications. Microelectron. J. **119**, 105321 (January 2022). https://doi.org/10.1016/j.mejo.2021.105321
10. Liang, Y., et al.: Influence of body effect on sample-andhold circuit design using negative capacitance FET. IEEE Trans. Electron Devices **65**(09), 3909–3914 (2018). https://doi.org/10.1109/TED.2018.2852679
11. Krivokapic, Z., et al.: 14nm Ferroelectric FinFET technology with steep subthreshold slope for ultra-low power applications. In: IEEE International Electron Devices Meeting (IEDM), pp. 15.1.1–15.1.4 (December 2017). https://doi.org/10.1109/IEDM.2017.8268393
12. Agarwal, H., et al.: Engineering negative differential resistance in NCFETs for analog applications. IEEE Trans. Electron Devices **65**(5), 2033–2039 (2018). https://doi.org/10.1109/TED.2018.2817238
13. Chauhan, N., Bagga, N., Banchhor, S., Datta, A., Dasgupta, S., Bulusu, A.: Negative-to-positive differential resistance transition in ferroelectric FET: physical insight and utilization in analog circuits. IEEE Trans. Ultrason. Ferroelectr. Freq. Control **69**(1), 430–437 (2022). https://doi.org/10.1109/TUFFC.2021.3116897
14. Das, D., Khan, A.I.: Ferroelectricity in CMOS-compatible hafnium oxides: reviving the ferroelectric field-effect transistor technology. IEEE Nanotechnol. Mag. **15**(5), 20–32 (2021). https://doi.org/10.1109/MNANO.2021.3098218
15. Böscke, T.S., Müller, J., Braeuhaus, D., Schroeder, U., Bottger, U.: Ferroelectricity in hafnium oxide thin films. Appl. Phys. Lett. **99**, 102903–102903 (September 2011). https://doi.org/10.1063/1.3634052

16. Hoffmann, M., Max, B., Mittmann, T., Schroeder, U., Slesazeck, S., Mikolajick, T.: Demonstration of high-speed hysteresis-free negative capacitance in ferroelectric Hf0.5Zr0.5O2. In: IEEE International Electron Devices Meeting (IEDM), pp. 31.6.1–31.6.4 (December 2018). https://doi.org/10.1109/IEDM.2018.8614677
17. Synopsys Inc. Version K-2015.06-SP1.2020
18. Darwish, M.N., Lentz, J.L., Pinto, M.R., Zeitzoff, P.M., Krutsick, T.J., Hong Ha Vuong: An improved electron and hole mobility model for general purpose device simulation. IEEE Trans. Electron Devices. **44**(9), 1529–1538 (September 1997). https://doi.org/10.1109/16.622611
19. Yadav, S., Upadhyay, P., Awadhiya, B., Kondekar, P.N.: Design and analysis of improved phase-transition FinFET utilizing negative capacitance. IEEE Trans. Electron Devices **68**(2), 853–859 (2021). https://doi.org/10.1109/TED.2020.3043222
20. Pahwa, G., Dutta, T., Agarwal, A., Chauhan, Y.S.: Designing energy efficient and hysteresis free negative capacitance FinFET with negative DIBL and 3.5X ION using compact modeling approach. In: 46th European Solid-State Device Research Conference (ESSDERC), pp. 41–46 (September 2016). https://doi.org/10.1109/ESSDERC.2016.7599584
21. Rathore, S., Jaisawal, R.K., Kondekar, P.N., Bagga, N.: Design optimization of three-stacked nanosheet FET from self-heating effects perspective. IEEE Trans. Device Mater. Reliab. (2022). https://doi.org/10.1109/TDMR.2022.3181672

i-MAX: Just-In-Time Wakeup of Maximally Gated Router for Power Efficient Multiple NoC

Neelkamal[1], Sonal Yadav[2](✉), and Hemangee K. Kapoor[3]

[1] Intel Technology India Pvt. Ltd., Bangalore, India
neelkamal@intel.com
[2] Computer Science and Engineering, National Institute of Technology, Raipur, India
syadav.cse@nitrr.ac.in
[3] Department of CSE, Indian Institute of Technology Guwahati, Guwahati, India
hemangee@iitg.ac.in

Abstract. Static power dissipation becomes a primary challenge for modern processor architects with the advancement of nanometer technology. Networks-on-Chip (NoC) contributes up to 42% of the total chip power, with routers using 50%–60% of that and static power comprising 76% of the total. The vast majority of routers remain idle in the low network traffic. These routers may be power gated to significantly reduce network static power. However, high-performance loss is a significant disadvantage with gated off routers. The Just-In-Time Wakeup of Maximally Gated Router (i-MAX) that we proposed in this research integrated power gating with multiple NoC. In the i-MAX design, we provide three methods for powering off routers in various NoC networks depending on workloads with high, moderate, and low traffic. When compared to standard NoC design, the advantages in static power have increased by more than 70% with the proposed architecture.

Keywords: Power gating · Multiple networks-on-chip · Router · Static power dissipation

1 Introduction

Energy-proportional computer systems are a need for today's technology because of the dark silicon problem [1]. It is possible to reduce the power consumption of a computer system by using energy proportional computing. Nanometer technology has made it possible to place billions of transistors on a single chip, leading to system on chip architecture, in which we can integrate heterogeneous components such as memory, controller, processor, and so on on a single chip and homogeneous manycore processors that is the foundation of modern processor architecture.

The on-chip network is the best possible solution to provide scalable and less complex communication network to these manycore processors. As the number of cores increases, a high proportion of the processor's power will be consumed

A. P. Shah et al. (Eds.): VDAT 2022, CCIS 1687, pp. 107–117, 2022.
https://doi.org/10.1007/978-3-031-21514-8_10

by its on-chip network. So, to design an energy proportional chip, first it is required to design an energy proportional on-chip network. An on-chip network is energy-proportionate if it consumes power proportional to network demand while having no effect on network latency. Real-time applications generate bursty network traffic, and even when all processing cores are engaged, network demand is not always approaching saturation. Static power becomes a critical problem in this instance since the number of routers and their complexity rises in order to scale up the bandwidth for processors with a high number of cores. The percentage of total power lost owing to static power is anticipated to rise. Even at network saturation, static power owing to network components may be as high as 39% in a 256-core system.

Power gating of underutilised network components may be very beneficial in reducing static power and obtaining an energy proportional on-chip network. Power gating may be used more successfully on multiple NoCs than on a single NoC. Because a whole subnet may be switched off in multiple NoC without losing network connection. It significantly contributes to the reduction of static power. It is also possible to reduce dynamic power consumption by efficiently distributing traffic over multiple NoCs, regardless of the traffic workload. Many-core processors need a high-bandwidth network. Because of the complex router design, the larger routers on single-plane NoC function at a high voltage. A bandwidth-equivalent, simpler router comprising multiple NoC operating on the same frequency, on the other hand, may overcome crossbar delay. Because power rises quadratically with respect to voltage, the power of a single wider router is greater than the aggregate power of multiple narrower routers in high-bandwidth networks. We have proposed Just-In-Time Wakeup of Maximally Gated Router (i-MAX) by integrating power gating approach on multiple NoC architectures. We have presented three different power gating strategies based on high, moderate, and low traffic workloads. These designs increase static power efficiency while incurring minimal performance penalty.

The rest of the paper is structured as follows. Section 2 discusses related work on multi-plane NoC and power gating approaches briefly. Section 3 explores how to integrate the power gating approach into a dual-plane NoC in various ways based on traffic workload. Section 4 compares the result metrics of the proposed power gating approaches to the conventional NoC. Section 5 concludes the results and discusses future research directions.

2   Motivation and Related Works

This section is broken into two subsections. The first provides a brief discussion of how multi-plane NoC design may improve NoC performance. The second part examines how power gating aids in the development of more energy-efficient NoC designs.

2.1   Multi-plane NoC

Initially, two approaches were proposed to increase NoC performance. The first technique uses virtual channels for maximum sustained throughput, whereas the second employs multiple physical networks in which resources are distributed over multiple independent and parallel physical networks or planes. Virtual Channels (VCs) offer logical channels for packet flow, which complicates router design, increasing critical path delay, occupying more area, and using more power. When total storage is limited, multi-plane routers are beneficial to use since they have a basic architecture that requires less area and power, making them more scalable than VCs and vice versa.

One plane in the multi-plane NoC is dedicated to efficient data transport, while others are dedicated to transport control messages. The performance improvement is dependent on the traffic pattern of running application. both the designs have their own benefits, we have used VCs with separate parallel physical networks by partitioning VCs across various physical networks [2]. Thus, multi-plane routers with fewer VCs have reduced hardware complexity and higher performance with lower latency than single-plane routers with a large number of VCs [3]. Multi-plane NoCs additionally provide separate parallel data flows via multiple NoC interconnects. They are more efficient in terms of power and energy than bandwidth equivalent single-NoCs due to their flexibility in traffic distribution and freedom of various hardware customization [4]. Multi-plane NoCs also provide improved bandwidth scalability and assure protocol-level deadlock freedom for various message classes.

This study indicates that routers perform a very crucial role in NoC performance and multi-plane virtual channel based router can be an effective design for Network-on-Chip to get better performance and lesser hardware complexity.

2.2   Power Gating

Power gating reduces static power usage. Routers contribute most of NoC's static power due to its buffers and complicated crossbar logic design. Whereas low traffic injection rate causes significant router idle time, approximately 70% [5]. Hence, switching off the router or its component reduces static power consumption in NoC but increases packet latency. As a result, packet detours or waiting for the downstream router to wake up. In this section, we examine several strategies suggested to enhance power gated NoC network performance.

An additional Duty Buffer (DB) structure may replace the need for VCs since it can hold incoming packets regardless of the number of VCs. As a result, VCs may be power gated with just a 9.67% increase in packet latency; nonetheless, this is not an efficient technique since it adds hardware cost, area overhead, and latency still has substantial value [6].

After investigating the characteristics of deterministic routing algorithms and mesh topology, it is discovered that at a router, packets are either forwarded in the same direction or ejected when the destination is reached, and they only make a few turns in the path. This is similar to X-Y routing, where only one

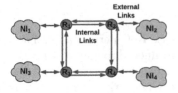
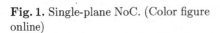
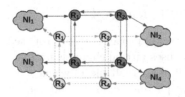

Fig. 1. Single-plane NoC. (Color figure online)

Fig. 2. Dual-plane Multiple NoC. (Color figure online)

turn is required for a packet to travel from source to destination. Based on these findings, a bypass latch and control unit is employed to prevent a router from turning on when it transmits a packet on a straight line or ejects a packet. When compared to standard power-gating, our method improves static power, performance, and network latency while incurring little area overhead [7].

Network latency can be reduced while still having advantage in static power consumption by using Power Punch approach [8]. Where wake-up signals generated at a router stay ahead of the data packet by few hops. All of these insights were gleaned through a thorough review of the literature. The research so far shows that the average network power of a power-gating optimized Multi-Plabe NoC design with four subnets could be 44% lower than a bandwidth equivalent single-network design [2]. Therefore, power gating and Multi-Plane NoC design are combined in our proposed approach to maximise the advantages of both techniques.

3   Implementation of Power Gated Dual-Plane NoC

Network interface (NI) (cloud form in light blue) is linked to a router (circle in light green colour) in the NoC architecture, as shown in Fig. 1. The controller of processor forwards messages to network interface, where these messages are split into flits (the size of which varies on the network link's width) and sent to an NI's local router through bi-directional external connections, where they are sent into the network (double headed arrow in dark green colour). Both the network interface and processing element get a response message from a local router through their respective bi-directional external connection. After receiving a flit, the router begins the pipeline process that is finished in one cycle.

Internal links are used to send the packet to the downstream router (single headed arrow in light green colour). A router performs a variety of functions including buffer write and route computation, switch allocation to determine which input port is selected in the event of output port contention. Virtual channel allocation determines which virtual channel this packet will be stored on the downstream router. The credits link is used to convey control information to the router, which is then utilised to implement the flow control mechanism.

Figure 1, represents the basic single-plane NoC structure as described for 2×2 Mesh topology. The dual-plane NoC architecture has the same resources

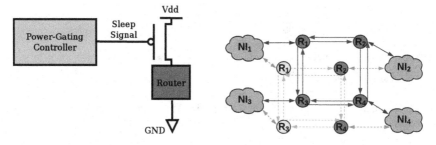

Fig. 3. Power-Gating Mechanism.   **Fig. 4.** Approach-1 NOC design (Color figure online)

as it's bandwidth-equivalent single-plane NoC, the only difference is that these resources are equally distributed between both planes. Fig. 2 represents the dual-plane NoC structure for 2×2 Mesh topology. Here, there is no link between plane-1 (NoC in light green colour) and plane-2 (NoC in light pink colour) that means the flit injected in one plane remains in the same plane until it reaches it's destination also both the planes (networks) function independently.

An additional piece of hardware is used to implement power gating for router. Every router has a power gating (PG) controller installed, and it is always operational. For example, PG controller monitors router components and different signals (which are sent via Pg links), it also stores information about neighbouring router status and conducts power-gating actions when specific event occur. A PG controller's fundamental architecture is shown in Fig. 3.

Pg signals are used to implement power gating. When all of a router's data paths are idle, it will wait for TIMEOUT cycles to check whether any of its neighbours are sending it a packet. The PG controller sends the Sleep signal if no neighbour sends a packet, and the router goes into sleep mode. Additionally, the controller informs all of the router's neighbours through pg connections that the router is in a sleep mode. Sending SWUREQ (Sleep to wakeup request) signals over pg connections is required before any router may deliver a packet to an idle router. As soon as PG controller gets a SWUREQ signal, the router is awakened. This process takes around TWU (time to wake up) cycles. A packet must wait in the sender's router throughout the sleep-to-awake transition phase, this increases packet delay. Here, the main cause of poor performance and an increase in average packet delay is long router waking times. Many strategies have been suggested to reduce the time it takes to wake up from a deep sleep. Our dual-plane NoC design employs the power punch [8] mechanism.

After implementing the dual-plane NoC design, we have established the injection rate criterion for low, moderate, and high network load. Through experimentation and analysis, we determined that for 100000 cycles, uniform random synthetic traffic types, 0.3, 0.7, and 0.9 injection rates are low, moderate, and high traffics.

Figure 4 shows Approach-1, where power gating is performed separately in both planes of a dual-plane NoC when network workload is high (power gated

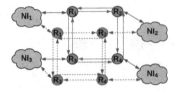 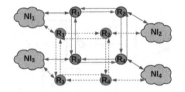

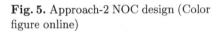

Fig. 5. Approach-2 NOC design (Color figure online)   **Fig. 6.** Approach-3 NOC design (Color figure online)

routers are depicted in grey colour). This behaviour is similar to that of a power gated single-plane NoC.

We have demonstrated Approach-2 in Fig. 5 where, depending on the network load, one plane is entirely power gated (NoC plane in gray colour) while all traffic is routed via another plane and all routers in another plane remain active.

In Fig. 6, we have demonstrated Approach-3, when one plane is entirely power gated (NoC plane in gray colour) and due to very low network load another plane behaves as power gated single-NoC (few routers are active - light green colour, power gated routers are in gray colour).

In the next section, we have experimented and compared results with the bandwidth-equivalent single-plane NoC.

4   Experimental Analysis

In this section, we shall discuss our experimental setup for *i-MAX*, simulation tools, and their configuration parameters, as well as various traffic patterns, traffic injection rates. We have used Approach-1 for high traffic (when injection rate is 0.9), Approach-2 for moderate traffic (when injection rate is 0.7) and Approach-3 for low traffic (when injection rate is 0.3). We have compared their result metrics including average packet network latency, static power, and dynamic power. The proposed power gated dual-plane NoC design is compared to a traditional single NoC architecture.

4.1   Experimental Set-up

Experiments are carried out on Gem5 [9] simulator aggregated with Garnet 2.0 [2], AGATE [10] and DSENT [11] simulator. Garnet provides a basic design of on-chip network, by making change in this module we have implemented dual-plane NoC architecture. The power gating technique is implemented on dual-plane NoC using AGATE simulator. We have used DSENT simulator to evaluate static and dynamic power at 11 nm.

Uniform random synthetic traffic patterns were used in the experiment. For 16 cores and 64 cores interconnected in 4×4 and 8×8 mesh topologies, three distinct injection rates are chosen: 0.3 (low traffic), 0.7 (moderate traffic), and 0.9 (high traffic). The simulation has run for 100000 cycles in both single-plane

Table 1. Network parameters

Parameter	Single-Plane NoC	Dual-Plane NoC
Topology	Mesh	Mesh
Routing Algorithm	XY	XY
Router Pipeline	1 Cycle	1 Cycle
Flow Control	VC Cut Through	VC Cut Through
Number of VCS per Vnet	4	2
Network Link Bandwidth	16 Byte	8 Byte
Network Link Latency	1 Cycle	1 Cycle
Credit Link Latency	1 Cycle	8 Cycle

and dual-plane NoC, without and with power gating. For power-gating controller we set wake-up latency (TWU) 20 cycles, time out period (TIMEOUT) 4 cycles.

The different network parameters that are either configured or present by default in Garnet2.0 are shown in Table 1. Throughout the result analysis, the following acronyms are used: PG means for power gated, NPG stands for not power gated, SP stands for single-plane, and DP/MP stands for dual-plane in all graphs and tables. In graphs, the Y-axis represents network metrics (average packet network latency, static power dissipation, dynamic power dissipation), the X-axis indicates simulation injection rates, and the four bars represent various entities stated in the graphs.

4.2 Latency Graph Analysis

As demonstrated in Figs. 7 and 8, the average packet network latency of Power gated NoC is higher than that of Non Power gated NoC for both single-plane and dual-plane NoC architectures with uniform random traffic (Table 2).

Table 2. Average packet network latency for power gated single-plane and dual-plane NoC for uniform random traffic pattern.

Injection rate	0.3	0.3	0.7	0.7	0.9	0.9
Mesh topology	4×4	8×8	4×4	8×8	4×4	8×8
Average packet network latency for PG SP	27.187	35.578	25.156	34.554	25.343	34.623
Average packet network latency for PG DP	31.812	44.007	30.312	44.609	30.531	44.664

Power gated dual-plane NoC has lower average packet latency than power gated single-plane NoC for a uniform random traffic pattern, as shown in Fig. 9. The traffic pattern has a significant impact on the average packet network latency

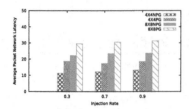

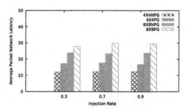

Fig. 7. Average packet network latency for non power gated single-plane NoC and power gated single-plane NoC for uniform random traffic.

Fig. 8. Average packet network latency for non power gated dual-plane NoC and power gated dual-plane NoC for uniform random traffic.

of single-plane NoC and dual-plane NoC. Power gated single-plane NoC's average packet network latency is higher than non-power gated single-plane NoC for uniform random traffic. Similarly, the power gated dual-plane NoC has a higher average packet network latency than the non-power gated dual-plane NoC.

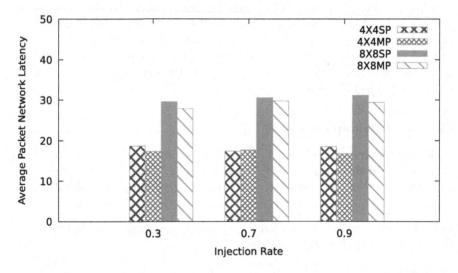

Fig. 9. Average packet network latency for power gated single-plane NoC and power Gated dual-Plane NoC for uniform random traffic.

4.3   Power Graph Analysis

The total network power is the sum of static and dynamic power. This section begins with a static power analysis of the router and then moves on to a dynamic power analysis of the router. Our focus is to reduce static power consumption in routers, which are the primary source of power dissipation in NoC.

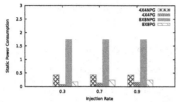

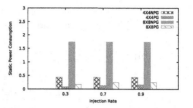

Fig. 10. All Router's Static Power Dissipation in Non Power Gated Single-Plane NoC and Power Gated Single-Plane NoC for Uniform Random Traffic.

Fig. 11. All Router's Static Power Dissipation in Non Power Gated Dual-Plane NoC and Power Gated Dual-Plane NoC for Uniform Random Traffic.

Static Power Analysis. The static power in power gated single-plane NoC is lowered by more than 50% when compared to non power gated single-plane NoC, as shown in Fig. 10.

When comparing in Fig. 11, the static power dissipation in power gated dual-plane NoC is reduced by more than 50% when compared to non power gated dual-plane NoC for uniform random. As a consequence, we have significantly reduced static power, which is one of the aims of proposed approach.

Dynamic Power Analysis. Table 3 shows that the dynamic power due to switching activity of the hardware by power gated dual-plane NoC is **0.35%** less for 4X4 and **0.5%** less for 8X8 configuration as compared to single-plane NoC design for uniform random traffic.

Table 3. All router's dynamic power dissipation in power gated single-plane NoC and dual-plane NoC for uniform random traffic.

Injection rate	4X4 SP	4X4 DP	8X8 SP	8X8 DP
0.3	0.231402	0.23069	0.928183	0.922761
0.7	0.2315	0.23069	0.928261	0.922761
0.9	0.231429	0.23069	0.928083	0.922761

Likewise, Table 4 shows that the dynamic power of non power gated dual-plane NoC is somewhat less than that of the single-plane NoC design. So we can conclude that dual-plane NoC dissipates less power than single-plane NoC. Also dynamic power consumption for dual-plane NoC with or without power-gating will be negligible as the power-gating mechanism affect static power component. This is compared for uniform random traffic.

Table 4. All router's dynamic power dissipation in non power gated single-plane NoC and dual-plane NoC for uniform random traffic

Injection rate	4X4 SP	4X4 DP	8X8 SP	8X8 DP
0.3	0.231474	0.23069	0.928528	0.922761
0.7	0.231589	0.23069	0.928445	0.922761
0.9	0.231434	0.23069	0.92838	0.922761

5   Conclusion

We have proposed Just-In-Time Wakeup of Maximally Gated Router (i-MAX) architecture by integrating power gating technique with dual plane NoC architecture. The dual-plane NoC is formed via partitioning of single-plane NoC architecture. Routers are power-gated according to high, moderate, and low traffic workloads in dual-plane NoC. In approach 1, the performance penalty is less severe since there is more traffic on the network. Because the packet passes through both planes of the dual-plane NoC throughout its journey. This means that packets have to wait a shorter amount of time for the downstream router to completely wake up. Because of this, there is less performance loss, and there are less advantages in terms of static power, because routers are power gated for a shorter period of time. When there is a moderate amount of traffic on the network, approach-2 may power gate one entire plane or NoC. As a result, the static power advantages are increased, and the performance cost is reduced. This is because half of the routers are power gated for the most of the time, and because packets flow over the active plane, reducing the number of gated routers they encounter. When traffic is very low, we have proposed approach 3, which results in static power benefits that are greater than 70% when compared to non-power gated single-plane and dual-plane NoC. This is possible because one NoC remains power gated and the majority of the routers in another NoC network are also power gated the majority of the time. On the other hand, there has been an increase of around 40% in the typical latency of packet networks.

Nevertheless, in the future, it will be possible to circumvent this cost by using effective routing strategies for approach-3. A control logic may be designed for general purpose processors in order to automatically transition between three distinct modes. These modes are determined by the amount of network traffic that is traversed through network and automate the process of activating planes in response to the detection of the workload on the network. We will also alter the power gating approach for dual-plane NoC with a simplified Leon power-gating controller [5]. This will further lower the average packet network latency without losing the advantages of static power.

References

1. Karkar, A., Dahir, N., Mak, T., Tong, K.: Thermal and Performance efficient on-chip surface-wave communication for many-core systems in dark silicon era. In: J. Emerg. Technol. Comput. Syst. **18**(3), 18 (2022)
2. Yadav, S., Raj, R.: Power efficient network selector placement in control plane of multiple networks-on-chip. J. Supercomputing **78**(5), 6664–6695 (2021). https://doi.org/10.1007/s11227-021-04098-4
3. Noh, S., Ngo, V., Jao, H., Choi, H.: Multiplane virtual channel router for network-on-chip design. In: First International Conference on Communications and Electronics, pp. 348–351 (2006)
4. Yadav, S., Laxmi, V., Gaur, M.: Multiple-NoC exploration and customization for energy efficient traffic distribution. In: IFIP/IEEE 28th International Conference on Very Large Scale Integration (VLSI-SOC), Salt Lake City, UT, USA (2020)
5. Neelkamal, Yadav, S., Kapoor, H.: Lightweight message encoding of power-gating controller for on-time wakeup of gated router in network-on-chip. In: 9th International Symposium on Embedded Computing and System Design (ISED), pp. 1–6 (2019)
6. Wang, P., Niknam, S., Wang, Z., Stefanov, T.: A novel approach to reduce packet latency increase caused by power gating in network-on-chip. In: Proceedings of the Eleventh IEEE/ACM International Symposium on Networks-on-Chip, pp. 1–8 (2017)
7. Farrokhbakht, H., Taram, M., Khaleghi, B., Hessabi, S.: Toot: an efficient and scalable power-gating method for NoC routers. In: Tenth IEEE/ACM International Symposium on Networks-on-Chip (NOCS), pp. 1–8 (2016)
8. Chen, L., Zhu, D., Pedram, M., Pinkston, T.: Power punch: towards non-blocking power-gating of NoC routers. In: IEEE 21st International Symposium on High Performance Computer Architecture (HPCA), pp. 378–389 (2015)
9. Qureshi, Y.M., Simon, W., Zapater, M., Olcoz, K., Atienza, D.: Gem5-x: a many-core heterogeneous simulation platform for architectural exploration and optimization. ACM Trans. Archit. Code Optim. (TACO) **18**(4), 1–27 (2021)
10. Chen, L., Zhu, D., Pedram, M., Pinkston, T.: Simulation of NoC power-gating: requirements, optimizations, and the agate simulator. J. Parallel Distrib. Comput. **95**, 69–78 (2016)
11. Sun, C., et al.: DSENT-A tool connecting emerging photonics with electronics for opto-electronic networks-on chip modeling. In: IEEE/ACM 6th International Symposium on Networks-on-Chip. IEEE, pp. 201–210 (2012)

Quantum Tunnelling and Themonic Emission, Transistor Simulation

Shivendra Yadav[1]($\boxtimes$), Deepak Joshi[1], Sanjib Kalita[2], and Tushita Singh[3]

[1] Sardar Vallabhbhai National Institute of Technology, Surat, Gujarat, India
shivendra.y@eced.svnit.ac.in
[2] RGM College of Engineering and Technology, Nandyal, AP, India
[3] Indian Institute of Information Technology Design and Manufacturing, Jabalpur, MP, India

Abstract. The novelty of the article is to bring the concept of thermionic emission and inter-band tunnelling together in the charge plasma tunnel FET (CP-TFET). The use of a thin n+ the doped layer which is placed under the channel in a dielectric box (SiO_2) injects extra electrons into the channel through the vertical thermionic emission process. The vertical thermionic emission causes a surplus to the electrons that are coming from horizontal tunnelling and that leads to six decades of furtherance in the drain current and ten decades of increment in the leakage current in the conventional CP-TFET structure. In addition, deposition of two metals of different work-function over the drain region is used for resolving the issues of higher leakage and ambipolar behavior of conventional TFET in the final state of art. The dual metal drain improves the reliability concern of CP-TFET at circuit level implementation and AS provides a good current driving ability.

Keywords: Charge plasma · Additional source (AS) · Ambipolarity · Thermionic emission · First Section

1 Introduction

High speed, low power consumption with high performance are the dire need of today's exponentially growing electronics era. Downscaling of MOSFET has played a vital role in the development of the semiconductor industry by providing superior device properties in terms of compactness, cost-effectiveness, low power supply and high operating speed [1]. But, as MOSFETs enter into nano regime, it leads to several short channel effects as channel length modulation, hot carrier effect, surface scattering, velocity saturation and more [2, 3]. Moreover, process variation as random dopant fluctuations (RDFs) is crucial at nano scale, which results in increment in standby power consumption because of high OFF state current and non abrupt junction [4, 5]. These shortcomings severely affect the performance of MOSFET. Therefore, researchers paying attention to various innovative devices like FinFET, Carbon nanotubes FET, carbon nanowire structure and 2D materials instead of conventional silicon. All of these have their pros and cons in their specific application domains [6]. In addition, tunnel FET is also one of the competing devices in

A. P. Shah et al. (Eds.): VDAT 2022, CCIS 1687, pp. 118–125, 2022.
https://doi.org/10.1007/978-3-031-21514-8_11

modern electronics, where Wentzel-Kramers Brillouin (WKB [7] is approximating the tunnelling current by the equation:

$$I_{tun} = exp\left(\frac{4\lambda\sqrt{2m}E_g^{3/2}}{3q\hbar(\Delta\varnothing + E_g)}\right)$$ (1)

where I_{tun} is approximated tunnelling current by WKB, E_g is energy band gap which varies upon material to material. Further, ^-h and q are having their standard notation. Whereas, φ is the overlapped energy of conduction and valence band, λ is shielding distance for potential. This (λ) is a critical parameter which contribute into tunnelling in two ways; by defining the doping profile at the tunnelling junction and dimension of channel [7]. TFETs have proven themselves as one of the most permissible and reliable device structures to overcome the constraints of CMOS technology. Due to its working mechanism of voltage-controlled band to band tunnelling of carriers [8] they have improved characteristics compared to the MOSFET. TFET deliver subthreshold swing (SS) below 60 mV/decade at 300 K, they are unaffected from short channel effects and provide a low leakage current (IOFF) and steeper slopes [9, 10]. But, in the nano region, physically doped TFET has their own issues (poor tunnelling) due to non-abrupt tunnelling junction caused by Random dopant fluctuation (RDFs) in the planer technology.

For resolving these issues doping less devices (charge plasma TFET and electrically doped TFET) come into the picture. Charge plasma TFET (CP-TFET) is based on work function (WF) engineering for creating the P-I-N structure [11]. Whereas, in electrically doped TFET the n+ and p+ regions are created by applying appropriate voltage on the source/drain electrodes [12, 13]. Arrangement of drain and source regions by charge plasma grips the merit of not using chemical implantation and reduced RDFs as well [13]. But, metal deposition (electrodes of different WF) causes weaker inversion in case of CP-TFET and leads to a barrier at the source/channel junction and causes poor DC/RF performance and lower current driving ability even in double gate structure [11]. In addition, CP-TFET further suffers from other reliability issues like ambipolarity, which represents shifting of tunnelling junction from source to drain side for negative VGS [14].

To resolve these issues, we have introduced a n+ film (AS) in the charge plasma based TFET as shown in the Fig. 1(b) that is symbolised as AS-CP-TFET. Additional source (AS) delivers extra free charge carriers in the channel region which increases ON state current of the device and transconductance; by virtue of higher transconductance the parameters of high frequency also get improved. But, vertical thermionic emission caused by AS in the channel region leads to higher leakage current in conventional CP-TFET. The insight physics is demonstrated in the subsequent sections through various means, where we can see the exact mechanism. Aforementioned issues are overcome by using two distinct workfunction over the drain region along with AS in the final structure ASDMD-CP-TFET as shown in the Fig. 1(c). As far as fabrication is concerned of dual metal drain, that can be done by interdiffusion of first metal into second one by putting them on the top of each other as reported in [15]. It offers higher work-function for the drain segment closer to the gate electrode which reduces tunnelling of the hole by increasing the barrier at the drain channel junction [16] in ambipolar state. Also causes quantum well under the drain electrode which prevents the flow of carriers from source to drain and channel to drain (by vertical thermionic emission) in the OFF-state. The whole manuscript is categorized into 4 sections. First one is introduction and Sect. 2 presents the device structure with models discussion. Important results and their discussions related to device calibration and characteristics have been presented in Sect. 3. Finally all findings are summarized in the last section.

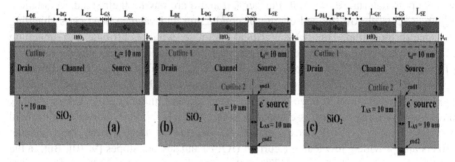

Fig. 1. Design of device (a) CP-Tunnel FET, (b) AS-CP-Tunnel FET and (c) AS-DMD-CP-Tunnel FET.

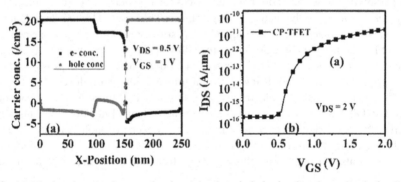

Fig. 2. (a) Black colour is electron density red colour is hole density along the device lateral length and (b) transfer characteristics of calibertaed device. (Color figure online)

2   Dimensions and Model Description

A 10 nm silicon wafer with $10^{15}/cm^{-3}$ n type doping used as a substrate body for all the three devices. A 2 nm thin layer of a dielectric material HfO_2 is grown as the oxide layer under the source, drain and gate electrodes in the devices to inhibit the silicide over source/drain regions [11, 17]. Figure 1(a–c) is visualizing the planer cross-sectional aspect of CP-TFET, additional source CP-TFET (AS-CP-TFET) and additional source dual metal drain CP-TFET (AS-DMD-CPTFET) respectively. Length (LAS) and thickness (TAS) of additional source (AS) is kept 10 nm and has been physically doped to the concentration of 10^{19} cm^{-3}. Length of gate and source electrodes (L$_{GE}$ and L$_{SE}$) are kept at 50 nm in all the three designs and L$_{DE}$ = 45 nm. Dual drain lengths in ASDMD-CP-TFET, LDE1 and L$_{DE2}$ are set at 25 nm and 20 nm respectively. Gate to drain and source spacer length is equal to 10 nm and 5 nm respectively in the three devices. Appropriate work functions of 3.3 eV (Hf), 4.5 eV and 5.93 eV (Pt) are applied on the drain (φ_{DE}), gate (φ_{GE}) and source (φ_{SE}) electrodes respectively to form the n + and p + regions by charge plasma [13]. Further, dual metal work function (φ_{DE2} = 4.0 eV) is applied at the drain electrode DE2 in AS-DMDCP-TFET. Nickel silicide (Nisi) has been used as the electrode for source and drain contacts. SILVACO 2D-TCAD 2014 version is typically used for simulations; here, nonlocal 2D BTBT model is accommodated by defining rigorous meshing for accounting the tunnelling at junction [7]. The model accounts generation rates at all the points of meshing. BGN is the model that is used to include the band gap alteration because of the heavily doped n+ region. Schottky is one of the SILVACO model which accounts the carrier flow at drain/source silicon end contacts with metal. Shockley-ReadHall (SRH) and Auger generation recombination models are activated by SRH and AUGER parameters for calculating the recombination probability in the channel region [18]. Field mobility in horizontal (lateral) and mobility depends upon concentration are critical measure which are covered by Fermi Dirac statical model. At last quantum confinement model is introduced to include trap assisted tunnelling in BTBT [19].

3   Result and Discussion

Before uncovering and establishing the simulation concepts, we need to authenticate and calibrate the used models. Here, first, the charge plasma formation is verified by work-function engineering near the surface of convention CP-TFET in comparison to [20, 21] and found approximately the same carrier concentration as shown in Fig. 2(a). It is important to note that the calibration of models is done at the same dimensions and other conditions as reported. Apart from achieving a similar carrier concentration, we are following the reference device in terms of transfer characteristics also through Fig. 2(b). The figure is illustrating the drain current with VGS in a comparative sense. The calibrated device is having diminished leakage due to charge plasma rather than physical doping [21]. For device analysis doping concentration and work functions over source/drain regions are kept constant along with the drain to source voltage (VDS) and only (VGS) changes over the device operation. Figure 3(a) exposing that the electric field at source and channel junction is nearly equal in all three devices; which is offering the same tunnelling probability for all three devices. By Fig. 3(b) the concept can be more confirmed which is depicting EBD in ON state with cutline 1, indicating the similar tunnelling width or barrier at the junction for carriers transport. Further, Fig. 3(c) depicts the vertical EBD in ON state along cutline 2, showing the movement of electrons from n+ doped AS into the channel region over the barrier. Since the channel is lightly n doped and it turns out to be more n-type when the device is in the ON state, whereas the AS is already heavily n+ doped.

In this condition, the barrier is very low between AS and channel, therefore the electrons started travelling from AS to channel through over the barrier. Here the importance

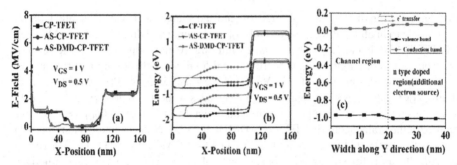

Fig. 3. (a) Electric field, (b) EBD along cutline 1 and (c) vertical EBD along cutline 2 in ON state.

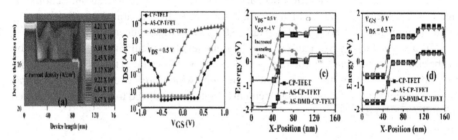

Fig. 4. (a) Contour plot of electron current density, (b) transfer characteristics, (c) EBD along cutline 1 in ambipolar condition and (d) distribution of energy bands with cut-line 1 in OFF state.

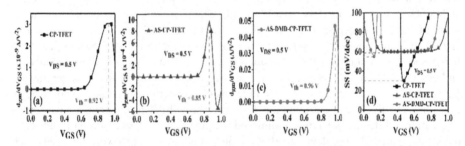

Fig. 5. Modelling of threshold voltage by transconductance first derivative method for individual devices. The peak of the graph reflects the threshold voltage of the device. (a) Vth of CP-TFET, (b) Vth of AS-CP-TFET, (c) Vth of AS-DMD-CP-TFET, (d) the graph shows comparative minimum point SS for all three devices as it is modelled as per the [23]. Since we are calculating the minimum SS therefor the lowest value of the curve is marked in the graph for all three devices

of AS can be understood in terms of addition carrier supplier from the opposite side of the gate electrode into the channel region. Figure 4(a) further strengthens the fact with the contour plot, indicating the high electron current density due to AS that is responsible for introducing extra carrier along with the tunnelling electrons in the channel region. Figure 4(b) shows the transfer characteristic of the devices, which reflects that ON-state current of AS-DMD-CP-TFET and AS-CP-TFET show a drastic improvement in drain current as compared to CP-TFET which is in the order of 10–4 A/um. It can also be noted that there is a hike in the leakage current in AS-CP-TFET due to thermionic emission as compared to CP-TFET. In addition, the problem of ambipolar current also persists; both of these issues are rectified by introducing the concept of drain work function engineering.

Table 1. DC characteristics

DC quantities/Unit	CP-TFET	AS-CP-TFET	AS-CP-TFET
V_{th} (V)	0.92	0.85	0.96
ON current (A/um)	7.793×10^{-11}	8.204×10^{-5}	1.984×10^{-4}
OFF current (A/um)	2.810×10^{-18}	7.308×10^{-15}	4.067×10^{-19}
Ambipolar current (A/um)	6.874×10^{-14}	7.312×10^{-13}	3.141×10^{-19}
SS (mV/dec)	29.773	60.204	59.72

Figure 4(c) and 4(d) show energy band diagram along cutline 1, which shows a notable upward shift in the energy bands under drain region-2 (DE2) for AS-DMD-CP-TFET in ambipolar as well as OFF- state respectively. As a result, the tunnelling barrier turns to be wider for the electrons that are trying to tunnel from the channel into the drain for negative V_{GS}, in the ambipolar state. Owing to the higher work function material ($\varphi_{DE2} = 4.0$ eV) as a part of the drain electrode leads to a decrement in tunnelling probability at drain/channel interface and causes suppression in ambipolar current. Further, the misalignment of energy bands under OFF state provides a restriction to the movement of electrons and suppresses the leakage as depicted in Fig. 4(b). Also, V_{th} of the devices have been calculated by the transconductance derivative method [22]. Figure 5(a–c) show the variation of transconductance derivative for CP-TFET, AS-CP-TFET and AS-DMD-CP-TFET respectively with gate voltage and the sharp peak of the curve reflects the threshold voltage of individual devices. Figure 5(d) is used to illustrate the minimum point subthreshold swing (SS) as reported in [23]; AS-CPTFET and AS-DMD-CP-TFET are suffering from higher SS due to the reason of thermionic emission. The mathematically modelled SS and V_{th} are further validated by simulation values which are given in Table 1.

4 Conclusion

The article first time proposes a state of art with the combined effect of band to band tunnelling and thermionic emission with drain electrode work-function engineering. A n+ doped additional source near the source-channel junction is deposited which leads to extra carriers (electrons) in the channel region through vertical thermionic emission along with horizontal tunnelling. AS-CP-TFET (second device) results in drastic improvement in the DC parameters due to the combined mechanism but, it contains issues of higher leakage and negative conductance. Therefore, a dual drain electrode is also introduced with AS in CP-TFET for making the device more secure and reliable. The dual work-function of the drain electrode not only causes misalignment in energy bands in ambipolar state but also forms a quantum well in the OFF-state. The aforementioned facts became reasons for suppressed leakage and ambipolar current in AS-DMD-CPTFET respectively.

References

1. Koswatta, S.O., Lundstrom, M.S., Nikonov, D.E.: Performance comparison between pin tunneling transistors and conventional MOSFETs. IEEE Trans. Electron Devices **56**(3), 456–465 (2009)
2. Damrongplasit, N., Kim, S.H., Liu, T.J.K.: Study of random dopant fluctuation induced variability in the raised-Ge-source TFET. IEEE Electron Device Lett. **34**(2), 184–186 (2013)
3. Duvvury, C.: A guide to short-channel effects in MOSFETs. IEEE Circuits Devices Mag. **2**(6), 6–10 (1986)
4. Damrongplasit, N., Shin, C., Kim, S.H., Vega, R.A., Liu, T.J.K.: Study of random dopant fluctuation effects in germanium-source tunnel FETs. IEEE Trans. Electron Devices **58**(10), 3541–3548 (2011)
5. Shin, C., Sun, X., Liu, T.J.K.: Study of random-dopant-fluctuation (RDF) effects for the trigate bulk MOSFET. IEEE Trans. Electron Devices **56**(7), 1538–1542 (2009)
6. Hajare, R., Lakshminarayana, C., Raghunandan, G.H., raj, C.P.: Performance enhancement of FINFET and CNTFET at different node technologies. Microsyst. Technol. **22**(5), 1121–1126 (2015). https://doi.org/10.1007/s00542-015-2468-9
7. ATLAS Device Simulation Software, Silvaco Int., Santa Clara (2014)
8. Royer, C.L., Mayer, F.: Exhaustive experimental study of tunnel field effect transistors (TFETs): from materials to architecture. In: Proceedings of the 10th International Conference Ultimate Integration of Silicon, pp. 53–56 (May 2009)
9. Choi, W.Y., Park, B.G., Lee, J.D., Liu, T.J.K.: Tunneling field effect transistor (TFETs) with subthreshold swing (SS) less than 60 mV/Dec. IEEE Electron Device Lett. **28**(8), 743–745 (2007)
10. Yadav, S.K., Sharma, D., Soni, D., Aslam, M.: Controlling ambipolarity with improved RF performance by drain/gate work function engineering and using high K dielectric material in electrically doped TFET: proposal and optimization. J. Comput. Electron. **16**(3), 721–731 (2017)
11. Kumar, M.J., Janardhanan, S.: Doping-less tunnel field effect transistor: design and investigation. IEEE Trans. Electron Devices **60**(10), 3285–3290 (2013)
12. Lahgere, A., Sahu, C., Singh, J.: PVT-aware design of dopingless dynamically congurable tunnel FET. IEEE Trans. Electron Devices **62**(8), 2404–2409 (2015)
13. Kumar, M.J., Nadda, K.: Bipolar charge-plasma transistor: a novel three terminal device. IEEE Trans. Electron Devices **59**(4), 962–967 (2012)
14. Zhang, Q., Zhao, W., Seabaugh, A.: Low-subthreshold-swing tunnel transistors. IEEE Electron Device Lett. **27**(4), 297–300 (2006)
15. Polishchuk, I., Ranade, P., King, T.J., Hu, C.: Dual work function metal gate CMOS technology using metal interdiffusion. IEEE Electron Device Lett. **22**(9), 444–446 (September 2001)
16. Mohankumar, N., Syamal, B., Sarkar, C.K.: Influence of channel and gate engineering on the analog and RF performance of DG MOSFETs. IEEE Trans. Electron Devices **57**(4), 820–826 (2010)
17. Nigam, K., Kondekar, P., Sharma, D.: DC characteristics and analog/RF performance of novel polarity control GaAs-Ge based tunnel field effect transistor. Superlattices Microstruct. **92**(C), 224–231 (April 2016)

18. Haug, A.: Auger recombination in direct-gap semiconductors: bandstructure effects. J. Phys. C: Solid State Phys. **16**(21), 4159–4172 (1983)
19. Schenk, A.: A model for the field and temperature dependence of Shockley-read-hall lifetimes in silicon. Solid State Electron **35**(11), 1585–1596 (1992)
20. Boucart, K., Ionescu, A.M.: Double-gate TFET with high-k gate dielectric. IEEE Trans. Electron Devices **54**(7), 1725–1733 (2007)
21. Wang, P.F., et al.: Complementary tunneling transistor for low power application. Solid State Electron. **48**(12), 2281–2286 (2004)
22. Raad, B.R., Tirkey, S., Sharma, D., Kondekar, P.: A new design approachof dopingless TFET for enhancement of device characteristics. IEEE Trans. Electron Devices **64**(4), 1830–1836 (2017)
23. Pahwa, G., et al.: Analysis and compact modeling of negative capacitance transistor with high on-current and negative output differential resistance part II: model validation. IEEE Trans. Electron Devices **63**(12), 4986–4992 (2016)

Electro-Thermal Analysis of Vertically Stacked Gate All Around Nano-sheet Transistor

Arvind Bisht[1] , Yogendra Pratap Pundir[1,2](✉) , and Pankaj Kumar Pal[1]

[1] Deptartment of Electronics Engineering, National Institute of Technology, Srinagar Garhwal, Uttarakhand 246174, India
y.pratap.iisc@gmail.com

[2] Deptartment of Electronics and Communication Engineering, HNB Garhwal University, Srinagar Garhwal, Uttarakhand 246174, India

Abstract. This paper presents optimization of drain/source extension length of 5 nm node Nano-sheet Transistor (NSHT) using a fully-calibrated TCAD platform. A 12 nm extension length shows a 49.5% increase in I_{ON}/I_{OFF} compared to NSHT with a 5 nm extension length. For the extension lengths longer than 12 nm, I_{ON}/I_{OFF} begins degrading. SHEs effects are worse for higher supply voltages (V_{DD}). An increase in V_{DD} from 0.7 V to 1.5 V results in a 50.89% increase in peak lattice temperature for the NSHT. Also, at $V_{DD} = 1.5$ V, the ON current (I_{ON}) degrades by 12.27% when SHEs are considered. Finally, the effect of different spacer dielectric materials on SHEs is studied for the optimized NSHT device. The I_{ON} degradations of 11.73%, 10.68%, and 12.27% are observed for HfO_2, Si_3N_4, and SiO_2, respectively. The use of spacer dielectric with larger thermal conductivity is observed as a possible remedy to tackle the I_{ON} degradation.

Keywords: Nano-sheet transistor · SHEs · Spacer dielectric material · Extension length

1 Introduction

Gate-all-around (GAA) stacked nano-sheet-field-effect transistor (NSHT) architecture has evolved as a key to carrying on the scaling toward the 5-nm technology node and beyond. It offers better electrostatic channel control and cell ratio modulation by continuously allowing the width to change [1]. Fabrication of the nano-sheet transistors (NSHTs) is possible by using the stacked active and sacrificial material as reported in [1]. NSHTs have the benefit of a GAA architecture and are a promising candidate as successors to Fin-FETs [1–4]. Moreover, the stacked nano-sheets with the {100} surface orientation potentially have higher electron mobility than Fin-FETs with the {110} sidewall orientation [5]. Several studies report on the performance of nano-sheet transistors [6–8]. Optimization of electro-thermal characteristics of NSHTs with a doping distribution of 0.8 nm/decade is reported in [9]. SHEs affect the performance of nanoscale transistors [10–12]. A study of electro-thermal effects in NSHTs with a doping distribution of 1.25 nm/decade is done in [12]. Various doping distribution rates have been reported

© The Author(s), under exclusive license to Springer Nature Switzerland AG 2022
A. P. Shah et al. (Eds.): VDAT 2022, CCIS 1687, pp. 126–136, 2022.
https://doi.org/10.1007/978-3-031-21514-8_12

by varying the Source/Drain and channel doping concentrations with a fixed extension length (L_{EXT}) of 5 nm. In the current work, we propose an NSHT device optimized at an extension length and investigate the optimized NSHT for SHEs effects (SHEs) for different supply voltage values (V_{DD}). Finally, using different spacer materials is explored to solve the SHE-related degradation of NSHT devices.

2   Device Structure and Simulation Setup

A 3D nano-sheet transistor structure is realized using the Sentaurus 3D technology-computer-aided-design (TCAD) tools [13–15]. Table 1 below displays the physical device dimensions and parameters used for the designed NSHT. Figure 1 shows a 2D prospect of the three-channel NSHT and the doping concentration distribution. A TCAD framework is calibrated with the reported experimental data [1] for N-type NSHT of a 5 nm technology node. Silicon material of transport orientation {100} is used. The gate dielectric stack comprises an interfacial layer of silicon dioxide (SiO_2) and the high-k dielectric layer of hafnium oxide (HfO_2). Side spacers use low-k dielectric material with relative permittivity of 5. For modeling the NSHT behavior, the density-gradient model and the basic drift-diffusion transport equation are solved, self-consistently, together with the Poisson and carrier-continuity equations [4]. The density-gradient model incorporates quantum-mechanical effects at nanoscale dimensions. The Old-Slot-Boom model considers Silicon bandgap narrowing effects. The Thin-Layer model considers the structural confinement of charge carriers in nano-sheets of 5 nm thickness. The effects of mechanical stress on carrier mobility are modeled using the Piezo model [4].

Table 1. Design parameters

Device dimensions/Parameters	values
Gate Length, L_g	12 nm
Width of Nano-sheet, W_{sh}	45 nm
Nano-sheet Thickness, T_{sh}	5 nm
Spacer Length, L_{ss}	5 nm
Effective oxide thickness, EOT	1.3 nm
High-k layer permittivity	22
Permittivity of interfacial layer	3.9
Source/drain doping concentration	1×10^{20} cm^{-3}
Channel Doping concentration	1×10^{15} cm^{-3}
Supply Voltage, V_{DD}	0.7 V
Number of Nanosheet channels	3

Figure 2 shows the calibrated results with experimental n-channel NSHT devices [1]. The drain currents plotted in Fig. 2 are normalized with the nano-sheet width, W_{sh}.

Drain voltage values for saturation and linear operation are kept at 0.7 V and 50 mV, respectively. The extracted threshold voltage (V_{TH}) values are 150 mV and 120 mV for the linear and saturation curves, respectively. The calibrated device's subthreshold swing (SS) and drain-induced barrier lowering (DIBL) are 70 mV/decade and 30 mV, respectively. These values are close to the reported experimental values and thus validate the calibrated TCAD simulation setup.

In the present study, the metal gate work function is tuned to achieve high-performance (HP) requirements, and the value of EOT is kept at 0.89 nm. Doping concentrations of 1×10^{20} cm^{-3} and 1×10^{16} cm^{-3} are used for source/ drain and channel regions, respectively.

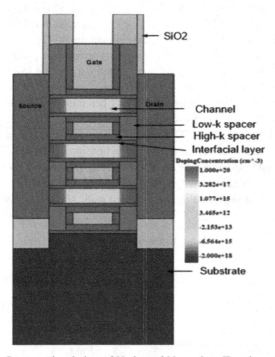

Fig. 1. Cross-sectional view of *N*-channel Nano-sheet Transistor (NSHT)

Multiple 3D nano-sheet Transistors (NSHTs) are designed with L_{EXT} of 5 nm, 7 nm, 10 nm, 12 nm, 13 nm, and 15 nm with a fixed width of 45 nm. Next, an Electro-thermal analysis is done on an NSHT with a L_{EXT} of 12 nm by varying the V_{DD}. Finally, an Electro-thermal study is done for NSHT with $L_{EXT} = 12$ nm, using spacer materials HfO$_2$, SiO$_2$, and Si$_3$N$_4$. The thermodynamic model is used to study the SHEs.

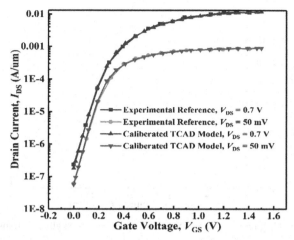

Fig. 2. Transfer characteristics for the calibrated TCAD model and the experimental reference results [1] for the *N*-channel NSHT device

3 Results and Discussions

The Transfer characteristics for the device under study are shown in Fig. 3 with different L_{EXT} values. Gate Voltage (V_{GS}) is varied from -0.04 V to 0.7 V with fixed Drain Voltage (V_{DS}) at 0.7 V. Figure 4, Fig. 5, and Fig. 6 display the ON-state current (I_{ON}), the OFF-state current (I_{OFF}), and the ON to OFF ratio (I_{ON}/I_{OFF}) variations, respectively, with different L_{EXT} values. Figures 3 and 4 show that the drain current (I_{DS}) values decrease as L_{EXT} increases. This decrease in I_{DS} is due to increased resistance for longer L_{EXT}.

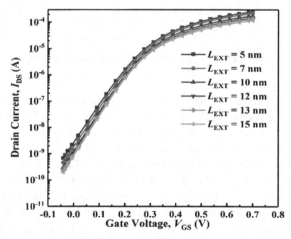

Fig. 3. I_{DS}-V_{GS} characteristics for *N*-channel NSHTs with extension length variations, $V_{DS} = 0.7$ V

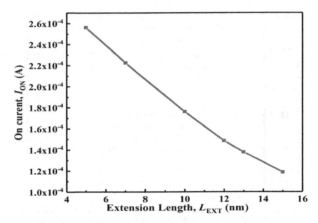

Fig. 4. ON current (I_{ON}) for N-channel NSHTs with extension length variations, $V_{DS} = 0.7$ V

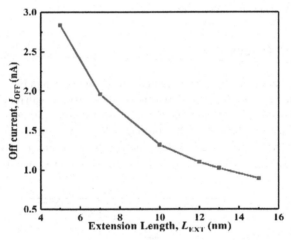

Fig. 5. OFF current (I_{OFF}) for N-channel NSHTs with extension length variations, $V_{DS} = 0.7$ V

However, it can be seen in Fig. 5 that the I_{OFF} decreases more rapidly at shorter L_{EXT}. Therefore, the decline in the I_{ON} begins to exceed the decline in I_{OFF} at longer L_{EXT} and the I_{ON}/I_{OFF} ratio falls, which can be noticed in Fig. 6.

As a result, We get the highest I_{ON}/I_{OFF} ratio around $L_{EXT} = 12$ nm. Therefore, the NSHT with $L_{EXT} = 12$ nm is considered for further study. Figure 7 shows the maximum lattice temperature variation with different V_{DD}. Figure 8, Fig. 9, and Fig. 10 show I_{ON} variation, I_{OFF} variation, and I_{ON}/I_{OFF} ratio variation, respectively, for different values of V_{DD}, considering the SHEs and without SHEs. It can be observed in Fig. 7 that the peak lattice temperature increases with V_{DD}. The effect of SHEs is observed in terms of drive current degradation, as observed in Fig. 8. A 50.89% increase in peak lattice temperature along with a 12.27% of decrement in I_{ON} is observed for 1.5 V V_{DD} due to SHEs. Figure 9 shows a negligible change in I_{OFF} when SHEs are considered. The I_{ON}/I_{OFF} ratio varies more or less like I_{ON}, as can be seen from Fig. 10.

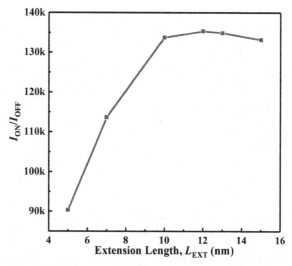

Fig. 6. ION/IOFF ratio for N-channel NSHTs with extension length variations, $V_{DS} = 0.7$ V

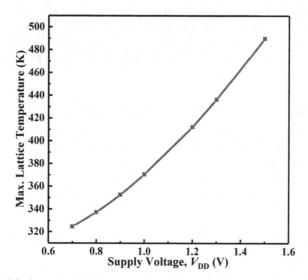

Fig. 7. Maximum Lattice Temperature variation with V_{DD}, considering SHEs.

Next, SHEs analysis is done for different spacers at a drain voltage of 1.5 V. Table 2 represents the relative permittivity and thermal conductivity of spacer dielectric materials used. Figure 11 shows transfer characteristics for different spacer materials considering the SHEs and without SHEs at $V_{DS} = 1.5$ V. Figure 12 portrays the I_{ON} variations of optimized NSHT with different spacer dielectric materials. From Fig. 11 and Fig. 12, it can be seen that the drain current degrades due to SHEs. I_{ON} degradations of 11.73%, 10.68%, and 12.27% are observed for HfO_2, Si_3N_4, and SiO_2 spacer dielectrics, respectively. Figure 13 shows the effect of different spacer dielectric materials on the I_{OFF} of

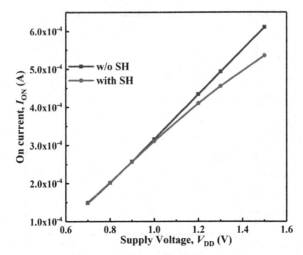

Fig. 8. ON Current (I_{ON}) variation with V_{DD}, considering SHEs and without SHEs

the optimized NSHT. I_{OFF} worsens slightly in the presence of self-heating for devices with Si_3N_4, or SiO_2 spacers. I_{OFF} changes negligibly for NSHT with HfO_2 spacers when self-heating is included. The extent of degradation of drain current is different for different spacer dielectric materials as they have different thermal conductivities [9] as shown in Table 2.

Table 2. Relative Permittivity and Thermal Conductivities of spacer materials [9].

Material	Relative permittivity	Thermal conductivity W/(m.K)
SiO_2	3.9	1.4
Si_3N_4	7.5	18.5
HfO_2	22	2.3

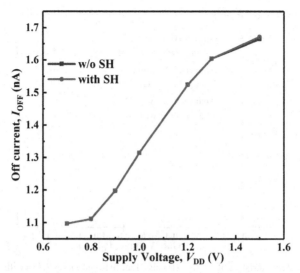

Fig. 9. OFF current (I_{OFF}) variation with different V_{DD}, considering SHEs and without SHEs.

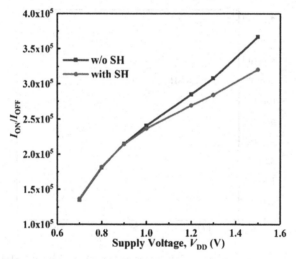

Fig. 10. ON to OFF current ratio (I_{ON}/I_{OFF}) variation with different V_{DD}, considering SHEs and without SHEs.

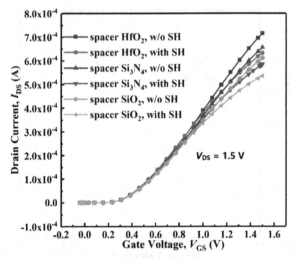

Fig. 11. Transfer characteristics of 12 nm extension length n-channel NSHTs with different spacer dielectric material considering SHEs and without SHEs.

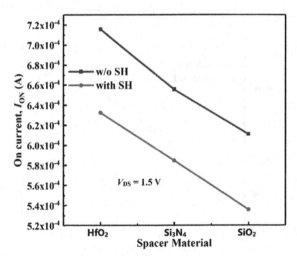

Fig. 12. ON current (I_{ON}) variation of 12 nm extension length N-channel NSHTs with different spacer dielectric material considering SHEs and without SHEs.

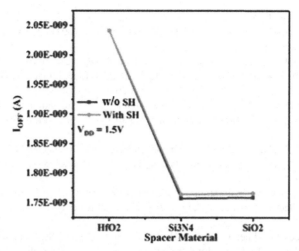

Fig. 13. OFF current (I_{OFF}) variation of 12 nm extension length N-channel NSHTs with different spacer dielectric material considering SHEs and without SHEs.

4 Conclusion

A calibrated TCAD setup has been used to design a three-channel nano-sheet transistor that shows optimized performance at 12 nm extension length. As extension length increases, the I_{ON} decreases due to the rise in resistance. The values of I_{OFF} decrease more rapidly at shorter extension lengths. As a result, at first, the I_{ON}/I_{OFF} ratio improves as the extension length increases. However, the decrements in the I_{ON} begin to outweigh the decrements in I_{OFF} at longer extension lengths, and, consequently, the I_{ON}/I_{OFF} ratio begins to fall. A 49.5% increase in I_{ON}/I_{OFF} is observed when extension length increases from 5 nm to 12 nm. And a decrement of 1.48% is observed when extension length increases from 12 nm to 15 nm. Therefore, a 12 nm extension length gives the optimum NSHT performance. Next, the thermodynamic model is applied to the optimized NSHT, and the V_{DD} is varied from 0.7 V to 1.5 V for electro-thermal performance investigation. It was observed that SHEs are more prominent for larger V_{DD}. A self-heating study for different spacer dielectric materials for supply voltage values up to 1.5 V is also reported. The study shows that the more the thermal conductivity of spacer dielectric material, the less I_{ON} degradation. The Si_3N_4 with the highest thermal conductivity shows the smallest degradation of I_{ON}.

References

1. Loubet, N., et al.: T17–5 (late news) stacked nanosheet gate-all-around transistor to enable scaling beyond FinFET T230 T231. VLSI Technol. **2017**(5), 14–15 (2017)
2. Yakimets, D., et al.: Power aware FinFET and lateral nano-sheet FET targeting for 3nm CMOS technology. Technical Digest International Electron Devices Meeting. IEDM, pp. 20.4.1–20.4.4 (2018). https://doi.org/10.1109/IEDM.2017.8268429

3. Seon, Y., Chang, J., Yoo, C., Jeon, J.: Device and circuit exploration of multi-nanosheet transistor for sub-3 nm technology node. Electron **10**, 1–14 (2021). https://doi.org/10.3390/electronics10020180
4. Yoon, J.S., Jeong, J., Lee, S., Baek, R.H.: Systematic DC/AC performance benchmarking of sub-7-nm node FinFETs and nanosheet FETs. IEEE J. Electron Devices Soc. **6**, 942–947 (2018). https://doi.org/10.1109/JEDS.2018.2866026
5. Young, C.D., et al.: Critical discussion on (100) and (110) orientation dependent transport: nMOS planar and FinFET. Digest of Technical Papers - Symposium on VLSI Technology, pp. 18–19 (2011)
6. Pundir, Y.P., Saha, R., Pal, P.K.: Effect of gate length on performance of 5nm node N-channel nano-sheet transistors for analog circuits. Semicond. Sci. Technol. **36** (2020). https://doi.org/10.1088/1361-6641/abc51e
7. Jang, D., et al.: Device exploration of nanosheet transistors for Sub-7-nm technology node. IEEE Trans. Electron Devices. **64**, 2707–2713 (2017). https://doi.org/10.1109/TED.2017.2695455
8. Yoon, J.S., Jeong, J., Lee, S., Baek, R.H.: Optimization of nano-sheet number and width of multi-stacked nano-sheet FETs for sub-7-nm node system on chip applications. Jpn. J. Appl. Phys. **58** (2019). https://doi.org/10.7567/1347-4065/ab0277
9. Liu, R., Li, X., Sun, Y., Shi, Y.: A vertical combo spacer to optimize electro-thermal characteristics of 7-nm nanosheet gate-all-around transistor. IEEE Trans. Electron Devices. **67**, 2249–2254 (2020). https://doi.org/10.1109/TED.2020.2988655
10. Prasad, C.: A review of self-heating effects in advanced CMOS technologies. IEEE Trans. Electron Devices. **66**, 4546–4555 (2019). https://doi.org/10.1109/TED.2019.2943744
11. Kim, H., Son, D., Myeong, I., Kang, M., Jeon, J., Shin, H.: Analysis on self-heating effects in three-stacked nanoplate FET. IEEE Trans. Electron Devices. **65**, 4520–4526 (2018). https://doi.org/10.1109/TED.2018.2862918
12. Cai, L., Chen, W., Du, G., Zhang, X., Liu, X.: Layout design correlated with self-heating effect in stacked nanosheet transistors. IEEE Trans. Electron Devices. **65**, 2647–2653 (2018). https://doi.org/10.1109/TED.2018.2825498
13. Yoon, J.S., Jeong, J., Lee, S., Baek, R.H.: Multi-Vth strategies of 7-nm node nanosheet FETs with limited nanosheet spacing. IEEE J. Electron Devices Soc. **6**, 861–865 (2018). https://doi.org/10.1109/JEDS.2018.2859799
14. Pundir, Y.P., Bisht, A., Saha, R., Pal, P.K.: Effect of temperature on performance of 5-nm node silicon nanosheet transistors for analog applications. SILICON (2022). https://doi.org/10.1007/s12633-022-01800-w
15. Synopsys: Sentaurus Device User Guide. (2019)

Sensors

Fabrication, Optimization and Testing of Photoconductively Tuned SAW Device Using CBD Method

Rahul Sharma$^{(\boxtimes)}$ and Harshal B. Nemade

Indian Institute of Technology Guwahati, Guwahati, India
{rahul.shsr,harshal}@iitg.ac.in

Abstract. In this paper, we explained the fabrication process of tunable surface acoustic wave (SAW) device. We have also demonstrated the photoconductivity of the material which is deposited over piezoelectric substrate. We have used an approach which is different from the conventional approach of using aluminium interdigital transducers (IDTs) which have a fixed frequency of operation. We do this by making SAW device programmable using light pattern IDTs (LiPIDTs) which allows us to vary the frequency of operation of SAW device by changing the width of the LiPIDTs. This process of tuning have been explained using a set of schematics and by building an equivalent electrical model of SAW resonator. We have optimized this fabrication process for the targeted application. In photoconductively tuned SAW we have measured I-V characteristics for the samples prepared with 1 mm, 2 mm, 3 mm and 5 mm electrode separation width. We find that 2 mm separation sample is best suited for this application in which we need to make LiPIDTs within this area. For 2 mm sample, we obtained $I_{on} = 3.36 \times 10^{-9}$ A (obtained by the light exposure) and $I_{dark} = 5.4 \times 10^{-12}$ A (in the absence of light). Thus we could achieve $I_{on}/I_{dark} > 10^3$. We have also obtained the X-ray diffraction (XRD) characteristics for the deposited photoconductive layer over piezoelectric substrate and we have found the main reflections at $2\theta = 26°$. In the study of Scanning electron microscopy (SEM), it has been observed that the clusters composed of nanoparticles have an average cluster size of 150 nm diameter.

Keywords: Photoconductive · Programmable · Tunable · SAW · Acoustics · SAW fabrication · CBD · LiPIDTs

1 Introduction

Surface acoustic wave (SAW) devices find their applications in electronic functional units (for example- delay lines), radios (mixer, oscillator etc.), microfluidics, flow measurement and for designing various electronics blocks in the communication system (amplifier, filters etc.) [1]. Applications like mobile phone use high Q bandpass filters that can be designed using SAW devices [2]. Apart from

Supported by Visvesvaraya PhD Scheme, Meity, GoI MEITY–PHD–1227.

its many advantages the SAW device is limited due to its fixed frequency characteristics. This limitation is due to fixed IDT structures which are made using metal such as Aluminium as shown in Fig. 1.

When SAW waves are generated in a SAW device, it is the pitch (loosely defined as distance between IDTs) and the acoustic wave velocity that decides the frequency of operation [1]. Similarly, filters are also designed for a particular center frequency due to the above reason. Thus, tuning of the filter is a major challenge with this device even though it has high-Q property. As it is clear from the above discussion we can get a high Q from SAW device but we are limited by the tunability of the operating frequency. In reality, there are tons of applications which can perform optimum if programmability can be added in the SAW device. The solution to make it programmable can be found in the above discussion and also in Refs. [3–6].

2 Theory and Proposed Device

SAW devices are made on piezoelectric substrates. This substrate material has a property due to which atoms change their relative position by applying external electric field to it. Consequently, the substrate feels vibration due to the generation of internal forces in the material as an effect of strain (generated electrically). This is how acoustic wave propagates in solids. For this process to happen, SAW velocity in material, electromechanical coupling coefficient and temperature coefficient delay are crucial parameters for selecting piezoelectric wafers [1].

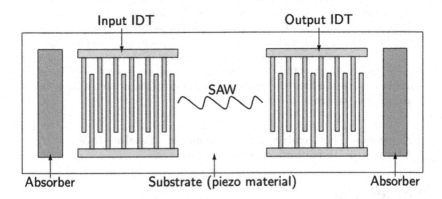

Fig. 1. Conventional surface acoustic wave device with two set of IDTs.

Since the IDTs are conventionally made using aluminium material in comb like structure as shown in Fig. 1, it limits the tunability of SAW. Generated SAW wave frequency (f) depends on the pitch size of IDTs in this manner, f = v/λ and pitch = λ/2. Here v is the SAW velocity in the material and λ is the wavelength of generated wave [7].

To eliminate these limitations, there are many ways available in literature such as use of variable material velocity [5], utilizing MEMS techniques [6], use of quantum well structure [8] and programmable SAW [3,4]. In this work, we have considered photoconductive technique for making tunable SAW device. In this technique we are making the IDTs (conventionally made using metal) using light pattern on a grown photoconductive layer over piezoelectric substrate as shown in Fig. 2. Before actually making these patterns, we need to fix the method for growing photoconductive layer over piezoelectric substrate for this phenomenon to happen.

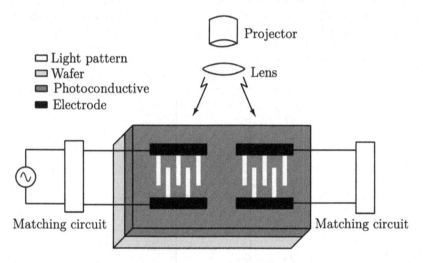

Fig. 2. Photoconductively tunned surface acoustic wave with light pattern IDT setup.

In the subsequent sections of this paper we will discuss how we have grown and optimized the photoconductive layer (cadmium sulphide) over piezoelectric (lithium niobate) substrate. As the proposed device structure Fig. 2 shows that the patterns are made using some projection unit and it is controlled according to the requirement of the application. We have taken the 128° Y-X lithium niobate (LiNbO$_3$) wafer and have deposited cadmium sulphide (CdS) layer. After this we have grown Aluminium (Al) electrodes over the CdS layer for connecting matching circuits and providing input along with making an intersection for LiPIDTs. Our main focus in this paper is to deposit CdS layer over LiNbO$_3$ and observe the I_{dark} and I_{on} by exposing white light to it before moving to the actual LiPIDTs in new device. Process of measuring on and dark current has been done recursively to achieve the best suited result for the targeted application.

We have taken some intuitive decisions based on basic physics and chemical understanding. At the end, we have measured the I-V characteristics of the fabricated devices and optimized the final design to proceed with.

3   Concept and Analysis

In Figs. 1 and 2 we have shown the conventional SAW delay line and programmable SAW delay line respectively which consists of input IDTs at one end and output IDTs at other end of the device. On the other hand if we take the example of simplest SAW device i.e. one port SAW resonator, it consists of one set of IDTs in the middle and reflectors on the either ends [1]. This one port SAW resonator can be represented with an equivalent RLC circuit, shown in Fig. 3. We can plot the resonance frequency (ω_r) and anti-resonance frequency (ω_a) of this resonator. These frequenciez can also be formulated in terms of inductance and capacitance of the equivalent circuit as shown in (1) and (2). Where L_m, C_m, R_m are the motional inductor, capacitor and resistor respectively and C_0 is the static capacitor.

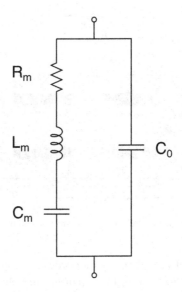

Fig. 3. Electrical equivalent circuit of one port SAW resonator.

$$\omega_r = 1/\sqrt{L_m C_m} \tag{1}$$

$$\omega_a = 1/\sqrt{L_m C_m C_0/(C_m + C_0)} \tag{2}$$

If we can measure the value of C_0, ω_r and ω_a from the finite element simulation plot then we can easily find the value of L_m and C_m from the (1) and

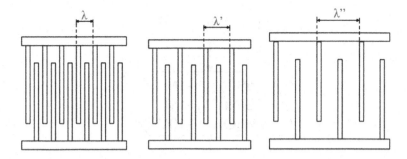

Fig. 4. Three different wavelength (depends of pitch size) LiPIDTs.

(2). In admittance Vs frequency plot, we have peak admittance at the resonance frequency. This value of admittance is nothing but $1/R_m$. This way, all the motional parameters can be obtained. Similarly, we are somehow changing the IDT pitches as shown in Fig. 4, the operational frequency also changes based on the concepts explained above. Figure 4 also shows IDTs for three different lambda value (directly proportional to pitch size). These different pitch size IDTs can be obtained using light pattern - LiPIDTs. Thus value of ω_r and ω_a changes for each set of IDTs and based on these values L_m, C_m and R_m comes out to be different which demonstrate the variable characteristics of resonator.

4 Device Fabrication

For making photoconductive devices, researchers have tried polymer such as PVK (polyvinyl carbazole) and other commonly used materials such as cadmium sulphide. These two materials have been used extensively on popular substrates such as glass, silicon and adhesive fiber etc. In our device the challenge is to deposit photoconductive material over the piezoelectric substrate. We have found few ways to deposit cadmium sulphide such as - physical vapour deposition [9], chemical vapour deposition (CVD) [10], metal organic chemical vapour deposition [11], chemical bath deposition (CBD) [12] and molecular beam epitaxy [13]. Since LiNbO$_3$ substrate does not tolerate high temperature (1000 °C) our main concern was to carry out deposition process at moderate temperature (in the range of 100 °C). Most of the deposition methods are done at very high temperature (for example CVD) which might damage the LiNbO$_3$ substrate. Thus, our first approach of selecting the method is to see the feasibility of process in our basic lab by following temperature compatibility. The other concern is the adhesiveness of cadmium sulphide over lithium niobate wafer. Therefore, we choose the CBD method for its simplicity and better adhesiveness.

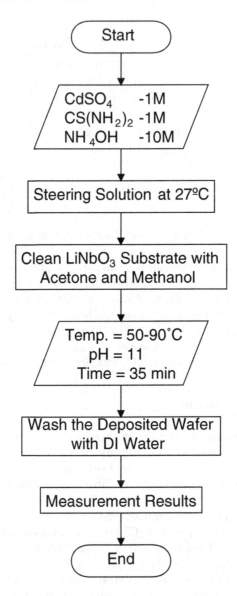

Fig. 5. Flow chart of chemical bath deposition of CdS over LiNbO$_3$ substrate

For depositing CdS over LiNbO$_3$ we have made a flow chart as shown in Fig. 5. To start with, we have selected few chemicals such as ammonium hydroxide, cadmium sulphate and thiourea. Next, we have made a solution by steering these chemicals along with deionized water (DI). After this process, another crucial process is to clean the lithium niobate substrate with acetone and methanol. We have placed the pieces of the substrate vertically in the solution and heated it gradually starting from 50 °C to 90 °C. This process has to be continued for roughly 35 min by maintaining the solution at pH=11. After deposition, substrates are washed with DI water and dried with air pump to remove loosely attached Cadmium sulphide particle. Initially powder weight is calculated for each of the chemical. It is required to sonicate these powders in DI water for mixing and when Solution is ready, steer it with the help of magnetic stirrer.

After this, it is required to test the basic photoconductive property of the deposited CdS layer over LiNbO$_3$. For this, first thing is to create the two electrodes at sufficient distance so that on shining light over the CdS coated LiNbO$_3$, it should conduct. Thus we have deposited the aluminum electrodes over the prepared sample. The distance between these electrodes is very crucial. One white light source is placed over the sample holder. This light source will shine the light over the substrate so that we can observe the photoconductive effect. Voltage is given to these electrodes from the source meter and I_{on}, I_{dark} currents are measured respectively. Value of I_{on}/I_{dark} decide the photoconductivity of the deposited material over piezoelectric substrate.

5 Optimization and Measurement Results

After iterative process of optimization in terms of temperature, time and chemical ratio, for above process, we could prepare few samples with a electrode separation distance of 5 mm, 3 mm, 2 mm and 1 mm as shown in Fig. 6. With these samples, I-V characteristics can be measured. We also did annealing for these samples to improve the results. We have measured transient characteristics of current while switching the light mode. A 5V DC Voltage is given to the device in all the measurements for first run. Figure 7 shows two level of currents for 2 mm device with a Higher level for the light being illuminated on the device and lower level for no light exposure. We find $I_{on} = 3.36 \times 10^{-9}$ A and $I_{dark} = 5.4 \times 10^{-12}$ A. Also Fig. 8 shows the current transient characteristics for 5 mm device and we find $I_{on} = 5.39 \times 10^{-11}$ A and $I_{dark} = 3.55 \times 10^{-12}$ A. We repeated the same process for 3 mm device and 1 mm device as well and find that for 3 mm device $I_{on} = 4.5 \times 10^{-10}$ A and $I_{dark} = 4.35 \times 10^{-12}$ A. On the other hand 1 mm device was providing the I-V characteristics similar to 2 mm device. In 2 mm device we also get an advantage of making LiPIDTs in better way as we get more vertical distance which gives us more liberty to play with the aperture of LiPIDTs. Thus, we can control our device in better way and ensure the accuracy.

Thus, 2 mm sample got us a 3 order change while going from dark current to on current by switching light. This change clearly demonstrate the photoconductivity of deposited sample. As discussed above, we have tried 1 mm, 2 mm, 3 mm and 5 mm electrode separation and obtained I_{on} and I_{dark} for each sample but 3 mm and 5 mm samples are not providing better phtoconductivity as compared to 1 mm and 2 mm sample. Due to above discussed reason finally we choose 2 mm sample as we need to make the LiPIDTs between this available space.

Figure 9 shows the XRD characteristics of deposited CdS. It is performed to study the bulk structure of the film which clearly shows the 2θ peak between

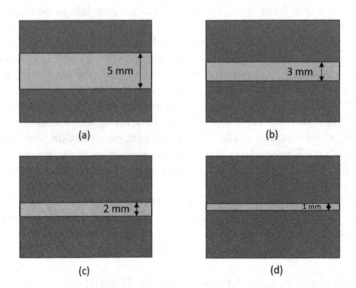

Fig. 6. Electrodes on Lithium Niobate substrate in gray color with spacing between electrodes (a) 5 mm (b) 3 mm (c) 2 mm (d) 1 mm; yellow color is showing deposited cadmium sulphide. We are calling these 5 mm device, 3 mm device, 2 mm device and 1 mm device respectively, for further references. (Color figure online)

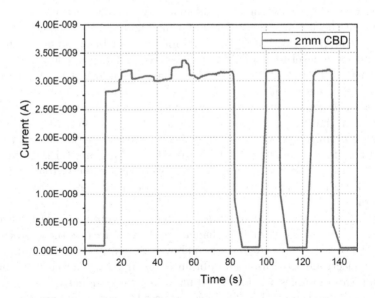

Fig. 7. Transient characteristics of current with respect to light switching for 2 mm device. $I_{on} = 3.36 \times 10^{-9}$ A and $I_{dark} = 5.4 \times 10^{-12}$ A.

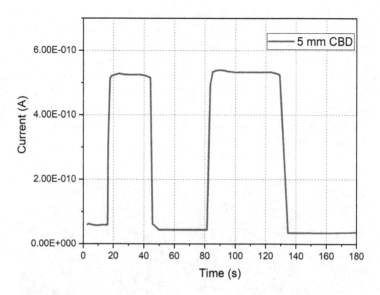

Fig. 8. Transient characteristics of current with respect to light switching for 5 mm device. $I_{on} = 5.39 \times 10^{-11}$ A and $I_{dark} = 3.55 \times 10^{-12}$ A.

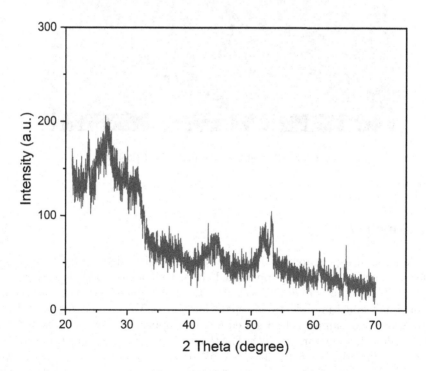

Fig. 9. XRD characteristics of CdS, deposited using CBD method.

20° n 30° and two small variation between 40° and 60°. The main reflection is assigned at $2\theta = 26°$. This will have orientation in [111] direction in case of cubic modification but if it is a hexagonal modification then it will be [002] direction. Similarly other peaks are shown $2\theta = 44°$ which have orientation in [220] direction for cubic modification and $2\theta = 51°$ which have orientiation [200] in case of hexagonal and [311] in case of cubic modification. We have also studied the surface morphology of thin film using SEM as shown in Fig. 10. It has been observed that the clusters composed of different sizes of nanoparticles with an average cluster size of 150 nm diameter.

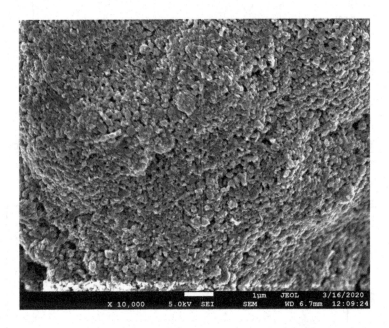

Fig. 10. SEM image of the deposited CdS layers.

6   Conclusion

All the critical aspects of tunable SAW are studied in details. By taking four different types of samples, we optimized the sample for the best desired performance. We have measured I-V characteristics for prepared samples with 1 mm, 2 mm, 3 mm and 5 mm electrode separation width. We demonstrated that the 2 mm separation sample is best suited for this application to make light pattern IDTs within this separation width. For this separation, we obtained, Ion = 3.36 $\times 10^{-9}$ A and Idark = 5.4 $\times 10^{-12}$ A. We have achieved $I_{on}/I_{dark} = 10^3$. We have also done structural characterization and surface morphology tests for the fabricated device. Through XRD we obtained main reflection at $2\theta = 26°$ and

SEM provide us the information regarding nanoparticles of CdS and have an average cluster diameter $= 150$ nm.

Acknowledgment. Authors are thankful to the Electronics and Electrical Engineering department and Center for Nanotechnology, IIT Guwahati for providing the facilities to conduct the experiments. This work is Supported by Visvesvaraya PhD Scheme, Meity, Government of India: MEITY–PHD–1227.

References

1. Morgan, D.: Surface Acoustic Wave Filters, Academic Press; 2 edition (2007)
2. Mohan, S.: The 5G effect on RF filter technologies. IEEE Trans Semiconductors Manuf. **30**(4), 494–499 (2017)
3. Robert, A., De, V.: Acousto-electric filter utilizing surface wave propagation in which the center frequency is determined by a conductivity pattern resulting from an optical image (1969) uS Patent 3,446,975. http://www.google.tl/patents/US3446975
4. Zhu, J., Lu, Y., Kosinski, J., Pastore, R.: Programmable surface acoustic wave (saw) filter (2003) uS Patent 6,541,893. https://www.google.co.in/patents/US6541893
5. Hong, J.: Method and apparatus for modifying acoustic wave characteristics, (2004) uS Patent 6,710,510. http://www.google.com.pg/patents/US6710510
6. Atkison, J.W., Candela, P., Gambino, T.J.: switchable filter structure and design (2016), cN Patent 103,187,947. https://www.google.co.in/patents/CN103187947B?cl=en
7. Navigator, T.Y.: Working principles and Applications of SAW/FBAR Devices (2016). http://docplayer.net/30770605-Working-principles-and-applications-of-saw-fbar-devices.html. Accessed 24 May 2022
8. Lu, Y., Emanetoglu, N.: Integrated tunable surface acoustic wave with quantum well structure technology and systems provided thereby (2003) uS Patent 6,559,736. https://www.google.com/patents/US6559736
9. He, X.Q., Brown, G., Rockett, A.: Microsturcutral and chemical investigation of PVD-CdS/ PVD-hetrojunctions: a transmission electron microscopy study. IEEE J. Photovoltaics **4**(6), 1625–1629 (2014)
10. Fainer, N.I., Losinova, M.L., Rumyantsev, Y.M., Salman, E.G., Kuzetsov, F.A.: Growth of PbS and CdS thin films by low-pressure chemical vapour deposition using dithiocarbamates. J. Thin Solid Films **280**(1–2), 16–19 (1996)
11. Uda, H., Fujii, T., Lkegami, S., Sonomura, H.: Polycrystalline CdS thin film prepared by metalorganic chemical vapour deposition. In: Proceedings IEEE Photovoltaic Specialists Conference (1997)
12. Moualkia, H., et al.: Growth and physical properties of CdS thin films prepared by chemical bath deposition. J. Phys. D: Appl. Phys. **42**, 135404 (2009)
13. Dauplaise, H.M., Vaccaro, K., Davis, A., Waters, W.D., Lorenzo, J.P.: Passivation of InP with thin layers of MBE-grown CdS. In: Proceedings IEEE ICIPRM, pp. 455–458 (1998)

High Resolution Temperature Sensor Signal Processing ASIC for Cryo-Cooler Electronics

Anuj Srivastava[1]([⊠])([iD]), Nishant Kumar[1], Nihar Ranjan Mohapatra[2], and Hari Shankar Gupta[1]

[1] Space Applications Centre, ISRO, Ahmedabad, India
{anuj918,nishnatsingh,hari}@sac.isro.gov.in
[2] Indian Institute of Technology Gandhinagar, Gandhinagar, India
nihar@iitgn.ac.in

Abstract. Infra-Red sensor requirements for high-resolution imaging satellites are increasing in future missions. IR sensors working in LWIR and MWIR regions have an inbuilt cryo-cooler as they operate at very low temperatures, generally < 100 K. The cooler requires precise temperature information for its better-controlled operation. Typically, IR sensors have a semiconductor temperature sensor. This paper presents details of low noise, high-performance ASIC front-end design to achieve high-temperature resolution for precise control of cryo-cooler. Designed temperature processing ASIC achieves ≈3 mK temperature resolution and consumes very low power around < 4 mW. The design has been carried out using 1.8 V SCL CMOS 180 nm technology.

Keywords: Constant bias current · Infrared · Opamp · STS · Temperature resolution

1 Introduction

The wide usage of Infra-Red (IR) payloads for thermal imaging is well known [1]. The IR remote sensing cameras consist of detectors that operate at cryo temperature, i.e., <100 K. The cryo-coolers are used to maintain them at such a low temperature. Generally, IR detectors are integrated with a cryo-cooler in close vicinity for precise temperature control. The IR detectors housed with a cryo-cooler are commonly referred to as Integrated Detector Dewar Cooling Assembly (IDDCA) [2]. Block schematic design of IDDCA is shown in Fig. 1(a).

Operating IR detector at low temperature reduces thermal noise and background offset, which helps in achieving better resolution and aids in identifying a target in worse conditions. Precise temperature control of IR detectors is also critical for imaging performance to deduce accurate image information. Therefore, the thermal stability requirement of upcoming IR payloads is becoming more stringent around < ±50 mK.

Q2N2222 diode based Semiconductor Temperature Sensor (STS), inbuilt in the Read-Out Integrated Circuit (ROIC) of the IR imaging sensor, is used to

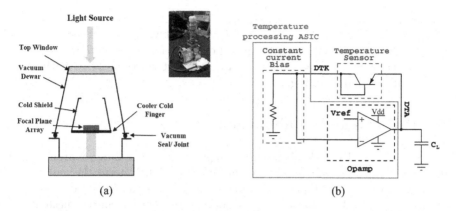

Fig. 1. Block diagrams of (a) IDDCA, and (b) temperature processing IC.

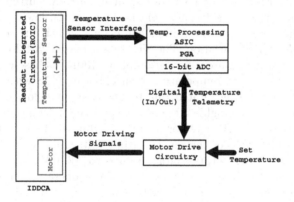

Fig. 2. TPIC interface with electronics circuits.

provide very precise and accurate temperature information[3]. The STS provides good accuracy and linearity for the payload operating temperature range (–15 °C to 60 °C). The STS measures the temperature of the imaging sensor and this temperature data is processed by the Temperature Processing IC (TPIC). In Fig. 1(b), block diagram of TPIC is shown. It provides a constant bias current to the STS for its operation and processes the temperature data. For constant bias current, resistors are matched with a combination of rnmpoly2t and rpplus_sal2t resistors having negative and positive temperature coefficient, respectively. Also variation of V_{ref} also has been taken into the account. The TPIC needs to be placed in close vicinity of the IR sensor for precise temperature information. Therefore, TPIC design becomes very critical with respect to its power dissipation. The opamp design for TPIC consumes very low power < 4 mW and provides a gain > 87 dB. Also, internal biases of opamp are tuned in such a way that opamp provides PSRR > 140 dB and CMRR > 100 dB for all test conditions.

Processed data is then digitized using 16-bit Analog-to-Digital Converter (ADC) and then provided to the motor drive circuitry. The cryo-cooler motor is driven through the signal generated based on the error between the set temperature and the STS processed temperature data. Interfaces of TPIC with other sub-systems are shown in Fig. 2.

2   TPIC Design Requirements

High-performance IR payloads require stringent thermal stability of around ±50 mK for 8 to 10 mins which is commonly known as short-term thermal stability. Hence, TPIC and further digitization of processed data demand temperature resolution of one order below i.e. ≈5 mK for a better thermal control mechanism. The STS requires constant current bias ranging from 10 μA to 1 mA. To achieve high-temperature resolution, STS is biased at a very low current of 25 μA ± 1% variation, maintaining safe operating margins at the lower end of biasing current. The diode base-emitter voltage can change either due to temperature variation or bias current variation. The STS sensor biased with low current provides the nearest temperature information of the ROIC as base-emitter voltage changes dominantly due to temperature. Hence, biasing STS with a low current (25 μA) keeps the noise generated due to bias current below the noise budget. The sensor provides roughly 500 mV voltage swing for temperature varying from 50 K to 280 K. The IR detector operates within the temperature range of 40 K to 100 K, which reduces the sensor output voltage range to 130 mV. After processing through PGA output voltage ranges to 300 mV. System-level specifications are shown in Table 1. Temperature sensor operating between 40 K to 100 K (close loop operation) yields a 60 K temperature range. With a required temperature resolution of 5 mK and sensor output voltage range around 300 mV (−55 °C to 125 °C), electronics resolution needs to be better than 25 μV. With 16-Bit ADC having 1 V swing, electronics resolution yields 15.25 μV, which fulfills our requirement for precise thermal control. After digitization, this temperature information is utilized to generate motor excitation signals to cool the IR detector.

TPIC design serves primarily two functions. First, it provides the constant current bias for STS and second, it processes the temperature information very precisely without adding any substantial noise. To serve both purposes, TPIC requires a low noise opamp design. The following section highlights the details of opamp specification and design.

Table 1. System level specifications

Parameters	Specifications
Temperature resolution	5 mK
Constant bias current variation	± 250 nA

3 Opamp Specifications & Design

The requirements for the opamp design are derived from the variation in constant current required for temperature sensor biasing. The reliazable electronic noise (N_E) depends on power supply, components and engineering noise. This can be represented as,

$$N_E = \sqrt{N_C^2 + N_P^2 + N_{EG}^2} \tag{1}$$

Here, N_C is the component noise, N_P is power supply noise and N_{EG} is the engineering noise. Total variation in constant current bias is allowed to be 500 nA. Apportioning equally among all the noise components, we get,

$$N_P = N_C = N_{EG} = 290nA \tag{2}$$

Further, components noise comprises the STS, current bias resistor & opamp. The variation due to the STS and current bias resistor can be large. Therefore, the noise due to opamp is targeted to have 1% of component noise variation. Hence amplifier gain requirement is estimated to keep the error < 2.9 nA.

$$e = \frac{1}{1 + A\beta} \tag{3}$$

For $\beta = 1$ (worst case) and $e < 2.9$ nA at $36\,\mathrm{K}$ bias resistor,

$$A \geq 9578.5 \quad (\geq 80\,dB) \tag{4}$$

There are various topologies of opamp such as telescopic, two stage, folded cacode etc. As per our requirement we have selected two stage opamp with differential input stage using PMOS as first stage and common source stage using NMOS with PMOS active load as second stage. Figure 3 presents the schematic of designed opamp [4,5]. It consists of startup circuit, bias circuit, differential input stage and single ended NMOS stage with active load. As soon as power supply is applied to the opamp, the startup circuit and bias circuit becomes operational. Bias circuit develop the current as per the sizing of MOSFET which is mirrored

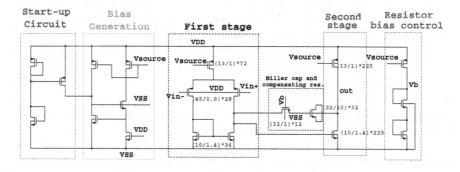

Fig. 3. Schematic of the designed two-stage opamp.

in both differential stage and single ended stage. The precision two-stage opamp is designed to operate at a single supply voltage of 1.8 V [6].

Different opamp parameters which impact the temperature sensor processing are evaluated for different test corners and conditions. The broad level opamp specifications are shown in Table 2 [7].

Table 2. Broad level opamp specifications

Parameters	Specifications
Supply range	1.8 V
DC Gain	> 80 dB
Phase margin	$> 60^0$
Input range	1.8 V
Output range	1.8 V
CMRR	> 80 dB
PSRR	> 100 dB
Power	< 10 mW

4   PSpice Model Integration

STS temperature sensor is a Q2N2222 diode-based temperature sensor. Q2N2222 Pspice models are readily available. Only vpnp BJT is available in cadence virtuoso to use BJT as a diode-based temperature sensor. Therefore, to have the closest results possible to the actual hardware, the Q2N2222 Pspice model is integrated with the cadence virtuoso library and then simulations are performed.

5   Results and Discussions

Figure 4 presents the opamp output voltage swing for supply-voltage variations, temperature variations and different corner conditions. The designed opamp gives almost full swing for a single power supply of 1.8 V.

Figure 5 presents gain and phase margin (PM) variation of the opamp for supply-voltage variations, temperature variations and different corner conditions. Since temperature processing close-loop action operates 1 Hz frequency and approximately 87 dB gain is achieved for all the test case scenarios for < 1 kHz frequency. This is sufficient for the desired application. PM of around 61^0 is achieved for all payload operational conditions.

Figure 6 shows the Monte Carlo (MC) results for constant bias current variation with respect to temperature, process and mismatch. MC simulations with

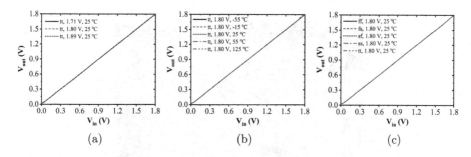

Fig. 4. Opamp swing relation with (a) supply variations (b) temperature variations, and (c) different corners.

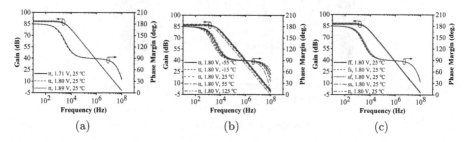

Fig. 5. Opamp gain and phase margin relation with (a) supply variations, (b) temperature variations, and (c) different corners.

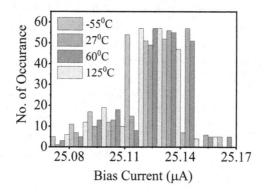

Fig. 6. 1000 point MC simulations at Constant Current Bias node variation with temperature, process and mismatch.

1000 points are performed to estimate the worst case scenario of constant current bias. The observed peak-to-peak current variation is $< \pm 50$ nA against the tolerance budget of ± 250 nA ($\pm 1\%$ of 25 μA) for bias current.

Figure 7 shows the hardware realization of Temperature Signal Processing Circuit using Discrete components to compare the TPIC design. Hardware consists of 4 number of Op-amps along with ADC & voltage regulators. Op-amps &

Fig. 7. Hardware realization of Temperature Signal Processing Circuit using Discrete components to compare the TPIC design.

Table 3. Achieved results

Parameters	Specifications	Achieved values
Temperature Resolution	5 mK	5 mK
Constant bias current variation	< ±250 nA	± 50 nA
Supply Range	1.8 ± 0.09 V	1.8 ± 0.09 V
DC Gain	80 dB	87 dB
Phase Margin	> 45^0	> 61^0
Input range	1.8 V	1.8 V
Output range	1.8 V	1.8 V
CMRR	> 80 dB	100 dB
PSRR	> 100 dB	140 dB
Power	< 10 mW	3.6 mW

ADC operates at 5 V supply. Approximate card size is 50 mm × 50 mm with power dissipation around 200 mW. Realized hardware achieved resolution is around 35 mK & provides around 50 nA variation in constant current bias. Table 3 shows the achieved simulation results and Table 4 shows the comparison of simulated design with discrete components based realized hardware in terms of weight volume and power.

Table 4. Comparison of simulated design and the discrete components based hardware

Parameters	Simulated (TPIC)	Discrete-Hardware
Number of Opamps	4	4
ASIC Layout Size (mm×mm)	3.5×3.5	–
PCB Size (mm×mm)	20×20	80×80
Mass (gm)	25	150
Total Power (mW)	100	200

6 Conclusion

Designed front-end temperature processing IC provides constant current bias of 25 μA with $< \pm 50$ nA variation against the total budget of $< \pm 250$ nA and achieves temperature resolution of 5 mK for 40 K to 100 K temperature range after digitization with 16-bit, 1 V swing ADC. Q2N2222 pspice model has been integrated with the cadence virtuoso for simulations. Discrete component-based temperature processing circuit hardware has been compared with our simulated design. TPIC performance w.r.t. weight, volume and power is much better compared to the discrete-based hardware. Further, this design will be integrated with 16-bit ADC for future designs.

Acknowledgements. We gratefully acknowledge the constant encouragement and guidance received from Shri Sanjeev Mehta, Shri A.Mishra, Shri S. S. Sarkar and Shri N.M. Desai (Director Space Applications Centre).

References

1. Chowdhury, A.R., et al.: Imaging Infrared Spectrometer (IIRS) onboard Chandrayaan-2 Orbiter-craft. Curr. Sci. **118**(3), 560 (2020)
2. Nagarsheth, H.H., Bhatt, J.H., Barve, J.J.: Cold-Tip temperature control of space-borne satellite stirling cryocooler: mathematical modeling and control investigation. IFAC-Papers OnLine **51**(1), 673–679 (2018)
3. Gupta, H.S., Kumar, A.S.K., Baghini, M.S., Chakrabarti, S., Sharma, D.K.: Design of high-precision ROIC for quantum dot infrared photodetector. IEEE Photonics Technol. Lett. **28**(15), 1673–1676, (2016). https://doi.org/10.1109/LPT.2016.2560804
4. Design of analog CMOS integrated circuits 2nd ed. California: McGraw Hill, pp. 539–571
5. Suman, S.: Two stage CMOS operational amplifier: analysis and design. SSRN Electron. J. **3**, 40–44 (2019). https://doi.org/10.2139/ssrn.3433181
6. Texas Instruments, Noise Analysis in Operational Amplifier Circuits, Application Report (2007) SLVA043B
7. Kouhalvandi, L., et al.: An improved 2 stage opamp with rail-to-rai! gain-boosted folded cascode input stage and monticelli rail-to-rail class AB output stage. In: 2017 24th IEEE International Conference on Electronics, Circuits and Systems (ICECS), pp. 542–545 (2017)

Analog/Mixed Signal

Low Power, Wideband SiGe HBT LNA Covering 57-64 GHz Band

Puneet Singh[1]📷, Saroj Mondal[2][✉]📷, and Krishnan S. Rengarajan[1]📷

[1] Department of Electrical and Electronics Engineering, Birla Institute of Technology and Science - Hyderabad Campus, Shamirpet-Keesara Road, Jawahar Nagar, Shameerpet, Hyderabad, Telangana 500078, India
[2] Department of Electrical Engineering, Indian Institute of Technology Dharwad, Dharwad, Karnataka 580011, India
saroj@iitdh.ac.in

Abstract. This work presents the design of a wideband two stage SiGe HBT LNA meant for a fully integrated RF front end millimeter-wave receiver covering 57 GHz to 64 GHz license free band. A cascode amplifier utilizing active and passive matching along with negative feedback is employed in the two-stage design of the LNA. The designed LNA exhibits 17 mW of power consumption, 20.2 dB gain, 3.7 dB noise figure, and 1-dB compression point (P1 dB) of -0.8 dBm all achieved simultaneously in the desired band. The LNA is realized in the $0.13\mu m$ SiGe BiCMOS technology node. In addition to that, the proposed LNA exhibits the 3-dB gain bandwidth of more than 21 GHz. A novel layout technique is used to reduce unnecessary parasitics so that the EM simulated response agrees well with the schematic response. Apart from that, a new figure of merit is proposed to fairly compare the performance of the proposed LNA with the state-of-the-art LNA operating around 60 GHz license free band. The designed LNA will form the RF front end of a battery-operated mm-wave receiver.

Keywords: Cascode · Figure of Merit (FOM) · Heterojunction Bipolar Transistor (HBT) · Low Noise Amplifier (LNA) · Millimeter Wave · Silicon Germanium (SiGe)

1 Introduction

Over the last few years, the 60 GHz band has been the focus of research into wireless applications. These include meeting the never ending requirement for increased data rates for personal hand held devices [3,5,9], faster downloading speeds, use in the automotive radar and personal networking spaces, and provision for greater security making it an ideal option for portable bio-medical devices. Greater security is because this band suffers from attenuation due to oxygen molecules. The 60 GHz band is not yet standardized and therefore, the transmission ranges from 57 GHz to 66 GHz in Europe (9 GHz range) and 57 GHz to 64 GHz in the United States (7 GHz range) are available as license free band

A. P. Shah et al. (Eds.): VDAT 2022, CCIS 1687, pp. 161–171, 2022.
https://doi.org/10.1007/978-3-031-21514-8_15

[2]. The channels in the 60 GHz band are 2 GHz wide and have guard bands of 240 MHz and 120 MHz, respectively.

At 60 GHz, the performance of a communication system heavily depends on low noise figure (NF), high linearity, and high gain at the receiver and one can achieve the same by carefully designing the LNA. However, designing a LNA with above mentioned features along with minimal process parameter variation at 60 GHz is not easy because the parameters cannot be controlled independently. Since the LNA is being designed for mm-wave frequencies, it would mainly be used in wireless body area network (WBAN) and in short range and high speed communication systems.

Due to the advancement of process technology, high electron mobility, and pronounced ballistic carrier transport SiGe HBT based LNAs are preferred over Si BJT in 60 GHz band. Moreover, same property makes it useful in the design of low power devices [1]. Apart from that, SiGe also has a high f_t and low NF compared with Si BJT.

In literature, Sun et al. [12] proposed a fully integrated 60 GHz LNA in SiGe technology using differential topology. However, differential topology has higher DC power consumption and a poor NF. The most preferred topology in the design of LNA's is the cascode topology because it achieves high gain, bandwidth, and better isolation simultaneously [6]. The LNA designed in [8] achieved high gain with low power consumption; however, spiral inductors for biasing and matching consumed a large chip area due to their high value of inductance. The cascode LNA in [7] also achieved a high gain and low NF but at the cost of a narrow 3 dB bandwidth. LNA's in literatures also have a poor P1 dB value [12,14] despite achieving high gain or low NF.

In this paper, a novel design technique is described that uses lumped components to match a two stage LNA. The proposed two-step design technique optimizes gain, noise figure, input and output return loss, IIP3, DC power consumption simultaneously and results in a compact chip size of 0.094 mm². First, a combination of series and shunt feedback is used along with device scaling so that the input and output impedance of the individual HBT's are matched to 50Ω as closely as possible as shown in Fig. 2. Finally, lumped and distributed components (interconnecting lines and via) are used to carry out matching of the input , output and interstage of the two stage LNA. Since all the layout parasitics are accounted into the matching network, the EM simulated response agrees well with the schematic response. To the best knowledge of the authors, this is the first time such a simple design technique is applied to mm-wave RFIC design. The same design technique is being applied by the authors in the design of a W-band LNA and the initial simulations results are quite encouraging.

The rest of the paper is organized as follows: Sect.-2 discusses the proposed LNA configuration and design steps. Section-3 discusses the layout approach taken so that there is a close match between schematic results and post layout EM simulation results. This section also suggests some good layout techniques and their impact on the EM response. Section-4 gives the post layout EM results and their correlation with schematic results. Also, a new Figure of Merit (FOM) is introduced that takes P1 dB into account. Sections 5 and 6 concludes with a performance comparison between the various published LNA results with the proposed LNA in the 60 GHz band using the proposed FOM.

2 Two-stage LNA Design

Most of the SiGe LNA designs reported in literature [10, 11, 13–15] try to optimize two or three design parameters. Our focus is to optimize all these parameters simultaneously by using a simple design technique. The first challenge is to choose an architecture for LNA that will help to optimize all the RF parameters mentioned earlier. A Common Emitter (CE) amplifier is difficult to match over a broad range of frequencies, although its well suited for low NF and high gain. A differential stage on the other hand consumes higher bias current resulting in high power dissipation. A cascode stage, though well suited to meet all the design goals needs higher collector voltage to bias two transistors that appears in series resulting in higher power dissipation compared to the single state CE amplifier but less compared to differential one.

The problem was overcome by biasing the two transistors close to saturation by using a lower supply voltage 1.3 V to get the desired performance as shown in Fig. 1. The price paid is a lower f_t and f_{max} compared to CE stage. A 1.6 V voltage source is required to bias the base of Q2 transistor as shown in Fig. 1. The use of lower collector bias voltage results in the base collector junction voltage, V_{bc}, of both transistors, Q1 and Q2, becoming positive by a minimum of 143 mV as shown in Fig. 1, which is still lower than the 800 mV required to forward bias the junction. As the base collector junctions of the two transistors are not fully turned on, they operate in soft saturation and still can be used to amplify small signals as in an LNA. As a result, the base collector junction capacitance, C_{bc}, increases beyond zero bias capacitance, C_{bco}, and the f_t of the cascode decreases. A small emitter degeneration inductor can help recovering back the f_t while keeping f_{max} nearly fixed. The inductor is realized using a high impedance transmission line Tx1. The HBT's in first stage cascode transistors were scaled to include ten emitter fingers. A parallel feedback was applied from output of the cascode to its input using discrete capacitors and resistor. This helps in stability and broadband match over the entire band. The final cascode with feedback before the input and output match is shown in Fig. 1. The f_t value is then plotted as a function of collector current, I_C, at different emitter inductor values as shown in Fig. 3. It is observed that increasing the transmission line length beyond 35 μm has no effect on f_t. Hence 35 μm was chosen as optimum inductor length. This along with chosen transistor size helps simplify the design of input and output matching network over a broad frequency range. The reason for improvement in f_t value is partial compensation provided by the emitter inductor for base emitter capacitance (C_{be}) of the lower transistor that degrades the f_t of the cascode. Similar compensation would be required for the upper transistor at higher frequencies of operation, say beyond 100 GHz. At 60 GHz emitter compensation of lower transistor is seen enough.

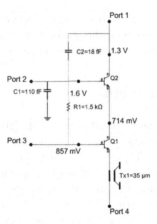

Fig. 1. Single stage SiGe HBT Cascode LNA with feedback.

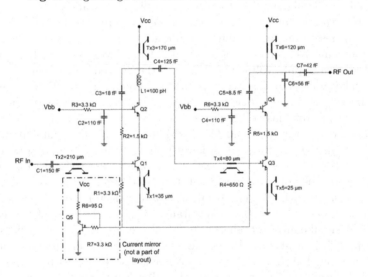

Fig. 2. Schematic of the proposed two-stage LNA.

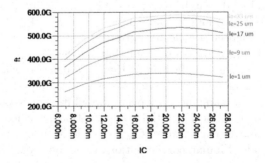

Fig. 3. f_t vs collector current with l_e as a parameter.

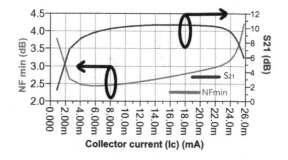

Fig. 4. NF_{min} and S_{21} vs collector current.

2.1 Biasing and Component Selection

As shown in Fig. 2, the peak value of f_t is around an I_C of 20 mA and decreases if one is further away from this value. The roll off is shallow on lower I_C side and steep on higher I_C side. A bias current of 6.3 mA was chosen for the first stage and 6.8 mA for the second stage in order to meet the goal of low DC power consumption. This selection of bias current is also suitable for lowest NF, as observed in Fig. 4. Finally a split inductor at the collector of the cascode was chosen for better gain and impedance match [4]. The second stage of the LNA is similar to the first stage except that the transistors sizes were scaled to seven emitter fingers and the split inductor at the collector of second stage was avoided for better match. Use of lumped inductors consumes a lot of chip area and hence most of the inductors were realized using high impedance transmission lines (see layout of the two-stage LNA as shown in Fig. 5). The simulated results of this two stage LNA are presented in Figs. 6, 7, 8 and also presented in Table 1.

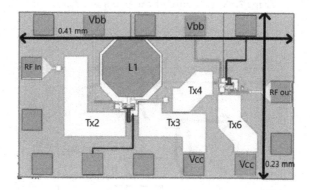

Fig. 5. Layout of the proposed two-stage LNA.

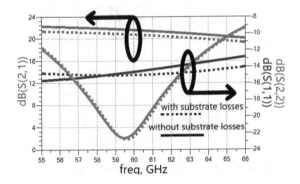

Fig. 6. S parameters of the two-stage LNA.

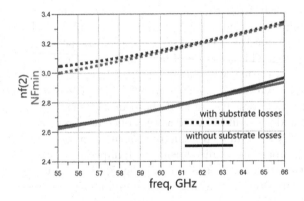

Fig. 7. Noise figure of the two-stage LNA.

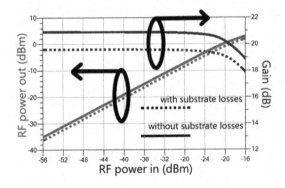

Fig. 8. 1 dB compression point of the two-stage LNA.

Table 1. Circuit simulation results of the two-stage LNA @ 60 GHz.

Gain (S_{21})	Input reflection coefficient (S_{11})	Output reflection coefficient (S_{22})	Noise figure	P1 dB
21.4 dB	−14.4 dB	−21.27 dB	2.7 dB	1 dBm

Table 2. Comparative study of state-of-the-art LNA

Reference	This work	[14]	[15]	[10]	[11]	[13]
Technology	0.13 µm SiGe	0.13 µm SiGe	0.13 µm SiGe	0.18 µm SiGe	90 nm CMOS	0.25 µm SiGe
	BiCMOS	BiCMOS	BiCMOS	BiCMOS		BiCMOS
Topology	Cascode	CE	CE + CC	Cascode	Cascode + CS	Cascode +CE
Stage	2	3	2	3	3	2
Frequency (GHz)	60	60	59	55	60	60
Gain (dB)	20.2	24	15	32.5	22	15.3
3 dB bandwidth (GHz)	21.3	9	14	24	5	7
Noise Figure (dB)	3.7	2.5	3.3	6	3.7	6.2
OP1 dB (dBm)	−0.8	−30 (in)	1.5	−6.5	−1	−20 (in)
Power (mW)	17	42.9	19.6	11.7	13.5	4
Chip Area (mm2)	0.094	0.098	0.105	0.39	0.593 (with pads)	0.9 (entire chip)
FOM (GHz/mW)	9.1	3.356	4.685	13.33	3.02	5.15
New FOM (GHz)	7.6	0.843	6.58	2.985	2.397	1.745

3   LNA Layout

The two-stage LNA was designed using IHP 130 nm SiGe BiCMOS process. Advanced Design System (ADS) was used to simulate and optimize the LNA. The IHP 130 nm process was used because of its high f_t value of around 500 GHz. The main challenge in the layout of the two-stage LNA was to create a good RF ground. Unfortunately, due to the absence of back via model in the IHP PDK the substrate ground at the back cannot be used and a finite ground is to be created on one of the metal layers. The PDK supports seven metal layers, and the two top metal layers thickness are much higher than other other metal layers. The HBT terminals appear on Metal1 and Metal2 layers. The ground was realized on Metal1 layer by splitting the Metal1 layer into ground and signal layer. The emitter inductor was realized using a thin metal track on metal3 layer. The length of this track along with via stacks at both its ends (emitter connection at one end and grounding at the other), was optimized to match the inductor value in schematic. All the transmissions lines were realized between TopMetal1 and Metal1 layers to minimize the via interconnects between layers thus minimizing the parasitic associated with vias. Lumped inductor was realized on TopMetal2 and TopMetal1 layer. Lumped capacitors are realized on TopMetal1 and Metal5 layers. The interconnect between components were realized using minimum track length. Probe pads were included at the RF input and output and pads for DC supply were also incorporated. First, the LNA was simulated using ideal circuit components and optimized to meet the desired specifications. Further, the ideal parts were replaced with PDK components and the simulations were performed. The PDK parts were tuned till the results obtained were found to be in close agreement with those obtained using ideal circuit components. The

PDK components account for a broader range of phenomena and hence produce more accurate set of results. Monte Carlo simulation was carried out on the LNA circuit using the process variations provided by the foundry and the yield was found to be better than 90% considering the gain and NF as the design goals. The LNA design was converted to a layout for a more accurate EM analysis and to include the effects of finite ground plane, component interconnects, and via holes. The layout was EM optimized for a response close to the circuit response. The optimized layout is shown in Fig. 5 and the layout optimized response is shown in Figs. 9, 10, 11.

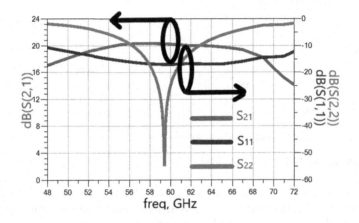

Fig. 9. S parameters of the two-stage LNA layout.

4   EM Simulation Results and Observations

The post layout EM simulation for two stage LNA is presented in Figs. 9, 10, 11 indicate that average gain in the band of interest (57 GHz to 64 GHz) is 20 dB and input and output return losses are better than -10 dB. Average NF in band is 3.7 dB and 3 dB bandwidth equals 21 GHz. Table 2 mention these parameters at band center of 60 GHz. Comparing with schematic results the average NF has increased by 1 dB and average gain has decreased by 1.5 dB in the band of interest. This can be explained by considering the losses due to via stacks and interconnects used. We can model these losses by introducing appropriate value resistors in series with emitter and base of the first stage cascode, as shown in Fig. 12. The schematic performance shown in Figs. 6, 7, 8 is now close to post layout EM results. The small difference is due to finite size of the ground plane and the pads used in the layout.

To compare this work with the state-of-the-art SiGe HBT LNA, we propose a new FOM. Unlike the FOM used in [11], we propose a new FOM which takes into account the output P1 dB. The FOM is a parameter of comparison which takes into account the gain, power consumed, bandwidth, and NF into account to give

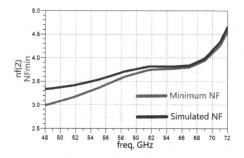

Fig. 10. Noise figure of the two-stage LNA layout.

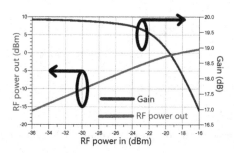

Fig. 11. 1 dB compression point of the two-stage LNA layout.

a number which would represent the overall performance of the RF system (in this case, the LNA). The conventional FOM as described in [7] is

$$FOM = \frac{Gain(dB) \times BW(GHz)}{P_D(mW) \times (NF - 1)(dB)} \tag{1}$$

However, the above formula does not consider factors like the chip area and output 1 dB compression point. So, we include these parameters in the FOM formula and modify it slightly to define a new FOM given by the formula

$$FOM_{new} = \frac{Gain(dB) \times BW(GHz) \times OP_{1dB}(mW)}{P_D(mW) \times (NF - 1)(dB)} \tag{2}$$

OP1 dB is part of the numerator in the above expression because of the requirement of higher P1 dB point (or dynamic range) while designing the LNA. The chip area cannot be used in the formula as the size of the pads often varies from one RF system design to another.

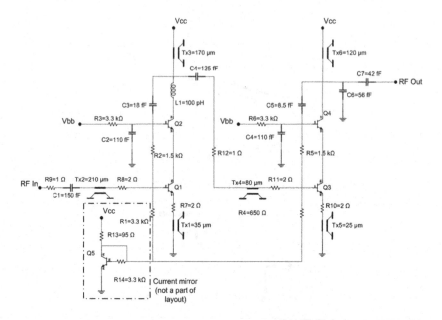

Fig. 12. Schematic of the proposed two-stage LNA incorporating losses.

5 Comparison with The-state-of-the-art LNA

On comparison with the-state-of-the-art LNA, it is observed that the LNA proposed in this paper has a high gain-bandwidth product, low DC power consumption of 17 mW, low NF, and a high output P1 dB. These results are all taken into account in the newly proposed FOM and its value of 7.6 indicates that the proposed LNA is the best amongst the LNA's it is compared against and possibly achieves one of the best design tradeoff's when compared with any LNA in this frequency of operation.

6 Conclusion

This paper proposes a two stage LNA having low power consumption and a large 3 dB bandwidth along with a high output P1 dB. The LNA operates in a frequency range of 57–64 GHz and achieves a peak gain of 20.2 dB at around 60 GHz. It has a 3 dB bandwidth of 21 GHz and has a NF of 3.7 dB in its frequency of operation. Its input and output reflection coefficient (S_{11} and S_{22}) is well below 10 dB and its output P1 dB has a value of -0.8 dBm. Overall, it achieves the best performance parameter tradeoffs when compared with other state-of-the-art LNA's and this has been shown with the help of a newly defined FOM. It can be used in short range and high speed communication systems.

References

1. Ashburn, P.: SiGe heterojunction bipolar transistors. Wiley Online Library (2003)
2. Božanić, M., Sinha, S.: Millimeter-Wave Low Noise Amplifiers. SCT, Springer, Cham (2018). https://doi.org/10.1007/978-3-319-69020-9
3. Chai, Y., Li, L., Cui, T.: Design of a 60 GHz LNA with 20 dB gain and 12 GHz BW in 65 nm LP CMOS. In: 2012 IEEE MTT-S IMWS on Millimeter Wave Wireless Technology and Applications, pp. 1–4. IEEE (2012)
4. Chen, H.K., Lin, Y.S., Lu, S.S.: Analysis and design of a 1.6-28-GHz compact wideband LNA in 90-nm CMOS using a π-match input network. IEEE Trans. Microwave Theory Tech. **58**(8), 2092–2104 (2010)
5. Cohen, E., Ravid, S., Ritter, D.: An ultra low power LNA with 15 dB gain and 4.4 dB NF in 90 nm CMOS process for 60 GHz phase array radio. In: 2008 IEEE RFIC Symposium, pp. 61–64. IEEE (2008)
6. Do, V.H., Subramanian, V., Boeck, G.: 60 GHz SiGe LNA. In: 2007 14th IEEE ICECS, pp. 1209–1212. IEEE (2007)
7. Fanoro, M., Olokede, S., Sinha, S.: A low noise and power consumption, high-gain LNA in 130 nm SiGe BiCMOS using transmission lines. In: 2017 XXXIInd URSI GASS, pp. 1–4. IEEE (2017)
8. Gordon, M., Voinigescu, S.P.: An inductor-based 52-GHz 0.18 μm SiGe HBT cascode LNA with 22 dB gain. In: Proceedings of the 30th ESSCIRC, pp. 287–290. IEEE (2004)
9. Heydari, B., Bohsali, M., Adabi, E., Niknejad, A.M.: Millimeter-wave devices and circuit blocks up to 104 GHz in 90 nm CMOS. IEEE JSSC **42**(12), 2893–2903 (2007)
10. Jang, S., Nguyen, C.: A high-gain power-efficient wideband V-band LNA in 0.18-μm SiGe BiCMOS. IEEE MWCL **26**(4), 276–278 (2016)
11. Kuo, H.C., Chuang, H.R.: A 60-GHz high-gain, low-power, 3.7-dB noise-figure low-noise amplifier in 90-nm CMOS. In: 2013 European Microwave Conference, pp. 1555–1558. IEEE (2013)
12. Sun, Y., Borngraber, J., Herzel, F., Winkler, W.: A fully integrated 60 GHz LNA in SiGe: C BiCMOS technology. In: Proceedings of the BBCTM, pp. 14–17. IEEE (2005)
13. Sun, Y., Scheytt, C.J.: Low-power 60 GHz receiver front-end with a variable-gain LNA in SiGe BiCMOS technology. In: 2010 IEEE BBCTM, pp. 192–195. IEEE (2010)
14. Völkel, M., Dietz, M., Hagelauer, A., Weigel, R., Kissinger, D.: A 60-GHz low-noise variable-gain amplifier in a 130-nm BiCMOS technology for sixport applications. In: 2017 IEEE ISCAS, pp. 1–4. IEEE (2017)
15. Zihir, S., Rebeiz, G.M.: A wideband 60 GHz LNA with 3.3 dB minimum noise figure. In: 2017 IEEE MTT-S IMS, pp. 1969–1971. IEEE (2017)

Four Differential Channels, Programmable Gain, Programmable Data Rate Delta Sigma ADC

Mohd Asim Saeed[1,2]($\boxtimes$) ![ID], Deep Sehgal[1] ![ID], and Surinder Singh[1] ![ID]

[1] Semi-Conductor Laboratory, S.A.S. Nagar, Mohali 160071, Punjab, India
[2] Electrical Engg. Department, IIT Ropar, Rupnagar 140071, Punjab, India
mohdasimsaeed@gmail.com, asim@scl.gov.in

Abstract. This paper presents a precision wide range Delta Sigma ADC SC1601 (SC1601 is the product number of ADC) with programmable gain amplifier (PGA) and programmable output data rate features. The ADC offers four fully differential input channels. Each channel can be programmed with a gain of 1 to 128 in binary steps i.e. in powers of 2. The ADC uses a second order delta sigma modulator (DSM) followed by a digital sinc^3 filter. The output data rate of the ADC is also programmable from 312.5 Hz to 2.5 kHz either to achieve higher accuracy or higher speed. The ADC also offers on chip offset and gain calibration features to reduce the offset and gain errors. The serial interface of ADC is SPI^{TM} compatible. The SC1601 ADC is fabricated in 0.18 µm CMOS process at Semi-Conductor Laboratory (SCL). The total power consumption of the ADC is 4 mW and it consumes total silicon area of 2.25 mm^2. SC1601 ADC achieves a maximum ENOB of 19.15 bits at a data rate of 312.5 Hz with a full scale range of 1.22 V. The ADC requires a supply voltage of 3.3 V and 1.8 V and can operate in a wide temperature range of $-55°$C to 125°C. SC1601 ADC is developed for the satellite launch vehicle telemetry system.

Keywords: Delta sigma modulator · Analog multiplexer · Programmable gain amplifier · Digital filter

1 Introduction

Delta Sigma ($\Delta\Sigma$) ADCs are one of the most popular candidate for high precision applications due to their inherent linearity. The principle of the $\Delta\Sigma$ ADCs is based on oversampling and noise shaping. Despite using inaccurate components, $\Delta\Sigma$ ADCs can achieve very high accuracy due to combined effect of oversampling and noise shaping. Their tolerance to the circuit non-idealities and component mismatch make them suitable for the on-chip very large scale integration (VLSI) implementation. The relaxed requirements of the anti-aliasing filter is an add on advantage of $\Delta\Sigma$ ADCs. Moreover by trading accuracy with data rate, $\Delta\Sigma$ ADCs allow very high performance to be achieved [1–3].

Supported by Semi-Conductor Laboratory.

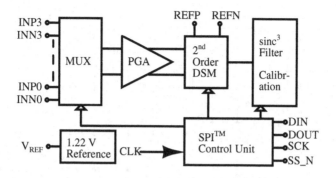

Fig. 1. Block Diagram of $\Delta\Sigma$ ADC SC1601

This paper presents a high precision $\Delta\Sigma$ ADC SC1601 with wide analog input range and programmable output data rate fabricated in 0.18 μm CMOS process. SC1601 ADC is a mixed-signal chip consisting of both analog and digital modules operating at a supply voltage of 3.3 V and 1.8 V respectively. SC1601 ADC is designed for the data acquisition of various sensors such as pressure sensors, temperature sensor etc., used in the telemetry systems of satellite launch vehicles [4,5]. SC1601 ADC consists of four differential input channels so that four different sensors can be connected at the input of ADC at the same time. The presence of the on chip PGA and programmable data rate feature of ADC make it suitable for a wide variety of sensors. The ADC is equipped with on-chip bandgap reference of 1.22 V. When on-chip bandgap reference is used, REFP input of the ADC can be shorted with V_{REF} externally and REFN to the analog ground. Also, the device can operate in a wide temperature range of -55°C to 125°C.

The rest of the paper is organized in the following manner: Sect. 2 presents the block diagram of the $\Delta\Sigma$ ADC SC1601 along with the implementation of various modules. The measurements results are discussed in Sect. 3 and Sect. 4 presents the conclusion.

2   Block Diagram and Implementation

The block diagram of the proposed ADC is shown in Fig. 1. The proposed ADC requires an external clock of 5.12 MHz. It consists of multiplexer to implement the four input differential channels followed by a PGA and a second order DSM. The DSM over samples the analog signal and converts it into a digital pulse train whose duty cycle represents the average value of the analog signal at any point of time. This digital pulse train is then processed by a digital sinc^3 filter to produce a 24 bits digital output. The offset and gain calibration is carried out on the 24 bits digital output of the filter to reduce offset and gain errors of the ADC or the input sensor. SC1601 ADC can communicate with the external world using SPI^{TM} serial interface. The control unit of SC1601 ADC consists

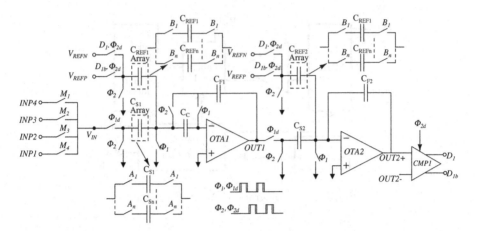

Fig. 2. Schematic of Second Order DSM along with Multiplexer and PGA.

of various control registers which can be written through SPI^{TM} to select any input channel of MUX or to set any gain of PGA or to set the required data rate. A detailed explanation of every block is given in the following sections.

2.1   Implementation of Multiplexer, PGA and DSM

The schematic of DSM along with the multiplexer and PGA is shown in Fig. 2. Figure 2 shows the single ended implementation of the DSM while actual implementation is fully differential. A 4X1 fully differential multiplexer is used to implement the four differential channels of the ADC. The multiplexer is implemented using CMOS switches in order to avoid any clipping of the input signal when the input signal is near to the supply rails. The maximum resistance of the CMOS switches used in the multiplexer will affect the settling error. Hence, the maximum resistance of the CMOS switches at highest temperature and worst design corner is chosen as 300 Ω to meet the settling requirements of the input signal when sampled onto sampling capacitor C_{S1}. Any of the channel can be selected externally by writing control registers of control unit through SPI^{TM}.

The multiplexer is followed by a PGA and the switched capacitor (SC) DSM. The PGA can be set to any value between 1 to 128 in binary steps i.e. in powers of 2, by writing appropriate value in the control unit registers using SPI^{TM}. The PGA helps to program the full scale range (FSR) of ADC to $\pm 1.22/PGA$ V. So, the sensors having full scale output between 1.22 V to 9.5 mV can be directly interfaced with the ADC without any need of external amplification. The PGA is implemented using the switchable capacitor array of input sampling capacitor C_{S1} and reference capacitors C_{REF1} and C_{REF2} of first and second integrator respectively as shown in Fig. 2. The programmable gain of the ADC can be give as,

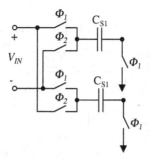

Fig. 3. Input Stage of SC1601 ADC

Table 1. Capacitor values for different PGA settings

PGA	C_{S1} (pF)	C_{REF1} (pF)	C_{REF2} (pF)
1	2	4	4
2	4	4	4
4	8	4	4
8	16	4	4
16	32	4	4
32	32	2	2
64	32	1	1
128	32	0.5	0.5

$$Gain = \frac{2 * C_{S1}}{C_{REF1}} \tag{1}$$

The switchable capacitor arrays of C_{S1}, C_{REF1} and C_{REF2} are implemented using a MIM capacitor with a unit capacitor value of 0.5 pF. The values of C_{S1}, C_{REF1} and C_{REF2} for different PGA settings are given in Table 1. Any of their values can be selected using the control signals A and B coming from the control unit. As shown in Fig. 3, a double sampling scheme is used to implement the input stage of the first integrator. Double sampling scheme helps in achieving an extra gain of 2 without increasing the thermal noise floor [6]. The resolution of any high precision ADCs is limited by the thermal noise [1]. A mathematical model of input referred thermal noise in DSM using SC integrator is presented in [3] and may be given as:

$$P_{CN,in} = \frac{2 * kT}{C_{S1}} \left(1 + \frac{C_{REF1}}{C_{S1}} \right) \frac{1}{OSR} + S_{op}^t \frac{GB_i}{2} \left(\left(1 + \frac{C_{REF1}}{C_{S1}} \right)^2 \frac{1}{OSR} \right) \tag{2}$$

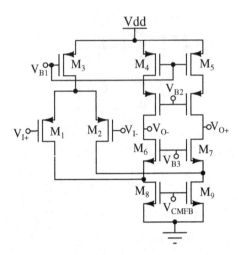

Fig. 4. Folded cascode OTA used in first and second integrator

where OSR: oversampling ratio; k: Boltzmann constant; T: absolute temperature; S_{op}^t: thermal noise PSD of OTA used in first integrator; GB_i: unity gain
bandwidth of OTA used in first integrator.

In the Eq. (2), the $1/f$ noise of OTA is ignored because of the correlated
double sampling (CDS) integrator. Using Eq. (2), the value of C_{S1} is selected
as 2 pF and the value of C_{REF1} is selected as 4 pF to keep the thermal noise
smaller than -120 dB of full scale voltage at a PGA value of 1 and an OSR value
of 2048.

A second order single loop switched capacitor (SC) based DSM is used to
implement the ADC. Several implementations of SC second order DSM are
recently reported in the literature [7,8]. The DSM is designed to operate at
a maximum modulator frequency f_{MOD} of 640 kHz. It samples the input analog
signal at a sampling rate of 640 kHz and produces a 1-bit digital stream whose
average duty cycle represents the digitized information. The external ADC clock
of 5.12 MHz is divided internally by a factor of 8 to generate f_{MOD}. A correlated
double sampling (CDS) integrator is used in the first stage to reduce the effect of
the offset voltage, offset voltage drift and $1/f$ noise of OTA. The CDS integrator
also helps in reducing the OTA gain errors [6,9]. The non-idealities of the second
integrator will get divided by the the gain of first integrator when referred to the
input. Hence, a simple integrator is used to implement the second integrator.
The coefficients of the DSM a (C_{S1}/C_{F1}), b (C_{REF1}/C_{F1}), c (C_{S2}/C_{F2}) and
a (C_{REF2}/C_{F2}) are chosen as 0.25, 0.25, 0.5 and 0.25 respectively. Hence, the
capacitor values of $C_{F1} = 16$ pF, $C_{S2} = 8$ pF and $C_{F2} = 16$ pF are selected for
the implementation of the DSM. Folded cascode OTA as shown in Fig. 4 is used
in first and second integrator. The key features for designing the OTA are open
loop DC gain, -3 dB bandwidth, slew rate and output swing. For the given
DSM coefficient values, the swing requirements of the integrators are slightly

larger than V_{REF}, which is feasible when operating with a 3.3 V supply voltage. In SC based DSMs, incomplete settling of integrator causes charge transfer error and affects the noise shaping of the DSM [3]. Charge transfer errors in SC integrator are mainly caused by three non-ideal characteristics of OTA - finite gain bandwidth, finite slew rate and finite DC gain. Single loop DSM are tolerant to the DC gain errors of the OTA. Also the CDS integrator helps to reduce the gain error effects on an SC integrator [6,9]. An open loop dc gain of 60 dB is enough to meet the accuracy requirements. The slew rate (SR) of the first CDS SC integrator is given as:

$$SR = \frac{I_{BIAS}}{C_{LT1}} \tag{3}$$

where I_{BIAS} is the tail current current of the $OTA1$ and C_{LT1} is the total loading capacitance during integration phase of the first integrator and is given as:

$$C_{LT1} = C_{L1} + \frac{C_{F1}\left(C_{S1} + C_{REF1} + \frac{C_C.C_{P1}}{C_C + C_{P1}}\right)}{C_{F1} + C_{S1} + C_{REF1} + \frac{C_C.C_{P1}}{C_C + C_{P1}}} \tag{4}$$

where C_{L1} is the parasitic loading capacitance at the out of $OTA1$ and C_{P1} is the parasitic capacitance at the input of $OTA1$.

The -3 dB bandwidth of integrator during integration phase f_{-3dB} is given as,

$$f_{-3dB} = \frac{\beta \times g_{m1}}{2\pi C_{LT1}} \tag{5}$$

The g_{m1} is the transconductance of the input differential pair of $OTA1$. The β is the feedback factor during the integration phase of first integrator and is given as:

$$\beta = \frac{C_{F1}}{\left(1 + \frac{C_{P1}}{C_C}\right)(C_{F1} + C_{S1} + C_{REF1}) + C_{P1}} \tag{6}$$

It can be seen from the Table 1 that the capacitive loading is highest at PGA value of 16. Hence, the capacitance values at PGA value of 16 are used when deciding the gain-bandwidth and slew rate requirements of the OTA. The behavioural simulations of DSM are carried out on $MATLAB^{TM}$ using analytical model of CDS SC integrator based DSM proposed in [10] to find the current in the $OTA1$ to meet the slew-rate and bandwidth requirements at f_{MOD} of 640 kHz. The tail current of the $OTA1$ comes out to 84 µA to meet the settling requirements of DSM. The output stage of the $OTA1$ shown in Fig. 4 is also biased at 84 µA to avoid any slew rate degradation. Hence, the total current required in $OTA1$ is 168 µA. The biasing voltage V_{B1} to V_{B4} of OTA shown in Fig. 4 are produced using wide swing cascode current mirrors. The capacitive loading in the second integrator is approximately same as in first integrator. Hence, same OTA is used in both the integrators. The summary of the OTA parameters used in the first integrator and second integrator is given in Table 2.

P-channel input MOS were employed on the OTA to reduce the flicker noise effects. An SC based common mode feedback (CMFB) is used to stabilize the common mode at the output of the OTA [11].

CMOS switches are used in both the integrators. The main design consideration for the switches are on resistance R_{ON} which affects the dynamic settling of SC integrator. CMOS switches with R_{ON} less than 300 Ω are used in multiplexer and switch matrix of capacitor arrays of C_{S1}, C_{REF1} and C_{REF2}. The R_{ON} of input switches sampling the input voltages onto C_{S1} and C_{S2} is kept smaller than 1 kΩ to meet the settling requirements. R_{ON} of switches used to sample the reference voltage on C_{REF1} and C_{REF2} is kept smaller than 4 kΩ. All the switches in the integrator are controlled using non-overlapping clocks $\Phi1$ and $\Phi2$ and their delayed version $\Phi1d$ and $\Phi2d$ are also used to avoid signal dependent charge injection.

A regenerative latch based comparator [12] with a pre-amplifier stage is used in DSM. The pre-amplifier stage is used to prevent any charge injection from the latch to the second integrator. The pre-amplifier is implemented using PMOS differential input pair and biased at 20 μA of biasing current.

Table 2. $OTA1$ and $OTA2$ specifications

Specifications	Value
Open Loop Gain (dB)	> 60
GBW (MHz)	> 2
Slew Rate (V/μs)	> 5
Output swing (V)	± 2
Total bias current (μA)	168

2.2   Implementation of Digital Filter, Calibration Unit, SPI and Control Unit

The digital module of the proposed ADC SC1601 comprises of digital filter, offset and gain calibration unit, SPI^{TM} and control unit. The block diagram of digital module of SC1601 ADC is shown in Fig. 5. The digital module operates at the voltage of 1.8 V. As mentioned in the previous section that analog module operates at 3.3 V supply voltage. Hence, level shifters are used between analog and digital modules to convert the voltage levels from 3.3 V to 1.8 V and vice-versa. The DSM over-samples the input signal at f_{MOD} which is much higher frequency than the Nyquist rate, f_N. The ratio of f_{MOD} and f_N is defined as the decimation factor (D) or oversampling ratio (OSR). The DSM produces a 1-bit pulse stream at f_{MOD} which is processed by a digital filter to produce higher bit data stream at a lower data rate (DR) which may be given as,

$$DR = \frac{f_{MOD}}{D} \qquad (7)$$

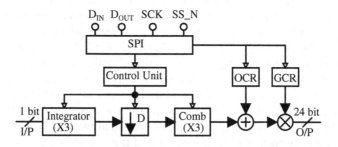

Fig. 5. Block Diagram of digital module of SC1601 ADC

The process of reducing the frequency from f_{MOD} to lower data rate is called decimation. The main purpose of the digital filter is to filter the noise which may aliased back into the base-band after decimation. The digital filter used in the SC1601 ADC is based on cascaded integrator-comb (CIC) structure [13]. A sinc^3 filter is adopted for the implementation of ADC. The decimation factor of the ADC is programmable and can be set to either 256, 512, 1024 or 2048 by writing its appropriate value in the control registers of control unit through SPI^{TM}. Hence, for a f_{MOD} of 640 kHz, the DR of the ADC can be set to any value of 312.5 Hz, 625 Hz, 1.25 kHz and 2.5 kHz .The ADC produces a 24-bit digital output at a set DR. Data rate programmability feature of the ADC make it versatile for the telemetry system of satellite launch vehicle. For higher frequency applications, data rate can be set to higher frequency and hence the integrated noise will also be higher as compare to application when lower data rate is set. The -3 dB bandwidth of the digital filter will be $0.262 * DR$. So, it is possible to trade between higher ENOB or higher bandwidth by varying the OSR [14]. The transfer function of the digital filter is given as,

$$H(S) = \frac{(1 - Z^{D*M})^N}{(1 - Z^{-1})^N} \qquad (8)$$

where N is the number of stages in filter and M is differential delay used in integrator and comb section. $M = 1$ is used to implement the CIC filter.

One important consideration in the design of CIC filter is the register growth or the register sizes of the filter. Register growth is directly proportional to number of stages of the filter and decimation factor. It is given as,

$$Register Length = N.(log_2 D.M) + B_{in} - 1 \qquad (9)$$

where B_{in} is the number of bits in input data stream.

In Eq. (9), the maximum value of the decimation factor D is used is calculate the Register Length. For $N = 3$, $D = 2048$, $M = 1$ and $B_{in} = 1$, the maximum $Register Length$ comes out to be 33 bits. Depending on the decimation factor, the $Register Length$ is controlled inside the filter. The output of the filter is the 24 bits MSBs which are selected from the output register of the filter. The rest of the LSBs are ignored. In order to remove the offset and gain errors of ADC and sensor, the offset and gain calibration is carried out on raw 24 bits filter output. The offset and gain errors are calibrated by applying a known input at the ADC and by comparing the obtained digital code with the expected value of digital code. The offset and gain calibration are to be carried out for a fixed configuration value of PGA and output data rate. For offset calibration of ADC, a zero differential voltage is to be applied at the the inputs of the ADC and the corresponding digital code is stored in the offset calibration register. It is also possible to digitally correct the offset voltage of the sensor. In this case, a voltage equal to the offset voltage of the sensor is to be applied at the input of the ADC and corresponding digital output code is stored in the offset calibration register (OCR). This offset calibration register value is subtracted from raw output of the 24 bit filter data in order to remove the offset. Gain calibration is carried out on the offset corrected data to remove the gain errors of ADC or sensor. During gain calibration, the offset corrected output of the ADC is multiplied with a scaling factor. For the gain correction, an input voltage equal to the full scale range of ADC at a particular value of PGA or the full scale voltage of the sensor is to be applied at the input of the ADC. The scaling factor is calculated based on the deviation obtained digital code from the expected digital code. A digital code correspond to the obtained scaling factor is stored on the gain calibration register (GCR). The offset corrected digital code is multiplied with this scaling factor to produce the offset and gain calibrated output. The offset and gain calibrated output of the ADC can be read from the ADC through SPI^{TM}. The serial interface of the ADC is standard four wire SPI^{TM} compatible. D_{IN} is the serial data input port and D_{OUT} is the serial data output port. SCK is the serial clock whose maximum value can be half of ADC external clock i.e. 2.56 MHz. The SS_N pin must be low during the communication with the ADC. Once it is high, the D_{OUT} pin will be in high impedance state.

3   Measurements Results

$\Delta\Sigma$ ADC SC1601 is designed and fabricated in SCL 0.18 μm CMOS process. The chip micrograph is shown in Fig. 6. SC1601 ADC consumes a total silicon area of 2.25 mm^2. The device is packaged in 64 pin CQFP package. The exhaustive testing the SC1601 ADC is carried out on the packaged device using a Mixed Signal tester. The proposed ADC is targeted for the low frequency applications, hence a DC characterization of the ADC is carried out. ENOB in $\Delta\Sigma$ ADCs for low frequency application, defines the usable resolution of ADC. It can be

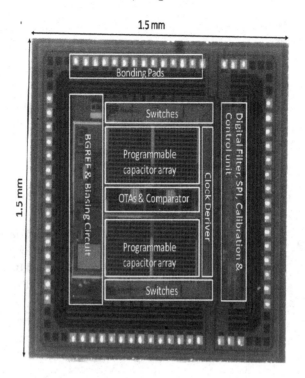

Fig. 6. Chip Micrograph of SC1601 ADC

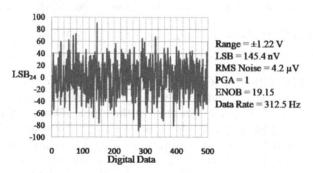

Fig. 7. Measured Noise performance at PGA = 1

measured by applying a fixed, known DC input to the analog input of ADC and calculating the standard deviation from several digital conversions [15]. ENOB in $\Delta\Sigma$ ADCs for low frequency application mat be given as:

$$ENOB = N - (log_2\sigma) \qquad (10)$$

where N : Number of converted bits (24 Bits; σ: Standard deviation of converted data.

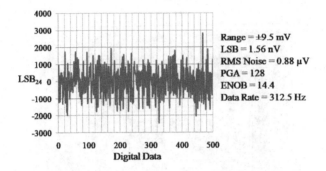

Fig. 8. Measured Noise performance at PGA = 128

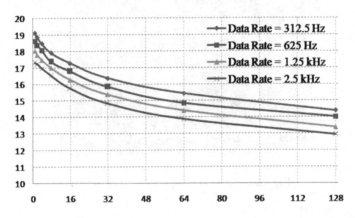

Fig. 9. Measured ENOB at various PGA and DR settings

The ENOB in SC1601 ADC is measured by shorting both the inputs of the ADC to the analog ground and by measuring the standard deviation of the 500 samples of collected digital code. Shorting of the input will prevent any external noise to enter the ADC and only the noise of the ADC will be measured. The ENOB is calculated by putting the value of measured standard deviation of 500 samples of digital code in Eq. (10). The above measurements is carried out at all the PGAs (1 to 128) values and a data rates of 312.5 Hz, 625 Hz, 1.25 kHz and 2.5 kHz. Figures 7 and 8 show the 500 digital code samples collected for PGA = 1 and PGA = 128 respectively at lowest data rate of 312.5 Hz. As, it can be seen from the Figs. 7 and 8 that rms noise of the ADC is reduced from 4.2 μV at PGA=1 to 0.88 μV at PGA = 128. Hence, higher value of the PGA is useful when sensor full scale output range is small. Figure 9 shows a plot of measured ENOB value at different PGA and data rates. It can be seen from Fig. 9 that as the data rate increases, the ENOB decrease. The noise of the ADC is dominated by the thermal noise, hence for every doubling of data rate, the ENOB goes down by approximately 0.5 bit. Hence, user can trade between the data rate and

ENOB value depending in the requirements. The ADC is also characterized for CMRR, PSRR, INL, offset, offset drift, gain error and gain error drift.

A commercially available ADC, ADS1218 from Texas Instruments is extensively used in telemetry systems of satellite launch vehicle for data acquisition of various sensor [4,5]. A comparison of various specifications of SC1601 ADC with ADS1218 is shown in Table 3.

Table 3. SC1601 ADC performance comparison with ADS1218 ADC

Specification	SC1601	ADS1218
Resolution (bits)	24	24
ENOB@PGA = 1 (bits)	19.15 @ DR = 312.5 sps	21 @ DR = 10 sps
ENOB@PGA = 128 (bits)	14.4 @ DR = 312.5 sps	18 @ DR = 10sps
Programmable Data Rate (DR) (Hz)	312.5 to 2.5 k	10 to 1 k
Bandwidth (Hz)	0.262 DR	0.262 DR
CMRR (dB)	> 100	> 100
PSRR (dB)	> 80	> 80
Offset Error (ppm of FSR)	< 2.5	< 7.5
Offset Drift (ppm of FSR/°C)	< 0.0013	< 0.02
Gain Error (ppm of FSR)	< 15	< 5
Gain Error Drift (ppm of FSR/°C)	< 2	< 0.5
INL (ppm of FSR)	< 20	< 15
Power (mW)	4	1
FOM_{SDNR} @PGA = 1 (pJ/conv)	42	91

$$FOM_{SNDR} = \frac{Power}{2 \times BW \times 2^{ENOB}};$$

4 Conclusion

A $\Delta\Sigma$ ADC SC1601 with 4 fully differential input channels, PGA, programmable data rate, offset and gain calibration, on-chip reference and SPI^{TM} compatible serial interface is fabricated in SCL 0.18 μm CMOS process. This device is indigenized for the data acquisition of variety of sensors placed all along the satellite launch vehicle. An exhaustive characterization including the temperature testing is carried out on more than 100 packaged devices of SC1601 ADC. SC1601 ADC meets all data acquisition requirements of satellite launch vehicle telemetry system. It achieves a better FOM_{SNDR} than ADS1218. The achieved ENOB values at PGA = 1 and PGA = 128 are lesser than ADS1218 ADC because of higher data rate of SC1601 ADC. SC1601 ADC will be used in satellite launch vehicle telemetry boards. The proposed ADC SC1601 can also be used in other sensor signal conditioning applications for data acquisition.

Acknowledgements. The authors are very grateful to S. N. Mittal of VLSI Test and Application Development Division (VTAD), Semi-Conductor Laboratory for carrying out rigorous testing of SC1601 ADC. In addition, the authors would like to thank Dr. Devarshi Mrinal Das of Electrical Engg. Dept., IIT Ropar for his fruitful discussions during the drafting of this paper.

References

1. de la Rosa, J.M., Schreier, R., Pun, K., Pavan, S.: Next-generation delta-sigma converters: trends and perspectives. IEEE J. Emerg. Sel. Top. Circuits Syst. **5**(4), 484–499 (2015). https://doi.org/10.1109/JETCAS.2015.2502164
2. Norsworthy, S.R., Schreier, R., Temes, G.C.: Delta-Sigma Data Converters: Theory, Design and Simulation, NewYork, NY. Wiley, USA (1997)
3. del Río, R., Mederio, F., Pérez-Verdú, B., de la Rosa, J.M., Rodríguez-Vázquez, Á.: CMOS Cascade Sigma-Delta Modulators for Sensors and Telecom. Springer, Netherlands (2006). https://doi.org/10.1007/1-4020-4776-2
4. Sreelal S. P., et al.: A versatile, software programmable telemetry system for satellite launch vehicles. In: Proceedings of 2006 International Telemetering Conference (ITC 06), San Diego, USA, pp. 06–18-04 (2006)
5. ADS1218: 8-Channel, 24-Bit Analog-to-Digital Converter Data sheet, Texas Instruments Inc., USA (2005)
6. Enz, C.C., Temes, G.C.: Circuit techniques for reducing the effects of op-amp imperfections: autozeroing, correlated double sampling, and chopper stabilization. Proc. IEEE **84**(11), 1584–1614 (1996)
7. Samadpoor Rikan, B., et al.: A sigma-delta ADC for signal conditioning IC of automotive piezo-resistive pressure sensors with over 80 dB SNR. Sensors **18**, 4199 (2018). https://doi.org/10.3390/s18124199
8. Benvenuti, L., Catania, A., Manfredini, G., Ria, A., Piotto, M., Bruschi, P.: Design strategies and architectures for ultra-low-voltage delta-sigma ADCs. Electronics **10**, 1156 (2021). https://doi.org/10.3390/electronics10101156
9. Nagaraj, K., Vlach, J., Viswanathan, T.R., Singhal, K.: Switched-capacitor integrator with reduced sensitivity to amplifier gain. Electron. Lett. **22**(21), 1103–1105 (1986)
10. Saeed, M.A., Gadhia, J., Jatana, H.S.: Accurate analysis of settling error in CDS integrator based sigma delta modulators. Annu. IEEE India Conf. (INDICON) **2015**, 1–6 (2015). https://doi.org/10.1109/INDICON.2015.7443484
11. Yao, L., Steyaert, M.S.J., Sansen, W.: A 1-V 140-/spl mu/W 88-dB audio sigma-delta modulator in 90-nm CMOS. IEEE J. Solid-State Circ. **39**(11), 1809–1818 (2004). https://doi.org/10.1109/JSSC.2004.835825
12. Yin, G.M., Eynde, F.O., Sansen, W.: A high-speed CMOS comparator with 8-b resolution. IEEE J. Solid-State Circ. **27**(2), 208–211 (1992)
13. Hogenauer, E.: An economical class of digital filters for decimation and interpolation. IEEE Trans. Acoust. Speech Signal Process. **29**(2), 155–162 (1981). https://doi.org/10.1109/TASSP.1981.1163535
14. Park, S.: Multi-stage decimation filter design technique for high-resolution sigma-delta A/D converters. IEEE Trans. Instrum. Meas. **41**(6), 868–873 (1992). https://doi.org/10.1109/19.199424
15. Baker, B.: A glossary of analog-to-digital specifications and performance characteristics. Texas Instruments Application Report, SBAA147B (2011)

Low Power Dual-Band Current Reuse-based LC-Voltage Controlled Oscillator with Shared Inductor for IoT Applications

Anshul Verma[(⊠)][ID] and Bishnu Prasad Das[ID]

Indian Institute of Technology, Roorkee, Roorkee, India
averma2@ec.iitr.ac.in, bishnu.das@ece.iitr.ac.in

Abstract. In this paper, a dual-band LC-voltage controlled oscillator (LC-VCO) is proposed, which employs the current reuse technique. The dual-band VCO can be operated at two frequencies such as 2.4 GHz and 5 GHz. The proposed VCO is designed at 0.6-V to reduce the power dissipation, which is a requirement for Internet-of-Things (IoT) applications. The active circuitry can be configured to generate the desired frequency of oscillation. The supply switching technique is used to operate the active circuitry of the design, which saves the power consumption. Due to the proposed supply switching technique, the VCO consumes around 53% less power than the conventional design at 5 GHz frequency of operation. As a single inductor is shared to generate dual-frequencies of the VCO, it makes the design more area-efficient. This approach saves around 46% area of the overall design. The proposed LC-VCO is simulated rigorously in 65 nm industrial process node to study the performance of the design. The parasitic extracted SPICE simulation results show that the proposed dual-band LC-VCO can generate output frequencies of 2.4 GHz and 5 GHz with power dissipation of 400 μW and 188 μW, respectively. The proposed VCO can achieve -122.16 dBc/Hz and -111.78 dBc/Hz phase noise and figure of merit (FOM) of -193.74 dB and -193.02 dB at a 1 MHz frequency offset for 2.4 GHz and 5 GHz, respectively. The area requirement of the proposed dual-band LC-VCO is 0.143 mm^2.

Keywords: Current-reuse · Clock generation · Figure of merit (FOM) · Low phase-noise · LC-VCO · Dual-band VCO · Low-power · Supply switching

1 Introduction

There are huge requirements for high-speed integrated circuits in many wireless applications such as wireless LAN (WLAN) and the Internet of Things (IoT) with low noise and low power to extend the battery life of the portable devices. The 2.4/5 GHz dual-band frequency synthesizers are required for WLAN standard 802.11 a/b/g/n [10]. The growth of IoT in various fields such as health

© The Author(s), under exclusive license to Springer Nature Switzerland AG 2022
A. P. Shah et al. (Eds.): VDAT 2022, CCIS 1687, pp. 185–198, 2022.
https://doi.org/10.1007/978-3-031-21514-8_17

care, home automation, smart farming, smart sensors, infrastructure monitoring are noticeable. These applications require high-speed communication channel between the sensor nodes and the central unit for video streaming, image transfer, and data processing, which rapidly change the requirement of wireless transceiver from single-band to multi-bands [3]. Circuits that can handle several frequency bands are becoming increasingly popular, as a results multi-band LC voltage-controlled oscillator (LC-VCO) have been reported in [4] - [5]. The dual-band LC-VCO is the core component of the RF wireless transceiver. In general, the varying capacitor (varactor) and inductor are used in the resonator tank to tune the LC-VCO, but the limited tuning range of the varactors makes the LC-tank challenging to obtain a different frequency band. Several design methods such as switched capacitors [9,16] and switched inductors [6,7] are introduced in the literature.

The typical LC-VCO topology can be modelled as shown in Fig. 1. This topology uses an active circuitry and a LC tank also known as LC resonator. In every cycle, the lossy LC-tank dissipates some of the tank energy, which causes an exponential decay in the oscillation amplitude. The active circuitry is used to compensate for the losses of the LC tank in each cycle. To maintain the frequency of oscillation, the LC tank losses resistance (R_P) must be compensated by the active circuitry generated negative resistance (R_{active}). The necessary condition can be defined as follows,

$$|R_{active}| = R_P \tag{1}$$

The major contributions of the paper are described as follows:

1. Design of 2.4/5 GHz dual-band LC-VCO with current reuse technique.
2. The design shares a common inductor, which makes the design more area efficient.
3. Supply switching technique for the active circuitry is used to generate the dual-band frequency, which provide low power for IoT applications and low phase noise for precise clock generation.

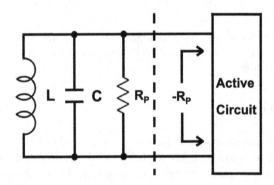

Fig. 1. LC-VCO model with active circuit [11]

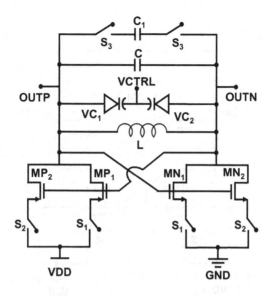

Fig. 2. Proposed Dual-Band LC-VCO architecture

This paper is organized as follows. The proposed dual-band LC-VCO with current reuse architecture is discussed in Sect. 2. Section 3 briefly discusses the post layout simulated results of the proposed LC-VCO. Finally, the conclusion is derived in Sect. 4.

2 Proposed Dual-Band LC-VCO Architecture

This section proposes a dual-band current reuse LC-VCO architecture, as shown in Fig. 2. The proposed LC-VCO can generate a 2.4 GHz and 5 GHz frequency band by switching the active circuitry and the capacitor. The proposed design shares a common resonator circuit (LC Tank) to generate the dual-band frequency, which saves the area of the design.

The two different active circuitry are used to maintain the desired frequency band oscillation. The requirement of two active circuitry is to compensate the positive resistance of the resonant tank at different frequency bands. A large current (large g_m) is required for the 2.4 GHz frequency because an additional capacitor switching is used to generate the 2.4 GHz frequency, which increases the tank loss resistance. In the case of 5 GHz frequency, capacitor switching is not used so that the tank loss resistance can be compensated by the small current (small g_m) compared to 2.4 GHz frequency operation. So, at a time, only one active circuitry is used to generate the corresponding frequency, and the other one is completely turned off to save the proposed design's power consumption.

The supply switching technique is used to operate the active circuitry of the design. This technique ensures that at a time, only one circuitry will operate. In Fig. 2, the cross-coupled transistors pairs $MP_1 - MN_1$ and $MP_2 - MN_2$

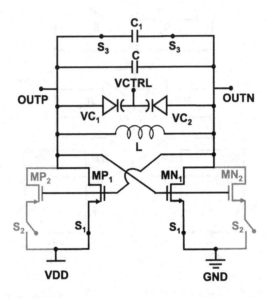

(a) Proposed dual-band LC-VCO in 2.4 GHz frequency operation

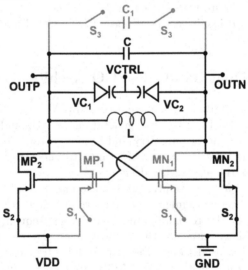

(b) Proposed dual-band LC-VCO in 5 GHz frequency operation

Fig. 3. Proposed Dual-Band LC-VCO architecture frequency operation

generate negative resistance to eliminate the positive resistance of the LC tank circuit at 2.4 GHz and 5 GHz frequency bands, respectively. A high-quality factor inductor with the value of 1.25 nH is used in the tank to achieve a better phase noise performance of the design with low power consumption. The equivalent circuits for 2.4 GHz and 5 GHz frequency oscillation are shown in Fig. 3(a) and (b), respectively.

For 2.4 GHz operation, the transistors MP_1 and MN_1 are connected to the supply through switch S_1, and capacitor C_1 is also connected between the output nodes of the LC-VCO through switch S_3. In this condition, the transistors MP_2 and MN_2 are disconnected from the supply, so there is no current flow through the transistors MP_2 and MN_2 in 2.4 GHz operation. The oscillation frequency for 2.4 GHz operation is given by,

$$f_{osc_{2.4GHz}} = \frac{1}{2\pi\sqrt{L(C + C_1 + C_{var})}} \tag{2}$$

where L and C are the resonator tank inductor and capacitor value, respectively. C_{var} is the varactor capacitance and C_1 is the additional capacitor required for 2.4 GHz frequency oscillation.

Similarly, for 5 GHz operation, switch S_2 is closed and provides the supply to the transistors MP_2 and MN_2. The Capacitor C_1 is disconnected from the output nodes of the LC-VCO by opening the switch S_3. The transistors MP_1 and MN_1 are turned off during 5 GHz operation. The oscillation frequency for 5 GHz operation is given by,

$$f_{osc_{5GHz}} = \frac{1}{2\pi\sqrt{L(C + C_{var})}} \tag{3}$$

Table 1. Aspect ratio of Transistors with passive element value of proposed dual band LC-VCO

	MP_1	MP_2	MN_1	MN_2	VC_1	VC_2	C (pF)	C_1 (pF)	L (nH)
Width (μm)	130	70	100	48	20	20	0.5	3.0	1.25
Length (nm)	90	125	60	80	800	800			

where L, C, and C_{var} are same as previously discussed. The aspect ratio of transistors and value of passive components are shown in Table 1.

2.1   Small Signal Analysis of Proposed Architecture

The small-signal analysis of the proposed dual-band LC-VCO is discussed in this subsection. Figure 4 illustrates a small-signal model of the proposed design. In the small-signal model, R_P represents the loss in the LC tank, L is the inductance of the tank, and C_T is the equivalent capacitance of the tank, including tank capacitance (C), varactor capacitance (C_{var}), and an additional capacitance (C_1) (only in the case of 2.4 GHz frequency operation).

$$C_T = C + C_{var} + C_1 \tag{4}$$

The g_{mP} and g_{mN} are the transconductance of the PMOS and NMOS transistors, respectively. The cross-coupled topology of PMOS and NMOS transistors are considered to have equal transconductances.

$$|g_{mP}| = |g_{mN}| \tag{5}$$

The V_{OUTP} and V_{OUTN} are the small signal differential output of the VCO.

$$V_{OUTP} = -V_{OUTN} \tag{6}$$

and,

$$V_X = V_{OUTP} - V_{OUTN}$$

From (6), the V_X can be written as,

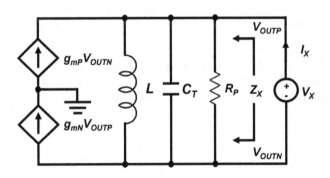

Fig. 4. Small signal model of proposed design with voltage stimulus

$$V_X = 2V_{OUTP} = -2V_{OUTN} \qquad (7)$$

The active circuitry must compensate for the tank losses R_P to maintain the stable frequency of the operation and ensure the reliable startup of the proposed design. To calculate the impedance Z_X of the design, a voltage stimulus V_X is applied between the output nodes V_{OUTP} and V_{OUTN}. From the KCL at node V_{OUTP},

$$I_X + g_{mP}V_{OUTN} = \frac{V_X}{SL} + \frac{V_X}{R_P} + V_X SC_T \qquad (8)$$

from (5), (7) and (8), the impedance Z_X can we written as,

$$Z_X(j\omega) = \frac{V_X}{I_X}(j\omega) = \frac{1}{\left(\frac{1}{R_P} - \frac{g_{mN}}{2}\right) + j\left(\omega C_T - \frac{1}{\omega L}\right)} \qquad (9)$$

For oscillation to occur, the resistive part of (9) must be satisfy the following condition,

$$\left(\frac{1}{R_P} - \frac{g_{mN}}{2}\right) \leq 0 \qquad (10)$$

or,

$$\frac{2}{g_{mN}} \leq R_P \qquad (11)$$

under this condition, the oscillation frequency of the VCO is given by (12),

$$f_{osc} = \frac{1}{2\pi\sqrt{LC_T}} \qquad (12)$$

from (11), it is clear that a large g_m is required to compensate the high tank losses R_P.

3   Post Layout Simulation Results of Proposed LC-VCO and Discussion

The proposed dual-band current reuse LC-VCO is implemented in 65 nm CMOS technology with an operating voltage of 0.6-V and simulated in Cadence Virtuoso. The parasitic extraction is performed with Caliber to validate the design performance after the layout design. The layout of the proposed architecture is shown in Fig. 5. The proposed architecture of LC-VCO occupies a total area of 0.143 mm^2 (340 μm x 422 μm). Exhaustive simulations have been carried out to study the performance of the proposed dual-band LC-VCO with current reuse architecture.

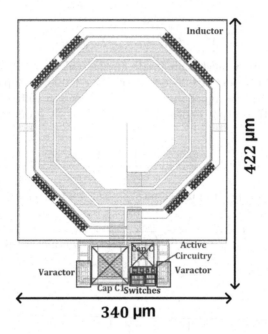

Fig. 5. Layout of proposed dual-band LC-VCO

3.1 Power Consumption

Author in [2] designed a current reused based VCO at a frequency of 2.4 GHz without the supply switching technique. In our proposed architecture the VCO is designed for two frequencies such as 2.4 GHz and 5 GHz. In this VCO we used current reused architecture with supply switching technique. Without supply switching technique, there is no improvement in the DC power dissipation. The circuit dissipates the same amount of DC power of $400\,\mu W$ for 2.4 GHz and 5 GHz frequencies. With the current reuse architecture and supply switching technique, the obtained power consumption of the proposed LC-VCO is $400\,\mu W$ and $188\,\mu W$ at 2.4 GHz and 5 GHz frequency operation, respectively. Around 53% power reduction is obtained for 5 GHz operation with the supply switching technique. Table 2 summarizes the power consumption of the design with and without supply switching technique.

Table 2. Power consumption comparison of designed LC-VCO with and without supply switching

	2.4 GHz	5 GHz	Power Reduction
Without supply switching	$400\,\mu W$	$400\,\mu W$	0 %
With supply switching (Proposed)	$400\,\mu W$	$188\,\mu W$	53 %

3.2 Frequency Tuning

The frequency variation with the control voltage of the proposed dual-band LC-VCO for 2.4 GHz and 5 GHz operation is shown in Fig. 6(a) and 6(b), respectively. For 2.4 GHz operation, LC-VCO can tune its frequency from 2.385-to 2.439 GHz for 0 to 600 mV control voltage. The 4.95-to 5.46 GHz tuning range is achieved for 5 GHz operation when the control voltage ranges from 0 to 600 mV. The tuning range of 2.25% and 10.2% is obtained for 2.4 GHz and 5 GHz frequency band, respectively.

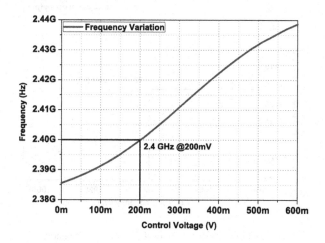

(a) Tuning range for 2.4 GHz LC-VCO operation

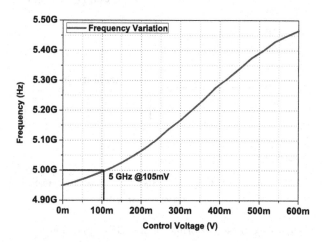

(b) Tuning range for 5 GHz LC-VCO operation

Fig. 6. Frequency variation with control voltage of Proposed dual-band LC-VCO

3.3   Phase Noise Performance

The proposed dual-band LC-VCO can achieve overall phase noise of -122.16 dBc/Hz and -111.78 dBc/Hz at a 1 MHz frequency offset from 2.4 GHz and 5 GHz, respectively. The phase noise variation for 2.4 GHz and 5 GHz output with respect to offset frequency is shown in Fig. 7(a) and (b), respectively. From the state-of-the-art, the phase noise performance improved by 10.05% for 2.4 GHz frequency operation and 1.16% for 5 GHz frequency operation.

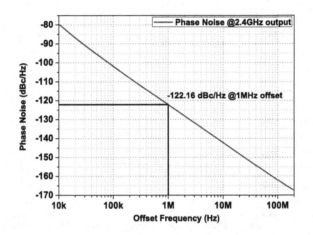

(a) Phase noise performance of 2.4 GHz operation

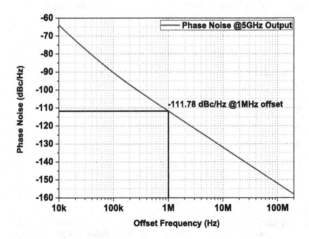

(b) Phase noise performance of 5 GHz operation

Fig. 7. Phase noise performance of Proposed dual-band LC-VCO

3.4 Frequency Spectrum of LC-VCO

To measure the spectral purity of the proposed VCO output, the frequency spectrum is plotted in MATLAB using the Hanning window. To plot the frequency spectrum, the frequency is first generated by tuning the control voltage of LC-VCO for 2.4 GHz and 5 GHz. Figure 8(a) and (b) show the proposed LC-VCO's frequency spectrum of 2.4 GHz and 5 GHz, respectively.

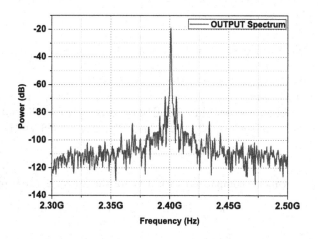

(a) Frequency spectrum for 2.4 GHz operation

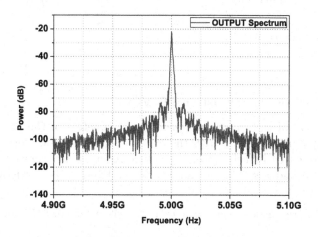

(b) Frequency spectrum for 5 GHz operation

Fig. 8. Frequency spectrum of Proposed dual-band LC-VCO

The frequency spectrum for 2.4 GHz and 5 GHz frequency operation is plotted for a 200 MHz frequency span. Figure 8(a) and (b) shows that the frequency spectrum is centered about the frequency of 2.4 GHz and 5 GHz, respectively.

3.5   Figure of Merit (FOM)

The FOM represents the most important performances of LC-VCO, such as power consumption, phase noise, and oscillation frequency. The FOM of LC-VCO is described as,

$$FOM = L\{\Delta f\} + 10\log(P_{DC}(mW)) - 20\log\left(\frac{f_{osc}}{\Delta f}\right) \qquad (13)$$

where $L\{\Delta f\}$ is the phase noise of the LC-VCO at frequency offset Δf, P_{DC} is the dissipated DC power of the LC-VCO, and f_{osc} is the oscillation frequency of the oscillator. The proposed dual-band current reuse LC-VCO obtained FOM at 1 MHz frequency offset is -193.74 dB and -193.02 dB for 2.4 GHz and 5 GHz, respectively.

Table 3. Performance comparison with State-of-the-art for 2.4 GHz operation

Parameter	ICECS '18 [1]*	IWS '16 [14]	ICECS '18 [2]*	APMC '13 [15]	This Work*
Technology (nm)	130	180	130	65	65
Supply Voltage (V)	0.6	0.5	1	0.3	0.6
Frequency Range (GHz)	2.34 – 2.38	2.25 – 2.52	2.30 – 2.55	2.22 – 2.43	2.385 – 2.439
Area (mm^2)	0.118	0.335	0.173	0.277	0.143
Phase Noise (dBc/Hz) @ 1 MHz Offset	−114.8	−119.4	−114.7	−111	−122.16
Power (mW)	0.411	3.23	0.262	0.576	0.400
FOM (dB) @ 1 MHz Offset	−186.26	−181.3	−188.15	−181.1	−193.74

*Post-layout simulated Results

3.6   Comparison with Existing LC-VCO

The comparison of the various performance parameters of the proposed dual-band current reuse LC-VCO with the existing state-of-the-art for 2.4 GHz and 5 GHz are presented in Tables 3 and 4, respectively. Table 3 shows the improvement of 10.05% and 6.98% in the phase noise and FOM, respectively with 30.56%

Table 4. Performance comparison with State-of-the-art for 5 GHz operation

Parameter	ARIS '20 [9]	URUCON '21 [13]	ECCTD '17 [12]*	TCAS-II '11 [8]	This Work*
Technology (nm)	180	180	65	65	65
Supply Voltage (V)	1	1	0.9	0.65	0.6
Frequency Range (GHz)	4.47 – 5.95	4.8 – 5.02	4.90 – 5.75	4.6 – 6.2	4.95 – 5.46
Area (mm^2)	0.489	0.207	0.100	0.330	0.143
Phase Noise (dBc/Hz) @ 1 MHz Offset	-115.8	-92	−110.5	−111.8	−111.78
Power (mW)	7	1.2	1.8	8.71	0.188
FOM (dB) @ 1 MHz Offset	-182.7	-165	−182.7	−176.38	−193.02

*Post-layout simulated Results

power reduction, compared to [15]. The phase noise and FOM shows the improvement of 1.16%, 5.65%, respectively with 89.56% power reduction for the 5 GHz operation compared to [12] as depicted in Table 4.

4   Conclusion

In this paper, a dual-band current reuse-based LC-VCO is proposed, which is optimized at a supply of 0.6-V in the industrial CMOS 65nm process. The proposed 2.4/5 GHz dual-band LC-VCO can be utilized to meet the frequency synthesizers' needs for the WLAN 802.11 a/b/g/n specifications. The operating frequency ranges from 2.385-to 2.439 GHz with a 2.25% tuning range for 2.4 GHz frequency operation and 4.95-to 5.46 GHz with a 10.2% tuning range for 5 GHz frequency operation. The DC power consumption was found $400\,\mu W$ and $188\,\mu W$, using the supply switching technique at 2.4 GHz and 5 GHz, respectively. This proposed LC-VCO also provides a low-power solution for battery-powered IoT devices. The proposed architecture can achieve phase noise of – 122.16 dBc/Hz and –111.78 dBc/Hz with –193.74 dB and –193.02 dB FOM at a 1 MHz frequency offset from 2.4 GHz and 5 GHz operations, respectively.

Acknowledgements. This work is supported and funded by Science and Engineering Research Board (SERB), Department of Science and Technology, Government of India under the project grant number CRG/2021/007437.

References

1. First, T., Mariano, A.A., Lacerda, P.C., Brante, G., Filho, O.C.G., Leite, B.: 2.4 GHZ reconfigurable low voltage and low power VCO dedicated to sensor networks applications. In: 2018 25th IEEE International Conference on Electronics, Circuits and Systems (ICECS), pp. 329–332 (2018). https://doi.org/10.1109/ICECS.2018.8617910

2. Haddad, F., Ghorbel, I., Rahajandraibe, W., Loulou, M., Slimane, A.: Current-reuse RF LC-VCO design for autonomous connected objects. In: 2018 25th IEEE International Conference on Electronics, Circuits and Systems (ICECS), pp. 473–476 (2018). https://doi.org/10.1109/ICECS.2018.8617894

3. Hsu, H.S., Duan, Q.Y., Liao, Y.T.: A low power 2.4/5.2 ghz concurrent receiver using current-reused architecture. In: 2016 IEEE International Symposium on Circuits and Systems (ISCAS), pp. 1398–1401 (2016). https://doi.org/10.1109/ISCAS.2016.7527511

4. Jia, L., Ma, J.G., Yeo, K.S., Yu, X.P., Do, M.A., Lim, W.M.: A 1.8-v 2.4/5.15-GHz dual-band LCVCO in 0.18-(μm) CMOS technology. IEEE Microwave Wirel. Compon. Lett.**16**(4), 194–196 (2006). https://doi.org/10.1109/LMWC.2006.872126

5. Kao, H.L., Yang, D.Y., Chin, A., McAlister, S.P.: A 2.4/5 GHZ dual-band VCO using a variable inductor and switched resonator. In: 2007 IEEE/MTT-S International Microwave Symposium, pp. 1533–1536 (2007). https://doi.org/10.1109/MWSYM.2007.380565

6. Kao, H.I., et al.: A 2.4/5 GHZ dual-band voltage-controlled oscillator using switched resonator. In: 2013 International Conference on Computational Problem-Solving (ICCP), pp. 20–22 (2013). https://doi.org/10.1109/ICCPS.2013.6893505

7. Kim, J.H., Han, J.H., Park, J.S., Kim, J.G.: A dual-band LC VCO with low phase noise in 0.18μm CMOS technology. In: 2017 IEEE International Symposium on Radio-Frequency Integration Technology (RFIT), pp. 168–170 (2017). https://doi.org/10.1109/RFIT.2017.8048261

8. Kytonaki, E.S.A., Papananos, Y.: A low-voltage differentially tuned current-adjusted 5.5-GHZ quadrature VCO in 65-nm CMOS technology. IEEE Trans. Circuits Syst. II Express Briefs **58**(5), 254–258 (2011). https://doi.org/10.1109/TCSII.2011.2149010

9. Lai, W.C.: Design of 1v CMOS 5.8 GHZ VCO with switched capacitor array tuning for intelligent sensor fusion. In: 2020 International Conference on Advanced Robotics and Intelligent Systems (ARIS), pp. 1–4 (2020). https://doi.org/10.1109/ARIS50834.2020.9205785

10. Nguyen, T.N., Agarwal, P., Heo, D.: A 5.8 GHZ and -192.9 DBC/HZ FOMT CMOS class-b capacitively-coupled VCO with gm-enhancement. In: 2016 IEEE MTT-S International Microwave Symposium (IMS), pp. 1–4 (2016). https://doi.org/10.1109/MWSYM.2016.7540351

11. Razavi, B.: RF Microelectronics (2nd Edition) (Prentice Hall Communications Engineering and Emerging Technologies Series), 2nd edn. Prentice Hall Press, USA (2011)

12. Sanchez-Azqueta, C., Aguirre, J., Royo, G., Aznar, F., Guerrero, E., Celma, S.: Design of a low-power quadrature LC-VCO in 65 nm CMOS. In: 2017 European Conference on Circuit Theory and Design (ECCTD), pp. 1–4 (2017). https://doi.org/10.1109/ECCTD.2017.8093330

13. Sola, F., Hernandez, H., Van Noije, W.: A bulk bias 1v 5ghz low power LC VCO with transconductance stabilization. In: 2021 IEEE URUCON, pp. 143–146 (2021). https://doi.org/10.1109/URUCON53396.2021.9647289

14. Wang, X., Yang, X., Xu, X., Yoshimasu, T.: 2.4-GHZ-band low-voltage LC-VCO IC with simplified noise filtering in 180-nm CMOS. In: 2016 IEEE MTT-S International Wireless Symposium (IWS), pp. 1–3 (2016). https://doi.org/10.1109/IEEE-IWS.2016.7585430

15. Yang, X., Uchida, Y., Xu, K., Wang, W., Yoshimasu, T.: 2.4 GHZ-band ultra-low-voltage class-c LC-VCO IC in 65 nm CMOS technology. In: 2013 Asia-Pacific Microwave Conference Proceedings (APMC), pp. 325–327 (2013). https://doi.org/10.1109/APMC.2013.6695134

16. Zhang, Y., et al.: A 5.8 GHZ implicit class-f VCO in 180-nm CMOS technology. In: 2019 IEEE Asia-Pacific Microwave Conference (APMC), pp. 1170–1172 (2019). https://doi.org/10.1109/APMC46564.2019.9038499

Aging Resilient and Energy Efficient Ring Oscillator for PUF Design

Anmol Verma, Shubhang Srivastava, and Ambika Prasad Shah$^{(\boxtimes)}$

IC-ResQ Laboratory, Department of Electrical Engineering, Indian Institute of
Technology Jammu, Jammu 181221, Jammu and Kashmir, India
ambika.shah@iitjammu.ac.in

Abstract. Hardware-based security primitives play an important role
in protecting and securing a system in Internet of Things (IoT) applications. The most important primitives are Physical Unclonable Functions
(PUFs) and True Random Number Generators (TRNGs), Cryptographic
Accelerators etc. Out of them, Physically Unclonable Functions (PUFs)
have come out to be most popular low-cost security primitives for authentication and cryptographic key generation. However, the PUF's stability with respect to variations over time still limits its usefulness and
widespread acceptance. One of the main problems limiting the performance of PUFs is their aging over time. Previous literatures focused
towards improving PUF robustness against aging but the power budget of the ring oscillator used in the design of these PUFs limits their
usage for low power applications, keeping this concern in mind a low
power variant of RO PUF is much needed. Hence in this paper, we propose a new energy efficient and aging resilient inverter and RO based
on aging resilient inverter design. The proposed inverter is 22.57% less
power consuming and 16% faster than the conventional Aging Resilient
inverter while showing nearly same aging characteristics. Also the Ring
Oscillator designed from the proposed inverter shows nearly 1.5% higher
frequency than the conventional Aging resilient Ring oscillator for same
number of inverter stages.

Keywords: Hardware security · Inverter · NBTI · Physically
Unclonable Function(PUF) · Ring Oscillator(RO)

1 Introduction

The Internet of Things (IoT) has become one of the key driver of the rapidly
growing electronic industry. Millions of new electronic devices are being connected to the Internet for a variety of uses [1]. With this massive increase in the
adoption and use of new technologies, security vulnerabilities are also increasing
exponentially. To secure the confidential data, cryptography offers an efficient
solution, but cryptographic encryption algorithms requires random numbers as

---

A. Verma and S. Srivastava—Equal Contribution.

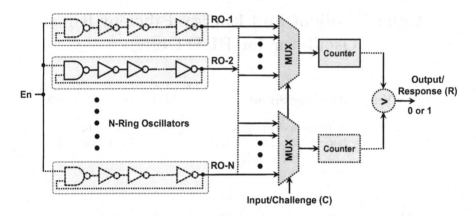

Fig. 1. Architecture for Ring Oscillator based Physically Unclonable Function [4]

their input. A truly random number can be thought of as a collection of unpredictable bits satisfying various statistical properties of randomness. If the bits generated are predictable with any degree of accuracy, it can lead to a device security failure that will cause enormous consequences and chances of possible sensitive data breach.

In the effort to design secure systems, the need for hardware security primitives like Physical Unclonable Functions (PUFs), True Random Number Generators (TRNGs) have surged in the recent years. Physically Unclonable Functions are of wide utility in the hardware security domain [2], Many PUF architectures [3] have been presented in the literature, such as Ring Oscillator (RO) PUF [4], Arbiter [5], SRAM PUF [6], DRAM PUF [7] and RS Latch PUF [8]. Under the category of elemental delay based PUF the RO based PUF which are one of the widely used security primitives due to their simple architecture and easy collection of responses as compared to other architectures of PUF [9]. In the architecture shown in Fig. 1, the frequency of RO is used as a function to generate challenge response pairs (CRP) in the PUF. The RO used inside the PUF is made up of chains of CMOS inverters. However in order to be useful in the cryptographic applications the security primitives should be reliable i.e., it should not change over time within an acceptable range of operating conditions, but it is well known that variations over time occur hence lead to IC performance degradation [10] and reliability issues popularly known as aging of the device. Figure 2 mentions the various systematic steps involved in the design of a RO based PUF, the figure clearly signifies that the most crucial step involved in the PUF designing is the selection of a reliable inverter, as the performance of RO inside the PUF is significantly affected by the aging related issues of the inverter.

There are various silicon related aging issues which include Negative Bias Temperature Instability (NBTI), Hot Carrier Injection (HCI), Time Dependent Dielectric Breakdown (TDDB) and Electromigration (EM) [10]. All these factors

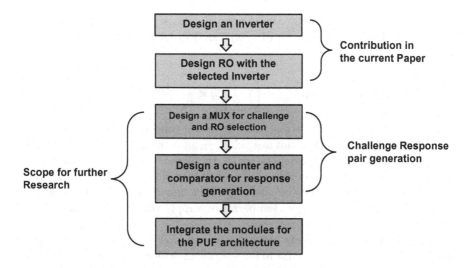

Fig. 2. Steps involved in a PUF design

shift the threshold voltage over time and increase the delay. Out these BTI and HCI are most significant. The two aging mechanisms of our concern are briefly described below:

HCI: Hot Carrier Injection (HCI) is the effect that a charge carrier gaining ample energy overcomes a potential barrier and is caged in the oxide layer hence limiting the voltages that can be used with these CMOS devices [11]. HCI is even more degrading and severe at these lower technology nodes and is a matter of concern. Gradually HCI leads to a change in transistor characteristics that typically increases the threshold voltage over time.

NBTI: Negative Bias Temperature Instability (NBTI) is a static mechanism. As stated in the previous literature, if $V_{GS} = -V_{DD}$ for a PMOS transistor, then the transistor is under stress. During this stress phase, some Si-H bonds are broken and trapped in the oxide layer [12]. As a result, this trapping changes the threshold voltage of the PMOS transistor which is mathematically expressed as [13]:

$$\Delta V_{TH_{stress}} = A_{NBTI} \times t_{ox} \times \sqrt{C_{ox}(V_{DD} - V_T)} \times e^{\frac{V_{DD} - V_T}{t_{ox}E_0} - \frac{E_g}{kT}} \times t_{stress}^{0.25} \quad (1)$$

where A_{NBTI} is the aging dependent constant, C_{ox} is the gate capacitance/area, t_{ox} is the thickness of oxide, t_{stress} is the stress time, E_a, E_0 are the device constants and k is the Boltzmann constant. During operation when $V_{GS} = 0$, some of the traps are eliminated and results in decrease of threshold voltage. This phenomenon is called the recovery phase. However not all trapped charges can be recovered and therefore the threshold voltage increases with time. The final threshold voltage change can be expressed in terms of stress and recovery time as [13]:

$$\Delta V_{TH} = \Delta V_{TH_{stress}} \times \left(1 - \sqrt{\eta \times \frac{t_{Recovery}}{t_{Recovery} + t_{Stress}}} \right) \qquad (2)$$

where t_{Stress}, $t_{Recovery}$ are stress time, recovery time respectively and η is a constant with value 0.3. BTI can degrade V_{TH} of a transistor by up to 10–15% in the first year of operation depending on the applied workload, resulting into a reduced drive current, reduced speed and degraded circuit performance [14]. The severity of the degradation caused by BTI and HCI is also dependent on signal probability, logic function, temperature, supply voltage, threshold voltage, technology node and device geometry.

Apart from the aging effects, since most of the IoT devices are battery powered therefore, the top priority for IoT-constrained devices is to consume minimal power. In this context, a low power implementation of these security primitives without sacrificing quality is required. Keeping this concern in mind, in this paper, we propose a new energy efficient and aging resilient inverter and RO design for a wide variety of RO based PUF design.

The rest of the paper is organized as follows. Section 1 presents the novel Aging resilient inverter. Section 3 focuses on the RO implementation from the inverter. Section 4 consists of associated results and discussion. Section 5 concludes our work.

2   Aging Resilient Inverter

Various inverter topologies like Conventional inverter (2T-INV), Conventional Aging Resilient inverter (ARI) [15] and Proposed Aging Resilient Transmission Gate based inverter (TG-ARI) are shown in Fig. 3. The proposed TG-ARI is made by modifying the ARI by adding an extra PMOS (M5) and thus converting the old pass transistor logic (M4) into the transmission gate logic. The working of proposed TG-ARI is discussed below:

Case 1: When V_{in} = '0' En = '0' and correspondingly $\overline{En}$ = '1', M3 and M4 goes to the cutoff state making V_{GS} of M2 in ARI and TG-ARI as V_{Tn} instead of $-V_{DD}$ as seen in the case of the 2T inverter.

Case 2: When En = '1' and correspondingly $\overline{En}$ = '0', M1 and M2 forms an inverter in all the three topologies.

Reliability analysis to find out the Threshold voltage variation due to NBTI under various stress times on our considered inverters is carried out on Cadence RelXpert available in Cadence environment using 40nm UMC technology. The threshold voltage variations for all the inverters for five years of stress time is shown in Fig. 4. Simulation results show that both the proposed TG-ARI and the conventional ARI show nearly same threshold voltage variation when stress is applied over time, also both of these inverters beat the 2T-INV by a large margin.

The reason for improved threshold value is that when $En = $ '0' or the RO made by the inverters is disabled, instead of 0, the V_{GS} of M2 is V_{Tn}, which in turn causes reduction of NBTI in the aging resilient inverters . This kind of NBTI protection is not possible in the 2T-INV. Hence we can safely conclude that both the conventional ARI and our proposed TG-ARI are far ahead from the traditional 2T-INV when it comes to aging resilience. However the main drawback in the conventional ARI is that when we use it as an inverter by making $En = $ '1' the input needs to pass through a pass transistor logic made by M4, if $V_{in} = V_{DD}$ the complete logic is not able to pass through M4 which causes power and speed related issues as presented in Sect. 4. Hence to resolve this issue we added a PMOS M5 as shown in Fig. 3(c) to the existing ARI design to convert

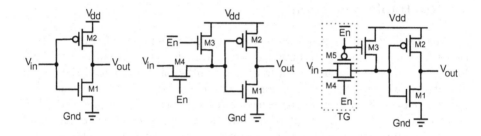

Fig. 3. Various inverter topologies (a) Conventional inverter (2T-INV) (b) Conventional aging resilient inverter (ARI) (c) Proposed aging resilient transmission gate based inverter (TG-ARI)

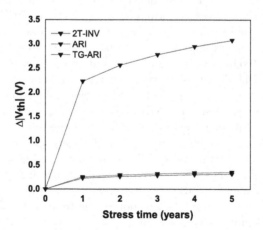

Fig. 4. Change in threshold voltage of various inverters with stress time

Table 1. Comparison between various inverter topologies

Parameter	2T-INV	ARI	TG-ARI
No. of Transistors	2	4	5
Aging Resilience	×	✓	✓
Input signal degradation	×	✓	×

the single pass transistor logic formed by M4 to the dual transistor transmission gate logic formed by M4 and M5. By doing this the logic degradation problem gets solved as evident from the results mentioned in Sect. 4. The above discussion and parameters are summarized in Table 1.

To further exploit the aging resilient property of the proposed inverter we designed and compared various parameters of the RO made by all the three mentioned inverters whose results are illustrated in the subsequent sections.

3   RO Implementation

A Ring Oscillator is a device consisting of an odd number of inverters in a ring whose output oscillates between two voltage levels representing high and low. This device can be used as a frequency synthesizing element in the digital circuits. A RO consists of a large number of identical delay elements usually an inverter, cascaded to form a closed feedback loop where the output of the last stage is connected to the input of the first stage, the oscillation frequency of an RO is a function of number of inverter stages present in it. A classical two transistor CMOS inverter based RO is shown in Fig. 5(a).

Although the RO circuit is a stable and power efficient design for frequency synthesis, aging mechanisms described in Sect. 1 severely degrade their performance, as gradually over the time their oscillation frequency dips considerably, which in turn deteriorates the performance of the RO based PUF making it unreliable for security applications. To overcome the aging issue, an aging resilient inverter based RO was proposed as shown in Fig. 5(b). Even though the aging resilience in this design is quite significant, but due to the high power budget and slower speed this design is unsuitable for low power applications specially IoT devices. Hence we propose a novel power efficient and aging resilient inverter based RO using our proposed TG-ARI as shown in Fig. 5(c).

The frequency dependent instability problem of the RO based PUF could be clearly seen in Fig. 6. To understand why a PUF generates erroneous response with time, we revisit the conventional RO-PUF shown in Fig. 1 and consider the frequency profile of a randomly selected RO pair shown in Fig. 6. For the given RO-pair, if the frequency of RO_x (f_{x_i}) is greater than that of RO_y (f_{y_i}), then '1' (otherwise '0') is generated as a response, the frequency difference must be maintained for the stable RO as shown in Fig. 6(a). However it fails to generate a reliable (i.e. same as before) response if a crossover happens (i.e. $f_{x_i} \leq f_{y_i}$) after possible frequency degradation due to aging as shown in Fig. 6(b). For

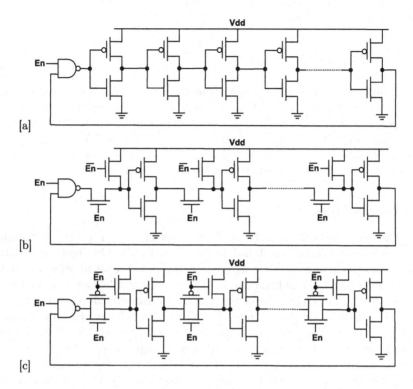

Fig. 5. Various RO typologies (a) Conventional inverter based RO (2T-RO) (b) Conventional aging resilient inverter based RO (ARO) (c) Proposed aging resilient inverter based RO (TG-ARO)

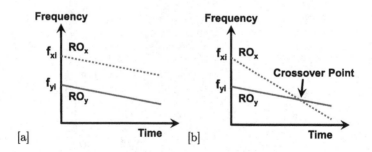

Fig. 6. Bit flip due to frequency degradation in RO pair with time (a) RO with moderate degradation (stable) (b) RO with high degradation (unstable). RO_x: fast aging RO, and RO_y: show aging RO.

maintaining maximum reliability, the two frequencies should never cross each other, maintaining a significant frequency difference.

4 Results and Discussions

All the simulations and analysis was done on Cadence Virtuoso analog design environment. The circuit simulation was carried out using Cadence Spectre simulation platform and the reliability analysis was carried out on Cadence RelXpert design simulator. The circuit schematic was designed at UMC 40nm process technology node for the inverters and the RO designs. Various results obtained for inverters and the Ring Oscillators are discussed below:

4.1 For Inverters

The dynamic power consumption of the inverter circuit with respect to supply voltage and temperature combined is shown in Fig. 7. The figure collectively depicts that with increase in temperature the power consumption of all the inverters is increasing, this behaviour could be easily justified as with increase in temperature the thermal energy of the carriers increases resulting in an exponential increase in number of collisions. The figure also indicates that the dynamic power tends to increase with an increase in supply voltage for all the inverter topologies as, with an increase in the supply voltage the current in the circuit increases. With the help of the comparison done in Fig. 7 we can easily observe that for low temperature and low supply voltage the TG-ARI consumes higher power than the other variants, if supply voltage is kept low and the temperature is increased the power consumption of all the inverters tends to increase. Here the TG-ARI consumes the maximum power followed by the conventional ARI,

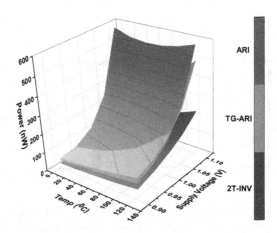

Fig. 7. Dynamic power dissipation of different inverter circuits with temperature and supply voltage variations.

if temperature is kept low and the supply voltage is increased the conventional ARI overtakes the TG-ARI in terms of power, a similar kind of behaviour is also observed when temperature is kept high and the supply is increased. For standard operating regions i.e. from 0.95V to 1.05V supply maximum power is consumed by the conventional ARI followed by the TG-ARI and finally the 2T-INV. Hence for low power applications the TG-ARI is far more preferable than the conventional ARI.

To study the performance of the inverters with respect to variations in supply voltage and temperature, we illustrated the variations of delay with changes in supply voltages and temperature, as shown in Fig. 8. As clearly indicated by both Fig. 8(a) and (b) the delay of all the inverters decrease with increase in the supply voltage and temperature respectively. This is mainly due to the increased mobility of the carries. The figures also indicates that the proposed TG-ARI is superior to the conventional ARI in terms of speed. Hence for high performance applications the TG-ARI is better choice instead of the conventional ARI.

For process variation analysis, we performed 2000 sets of Monte Carlo simulations on power for all the considered inverters as shown in Fig. 9. The mean and $\pm 3\sigma$ deviation on dynamic power dissipation is calculated for all the three considered inverter circuits. From the results it is observed that the proposed TG-ARI shows less process variations when compared to the ARI.

To mathematically rate and better visualize the different inverter circuits considering various parameters we propose a Figure of Merit:

$$\text{FOM} = \frac{1}{P_d \times t_d \times A \times \text{Aging}_{\text{Factor}}} \tag{3}$$

This FOM included characterization parameters which are power (P_d), delay(t_d), area (A), aging $(\text{Aging}_{\text{Factor}})$ which we calculated for each configuration, all the parameters are normalized with the conventional 2T Inverter circuit. The key comparison results of all the three inverters are summarised in Table 2. Results demonstrate that the proposed inverter has 1.35x better FOM as compared to the conventional 2T-INV circuit.

All the results were taken at standard operating regions i.e. 1V to supply and 25°C.

4.2   For Ring Oscillator

For the analysis of the RO designed with proposed TG-ARI (TG-ARO), the conventional Aging Resilient Inverter based RO (ARO) and the conventional 2T-INV based RO (2T-RO), we compared the deviation of the oscillation frequency from their base frequency with respect to stress time as shown in Fig. 10. This figure shows that the ARO surpasses our proposed TG-ARO in terms of frequency degradation with time. But proposed TG-ARO defeats the conventional 2T-RO by a large margin.

We also observed dependency of RO frequency with number of inverter stages. The frequency variation of RO with the number of stages for all the three designs

Table 2. Performance analysis of various inverters

Parameter	2T-INV	ARI	TG-ARI
Dynamic Power, P_d(nW)	59.08	122.8	95.08
Delay, td (ps)	43.36	115.91	96.49
Area, A (μm^2)	0.0162	0.0270	0.0324
Change of threshold Voltage (mV)	3.075	0.353	0.317
Normalised (FOM)	1.00	0.94	1.35

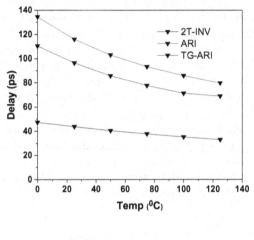

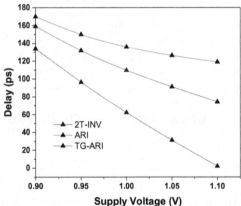

Fig. 8. Delay of the different inverter circuits with (a) Temperature variations, (b) Supply variations

is shown in Fig. 11. As clearly illustrated in the figure the oscillation frequency of RO degrades as the number of stages of inverter are increased. This decrement occurs due to an increase in the overall delay with increase in the number of

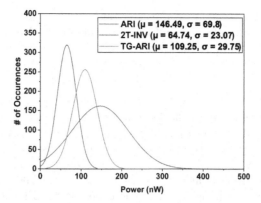

Fig. 9. Monte Carlo simulation for power of various inverter circuits.

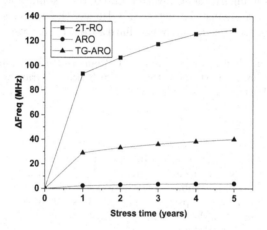

Fig. 10. Change in oscillation frequency of different RO circuits with stress time.

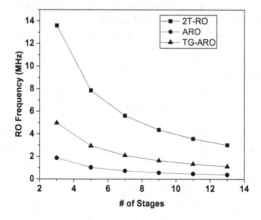

Fig. 11. Change in oscillation frequency of various Ring Oscillators with number of inverter stages

inverter units. From result we can easily conclude that the proposed TG-ARO gives a higher oscillation frequency for the same number of inverter stages, when compared with 2T-RO and ARO.

5   Conclusion

In this paper, we presented a novel aging resistant, low-power inverter design for hardware security-based applications. We have further exploited the aging resistant properties of inverters by using them to construct a ring oscillator . The results shows that the proposed inverter is both faster and consumes less power than the conventional aging resistant inverter while possessing similar aging characteristics. Further the RO based on proposed inverter has a higher oscillation frequency for the same number of inverter stages, when compared with the conventional aging resilient inverter based RO, simultaneously possessing considerable aging resilience characteristics. Hence, the proposed inverter design is best suited for high speed, low power hardware security applications.

Acknowledgement. The authors would like to thank the SERB, Government of India for providing financial support under the Startup Research Grant Scheme with grant no. SRG/2021/001101.

References

1. Kumar, S., Tiwari, P., Zymbler, M.: Internet of things is a revolutionary approach for future technology enhancement: a review. J. Big Data **6**, 12 (2019)
2. Gao, Y., Al-Sarawi, S.F., Abbott, D.: Physical unclonable functions. Nature Electron. **3**(2), 81–91 (2020). https://doi.org/10.1038/s41928-020-0372-5
3. McGrath, T., Bagci, I.E., Wang, Z.M., Roedig, U., Young, R.J.: A PUF taxonomy. Appl. Phys. Rev. **6**(1), 011303 (2019). https://doi.org/10.1063/1.5079407
4. Suh G.E., Devadas, S.: Physical unclonable functions for device authentication and secret key generation. In: Proceedings of the 44th Annual Design Automation Conference, ser. DAC 2007. New York, NY, USA: Association for Computing Machinery, pp. 9–14 (2007). https://doi.org/10.1145/1278480.1278484
5. Lim, D., Lee, J., Gassend, B., Suh, G., van Dijk, M., Devadas, S.: Extracting secret keys from integrated circuits. IEEE Trans. Very Large Scale Integr. (VLSI) Syst. **13**(10), 1200–1205 (2005)
6. Holcomb, D.E., Burleson, W.P., Fu, K.: Power-up SRAM state as an identifying fingerprint and source of true random numbers. IEEE Trans. Comput. **58**(9), 1198–1210 (2009)
7. Tehranipoor, F., Karimian, N., Yan, W., Chandy, J.A.: Dram-based intrinsic physically unclonable functions for system-level security and authentication. IEEE Trans. Very Large Scale Integr. (VLSI) Syst. **25**(3), 1085–1097 (2017)
8. Habib, B.: Efficient SR-latch PUF (2015)
9. Herder, C., Yu, M.-D., Koushanfar, F., Devadas, S.: Physical UNCLON able functions and applications: a tutorial. Proc. IEEE **102**(8), 1126–1141 (2014)
10. Nigam, T., Parameshwaran, B., Krause, G.: Accurate product life time predictions based on device-level measurements. In: IEEE International Reliability Physics Symposium, pp. 634–639 (2009)

11. Shan, W., Song, Y., Wu, J., Zhao, A., Chien, K.: Investigations of hot carrier injection on NMOSFET with high VDS and low VGS stress. In: China Semiconductor Technology International Conference (CSTIC), pp. 1–3 (2016)
12. Wu, Z., et al.: A physics-aware compact modeling framework for transistor aging in the entire bias space. In: 2019 IEEE International Electron Devices Meeting (IEDM), pp. 21.2.1-21.2.4 (2019)
13. Tiwari, A., Torrellas, J.: Facelift: hiding and slowing down aging in multicores. In: 2008 41st IEEE/ACM International Symposium on Microarchitecture, pp. 129–140 (2008)
14. Rahman, M.T., Rahman, F., Forte, D., Tehranipoor, M.: An aging resistant RO-PUF for reliable key generation. IEEE Trans. Emerg. Top. Comput. 4(3), 335–348 (2016)
15. Rahman, M.T., Xiao, K., Forte, D., Zhang, X., Shi, J., Tehranipoor, M.: TI-TRNG: technology independent true random number generator. In: 2014 51st ACM/EDAC/IEEE Design Automation Conference (DAC), pp. 1–6 (2014)
16. Khan, S., Shah, A.P., Gupta, N., Chouhan, A.P., Pandey, J.G., Vishvakarma, S.K.: An ultra-low power, reconfigurable, aging resilient RO PUF for IOT applications. Microelectron. J. **92**, 104605 (2019). https://www.sciencedirect.com/science/article/pii/S0026269219303593

A GaN Based Reverse Recovery Time Limiter Circuit Integrated with a Low Noise Amplifier

Neha Bajpai$^{(\boxtimes)}$ ⓘ and Yogesh Singh Chauhan

Department of Electrical Engineering, Indian Institute of Technology Kanpur,
Kanpur 208016, India
{bajpai,chauhan}@iitk.ac.in

Abstract. This article presents the design of a GaN-only robust low noise amplifier (LNA) monolithic microwave integrated circuit (MMIC) integrated with a reverse recovery time compensation (RRTC) circuit at the input. We use the **0.25 μm** GaN HEMT process from UMS in the complete design of robust LNA MMIC in the 5.8–6.2 GHz band. The proposed MMIC design is compact and requires a single substrate to fabricate LNA and RRTC circuits. To test the design, we apply a high power RF pulse of 40 dBm for 250 nsec and achieve a 16.8 dB reduction in gain S_{21} with an RRT limiter circuit in place. The simulated LNA takes less than 100 nsec to get back to its normal operating condition after applying a wideband (4–10 GHz) and high power (10–40 dBm) RF pulse for 250 nsec.

Keywords: Gan-HEMT · Low Noise Amplifier (LNA) · Monolithic Microwave Integrated Circuit (MMIC) · Reverse recovery time

1 Introduction

The receivers in radar are some times subjected to high input drive levels due to jamming signals, transmitter leakage and/or close-range target reflections [17]. This phenomenon leads to receiver deactivation for some time and hence in loss of information sent during receiver deactivation. Thus, high power limiters are used in wireless receivers to prevent significant incoming signals from permanently damaging or momentarily over-driving the sensitive RF front end stages such as low noise amplifier (LNA) [9]. A low noise amplifier (LNA) in an RF front end module (FEM) is mainly responsible for signal quality and a receiver's sensitivity [7]. For improved signal quality and enhanced sensitivity of an LNA, low noise figure (NF) and high power survivability are desired, respectively.

LNA designed using gallium arsenide (GaAs) has a low noise figure compared to gallium nitride (GaN) [6]. Since GaAs has a small bandgap (1.42 eV), it has low survivability, i.e., a breakdown field of 40 $V/\mu m$ only. Thus, LNAs made up of GaAs can not sustain in high power applications like – military microwave systems, anti-electromagnetic interference, and signal detection regions [5,14]. In case, GaAs LNA is used in high power applications, RF designers use a high power limiter at the input of LNA, but this increases the system noise figure [16].

© The Author(s), under exclusive license to Springer Nature Switzerland AG 2022
A. P. Shah et al. (Eds.): VDAT 2022, CCIS 1687, pp. 212–221, 2022.
https://doi.org/10.1007/978-3-031-21514-8_19

To improve the sustainability of an LNA in a FEM for high power applications, recently GaN LNAs have gained much interest. Due to the wide bandgap of GaN (3.5 eV), their breakdown field is almost eight times the GaAs breakdown field [2,13]. Moreover, GaN LNA has much higher linearity, enabling a more complicated modulation mode and broader bandwidth while having a slightly higher noise figure than GaAs [8]. One of the critical RF parameters of using GaN to design an LNA is the time it takes to return to its normal mode of operation when high power RF pulse diminishes – known as reverse recovery time (RRT) [15].

Alteration in RF performance and destruction mechanism in a robust GaN LNA due to input power overdrive are presented in [3], experimentally. Ref. [26] showed a 16 W continuous wave (CW) input power survivable GaN LNA using active limiter with noise figure of 1.75 dB. A single chip X-band transceiver for RF front end module using GaN technology is presented in [21]. In this work, author uses an increased value of DC feed resistor in the gate to limit the increase in the gate current occurs during input overdrive.

Several works have been reported to reduce RRT using limiters at the input of GaN LNA [10,19,20,25]. Predominantly conventional high power reflectors are used to increase the robustness of a GaN LNA against significantly higher input power. A conventional high-power reflector circuit has a parellel combination of a PIN diode and an inductor for DC short, known as a self-biased limiter [18]. PIN diode turns on when the magnitude of high power pulse exceeds the PIN diode cut-in voltage. As soon as the diode turns on, it starts offering low impedance that reflects high power signal to the source [24]. This approach has two drawbacks, (1) it requires large size devices between the signal path, resulting in the rise of insertion loss in the signal path, and (2) the maximum power of undesired jammer signals is limited by the diode's maximum power handling. To overcome the above two problems in this article, we present a novel approach to absorbing the high-power jammer signals directly to the ground.

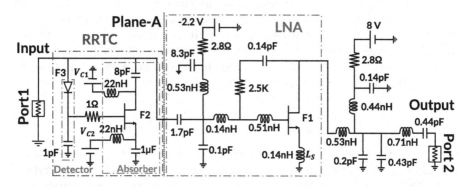

Fig. 1. Schematic of a single-stage GaN LNA MMIC integrated with a reverse recovery time compensation circuit at the input.

We use 0.25 μm GaN process from United Monolithic Semiconductors (UMS) to implement complete RRT compensation (RRTC) circuit and an LNA in 5.8 to 6.2 GHz band. The proposed design solution can be tuned to operate in any frequency band but we choose frequency band of 5.8 to 6.2 GHz because we targeted to design an LNA in FR1 bands of 5G. For example, n47, n96 and n102 are the three sub bands of 5G FR1 band which are covered by our design [12]. The schematic of single-stage LNA along with the RRTC circuit at the input is shown in Fig. 1. MMIC comprises of a D-mode GaN device of 0.2 mm gate width (4×50 μm) in common source topology, RC feedback stabilizing network, and an integrated RRTC circuit. To the best of the author's knowledge, no one has yet provided a solution for the RRTC circuit using GaN-only devices.

2   MMIC Design

This section explains the design of complete MMIC, which can be best understood by dividing it into two parts (1) an RRT compensation circuit and (2) a GaN LNA. We first explain the design and working of the RRTC circuit, followed by the design of LNA. In the next section, we analyze the RF performance of complete MMIC by applying a high-power interfering signal.

2.1   Reverse Recovery Time Compensation Circuit

RRTC circuit works in two modes (1) Linear mode (RRTC OFF) and (2) Non-linear mode (RRTC ON). In linear mode, i.e., when no jamming pulse is applied, RRTC remains in the OFF state, and in this state, it should not impact the RF performance of LNA. Thus, the off-state capacitance of device F2 in RRTC should be as small as possible, see Fig. 1. Whereas, in the case of non-linear mode, RRTC should provide a very low impedance path for high power signal to the ground, i.e., ON-state resistance of device F2 should be small. Therefore, the size of device F2 is critical in implementing an efficient RRTC circuit. The size of F2 is decided based on the best compromise among the following parameters: the minimum off-state capacitance, minimum insertion loss, and appropriately large size to bypass larger currents generated due to high power RF signals.

As shown in Fig. 1, the voltage transfer function from port-1 to plane-A of LNA MMIC after passing through the RRTC circuit is:

$$\frac{V_A}{V_{in}} = \frac{R_{par}}{R_{par} + R_A} \frac{1}{1 + sC_{par}(R_{par}||R_A),} \tag{1}$$

where R_A is the total input impedance at plane-A, R_{par} and C_{par} are the equivalent parasitic shunt resistance and capacitance of the input RRTC circuit, respectively. The parasitic capacitance (C_{par}) and passband frequency of the equivalent RRTC circuit, both are inversely propositional to each other. Below the roll-off frequency, noise figure (NF) also increases due to the parasitic shunt resistance of the RRTC circuit. The NF depends on ($1 + R_A/R_{par}$), and it increases by

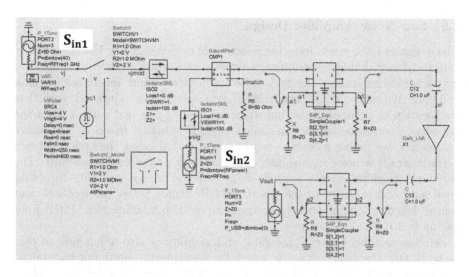

Fig. 2. Block diagram to simulate RRT of an LNA with the application of low power CW desired signal (S1) along with high power RF signal pulse (S2).

$\sim$0.2 dB with a decrease in R_{par} by $\sim$ 500 Ω [23]. The design objective is to absorb the parasitic capacitance in the matching network to mitigate losses.

The RRTC circuit comprises of a high-power detector and a high-power absorber. Both the circuits are analyzed separately and then combined to form an RRTC circuit.

High power detectors are based on a GaN Schottky diode (F3) and a 1 pF capacitor, which is used to extract the envelope of the high power input RF signal. With the increase in the high power input signal S_{in2} (see Fig. 2), the threshold voltage of the diode (1.5 V in our case) exceeds a specific limit, the diode starts conducting and provides the envelope of the RF signal applied at its cathode. Thus, the dependence on input power level is estimated by the output of envelop detector.

The output of the detector is coupled to the high power absorber consisting of a GaN-based D-mode HEMT device (F2) of 8 × 100 μm gate width, shown in Fig. 1. Gate bias for device F2 comes from the output of envelope detector. External voltage sources V_{c1} and V_{c2} are used to bias the drain and source side of device F2 through two 22 nH bias inductors, as shown in Fig. 1. The conduction current of power absorber is controlled by the gate voltage of device F2. The anode and cathode of diode F3 are connect to the input signal and to the gate of device F3, respectively. This connection ensures dependence of conduction current of F3 on input power level. The conduction current of F3 increase with the increase in input power level. As soon as the envelope signal is applied to the gate of the F2 device, it turns on and starts conducting. F2 bypasses the high power input signal to the ground and protects the primary LNA device, F1, from unexpected damage by high power signals.

2.2   Low Noise Amplifier Design

The design of LNA starts from the selection of device size. For low noise figure, gate resistance should be minimal; we divide gate width in multiple fingers to have low gate resistance. The device size also impacts input impedance for noise and gain. We choose device size and source degeneration inductance such that the location of optimum noise impedance is close to the real part of the input impedance corresponding to maximum gain. Eventually, based on the above parameters, we choose a device size of 4 × 50 μm, balancing the high-frequency performance, low noise figure, high gain, and high power handling ability. The low noise amplifier adopts a single-stage common source structure to obtain good gain and stability in the 5.8 to 6.2 GHz band. Series RC feedback and source degeneration inductor techniques are used to stabilize the MMIC from DC up to 10 GHz.

Minimum noise figure F_{min}, gain, and stability is also a function of bias point [1,11]. The bias voltage is swept for selecting the optimum bias point, and various device parameters (NF, stability factor, trans-conductance, voltage swing, and maximum available gain) are observed. We prioritize NF and consider the other trade-offs. The selected operating point for transistor is $V_{DD} = 16$ V, $V_{GG} = -2$ V and $I_{DD} = 45$ mA. RF chokes at the drain and gate are used to bias, and capacitors parallel to the ground are used to bypass the RF signal leaking to bias arms. The resistance and inductor in bias arms can further improve the amplifier's stability.

A narrowband passive LC matching network is used at the output sides to transform the LNA device impedance to 50 Ω. Whereas, at the input side MN is designed considering RRTC circuit Off-state capacitance is absorbed in the input match while transforming to 50 Ω terminations [4].

Simulated small-signal s-parameters are shown in Fig. 3. The maximum gain S_{21} is 12 dB while input and output reflections are less than -10 dB see Fig. 3(a).

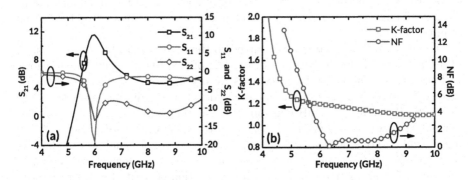

Fig. 3. Linear mode, small-signal (a) Gain S_{21} and input and output reflections S_{11} and S_{22}, respectively and (b) Stability factor (k) and noise figure, with respect to frequency.

3   RRT Simulation Setup and Results

Reverse recovery time is defined as the time in which the gate bias returns to its original bias when high power input stress is removed. Before calculating the RRT, we need to observe LNA's large-signal S-parameters to check if the RRTC circuit is making LNA unstable. The Block diagram for the test setup we use for the simulation of large-signal s-parameter (LSSP) and recovery time is shown in Fig. 2. Large signal s-parameters are the same as small-signal s-parameters but at high input power.

The high power robust LNA with RRT compensator (LNA-C) designed is first tested for a linear mode of operation. S-parameter simulations are done first in the off state of the compensator to check the loading on LNA's RF performance. LNA-C has maximum linear gain S_{21} of 12 dB while input and output reflections are less than -10 dB, see Fig. 3(a). Figure 3(b) shows the unconditional stability of LNA design up to 10 GHz. We achieve a noise figure between 1.38 to 0.2 dB at the two extremes of the band.

The compensator's recovery time is measured by combining the continuous low power desired signal S_{in1} (from PORT-1) with a high power RF signal pulse S_{in2} (from PORT-3), as shown in Fig. 2. A dual directional coupler (CMP-1) combines the above two signals. Directional coupler has four ports coupling, thru, isolation and reflection port. Desired low power signal S_{in1} and undesired pulsed high power signal S_{in2} are applied at reflect and thru port, respectively. The reverse isolation between reflect and thru port helps in separating the two signals. We use a switch (SWITCHV-1) controlled by a pulse (SRC-4) to generate the pulse of the high-power RF signal from a continuous RF signal source S_{in2}. Then, using 4-port directional couplers to record the power transmitted and reflections at each port of LNA-C under test. Isolators are used to avoid any further reflections generated. Consequently, a system to measure large signal S-parameter (LSSP) and recovery time using two RF tones has been developed, see Fig. 2.

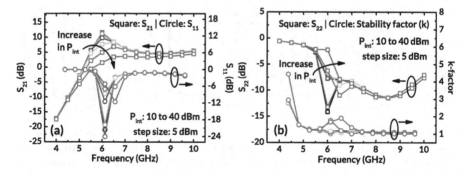

Fig. 4. Non-Linear mode, small-signal (a) Gain S_{21} and input and output reflections S_{11} and S_{22}, respectively and (b) Stability factor (k) and noise figure, with respect to frequency.

Figure 4(a) shows the gain S_{21} and reflections S_{11} and S_{22} in the presence of high power pulse. From the Fig. 4(a) it is seen that gain varies from 5 to 12 dB the variations in large signal gain and reflections are in acceptable limit. Usually, LNAs become unstable with the application of high power signals. Our LNA's stability factor is found to be greater than one up to 10 GHz in the presence of high power signal, as shown in Fig. 4(b). This indicates that our LNA design is not oscillating with high input power.

Next, we move on to the calculation of RRT. First, we generate the pulse of 10 nsec high power RF signal (or interferer) from a CW 2 GHz high power signal using an RF switch as shown in Fig. 5(a). When this high-power RF signal is superimposed on a CW small-signal (S_{in1}) 0 dBm at 6 GHz, the modulated waves are achieved at the input (gate) and the output (drain) of LNA-C are shown in Fig. 5(b). Figure 5(b) shows that LNA-C takes around 2.5 nsec to get back to the normal operating mode after the application of modulated wave at its input.

Using envelop simulator, it is possible to simulate the response time of LNA-C as the RF input power level drops back to the normal operating level. Transient plots for gain (S_{21}) with and without the RRTC circuit are shown in Fig. 5(c). For transient gain plots, the desired signal is kept at 6-GHz, 0-dBm CW, and the interferer is a pulse of 250-ns pulse width, with 41% duty cycle having frequency and power varied from 4–10 GHz, 10–40-dBm, respectively. LNA-C returns back to its average operating level in less than 100 nsec if we use the RRT compensation circuit at the input of LNA MMIC. Figure 5(c) depicts that with the use of RRT compensation, the peak power applied to the LNA device also drops significantly from 29.3 dB to 10.9 dB.

To quantify the RF performance of our LNA design, we present comparison with other state of the art robust multi-stage GaN LNAs working near our design band, as listed in Table 1. Our LNA design has best compromise between low noise figure and high power survivability compared with other contemporary LNA designs.

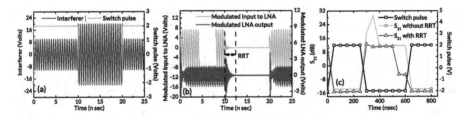

Fig. 5. Transient waves of (a) CW high power RF signal (interferer) (S2) and switch control voltage (SRC4 in Fig. 2), (b) modulated input and output voltage to and from LNA and (c) Magnitude of transient gain (S_{21}) with and without RRT compensator and RF high power switching pulse voltage, with respect to time.

Table 1. Summary of comparison with other LNA designs for the 5.8 – 6.2 GHz band in the literature.

Parameters	[3]	[26]	[21]	[17]	[22]	This work
Process	GaN 250nm	GaN 250nm	GaN 250nm	GaN 250nm	GaN 250nm	GaN 250nm
Frequency (GHz)	5–6	8–11	8–12	8–10	6	5.8–6.2
V_{DD} (V)	15	10	10	15	10	16
Gain (dB)	12	23.5	14.5	18	21	12
NF (dB)	6	1.75	3.2	2.8	1.2	1.38
CW Survivability (dBm)	43	42	37	40	28	40
RRT	50 s	40 ms	–	30 ns	–	2.5 ns
Topology	2-stage Cascode-CS	2-stage CS	2-stage CS	2-stage CS	3-stage CS	1-stage CS

4 Conclusion

In this article, we have shown that GaN outperforms as a transmitter and hence can also be used as a receiver. We reported a circuit to reduce one of the most critical RF performance parameters of GaN LNA, i.e., reverse recovery time using GaN-only devices. GaN only solution of reverse recovery compensator helps in increasing the packaging density in an RF front end module. The robust low power LNA with compensator design has a band-pass response in S-parameter simulations with 12 ± 1 dB of small-signal gain while consuming only 0.36 W of dc power. The designed solution is compact and allows large-scale integration on a single GaN substrate.

Acknowledgement. The work was funded in part by the IUSSTF/USISTEF/9th call/EC-059/2018/2019–20, SwarnaJayanti Fellowship under Grant DST/SJF/ETA-02/2017–18 and in part by the FIST Scheme of the Department of Science and Technology under Grant SR/FST/ETII-072/2016.

References

1. Aamir Ahsan, S., Ghosh, S., Khandelwal, S., Chauhan, Y.S.: Physics-based multi-bias RF large-signal GaN HEMT modeling and parameter extraction flow. IEEE J. Electron Devices Soc. **5**(5), 310–319 (2017). https://doi.org/10.1109/JEDS.2017. 2724839

2. Aamir Ahsan, S., Ghosh, S., Sharma, K., Dasgupta, A., Khandelwal, S., Chauhan, Y.S.: Capacitance modeling in dual field-plate power GaN HEMT for accurate switching behavior. IEEE Trans. Electron Devices **63**(2), 565–572 (2016). https:// doi.org/10.1109/TED.2015.2504726

3. Andrei, C., Bengtsson, O., Doerner, R., Chevtchenko, S.A., Heinrich, W., Rudolph, M.: Dynamic behaviour of a low-noise amplifier GAN MMIC under inputpower overdrive. In: 2015 European Microwave Conference (EuMC), pp. 231–234 (2015). https://doi.org/10.1109/EuMC.2015.7345742

4. Bahl, I.: Matching network components, chap. 6, pp. 125–148 John Wiley Sons, Ltd (2009). https://doi.org/10.1002/9780470462348.ch6. https://onlinelibrary.wiley. com/doi/abs/10.1002/9780470462348.ch6

5. Bajpai, N., Chauhan, Y.S.: A broadband power amplifier MMIC to compensate the frequency dependent behaviour. In: 2021 IEEE MTT-S International Microwave and RF Conference (IMaRC), pp. 1–4 (2021). https://doi.org/10.1109/IMaRC49196.2021.9714648

6. Bajpai, N., Pampori, A., Maity, P., Shah, M., Das, A., Chauhan, Y.S.: A low noise power amplifier MMIC to mitigate co-site interference in 5G front end modules. IEEE Access 9, 124900–124909 (2021). https://doi.org/10.1109/ACCESS.2021.3108596

7. Bera, S.C.: Microwave Active Devices and Circuits for Communication. LNEE, vol. 533. Springer, Singapore (2019). https://doi.org/10.1007/978-981-13-3004-9

8. Bettidi, A., et al.: X-band T/R module in state-of-the-art GAN technology. In: 2009 European Radar Conference (EuRAD), pp. 258–261 (2009)

9. Chaturvedi, S., Badnikar, S.L., Naik, A.A.: Ultra wideband receiver protection limiter using $0.13\mu m$ pHEMT technology. In: IEEE MTT-S International Microwave and RF Conference (2017). ISBN: 978-1-586-120-717/31.00

10. Cui, L., Zhou, X., Li, Y.P., Wei, H.T.: Codesign of 12–22 GHz integrated pin-diode limiter and low noise amplifier. In: 2018 14th IEEE International Conference on Solid-State and Integrated Circuit Technology (ICSICT), pp. 1–3 (2018). https://doi.org/10.1109/ICSICT.2018.8564886

11. Dasgupta, A., Chauhan, Y.S.: Modeling of induced gate thermal noise in HEMTs. IEEE Microwave Wirel. Compon. Lett. 26(6), 428–430 (2016). https://doi.org/10.1109/LMWC.2016.2562642

12. ETSI: TS 138 521-2 - V15.3.0 - 5G; NR; User Equipment (UE) conformance specification; Radio transmission and reception; Part 2: Range 2 standalone (3GPP TS 38.521-2 version 15.3.0 Release 15). 3GPP TS 38.101-1 version 15.2.0 Release 15 15.3.0, 1–72 (2018). https://portal.etsi.org/TB/ETSIDeliverableStatus.aspx

13. Ghosh, S., Dasgupta, A., Khandelwal, S., Agnihotri, S., Chauhan, Y.S.: Surface-potential-based compact modeling of gate current in ALGaN/GaN HEMTs. IEEE Trans. Electron Devices 62(2), 443–448 (2015). https://doi.org/10.1109/TED.2014.2360420

14. van Heijningen, M., et al.: C-band single-chip radar front-end in ALGaN/GaN technology. IEEE Trans. Microw. Theory Tech. 65(11), 4428–4437 (2017). https://doi.org/10.1109/TMTT.2017.2688438

15. Huang, T., Axelsson, O., Bergsten, J., Thorsell, M., Rorsman, N.: Achieving low-recovery time in ALGaN/GaN HEMTs with AlN interlayer under low- noise amplifiers operation. IEEE Electron Device Lett. 38(7), 926–928 (2017). https://doi.org/10.1109/LED.2017.2709751

16. Huang, T., Axelsson, O., Bergsten, J., Thorsell, M., Rorsman, N.: Impact of ALGaN/GaN interface and passivation on the robustness of low-noise amplifiers. IEEE Trans. Electron Devices 67(6), 2297–2303 (2020). https://doi.org/10.1109/TED.2020.2986806

17. Liero, A., Dewitz, M., kuhn, S., Chaturvedi, N., Xu, J., Rudolph, M.: On the recovery time of highly robust low-noise amplifiers. IEEE Trans. Microw. Theory Tech. 58(4), 781–787 (2010). https://doi.org/10.1109/TMTT.2010.2041519

18. Lim, C.L.: Recovery time of the schottky-pin limiter. Microw. J. 55(11), 66–72(2012)

19. Looney, J., Conway, D., Bahl, I.: An examination of recovery time of an integrated limiter/LNA. IEEE Microwave Mag. 5(1), 83–86 (2004). https://doi.org/10.1109/MMW.2004.1284947

20. Provost, Z.O., et al.: High robustness S-band GaN based LNA. In: 2019 14th European Microwave Integrated Circuits Conference (EuMIC), pp. 243–246 (2019). https://doi.org/10.23919/EuMIC.2019.8909569
21. Schuh, P., Sledzik, H., Reber, R.: Gan-based single-chip frontend for next-generation x-band AESA systems. Int. J. Microw. Wirel. Technol. **10**(5–6), 660–665 (2018). https://doi.org/10.1017/S1759078718000557
22. Suijker, E.M., et al.: Robust ALGaN/GaN low noise amplifier MMICs for c-, ku- and ka-band space applications. In: 2009 Annual IEEE Compound Semiconductor Integrated Circuit Symposium, pp. 1–4 (2009). https://doi.org/10.1109/csics.2009.5315640
23. Sun, M., Lu, Y., Huai, Y.: Low capacitance ESD protection circuits for GaAs RF ICs. J. Electrostat. **65**(3), 189–199 (2007). https://doi.org/10.1016/j.elstat.2006.07.016
24. Wanum, M., Vliet, F.: A 58-dBm S-band, pp. 3034–3042 (08 2013)
25. Yagbasan, C., Aktug, A.: Robust x-band GaN LNA with integrated active limiter. In: 2018 48th European Microwave Conference (EuMC), pp. 1205–1208 (2018). https://doi.org/10.23919/EuMC.2018.8541779
26. Yagbasan, C., Aktuğ, A.: Robust x-band GaN LNA with integrated active limiter. In: 2018 13th European Microwave Integrated Circuits Conference (EuMIC), pp. 237–240 (2018). https://doi.org/10.23919/EuMIC.2018.8539928

Novel Configuration of Multi-mode Universal Shadow Filter Employing a New Active Block

Divya Singh and Sajal K. Paul$^{(\boxtimes)}$

Department of Electronics Engineering, (Indian School of Mines), Indian Institute of
Technology, Dhanbad 826004, India
sajalkpaul@rediffmail.com

Abstract. The differential current conveyor cascaded transconductance amplifier
(DCCCTA), a new active block, is presented in this study, along with its implementation in a multi-mode biquadratic universal shadow filter. The proposed circuit
can operate in the two modes of operation such as transadmittance mode (TAM)
and current mode (CM). High-pass (HP), low-pass (LP), band-pass (BP), band-
reject (BR), and all-pass (AP) universal filter responses are all realized simultaneously. As desired, the low input impedance for CM and high input impedance for
TAM while high output impedance for both the modes of operations are obtained.
Moreover, Monte Carlo analysis, inter-modulation distortion (IMD), and percentage total harmonic distortion (%THD) responses are obtained. The theoretical
results are validated through TSMC 180 nm technology using Cadence Virtuoso.

Keywords: DCCCTA · Current mode · Transadmittance mode · Biquadratic
filter · Shadow filter

1 Introduction

Current mode (CM) active filters have reached a new dimensions due to the introduction of a variety of active building blocks (ABBs). These ABBs are expected to have
superior features such as low power consumption, low supply, increased CMRR, wide
bandwidth, increased signal to noise ratio, and better signal linearity in comparison to
the conventional op-amp. Due to these advantages, researchers have developed a wide
variety of CM single input multiple output (SIMO) filters due to their wide range of
appreciations. Another, important aspect, of the active filters is the electronic tunability
of their various performance parameters. The conventional way of tuning these parameters is by altering the values of passive components or by the DC current or voltage
electronically. The frequency-agile filter, commonly known as the shadow filter, is a
new family of second-order filters [1], that was recently introduced and shown in Fig. 1.
The gain (A) of the external amplifier can readily change the filter's parameters. The
inclusion of an additional amplifier to the filter's feedback loop improves tunability.

A. P. Shah et al. (Eds.): VDAT 2022, CCIS 1687, pp. 222–233, 2022.
https://doi.org/10.1007/978-3-031-21514-8_20

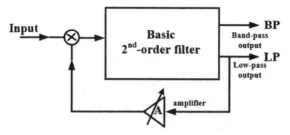

Fig. 1. Scheme of the shadow filter [1].

An extensive study of literature [2–10] has been compared in Table 1. In [2–4, 6], only BP response through the shadow filter is obtained by employing a current differencing transconductance amplifier (CDTA). Four operational floating current conveyors (OFCCs), along with the five resistors and two capacitors are required to obtain a BP shadow response also it does not have full-cascadability [5]. Another implementation of BP response [7] with lots of MOSs requirements is proposed by employing four electronically controllable second-generation current conveyors (ECCIIs). Two different variants of shadow filters are proposed in [8] which are multifunctional and universal employing current controlled current differencing cascaded transconductance amplifier (CC-CDCTA) and second-generation current conveyor (CCII). In Ref. [9], a universal shadow filter is proposed again with two different types of ABBs, namely extra-X current controlled conveyor transconductance amplifier (EX-CCCTA) and current conveyor cascaded transconductance amplifier (CCCTA). Multi-mode, transimpedance mode (TIM) and transadmittance mode (TAM) shadow filter to realize only BP response is reported in Ref. [10] with the two different structures for both the modes which explain a lot of requirements of MOSs and so as the passive elements. As per the authors, this work presents the first multi-mode universal shadow filter in a single configuration, which makes the simple circuitry as well.

2 Proposed Circuit

2.1 Differential Current Conveyor Cascaded Transconductance Amplifier (DCCCTA)

The differential current conveyor cascaded transconductance amplifier (DCCCTA) is derived from the differential second generation current conveyor (DCCII) [11]. DCCCTA is formed by the addition of DCCII with transconductance amplifier (TA) in the cascaded form such as the input terminal of first TA is connected with the Z terminal of DCCII, similarly output of the first TA is connected with the input of the second TA. It consists of two low input impedance terminals, namely X_P, X_N and Y with high input impedance and three high output impedance terminals Z, O_1 and O_2 which makes it suitable for cascading for current mode circuits. Figure 2 shows the symbol of DCCCTA and its CMOS based internal structure is shown in Fig. 3.

The aspect ratio of the proposed DCCCTA is given in Table 2. The basic features of DCCCTA can be verified through the simulation using TSMC 180 nm through Cadence

Table 1. Comparative study of the available CM and TAM shadow filters.

Ref	No. & type of ABB	Total no. of MOSs req	No. of passive elements (R/C), all grounded	Filter Functions	Mode	Independent tuning of f_O and Q_O	Electronic tuning	Fully Cascadable	P.C. (mW)	SNR (dB)
2	2 CDTA	52	2/2, No	BP(C)[c]	CM	Yes	No	No	7.79	21.8
3	2 CDTA, 1TA	58	1/2, Yes	LP(R), BP[b]	CM	Yes	Yes	No	21.2	135.3
	2 VDTA	57	0/2, Yes	LP, BP(C)[c]	CM	Yes	Yes	No	17.4	171.6
4	3 CDTA	48	1/2, Yes	BP	CM	Yes	Yes	No	5.9	NA
5	4 OFCC	100	5/2, Yes	BP	CM	Yes	No	Yes	NA	NA
6	2 CDTA, 1 CA	56 + 1 CA	0/2, Yes	BP	CM	Yes	Yes	Yes	NA	NA
7	4 ECCII	96	2/2, No	BP	CM	Yes	No	No	NA	NA
8	2 CC-CDCTA (Fig. 9)	94	0/2, Yes	LP, HP(C), BP[c]	CM	Yes	Yes	No	1.5	64.1
	3 CC-CDCTA, 1 CCII	146	0/2, No	UF	CM	Yes	Yes	Yes	2.23	64.1
9	1 CCCTA, 1 EX-CCCTA	98	0/2, Yes	UF	CM	Yes	Yes	Yes	4.1	71.5
10[a]	4 OFCC	100	5/2, Yes	BP	TAMTIM	No	No	Yes	NA	NA
This work	2 DCCCTA	76	4 MOSs/2, Yes	UF	CM, TAM	Yes	Yes	Yes	2.5	67.3

PC power consumption

[a] Different structures for the different mode of operation

[b] Response is obtained through resistor

[c] Responses are obtained through capacitor

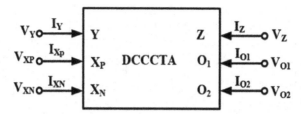

Fig. 2. Symbol of the proposed DCCCTA.

Virtuoso. Figure 4(a) shows the DC transfer characteristics, the DC current characteristics I_Z versus I_{XP} and I_Z versus I_{XN} shows the linearity for 400 μA to − 380 μA. The DC voltage characteristics V_{XP}, V_{XN} versus V_Y is shown in Fig. 4(b) which explains the linear region of − 600 to 587 mV. Figure 5 shows the ac transfer characteristics for the current gain at the output terminals of Z, O_1 and O_2 with a − 3 dB bandwidth of 980, 45.7 and 45.7 MHz, respectively.

The port relationships of DCCCTA are as follows:

$$
\begin{bmatrix} I_Y \\ V_{XP} \\ V_{XN} \\ I_Z \\ I_{O1} \\ I_{O2} \end{bmatrix} = \begin{bmatrix} 0 & 0 & 0 & 0 & 0 & 0 \\ 1 & 0 & 0 & 0 & 0 & 0 \\ 1 & 0 & 0 & 0 & 0 & 0 \\ 0 & 1 & -1 & 0 & 0 & 0 \\ 0 & 0 & 0 & g_{m1} & 0 & 0 \\ 0 & 0 & 0 & 0 & g_{m2} & 0 \end{bmatrix} \begin{bmatrix} V_Y \\ I_{XP} \\ I_{XN} \\ V_Z \\ V_{O1} \\ V_{O2} \end{bmatrix} \tag{1}
$$

The transconductances of the first and second transconductance amplifiers (TAs) are, g_{m1} and g_{m2}, respectively.

$$
g_{m1} = \sqrt{\mu_n C_{ox} \left(\frac{W}{L}\right)_{M_{22,23}} I_{O1}}, \, g_{m2} = \sqrt{\mu_n C_{ox} \left(\frac{W}{L}\right)_{M_{28,29}} I_{O2}} \tag{2}
$$

where W/L, μ, and C_{ox} are the aspect ratio, mobility, and gate oxide-capacitance of the respective MOSs. I_{O1} and I_{O2} are the bias currents of the transconductance amplifiers.

Table 2. Aspect ratios of DCCCTA (Fig. 3).

MOS transistors	W (μm)/L (μm)	MOS transistors	W (μm)/L (μm)
M_{1-4}	20.5/0.36	M16, 17	10/2.0
M_{5-8}	50/0.36	M18–20	10/1.0
M_{9-11}	30/2.0	M21	2.0/2.0
M12–14	30/1.0	M22–33	10.8/0.36
M15	50/2.0	–	–

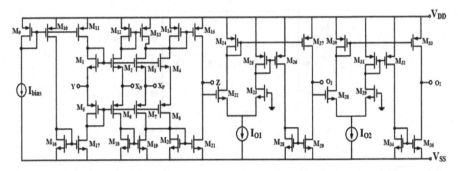

Fig. 3. CMOS based internal structure of DCCCTA.

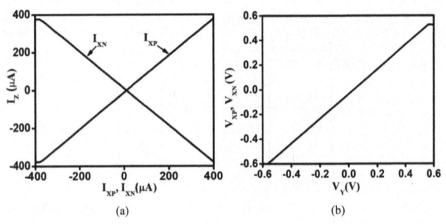

(a)   (b)

Fig. 4. DC transfer characteristics: (a) I_Z versus I_{XP} ($I_{XN} = 0$) and I_Z versus I_{XN} ($I_{XP} = 0$) (b) V_{XP} and V_{XN} versus V_Y.

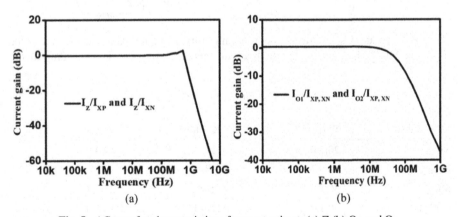

(a)   (b)

Fig. 5. AC transfer characteristics of current gain at: (a) Z (b) O_1 and O_2.

2.2 Multi-mode Universal Shadow Filter

Figure 6(a) depicts the proposed multi-mode universal shadow filter implementation which employs the approach outlined in Fig. 1 [1] to improve the filter response. The DCCCTA-1 functions as the basic second order filter and DCCCTA-2 as amplifier of variable gain A. The low pass response is fed-back to the basic filter through the amplifier with the gain A. The basic filter is made up of one resistor Rin, one active building block DCCCTA, and two grounded capacitors. Another DCCCTA and one grounded resistor are used to build the feedback. Resistors used in Fig. 6(a) can be implemented as shown in Fig. 6(b) using MOSs and expressed as:

$$R = \frac{L}{2\mu C_{ox} W (V_{DD} - V_T)} \tag{3}$$

where W/L, μ, C_{ox}, and V_T have their usual meaning for the MOSs, M_a and M_b.

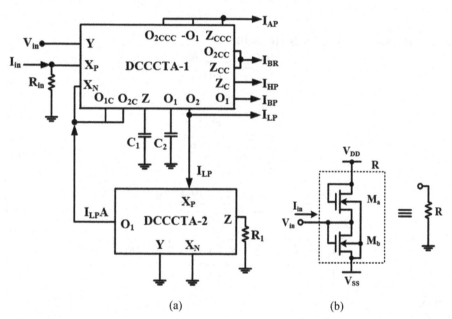

(a)   (b)

Fig. 6. (a) Proposed multi-mode universal shadow filter and (b) Resistor implementation using MOS implementation.

In Fig. 6(a), the Z_C, Z_{CC} and Z_{CCC} are the copies of the Z terminal. The O_{1C} and $-O_1$ are the copy terminal and 180° phase shift of the O_1 terminal, respectively. Also, the O_{2C}, O_{2CC} and O_{2CCC} are the copy terminals of O_2. Since two DCCCTA blocks have been used, therefore $g_{m1}^{(1)}$ and $g_{m2}^{(1)}$ are the transconductances of the first block which has been used for the implementation of the basic filter, while $g_{m1}^{(2)}$ is the transconductance of the second block which has been used for the amplifier.

The routine analysis of Fig. 6(a) results in the following transfer functions:

2.2.1 Current Mode ($V_{in} = 0$, $R_{in} = 0$)

$$\frac{I_{LP}}{I_{in}} = \frac{g_{m1}^{(1)} g_{m2}^{(1)}}{D(s)} \tag{4}$$

$$\frac{I_{BP}}{I_{in}} = \frac{g_{m1}^{(1)} s C_2}{D(s)} \tag{5}$$

$$\frac{I_{HP}}{I_{in}} = \frac{s^2 C_1 C_2}{D(s)} \tag{6}$$

$$\frac{I_{BR}}{I_{in}} = \frac{s^2 C_1 C_2 + g_{m1}^{(1)} g_{m2}^{(1)}}{D(s)} \tag{7}$$

$$\frac{I_{AP}}{I_{in}} = \frac{s^2 C_1 C_2 - g_{m1}^{(1)} s C_2 + g_{m1}^{(1)} g_{m2}^{(1)}}{D(s)} \tag{8}$$

2.2.2 Transadmittance Mode ($I_{in} = 0$)

$$\frac{I_{LP}}{V_{in}} = \frac{g_{m1}^{(1)} g_{m2}^{(1)} R_{in}}{D(s)} \tag{9}$$

$$\frac{I_{BP}}{V_{in}} = \frac{g_{m1}^{(1)} s C_2 R_{in}}{D(s)} \tag{10}$$

$$\frac{I_{HP}}{V_{in}} = \frac{s^2 C_1 C_2 R_{in}}{D(s)} \tag{11}$$

$$\frac{I_{BR}}{V_{in}} = \frac{\left(s^2 C_1 C_2 + g_{m1}^{(1)} g_{m2}^{(1)} \right) R_{in}}{D(s)} \tag{12}$$

$$\frac{I_{AP}}{V_{in}} = \frac{\left(s^2 C_1 C_2 - g_{m1}^{(1)} s C_2 + g_{m1}^{(1)} g_{m2}^{(1)} \right) R_{in}}{D(s)} \tag{13}$$

where

$$D(s) = s^2 C_1 C_2 + g_{m1}^{(1)} s C_2 + g_{m1}^{(1)} g_{m2}^{(1)} (1 + A) \tag{14}$$

$$A = g_{m1}^{(2)} R_1$$

The pole frequency (ω_o) and quality factor (Q_o) are:

$$\omega_o = \sqrt{\frac{g_{m1}^{(1)} g_{m2}^{(1)} (1 + A)}{C_1 C_2}}, Q_o = \sqrt{\frac{C_1 g_{m2}^{(1)} (1 + A)}{C_2 g_{m1}^{(1)}}} \tag{15}$$

If $C_1 = C_2$, Eq. (15) gives:

$$\omega_o = \frac{1}{C}\sqrt{g_{m1}^{(1)}g_{m2}^{(1)}(1+A)}, Q_O = \sqrt{\frac{g_{m2}^{(1)}(1+A)}{g_{m1}^{(1)}}} \tag{16}$$

The above Eq. (16) indicates that pole frequency (ω_o) and quality factor (Q_O) are electronically tunable. ω_o is also independently tunable by C. While gain (A) is capable of tuning both the pole frequency (ω_o) and quality factor (Q_O) externally via $g_{m1}^{(2)}$ and R_1.

3   Simulated Results

The functional verification of the biquadratic multi-mode universal shadow filter is done through TSMC 180 nm technology using Cadence Virtuoso. The DC biasing levels are taken as $V_{DD} = 1.7$ V, $V_{SS} = -1.7$ V, $I_{bias} = 200$ μA, and $I_{O1} = I_{O2} = 50$ μA. The transistors' aspect ratios are listed in Table 2. Figure 7 shows the layout of the proposed multi-mode universal shadow filter for $C_1 = C_2 = 2$ pF, $R_{in} = 1$ Ω, and $R_1 = 1.38$ kΩ, comprising an area of 187 μm x 85 μm.

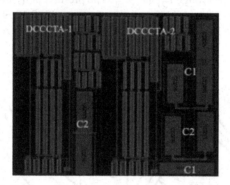

Fig. 7. Layout of the multi-mode universal filter (Fig. 6(a)).

3.1   AC Simulations

The pre-layout and the post-layout gain responses of HP, LP, BP, and BR are shown in Fig. 8(a), while the gain and phase responses of AP are presented in Fig. 8(b) for both the CM and TAM modes of operations. It is noted that the same responses have been obtained for both the modes. The calculated pole frequency and the quality factor are 6.57 MHz and 1, respectively. The pre-layout and post-layout frequencies are 6.8 and 6.45 MHz, respectively.

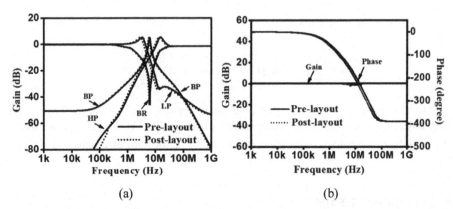

Fig. 8. Simulated results for (a) gain responses of HP, LP, BP, BR (b) gain and phase responses of AP.

The independent tunability of f_O can be obtained in line with (16) by varying $C_1 = C_2 = C$ is shown in Fig. 9(a). The f_O for pre-layout simulated responses are obtained as 13.6, 6.8 and 3.5 MHz and for post-layout responses are 13.13, 6.3 and 3.21 MHz for C = 1, 2, and 4 pF, respectively. Figure 9(b) shows the tunability of f_O as well as Q_O via gain (A) of the amplifier through $I_{O1}^{(2)}$ i.e. $g_{m2}^{(2)}$. The pre-layout f_O are 6.8, 8.48, 9.59 MHz and Q_O are 1.48, 1.83, 2.08 while post-layout f_O are 6.45, 8.13, 9.21 MHz and Q_O are 1.43, 1.79, 1.99 for the bias current I_{O1} = 50, 200, and 400 μA, respectively.

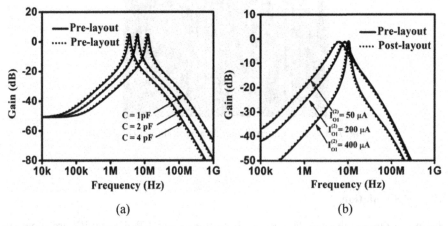

Fig. 9. Simulated results of tuning of: (a) f_O via capacitance value C (b) f_O and Q_O via gain (A).

3.2 Monte Carlo Simulation and Process Corner Analysis

The considered deviation of standard parameters of MOSs is used to generate Monte Carlo (MC) simulation for 200 runs in order to check the effect of the fabrication process and mismatch deviation on the circuit's performance. Figure 10(a) shows the histogram plot for center frequency. The standard deviations are obtained as 4.1 MHz from the center frequency statistical results. The PVT analysis has been done for the Fast Fast (FF), nominal, and Slow Slow (SS) corners. The voltage variations have been taken as 1.7 ± 10% while temperatures are taken as − 40, 27, and 125 °C for all the respective corners FF, nominal, SS. Figure 10(b) shows the BP responses which gives the resultant frequency of 6.8 MHz for the nominal, 8.56 MHz for FF, and 4.23 MHz for SS corners.

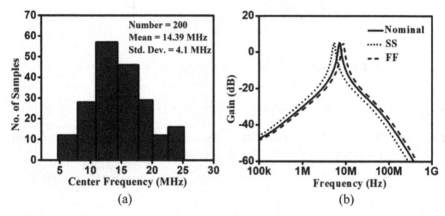

Fig. 10. (a) Histogram for BP center frequency (b) BP responses in FF, nominal, and SS.

3.3   Total Harmonic Distortion and Inter-modulation Distortion

Figure 11 shows the % total harmonic distortion (% THD) as a function of input current Iin for the high pass and low pass filters at 10 MHz. Up to 800 μA, the percent THD is determined to be low. The intermodulation distortion (IMD) findings for the band-pass filter of the current mode for the relevant frequencies reported in Table 3 were obtained for sinusoidal input signals of 100 μA at 6 MHz with a parasitic signal of 10 μA.

Table 3.   IMD results for the BP response

Frequency (MHz)	1	2	4	6	8	10
%THD	1.51	0.71	1.32	1.91	1.47	2.1

Table 4 shows the summarized results of all the calculated parameters in both the modes of operations current mode transadmittance mode.

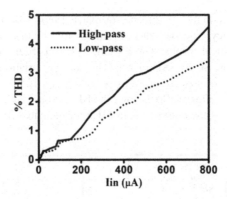

Fig. 11. %THD of the HP and LP response for the current-mode.

Table 4. Calculated parameters for CM and TAM

Parameters	Req. Passive component (R/C)	Freq. (MHz)	Power Consumption (mW)	SNR (dB)	% THD at 500 μA
CM	1/2	6.8	2.5	67.3	2.1
TAM	2/2	6.8	2.69	63.4	2.5

4 Conclusion

This paper introduces a differential current conveyor cascaded transconductance amplifier (DCCCTA) as a new active building block along with a novel configuration of multimode universal shadow filter. The basic filter uses one grounded resistor, one active block DCCCTA, and two grounded capacitors. All the standard responses of the universal filter are obtained in both the modes of operations, current mode and transadmittance mode..

References

1. Lakys, Y., Fabre, A.: Shadow filters – new family of second order filters. Electron Lett. **46**(4), 985–986 (2010)
2. Pandey, N., Pandey, R., Choudhary, R., Sayal, A., Tripathi, M.: Realization of CDTA based frequency agile filters. In: IEEE International Conference on Signal Processing, Computing and Control, pp. 1–8 (2013)
3. Pandey, N., Sayal, A., Choudhary, R., Pandy, R.: Design of CDTA and VDTA based frequency agile filters. Adv. Electron. **2014**, 1–14 (2014)
4. Atasoyu, M., Kuntman, H., Metin, B., Herencsar, N., Cicekoglu, O.: Design of current-mode class 1 frequency agile filter employing CDTAs. In: European Conference on Circuit Theory and Design, pp. 1–4 (2015)
5. Nand, D., Pandey, N.: New configuration for OFCC-based CM SIMO filter and its application as shadow filter. Arab. J. Sci. Eng. **43**(6), 3011–3022 (2018)

6. Yesil, A., Kacar, F.: Band-pass filter with high quality factor based on current amplifier. AEU-Int. J. Electron. Commun. **75**, 63–69 (2017)
7. Atasoyu, M., Metin, B., Kuntman, H., Herencsar, N.: New current-mode class 1 frequency-agile filter for multi-protocol GPS application. Elektronica ir Elektrotechnika **21**(5), 35–39 (2015)
8. Singh, D., Paul, S.K.: Realization of current mode universal shadow filter. AEU-Int. J. Electron. Commun. **117**, 1–16 (2020)
9. Singh, D., Paul, S.K.: Improved current mode biquadratic shadow universal filter. Inf. Midem-J. Microelectron. Electron. Compon. Mater. **52**(1), 51–66 (2022)
10. Nand, D., Pandey, N., Bhanoo, V., Gangal, A.: Operational floating current conveyor based TAM & TIM shadow filter. In: Proceedings of 4th International Conference on Computer and Management ICCM, pp. 103–115 (2018)
11. Vijay, V., Srinivasulu A.: A square wave generator using single CMOS DCCII. In: 2013 International SoC Design Conference (ISOCC), pp. 322–325 (2013)

Highly Non-linear Feed-Forward Arbiter PUF Against Machine Learning Attacks

Aranya Gupta$^{(\boxtimes)}$, Sanjeev Manhas, and Bishnu Prasad Das

Indian Institute of Technology, Roorkee, Uttrakhand 247667, India
aranya_g@ec.iitr.ac.in,
{sanjeev.manhas,bishnu.das}@ece.iitr.ac.in

Abstract. Arbiter PUFs (APUFs) are a good choice for their lightweight configuration but vulnerable to Machine Learning (ML) based attacks. This paper presents a feed-forward PUF (FF PUF) to increase the resistivity by adding a non-linear component in the feed-forward loop. The non-linear component is designed by XORing the response of two consecutive stages of conventional FF PUF and feeding it as a challenge to an intermediate stage. To decrease the susceptibility to various ML-based attacks, the proposed feed-forward XOR PUF (FFXOR PUF) is designed by XORing the response of multiple FF PUFs. The performance of the proposed FFXOR PUF is compared with the existing APUF and XOR APUF. The minimum prediction accuracy of the proposed FFXOR PUF with 5 levels is achieved 51.6%(SVM) and 50.43%(ANN). Also, the training time is increased by 3.1 times in comparison with the conventional XOR APUF. Different PUF architectures such as APUF, XOR APUF and the proposed FFXOR PUF with 32-stages are implemented on Xilinx Zynq-7000 (Zedboard) FPGA.

Keywords: Hardware security · PUFs · Attack-resilient · Feed-Forward PUFs · FPGA PUFs

1 Introduction

Nowadays, the Internet of Things (IoT) has become so popular for developing the next-generation communication between wireless sensor networks, including smart homes, smart meters, health and social security cards, electronic passports etc. [6]. Communication security among the IoT devices is critically essential, and device authentication is one of the conventional ways to secure the communications between the devices. Conventional authentication technique like key-based cryptographic algorithms that utilize the non-volatile memories to store the keys, are heavily resource hungry and increase the chip production cost and complexity [25]. Many IoT devices are resource-constrained for their compact size and low power consumption. Therefore, the conventionally available key-based authentication protocols are unsuitable for portable and battery-powered applications. Also, the IoT devices can be accessed easily within close physical

© The Author(s), under exclusive license to Springer Nature Switzerland AG 2022
A. P. Shah et al. (Eds.): VDAT 2022, CCIS 1687, pp. 234–248, 2022.
https://doi.org/10.1007/978-3-031-21514-8_21

distances, making them vulnerable to side-channel attacks [21], and the secret keys can be exposed more effectively when they are in the range of physical access.

Physically Unclonable Functions (PUFs) were introduced [13] as low-cost cryptographic primitives for generating the secret keys and authenticating the edge devices. By exploiting the inherent silicon variations due to manufacturing process variations, PUF generates a unique response with a set of challenges. The generated responses are different for an individual Integrated Circuit (IC) and can not be cloned by the manufacturers [12,15]. With the inevitable process-dependent variations, many circuit-dependent combinations of keys can be produced from the different locations of the chip [17]. With the ability to generate a large number of challenge-response pairs (CRPs), low manufacturing cost and power consumption, PUF has become a suitable security alternative for low resource-oriented IoT devices [14,23].

Theoretically, being physically unclonable, the response of the PUFs can be predicted accurately with Machine Learning (ML) models, which make PUFs 'mathematically clonable' [19]. Adversaries can snoop on the communication channel between the trusted partner and the edge devices where PUF is located and collect the CRPs for training the multiple ML models [20]. Several PUF designs [2,14,23] have been proposed to showcase the PUFs acceptability as a secure, lightweight authentication protocol for IoT applications. The Arbiter PUF (APUF) and its variants like XOR PUFs, Lightweight Secure PUFs, Feed-Forward PUFs (FF PUFs), Interpose PUFs and multiplexer PUFs have been suggested as a low-cost and trusted lightweight authentication protocol. However, it has been proved that APUF and its variants are susceptible to various ML attacks like Support Vector Machine (SVM) [17,20], Logistic Regression (LR) [20], Artificial Neural Network (ANN) [2] etc. Many PUF designs [10,11,18,22,26] proposed in the state-of-the-art have low circuit complexity and operation power. However, the studies [2,9] show that they are vulnerable to various ML-based attacks due to their moderate resiliency.

The main contribution of this work is to improve the resiliency of the FF APUFs from ML-based attacks by increasing the complexity in the feed-forward loops and XORing the different levels of FF PUFs. The paper is organised as follows. Section 2 explains the conventional architectures of APUF and its variants. Section 3 presents the proposed architecture of highly non-linear FFXOR PUF. Section 4 describes the experimental setup and the approaches of the ML-based attacks. The prediction accuracy and other parameters are presented in Sect. 5. Finally, we conclude in Sect. 6.

2   Architecture of the Conventional Arbiter PUF and Its Variants

2.1   Arbiter PUF

The architecture of a k-stage Arbiter PUF consists of k pairs of 2-to-1 multiplexers as shown in Fig. 1 and takes the same challenge bit for the same stage [14].

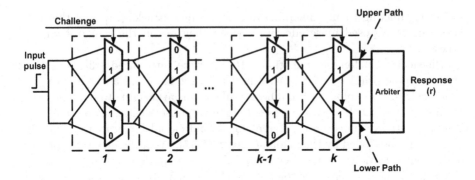

Fig. 1. Architecture of the conventional Arbiter PUF

At the input stage, an input pulse propagates through nominally identical delay paths of both the multiplexers of a stage. The applied challenge bit controls the paths of the input signal. Due to the manufacturing process variations [7], there is a delay difference (Δp) between the two propagation paths (upper and lower). An arbiter block is placed after the delay path to determine the faster path. Generally, a D-latch generates a response '0' or '1' by comparing the arrival time of the upper and lower paths. The input pulse can propagate through 2^k possible paths for a k-stage APUF. The functionality of the Arbiter PUF satisfies the additive linear model. Depending on challenge $C(c_1, c_2, ...c_k)$, the total delays of both paths can be modelled as the sum of the delay of the individual stage [17]. The total delay difference (Δ_D) at the final stage of a k-stage APUF can be described as:

$$\Delta_D = \sum_{i=1}^{k} \Delta p_i X_i \tag{1}$$

where, Δp_i denotes the difference between the upper and lower path delays at i^{th} stage and X_i denotes the transformed challenge bit applied to i^{th} stage. The procedure of ML attacks [2] is divided into two phases: the training phase and the classification phase. At the beginning of the training phase, a number of CRPs are collected from the targeted APUF by the attackers. The challenge (C) is transformed to improve the training efficiency [17]. The process of this transformation can be described as follows. Let c_n is the nth bit of the k-bit long challenge, where $n = 1,2,...,k$. Now, let X_m be the mth bit of the transformed challenge. The challenge is transformed from $c \in \{0,1\}^k$ to $X = \{-1,1\}^{k+1}$. This transformation model [17] is expressed as below in (2):

$$X_m = \begin{cases} \prod_{n=m}^{k} (1 - 2c_n) & (m = 1, 2, ..., k) \\ 1 & (m = k + 1) \end{cases} \tag{2}$$

After this transformation, the additive delay model is constructed with delay parameter (Δp) and the transformed challenge (X) to calculate the final response as described in (3). The response of the APUF can be modelled with a sign function and the sum of the total delay difference between the two paths at the final stage(Δ_D) and delay of the arbiter (D_{arb}). Therefore, the final response (r) can be described as follows:

$$r = \text{sgn}[\sum_{i=1}^{k} \Delta p_i X_i + D_{arb}] \tag{3}$$

In practice, a large number of collected CRPs are used to train the ML models for accurately predicting the response to an unseen challenge. Therefore, we can say that the Arbiter PUF is vulnerable to ML attacks due to its linear relation between the generated response (r) and challenge (C) [17,20].

2.2 XOR Arbiter PUF

The concept of generating the final response by XORing outputs of multiple APUFs was introduced in [2,19]. An n-XOR APUF consists of n separate APUF, as shown in Fig. 2. The same challenges are applied to the n APUFs with n stages. For a particular challenge, n responses from n individual APUF are XORed to get the final response. Therefore, the final XORed response (r_{XOR}) can be expressed with the help of the following expression:

$$r_{XOR} = \bigoplus_{j=1,2..n} r_j \tag{4}$$

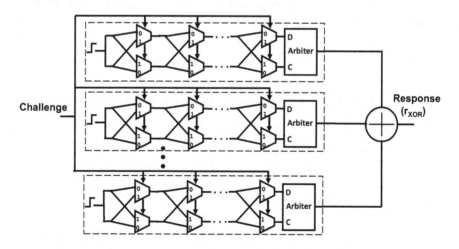

Fig. 2. Architecture of the XOR arbiter PUF

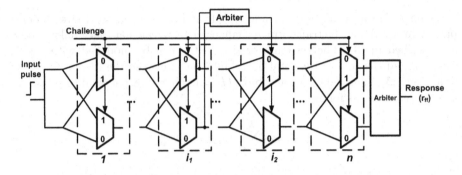

Fig. 3. Architecture of the conventional FF PUF

The purpose of XORing the individual PUF response is to increase the degree of non-linearity between the applied challenge and the final response. This XOR configuration of APUFs increases the dimensionality of the parameters to be used to train ML algorithms [24] while compromising the chip implementation area and power.

2.3   Feed-Forward Arbiter PUF

The architecture of the feed-forward PUF (FF PUF) is illustrated in Fig. 3. The complexity between the response and challenge is increased by adding an intermediate feed-forward stage to generate a challenge for an intermediate stage [3, 26].

Suppose, the feed-forward loop starts at stage i_1 and terminates at stage i_2 where $(i_2 < n)$ for an n-stage PUFs, the response of a single-loop FF PUF can be modelled by the following equations:

$$r_{ff} = \text{sgn}\left[\left(\sum_{i \neq i_2}^{n} \Delta p_i X_i + \Delta p_{i_2} X_{i_2}\right) + D_{arb}\right] \tag{5}$$

where, the challenge transformation can be defined as follows:

$$\begin{cases} X_n = (1 - 2C_n), \\ X_{i_i} = (1 - 2C_{i_1}), \\ X_{i_2} = \text{sgn}\left[\sum_{i=1}^{i_1} \Delta p_i X_i + D_{arb}\right], \\ X_i = (1 - 2C_i)X_{i+1} \; for \, i \neq i_1, i_2 \, and \, i < n \end{cases}$$

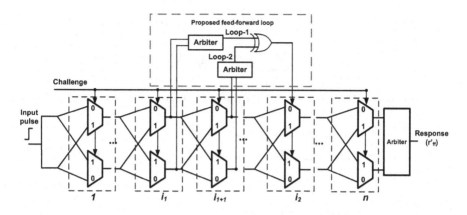

Fig. 4. Architecture of the proposed FF PUF

The sign function adds more non-linearity to the PUF model, which is not easily non-differentiable by the ML algorithms. Therefore, the transformed challenge (X_{i_2}) also adds non-linearity to the response of the PUFs. This non-differentiability of FF PUF converts the linearly separable hyperplane of a conventional APUFs into a complex non-linear hyperplane. Due to the inability of the ML algorithms to model the non-linear separable classes, the FF PUFs are more resilient to ML attacks [3].

3   Proposed Highly Non-linear Feed-Forward XOR PUF

The architecture of the proposed FF PUF is shown in the following Fig. 4. As mentioned above, a feed-forward loop increases the non-linearity between the challenge-response pairs. Our idea behind this modification is to increase the level of non-linearity of the existing feed-forward loop shown in Fig. 3. In our proposed architecture, two consecutive feed-forward loops are used to generate a challenge bit for an intermediate stage. For a n-stage APUF, let say two intermediate feed-forward loops are originated from i_1^{th} and $(i_1 + 1)^{th}$ stages and the outputs of the intermediate arbiters are XORed to generate the intermediate challenge for i_2^{th} stage.

The output of the intermediate feed-forward loops can be expressed as follows:

$$r_{loop_1} = \text{sgn}\big[\sum_{i=1}^{i_1} \Delta p_i X_i + D_{arb}\big] \tag{6}$$

$$r_{loop_2} = \text{sgn}\big[\sum_{i=1}^{i_1+1} \Delta p_i X_i + D_{arb}\big] \tag{7}$$

The response r'_{ff} of this proposed FF PUF can be modelled as follows:

$$r'_{ff} = \text{sgn}\left[\left(\sum_{i \neq i_2}^{n} \Delta p_i X_i + \Delta p_{i_2} X'_{i_2}\right) + D_{arb}\right] \tag{8}$$

where, transformed challenge (X'_{i_2}) for the i_2-th stage can be expressed as follows (9):

$$\begin{aligned}
X'_{i_2} &= (r_{loop_1} \oplus r_{loop_2}) \\
&= (\text{sgn}\left[\sum_{i=1}^{i_1} \Delta p_i X_i + D_{arb}\right] \oplus \text{sgn}\left[\sum_{i=1}^{i_1+1} \Delta p_i X_i + D_{arb}\right])
\end{aligned} \tag{9}$$

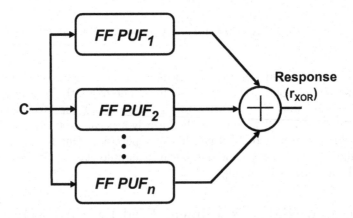

Fig. 5. Architecture of the proposed FFXOR PUF

The response of the proposed FF PUF in (8) contains more non-linear terms due to the transformed challenge expressed in (9) in comparison with the response of the conventional FF PUF in (5). A linear approximation is invalid when the proposed FF PUF is used as a component in XOR PUF. Hence, the proposed FFXOR PUF architecture is more resilient to ML-based attacks. In this work, we proposed a feed-forward loop architecture which originated from the 8th and 9th stage and terminated at 24th stage of a 32-stage MUX-based APUF. Further, we designed FFXOR PUF by XORing the outputs of the individual proposed FF PUFs to decrease the susceptibility to the ML attacks [3,4]. By changing the levels or component PUFs in FFXOR PUF, different configurations are implemented for testing, as shown in Fig. 5, and the performance of the proposed architecture is described in Sect. 5.

4   Experimental Setup for ML Attacks on PUFs

This section describes the experimental setup for the generation of CRPs, the structure of the ML algorithms and various attacks performed on the PUFs.

4.1   Generation of Challenge-Response Pairs (CRPs)

The proposed PUF and other PUFs explained in the previous section are designed in Verilog HDL using Xilinx Vivado 2019.1 and implemented on Xilinx Zedboard (Zynq-7000, xc7z020clg484-1). We conducted all the experiments at room temperature. The random challenge generation and response extraction from the PUF is done using Vivado Software Development Suite with the help of the Zynq Processing System (PS) and UART module. For our analysis, a 32-bit challenge is applied to the PUF to generate 1 bit of response. Thus, 100K CRPs were extracted within a shorter time duration. These CRPs are processed further to analyse the ML attacks described in later sections.

4.2   ML Models for Attacks on PUFs

In this paper, we have deployed two ML attacks such as the Support Vector Machines (SVM) and Artificial Neural Networks (ANN). The SVM classifier is widely used in literature to test the resiliency of the Strong PUFs [2,26]. By finding the optimum hyperplane, the SVM algorithm is efficient enough to separate the two binary classes (class '0' and class '1'). The ANN is also considered for testing the PUF models due to its capability of modelling non-linear datasets. A multi-layered perceptron (MLP) method is used to form the ANN model, as shown in Fig. 6 [8]. In the training phase, input data is applied to the neurons of the input layers of MLP. Each neuron provides an output based on the result of the activation function working on that neuron. The activation function calculates the output by multiplying the input data with the weight vector and adds a bias for that particular neuron.

In the training phase, the error caused by the difference between the predicted value and observed value is minimized by the back-propagation technique. For each data point, the weight parameter and bias for a neuron are adjusted and updated. The process of training ends when a particular number of epochs are completed. We have chosen resilient back-propagation [3] as a training algorithm due to its fast convergence time and prediction accuracy .

4.3   Study of Attacks on APUFs, XOR APUFs and Proposed FFXOR PUFs

As we explained in Sect. 2.1, the delay difference of APUFs linearly correlates with the transformed challenges. The attack methodology shown in [16] described that the raw CRPs as input feature results in very poor accuracy in the case of a normal APUF. Therefore, we transformed the challenges using (3) before

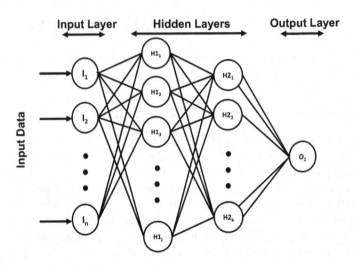

Fig. 6. Standard architecture of the neural network for attacking PUFs

Table 1. Description of the neural network For ML attacks on APUF, XOR APUF & proposed FFXOR PUF

Neural network parameters	Descriptions
Hidden layers	3 (32,64,32)
Activation function (Hidden layer)	Relu
Activation function (Output layer)	Softmax
Loss function	Binary cross entropy
Name of optimizer	ADAM
Learning rate	Adaptive
Batch size	1000

applying them to the different PUFs to ensure a fair comparison of the proposed PUF architecture with the existing PUFs. The ANN and SVM modelling attacks were implemented in Python 3.8 with the help of the TensorFlow [1] backend and Keras [5] framework. The attacks on the PUFs were executed on a workstation with a 4.2 GHz 20-core Intel Xeon 4200 processor and 64 GB RAM. To evaluate the performance metrics, we split the total CRPs as 80% for training and 20% for testing. To find the best kernel for an SVM attack, we tested a dataset with 5-fold cross-validation. We chose a quadratic SVM kernel for attacking the PUF models. The parameters used for the neural network for APUF, XOR APUF and proposed FFXOR PUF are listed in Table 1. We trained and validated the ML attack models for 200 epochs.

5   Result and Discussion

In this section, we analysed the prediction accuracy, loss and training time of different PUF models such as APUF, XOR APUF, and proposed FFXOR PUF. The prediction accuracy and training time for the conventional APUF are shown in Table 2. Due to the linear additive delay model, very high prediction accuracy with lesser training time is achieved for both SVM and ANN-based attacks. Therefore, the conventional APUF is vulnerable to ML-based attacks.

Table 2. Prediction accuracy and training time for APUF

Attack method	Prediction accuracy(%)	Training time (sec)
SVM	99.05	20
ANN	99.20	11

5.1   Analysis of Prediction Accuracy

Table 3 presents the comparison of the prediction accuracy between the conventional XOR APUF and proposed FFXOR PUF for both ANN and SVM attacks. The total number of CRPs used is 100K and the number of levels in the XOR is varied from 2 to 5. The range of the prediction accuracy of the conventional XOR APUF is 85.50% to 92.20% for SVM and 95.80% to 98.40% for ANN attacks which are very high. However, the range of the prediction accuracy of the proposed FFXOR PUF is 51.6% to 68.25% for SVM and 50.43% to 67.75% for ANN attacks. The minimum prediction accuracy is achieved 51.6% for SVM and 50.43% for ANN attack with 5 levels of proposed FFXOR PUF. Therefore, the reduction in the prediction accuracy for the proposed FFXOR PUF with 5 levels compared to conventional XOR APUF is very significant as 33.90% for SVM and 45.37% for ANN-based attacks.

For an ML attack-resistant PUF, the prediction accuracy should be as low as possible so that the attackers can not easily guess the response of the PUF to an unseen challenge. As the proposed FFXOR PUF architecture achieves as low accuracy ($\sim$50%) as random guessing, it could be a good choice for ML resilient PUF.

5.2   Analysis of Training Time

The comparison of the training time of the conventional XOR APUF and proposed FFXOR PUF for different levels are shown in Table 4. The training time for the proposed FFXOR PUF with 5 levels is increased 3.1 times for SVM and 2.1 times for ANN attack compared with the conventional XOR APUF. In reality, the attackers get a chance to access the communication channel by snooping/eavesdropping for a limited time. If the training time is significantly higher, the attackers will not be able to perform ML-based attacks and clone the PUF model.

Table 3. Comparison of the prediction accuracy between the conventional XOR APUF and proposed FFXOR PUF

Attack method	No. of levels in XOR	Prediction accuracy (%)		Reduction in accuracy (%) (A-B)
		Standard XOR APUF (A)	Proposed FFXOR PUF (B)	
SVM	2	92.20	68.25	23.95
	3	88.51	64.30	24.21
	4	86.31	55.79	30.52
	5	**85.50**	**51.60**	**33.90**
ANN	2	98.40	67.75	30.65
	3	97.65	63.01	34.64
	4	96.20	53.83	42.37
	5	**95.80**	**50.43**	**45.37**

Table 4. Comparison of the training time between the conventional XOR APUF and proposed FFXOR PUF

Attack method	No. of levels in XOR	Training time (min)		Increment in training time (D/C)
		Conventional XOR APUF (C)	Proposed FFXOR PUF (D)	
SVM	2	2.47	4.68	1.9x
	3	2.93	6.95	2.4x
	4	3.08	9.25	3.0x
	5	3.75	11.57	**3.1x**
ANN	2	0.80	1.85	2.3x
	3	1.65	2.37	1.4x
	4	2.18	4.88	2.2x
	5	2.62	5.53	**2.1x**

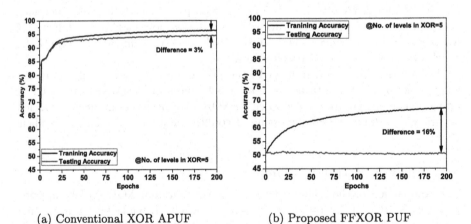

(a) Conventional XOR APUF   (b) Proposed FFXOR PUF

Fig. 7. Comparison of prediction accuracy using ANN Attack between the conventional XOR APUF and proposed FFXOR PUF.

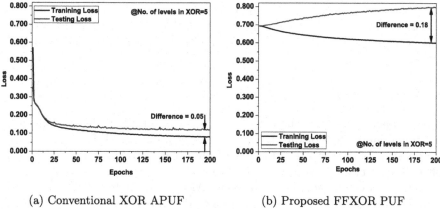

(a) Conventional XOR APUF   (b) Proposed FFXOR PUF

Fig. 8. Comparison of loss using ANN Attack between the conventional XOR APUF and proposed FFXOR PUF.

Table 5. Comparison with the recent state-of-the-art PUFs

	This work	[18] iSES'20	[10] VLSID'21	[22] JETCAS'21
FPGA	Zynq-7000	Artix-7	Artix-7	Artix-7
PUF Type	Feed-Forward XOR PUF	XOR-mesh PUF	Obfuscated PUF	Rec-DA PUF
Size of CRPs	100K	10K	100K	140K
Minimum prediction accuracy(%)	50.43	62.4	58.4	64.9

5.3   Performance Evaluation of Proposed FFXOR PUF

Fig. 7 shows the comparison of the prediction accuracy with respect to different number of epochs between the conventional XOR PUF and the proposed FFXOR PUF. As we can see, the difference between the training and testing accuracy (Fig. 7(a)) is very close (3%) for the conventional XOR APUF. In contrast, this difference becomes significant (16%) in the case of our proposed FFXOR PUF (Fig. 7(b)). For ML attack resilient PUF, the difference between the training vs testing accuracy/loss should be as high as possible so that the ML attacks models can not predict the response correctly. The comparison between training and testing loss with respect to different number of epochs is shown in Fig. 8. For the conventional XOR APUF, the difference between the training and testing loss is only 5%, as shown in Fig. 8(a). However, the results in Fig. 8(b) show that the difference between the training and testing loss of the proposed FFXOR PUF is increased to 18%, which is very favourable to resist the ML-based attacks on PUFs.

Table 5 shows the comparison in terms of the ML resiliency of the proposed FFXOR PUF with recently published state-of-the-art PUFs tested on FPGA.

The proposed FFXOR PUF demonstrates a higher resistance against ML-based attacks than the work presented in [10,18,22]. The resistivity of the proposed work is increased by 22.3% in comparison with [22] with a training set of 100K CRPs.

6 Conclusion

In this paper, we implemented an ML resilient strong PUF by introducing a highly non-linear feed-forward loop. To make the proposed FF PUF more robust against state-of-the-art ML attacks, FFXOR PUF is designed and tested. The different performance metrics of the proposed FFXOR PUF architecture are extracted and compared with the existing APUF and XOR APUF. The experimental attack results show that the proposed non-linear FFXOR PUF with 5 levels in XOR is more resilient against ML attacks due to its low prediction accuracy ($\sim$50%) and 3 times increment in the training time. Also, the proposed FFXOR PUF significantly increases the differences between the training and testing accuracy/loss so that classification-based (SVM) and ANN-based attacks can not accurately predict the response of the PUF. Moreover, the extra non-linear element in the feed-forward loop incurs lesser resource utilization on FPGA, making our proposed design a suitable candidate for lightweight IoT applications.

Acknowledgements. This work is supported and funded by Science and Engineering Research Board (SERB), Department of Science and Technology, Government of India under the project grant number CRG/2021/007437.

References

1. Abadi, M., et al.: Tensorflow: a system for large-scale machine learning. In: Proceedings of the 12th USENIX Conference on Operating Systems Design and Implementation, pp. 265–283. OSDI 2016, USENIX Association, USA (2016)
2. Aseeri, A.O., Zhuang, Y., Alkatheiri, M.S.: A machine learning-based security vulnerability study on XOR PUFS for resource-constraint Internet of Things. In: 2018 IEEE International Congress on Internet of Things (ICIOT), pp. 49–56 (2018). https://doi.org/10.1109/ICIOT.2018.00014
3. Avvaru, S.V.S., Zeng, Z., Parhi, K.K.: Homogeneous and heterogeneous feed-forward xor physical unclonable functions. IEEE Trans. Inf. Forens. Secur. **15**, 2485–2498 (2020). https://doi.org/10.1109/TIFS.2020.2968113
4. Avvaru, S.S., Parhi, K.K.: Effect of loop positions on reliability and attack resistance of feed-forward pufs. In: 2019 IEEE Computer Society Annual Symposium on VLSI (ISVLSI), pp. 366–371 (2019). https://doi.org/10.1109/ISVLSI.2019.00073
5. Chollet, F., et al.: Keras (2015). https://keras.io
6. Daniele, M., Sabrina, S., Francesco, D.P., Imrich, C.: Internet of things: Vision, applications and research challenges. Ad Hoc Netw. **10**(7), 1497–1516 (2012)
7. Das, B.P., Amrutur, B., Jamadagni, H.S., Arvind, N.V., Visvanathan, V.: Within-die gate delay variability measurement using reconfigurable ring oscillator. IEEE Trans. Semiconduct. Manufact. **22**(2), 256–267 (2009). https://doi.org/10.1109/TSM.2009.2017662

8. Das, B.P., Amrutur, B., Jamadagni, H.S., Arvind, N.V., Visvanathan, V.: Voltage and temperature-aware SSTA using neural network delay model. IEEE Trans. Semiconduct. Manufactur. **24**(4), 533–544 (2011). https://doi.org/10.1109/TSM. 2011.2163532

9. Delvaux, J.: Machine-learning attacks on polypufs, ob-pufs, rpufs, lhs-pufs, and puf-fsms. IEEE Trans. Inf. Forens. Secur. **14**(8), 2043–2058 (2019). https://doi. org/10.1109/TIFS.2019.2891223

10. Ebrahimabadi, M., Younis, M., Lalouani, W., Karimi, N.: A novel modeling-attack resilient arbiter-PUF design. In: 2021 34th International Conference on VLSI Design and 2021 20th International Conference on Embedded Systems (VLSID), pp. 123–128 (2021). https://doi.org/10.1109/VLSID51830.2021.00026

11. Gao, Y., et al.: Obfuscated challenge-response: a secure lightweight authentication mechanism for PUF-based pervasive devices. In: 2016 IEEE International Conference on Pervasive Computing and Communication Workshops (PerCom Workshops), pp. 1–6 (2016). https://doi.org/10.1109/PERCOMW.2016.7457162

12. Gassend, B., Clarke, D., van Dijk, M., Devadas, S.: Controlled physical random functions. In: Proceedings of 18th Annual Computer Security Applications Conference, 2002, pp. 149–160 (2002). https://doi.org/10.1109/CSAC.2002.1176287

13. Gassend, B., Clarke, D., van Dijk, M., Devadas, S.: Silicon physical random functions. In: Proceedings of the 9th ACM Conference on Computer and Communications Security, pp. 148–160. CCS 2002. Association for Computing Machinery, New York, NY, USA (2002). https://doi.org/10.1145/586110.586132

14. Halak, B., Zwolinski, M., Mispan, M.S.: Overview of PUF-based hardware security solutions for the Internet of Things. In: 2016 IEEE 59th International Midwest Symposium on Circuits and Systems (MWSCAS), pp. 1–4 (2016). https://doi. org/10.1109/MWSCAS.2016.7870046

15. Herder, C., Yu, M.D., Koushanfar, F., Devadas, S.: Physical unclonable functions and applications: a tutorial. Proc. IEEE **102**(8), 1126–1141 (2014). https://doi. org/10.1109/JPROC.2014.2320516

16. Ikezaki, Y., Nozaki, Y., Yoshikawa, M.: Deep learning attack for physical unclonable function. In: 2016 IEEE 5th Global Conference on Consumer Electronics, pp. 1–2 (2016). https://doi.org/10.1109/GCCE.2016.7800478

17. Lim, D., Lee, J., Gassend, B., Suh, G., van Dijk, M., Devadas, S.: Extracting secret keys from integrated circuits. IEEE Trans. Very Large Scale Integr. (VLSI) Syst. **13**(10), 1200–1205 (2005). https://doi.org/10.1109/TVLSI.2005.859470

18. Rajan, A., Sankaran, S.: Lightweight and attack-resilient PUF for Internet of Things. In: 2020 IEEE International Symposium on Smart Electronic Systems (iSES) (Formerly iNiS), pp. 139–142 (2020). https://doi.org/10.1109/iSES50453. 2020.00039

19. Rostami, M., Majzoobi, M., Koushanfar, F., Wallach, D.S., Devadas, S.: Robust and reverse-engineering resilient PUF authentication and key-exchange by substring matching. IEEE Trans. Emerg. Top. Comput. **2**(1), 37–49 (2014). https:// doi.org/10.1109/TETC.2014.2300635

20. Rührmair, U., Sehnke, F., Sölter, J., Dror, G., Devadas, S., Schmidhuber, J.: Modeling attacks on physical unclonable functions. In: 17th ACM Conference on Computer and Communications Security, pp. 237–249. CCS 2010. Association for Computing Machinery, New York, NY, USA (2010). https://doi.org/10.1145/1866307. 1866335

21. Rührmair, U., et al.: Efficient power and timing side channels for physical unclonable functions. In: Batina, L., Robshaw, M. (eds.) CHES 2014. LNCS, vol. 8731, pp. 476–492. Springer, Heidelberg (2014). https://doi.org/10.1007/978-3-662-44709-3_26

22. Shah, N., Chatterjee, D., Sapui, B., Mukhopadhyay, D., Basu, A.: Introducing recurrence in strong PUFS for enhanced machine learning attack resistance. IEEE J. Emerg. Select. Top. Circ. Syst. **11**(2), 319–332 (2021). https://doi.org/10.1109/JETCAS.2021.3075767

23. Suh, G.E., Devadas, S.: Physical unclonable functions for device authentication and secret key generation. In: 2007 44th ACM/IEEE Design Automation Conference, pp. 9–14 (2007)

24. Wang, S.J., Chen, Y.S., Li, K.S.M.: Adversarial attack against modeling attack on PUFS. In: 2019 56th ACM/IEEE Design Automation Conference (DAC), pp. 1–6 (2019)

25. Yu, M.D., Hiller, M., Delvaux, J., Sowell, R., Devadas, S., Verbauwhede, I.: A lockdown technique to prevent machine learning on PUFS for lightweight authentication. IEEE Trans. Multi-Scale Comput. Syst. **2**(3), 146–159 (2016). https://doi.org/10.1109/TMSCS.2016.2553027

26. Zhuang, Y., Mursi, K.T., Li, G.: A challenge obfuscating interface for arbiter PUF variants against machine learning attacks. CoRR abs/2103.12935 (2021). https://arxiv.org/abs/2103.12935

An Online Testing Technique for the Detection of Control Nodes Displacement Faults (CNDF) in Reversible Circuits

Bappaditya Mondal[1], Udit Narayana Kar[2], Chandan Bandyopadhyay[3,4,6(✉)], Debashri Roy[5], and Hafizur Rahaman[6]

[1] Department of Computer Science and Engineering, Academy of Technology, Sarisha, West Bengal, India
bappa.arya@gmail.com
[2] School of Computer Science and Engineering, Vellore Institute of Technology-AP, Amaravati, India
uditnarayana.k@vitap.ac.in
[3] Department of Computer Science and Engineering, University of Bremen, Bremen, Germany
[4] Department of Computer Science and Engineering, Dr. B. C. Roy Engineering College, Durgapur, West Bengal, India
chandanb.iiest@gmail.com
[5] Department of Electrical and Computer Engineering, Northeastern University, Boston, MA, USA
debashri.roy.08@gmail.com
[6] Department of Information Technology, Indian Institute of Engineering, Science and Technology Shibpur, Shibpur, India
rahaman_h@yahoo.co.in

Abstract. With the advancements of Quantum Computing and its implementing technologies like NMR, IoN trap, the necessity of constructing fault-free quantum circuit is observed. But in way to ensure fault-free circuit, appropriate testing model to be invoked and here in this paper we present an online testing technique that effectively detects control node displacement fault (CNDF) in quantum circuit designed with reversible gates.

Our testing approach involves two steps. In the very first step, the input circuit is transformed to its corresponding testable design by appending additional gates and lines (auxiliary lines). Next, appropriate test vectors are generated and subsequently are applied to find possible node displacement faults in the circuit. The proposed online testing approach is suitable for all type of quantum circuits built with reversible gates (MCT gates). More interestingly, some small changes in the design turn this scheme very effective for ESOP based representation as well. We have extensively tested our approach over a large spectrum of benchmarks and comparison with existing testing algorithms is also summarized in the result tables.

Keywords: Multi control toffoli (MCT) · Reversible circuit · ESOP circuit · Control node displacement fault · Online testing · Auxiliary lines

A. P. Shah et al. (Eds.): VDAT 2022, CCIS 1687, pp. 249–261, 2022.
https://doi.org/10.1007/978-3-031-21514-8_22

1   Introduction

With the advancements of the fabrication technologies, the necessity of the developing high end circuit and the computing devices is observed. Quantum computing [1, 2] has evolved as one of such solutions that have the capacity to meet the asked challenges. Nowadays, it (quantum technology [3, 4]) is considered as one of the most promising research domains due not only its computing capacity but also for its wide range of applications in different fields like nanotechnology, cryptography, machine learning and bioinformatics. This highly emerging filed is not restricted to theoretical concepts only, enormous progress [5–7] has been made towards developing quantum circuit implementing technologies like NMR, IoN Trap and Super Conducting qubit. Successful implementation of the 2-qubit quantum gate in silicon [8], the conceptualization of lower qubit quantum computers [9] had again advanced this highly emerging computing field to a new dimension. Reversible circuit is one of the most promising means which can design quantum circuit as all the quantum operations are inherently reversible. In recent time, this filed has progressed significantly, where different well-established algorithms are proposed for the efficient synthesis and design of reversible logic, such as ESOP [10], BDD [11] and Reed-Muller [12]. In addition to circuit synthesis, identification of faults [13] in reversible circuits has also become a significant issue to fabricate the fault-free circuit. For example, some well-known fault models are Single Missing Gate Fault (SMGF), Partial Missing Gate Fault (PMGF), Multiple Missing Gate Fault (MMGF), and Repeated Gate Fault (RGF).

Several researches are ongoing in the domain of reversible circuit testing for the design of efficient fault detection and diagnosis algorithms. Here, we are presenting some well-known algorithms to perform the test operation in reversible circuits.

The test vector generation mechanism for the reversible circuit to detect the fault and also to localize the fault for different fault models is presented in [14]. Here, the deterministic approach and probabilistic approach of fault detection are described and compared. Special measurement of the internal states of gates is used to establish the probabilistic mechanism of fault detection. An efficient and complete test vector generation mechanism for the reversible circuit is reported in [15]. Apart from that, finding out minimal test set by integer linear programming for smaller circuits has been described in the work. The derivation of the optimal test set (OTS) and its effective use in the detection of missing gate faults in k-CNOT gate based reversible circuits is introduced in [16], where the authors have find out that the OTS is sufficient to detect all SMGFs and all detectable repeated gate faults (RGFs) in the circuit. Another approach of SMGF and RGF detection has been proposed in [17]. In this work, test vectors are generated with minimum test time to find out any kind of SMGF and RGF in the circuit. Here, 100% fault coverage has also been achieved. Apart from test vector generation and fault detection in reversible circuits, another aspect of testing is fault localization. The mechanism of fault localization for the reversible circuit is proposed in [18]. Here in this approach, the reversible circuit is divided into two parts. The first part of the circuit is represented as a symmetric adaptive tree and another part of the circuit is represented as a mirror image of the first part. Hence, it is quite easy to locate the exact fault in the circuit so that the fault can be corrected as early as possible. A new test vector generation technique is introduced in [19] where the concept of Boolean generator is used. An approach of fault diagnosis is also presented in [20]. Till so far we have talked on different developments over offline testing techniques, now here we are discussing on progressed made over online testing. An online testing technique for all ($n \times n$) and d depth reversible circuits using $2d$ garbage outputs along with ($2d + 1$) auxiliary lines has been proposed in [21]. The formation of testable design for effectively finding faults is discussed in [22], where some redundant gates are added in the input side of the testable design to make the design simpler. Another approach of online testing using testable design approach has been presented in [23], where the existing gates are modified to design two new gates which efficiently detects faults in online circuits. As the testable design is formed with additional lines and gates, it creates design overhead in the testing process. Hence to minimize the design overhead in the testable design, an online testing scheme has been proposed in [24], where no auxiliary lines are used to detect the possible SMGFs in reversible circuits in online mode. So far, we mainly have talked about different offline and online testing algorithms for SMGF, PMGF, MMGF, and RGF. Apart from that, a reversible circuit may incur the control node displacement fault (CNDF) in a gate of the circuit. To deal with such a type of fault, here in this proposed approach, we have proposed an online fault detection mechanism of CNDF in reversible circuits.

The rest of the paper is presented as follows. Introduction to reversible circuit and the different fault variations are stated in Sect. 2. The proposed fault detection model with example is explained in Sect. 3. The different benchmarking and experimental evaluations are reported in Sect. 4 and finally, the paper is concluded in Sect. 5.

2 Preliminaries

Some basic concepts regarding reversible circuits and different fault models related to the reversible circuits are introduced in this section.

Definition 1: *A circuit that exhibits objective mapping between inputs to outputs and has equal number of input-output lines is known as reversible circuit.*

The circuit must also need to satisfy the fan-out free condition and all the gates in the circuit must be reversible only.

Some Familiar gates in the reversible domain are Feymen [25], Toffoli [26], Fredkin [27].

Definition 2 [2]: *ESOP (Exclusive Sum-Of-Products) based circuit can be expressed in Boolean function represented by the operator '$\oplus$'.* Here, we will discuss some of the fault models for the reversible circuits.

Definition 3: *When a gate completely disappears or goes missing from a circuit then the infused fault is termed as Single Missing-Gate Fault (SMGF).*

Definition 4: *Unwanted occurrence of a gate by multiple times is known as repeated gate fault (RGF).*

Definition 5: *When a circuit has multiple and consecutive SMGFs in a circuit then the intensity of the fault in the circuit goes high which is known as multiple missing-gate faults (MMGF).*

Definition 6: *A fault is categorized as Partial missing gate fault (PMGF), when control nodes from gates go missing by causing change in functional behavior of the circuit then the infused fault is termed as Partial missing gate fault (PMGF).*

Definition 7 [28]: *Unlike PMGF, when control nodes of a gate get misplaced over different circuit lines but size of the gate remain same then the incurred fault in the circuit is termed as control node displacement fault (CNDF).*

For an example, If the control node at the line x in any gate G_i of the circuit is displaced to the through line y then the *CNDF* is denoted as $D_{G_i}^{x \to y}$, where $0 \le i \le (N\text{-}1)$ and N represent total gates in the circuit. Whereas the test vectors needed to detect any $D_{G_i}^{x \to y}$ are represented as $T(D_{G_i}^{x \to y})$ [28]. Here it is assumed that the target node is always fixed to its original position.

3   Proposed Technique

Here, we introduce two different variations in CNDF testing technique – 1) generalised CNDF testing scheme in any arbitrary reversible circuit, and 2) ESOP design specific CNDF detection procedure. Both the testing processes are divided into the following four phases: formation of circuit under test, establishment of fault detection mechanism, test vector generation, detection of the fault. We explain all the phases of this CNDF detection using a model circuit.

3.1   CNDF Testing Scheme for Any Reversible Circuit

3.1.1   Formation of Circuit Under Test

To transform a Toffoli circuit to the form of circuit under test, at first an extra circuit line is added in the input design and then a series of copy gates are added (for all the existing gates in the circuit). Hence after, a list of CNOT gate is placed in the beginning and at the end of the circuit where the number of newly added CNOT gate is twice the number of circuit lines in the Toffoli network. The steps involving this transformation are outlined in Algorithm 1.

Let us take the circuit (C_{input}) of Fig. 1(a) and transform it to circuit under test ($C_{under-test}$) using Algorithm 1. From the circuit configuration, we see that the design has 5 CNOT/Toffoli gates placed over 3 circuit lines. Now in the initial step, an auxiliary line (having input as I_{aux} and output as O_{aux}) is appended after the input line z and place five copy gates for all the five gates in the circuit. As the initial circuit had three circuit lines, accordingly we add CNOT gates at beginning and end of the design. Finally, we obtain the testable design ($C_{under-test}$) as depicted in Fig. 1(b) and this transformed design also preserve the same logic functionality as the initial circuit had.

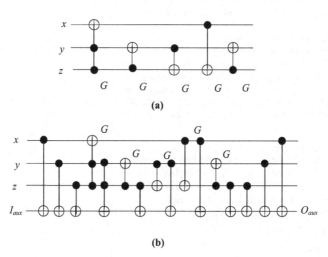

(a)

(b)

Fig. 1. (a) Input Circuit (C_{input}) "ham3\design#1" and (b) Circuit Under Test ($C_{under-test}$) for (a).

ALGORITHM 1: Online Detection of CNDF in
Reversible (*Toffoli* gate based) Circuit

Input: Reversible (*Toffoli* gate based) Circuit C_{input}
Output: Detection of any CNDF in the $C_{under\text{-}test}$
begin

    Step1: Formation of Circuit Under Test:
        Transform the input circuit C_{test} to the testable form
    ($C_{under\text{-}test}$) using the ***circuit-under test()*** function.

    Step2: Test Vector Formation:
    For any control node displacement fault in gate
    G_i ($D_{G_i}^{x\to y}$), the test vector $T(D_{G_i}^{x\to y})$ is detected by fixing
    0 at the original position of the control node and 1 at
    the current position of the control node of the circuit
    under test. Also 1 is set to others control node and 0/1
    to the target line and through line of the circuit under
    test respectively.

    Step3: Fault Detection Phase:
    For any control node displacement fault in any gate
    $G_i(D_{G_i}^{x\to y})$, the test vector $T(D_{G_i}^{x\to y})$ is applied to the test
    able circuit and if $O_{aux} = I_{aux}$ then it can be confirmed
    that CNDF is present in the testable circuit.

            //Detection of CNDF//

    Step4: ***circuit-under test()***

        begin

            4.1 Add auxiliary line to the input circuit C_{test}
            4.2 Copy each gate of C_{test} in such a way that
                  target would be fix to the line I.
            4.3 Before the first gate and after the last
                  gate, add n number of CNOT gate whose
                  target is fixed to line I from each n line
                of the circuit.

3.1.2 CNDF Detection Mechanism

Any CNDF in any gate of the circuit is detected if and only if the following condition is true $O_{aux} = \overline{I_{aux}}$.

Lemma 1: For any CNDF in any gate $G_i(D_{G_i}^{x\to y})$, the test vector $T(D_{G_i}^{x\to y})$ can detect the CNDF if and only if $O_{aux} = \overline{I_{aux}}$.

Proof: From any input circuit (C_{input}), the circuit under test (C_{under_test}) is designed in such a way that it always satisfies the statement $O_{aux} = I_{aux}$ for any fault free circuit C_{under_test}.

To illustrate trueness of the statement, let us consider the fault free circuit C_{under_test} of Fig. 1(b). Now, it can be observed that $O_{aux} = I_{aux} \oplus z \oplus y \oplus x \oplus yz \oplus z \oplus y \oplus z \oplus x \oplus yz \oplus y \oplus x \oplus yz \oplus z \oplus y \oplus z \oplus x \oplus yz \oplus y \oplus z \oplus x \oplus yz \oplus y \oplus x \oplus yz = I_{aux}$.

So, for any fault free circuit C_{under_test}, it is always true that $O_{aux} = I_{aux}$. Now for any occurrence of CNDF in the circuit C_{under_test}, it is always true that $O_{aux} = \overline{I_{aux}}$. To check the accuracy of the statement, it is assumed that a CNDF $(D_{G_2}^{y \to x})$ has occurred in the circuit C_{under_test} of Fig. 1(b). Now, $O_{aux} = I_{aux} \oplus z \oplus y \oplus x \oplus yz \oplus z \oplus y \oplus z \oplus x \oplus yz \oplus z \oplus z \oplus y \oplus x \oplus yz = I_{aux} \oplus x \oplus y \oplus z \oplus yz$.

At the time of the fault detection, as the control node moves from y to x, the node x always need to set to 1 and other terms would be nullified by default. Now, O_{aux} becomes $O_{aux} = I_{aux} \oplus 1 = \overline{I_{aux}}$. Hence, faults are detected when $O_{aux} = \overline{I_{aux}}$.

■

3.1.3 Test Vector Formation Method for the CNDF

Any CNDF is detected by fixing 0 at the original position of the control node and 1 at the current position of the control node of the circuit under test. Also 1 is set to others control node and 0/1 to the target line and through line of the circuit under test respectively.

Let us consider the circuit of Fig. 2(a) to evaluate the test vector formation method for the CNDF. According to the CNDF detection rule as discussed, the CNDF of $C_{G_0}^{y \to z}$ Fig. 2(a) is detected by $< xyzT > = < 1\,0\,1\,0 >$ and $< xyzT > = < 1\,0\,1\,1 >$. So, $T(D_{G_0}^{y \to z}) = \{<1\,0\,1\,0 >, < 1\,0\,1\,1 >\}$.

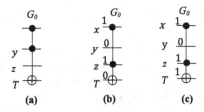

Fig. 2. Formation of Test Vector shown in (b), (c) for the $C_{G_0}^{y \to z}$ in (a).

3.1.4 Detection of the CNDF

Let us take the circuit of Fig. 1(b) which is the circuit under test of Fig. 1(a) to observe the detection mechanism of CNDF in Fig. 1(b). Different possible CNDF in Fig. 1(b) are $C_{G_1}^{z \to x}, C_{G_2}^{y \to x}, C_{G_3}^{x \to y}$ and $C_{G_4}^{z \to x}$. Based on the test vector formation method discussed earlier, generated test vectors for all the CNDF are $T(D_{G_1}^{z \to x}) = <1\,3\,4\,7>$, $T(D_{G_2}^{y \to x}) = <1\,2\,4\,6>$, $T(D_{G_3}^{x \to y}) = <1\,2\,4\,6>$, $T(D_{G_4}^{z \to x}) = <2\,3\,6\,7>$.

Let us assume that the fault $C_{G_2}^{y \to x}$ occurs in G_2 of the C_{under_test} in Fig. 1(b) where the control node moves to input line x from the input line y.

So, $O_{aux} = I_{aux} \oplus z \oplus y \oplus x \oplus yz \oplus z \oplus y \oplus z \oplus x \oplus yz \oplus z \oplus z \oplus y \oplus x \oplus yz = I_{aux} \oplus x \oplus y \oplus z \oplus yz$.

To detect the CNDF ($C_{G_2}^{y \to x}$), any test vector from the list $< 1, 2, 4, 6 >$ can be used. The vector 2 ($<xyz> = < 100 >$) is chosen from the list and applied over the C_{under_test}. Now, $O_{aux} = I_{aux} \oplus x \oplus y \oplus z \oplus yz = I_{aux} \oplus 1 \oplus 0 \oplus 0 \oplus 0.0 = \overline{I_{aux}}$.

Here, it is observed that $O_{aux} = = \overline{I_{aux}}$ which reveals that there is CNDF in the circuit of Fig. 1(b). Similarly, any CNDF in the circuit under test can be detected in online mode.

Till now, we have seen the behaviour of Algorithm 1 on any reversible circuit constructed with k-CNOT gates. The Example 1 is used to analyse the behaviour of the Algorithm 1 on the ESOP based reversible circuit..

Example 1: Let's consider an ESOP circuit as shown in Fig. 3(a) to see the outcome of Algorithm 1 on the ESOP circuit. The testable circuit implemented by Algorithm 1 is shown in Fig. 3(b).

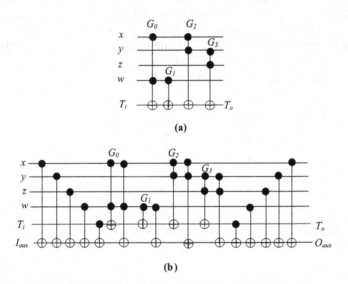

(a)

(b)

Fig. 3. (a) Input *ESOP* circuit (C_{input}) and (b) Circuit Under Test ($C_{under-test}$).

Let us assume that the CNDF ($D_{G_2}^{y \to z}$) has occurred in G_2 of Fig. 4(b). The said CNDF can be detected by $T(D_{G_2}^{y \to z}) = \{ <xyzw> = < 10 1 0 > \text{ or } < xyzw > = < 1 0 1 1 > \}$. Due to the fault in the circuit, O_{aux} becomes $O_{aux} = I_{aux} \oplus x \oplus y \oplus z \oplus w \oplus T_i \oplus xw \oplus w \oplus xy \oplus yz \oplus T_i \oplus xw \oplus w \oplus xy \oplus yz \oplus w \oplus z \oplus y \oplus x = I_{aux} \oplus xy \oplus xz$.

Now, for the test vector $< xyzw > = < 1\ 0\ 1\ 0 >$, $O_{aux} = I_{aux} \oplus 1.0 \oplus 1.1 = \overline{I_{aux}}$. Hence, the fault $C_{G_2}^{y \to z}$ in the testable circuit of Fig. 4(b) is detected.

Here, in this example, it can be observed that total $(2n + G)$ number of more gates (circuit overhead) are required to design the circuit under test to detect CNDF for the ESOP circuit using the Algorithm 1, where n represents total input lines of the input circuit and G means all gates of the input circuit.

3.2   CNDF Testing Scheme Only for ESOP Circuit

It has been experimented that the circuit overhead can be reduced to perform the CNDF test on the ESOP circuit and that is the primary motivation to develop the Algorithm 2 that describes the CNDF detection only in ESOP circuit with minimized circuit overhead. Algorithm 2 is explained in detail in the next section.

3.2.1   Formation of Circuit Under Test

The very same fault detection condition $(O_{aux} = \overline{I_{aux}})$ discussed in Algorithm 1 is also used in Algorithm 2 for the detection of a fault in the testable circuit.

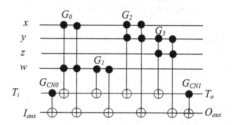

Fig. 4. (a). Final testable circuit $C_{testable}$

ALGORITHM 2: Online Detection of CNDF in
ESOP Based Circuit

Input: ESOP based Reversible Circuit C_{test}

Output: Detection of any CNDF in the $C_{testable}$ Circuit

begin

> **Step1: Formation of the Circuit Under Test:**
>
> > Transform the input circuit C_{input} to the testable
>
> form ($C_{under-test}$) using the ***circuit-under test()*** function.
>
> **Step2: Test Vector Formation:**
> For any control node displacement fault in gate
> $G_i(D_{G_i}^{x \to y})$, the test vector $T(D_{G_i}^{x \to y})$ is detected by fixing
> 0 at the original position of the control node and 1 at
> the current position of the control node of the circuit
> under test. Also 1 is set to others control node and 0/1
> to the target line and through line of the circuit under
> test respectively.
>
> **Step3: Fault Detection Phase:**
> For any control node displacement fault in any gate
> $G_i(D_{G_i}^{x \to y})$, the test vector $T(D_{G_i}^{x \to y})$ is applied to the
> testable circuit and if $O_{aux} = I_{aux}$ then it can be con
> firmed that CNDF is present in the testable circuit.
>
> > **//Detection of CNDF//**
>
> **Step4:** ***circuit-under test()***
>
> > **begin**
> >
> > > 4.1 Add line (ANC) to the input circuit C_{test}.
> > > 4.2 Copy each gate of C_{test} in such a way that
> > > > target would be fixed to the line ANC.
> > > 4.3 Before the first gate and after the last
> > > > gate, add a CNOT gate whose target is
> > > > fixed to ANC line from each n line of
> > > > the circuit.

3.2.2 Test Vector Formation Method for the CNDF

All possible CNDF for the circuit in Fig. 4(a) are $D_{G_0}^{x \to y}, D_{G_0}^{x \to z}, D_{G_0}^{w \to y}, D_{G_0}^{w \to z}, D_{G_1}^{w \to x}, D_{G_1}^{w \to y}, D_{G_1}^{w \to z}, D_{G_2}^{x \to z}, D_{G_2}^{x \to w}, D_{G_2}^{y \to z}, D_{G_2}^{y \to w}, D_{G_3}^{y \to x}, D_{G_3}^{y \to w}, D_{G_3}^{z \to x}$ and $D_{G_3}^{z \to w}$. Required test vectors needed for all the respective CNDFs are $T(D_{G_0}^{x \to y})$ = $< 5, 7 >$, $T(D_{G_0}^{x \to z})$ = $< 3, 7 >$, $T(D_{G_0}^{w \to y})$ = $< 12, 14 >$, $T(D_{G_0}^{w \to z})$ = $< 10, 14 >$, $T(D_{G_1}^{w \to x})$ = $< 8, 10, 12, 14 >$, $T(D_{G_1}^{w \to y})$ = $< 4, 6, 12, 14 >$, $T(D_{G_1}^{w \to z})$ = $< 2, 6, 10, 14 >$, $T(D_{G_2}^{x \to z})$ = $< 6, 7 >$, $T(D_{G_2}^{x \to w})$ = $< 5, 7 >$, $T(D_{G_2}^{y \to z})$ = $< 10, 11 >$, $T(D_{G_2}^{y \to w})$ = $< 9, 11 >$, $T(D_{G_3}^{y \to x})$ = $< 10, 11 >$, $T(D_{G_3}^{y \to w})$ = $< 3, 11 >$, $T(D_{G_3}^{z \to x})$ = $< 12, 13 >$, $T(D_{G_3}^{z \to w})$ = $< 5, 13 >$.

3.2.3 Detection of the CNDF

Let's consider the CNDF $(D_{G_0}^{x \to y})$ that occurs in G_0 of Fig. 4(a). Hence, the $C_{testable}$ circuit becomes faulty and the expression from O_{aux} becomes $O_{aux} = (I_{aux} \oplus T_i) \oplus (xw \oplus w \oplus xy \oplus yz) \oplus (yw \oplus w \oplus xy \oplus yz) \oplus T_i = I_{aux} \oplus xw \oplus yw$.

The fault $D_{G_0}^{x \to y}$ is identified by $T(D_{G_0}^{x \to y}) = \ <5, 7>$. Now apply the test vector5 i.e. $<xyzw> = \ <0101>$ over the circuit $C_{under\text{-}test}$ then $O_{aux} = I_{aux} \oplus 0.1 \oplus 1.1 = \overline{I_{aux}}$ is observed. As $O_{aux} = \overline{I_{aux}}$, hence it is confirmed that a CNDF occurred in the circuit of Fig. 4(b). Similarly, the other CNDFs in the circuit can be detected by the described mechanism.

4 Experimental Results

We have tested our technique over a wide range of benchmarks [29] and the obtained results are summarized in Tables 1 and 2 respectively. In Table 1, the overhead calculation (Garbage Output (GO) and Quantum Cost (QC)) of the testable design over non-testable design of our approach (Algorithms 1 and 2) is compared and tabulated for any reversible circuit.

Similarly, in Table 2, Algorithms 1 and 2 of our proposed work is compared to justify the efficiency algorithm when it works only for the ESOP circuit. It has been observed from Table 2 that the ESOP circuit can be tested with the reduced design overhead using Algorithm 2.

Table 1. Overhead calculation of the circuit-under test over the input circuit

Approach	Average overhead for testability feature	
	GO	QC
Approach in [24]	0%	300.67%
Approach in [23]	63409.48%	312.28%
Approach in [30]	5163.03%	388.67%
Approach in [22]	63409.48%	312.28%
Our approach (Algorithm 1)	0%	$(100 + 2n)$%, n is the number of input lines
Our approach (Algorithm 2)	0%	102%

GO, Garbage Outputs; *QC*, Quantum Cost.

Table 2. Comparison of Algorithms 1 and 2 only on ESOP circuit

Benchmark name	GC	Algorithm 1		Algorithm 2			
		GC	Circuit Overhead (%)	GC	Improvement in Circuit Overhead (%)	Reduced GC	Reduced Circuit Overhead (%)
Z4ml	48	110	130	98	102	12	28
Sym9	28	74	164	58	102	16	62
Ex2	15	40	166	32	102	8	64
Frg2	3724	7594	110	7450	102	44	8
apex5	2909	7868	171	5820	102	2048	49

5 Conclusion

Several well-established algorithms are available for fault models like SMGF, PMGF, and MMGF. But, till now no such algorithms are for the detection of the control node displacement fault in online mode. Here in this work, we have implemented a fault detection mechanism to detect the control node displacement fault in the running time of the circuit. The developed fault detection method has been successfully tested over different benchmark circuits and the obtained results have been disclosed in different tables.

References

1. Bhattacharjee, A., Bandyopadhyay, C., Niemann, P., Mondal, B., Drechsler, R., Rahaman, H.: An improved heuristic technique for nearest neighbor realization of quantum circuits in 2D architecture. Integration **76**, 40–54 (2021)
2. Niemann, P., Bandyopadhyay, C., Drechsler, R.: February. Combining SWAPs and remote toffoli gates in the mapping to IBM QX architectures. In 2021 Design, Automation & Test in Europe Conference & Exhibition (DATE), pp. 200–205. IEEE (2021)
3. Shor, P.W.: Algorithms for quantum computation: discrete logarithms and factoring. In Foundations of Computer Science, pp. 124–134 (1994)
4. Grover, L.K.: A fast quantum mechanical algorithm for database search. In Theory of Computing, pp. 212–219 (1996)
5. Haffner, H., et al.: Scalable multiparticle entanglement of trapped ions. Nature **438**, 643–646 (2005)
6. Laforest, M., et al.: Using error correction to determine the noise model. Phys. Rev. A **75**, 133–137 (2007)
7. Ghosh, J., et al.: High-fidelity CZ gate for resonator based superconducting quantum computers. Phys. Rev. A **87**, 022309 (2013)
8. Veldhorst, M., et al.: A two qubit logic gate in silicon. Nature **526**, 410–414 (2015)
9. Kane, B.: A silicon-based nuclear spin quantum computer. Nature **393**, 133–137 (1998)
10. Fazel, K., Thornton, M., Rice, J., E.: ESOP-based Toffoli gate cascade generation. In IEEE Pacific Rim Conference on Communications, Computers and Signal Processing, pp. 206–209. Citeseer (2007)

11. Wille, R., Drechsler, R.: BDD-based synthesis of reversible logic for large functions. In DAC 2009, 270–275 (2009)

12. Gupta, P.A., Agrawal, A., Jha, N.K.: An algorithm for synthesis of reversible logic circuits. IBM Res. Develop. **25**(11), 2317–2329 (2006)

13. Hayes, J.P., Polian, I., Becker, B.: Testing for missing-gate faults in reversible circuits. In IEEE Asian Test Symposium, pp. 100–105 (2004)

14. Perkowski, M., Biamonte, J., Lukac, M.: Test generation and fault localization for quantum circuits. In International Symposium on Multi-Valued Logic, pp. 62–68 (2005)

15. Patel, K.N., Hayes, J.P., Markov, I.L.: Fault testing for reversible circuits. In IEEE VLSI Test Symposium, pp. 410–416 (2003)

16. Kole, D.K., Rahaman, H., Das, D.K., Bhattacharya, B.B.: Derivation of optimal test set for detection of multiple missing-gate faults in reversible circuits. In IEEE Asian Test Symposium, pp.33–38 (2010)

17. Zamani, M., Tahoori, M.B., Chakrabarty, K.: Ping-pong test: Compact test vector generation for reversible circuits. In IEEE VLSI Test Symposium, pp. 164–169 (2012)

18. Ramasamy, K., Tagare, R., Perkins, E., Perkowski, M.: Fault localization in reversible circuits is easier than for classical circuits. In IEEE Asian Test Symposium (2004)

19. Mondal, B., Kole, D.K., Das, D.K., Rahaman, H.: Generator for Test Set Construction of SMGF in Reversible Circuit by Boolean Difference method. In IEEE 23rd Asian Test Symposium, pp. 68–73 (2014)

20. Rahaman, H., Kole, D.K., Das, D.K., Bhattacharya, B.B.: Fault diagnosis in reversible circuits under missing-gate fault model. Comput. Electr. Eng. **37**(4), 475–485 (2011)

21. Mahammad, S.N., Hari, S.K., Shroff, S., Kamakoti, V.: Constructing online testable circuits using reversible logic. In International Symposium on VLSI Design and Test, pp. 373–383 (2006)

22. Vasudevan, D.P., Lala, P.K., Jia, D., Parkerson, J.P.: Online testable reversible logic circuit design using NAND blocks. In International Symposium on Defect and Fault-Tolerance in VLSI Systems, pp. 324–331 (2004)

23. Vasudevan, D.P., Lala, P.K., Jia, D., Parkerson, J.P.: Reversible logic design with online testability. IEEE Trans. Instrum. Measur. **55**, 406–414 (2006)

24. Kole, D.K., Rahaman, H., Das, D.K.: Synthesis of Online Testable Reversible Circuit. In International Symposium on Design and Diagnostic of Electronic Circuits and Systems, pp. 277–280 (2010)

25. Feynman, R.: Quantum mechanical computers. In Foundations of Physics, pp. 507–531 (1986)

26. Toffoli, T.: Reversible computing. In: de Bakker, J., van Leeuwen, J. (eds.) ICALP 1980. LNCS, vol. 85, pp. 632–644. Springer, Heidelberg (1980). https://doi.org/10.1007/3-540-10003-2_104

27. Fredkin, E., Toffoli, T.: Conservative logic. Int. J. Theor. Phys. **21**, 219–253 (1982)

28. Mondal, B., Bhattacharjee, A., Bandyopadhyay, C., Rahaman, H.: An approach for detection of node displacement fault (NDF) in reversible circuit. In IEEE Symposium on VLSI Design and Test, pp. 605–616 (2019)

29. Wille, R., Grosse, D., Teuber, L., Dueck, G., W., Drechsler, R.: Revlib: An online resource for reversible functions and reversible circuits. In 38th ISMVL, pp. 220–225 (2008)

30. Farazmand, M., Zamani, M., Tahoori, M.B.: Online fault testing of reversible logic using dual rail coding. In Proceedings of International On-Line Testing Symposium, pp. 204–205 (2010)

An Approach Towards Analog In-Memory Computing for Energy-Efficient Adder in SRAM Array

S Kavitha[1]($\boxtimes$) (iD), S. K. Vishvakarma[2], and B. S. Reniwal[1] (iD)

[1] Indian Institute of Information Technology, Design and Manufacturing, (IIITDM), Kancheepuram, India
edm20d014@iiitdm.ac.in
[2] Indian Institute of Technology, Indore, India

Abstract. To conquer the drawback of von Neumann architecture, research has been carried out on the computational methods in the memory array itself to achieve near-memory or in-memory computations (IMC). This paper for the first time proposed an analog IMC approach for full adder design using 8^+T Static Random Access Memories (SRAM). In conventional FA, addition is executed as a sequence of digital boolean operations inside the memory array and there is a need for external logic gates to compute the FA outputs. The proposed analog adder exploits the bit-line voltage discharge (V_{BL}) with respect to the data stored in the 8^+T memory cell for the bit addition. The bit-line discharge voltage is accumulated using a voltage accumulation circuit (VAC) and acts as an input to an analog to digital converter (ADC). The digital output obtained is the Sum of a single bit FA. Multi-bit FA is computed from this single-bit analog FA. Extensive simulation results, referring to an industrial hardware-calibrated UMC 65-nm CMOS technology indicate 27× improvement in power and 36× improvements in throughput leading to a reduction of 972× in energy-delay product.

Keywords: Full adder · Analog adder · In memory computing · 8^+T SRAM · Computing logic

1 Introduction

In this big data era where huge data are being generated and processed, high speed computation becomes an essential requirement. However, the traditional von Neumann architectures possess a performance gap due to fetching the data from memory and processing the data in the processor. This becomes the major impediment in von Neumann architecture. A wide area of research concerning in-memory computing architecture is aimed to mitigate this drawback. In this architecture, initially some processing units are added close to main memory and it is named as memory accelerators [1]. In the late 1990s, (Processor in memory) PIM evolved based on dividing the main memory into different parts, each consisting of computational blocks near to the memory [2]. To address the advent of data-intensive applications such as artificial intelligence [3], neural network [4],

A. P. Shah et al. (Eds.): VDAT 2022, CCIS 1687, pp. 262–274, 2022.
https://doi.org/10.1007/978-3-031-21514-8_23

machine learning [5,6] and big data, many studies have been conducted to bring computations to different level of memory hierarchies. To speed up the computations and improve the performance, parallelism is employed. SRAM based IMC effectively allows significant parallelism. Addition (boolean or arithmetic) is the basic operation from which any complex computations can be achieved. A digital Boolean logic and an arithmetic operation can both be executed in SRAM by either altering the memory array or adding some peripheral circuit, or both. Arithmetic circuits like adders are implemented using logic gates that are computed using IMC [7]–[9].

Many types of analog IMC architectures have been proposed with computations being performed in either current or voltage domain. In case of current domain, we pre-store one operand in the SRAM memory cell while other operand is modulated into the word line voltage level [10] or pulse width of the word line enable signal [11]. The variation in discharge currents of the bits cells results in multiplication of the two operands. To achieve higher order multiplication, multiple word lines are activated and the current flow or voltage discharge is accumulated to obtain the result. The 8T SRAM cell has been used as a rudimentary for analog-like dot product computations, without modifying the bit-cell circuitry [12]. The analog dot product of the required bits are obtained by subjecting the read ports of the 8T SRAM to suitable analog voltages and discerning the output current. The use of time-domain computations was proposed in [13], where operands are modulated into reference voltage applied to voltage controlled oscillator and pulse widths are sensed to obtain multiplication result. The use of digital logic gates for computing the adders includes need of more peripheral circuits to achieve the addition operation. To obtain the FA digital outputs, more switching of data is required, which increases the chance of erroneous output. To mitigate the higher number of switching data and to perform the addition with minimum peripheral circuits, we propose a new technique to design Full Adder using analog addition. Using the accumulation of voltage or current, analog addition is performed with fewer peripheral circuits and the final accumulated voltage will be sent to the ADC to get the final digital output (Sum and Carry). Traditional 6T SRAM has read stability issues as well as low read noise margins. These concerns are alleviated by 8T SRAM with separate decoupled read port. The 8^+T SRAM has differential dual-read port, thus making it ideal for IMC.

In this paper, we describe analog accumulation based FA in 8^+T SRAM. Then a four-bit ripple carry design is elaborated from the one-bit FA design. In both the cases, faster computation was obtained. The rest of this paper is organized as follows. Sect. 2 describes the full adder computations in 8^+T SRAM cell. Sect. 3 describes the proposed Analog adder for in-memory computation. Sect. 4 shows the simulation and analysis results. Finally, Sect. 5 concludes this paper.

2 Full Adder Computations in 8⁺T SRAM

The architecture for IMC in c is shown in Fig. 1, which consists of 256×256 SRAM arrays. Using horizontal word lines and vertical bit lines, the data are being written or stored conventionally. A row decoder, column decoder, write driver, bit-line pre-charge, sense amplifier (SA) and computing logic are the SRAM peripherals. In Fig. 1, RBL and RBLB are the read bit-lines and WBL and WBLB are the write bit-lines for reading and writing the data in the memory cell.

Figure 2 a and b shows the conventional FA circuit diagram with Sum and Carry outputs and truth table of the FA. The Sum and Carry are given by

$$Sum = A \oplus B \oplus Cin \tag{1}$$

$$Carry = A.B + B.Cin + Cin.A \tag{2}$$

where A, B, Cin are the inputs of the Full Adder;
Sum, Carry are the outputs of the Full Adder.

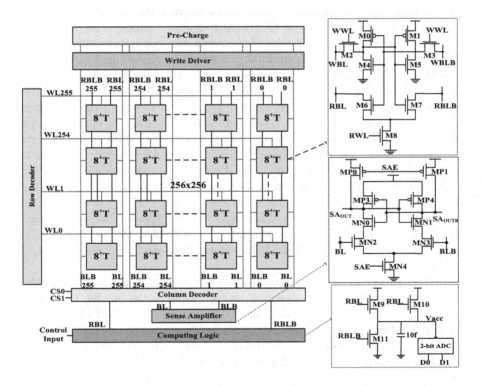

Fig. 1. IMC architecture for 8⁺T SRAM

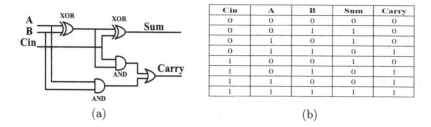

Cin	A	B	Sum	Carry
0	0	0	0	0
0	0	1	1	0
0	1	0	1	0
0	1	1	0	1
1	0	0	1	0
1	0	1	0	1
1	1	0	0	1
1	1	1	1	1

(a)   (b)

Fig. 2. a) Conventional full adder using logic gates b) Truth table of Full Adder

An asymmetric SA was introduced by skewing the transistors. Skewing can be realized by modifying the size of the transistor, the potential of the body bias or the threshold voltage of the transistor. Asymmetrical SA is used to obtain AND/NAND, OR/NOR between two inputs (say A and B). Further XOR is obtained by NORing the NOR and AND output from SA. Cin and previous XOR output (i.e., $A \oplus B$) are given as inputs to XOR gate to obtain the sum. For obtaining carry out, external logic gates, namely NAND, AND are used [9].

Another method of obtaining XOR in IMC is using Muller-C element [8]. NAND and OR is obtained from the discharge of RBL/RBLB by connecting an inverter. These outputs obtained from IMC are fed as inputs to the external logic gates to obtain Sum and Carry.

The above mentioned digital IMC works as simple bit-wise logic operations. These are carry less operations that do not require interaction between bit-lines. To encourage complete in-memory computations, there is a need of performing carry propagation between the bit-lines. We propose an analog adder performing addition of the stored bits based on the discharge of the bit-lines.

3   Proposed Analog Adder

The proposed Analog adder is designed to demonstrate the basic arithmetic block in the IMC architecture. Figure 1 shows the architecture for IMC consisting of SRAM arrays, control inputs and near memory peripherals required to perform analog addition. The data bits of the same vectors are placed spreading across a single row from least significant bit (LSB) to most significant bit (MSB). Corresponding bits to be operated upon from the vectors are placed in the same column with common bit-lines. In order to perform bit serial addition, the same bit position needs to be activated and fetched at the output of the column decoder through the bit-line/bit-line bar (BL/BLB) or RBL/RBLB. This discharged RBL/RBLB voltage is fed to the computational logic block to accumulate the analog voltage. For example, in the first cycle, the read word lines of the LSB of the two vectors stored are simultaneously activated. Then computation is performed in a compute logic block based on RBL/RBLB discharge. The accumulated analog voltage is sent to ADC to compute the digital output.

3.1   Full Adder

Fig. 3 a) shows the proposed IMC based approach and its implementation for the FA design. The input A and B are stored in row 1 and 2 respectively. Using Write Driver (WD), the write cycle starts with Cin input written into the Q00 cell as Write Driver Enable (WDE) is turned ON. Then the IMC cycle starts by turning ON Read Word Lines (RWL) of Row 0, 1 and 2 simultaneously, which in turn leads to discharge of RBL and RBLB based on the value stored in the memory cells Q00, Q10 and Q20 as shown in fig. 3. The voltage developed at bit-lines based on the data stored in the memory cell appears as the input to the analog computing logic to accumulate the voltage based on the discharge. Subsequently, an ADC is designed to convert into digital output. These execution cycles are tabulated in Table 1.

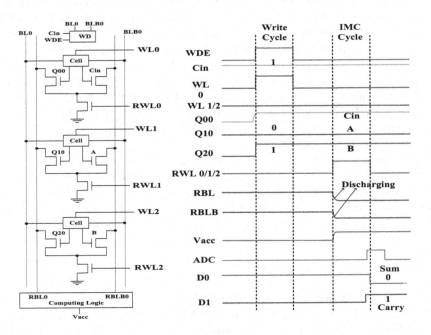

Fig. 3. One-bit full adder using 3 × 1 SRAM array and control signal for computing full adder

Table 1. Execution table for one-bit full adder

Cycle	Inputs	ADC inputs	ADC outputs
Write	Q00 <– Cin	–	–
IMC	Q00 = Cin;Q10 = A;Q20 = B	Vacc	D0 = Sum, D1 = Carry

3.2 4-Bit Ripple Carry Adder

To demonstrate more complex calculations in arithmetic block design, four bit ripple carry is developed based on the FA design. Figure 4 illustrates four bit ripple carry addition. Figure 5 shows the schematic of 4 bit FA in IMC, with 1-bit FA structure getting repeated 4 times to compute 4 bit operations. The execution cycles of operations are listed in the Table 2. From table, it is clear that the previous carry out is propagated as carry in to the current execution state. Thus the proposed 4 bit ripple carry adder takes 4 cycle of operations to get the final sum [s3, s2, s1, s0] and carry [c3, c2, c1, c0] from binary inputs [a3, a2, a1, a0 + b3, b2, b1, b0]. Similarly n bit addition can be performed with n cycle of iterations. The algorithm for n bit ripple carry is explained in Algorithm 1. This algorithm shows how to implement two n-bit numbers A and B on a 3 × n SRAM array. The bits A [an...., a3, a2, a1, a0] are written into second row by turning on WL1 and bit B [bn,...b3, b2, b1, b0] are written into third row by turning on WL2. The memory cells in Row 1 are reserved for carry bit iterations. Sum S_n and Carry C_n will be produced for n iterations.

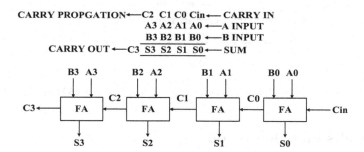

Fig. 4. A four-bit ripple carry adder

Table 2. Execution table for 4-bit ripple carry adder

n	Cycle	Inputs Q2n Q1n Q0n	ADC inputs	ADC outputs D1 D0
1	Write	– Cin	–	
1	IMC	B0 A0 Cin	Vacc0	C0 S0
2	Write	– C0	–	
2	IMC	B1 A1 C0	Vacc1	C1 S1
3	Write	– C1	–	
3	IMC	B2 A2 C1	Vacc2	C2 S2
4	Write	– C2	–	
4	IMC	B3 A3 C2	Vacc3	C3 S3

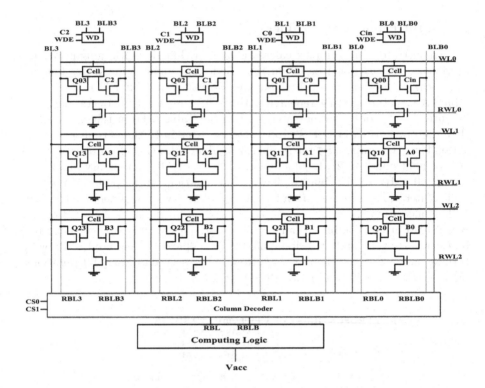

Fig. 5. A four-bit ripple carry adder using 3 × 4 SRAM array

4   Results and Discussion

Fig. 6 shows the transient simulation for addition of 1-bit for different input combinations. RBL/RBLB discharge for different input combinations for inputs Cin, A, B are 0, 0, 0; 0, 0, 1; 1, 0, 1 and 1, 1, 1 at 8 to 10 ns, 20 to 22 ns, 32 to 35 ns and 44 to 46 ns respectively is shown in Fig. 6. The voltage accumulation and the outputs of the ADC are also shown. The sharing of bit-lines by large column of memory cells leads to parasitic capacitance effects. To in-corporate the parasitic capacitance, the bit-lines were loaded with 1pF capacitor each. The operating temperature was set to 27°C and simulations were performed with statistical variation of process and mismatch for all transistors of the circuit in nominal process corner. Monte Carlo simulations were performed for 1000 iterations. The primary supply voltage was set to 1 V.

The benchmarks circuits of Full Adder using Muller-C element [8], asymmetrical sense amplifier (ASA) [9] and the proposed circuit are implemented in 65nm UMC CMOS bulk technology. The designs are analyzed with figure of merits like delay, average power consumption, product of delay and power (PDP) and area. The sizing of the 8^+T SRAM, sense amplifier and write driver are identical.

Algorithm 1. Algorithm for n-bit Ripple Carry Adder

Data: n-bit of two integers: $a_n,a_{n-1},a_{n-2},....,a_1,a_0$; $b_n,b_{n-1},b_{n-2},....,b_1,b_0$, where a and b are the inputs to FA. An array of SRAM with size $3 \times n$, voltage source V_{DD}, Compute Logic, ADC.

WL0 is the word line control at row 0.

RWL0,1 and 2 is the read word line control at row 0,1 and 2 respectively.

Q0i, Q1i and Q2i - is the value stored at array position (0,i), (1,i) and (2,i) respectively.

Result: Final sum bits S_i, $0 \leq i \leq n$ and Carry out C_i; where S_i is the Sum output of the FA at i^{th} position, C_i is the carry out the n-bit FA.

initialize Carry = Cin;

for i = 0 to n-1 **do**

        WL0 < − Turn on % Write - propagating carry

        Q0i < − Carry

        RWL0,1,2 < − Turn on % IMC

        S_i,C_i = Q0i + Q1i + Q2i;

        Carry = C_i;

end

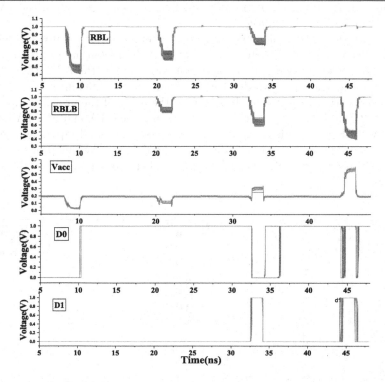

Fig. 6. Monte Carlo simulations for SA_{OUT} and SA_{OUTB} outputs for input cases - 00, 01/10, 11 for a) b) c) NOR/OR logic operations.

4.1 Delay

Delay is calculated in terms of time taken for propagation of the input to get the final outputs. In our proposed circuit, the total delay is the sum of the time taken for the RBL/RBLB to discharge to 50% of its required voltage when RWL is enabled and the minimum time taken to convert the analog signal to digital output. For the Muller-C element circuit, the total delay is calculated as the sum of RBL/RBLB discharge delay, sum delay (XOR output delay by Muller-C and XOR logic gate delay for input Cin) and carry delay (delay in the logic gates used to calculate carry). For asymmetrical SA circuit, the total delay is calculated as the sum of RBL/RBLB discharging, sense amplifier delay for generating AND/OR logic, NOR gate delay (XOR output of input A and B), sum delay (XOR output delay for input Cin) and carry delay.

The delay for the Muller-C FA circuit is higher than other FA, since there is a need of maximum discharge of RBL/RBLB for getting the XOR output, while in case of ASA FA the XOR output depends on SA, there is no need of maximum discharge. A minimum voltage difference can be sensed by the SA and the delay of ASA FA is reduced.

The proposed circuit does not require any external logic gates for getting the FA output. Thus these logic gates delays are eliminated in our proposed FA and we are achieving minimum delay when compared to the ASA FA and MC FA. Figure 7 a) and b) shows the delay distribution for different supply voltage and process corner respectively. In Fig. 7 a), the delay of the proposed circuit is about 19.2% and 36.43% lower than the asymmetrical FA and MC FA circuit respectively. This delay is calculated at the worst case of all inputs as one and SS (slow-slow) process corner. In Fig. 7 b), the delay at various process corner like SS, FS (fast-slow), TT (typical-typical), FF (fast-fast) and SF (slow-fast) are shown.

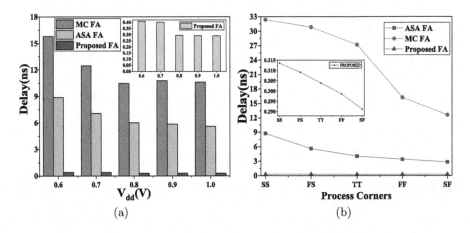

Fig. 7. a) Delay distribution at different supply voltage b)Total delay at different process corners for MC FA, ASA FA and the proposed FA.

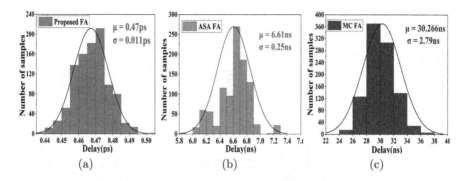

Fig. 8. Monte Carlo Simulation across SS process corner for the proposed FA, ASA FA and MC FA under 3 sigma variation in nominal V_{DD}.

The fast process corner has the shortest delay, whereas the typical and slow process corners has nominal and worst delay respectively. Thus at SS process corner, the delay is maximum.

Figure 8 shows the delay distribution of the proposed circuit, MC FA and ASA FA for 1000 iterations of Monte-Carlo analysis. The statistical variations of process and mismatch were applied to all the transistors in the circuit with 3 sigma variations for the SS process corner. With this regards to variability, the proposed circuit has least standard deviation of 0.011 ps when compared to the ASA FA and MC FA with standard deviation of 0.25 ns and 2.79 ns respectively.

4.2   Power Dissipation and PDP

The average power consumed during the read and write cycle is measured as power dissipation. For different V_{DD}, the average power consumption are measured for Muller-C, ASA and the proposed FA circuit. The total number of transistors required for computing 1-bit FA is around 44 (which includes two SAs, NOR gate, XOR gate for getting final sum with Cin, NAND and AND gates for carry output and two memory cell for storing the input) and 32 (which includes Muller-C circuit for XOR, inverters for getting NAND and NOR, XOR gate for Sum and NAND, AND gates for carry output and two memory cells to store the inputs) for ASA and Muller-C circuit respectively. The proposed FA circuit needs three memory cells, three transistors for the compute logic and two-bit ADC. Since MC FA has higher number of transistors, and more switching of data happens from RBL discharge to XOR output from Muller-C element and then to XOR gate output, the power consumption is greater than ASA FA and proposed FA. In case of ASA FA, the number of transistors is more than the proposed FA circuit. Thus ASA FA has greater power consumption when compared to proposed FA. Fig 9 a) shows the average power consumption at different supply voltage for the MC FA, ASA FA and proposed FA.

PDP is calculated as the product of delay and power. PDP is correlated with energy efficiency or the switching energy of the circuit. From Fig. 9 b), we con-

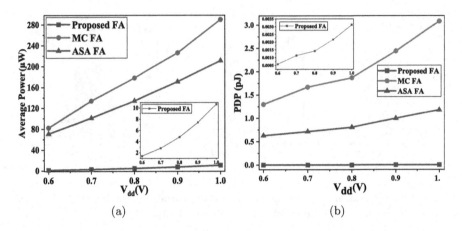

Fig. 9. a) Average power consumption b) PDP of MC FA, ASA FA and the proposed FA circuit at different supply voltage.

clude that proposed FA circuit consumes less switching energy when compared to ASA FA and MC FA.

4.3   Area Analysis

The custom layout for the proposed FA has been designed, and the array has been created using the 65nm UMC technology process, as shown in Fig. 10. The circuit's area is 36.33 μm^2, with three memory cells and an accumulating circuit. The ASA FA (MC FA) has a surface area of 209.81 μm^2 (113.19 μm^2), which is 5.77× (3.12×) that of the proposed circuit. The proposed FA requires an ADC to transform the accumulated analog voltage to digital output in order to compute the FA Sum and Carry. ADC functionality is emulated using VerilogA code. Even after taking ADC into consideration, the suggested FA takes up less space because only one ADC is required for each cycle. When we envision it for more than a single bit, the logic gates take up more space.

The performance comparison of the MC FA [8], ASA FA [9] and the proposed FA are listed in Table 3.

Table 3. Performance Comparison with Cell Type, Delay, Power , PDP and Area for all three designs

	Cell Type, XOR Method	Delay (ns)	Power (μ W)	PDP (pJ)	Area (μm^2)
[8]	8$^+$T, Muller-C Element	10.60	290	3.08	113.19
[9]	8$^+$T, 2 SAs per column	5.60	211	1.18	209.82
This work	8$^+$T, –	0.29	10.70	0.00312	36.33

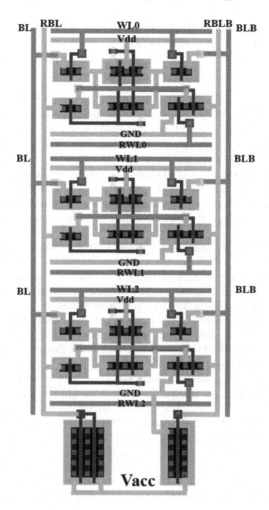

Fig. 10. Layout of proposed analog FA.

5 Conclusion

In this work, we have presented a novel method to perform Full Adder based on analog addition in 8^+T SRAM to obtain IMC and have compared the proposed FA design with Muller-C FA and ASA FA. The output logic is determined based on the voltage discharge in bit-lines with respect to value stored in the memory cell. A simple computing logic has been implemented to accumulate the discharged voltage and an ADC is used to determine the output. n-bit adders are implemented using single bit FA. The proposed FA has fast computational speed. The reliability of proposed FA circuit is compared with MC FA and ASA FA with different paramaters like delay, power consumption, PDP and area.

From all these comparisons, proposed FA stands superior than other FAs and eliminates the need of more peripheral logic gates.

References

1. Kautz, W.H.: Cellular logic-in-memory arrays. IEEE Trans. Comput. C-18(8), 719–727 (1969). https://doi.org/10.1109/T-C.1969.222754
2. Kogge, P.M., Bass, S.C., Brockman, J.B., Chen, D.Z., Sha, E.: Pursuing a petaflop: point designs for 100 TF computers using PIM technologies. In: Proceedings of 6th Symposium on the Frontiers of Massively Parallel Computation (Frontiers 1996), pp. 88–97 (1996). https://doi.org/10.1109/FMPC.1996.558065
3. Bavikadi, S., et al.: A review of in-memory computing architectures for machine learning applications. In: Proceedings of the 2020 on Great Lakes Symposium on VLSI (2020)
4. LeCun, Y., Bengio, Y., Hinton, G.: Deep learning. Nature **521**(7553), 436–444 (2015)
5. Ankit, A., Chakraborty, I., Agrawal, A., Ali, M., Roy, K.: Circuits and architectures for in-memory computing-based machine learning accelerators. IEEE Micro. **40**(6), 8–22 (2020). https://doi.org/10.1109/MM.2020.3025863
6. Biswas, A., Chandrakasan, A.P.: Conv-RAM: an energy-efficient SRAM with embedded convolution computation for low-power CNN based machine learning applications. In: 2018 IEEE International Solid-State Circuits Conference-(ISSCC), pp. 488–490 Tech. Papers (2018)
7. Dutt, S., Nandi, S., Trivedi, G.: Analysis and design of adders for approximate computing. ACM Trans. Embedd. Comput. Syst. (TECS) **17**(2), 1–28 (2017)
8. Song, S., Kim, Y.: Novel in-memory computing circuit using muller C-element, In: Proceedings of the 2021 18th International SoC Design Conference (ISOCC), Jeju Island, Korea, 6–9 October, pp. 81–82 (2021)
9. Song, S., Kim, Y.: Novel in-memory computing adder using 8+T SRAM. Electronics **11**(6), 929 (2022). https://doi.org/10.3390/electronics11060929
10. Zhang, J., Wang, Z., Verma, N.: In-memory computation of a machine-learning classifier in a standard 6T SRAM array. IEEE J. Solid-State Circ. **52**(4), 915–924 (2017)
11. Kang, M., Gonugondla, S.K., Patil, A., Shanbhag, N.R.: A multi-functional in-memory inference processor using a standard 6T SRAM array. IEEE J. Solid-State Circ. **53**(2), 642–655 (2018). https://doi.org/10.1109/JSSC.2017.2782087
12. Jaiswal, A., Chakraborty, I., Agrawal, A., Roy, K.:8T SRAM cell as a multi-bit dot product engine for beyond von-Neumann computing (2018). arXiv:1802.08601. http://arxiv.org/abs/1802.08601
13. Yang, J., et al.: 24.4 Sandwich-RAM: an energy-efficient in-memory BWN architecture with pulse-width modulation. In: 2019 IEEE International Solid- State Circuits Conference - (ISSCC), pp. 394–396 (2019). https://doi.org/10.1109/ISSCC.2019.8662435

Digital Design

MANA:Multi-Application Mapping onto Mesh Network-on-Chip using ANN

Jitesh Choudhary[1,2]([⊠]) [ID], Vishesh Bindal[3] [ID], and J. Soumya[1] [ID]

[1] BITS-Pilani, Hyderabad Campus, Hyderabad, India
soumyaj@hyderabad.bits-pilani.ac.in
[2] Centre for Development of Advanced Computing, Pune, India
jiteshchoudhary@gmail.com
[3] National Institute of Technology, Kurukshetra, India

Abstract. Parallel computing and many-core Network-on-Chip (NoC) technology are increasingly popular to accelerate performance. One way to accomplish this is by simultaneously deploying multiple applications on the NoC. Applications are deployed in NoCs using application mapping, which is considered a critical design process due to its NP-hard nature. The application mapping problem has been addressed in many ways. However, most of the efforts have focused on single application mapping, and only a few multi-application mapping approaches have been developed. This work proposes a multi-application mapping approach based on Artificial Neural Networks (ANN) for mesh NoC. In order to evaluate the mapping strategy, communication costs and CPU runtime are taken into account. Our approach is able to reduce communication costs by 80% or more than the communication cost reported in the literature.The proposed approach results demonstrated that the proposed approach could solve application mapping problems without high complexity or computational cost. In future works, the proposed approach will be integrated with a reconfigurable approach for solving multi-application problems with better performance parameters.

Keywords: Network-on-chip · Multi-application mapping · Optimization · Artificial neural network

1 Introduction

In last few decades, System-on-Chip (SoC) has revolutionized the electronic system design and enhanced the computing power manifold. A single SoC can integrate hundreds of cores and have multiple applications integrated on the same chip to be cost-effective [13]. In a multi-application system despite sharing many hardware components, different applications on SoC may have very different communication requirements and design constraints [13]. To fulfill the communication requirements of SoCs, a communication-centric paradigm, i.e., Network-on-Chip (NoC), has been adopted and has become the basic building block of SoC design in quick time [13].

© The Author(s), under exclusive license to Springer Nature Switzerland AG 2022
A. P. Shah et al. (Eds.): VDAT 2022, CCIS 1687, pp. 277–291, 2022.
https://doi.org/10.1007/978-3-031-21514-8_24

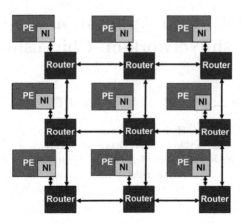

Fig. 1. NoC Architecture [5]

As shown in Fig. 1, NoCs are integrated networks that use routers to connect the various processing elements (PE) in a computation network through network interfaces (NI). Data packets from PE get converted into fixed-length flow-control digits (flits) by NI. The array of flits is routed hop-by-hop from one router to another router [16]. Computing in the present and future will be largely parallelized on many cores SoC [13]. To support parallelism, multiple applications can be deployed on different regions of the NoC [8]. Increasing PEs and data traffic between them on the SoC present newer challenges for optimizing application mapping, routing, scheduling, power management, and reliability in NoC design [5].

Application mapping is considered as one of the most critical design processes in the NoC design. It directly impact the communication cost, traffic congestion and latency in multi-core processors. It has been shown that optimizing the mapping may enhance NoC performance by up to 60 % [4]. The application mapping problem is known as an NP-hard quadratic assignment problem because with increasing system size, the search space for the problem grows exponentially [5]. An efficient SoC supports all the requirements of the applications running on it. As the SoC has more than one application requirement, it is necessary to allocate the cores to the network routers in an efficient manner so that the performance metrics of all applications are optimized.

Various mathematical formulations, heuristics, and meta-heuristic methods have been investigated to solve the application mapping problem. The most precise technique is mathematical programming, but increase in execution time as the size of the network increases poses a serious disadvantage. The heuristic approach takes the least amount of time to execute, but it is prone to get stuck in local minima. Researchers are exploring novel techniques to overcome the limitations of existing approaches, and Artificial Neural Networks (ANN) models have shown promising results in addressing problems like application mapping [3].

During the search process, heuristics generate a large volume of data that carry useful knowledge, such as the properties of good and bad solutions, the performance of different operators at different stages of the search process, precedence of search operators, etc. Classical heuristic does not use any of the knowledge hidden in these data. Machine Learning (ML) techniques can extract useful knowledge from data generated during the search process. Incorporating such knowledge into the search process improves model performance in terms of solution quality, convergence rate, and robustness. On the basis of above discussion, our novel contributions in this work are as follows:

- Proposing an ANN model for Multi-application mapping on Mesh NoC.
- Developing an ANN model for Multi-application mapping with optimum communication cost.

This paper presents related work in Sect. 2. Section 3 presents the problem formulation, followed by proposed method in Sect. 4. The experimental results along with their analysis are discussed in Sect. 5. Section 6 has the conclusion of the presented work.

2   Related Work

Several studies on the application mapping problem have been conducted in recent years. However, most of these studies have focused on single application mapping, and only a few multi-application mapping approaches have been developed.

The problem of multi-application NoC mapping is addressed in [12] using an adaptive multi-objective algorithm. Latency and power consumption are the targeted objective functions. A platform-aware design flow for multi-application mapping onto tiled NoCs is presented in [18]. Single application heuristics are incorporated into the proposed methodology to provide accurate mapping for multi-applications. In [11] author proposes an approach to map multi-application on NoC using reliability-aware techniques. Three steps are outlined in this technique. First, generate a new core graph with spares from a given application core graph. Then, a heuristic algorithm is used to find the smallest rectangular area where the application should be placed. Finally, a region is selected with optimal overall performance and the lowest amount of communication energy during the search.

In [7], the author proposes a meta-heuristic-based approach for mapping applications onto a multiprocessor platform based on NoCs. In [9], a mesh topology-based reconfigurable NoC architecture is proposed for application mapping. A two-phase procedure where the cores of the combined application set are tentatively mapped to individual routers in the first phase. In second phase individual core positions are decided for each application. A reconfigurable architecture based on configuration switches is proposed in [14]. Integer Linear Programming (ILP) and Particle Swarm Optimization (PSO) based reconfiguration strategies and mapping have been developed for the proposed architecture. For

NoC design, a multi-phase, multi-application mapping strategy is presented in [8]. Rectangle analysis is first performed on a variety of prospective application areas. Then, using a genetic algorithm, all application tasks are mapped into these prospective zones, and the best performing one is identified. A simulated annealing approach is utilised to establish the ideal multi-application map layout after identifying the packeted zones for each application.

For multi-application mapping, all of the studies mentioned above used either heuristic, meta-heuristic, nature-inspired, or genetic approaches and could produce optimal solutions with high accuracy. However, ANN was also used for solving NP-Hard problems by several researchers in the previous decade to achieve high accuracy at a lower cost of computation than the heuristic. It enables model to learn the parameters of a function from a small number of optimization trials and could result in novel approaches in solving optimization problems [1].

3   Problem Formulation

This work uses ANN for multi-application mapping on a mesh NoC with an objective of minimizing communication cost. Communication cost is defined as the sum of the product of the number of bits transferred per second between the source and destination routers and the number of hops between them [5]. The XY routing algorithm determines the path and distance (number of hops) between the source and destination routers for data communication [5]. The objective of mapping a single application is to determine an appropriate position for each application task based on specific performance metrics. However, in multi-application scenarios, the problem is extended to include searching for the best placement for all individual applications. To formulate the mapping problem, we require the following definitions.

3.1   Definition 1: Combined Application Core Graph

The communication information in application is represented by communication graph (CG). CG is a directed graph and can be used to represent a single application communication graph $G(C, E)$. Each edge $e_{ij} \in E$ represents the logical link between the two processing cores in application which are represented by vertex $c_i, c_j \in C$. Every edge has a single attribute, B, represents the amount of communication bandwidth in bits per seconds(bps). The combined application core graph is defined as a set of applications $S = (CG_1, CG_2, \ldots CG_n)$, where n is the number of given applications in multi-application environment. The node set $C = (C_1 \cup C_2 \cup \ldots \cup C_n)$ is the set of cores required for the entire set of applications. An edge e is included in E only if $e \in E_i$ for at least one application CG_i. The total weight of an edge e is equal to the sum of weights of all such edges in the whole application set as shown in Eq. (1) [14].

$$Weight\,(e) = \sum_{i=1}^{n} (Weight\,of\,e\,in\,E\,_i) \tag{1}$$

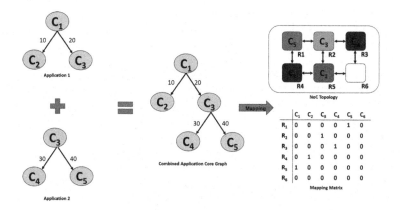

Fig. 2. Multi-application Mapping

Fig. 2 is an example of a combined application core graph. The purpose of creating combined application core graph is to identify the cores requiring high bandwidth for communication so that they can be placed as close as possible.

3.2   Definition 2: NoC Topology

The targeted NoC platform is a homogeneous 2-D m × n mesh, consists of routers R and physical links L. In mesh topologies, all routers are linked to one another in a grid like structure. An NoC platform is modeled as a Topology Graph (TG). A TG is a directed graph $TG(R, L)$, where R denotes the set of routers in NoC corresponding to vertices of the TG and L denotes the set of physical links l_{ij} between nodes i and j in NoC corresponding to edges of the TG. X-Y deterministic routing allows data to be moved in the X-direction first, and then in the Y-direction over the NoC. Under these assumptions, the communication distance D_{ij} is calculated using Eq. (2) [5].

$$d_{ij} = \mid x_i - x_j \mid + \mid y_i - y_j \mid \tag{2}$$

where (x_i, y_i) and (x_j, y_j) represent the coordinates of the routers r_i and r_j respectively. A mesh topology of 2×3 is shown in Fig. 2.

3.3   Definition 3: Objective Function

The proposed multi-application mapping algorithm aims to achieve optimal communication costs for each application when multiple applications are mapped on the NoC. Minimizing the communication cost can reduce network delay and energy usage for any application [17]. The Communication cost of multiple applications in this work is the sum of the communication cost of all applications on the NoC, i.e., the sum of products of communication bandwidth $b_{i,j}$, it represents the communication bandwidth between the nodes c_i to c_j in CG and the

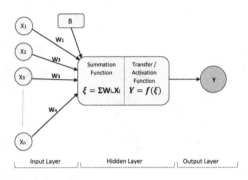

Fig. 3. Generic ANN model [2]

communication distance $d_{i,j}$ within each application. The communication cost is defined as follows:

$$Comm.Cost = \sum_{i=1}^{n}(No.\,of\,Hops\,*\,Bandwidth)$$

$$= (\sum_{i=1}^{n}\sum_{i=1}^{n}d_{ij}*l_{ij})*(\sum_{k=1}^{n}\sum_{m=1}^{n}e_{km}*b_{km}) \qquad (3)$$

It is implied by Eq. (3) that to minimize communication cost we have to minimize distance between cores of each application. Figure 2 shows an example of multi-application mapping on mesh NoC.

The multi-application mapping problem can be defined as follows: Given a set of applications $S = (CG_1, CG_2, CG_3, ...CG_n)$ and an NoC platform, identify a mapping region on the NoC for each CG where all cores in CG can be placed such that the best performance in terms of minimized communication cost is achieved. Consequently, all applications are placed at the optimal mapping regions, so that the space required to accommodate all applications is reduced. Mapping is a type of sequence-to-sequence modelling that uses sorting to find the best core placement in an NoC topology. The number of cores in combined application core graph should be less than the number of routers in TG and each core can be mapped to only one router for a correct application mapping. The process of multi-application mapping is depicted in Fig. 2. S has two applications represented by application 1 (CG1) and application 2 (CG2). Both the CGs have three cores each, and TG has a 2×3 mesh topology. The mapping is done by rearranging the application cores c_1 to c_5 in the combined application core graph onto the routers r_1 to r_6 of NoC topology to reduce communication costs.

4 Proposed Method

To achieve the goals of minimum communication cost and minimum mapping area for the applications on the NoC platform in a multi-application scenario,

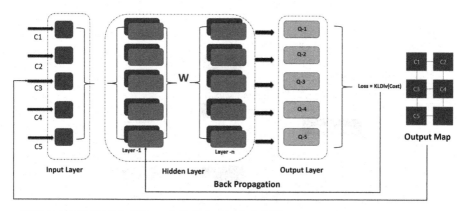

Where, C_i = Core; W =Weights for ANN layers; Q_i= Router-Core Mapping Probability

Fig. 4. Proposed ANN Model Architecture

we proposed an *ANN-based multi-application mapping* approach. The proposed approach is a static application mapping approach and is described in the Algorithm 1 and shown in Figs. 4 and 5. The proposed approach consists of three phases: Data preparation, Mapping Search and Optimization. Data preparation analyzes the input applications and NoC topology for a given multi-application environment and transforms them into the required input format. The ANN model is used to find optimal application mapping with minimized communication costs in the mapping search phase. After the search phase is over, the resultant mapping is further checked for any possible optimization using heuristic method.

Artificial Neural Network: ANN has been successfully applied to various optimization problems. ANN is a good alternative for traditional heuristic and metaheuristic algorithms [1]. The ANNs are a set of algorithms that intent to identify patterns, relationships, and information in data using a process inspired by the human brain's approach of learning. In a mapping process, ANN adjusts its weights with each iteration to find the best placement for cores in the application. The essential components of an ANN consists of the input layer, hidden layers, and output layer. In the ANN, the data processing part happened in the hidden layer. The summation and the activation are the two functions performed by a hidden layer. The summation function is the first task where sum of the product of each input (X) to ANN with its respective weight (W) is added with bias of the ANN model. The bias and weighted sum of the inputs together regulate the neuron's output. The activation function is the second task; which transformed output of summation function module into an output of a node in ANN model. Figure 3 shows a generic ANN model.

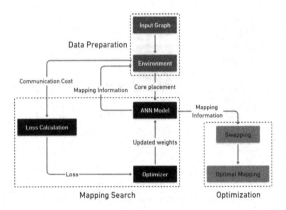

Fig. 5. Proposed ANN Model Flowchart

4.1 Data Preparation

The multi-application communication graph is initially transformed into an appropriate input for ANN; otherwise, the neural network will not produce accurate results. Data preparation entails combining multiple raw data inputs into a single ANN input. Bandwidth and adjacency matrix are also prepared, and a random mapping of cores on NoC is generated to give as input to the next stage, i.e., the mapping search stage.

4.2 Mapping Search

In the proposed approach, ANN is provided with application mapping data but not the desired outputs. ANN itself decides which features must transform the input data into the desired output. This type of learning is often referred to as self-organization or adaptation. In this phase, the weights of the neural connections are calibrated using a feedback loop. All neurons of a given layer generate an output, but they do not have the same weight for the next layer. A high weight indicates that input is significant, while a low weight indicates less significant input. There are two main types of neural networks: batch updating and incremental updating. A batch updating neural network needs all the data at once, whereas an incremental network requires one data point at a time.

Our proposed work uses incremental neural networks, in which each mapping generated in the previous iteration becomes the input for the next iteration. The loss is back-propagated into the ANN to adjust the weights of ANN for the next iteration and update the mapping data. Loss is the function of difference between ideal cost and observed cost and calculated using KL Divergence loss function [10]. The network processes the initial mapping data as the training data, using the weights and functions in the hidden layers and generates the probability matrix for different router-core pairing. Model uses probability matrix to predict the next mapping and calculate the communication cost. Calculated loss is then

---

Algorithm 1: Multi-application Mapping

Input : Combined Application Core Graph and
Mesh NoC Topology
Output: Mapping of Routers and Cores

---

1 Initialize $Map = 0$, Obs = 0, Comm.Cost = 0, Best.cost = min. cost of
application, loss = 0, I = No. of Iterations
2 Initialize ANN model and NoC Topology
3 $Map \leftarrow$ Random(Cores,Routers)
4 **for** $i \leftarrow 1$ **to** I **do**
5     $Obs \leftarrow$ model (Map)
6     $Map \leftarrow$ prob2map (Obs)
7     $Comm.Cost \leftarrow$ Cost(Map)
8     $loss \leftarrow$ KLDiv(Best.Cost - Comm.Cost)
9     $Model \leftarrow$ Optimize (loss)
10 $Map \leftarrow$ Swap (Map)
11 $Comm.Cost \leftarrow$ Cost(Map)
12 **return** Map, Comm.Cost

---

back propagated into the model, forcing the model to adjust its weights. This
process is repeated and weights are continually updated till all the iterations get
completed.

4.3 Optimization

During the optimization process, the loss function in ANN encounters two types
of issues: saddle points and local minima, and sometimes the loss function does
not improve and gets stuck in solution space. As a result, we used heuristics to
ensure that the solution arrived was optimal, and if it is not, heuristics would
improve the outcome. As a result, the near optimal mapping obtained after the
search phase is further optimized for any potential reduction in communication
costs and core placement area using core swapping.

5 Experimental Results

This section discusses the results obtained from the proposed method and analyzes them. Experiments are performed on both embedded and synthetic benchmark applications to evaluate the proposed multi-application mapping approach.
To verify the efficiency of our approach, we used the approach described in [14]
as a reference.

Table 1. Comparison of Communication Cost of Proposed Approach with Approach [14] for Benchmark Applications

Multi-Application	Combined Core Graph Size	Common Core	NoC Mesh Size	No. of Cores	Parameter	Before Reconfiguration ILP [14]	Before Reconfiguration PSO [14]	Our Approach
MPEG + MWD	21	3	5 X 5	MPEG = 12	Cost (Mb/s)	22386	21882	3570
					Normalized Cost to PSO	1.02	1.00	0.16
					Time (s)	91.75	0.45	14.10
				MWD = 12	Cost (Mb/s)	10560	9792	1920
					Normalized Cost to PSO	1.08	1.00	0.20
					Time (s)	91.69	0.40	14.10
MP3_ENC + 263_DEC + 263_ENC	39	13	5 x 6	MP3_ENC= 13	Cost (Mb/s)	106.44	103.00	19.97
					Normalized Cost to PSO	1.03	1.00	0.19
					Time (s)	247.23	0.87	37.11
				263_DEC = 14	Cost (Mb/s)	133.62	131.00	23.94
					Normalized Cost to PSO	1.02	1.00	0.18
					Time (s)	265.86	1.03	37.11
				263_ENC = 12	Cost (Mb/s)	1382.88	1392.00	231.52
					Normalized Cost to PSO	0.99	1.00	0.17
					Time (s)	239.03	0.49	37.11

Table 2. Comparison of Communication Cost of Proposed Approach with Approach [14] for Synthetic Graphs

Multi-Application	Combined Core Graph Size	Common Core	NoC Mesh Size	No. of Cores	Parameter	Before Reconfiguration ILP [14]	Before Reconfiguration PSO [14]	Our Approach
G_1 + G_2 + G_3	30	2	6 x 5	G_1 = 19	Cost (Mb/s)	-	185574	30512.40
					Normalized Cost to PSO	-	1.00	0.16
					Time (s)	-	11.92	56.78
				G_2 = 11	Cost (Mb/s)	-	87950	13916.62
					Normalized Cost to PSO	-	1.00	0.16
					Time (s)	-	0.72	56.78
				G_3 = 10	Cost (Mb/s)	-	74370	12925
					Normalized Cost to PSO	-	1.00	0.17
					Time (s)	-	0.53	56.78
G_1 + G_2 + G_4	60	17	7 x 7	G_1 = 19	Cost (Mb/s)	-	198498	38437.13
					Normalized Cost to PSO	-	1.00	0.19
					Time (s)	-	13.02	88.18
				G_2 = 11	Cost (Mb/s)	-	163593	17833.91
					Normalized Cost to PSO	-	1.00	0.11
					Time (s)	-	1.01	88.18
				G_4 = 30	Cost (Mb/s)	-	439299	79341.28
					Normalized Cost to PSO	-	1.00	0.18
					Time (s)	-	25.27	88.18

- Data Not Available

Table 3. Communication Cost of Random Graphs for Scalability

Multi Applica-tion	Combined Core Graph Size	Common Core	NoC Mesh Size	No. of Cores	Ideal Cost (Mb/s)	Cost (Mb/s)	Time (s)
G_5 + G_6	100	88	10x10	G_5 = 60	23283	53244	851
				G_6 = 40	34808	82600	851
G_7 + G_8	250	215	16x16	G_7 = 100	57936	499708	18751
				G_8 = 150	81153	808881	18751

5.1   Experimental Setup

Python is used to develop and simulate the proposed work, and it is executed on a computer with a 2.0 GHz Intel(R) Core(TM) i7-4790 processor and 16 GB of RAM. The embedded benchmark applications used for evaluation are MPEG, MWD, 263ENC, MP3ENC, and 263DEC [15], and synthetic applications are generated using TGFF Tool [6]. Many multi-applications are evaluated using the proposed approach, and the sequence of input applications is randomly created using embedded benchmark and synthetic applications. In order to conduct the experiments, the following NoC configuration was considered:

- Traffic: Application Specific
- Channel width: 32 bits
- Packet size: 64 flits
- Buffer Length: 8 flits
- Flit size: 32 bits
- Router Type: Wormhole

5.2   Results and Performance Analysis

The results of the proposed approach as well as the results of the reconfiguration approach in [14] , are presented in Tables 1 and 2. Synthetic benchmarks G1, G2, G3, and G4 generated using the TGFF tool are combined with the well-known embedded benchmarks MP3 ENC, 263 DEC, 263 ENC, MPEG4 and MWD for evaluation. For example, by combining the application graphs of MPEG4 and MWD, a new application MPEG4 + MWD, has been created. "MPEG4 (MPEG4 + MWD)" in the table denotes the scenario in which the applications MPEG4 and MWD are merged, and the communication cost for MPEG4 is indicated. The same notation applies to all other table entries. The results of the reconfiguration approach in [14] have been taken as a reference for evaluating the performance of the proposed approach.

During literature survey we are unable to find similar type of work for comparison. In most of the multi-application mapping approaches network latency and power consumption have been used as the performance metrics instead of communication cost. In [14] although the reconfiguration approach is used to improve the communication cost but before doing the reconfiguration, authors have created an optimized mapping for the given applications and then the reconfiguration is done at hardware level. The proposed work can replace the optimization algorithm used in before reconfiguration case of [14] to improve the results. The presented work can be extended and integrated with reconfigurable approach for solving multi-application problem with better performance parameters. Comparison with before reconfiguration results of [14] is done to evaluate performance of proposed approach. Before reconfiguration results mentioned in the [14] are relevant for comparison with proposed approach as it calculated communication cost in similar manner using optimization algorithm like ILP and PSO.

The mesh sizes for the applications mapping are not disclosed by the authors in [14]. Hence the smallest mesh topology results are assumed for evaluation. In all circumstances, the approach presented in this study produces better results than the results of approach proposed in [14]. This is because the proposed solution employs an ANN model that does not require explicit programming and unlike ILP and PSO, proposed ANN model extracts useful knowledge from search data and incorporate such knowledge into the search process which improves the model's solution quality, convergence rate, and robustness. Table 1 compares the communication costs of the proposed technique to the ILP and PSO before reconfiguration approaches described in [14].

As the size of the problem increases, ILP fails to produce output and consumes a large amount of CPU time. PSO delivered satisfactory results in a reasonable amount of time. For every benchmark application, the suggested technique is able to reduce communication cost by 80% or more than the communication cost generated with PSO before reconfiguration in [14]. The CPU time required to run the proposed technique is shown in Table 1 for reporting purpose. We cannot compare the run time results of our approach with the run time results of approach in [14] because both the approaches are evaluated on CPUs with different configuration.

Nodes and edges determine the mapping solution. As a result, random communication networks with various node degrees are also used to assess the scalability of the suggested approach and results are presented in Table 3. The suggested approach successfully maps random task graphs using the lowest mesh topology that can accommodate graph nodes. Table 2 presents the communication costs and run-time for random task graphs obtained with reconfiguration approaches in [14] and the proposed approach.

6   Conclusion and Future Scope

A multi-application mapping technique based on ANN is proposed in this paper, and communication cost is used as a performance indicator for evaluating it. The performance of several embedded benchmark applications is compared with the reconfiguration approach presented in [14]. The suggested method is scalable, as random application graphs of the size up to 250 nodes are also evaluated. The proposed method can find a solution for unseen graphs without prior training.

It indicates that the leanings of the model are generalized and suitable for any similar type of problem. Compared to the results presented in [14] proposed technique resulted in considerable reductions (more than 80%) in communication cost. The findings of the suggested technique showed that it could handle application mapping difficulties without requiring a high level of complexity or processing expenses. By simplifying and shrinking the search space, the suggested method can enhance the design exploration process and be used as a component for other optimization algorithms. In Future work, proposed approach can be integrated with the reconfigurable approach for solving multi-application problem to achieve better performance parameters.

Acknowledgements. Authors thank the Center for Development of Advanced Computing, India for their support and encouragement in doing this work.

References

1. Abdolrasol, M., et al.: Artificial neural networks based optimization techniques: a review. Electronics **10**, 2689 (2021). https://doi.org/10.3390/electronics10212689
2. Alaloul, W.S., Qureshi, A.H.: Data processing using artificial neural networks. In: Harkut, D.G. (ed.) Dynamic Data Assimilation, chap. 6. IntechOpen, Rijeka (2020). https://doi.org/10.5772/intechopen.91935. https://doi.org/10.5772/intechopen.91935
3. Amin, W., et al.: Performance evaluation of application mapping approaches for network-on-chip designs. IEEE Access **8**, 63607–63631 (2020). https://doi.org/10.1109/ACCESS.2020.2982675
4. Benini, L., Bertozzi, D.: Network-on-chip architectures and design methods. computers and digital techniques. In: IEEE Proceedings, vol. 152, pp. 261–272 (2005). https://doi.org/10.1049/ip-cdt:20045100
5. Choudhary, S.J.J., Cenkeramaddi, L.R.: Raman: reinforcement learning inspired algorithm for mapping applications onto mesh network-on-chip. In: 2021 ACM/IEEE International Workshop on System Level Interconnect Prediction (SLIP), pp. 52–58 (2021). https://doi.org/10.1109/SLIP52707.2021.00019
6. Dick, R., Rhodes, D., Wolf, W.: TGFF: task graphs for free. In: Proceedings of the Sixth International Workshop on Hardware/Software Codesign. (CODES/CASHE1998), pp. 97–101 (1998). https://doi.org/10.1109/HSC.1998.666245
7. Farias, M., Barros, E., Araújo, A.: An approach for multi-task and multi-application mapping onto NoC-based MPSoC. In: 2014 IEEE 57th International Midwest Symposium on Circuits and Systems (MWSCAS), pp. 205–208 (2014). https://doi.org/10.1109/MWSCAS.2014.6908388
8. Ge, F., Cui, C., Zhou, F., Wu, N.: A multi-phase based multi-application mapping approach for many-core networks-on-chip. Micromachines **12**(6), 613 (2021). https://doi.org/10.3390/mi12060613, https://www.mdpi.com/2072-666X/12/6/613
9. Sharma, A., Chattopadhyay, S.: Multi-application network-on-chip design using global mapping and local reconfiguration. ACM Trans. Reconfig. Technol. Syst. **7**(2), 1–24 (2014). https://doi.org/10.1145/2556944
10. Joyce, J.: Kullback-Leibler Divergence, pp. 720–722 (2011). https://doi.org/10.1007/978-3-642-04898-2_327

11. Khalili, F., Zarandi, H.R.: A reliability-aware multi-application mapping technique in networks-on-chip. In: 2013 21st Euromicro International Conference on Parallel, Distributed, and Network-Based Processing, pp. 478–485 (2013). https://doi.org/10.1109/PDP.2013.77

12. Sepúlveda, M.J., Chau, W.J., Gogniat, G., Strum, M.: A multi-objective adaptive immune algorithm for multi-application NoC mapping. Analog Integr. Circ. Sig. Process **73**(3), 851–860 (2012). https://doi.org/10.1007/s10470-012-9869-9

13. Sepúlveda, J., Strum, M., Chau, W.J., Gogniat, G.: A multi-objective approach for multi-application NoC mapping. In: 2011 IEEE Second Latin American Symposium on Circuits and Systems (LASCAS), pp. 1–4 (2011). https://doi.org/10.1109/LASCAS.2011.5750275

14. Soumya, J., Babu, K.N., Chattopadhyay, S.: Multi-application mapping onto a switch-based reconfigurable network-on-chip architecture. J. Circuits Syst. Comput. **26**(11), 1750174 (2017). https://doi.org/10.1142/S0218126617501742

15. Tosun, S., Ozturk, O., Ozkan, E., Ozen, M.: Application mapping algorithms for mesh-based network-on-chip architectures. J. Supercomput. **71**(3), 995–1017 (2014). https://doi.org/10.1007/s11227-014-1348-x

16. Tsai, W.C., Lan, Y.C., Hu, Y.H., Chen, S.J.: Networks on chips: structure and design methodologies. J. Electr. Comput. Eng. **2012**, 509465 (2011). https://doi.org/10.1155/2012/509465

17. Yang, B., Xu, T., Säntti, T., Plosila, J.: Tree-model based mapping for energy-efficient and low-latency network-on-chip, pp. 189–192 (2010). https://doi.org/10.1109/DDECS.2010.5491789

18. Zhu, G., Wang, Y.: A multi-application mapping case study for NoC-based MPSoCs, pp. 1–6 (2013). https://doi.org/10.1109/ICSPCC.2013.6664092

Metastable SR Flip-Flop Based True Random Number Generator Using QCA Technology

Abhishek Maurya, Ayush Singh, Syed Farah Naz,
and Ambika Prasad Shah$^{(\boxtimes)}$ (iD)

IC-ResQ Laboratory, Department of Electrical Engineering, Indian Institute
of Technology Jammu, Jammu 181221, Jammu and Kashmir, India
ambika.shah@iitjammu.ac.in

Abstract. In today's modern world, when security of hardware devices is a must, then hardware-based encryption architectures like physically unclonable functions (PUF) and true random number generators (TRNG) are playing a very crucial role in hardware security. These hardware security architectures are able to generate random and unpredictable keys for encryption and decryption of data. This paper proposes a new architecture of QCA technology based TRNG using SR Latch and metastability. 4 statistical NIST test have been performed on proposed TRNG. Results of the NIST test shows that proposed TRNG is generating truly random sequences.

Keywords: Hardware security · QCA · TRNG · PUF · Metastability

1 Introduction

The evolution of modern-day chip from basic few transistors to billions of transistors has been consistent with Moore's law. Things were working quite natural until the size of 5 nm, but as the technology advances, and further increases transistor density, has brought us to undesired quantum effects which are well observed when electrons tunnels less than 2 nm gate size [1]. To further increase the transistor density, the search for alternate technology had brought us to Quantum-dot cellular automata (QCA). So in QCA, the concept of polarization share between the neighboring atoms is used rather than the direct flow. QCA is the best to counter the problems like high power dissipation, hot electron effect, etc. unlike the traditional CMOS technology [2].

The most fascinating architecture is where quantum physical properties are utilized in the QCA cell architecture. As illustrated in Fig. 1, each cell is made up of four quantum dots enclosed in a square form box. $4n + 2$ numbers of electrons are entangled in dots in each cell. The excess electrons can't leave the cell, but they can tunnel between the dots inside it. Due to columbic repulsion, extra electrons are placed in two farthest dots of a cell, i.e. in a diagonal position, whenever external biasing affects the cell. A bi-stable condition exists in each QCA cell. When cell polarization is "+1", then it denotes logic "1" and when cell polarization is "-1", then it denotes logic "0" as shown in Fig. 1 [3].

A. P. Shah et al. (Eds.): VDAT 2022, CCIS 1687, pp. 292–304, 2022.
https://doi.org/10.1007/978-3-031-21514-8_25

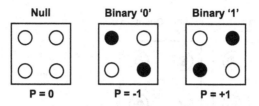

Fig. 1. QCA cells (a) No polarized, (b) +1 Polarized, (c) -1 Polarized [5].

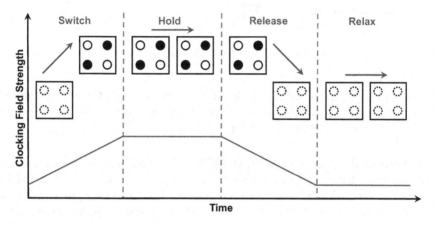

Fig. 2. Four Clocking Phases in QCA Cell [6].

1.1 Switching and Clocking in QCA

Once electrons are given enough tunneling energy, they tunnel through the inter-dot barrier; this is basically called switching the QCA technology. The clock is used to control QCA circuits. Four separate clocks are used to synchronize the modulation of distinct interdot barriers. While altering the cell states, the barriers are first decreased to achieve a ground state. The switching occurs in the ground state, resulting in minimal energy loss. The barriers are then raised, allowing cells to maintain their new state. Hence, we divide the clock in four phases: Relax Phase, Hold Phase, Release Phase and Switch Phase as shown in Fig. 2.

The barriers are lowered during the relaxing phase, allowing electrons to tunnel through junctions. The barriers begin to rise during the switch phase, and the cells begin to achieve a definite polarization. In the hold phase, potential barriers are at their highest, and cells have a distinct polarization state. Finally, in the release phase, potential barriers are reduced and cells achieve a ground state [4].

Cell Count: The number of cells employed in device modeling is revealed by this parameter. Any circuit is expected to implement any function with the

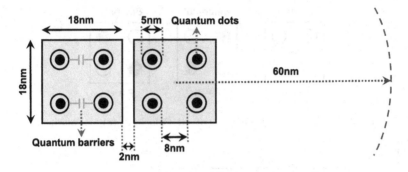

Fig. 3. Cell area and radius of effect [7].

fewest number of cells possible. The fewer the cells, however, the more prone the circuit is to failures. As a result, more cells are used to strengthen polarization, raising the value of this parameter [8].

Cell Area and Radius of Effect: QCA cells which are commonly used to design circuits have an area of 18×18 nm^2. Cell area can be calculated by multiplying area of a cell and total cell count. The perimeter under which a polarised QCA cell can show its polarisation effect to nearby QCA cells, is known as radius of effect as shown in Fig. 3.

Total Area: It determines the final chip size by providing an accurate estimate of how much space a certain cell layout would take up on a die. The area occupied by the cellular structure is just the whole length multiplied by total breadth. This measure differs from cell area in that it takes into account the 2 nm inter-cellular gap.

1.2   Hardware Security Primitives

There is always a demand to make communication systems more secure, this security in our communication system comes from encryption keys, which are none other than unpredictable, non-repeating, and highly random numbers generated by the True Random Number Generator. The highly nondeterministic and probabilistic nature of QCA cells is exploited for this purpose. Some of the hardware security primitives are:

Random Number Generator (RNG): RNG is one of the most important hardware-based encryption architecture for a secure communication system. The unpredictability of generated random numbers determines whether this RNG is generating truly random number or not. The unpredictability of generated numbers improve the device or communication's security. TRNG are used to get non-deterministic bit-stream that can be used to form a encryption key for a secure communication system [9].

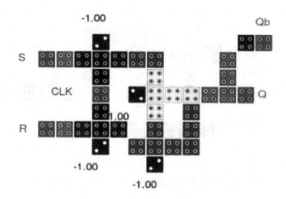

Fig. 4. SR flip-flop used for TRNG implementation [10].

Physically Unclonable Function (PUF): A unique and creative technique for encrypting data uses physically unclonable functions as hardware security primitives. Identification of identical devices can be done using PUF by creating challenge-response pairs. PUFs are made by exploiting the defects in QCA designs during fabrication [9].

The organization of this paper is as follows: Sect. 2 presents the SR Flip Flop and the metastability used for proposed 8-bit TRNG. Section 3 presents the TRNG unit and architectural circuit diagram model and the QCA circuit design. Section 4 discusses the results and discussion of the proposed circuit design. Section 5 presents the conclusion.

2 SR Flip Flop and the Metastability

There is a lot of research going on to get new designs of TRNG using different methods. In this paper, a TRNG is designed using SR Flip-Flop and metastability of QCA is used to increase randomness.

2.1 SR Flip Flop

SR Flip Flop proposed in [10], shown in Fig. 4, is used to design the proposed 8-bit TRNG. It is observed that for input S = 1 and R = 1, SR Flip Flop is generating non-deterministic output on different simulations. Modified QCA structure of SR Flip Flop asshown in Fig. 5 [10] is used to construct proposed 8-bit TRNG in this paper. The simulated outputs of the modified QCA structure is shown in Fig. 6. The outputs are different after each run which indicate the variability and can be used for TRNG designs. This SR Flip Flop is constructed of 41 QCA cells with area 0.05 μm^2. The peak polarisation of Q and Qb are 0.952 and 0.948, respectively.

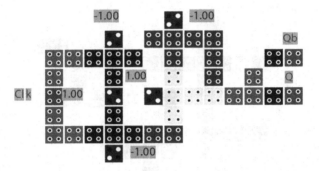

Fig. 5. Modified QCA design of SR flip-flop [10] used for proposed 8-bit TRNG implementation

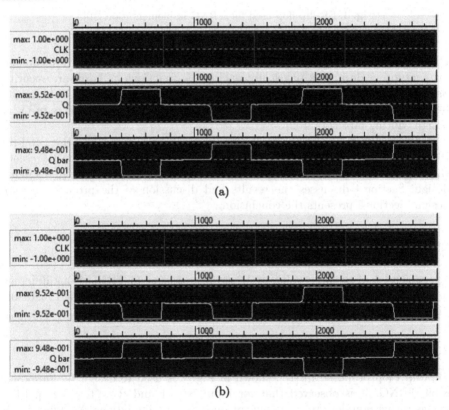

Fig. 6. Simulation results of modified QCA structure of SR flip-flop (a) output type 1 (b) output type 2 [10].

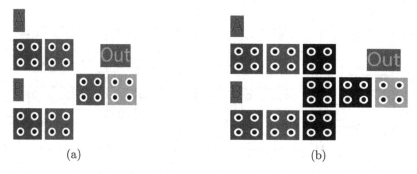

(a)   (b)

Fig. 7. (a) Metastable block A (b) Metastable block B.

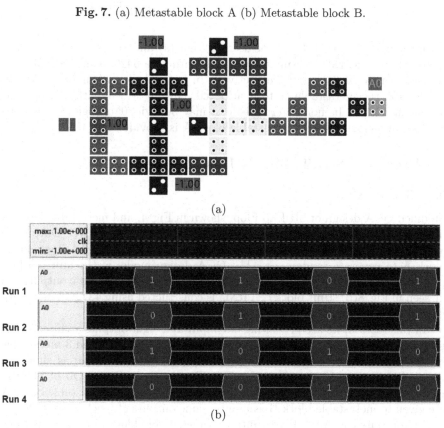

Fig. 8. (a) QCA design model of unit block of propose 8-bit TRNG, (b) Outputs of different simulations of the proposed 8-bit TRNG unit.

2.2 Metastable Blocks

Metastability of QCA is used to increase randomness in output. Two types of metastable blocks have been used in the proposed 8-bit TRNG. Metastable block

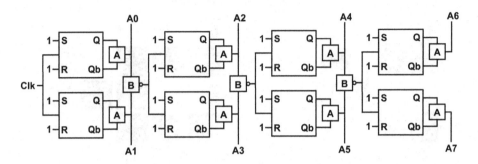

Fig. 9. Architecture model of proposed 8 bit TRNG

A and metastable block B can be seen in Fig. 7(a) and (b) respectively. Block A and B are constructed using 6 QCA cells with area 6429.57 nm^2 and 9 QCA cells with area 7966.34 nm^2, respectively. In both blocks, when AB = '01' or AB = '10', the metastable state is achieved. Output will be either A or B. It means output will be non-deterministic, it may be logic '0' or logic '1'. Detailed analysis of metastability in metastable block A is provided in [11].

3   Proposed 8-BIT TRNG Design

3.1   TRNG Unit

Modified QCA design of SR Flip Flop, shown in Fig. 4, and metastable block A of Fig. 7 are used to construct unit blocks of proposed 8-bit TRNG. Outputs Q and Qb of modified QCA design of SR Flip Flop are used as input to metastable block A to generate randomness. The QCA design model of the unit block of proposed 8-bit TRNG is given in Fig. 8(a) and its non-deterministic outputs can be seen in Fig. 8(b). Unit block of TRNG is constructed using 43 QCA cells with cell area of 0.05 μm^2. Peak polarisation of output A0 is 0.951 V.

In this section, we are presenting one input and eight outputs architecture of proposed 8 bit TRNG. 8 SR Flip Flops, 8 metastable block A and 3 metastable block B are used to construct the proposed TRNG architecture as shown in Fig. 9. Clock input is given to 2 SR Flip Flops, output Q and Qb of SR Flip Flops are given as input to metastable block A. Outputs of metastable block A are given to metastable block B as inputs, same outputs of block A are taken as TRNG outputs e.g. A0, A1 etc. Output of metastable block B is given as clock input to the next 2 SR Flip Flops. Similar process is followed to construct the proposed 8-bit TRNG.

3.2   Architecture Model

3.3   QCA Design Model of Proposed 8-Bit TRNG

In this section we have designed the QCA model of the proposed 8-bit TRNG as shown in Fig. 10. It has been constructed by cascading 8 TRNG units as shown

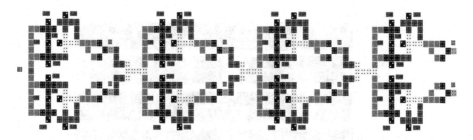

Fig. 10. QCA design model of proposed 8 bit TRNG.

Table 1. Simulation parameters of bistable approximation

Parameter	Value
Number of samples	12800
Convergence tolerance	0.001
Radius of Effect	65 nm
Relative permittivity	12.9
Clock high	9.800000e–022 J
Clock low	3.800000e–023 J
Clock shift	0.000000e+000
Clock amplitude Factor	2.000000
Layer separation	11.500000 nm
Maximum iterations per sample	100

in Fig. 8(a). 3 metastable block B are used to connect TRNG units, output of metastable block B, which is random, is given as clock input to other TRNG units. Due to non-deterministic clock input to TRNG units it generates random outputs. The proposed 8-bit TRNG design is constructed with the help of 395 QCA cells and require a total area of 0.54 μm^2.

4   Results and Discussion

The proposed QCA structures is simulated with QCADesigner version 2.0.3 using bistable approximation simulation engine [12]. The simulation parameters of bistable approximation simulation engine are kept at default values and are listed in Table 1.

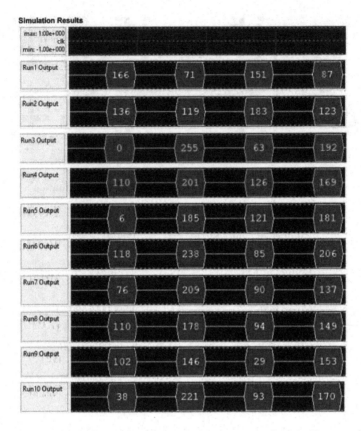

Fig. 11. Simulation waveform of random numbers generated after 10 runs of the proposed 8- bit TRNG QCA design model.

Table 2. NIST statistical test results

Statistical test	p-value
Frequency	0.772830
Block frequency	0.727272
Runs	0.470560
Longest run of ones	0.856871

4.1   Performance Analysis

We performed ten simulation runs for the output of the proposed TRNG circuit as shown in Fig. 11. From results it is observed that the proposed circuit generates random outputs for all ten simulation runs. We also performed statistical tests, proposed by the NIST [13] on generated random sequences by the proposed QCA TRNG. Proposed 8-bit TRNG was simulated multiple times to collect enough random sequences for NIST statistical tests. Bit streams of 192

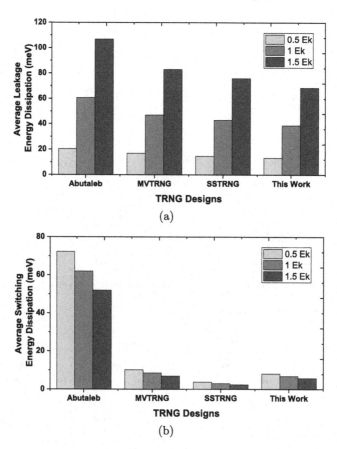

Fig. 12. Comparison with existing QCA TRNGs, Abutaleb [11], MVTRNG [5], SSTRNG [7] for (a) average leakage energy dissipation (b) average switching energy dissipation.

bits, 384 bits and 576 bits were generated by proposed 8-bit TRNG and different statistical tests were performed on these output bit streams in NIST statistical test suite. According to NIST test suite documentation, if the calculated p-value is greater than 0.01 for various statistical tests, then it means that proposed TRNG is generating random sequences. 4 out of 16 statistical tests were performed and obtained p-values are tabulated in Table 2. It is observed that p-values for all 4 performed tests is more than 0.01. Hence, it can be concluded that the proposed QCA 8-bit TRNG is generating truly random sequences.

4.2 Energy Dissipation Analysis

The energy dissipation analysis of proposed QCA 8-bit TRNG is performed on QCA Pro tool [14]. The energy dissipation per bit of various TRNG are compared in Fig. 12. It is observed that average leakage energy dissipation and average

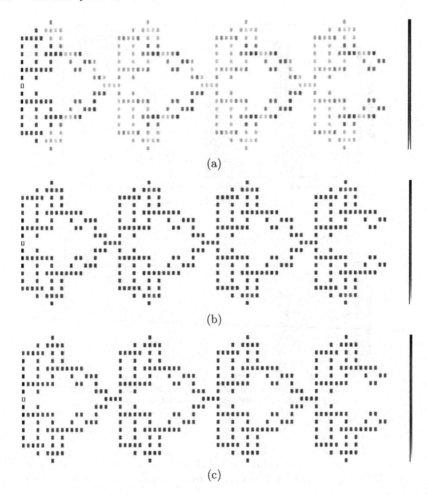

Fig. 13. Energy dissipation map at (a) 0.5 Ek (b) 1 Ek (c) 1.5 Ek.

switching energy dissipation are 38.841 meV/bit and 6.95 meV/bit, respectively at 1 E_k. Here E_k is the kink energy.

The average leakage energy dissipation and average switching energy dissipation of all the considered QCA based TRNG designs are shown in Fig. 12(a) and (b), respectively. It is observed that the proposed model has minimum average leakage energy dissipation and it is dissipating lesser average switching energy than Abutaleb [11] and MVTRNG [5]. We also evaluated the energy dissipation map of the proposed 8-bit TRNG at different kink energy $0.5E_k$, $1E_k$, and $1.5E_k$ as shown in Fig. 13. Results indicate that the average leakage energy dissipation increases with E_k. Results also indicate that the energy dissipation is maximum at the cells where seed input is applied.

5   Conclusion

A 8-bit TRNG using QCA technology is proposed in this paper. Modified QCA structure of an existing SR Flip Flop and metastable blocks are used to construct proposed 8-bit TRNG. The randomness of the proposed 8-bit TRNG is validated with the NIST statistical test suite, and the results are indicating that proposed 8-bit TRNG is generating truly random sequences. Hence, it can be used for cryptographic key generation and other security applications. Energy dissipation analysis shows that proposed TRNG is not consuming more power than existing TRNGs.

Acknowledgement. The authors would like to thank the SERB, Government of India for providing financial support under the Startup Research Grant Scheme with grant no. SRG/2021/001101.

References

1. Mann, C.C.: The End of Moore's Law?. MIT Technology Review (2000)
2. Lent, C.S. , Tougaw, P.D., Porod, W., Bernstein, G.H.: Quantum cellular automata. Nanotechnology **4**(1), 49 (1993). https://doi.org/10.1088/0957-4484/4/1/004
3. Tougaw, P., Lent, C.: Dynamic behavior of quantum cellular automata. J. Appl. Phys. **80**(8), 4722–4736 (1996)
4. Tóth, G., Lent, C.S.: Quasiadiabatic switching for metal-island quantum-dot cellular automata. J. Appl. Phys. **85**(5), 2977–2984 (1999). https://doi.org/10.1063/1.369063
5. Sadhu, A., Das, K., De, D., Kanjilal, M.R.: MVTRNG: majority voter-based crossed loop quantum true random number generator in QCA nanotechnology. In: Maharatna, K., Kanjilal, M., Konar, S., Nandi, S., Das, K. (eds.) Computational Advancement in Communication Circuits and Systems. Lecture Notes in Electrical Engineering, vol. 575. Springer, Singapore (2020). https://doi.org/10.1007/978-981-13-8687-9-22
6. Zang, H., Yuan, Y., Wei, X.: Research on pseudorandom number generator based on several new types of piecewise chaotic maps. Math. Probl. Eng. **2021**, 1–12 (2021). https://doi.org/10.1155/2021/1375346
7. Sadhu, A., Das, K., De, D., Kanjilal, M.R.: SSTRNG: self starved feedback SRAM based true random number generator using quantum cellular automata. Microsyst. Technol. **26**(7), 2203–2215 (2019). https://doi.org/10.1007/s00542-019-04525-w
8. Fazili, M.M., Shah, M.F., Naz, S.F., Shah, A.P.: Survey, taxonomy, and methods of QCA-based design techniques part II: reliability and security. Semiconduct. Sci. Technol. **37**(6), 063002 (2022)
9. Fazili, M.M., Shah, M.F., Naz, S.F., Shah, A.P.: Survey, Taxonomy, and Methods of QCA based Design Techniques - Part II: Reliability and Security (2022)
10. Chakrabarty, R., Mahato, D.K., Banerjee, A., Choudhuri, S., Dey, M., Mandal, N.K.: A novel design of flip-flop circuits using quantum dot cellular automata (QCA). In: 2018 IEEE 8th Annual Computing and Communication Workshop and Conference (CCWC), pp. 408–414 (2018). https://doi.org/10.1109/CCWC.2018.8301775

11. Abutaleb, M.: A novel true random number generator based on QCA nanocomputing. Nano Commun. Netw. **17**, 14–20 (2018). https://doi.org/10.1016/j.nancom.2018.04.001
12. Walus, K., Dysart, T., Jullien, G., Budiman, R.: QCADesigner: a rapid design and simulation tool for quantum-dot cellular automata. IEEE Trans. Nanotechnol. **3**, 26–31 (2004)
13. National institute of standards and technology (NIST), A Statistical test suite for random and pseudorandom number generators for cryptographic applications, Special Publication 800–22 (2010)
14. Srivastava, S., Asthana, A., Bhanja, S., Sarkar, S.: QCAPro-an error power estimation tool for QCA circuit design. In: IEEE International Symposium of Circuits Systems, pp. 2377–2380 (2011)

Hardware Design of Two Stage Reference Free Adaptive Filter for ECG Denoising

Priyank Prajapati$^{(\boxtimes)}$ and Anand Darji

Sardar Vallabhbhai National Institute of Technology, Surat, India
priyank.prajapati@rediffmail.com, add@eced.svnit.ac.in

Abstract. Recent trends in wearable ECG monitoring devices are focused on the early diagnosis of heart diseases. However, the artifact generated during ECG signal acquisition reduces the performance of these devices. Many methods available for artifact suppression have a limitation on hardware implementation due to high complexity. This paper analyzes a two-stage reference-free active noise cancellation (ANC) adaptive filter for optimum step-size and filter length selection to denoise the ambulatory ECG signal. The ECG denoising results show that the proposed method gives 16.04% more average output SNR and 10.61% more average MSE reduction than the existing reference-free adaptive filter design. Further, the analysis is carried out for a two-stage adaptive filter hardware design. The real-time hardware testing is performed on a spartan3E FPGA board. The results show that implemented hardware only occupies 465 slices, which is 9.46% lower resource utilization compared to the existing method on Virtex-7 FPGA. Moreover, the hardware ASIC implementation shows only 0.66 $(mm)^2$ area utilization and total 0.5 mW power consumption at 1.8 V supply and 5 kHz sampling frequency.

Keywords: Electrocardiogram · Artifact suppression · Adaptive filter · FPGA

1 Introduction

The continuous monitoring and early diagnosis of heart diseases are essential as they are the leading cause of death [1]. The portable/wearable electrocardiogram (ECG) devices are used to continuously monitor the signal and early diagnosis of cardiovascular diseases (CVDs) [19]. However, in daily life activity, ECG signal is contaminated with various artifacts due to body movement, muscle contraction, and body capacitance. The Baseline Wander (BW), Motion Artifact (MA), Electrocardiographic (EMG) and Power line noise are prevalent in wearable ECG [14,15]. The change in ECG amplitude due to noise may create vital information loss or difficulty in ECG diagnosis. Hence, artifact suppression of ECG signals has prime importance in wearable devices.

Many artifact suppression techniques are available for ECG denoising [19] such as conventional methods like FIR-IIR filters, statistical moving average filter, RLS and Kalman based adaptive filter, S-Golay filter, signal decomposition

© The Author(s), under exclusive license to Springer Nature Switzerland AG 2022
A. P. Shah et al. (Eds.): VDAT 2022, CCIS 1687, pp. 305–319, 2022.
https://doi.org/10.1007/978-3-031-21514-8_26

techniques like discrete wavelet transform (DWT), empirical mode decomposition (EMD) [3,7,14]. Further, hybrid methods such as DWT and EMD with adaptive filter variants were developed to enhance signal quality over conventional methods for ECG denoising [9,15]. The traditional methods such as FIR filter, zero-phase IIR filter, moving average filter, moving median filter, wavelet, EMD, and RLS adaptive filtering were compared for motion artifacts suppression and concluded that RLS-based adaptive filtering gives the best result among all [21]. Further, a wearable dynamic ECG system is implemented with NLMS adaptive algorithm [5] under various actions like standing still, walking slowly, squatting, and chest expanding.

The conventional filter-based method often suffers from less quality improvement due to low in-band noise reduction. The signal decomposition and hybrid methods have high computational complexity. Hence, they are not easy to implement on hardware or limited to software-based simulations as they require large storage capacity and complex hardware implementation strategy for low-power design. The hardware co-simulation plays an essential role in the fast system design cycle [2,4]. The main issue in wearable ECG denoising arises due to often occurrence of noise/artifact during activity, which highly overlaps with the ECG frequencies. Further, the low power, cost-effective, and compact stringent hardware design requirements for wearable ECG devices make it challenging. Most of the known ECG denoising hardware either utilizes huge hardware resources due to high complexity or gives poor artifact reduction results at low hardware complexity [12]. Hence, a sophisticated algorithm is required to denoise the signal effectively.

The adaptive filter-based active noise cancellation (ANC) method can be helpful for wearable hardware design because of its low computational complexity. Further, an adaptive filter without the use of an external reference (such as an accelerometer signal for low frequency (LF) artifact reduction) can be able to remove the artifact from ECG as shown in [11,15,16]. These methods will further reduce the hardware cost of wearable design. Hence, in this work, the two-stage reference-free adaptive filter technique of [11] with LMS filter is used to denoise ECG for hardware design. Further, the hardware is tested on a spartan3E FPGA board for real-time testing. Moreover, its ASIC is also designed for its post-layout verification.

The work is organized as follows; Sect. 2 briefly describes the background of the two-stage ANC structure for artifact suppression and the basics of the LMS algorithm. Section 3 shows the analysis work proposed for hardware efficient ECG denoising design. The proposed reference-free two-stage adaptive filter hardware design is discussed in Sect. 4. Further, it describes the software simulation results and comparison with existing reference-free adaptive filter-based methods. Section 5 shows the FPGA/ASIC implementation and its comparison with existing hardware. The work is concluded in the last section.

2   Background of the Methods

2.1   Reference Free Two Stage ANC Adaptive Filter Design

In the ANC technique, the reference signal is essential to denoising the signal using adaptive algorithms [6]. The reference signal is generated- through external hardware like accelerometer [13], fabric electrodes [5], FIR filtering. However, adding an external hardware interface increases the cost of wearable system design and may introduce inaccuracy if it malfunctions [21]. Hence, it is better to produce the reference signal from the noisy signal itself [12, 15]. Further, constant input as a reference with novel algorithm design can significantly reduce the hardware cost. Two-stage ANC, as shown in Fig. 1 is used in this work to reduce low frequency (LF) artifacts (i.e., BW, MA) and High frequency (HF) artifacts (i.e., in-band ECG Gaussian noise, EMG) from ECG signal [11]. The adaptive filter 1 suppresses the LF frequency artifact at $e_1(n)$ and filter 2 suppresses the HF artifact at its output $y_2(n)$ using constant step-input as a reference [11].

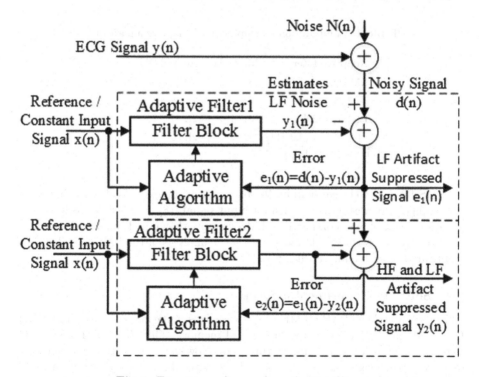

Fig. 1. Two stage reference free adaptive filter

2.2 Least Mean Squares (LMS) Adaptive Algorithm

LMS is an adaptive algorithm [6] in which the weights of the filter are updated as follows:

$$\mathbf{w}(n+1) = \mathbf{w}(n) + \mu \cdot \mathbf{x}(n) \cdot e(n) \tag{1}$$

Here, $\mathbf{w}(n)$ is the weight, μ is the step size, $e(n)$ is the error, $\mathbf{x}(n)$ is the input signal. LMS has low complexity and good signal tracking capability. Hence, it is useful for ECG signal denoising [17].

3 Two Stage Adaptive Filter Analysis

3.1 Analysis for Adaptive Filter Selection

In two-stage adaptive filter hardware design, the types of adaptive filters, their order $L-1$ (filter length L), and the step-size μ selections are crucial to denoise the signal with low complexity. For cost-effective hardware design, a computationally efficient adaptive algorithm is chosen based on Table 1.

Table 1. Computational complexity of adaptive algorithms

Adaptive filter	Multiplier	Adder	Division
LMS [6]	2L+1	2L	0
NLMS [6]	2L+1	2L+1	1
ENLMS [20]	2L+1	2L+1	1
Step-size scaler [11]	2L+2	2L+2	1

L is the filter length

LMS filter was chosen mainly due to its low complexity for hardware reduction and good denoising with constant input signal [18]. Further, it has less computational complexity compared to LMS variants shown in Table 1 and recursive least square (RLS) filter [6]. The convergence analysis of the LMS filter for constant input is stable and is shown in [11].

3.2 Software Experimental Setup

This work uses MATLAB (R2015b) software for simulation, running on Intel(R) Core(TM) i5 CPU 2.50 GHz with 6 Gb of memory. The entire MIT-BIH ECG database is used for simulation in this work. However, due to the unavailability of ground truth signals, 4000 samples of noise-free database records are used to calculate signal quality check parameters, i.e., signal to noise ratio (SNR) and mean square error (MSE). The 4000 samples (10 s) of 5 popular MIT-BIH ECG records (100, 103, 109, 115, 203) [10] and a synthetic MATLAB ECG records are used in this work at $F_s = 360$ Hz. In this work, calibrated amount of noise from noise-stress database signal BW, MA, EMG, and Gaussian noise is added to generate an experimental noisy signal [16].

3.3 Analysis for Adaptive Filter Length and Step-Size Selection

For this analysis, filter length has been varying from $1 - 200$, and step-size is chosen in integer power of 2 that reduces multiplication in hardware, i.e., $\mu = 2^{-i}$, where i is varying from $0 - 15$. Figure 2 shows the SNR analysis result for LF artifact suppression of adaptive filter 1. Maximum values annotated in the plot show the largest SNR achieved for filter length and step size in the analysis.

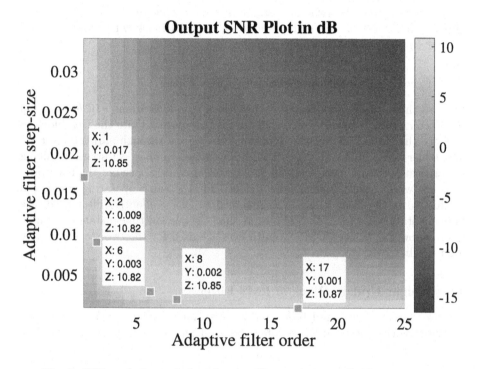

Fig. 2. SNR analysis result for adaptive filter step-size and order variations

Adaptive Filter Length Selection: This analysis is critical since the filter length of any adaptive filter decides the hardware computation, area, and power to implement it on hardware. Hence, the filter length should be taken such that it is not too costly on hardware, and denoising should also be satisfactory.

Adaptive Filters Step-Size Selection: If the adaptive filter's step size is large, it converges fast, but the error can shoot up rapidly. The filter can take a long time to converge if it is too small. Hence, the value of step size should be chosen such that there is a balance between the convergence time and error minimization.

Based on the above discussion for adaptive filter1, hardware implementation filter length $L_1 = 9$ (order 8) is selected, and the step-size $\mu_1 = 2^{-9}$ is chosen from Fig. 2. A similar analysis is carried out for adaptive filter2 for HF artifact reduction and chosen adaptive filter length $L_2 = 9$ (order 8) and step-size $\mu_2 = 2^{-4}$. The adaptive filters' step-size is converted to 2^{-i} to replace multiplication by shift, reducing the design hardware. The integer i represents the number of shift operations for multiplication.

4   Hardware Design of Two Stage Adaptive Filter

This section deals with the hardware design of the LMS adaptive filter, which is extended to realize the two-stage adaptive filter hardware of Fig. 1. It consists of two main block, i.e., *Error Computation*, i.e., FIR block with subtractor and *Weight Update Blocks*, i.e. adaptive algorithm.

4.1   Error Computational Block of LMS Filter

Figure 3 shows the Error Computational Block mainly contains *FIR block* and *a Subtractor Block*. The adder tree structure is incorporated into the FIR block to improve the speed and power reduction of the design through parallel addition. The adder tree reduces the $N - 1$ addition stages to $\lceil \log_2 N \rceil$ stages reducing the critical path and increasing the maximum operating speed of the hardware. In other words, the power will be reduced for the same operating frequency. In this work, the filter length L is renamed to N for adaptive filter hardware implementation, i.e., $N = 9$. The n represents the current time instance. A built-in area-power optimized DSP48 multipliers are used for the two-stage adaptive filter hardware design.

4.2   Weight Update Block of LMS Filter

The weights are calculated based on adaptive algorithm Eq. (1) and fed into the FIR block of the adaptive filter. Figure 4 shows that the weight update

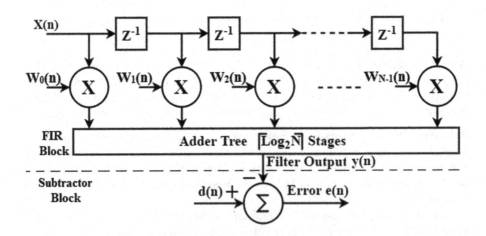

Fig. 3. Block diagram of error computational block

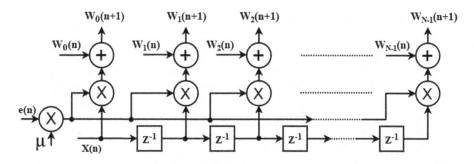

Fig. 4. Weight update block diagram

block consists of input signal delay block, multipliers, and adders. The delay block is shared with the FIR block's delays to reduce the hardware. Further, the multiplication of error e and the step-size μ is implemented using a shifter to reduce hardware. The step size of the two-stage adaptive filter hardware is configurable through a shifter that can be dynamically varying to control its filtering performance.

4.3   Analysis for Hardware Design of LMS Filter

Extensive analysis has been carried out with the sampling frequency and different fixed-point hardware architecture to implement the proposed ANC filter.

Analysis of Sampling Frequency. The sampling frequency decides the filter's operating frequency, which would ultimately affect the power consumption of the filtering device. Moreover, the sampling frequency of the ECG signal should be higher than the Nyquist sampling rate since most of the ECG signal power is in the range of $0.25 - 35$ Hz[8]. The SNR and MSE values for different MIT-BIH records are noted in this analysis for various sampling frequencies ranging from 180 Hz to 1080 Hz. HF and LF, both the artifacts, are used in this simulation with the same setup discussed in Sect. 3.2.

Table 2 shows the analysis results. It has been noted that the sampling rate of 360 samples per second (SPS) gives the highest performance in terms of SNR and MSE minimization. Increasing the signal's sampling rate would decrease the SNR of the proposed adaptive filter. The reason of decreases in SNR is due to increases in high-frequency noise components. This high frequency can be reduced by changing the step size of the adaptive filter. The 360 SPS sampling rate is adequate and minimizes the operating frequency requirements of the filter, which would ultimately reduce the power and maintain the signal quality. Hence, it is chosen for the hardware implementation.

Analysis of Fixed-Point Hardware Design. This analysis shows the direct dependency of the system's chosen bit resolution/ fixed-point representation on

Table 2. Software based analysis of sampling frequency for adaptive filter hardware design

Record	Input SNR	180SPS		360SPS		540SPS		720SPS		1080SPS	
		SNR	MSE	SNR	MSE	SNR	MSE	SNR	MSE	SNR	MSE
100	−6.06	5.58	−20.97	9.28	−24.69	9.72	−25.09	9.19	−24.56	7.82	−23.28
103	−0.91	11.45	−21.67	12.39	−22.60	10.74	−20.97	9.24	−19.47	7.14	−17.35
109	0.81	9.38	−17.88	6.51	−15.02	5.11	−13.62	4.20	−12.71	3.04	−11.54
115	−1.22	10.03	−20.56	10.30	−20.81	9.27	−19.79	8.37	−18.89	7.01	−17.54
203	2.96	7.29	−13.65	6.16	−12.52	5.27	−11.62	4.56	−10.91	3.51	−9.87
Average	−0.88	8.75	−18.94	8.93	−19.13	8.02	−18.22	7.11	−17.31	5.70	−15.92

Output SNR (in dB) and MSE (in dB)

the power. As the number of bits required for the adaptive filter increases, its implementation cost, i.e., area of implementation and processing power, also increases. So, this analysis provides how many bit resolutions or fixed-point systems to choose wisely. With the negligible cost of SNR degradation, more area and power can be reduced and targeted for the low area-power devices. For this analysis, the 24-bit hardware system is designed. From this hardware, other 18-bit, 16-bit, 14-bit, and 12-bit system architectures are simulated, and results are exported in the MATLAB software environment.

Table 3. Hardware analysis of different fixed point system architecture for adaptive filter design

Record	Input SNR	SNR(dB)					MSE (dB)				
		12-bit	14-bit	16-bit	18-bit	24-bit	12-bit	14-bit	16-bit	18-bit	24-bit
100	−6.06	8.99	9.36	9.43	9.43	9.43	−23.77	−24.75	−24.95	−24.95	−24.95
103	−0.91	12.06	12.44	12.50	12.50	12.50	−21.93	−22.62	−22.74	−22.74	−22.74
109	0.81	5.30	5.29	5.33	5.33	5.33	−14.92	−14.90	−15.01	−15.01	-15.01
115	−1.22	9.86	10.14	10.17	10.17	10.17	−20.18	−20.76	−20.81	−20.81	-20.81
203	2.96	5.78	5.78	5.77	5.77	5.77	−12.49	−12.50	−12.48	−12.48	-12.48
Average	−0.88	8.40	8.60	8.64	8.64	8.64	−18.65	−19.11	−19.19	−19.19	−19.19

Table 3 shows the analysis carried out on different records and the impact of changing bit resolution of ADC/fixed-point hardware architecture on output SNR. It is noted that the 24-bit system has the highest SNR and noted least MSE values. A 14-bit fixed-point system has been chosen for proposed hardware implementation since it just drops 0.04 dB SNR giving an adequately high SNR of 8.60 dB. Further, it will be helpful to reduce the are-power of the design compared to 16-bit hardware. Hence, it has been chosen a 14-bit hardware system. The proposed 14-bit hardware design and software implementation results Table 4 show only a 0.33 dB average output SNR reduction.

Table 5 shows the comparison of the reference-free adaptive methods. The SNR and MSE improvement of the two-stage LMS adaptive filter with chosen

Table 4. Software and 14-bit hardware architecture implementation results comparison

Record	Input SNR	SNR(dB)		MSE (dB)	
		Software	Hardware	Software	Hardware
100	−6.06	9.28	9.36	−24.69	−24.75
103	−0.91	12.39	12.44	−22.60	−22.62
109	0.81	6.51	5.29	−15.02	−14.90
115	−1.22	10.30	10.14	−20.81	−20.76
203	2.96	6.16	5.78	−12.52	−12.50
Average	−0.88	8.93	8.60	−19.13	−19.11

Table 5. Comparison of artifact noise cancellation techniques

Reference free adaptive methods	Complexity of algorithm	Result A		Result B		Result C	
		SNR (dB)	MSE (dB)	SNR (dB)	MSE (dB)	SNR (dB)	MSE (dB)
EMD+LMS [14]	High	2.24	−10.41	−0.57	−2.94	0.84	−6.68
DWT+LMS [15]	high	8.48	−16.58	6.31	−8.20	7.40	−12.39
DWT+NLMS [12]	High	7.65	−15.85	9.83	−16.04	8.74	−15.94
Step-size scaler [11]	Medium	9.35	−20.36	6.00	−5.49	7.68	−12.93
Two stage adaptive LMS (this work)	Low	10.85	−22.52	7.00	−11.06	8.93	−16.79

Avg. Result A: LF artifact reduction for Avg. input $SNR = −4.25$ dB
Avg. Result B: HF artifact reduction for Avg. input $SNR = 2.5$ dB
Avg. Result C: LF & HF artifact reduction for Avg. input $SNR = −0.88$ dB

parameters gives the highest SNR and Lowest MSE compared to all other existing methods for LF and HF artifact reduction. Further, the two-stage LMS filter has less computational complexity as other methods use signal decomposition and division operation in their computation unlike proposed method. It has been noted that 16.043% average output SNR increment and 10.61% average MSE decrement compared to the existing method for LF artifact reduction. For LF and HF artifact reduction, the output average SNR and MSE are improved by 2.17% and 5.33%, respectively.

5   FPGA/ASIC Implementation and Results

5.1   FPGA Hardware Test Setup

The Verilog language is used for RTL design. Xilinx ISE 14.7, MATLAB 2105b, and ArbExpress 3.4 software are used for experimentation. Spartan3E FPGA board, arbitrary function generator AFG1022, and digital storage oscilloscope (DSO) are used for the hardware testing as shown in Fig. 5. The two-stage adaptive filter design is interfaced with SPI in a top module to get the ADC data for processing on FPGA. The noisy synthesized ECG signal is simulated from an arbitrary function generator with an SNR of 2.5 dB. The sampling frequency of

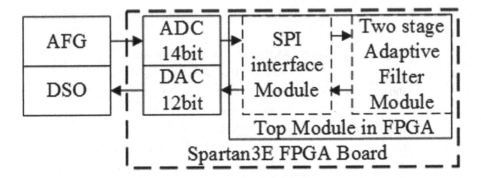

Fig. 5. Interfacing block diagram of implemented adaptive filter on FPGA

ADC (400 KHz) is downsampled 360 Hz in the hardware top module. It passes through the adaptive filter. The generated filtered signal has been sent to DAC via SPI interfacing and sent to the DSO for display. Figure 6(A) shows the experimental setup for the real-time hardware testing of filter on FPGA for synthetic ECG data. Figure 6(B) and Fig. 6(C) show the real-time ECG LF and HF noise

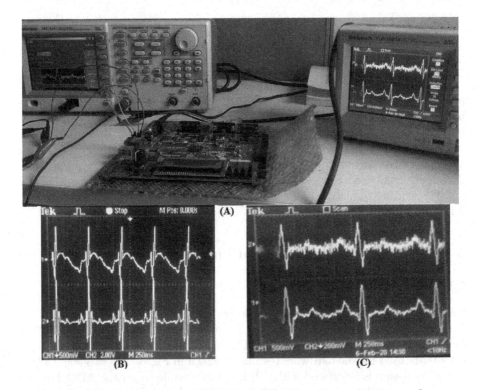

Fig. 6. (A) Hardware setup, (B) LF and (C) HF artifact reduction results

Table 6. Summary report of spartan3E FPGA implementation

Parameters	Flip flops	LUTs	Slices	Multiplier	Synthesis Max. Clk. Freq. (MHz)	Power (mW) @ 3.3V 25°C
LMS filter	252	1184	684	18	75.569	10 @ 50 MHz
System	1215	6315	3571	20	31.46	0.010 @360 SPS

removal results on spartan 3E FPGA. It has been noted that the two-stage adaptive filter algorithm removes the ECG noise using a designed hardware system.

Table 6 summarizes the hardware utilization report of designed hardware implementation on the spartan3E FPGA board. It has been observed that the hardware design only occupies 1184 LUTs and 684 slices. The implemented hardware architecture takes an 18 built-in DSP multiplier with a 2 global buffer. One buffer is utilized in the design for clock tree synthesis, and another is a driver in the external clock 50 MHz coming from the FPGA board. The implemented design can run at a max of 75.569 MHz frequency. Moreover, the implemented hardware can only utilize 10 mW of power on an FPGA chip when running on a 50MHz clock. The power consumption of the filter is measured using the Xilinx power analyzer tool after the place and route of the design. Further, the system power is estimated at a sampling rate of 360 SPS after getting the power report from the tool. A proposed ANC filter system utilizes 6315 LUTs, has a maximum clock frequency of 31.46 MHz, and consumes only 10 μW power at a sampling rate of 360 SPS, which can be easily targeted on a wearable device. The system power consumption is estimated at a practical sampling frequency of 360SPS, hence showing less power consumption than LMS adaptive filter power computed at 50 MHz FPGA board operating frequency.

5.2 ASIC Implementation of Proposed Adaptive Filter

This work performs the VLSI back-end flow of RTL to GDS using the 180nm SCL library for the proposed design. Before the ASIC design, the proposed adaptive filter is integrated with the SPI interface module to minimize the number of I/O pins and power consumption. The filter's chip Layout and its post-layout simulation results are shown in Fig. 7 and Fig. 8 respectively. Results show that the proposed hardware filter out the ECG signal, and its output SNR is 8.60 dB. The proposed chip utilizes only 0.66 $(mm)^2$ area and has a total of 0.5 mW power consumption at supply $Vdd = 1.8$ V, and a maximum sampling rate of design is 5 KSPS. The sampling rate is reduced due to SPI interfacing. This sampling rate is sufficient for ECG signal processing. Figure 8 shows that the filtered signal amplitude is changed due to the fixed step size selected for filter performance. Hence, the amplitude correction or the dynamical variation of adaptive filter step-size with an additional control algorithm is essential for

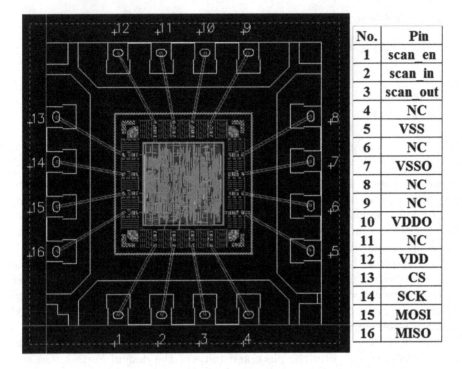

No.	Pin
1	scan_en
2	scan_in
3	scan_out
4	NC
5	VSS
6	NC
7	VSSO
8	NC
9	NC
10	VDDO
11	NC
12	VDD
13	CS
14	SCK
15	MOSI
16	MISO

Fig. 7. Proposed chip layout

reference-free adaptive filter design [11]. The future part of the work will be optimizing the adaptive filter through the chip interfacing with an embedded controller to dynamically vary the adaptive filter's step-size.

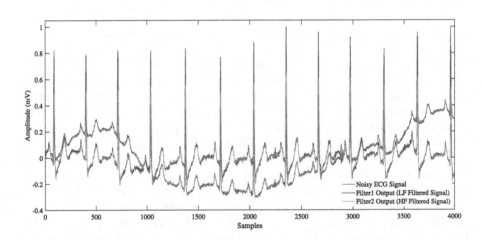

Fig. 8. PostLayout simulation over Noisy ECG signal

Table 7. Comparison of FPGA implemented hardware

Parameters	DWT+LMS [16]	This work	DWT+NLMS [12]	This work
FPGA part	Virtex-6 XC6VL240TFF1156-1		Virtex-7 XC7VX485TFFG1761-1	
LUTs	8953 (5.94%)	1299 (0.86%)	7688 (5.77%)	1292 (0.43%)
Registers	1227 (0.41%)	593 (0.20%)	5919 (2.2%)	593 (0.10%)
Slices	4796 (12.73%)	518 (1.38%)	3368 (10.07%)	465 (0.61%)
Avg. SNR (dB)	7.40	8.60	8.74	8.60

The values inside ( ) indicate the percentage resource utilization of FPGA

5.3   Hardware Results and Comparison with Existing Work

The proposed hardware is designed over 14 bit (Q2.12) fixed-point system. Hence, it introduces the hardware's floating-point to fixed-point conversion quantization error compared to the software simulation results. It has been noted that the average value of output SNR is reduced by 0.33 dB. This difference is negligibly small. Hence proposed fixed-point hardware can be helpful for ECG denoising.

Table 7 compares proposed hardware implementation results with existing work on various FPGA platforms. The proposed hardware implementation occupies 5.08% fewer LUTs, 0.21% fewer registers, 11.35% fewer hardware resources, and higher average output SNR compared to optimized reference-free hardware implementation [16]. The designed hardware has lower average output SNR than DWT+NLMS method [12]. However, this work occupies significantly fewer hardware resources than the existing work of [12] because of its low computation complexity.

6   Conclusion

This paper proposes a two-stage reference-free efficient adaptive LMS algorithm for ECG denoising and compares it with existing adaptive filter-based methods. It gives better performance for both low and high-frequency artifacts. The two-stage adaptive filter design is implemented through various analyses for its better performance on hardware. The software simulation shows that the 360SPS achieves a maximum of 8.93 dB output SNR and -19.13 dB MSE minimization for ECG denoising among various experimented sampling frequencies. The software implementation of the two-stage reference-free adaptive LMS method gives 16.04% more average output SNR and 10.61% more average MSE minimization compared to existing methods. The hardware simulation shows that the 14-bit fixed-point system architecture shows just a 0.33 dB output SNR drop compared to software-based implementation. Further, it is successfully realized on a spartan3E FPGA board showing it can remove real-time artifacts from ECG signals.

References

1. The top 10 causes of death. https://www.who.int. Accessed 10 July 2020
2. Ug897 vivado design suite user guide model-based DSP design using system generator. https://www.xilinx.com
3. Aqil, M., Jbari, A., Bourouhou, A.: ECG signal denoising by discrete wavelet transform. Int. J. Online Eng. **13**(9) (2017)
4. Bahoura, M., Ezzaidi, H.: FPGA-implementation of discrete wavelet transform with application to signal denoising. Circ. Syst. Sign. Process. **31**(3), 987–1015 (2012)
5. Gong, Z., Ding, Y.: Design and implementation of wearable dynamic electrocardiograph real-time monitoring terminal. IEEE Access **8**, 6575–6582 (2019)
6. Haykin, S.S.: Adaptive Filter Theory. Pearson Education India (2007)
7. Kim, B.H., Noh, Y.H., Jeong, D.U.: A wearable ECG monitoring system using adaptive EMD filter based on activity status. In: 2015 IEEE 29th International Conference on Advanced Information Networking and Applications Workshops, pp. 11–16. IEEE (2015)
8. Li, J., Deng, G., Wei, W., Wang, H., Ming, Z.: Design of a real-time ECG filter for portable mobile medical systems. IEEE Access **5**, 696–704 (2017). https://doi.org/10.1109/ACCESS.2016.2612222
9. Liu, Z.l., Xu, S., Quan, H.Y., Guo, Y.G.: Study of spectrum analysis based on EMD adaptive filter. In: 2009 International Conference on Computational Intelligence and Security, vol. 2, pp. 598–600. IEEE (2009)
10. Moody, G.B., Mark, R.G.: The impact of the MIT-BIH arrhythmia database. IEEE Eng. Med. Biol. Mag. **20**(3), 45–50 (2001). https://doi.org/10.1109/51.932724
11. Prajapati, P.H., Darji, A.D.: Two stage step-size scaler adaptive filter design for ECG denoising. In: 2021 IEEE International Symposium on Circuits and Systems (ISCAS), pp. 1–5. IEEE (2021)
12. Mathuria, R., Potla, V.V., Prajapati, P., Gupta, S., Kakkireni, N., Darji, A.: Hardware co-simulation of an efficient adaptive filter based ECG denoising system with inbuilt reference generator. In: IEEE Region 10 symposium (TENSYMP), pp. 1–6. IEEE (2022)
13. Rahman, M.Z.U., Shaik, R.A., Reddy, D.R.K.: Efficient and simplified adaptive noise cancelers for ECG sensor based remote health monitoring. IEEE Sens. J. **12**(3), 566–573 (2011)
14. Rakshit, M., Das, S.: An efficient ECG denoising methodology using empirical mode decomposition and adaptive switching mean filter. Biomed. Sign. Process. Control **40**, 140–148 (2018)
15. Salman, M.N., Rao, P.T., Rahman, M.Z.U.: Novel logarithmic reference free adaptive signal enhancers for ECG analysis of wireless cardiac care monitoring systems. IEEE Access **6**, 46382–46395 (2018)
16. Saripalli, G., Prajapati, P.H., Darji, A.D.: CSD optimized dwt filter for ECG denoising. In: 2020 24th International Symposium on VLSI Design and Test (VDAT), pp. 1–6. IEEE (2020)
17. Saxena, S., Jais, R., Hota, M.K.: Removal of powerline interference from ECG signal using FIR, IIR, DWT and NLMS adaptive filter. In: 2019 International Conference on Communication and Signal Processing (ICCSP), pp. 0012–0016. IEEE (2019)
18. Thakor, N.V., Zhu, Y.: Applications of adaptive filtering to ECG analysis: noise cancellation and arrhythmia detection. IEEE Trans. Biomed. Eng. **38**(8), 785–794 (1991). https://doi.org/10.1109/10.83591

19. Tompkins, W.J.: Biomedical Digital Signal Processing. Editorial Prentice Hall (1993)
20. Venkatesan, C., Karthigaikumar, P., Varatharajan, R.: A novel LMS algorithm for ECG signal preprocessing and KNN classifier based abnormality detection. Multimedia Tools Appl. **77**(8), 10365–10374 (2018). https://doi.org/10.1007/s11042-018-5762-6
21. Zou, C., Qin, Y., Sun, C., Li, W., Chen, W.: Motion artifact removal based on periodical property for ECG monitoring with wearable systems. Pervasive Mob. Comput. **40**, 267–278 (2017)

A Reconfigurable Arbiter PUF Based on VGSOT MTJ

Kunal Kranti Das[1][✉], Aditya Japa[2], and Deepika Gupta[1]

[1] Department of Electronics and Communication Engineering, Dr. Shyama Prasad Mukherjee International Institute of Information Technology, Naya Raipur, Chhattisgarh, India
kunalkrantidas@gmail.com
[2] Department of Electronics and Communication Engineering, Koneru Lakshmaiah Education Foundation, Hyderabad, Telangana, India

Abstract. With the serious scaling limitations of complementary metal-oxide-semiconductor technology, emerging spintronic devices have attracted recent attention for next-generation energy-efficient and secure systems. Voltage-Gated Spin-Orbit Torque (VGSOT) based Magnetic Tunnelling Junction (MTJ) device is proved to show lower energy consumptions with stochastic switching, process variations, and chaotic magnetization. Exploiting these intrinsic variations, this paper for the first time presents a reconfigurable arbiter physically unclonable function (PUF). Further, the PUF functionality is validated considering VGSOT MTJ and 45nm CMOS technology. Considering the state of VGSOT devices, the proposed PUF is observed to be fully reconfigurable. Considering the abilities of VGSOT, PUF shows higher uniqueness of 50.2% at a supply voltage of 0.8V. Additionally, PUF achieves high reliability of 95.8% considering supply voltage and temperature variations. Moreover, at a supply voltage of 0.8V, the proposed PUF achieves lower energy consumption of 24fJ/bit.

Keywords: Spintronics · Voltage-Gated Spin-Orbit Torque (VGSOT) · Magnetic Tunnelling Junction (MTJ) · Hardware Security · Physically Unclonable Function (PUF)

1 Introduction

With complementary metal oxide semiconductor (CMOS) technology scaling, increased leakage current has become a key barrier for modern CMOS-based integrated circuits [1–3]. Furthermore, CMOS-based memories have shown increased write and read energy consumption with degraded performance. To address these issues, researchers have proposed several emerging magnetic devices to replace traditional CMOS technology. Because of its promising characteristics like nonvolatility, 3-D incorporation, and scalability, spintronic devices have attracted recent attention [4, 5]. Spintronic memories have the ability to outperform CMOS-based Static Random Access Memory (SRAM) or Dynamic Random Access Memory (DRAM) due to their zero static power consumption, and nonvolatility [6]. Despite the promising nature of perpendicular magnetic tunnel

A. P. Shah et al. (Eds.): VDAT 2022, CCIS 1687, pp. 320–330, 2022.
https://doi.org/10.1007/978-3-031-21514-8_27

junction (p-MTJ) based on spin-transfer torque (STT) MTJ devices, it still suffers from many issues, including a long incubation time, high switching current densities, and read current disturbance. Recent experiments have shown that a three terminal p-MTJ based on a ferromagnetic (FM)/antiferromagnetic (AFM)/oxide structure shows field-free spin orbit torque (SOT) switching. This is because the AFM is not only able to create the SOT but also offer an exchange bias (H_{EX}) to substitute the external field [7, 8]. However, the H_{EX} given by these structures is insufficient to perform a full switch, leading to low dependability and a high critical switching current. To address these challenges, researchers developed a novel switching mechanism based on the VGSOT effect, which employs the voltage-controlled magnetic anisotropy (VCMA) to aid the SOT. The energy barrier of MTJ between parallel (P) and anti-parallel (AP) is lowered due to the VCMA effect, while the bias voltage supplied to the oxide layer of the MTJ is positive [9]. As a consequence of adding the VCMA effect in the p-MTJ based on the FM/AFM/oxide structure, the crucial critical SOT current reduces, resulting in improved switching reliability and lower switching energy consumption [10].

Apart from this, VGSOT MTJ shows large process variations that can be explored to design hardware security primitives like physically unclonable function (PUF). PUF is a function that generates on-the-fly security keys by exploring process variations [11, 12]. Also, the actual manufacturer cannot perfectly clone or replicate two indistinguishable PUFs since manufacturing process variances are intrinsically unpredictable. PUF's challenge-response method is used to verify the identity of devices and systems [13]. PUFs of many varieties have been proposed in recent years, including delay PUFs [14], memory PUF (MPUF) [15], flash PUFs [16], and flip-flop PUFs [17]. These PUFs show a huge area overhead due to the enormous number of components in their memory cells whereas a typical PUF employs many kilobits of memory cells. Designing a CMOS-based PUF with a lower footprint, and low energy consumption with higher reliability is always a challenge. To avoid this, a unique VGSOT MTJ-based reconfigurable arbiter PUF is designed. Importantly, the reported design is evaluated for reliability, uniqueness, and uniformity characteristics. The design has been examined by exploring 45nm CMOS technology and the VGSOT MTJ model. The remainder of the paper is laid out in the following manner. Section 2 presents the device structure, models explored, and characteristics of VGSOT MTJ. Further, the VGSOT-based proposed PUF design is introduced in Sect. 3. Apart from this, the proposed PUF is analyzed and several performance parameters including uniqueness, uniformity, and reliability have been calculated in Sect. 4. Further, the performance of the proposed PUF is compared with other latest PUF designs in the literature. Finally, conclusions are offered in Sect. 5.

2 VGSOT MTJ Device and Characteristics

The VGSOT MTJ is a three-terminal device that comprises two ferromagnetic layers (CoFeB) placed on top of the AFM layer (IrMn) and divided by an extreme-thin oxide layer (MgO) as shown in Fig. 1(a). This thin oxide layer works as a barrier for currents. The two FM layers are called as a fixed layer and a free layer. The fixed layer magnetization is often static in one direction, whereas the magnetization of the free layer is changeable. If the ferromagnetic directions of both the layers are the same

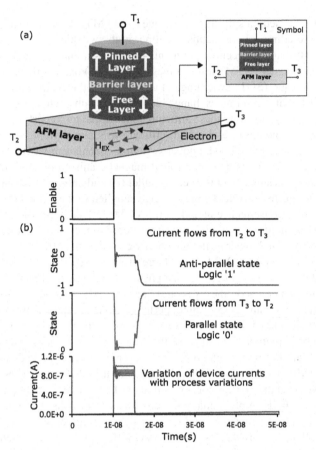

Fig. 1. (a) VGSOT device structure with the symbol (b) Switching characteristics demonstrating anti-parallel and parallel states.

then the MTJ enters into a parallel state and shows lower resistance (R_P). Otherwise (if the ferromagnetic directions of both the layers are opposite), MTJ enters into an anti-parallel state and shows higher resistance (R_{AP}). When a current (I_{SOT}) travels through the anti-ferromagnetic metal, the spin-orbit coupling formed by the spin-hall effects (SHE)occurs. Due to SHE, a vertically spin current will be induced on the free layer's magnetization. Further, AFM metal provides in-plane exchange bias (H_{EX}) due to which no outer magnetic field is required for the switching of the MTJ. Upon supplying a positive voltage (V_b) across the p-MTJ, its energy barrier can be reduced temporarily during the switching according to the VCMA effect.

This paper explores a VGOST MTJ Verilog-A model with perpendicular magnetic anisotropy [9]. This model captures complete switching behaviour with process variation effects. The important parameters of VGOST MTJ have been summarized in Table 1. More details of the VGSOT MTJ Verilog-A model, device parameters, and characteristics can be found in [9, 10]. Figure 1(b) shows the switching characteristics of VGSOT MTJ whereas MTJ shows both parallel and antiparallel states. When current flows through

Table 1. VGSOT MTJ device parameters

Parameter	Description	Unit	Default Value
tsl	Free layer thickness	nm	1.1
t_{ox}	MgO barrier thickness	nm	1.4
TMR	TMR ratio under zero bias voltage	%	100
a, b, r	MTJ surface length, width, radius	nm	50, 50, 25
d, w, l	AFM strip thickness, width, length	nm	3, 50, 60
rho	AFM strip resistivity	Ω-m	278e-8
shape	MTJ surface shape	-	Circle

the AFM layer from T_2 to T_3, MTJ enters into an anti-parallel state. In contrast, if the current flow through the AFM layer from T_3 to T_2, MTJ enters into a parallel state. The actual thickness of the oxide layer and free layer cannot be kept at one constant amount as a result of natural fabrication process variations. As a result, MTJ exhibits significant variation in switching resistance. The range of parallel MTJ resistance and anti-parallel MTJ resistance can be observed from the complete stochastic switching operation from parallel to anti-parallel and from anti-parallel to parallel respectively [18]. These changes in the value of the resistance cause the change in device current as shown in Fig. 1(b). Due to the above process-dependent characteristics, the VGSOT device can be explored to construct a resilient PUF design. Exploiting VGSOT MTJ device process variations, this paper proposes arbiter MPUF which is explained in the next sections. The Verilog-A based VGSOT model has been plugged into the Cadence virtuoso environment to design and analyze the VGSOT MTJ based PUF.

3   Proposed PUF Design and Operation

The proposed design of the arbiter MPUF is shown in Fig. 2. It consists of two delay paths (delay path1 and delay path2) that are designed using emerging VGSOT devices. Each delay path is controlled using source lines (SLs are S_0, S_1..., S_{n-1}) and bit lines (BLs are B_0, B_1, ... B_{n-1}) as shown in Fig. 2. Moreover, the selection of SL and BL signals decides the state of VGSOT. Further, each delay path consists of control signals (C_0, C_1, ... C_{n-1}) that operate access transistors and act as challenges to PUF. The pre-charge sense amplifier (PCSA) circuit [19] used in the proposed MPUF compares current discharge speeds to obtain an output response (Q_m). The signal propagation delays are compared for traditional arbiter PUFs to produce the output response. This makes MPUF a more suitable security application for high-speed circuits. Interestingly, the proposed MPUF exploits the intrinsic randomness of the VGSOT MTJ device to produce a difference in delays of two paths and hence, obtain the output response. This delay difference makes MPUF produce a unique1-bit response, upon applying different challenges. To get a larger bit response we can repeat the same circuit multiple times.

Figure 3(a) shows an arbiter MPUF circuit with 4 VGSOT MTJ devices to demonstrate the functionality of the proposed PUF. There are two delay paths, each with four

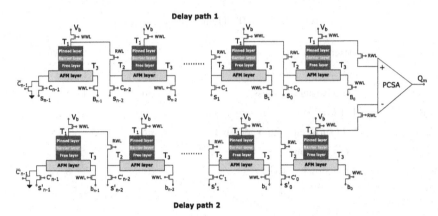

Fig. 2. VGSOT MTJ-based proposed arbiter MPUF architecture.

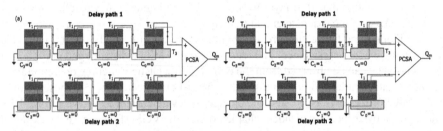

Fig. 3. Proposed arbiter MPUF architecture (a) With similar challenges for both delay paths (b) With dissimilar challenges for both delay paths.

VGSOT MTJ cells. The proposed PUF design is explained in two different phases. These are the writing phase and followed by the read phase. In the writing phase of operation, read enable (RWL) is low and all RWL driven transistors are turned off. On the other hand, the write enables (WWL) and all challenges (C_0-C_3 and C'_0-C'_3) of PUF become logic high. All SLs and BLs can be used to set each VGSOT cell into the parallel (P) or anti-parallel (AP) state separately. When BL is high and SL is low, the VGSOT switches from P to AP. In contrast, when SL is high and the BL line is low, VGSOT is switched from AP to P. The antiparallel VGSOT state denotes logic 1, while the parallel VGSOT state denotes logic 0. The proposed PUF can act as a reconfigurable design that is highly suitable for encryption applications. This is due to the fact that in the write phase all VGSOT devices have been set into either P or AP state that can be reconfigured every time. Thus, the PUF achieves a unique response by setting the VGSOT states.

During the read phase, RWL is high and all RWL-controlled transistors are switched ON. As a result, all the VGSOT devices form a delay path that produces a fixed propagation delay depending on the challenges applied. When all of the challenges are low for two delay paths, VGSOT devices form a unique delay path as shown in Fig. 3(a) (red line). Further, output Q_m is produced by exploiting the different propagation delays caused by the process variations of VGSOT devices and their respective states. Following another method, upon applying different challenges to delay paths, MPUF produces

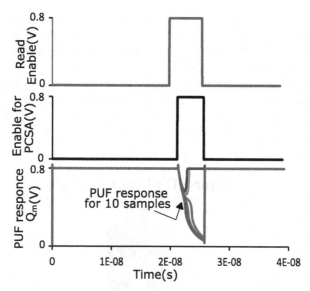

Fig. 4. Transient characteristics of proposed PUF design for 10 samples.

a unique equivalent propagation delay as shown in Fig. 3(b). Figure 4 shows the transient characteristics of the proposed PUF for 10 different samples considering process variations at a supply voltage of 0.8V. It can be observed that out of 10 samples, 5 PUFs produce 0V (logic '0'), and the other 5 produce 0.8V (logic '1'). The proposed MPUF consists of two delay paths and each delay path has "m" number of MRAM cells. Each MRAM cell state (P or AP) indicates a challenge value. For example, consider "m" VGSOT cells that show a 2^m number of distinct potential configurations. Furthermore, each delay path does not need to have the same challenge value. For example, if delay path 1 has an "m" MRAM cells and delay path 2 has "n" MRAM cells, there might be $2^m \times 2^n$ potential challenge response pairs (CRPs). Further, if "p" and "q" distinct BL access transistor challenge values are used for delay path 1 and delay path 2, the number of CRPs can be increased. Therefore, the proposed arbiter MPUF shows a large CRPs of $2^m \times 2^n \times p \times q$ number. The large number of CRP becomes the exclusive property of MPUF.

4 Results and Discussion

In this paper, arbiter MPUF is proposed that explore a compact VGSOT MTJ model with 45 nm CMOS technology [9]. Significantly, MPUFs are simulated and analyzed to obtain three important performance parameters i.e. uniqueness, uniformity, and reliability. Specifically, the uniqueness of the PUF has resulted from their ability to generate output differently when the same challenge is applied. The presented arbiter MPUF is analyzed to obtain several different performance parameters including uniqueness, uniformity, and reliability. To model the process variations and mismatch, monte carlo simulations were run on the design for 25 separate PUF instances with 200 challenges.

The simulation is run at a supply voltage of 0.8V and a nominal temperature of 27^0 C. The inter-hamming distance (inter-HD) or uniqueness [21] of the proposed MPUF is found to be 50.21%, as shown in Fig. 5. As a result, the proposed MPUF can produce distinct CRPs to identify various chips.

Uniformity is used to estimate the unpredictability of the response of the PUFs even if one has the previous circuit information. The uniformity of the proposed MPUF is found to be 50.75% as shown in Fig. 6. It means that the response contains almost an equal number of 1's and 0's. The result shows that our proposed MPUF is highly unpredictable and random.

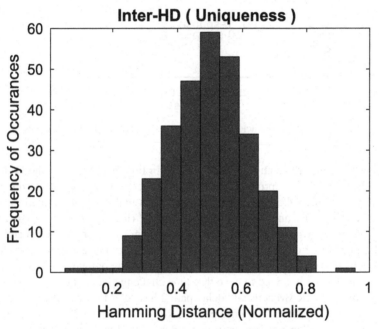

Fig. 5. Distribution of normalized Inter HD of proposed PUF.

To calculate the reliability, the proposed PUF is simulated at a supply voltage of 0.8V with a nominal operating temperature of 27 °C, and the response is recorded as "R_i". Further, the same procedure is repeated on the chip under various operating conditions for the same challenge and noted in the response termed "R'_i". Then, the average intra-hamming (intra-HD) distance of several samples of "R'_i" at varying temperatures (-20 °C to 70 °C) and voltages (0.8V to 1.2V) has been calculated. The intra-HD of the proposed PUF is 0.043 and the average reliability is found to be 95.7% as shown in Fig. 7. Thus, the proposed PUF is proved to be robust against environmental variations.

At a supply voltage of 0.8V, the proposed MPUF shows read and write power consumption of 16.12 nW and 1.189 μW. Further, the propagation delays of the proposed PUF for reading and writing operations resulted in 5ns and 10ns respectively. Table 2 compares the performance of the proposed arbiter PUF with recent literature. It can be observed that the proposed arbiter MPUF has shown higher reliability and

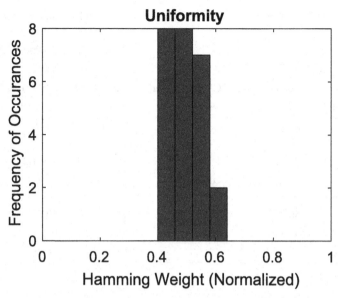

Fig. 6. Distribution of normalized Hamming Weight of proposed PUF.

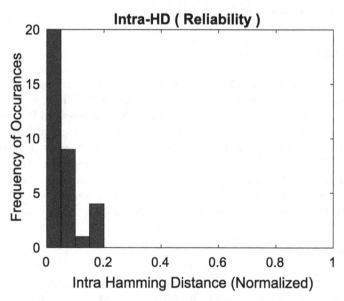

Fig. 7. Distribution of normalized Intra HD of proposed PUF.

uniqueness. The proposed PUF exploits the characteristics and strong process variations of VGSOT MTJ which enable the PUF to enhance its performance. Further, exploiting the characteristics of VGSOT MTJ, the proposed PUF achieved a large amount of CRP

Table 2. Performance comparison of proposed PUF with recent literature

Parameters	[21]	[23]	[24]	Proposed Work
Technology (nm)	65	180	40	45
Type of PUF	Voltage array	CMOS Arbiter	STT-MRAM	VGSOT MTJ arbiter
Possible CRPs	1.15×10^{18}	2^m	–	$2^m \times 2^n \times p \times q$
Energy consumption/bit	0.3pJ	–	6.60 pJ	24 fJ
Voltage range (V)	0.8–1	1.75–1.85	0.9–1.1	0.8–1.2
Temperature range (°C)	0–50	20–70	-45 to 100	0–50
Uniqueness (%)	50.26	40	50.1	50.2
Reliability (%)	95.34	96.5	96.73	95.7
Unifomity (%)	–	–	51	50.75

space compared to other designs. The proposed PUF has achieved a lower energy consumption of 24fJ/bit at a supply voltage of 0.8V. This shows that it can be used in low power and lightweight security for digital devices.

5 Conclusion

This paper proposed a novel ultra-low power arbiter PUF with high-quality metrics. The proposed arbiter MPUF explores the innate process variations of VGSOT MTJ. Furthermore, in comparison to traditional arbiter PUFs, the proposed PUF is reconfigurable and can generate a large amount of CRP space. The proposed PUF has shown higher uniqueness of 50.2% at a supply voltage of 0.8V. Moreover, PUF has shown high reliability of 95.7% considering supply voltage and temperature variations. At a supply voltage of 0.8V, the proposed PUF has shown a lower energy consumption of 24fJ/bit. The proposed arbiter PUF based on VGSOT MTJ is highly suitable for device authentication and key generation for low-power devices.

References

1. Zhang, D., Zeng, L., Zhang, Y., Klein, J.O., Zhao, W.: Reliability enhanced hybrid CMOS/MTJ logic circuit architecture. IEEE Trans. Mag. **53**(11), 1–5 (2017)
2. Bohr, M.T., Young, I.A.: CMOS scaling trends and beyond. IEEE Micro. **37**(6), 20–29 (2017)
3. Zhang, D., et al.: Reliability-enhanced separated pre-charge sensing amplifier for hybrid CMOS/MTJ logic circuits. IEEE Trans. Mag. **53**(9), 1–5 (2017)
4. Chun, K.C., Zhao, H., Harms, J.D., Kim, T.H., Wang, J.P., Kim, C.H.: A scaling roadmap and performance evaluation in in- plane and perpendicular MTJ based STT-MRAMs for high-density cache memory. IEEE J. Solid State Circuits **48**(2), 598–610 (2013)

5. Augustine, C., Mojumder, N., Fong, X., Choday, H., Park, S.P., Roy, K.: STT-MRAMs for future universal memories: Perspective and prospective. In: 28th International Conference on Microelectronics Proceedings, pp. 349–355. IEEE, Nis, Serbia (2012)
6. Kitagata, D., Sugahara, S.: Design and energy-efficient architectures for nonvolatile static random access memory using magnetic tunnel junctions. Jpn. J. Appl. Phys. **58**(SB), SBBB12 (2019)
7. Ikeda, S., et al.: Perpendicular-anisotropy CoFeB-MgO based magnetic tunnel junctions scaling down to 1X nm. In: IEEE International Electron Devices Meeting, 2014, pp. 33.2.1–33.2.4. IEEE, San Francisco, CA, USA (2014)
8. Sarkar, M.R., Bappy, M.M.A., Azmir, M.M., Rashid, D.M., Hasan, S.I.: VG-SOT MRAM Design and Performance Analysis. In: IEEE 12th Annual Information Technology, Electronics and Mobile Communication Conference, pp. 715–719. IEEE, Vancouver, BC, Canada (2021)
9. Zhang, K., Zhang, D., Wang, C., Zeng, L., Wang, Y., Zhao, W.: Compact modeling and analysis of voltage-gated spin-orbit torque magnetic tunnel junction. IEEE Access **8**, 50792–50800 (2020)
10. Wang, C., et al.: Magnetic nonvolatile SRAM based on voltage-gated spin-orbit-torque magnetic tunnel junctions. IEEE Trans. Electron Dev. **67**(5), 1965–1971 (2020)
11. Devadas, S., Suh, E., Paral, S., Sowell, R., Ziola, T., Khandelwal, V.: Design and implementation of PUF-based unclonable RFID ICs for anti-counterfeiting and security applications. In: IEEE International Conference on RFID, pp. 58–64. IEEE, Las Vegas, NV, USA (2008)
12. Lee, J.W., Lim, D., Gassend, B., Suh, G.E., Van Dijk, M., Devadas, S.: A technique to build a secret key in integrated circuits for identification and authentication applications. In: Symposium on VLSI Circuits. Digest of Technical Papers, pp. 176–179. IEEE, Honolulu, HI, USA (2004)
13. Suh, G.E., Devadas, S.: Physical unclonable functions for device authentication and secret key generation. In: 44th ACM/IEEE Design Automation Conference, pp. 9–14. IEEE, San Diego, CA, USA (2007)
14. Wang, Y., Wang, C., Gu, C., Cui, Y., ONeill, M., Liu, W.: Theoretical analysis of delay-based pufs and design strategies for improvement. In: IEEE International Symposium on Circuits and Systems, pp. 1–5. IEEE, Sapporo, Japan (2019)
15. Garg, A., Kim, T.T.: Design of SRAM PUF with improved uniformity and reliability utilizing device aging effect. In: IEEE International Symposium on Circuits and Systems (ISCAS), pp. 1941–1944. IEEE, Melbourne, VIC, Australia (2014)
16. Sakib, S., Rahman, M.T., Milenković, A., Ray, B.: Flash memory based physical unclonable function. In: 2019 SoutheastCon, pp. 1–6. IEEE, Huntsville, AL, USA (2019)
17. Sushma, R., Murty, N. S.: Feedback oriented XORed flip-flop based arbiter PUF. In: International Conference on Electrical, Electronics, Communication, Computer, and Optimization Techniques (ICEECCOT), pp. 1444–1448. IEEE, Msyuru, India (2018)
18. Manual of Compact Model of Voltage-Gated SOT, http://www.spinlib.com
19. Zhao, W., Chappert, C., Javerliac, V., Noziere, J.P.: High speed, high stability and low power sensing amplifier for MTJ/CMOS hybrid logic circuits. IEEE Trans. Mag. **45**(10), 3784–3787 (2009)
20. Japa, A., Mujumdar, M.K., Sahoo, S.K., Vaddi, R.: Tunnel FET-based ultra-lightweight reconfigurable TRNG and PUF design for resource-constrained internet of things. Int. J. Circuit Theory Appl. **49**(8), 2299–2311 (2021)
21. Venkatesh, A., Venkatasubramaniyan, A. B., Xi, X., Sanyal, A.: 0.3 pJ/bit machine learning resistant strong PUF using subthreshold voltage divider array. IEEE Trans. Circuits Syst. II: Express Briefs **67**(8), 1394–1398 (2019)
22. Tanaka, Y., et al.: Physically unclonable functions with voltage-controlled magnetic tunnel junctions. IEEE Trans. Mag. **57**(2), 1–6 (2021)

23. Lim, D., Lee, J. W., Gassend, B., Suh, G. E., Van Dijk, M., Devadas, S.: Extracting secret keys from integrated circuits. IEEE Trans. Very Large Scale Integr. Syst. **13**(10), 1200–1205 (2005)

24. Dodo, S. B., Bishnoi, R., Nair, S. M., Tahoori, M. B.: A Spintronics memory PUF for resilience against cloning counterfeit. IEEE Trans. Very Large Scale Integr. Syst. **27**(11), 2511–2522 (2019)

Pass Transistor XOR Gate Based Radiation Hardened RO-PUF

Syed Farah Naz[1], Sajid Khan[2], and Ambika Prasad Shah[1]([✉]) [iD]

[1] IC-ResQ Laboratory, Department of Electrical Engineering, Indian Institute of Technology Jammu, Jammu 181221, Jammu and Kashmir, India
ambika.shah@iitjammu.ac.in
[2] Indian Institute of Technology Indore, Indore 453552, MP, India

Abstract. Hardware security is important and need of the hour particularly for low cost electronic devices. Hardware-based encryption designs such as physically unclonable functions (PUFs) outperform any known software-based cryptography technique in terms of attack deterrence. This paper proposes a novel design of Three-Transistor (3T) XOR gate based ring-oscillator (RO) PUF. This XOR gate is used as its main element because of its high critical charge than those present in the literature. The critical charge of this XOR gate being 35.52% higher as compared to the inverter. The 3T XOR gate based PUF is then designed with improved uniqueness and reliability at different operating temperatures. The uniqueness of the proposed PUF design is 0.4958 which is better as compared to other counterparts.

Keywords: Physically unclonable function · Hardware security · RO · Uniqueness

1 Introduction

Physical Unclonable Function (PUF) based designs have potential to promise security primitive in the endeavor to create secure systems [1,2]. A PUF is a block in an cryptography secured integrated circuit capable of generating unique responses by taking advantage of the inherent physical variances in the keys manufacturing. PUFs increase the security of the crypto-system by preventing it from being hacked. Traditional way of using secret bits stored in some memory either volatile or non-volatile is replaced by an intrinsic mapping behavior of a PUF. The PUF maps a challenge in terms of functionality (the PUF input) to the response (the PUF output). Even, the designs are resistant to cloning as well. The identical PUFs with same manufacturing conditions provide different responses because of the internal process variations and the prediction of the output becomes a very challenging task. This makes it very feasible to use as key generator for cryptography secured system. The advantages over the usage of a PUF are prominent as it offer dynamic, eavesdropping-resistant key storage as compared to traditional systems storing keys in memory.

A. P. Shah et al. (Eds.): VDAT 2022, CCIS 1687, pp. 331–344, 2022.
https://doi.org/10.1007/978-3-031-21514-8_28

Various PUF based designs are proposed with vital components such as certified execution, hardware metering, key generation, identification and authentication for encryption within IC [1–4]. Another advantage of PUFs is that they are highly inexpensive and tremendously secure as they provide the keys which do not need to be stored anywhere. In addition to that, PUFs do not need a special fabrication and manufacturing process. PUF is typically characterized by having two phases viz enrollment phase and the authentication phase.

The radiation effects of PUF are a necessary issue when it is used in space. A soft error occurs due to charged particle strikes on sensitive nodes and the circuit becomes more vulnerable to reliability issues as a result of the technology scaling due to the decreasing supply voltage, decreased critical charge (Qcrit), and higher transistor density [5]. This exposes these circuits to external particle radiations that result in soft errors [6]. The main failure mechanism that destroys electronics devices by momentarily flipping the recorded data is the single event upset (SEU) generated by radiation particles in terrestrial and aircraft applications [7]. The induced charge is gathered and accumulated through the drift process when a high energy particle strikes a circuit's sensitive node. The sensitive node's stored information flips once the generated voltage pulse from accumulated charge reaches a level over the switching threshold [8].

The organization of this paper is as follows: Sect. 2 discusses the characteristics and properties of PUFs. Section 3 discusses the classification of PUFs and Sect. 4 discusses the radiation effect on PUFs, Sect. 5 presents the pass transistor XOR gate based RO-PUF and its working. Section 6 presents the results and discussions of the proposed circuit. Section 7 presents the conclusion.

2   Characteristics and Properties of PUFs

The characteristics of the PUFs are determined by a number of parameters. Some of them are briefly described as follows:

2.1   Challenge-Response Pair

The PUF is subjected to a particular input also termed as challenge. The output of PUF obtained from internal process variations also termed as response is unique for each challenge. The different responses are differentiated from each other using a popular metric called Hamming distance [9]. Depending upon the source of response, this Hamming distance is of two types namely, Inter and Intra Hamming distance. For a particular challenge, the inter-hamming distance is defined as the distance between the two response bit strings of two different PUFs and the ideal value of Inter-Hamming distance is 0.5 (50%). The variation in expected value for distinct PUFs spans over 20% to 50%, subjected to presence of bias effect. The Intra Hamming Distance can be calculated using bit-wise XOR operation followed by average over the entire result.

When the same challenge is given to a particular PUF then the difference between the two responses of the PUF measured by Hamming distance is known as the Intra-Hamming distance. Thus, Intra-Hamming distance is a measure to quantify the responses of a same PUF under same challenge. For a reliable PUF, it should be as small as possible [9]. Ideally, 0% is the Intra-Hamming Distance between the two responses of a PUF for the same challenge.

2.2 Uniqueness

Uniqueness is a metric to define the two response bit strings differ from each other. In order to distinguish the two responses from two PUF instances, the Uniqueness is standard reference parameter defined as inter-die hamming distance. The optimal value of uniqueness is 50%, that signifies for an identical input to any of the two PUF instances, the response string bit vector differ from each other at half of indices. Consider two bit string responses R_p and R_q randomly picked chip p and q out of m number of accessible chips, and that corresponds to a specific challenge C. As a result, the uniqueness (U) of m chips can be expressed in Eq. 1 [10] as:

$$U = \frac{2}{m(m-1)} \sum_{p=1}^{m-1} \sum_{q=p+1}^{m} \frac{HD(R_p, R_q)}{n} \times 100 \qquad (1)$$

Here $HD(R_p, R_q)$ is the inter-hamming distance between responses R_p and R_q of chips p and q respectively.

2.3 Randomness

Randomness implies the unpredictability of the response of a particular chip. It also implies that, even if all other response bits are known in advance, current bit in the response is random. The definite predictable order in a sequence of bits corresponds to non-randomness and various tests target in detection of such patterns [11] for randomness test. Specifically, randomness corresponds to failure of prediction which is build on some pre-assumption of pattern from past bit strings. A controlled biased variations in PUF results in biased bit responses (proportion of 1's and 0's in the response bit string) seemingly from same PUF.

2.4 Reproducibility

The average number of bit difference between each subsequent response regeneration quantified using Hamming distance is termed as Reproducibility. Reproducibility expresses the average noise present in the consecutive responses. The constancy in the challenge-response pair of a PUF over repeated operations under certain environmental conditions. The PUF is fundamentally based on process variations and these variations are sensitive to environmental setup. Thus, PUF response requires to guarantee its one to one mapping of challenge and response pairs. These environmental conditions include environmental fluctuations, ambient noise, and aging [12]. Although the majority of the generated response bits of PUF are highly reliable, few lack sufficient bias to land in expected state that is either of the two states, a '1' or a '0.' In applications like encryption key generation with high reliability is vital as it directly impacts accuracy of encryption performance. A classical method to achieve better reproducibility of any PUF is to use the Error Correction Codes (ECC) but at the cost of increase in area overheads [13]. Moreover the use of ECC also requires to be implemented carefully as they may introduce security threats by the leakage of the responses of these PUFs [14] and is given as in [15]:

$$\text{Reproducibility} = \text{HDintra} \times 100\% \tag{2}$$

2.5   Reliability

Reliability is used to measure the stability of a PUF in various environmental conditions. These environmental conditions include change in temperature or supply voltage. Ideally, the difference between any two responses of the same challenge under different environmental conditions should be zero. The PUF reliability can be comparable to the process variations. Reliability has been measured by comparing the two responses taken at different time instances. The reliability R of a chip can be measured by:

$$R = 1 - \frac{1}{k} \sum_{m=1}^{k} \frac{\text{HD}\left(R_m, R'_m\right)}{n} \times 100\% \tag{3}$$

where k is the number of samples, n is the number of generated bits, and $HD(R_m, R'_m)$ is the hamming distance between R_m and R'_m.

2.6   Bit Error Rate (BER)

In a particular chip (PUF), the number of bits in the response bit string that are differed between the two consecutive bit-responses for a particular challenge gives the parameter called as BER. This is mathematically calculated as shown in Eq. 4 [16] as:

$$\text{BER} = \frac{1}{r} \sum_{j=1}^{r} \frac{\text{HD}\left(R_i, R_j\right)}{n} \times 100\% \tag{4}$$

where R_j is j^{th} n-bit response sample when the measurement is repeated r times, R_i is the n-bit PUF response from the ith chip.

2.7   Key Error Rate (KER)

Key Error rate indicates a performance index of the PUF to be used as the key in the authentication or cryptographic applications [17]. Mathematically, it is calculated as shown in Eq. 5 [18] as:

$$\text{KER} = 1 - \sum_{i=0}^{K} {}^{N}C_K (1 - \text{BER})^{(N-i)} \text{BER}^{i} \tag{5}$$

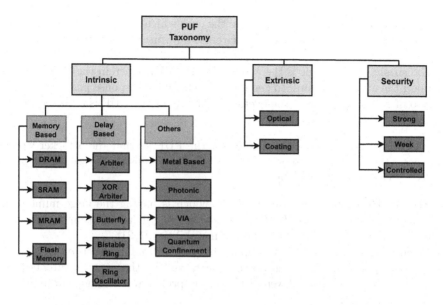

Fig. 1. Taxonomy of Physically Unclonable Function.

where K is the error correction capability of Error Correction Code, and N is the code bit string length.

2.8   Figure of Merit (FOM)

In PUF based designs, the reliability and uniqueness are vital criteria for it's functionality. The values are expected to remain around ideal values as mentioned earlier. While the circuit's primary concerns are power, latency, and area. An exponential term has been used to focus on uniqueness even further and thus FOM is defined as parameter to evaluate all other parameters. Mathematically, it is calculated as shown in Eq. 6 [19] as:

$$\text{FOM} = \frac{R_{WT} + R_{WS}}{2 \times n \times P \times D} \times e^{-\frac{0.5U}{\pi \cdot 02}} \tag{6}$$

where R_{WT} represent worst-case thermal reliability, R_{WS} represent worst-case supply voltage reliability, U is uniqueness and n is the number of the transistors, P is the total power in micro-watts, and D is the delay in ns.

3   Types of PUFs

PUFs can be classified on various parameters as depicted in Fig. 1. Depending upon the stimuli given to the PUFs, they are broadly classified as intrinsic and extrinsic PUFs. These are briefly explained as follows:

a **Intrinsic PUFs:** Intrinsic PUFs are the ones which rely/depend on the internal process variations of the PUF circuits and further classified into various types.
b **Extrinsic PUFs:** This is the category of the PUF wherein the PUF depend upon the external stimuli to generate the challenge-response pairs. These are also of further types and the overall taxonomy of the PUF is depicted in the Fig. 1.

Secure key generation is important for the PUF so that the attacker would not access the key generated or stored in PUF. Depending on the security aspect, PUFs are characterized as [20]:

a **Strong PUF:** It is the type of PUF, which is having the large number of challenge-response pairs (CRPs), thereby making it harder from any cryptographic adversary and environmental instabilities [1,21].
b **Weak PUF:** Weak PUFs support only a limited number of challenge-response pairs and thus can be easily attacked by the security threats [22]. However, the responses of weak PUFs are unpredictable and depend upon the process variations.
c **Controlled PUF:** Modeling attacks are mostly prevented with controlled PUFs [23]. Controlled PUFs use a wrapper logic built around a strong PUF to prevent challenges from being applied directly to the strong PUF, as well as to prohibit direct access to the PUF's responses.

4   Radiation Effect on PUF

Nanoscale electronics is more susceptible to radiation-induced errors, which exacerbates the circuits' noise immunity [24]. Furthermore, modern technology generation operates at low supply voltages, which can minimise circuit node capacitances while also increasing the likelihood of soft errors [25]. In general, smaller feature sizes, lower operating voltages, and higher operating frequencies, along with smaller noise margins, result in a higher soft error rate in integrated circuits [26]. Furthermore, the secure circuits such as PUFs that are needed for applications which are prone to high energy particles such as alpha particles need to have high critical charge so that these particles will not be able to flip the bit value and the PUF will operate correctly even at radiation prone applications. For this, we have used the pass transistor based XOR gate for designing PUF which is having higher critical charge as discussed in next section.

5   Three Transistor (3T) XOR Gate Based RO PUF

We have considered three designs which function as inverter for critical charge analysis as shown in Fig. 2. Only sensitive nodes can experience single even transients. A sensitive node is essentially a reverse biased pn-junction. Normally, transistors in the OFF state's drain junctions experience this circumstance. In

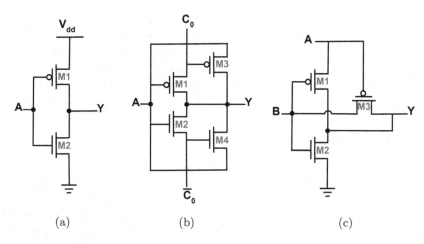

Fig. 2. (a) Conventional Inverter (b) 4T XOR Gate [16] (c) Pass Transistor (3T) based XOR gate [27].

actuality, the voltage drop across the junction, which determines the electric field across that junction, is at its highest value in this instance. The two scenarios below can happen while using a typical CMOS inverter. First, the NMOS transistor is in its OFF state and its drain junction is the sensitive one when the input is logic 0 and the output is logic 1. An energetic particle striking this area has the potential to generate enough charge to result in a temporary $1 \rightarrow 0$ transition at the inverter output, known as a negative glitch. Second, the PMOS transistor is in its OFF state and its drain junction is the sensitive one when the input is logic 1 and the output is logic 0. The inverter output may experience a positive glitch, or a temporary $0 \rightarrow 1$ change, as a result of an energetic particle striking this area [28]. Similar operation occurs in $M1$ and $M2$ transistors of Fig. 2(b). The third design consists of a pmos pass transistor in addition to the CMOS inverter. Feedback present in the circuit enhances the critical charge of the circuit, and thus higher soft error robustness.

The proposed RO-PUF is based on the 3T XOR gate as shown in Fig. 2(c). The total of 25 XOR gates are used as inverters in the design of the RO which is then used to design the PUF.

5.1   Transmission Gate Based XOR Gate

A modified CMOS inverter and a PMOS pass transistor are used in the design as shown in Fig. 2(c). The inverter on the left behaves like a conventional CMOS inverter when input A is at logic high. As a result, the output Y is equal to the complement of the input B. The CMOS inverter output is in high impedance when input A is at logic low. The pass transistor M3, on the other hand, is enabled, and the output Y receives the same logic value as the input B. As a result, the entire circuit works like a two-input XOR gate. When A = 0 and B =

1, however, voltage degradation occurs owing to threshold drop across transistor M3, and the output Y degrades in comparison to the input. Thus, to function this XOR gate as an inverter, needed for the construction of ring oscillator (RO), input A is set at high logic and B input is kept as a variable so that whatever we give at the input B, output is always its complemented form. Thus, forming the basic block for the RO design.

5.2   Proposed RO-PUF

A number of RO-PUF configurations are present in the literature as shown in Fig. 3 which are using different configurations to generate unique responses for same challenges. The pass transistor based XOR gate (here used as inverter) is used as a basic building block for the design of RO-PUF. 'A' input of the XOR gate is set to V_{dd} and 'B' is kept as variable input to function it as an inverter. The B input in the RO-PUF design in the output of the NAND gate used for enabling the PUF circuit. 25 such XOR gates are connected back to back to make the chain of these gates and the output is fed back to the input to make it function as a RO. The output from these ROs is fed to the multiplexers to select the RO for comparison. The functionality of the multiplexers is decided by the challenge/input given and then the counter counts the number of times the faster RO obtains its upper limit as shown in Fig. 4. The comparator finally compares the frequency of these ring oscillators and gives it to the output and thus the 1-bit PUF response is generated. This configuration can be instantiated n times so obtain n-bit PUF response. This RO-PUF design is soft-error tolerant and consumes low area as we have used the soft-error tolerant and low area XOR gate as its basic building block.

6   Results and Discussions

The reason behind taking this XOR gate as the basic building block of the RO-PUF is that this XOR gate is having high critical charge as compared to the conventional inverter as well as other XOR gates present in the literature considered. The high critical charge of this 3T-XOR gate is depicted in Fig. 5. The critical charge is the minimum charge required for the cell to flip the stored data on the cell. For giving some disturbance on the node we will give the exponential current source. In the case of CMOS circuits, the SEUs are modeled by injecting the double exponential current pulse at the sensitive nodes of the circuit. The given pulse will be having fleeting rise time and moderate fall time. This increase in critical charge can be depicted and validated from Fig. 5 and the reason behind this increase is the presence of feedback at the output which leads to the increase in the node capacitances and hence increase in the critical charge. The injection of the current pulse (SEU) at the output node of this gate is shown in Fig. 6 and the bit does not flip until the radiation particle having critical charge greater that the 11.74 fC strikes on the 3T XOR gate. However, the bit flip can easily occur in the inverter and the 4T XOR [16] gate, below this

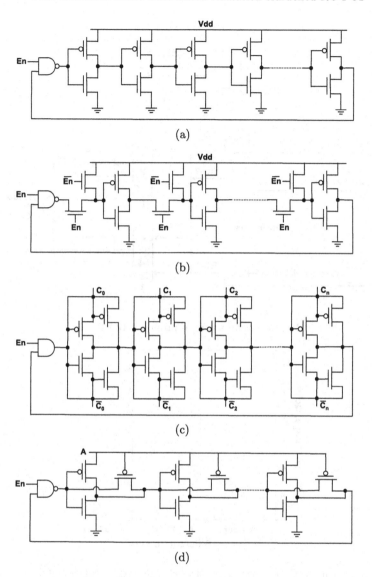

Fig. 3. Different RO structures: (a) Conventional inverter based, (b) Aging Resilient RO (ARO), (c) Low Power XOR based and (d) Proposed radiation hardened 3 transistors XOR based RO.

value because of their low critical charge. Thus, the XOR gate will be resilient to the soft errors occurring due to high energy particles present in the higher altitudes especially in the space applications. In addition to this, the 3T XOR gate is consuming less area as compared to the 4T XOR gate because it uses only three transistors. Thus, in addition to being radiation hardened, it is area

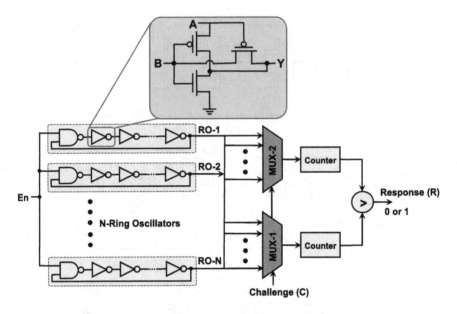

Fig. 4. Architecture of proposed RO-PUF.

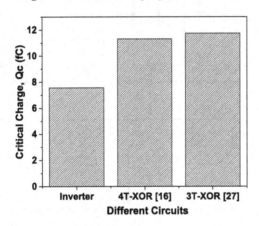

Fig. 5. Comparison of critical charge of different circuits.

efficient as well. Thus, the 3T XOR gate is the better candidate for the radiation hardened as well as low area applications.

The 3T XOR gate and the proposed PUF structure are designed in the Cadence Virtuoso at 40 nm technology node. The proposed RO-PUF is a delay based PUF which consists of 32 ring oscillators whose output is given to the multiplexers so that the particular ring oscillator gets selected and the frequency of the ring oscillators is compared and finally a particular response is obtained. The same design can be replicated to obtain the n-bit response. The RO-PUF design

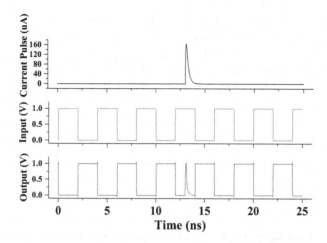

Fig. 6. Injection of current pulse at the output node of pass transistor XOR gate.

Table 1. Simulation results for uniqueness and reliability of various PUF designs.

Design	No. of inverters	Uniqueness	Reliability			
			Temperature (in °C)			
			50	75	100	125
Conventional RO PUF [1]	25	0.486	0.9923	0.9912	0.9815	0.9784
ARO PUF [29]	25	0.490	0.9903	0.9871	0.9783	0.9681
Low power RO PUF [16]	21	0.471	0.9922	0.9831	0.9831	0.9521
Proposed RO PUF	25	0.4958	0.9926	0.9928	0.993	0.9928

is based on the 3T XOR gate which is having higher critical charge and thus is radiation hardened. The critical charge of the 3T XOR gate is 35.52% greater than the inverter as depicted in Fig. 5. The PUF parameters such as uniqueness is calculated at a supply voltage of 0.4V and an operating temperature of 27 °C. The reliability of all the considered PUFs is calculated at different temperatures of 50 °C, 75 °C, 100 °C and 125 °C as listed in Table 1. From results, it is observed that the proposed PUF outperforms the other PUF designs in terms of reliability also. The uniqueness of the proposed PUF design is 0.4958 which is greater than those present in the literature considered as shown in Table 1.

7   Conclusion

A pass transistor XOR gate based RO-PUF is proposed in this paper which is resilient to soft error because of the high critical charge of the 3T XOR gate. The proposed RO-PUF also consumes less area because of the low area 3T transistor used as a building block for its design. The critical charge of this XOR gate being 35.52% higher as compared to the inverter. Thus, the PUF designed is having high critical charge and is resilient to soft error. In addition to this, the proposed PUF is having higher uniqueness of 0.4958 as compared to conventional RO-PUF, ARO PUF and Low Power RO-PUF at a supply voltage of 0.4V and operating temperature of 27 °C. The proposed PUF is also having higher reliability at different operating temperatures of 50 °C, 75 °C, 100 °C and 125 °C as compared to other considered RO-PUFs. Thus, the proposed PUF can be used for the radiation hardened and secure applications.

Acknowledgements. The research leading to this work has received substantial funding from the Prime Minister's Research Fellows (PMRF) Scheme, Government of India.

References

1. Suh, G.E., Devadas, S.: Physical unclonable functions for device authentication and secret key generation. In: 2007 44th ACM/IEEE Design Automation Conference, pp. 9–14. IEEE (2007)
2. Herder, C., Meng-Day, Yu., Koushanfar, F., Devadas, S.: Physical unclonable functions and applications: a tutorial. Proc. IEEE **102**(8), 1126–1141 (2014)
3. Guajardo, J., et al.: Anti-counterfeiting, key distribution, and key storage in an ambient world via physical unclonable functions. Inf. Syst. Front. **11**(1), 19–41 (2009)
4. Katzenbeisser, S., Kocabaş, Ü., Rožić, V., Sadeghi, A.-R., Verbauwhede, I., Wachsmann, C.: PUFs: myth, fact or busted? a security evaluation of physically unclonable functions (PUFs) cast in silicon. In: Prouff, E., Schaumont, P. (eds.) CHES 2012. LNCS, vol. 7428, pp. 283–301. Springer, Heidelberg (2012). https://doi.org/10.1007/978-3-642-33027-8_17
5. Shah, A.P., Yadav, N., Beohar, A., Vishvakarma, S.K.: An efficient NBTI sensor and compensation circuit for stable and reliable SCRAM cells. Microelectron. Reliabil. **87**, 15–23 (2018)
6. Ibe, E., Taniguchi, H., Yahagi, Y., Shimbo, K., Toba, T.: Impact of scaling on neutron-induced soft error in SRAMS from a 250 nm to a 22 nm design rule. IEEE Trans. Electron Devices **57**(7), 1527–1538 (2010)
7. Dodd, P.E., Massengill, L.W.: Basic mechanisms and modeling of single-event upset in digital microelectronics. IEEE Trans. Nuclear Sci. **50**(3), 583–602 (2003)
8. Guo, J., et al.: Design of area-efficient and highly reliable RHBD 10t memory cell for aerospace applications. IEEE Trans. Very Large Scale Integr. (VLSI) Syst. **26**(5), 991–994 (2018)
9. Maes, R., Ingrid, V.: Physically unclonable functions: a study on the state of the art and future research directions. In: Towards Hardware-Intrinsic Security, pp. 3–37. Springer (2010)
10. Gu, C., Hanley, N., O'Neill, M.: FPGA-based strong puf with increased uniqueness and entropy properties. In 2017 IEEE International Symposium on Circuits and Systems (ISCAS), pp. 1–4. IEEE (2017)
11. van der Leest, V., van der Sluis, E., Schrijen, G.-J., Tuyls, P., Handschuh, H.: Efficient implementation of true random number generator based on SRAM PUFs. In: Naccache, D. (ed.) Cryptography and Security: From Theory to Applications. LNCS, vol. 6805, pp. 300–318. Springer, Heidelberg (2012). https://doi.org/10.1007/978-3-642-28368-0_20

12. Maiti, A., Schaumont, P.: The impact of aging on a physical unclonable function. IEEE Trans. Very Large Scale Integr. (VLSI) Syst. **22**(9), 1854–1864 (2013)

13. Meng-Day, Yu., Devadas, S.: Secure and robust error correction for physical unclonable functions. IEEE Des. Test Comput. **27**(1), 48–65 (2010)

14. Vivekraja, V., Nazhandali, L.: Circuit-level techniques for reliable physically uncloneable functions. In: 2009 IEEE International Workshop on Hardware-Oriented Security and Trust, pp.30–35. IEEE (2009)

15. Amsaad, F., Chaudhuri, C.R., Niamat, M.: Reliable and reproducible PUF based cryptographic keys under varying environmental conditions. In: 2016 IEEE National Aerospace and Electronics Conference (NAECON) and Ohio Innovation Summit (OIS), pp. 468–473. IEEE (2016)

16. Khan, S., Shah, A.P., Gupta, N., Chouhan, S.S., Pandey, J.G., Vishvakarma, S.K.: An ultra-low power, reconfigurable, aging resilient RO PUF for IoT applications. Microelectron. J. **92**, 104605 (2019)

17. Taneja, S., Alvarez, A.B., Alioto, M.: Fully synthesizable PUF featuring hysteresis and temperature compensation for 3.2% native ber and 1.02 fj/b in 40 nm. IEEE J. Solid-State Circ. **53**(10), 2828–2839 (2018)

18. Delvaux, J., Dawu, G., Schellekens, D., Verbauwhede, I.: Helper data algorithms for PUF-based key generation: overview and analysis. IEEE Trans. Comput.-Aid. Des. Integr. Circ. Syst. **34**(6), 889–902 (2014)

19. Khan, S., et al.: Utilizing manufacturing variations to design a tri-state flip-flop PUF for IoT security applications. Analog Integr. Circ. Sign. Process. **103**(3), 477–492 (2020)

20. Orshansky, M., Milor, L., Chenming, H.: Characterization of spatial intrafield gate cd variability, its impact on circuit performance, and spatial mask-level correction. IEEE Trans. Semiconduc. Manufact. **17**(1), 2–11 (2004)

21. Gassend, B., Dijk, M.V., Clarke, D., Devadas, S.: Controlled physical random functions. In: Proceedings on 18th Annual Computer Security Applications Conference 2002, pp. 149–160. IEEE (2002)

22. Škorić, B., Tuyls, P., Ophey, W.: Robust key extraction from physical uncloneable functions. In: Ioannidis, J., Keromytis, A., Yung, M. (eds.) ACNS 2005. LNCS, vol. 3531, pp. 407–422. Springer, Heidelberg (2005). https://doi.org/10.1007/11496137_28

23. Guajardo, J., Kumar, S.S., Schrijen, G.-J., Tuyls, P.: FPGA intrinsic PUFs and their use for IP protection. In: Paillier, P., Verbauwhede, I. (eds.) CHES 2007. LNCS, vol. 4727, pp. 63–80. Springer, Heidelberg (2007). https://doi.org/10.1007/978-3-540-74735-2_5

24. Bol, D., Ambroise, R., Flandre, D., Legat, J.D.: Interests and limitations of technology scaling for subthreshold logic. IEEE Trans. Very Large Scale Integr. (VLSI) Syst. **17**(10), 1508–1519 (2009)

25. Lin, S., Kim, Y.-B., Lombardi, F.: Analysis and design of nanoscale CMOS storage elements for single-event hardening with multiple-node upset. IEEE Trans. Dev. Mater. Reliabil. **12**(1), 68–77 (2011)

26. Mavis, D.G., Eaton, P.H.: Soft error rate mitigation techniques for modern microcircuits. In: 2002 IEEE International Reliability Physics Symposium. Proceedings. 40th Annual (Cat. No. 02CH37320), pp. 216–225. IEEE, (2002)

27. Chowdhury, S.R., Banerjee, A., Roy, A., Saha, H.: A high speed 8 transistor full adder design using novel 3 transistor xor gates. Int. J. Electron. Circ. Syst. **2**(4), 217–223 (2008)

28. Shah, A.P., Rossi, D., Sharma, V., Vishvakarma, S.K., Waltl, M.: Soft error harden-
    ing enhancement analysis of NBTI tolerant schmitt trigger circuit. Microelectron.
    Reliabil. **107**, 113617 (2020)
29. Rahman, M.T., Rahman, F., Forte, D., Tehranipoor, M.: An aging-resistant RO-
    PUF for reliable key generation. IEEE Trans. Emerg. Top. Comput. **4**(3), 335–348
    (2015)

QCA Technology Based 8-Bit TRNG Design for Cryptography Applications

Prateek Sinha, Aniket Sharma, Nilay Naharas, Syed Farah Naz,
and Ambika Prasad Shah[✉] [iD]

IC-ResQ Laboratory, Department of Electrical Engineering,
Indian Institute of Technology Jammu, Jammu 181221, J&K, India
ambika.shah@iitjammu.ac.in

Abstract. Hardware Security is very important considering the extensive usage of hardware devices and data security. In this paper, the structure of a hardware security primitives namely the True Random Number Generator (TRNG) is proposed using Quantum Cellular Automata (QCA) technology. The AND gate, XOR gate and a gate with irregular behavior are used to generate random output depending upon the metastability of the QCA structure. Furthermore, the structure is cross looped and asymmetrically inverted for extra randomness. The energy calculations of the structure were performed using QCA Designer Pro and the randomness of the output was tested in the NIST Test Suite.

Keywords: Quantum dot cellular automata · Metastability · TRNG · Randomness · NIST Test

1 Introduction

Hardware security is an important area of work in the digital world which is hardware intensive; secure hardware is the key in making reliable computers and other essential devices. It is important for security that the data transmitted between various points is encrypted and the secure encryption key is needed for such encryption purposes. The Random Number Generators (RNGs) acts as the encryption locks and keys to help securing the data communication between sender and receiver. For accomplishing an end-to-end encrypted communication between the two stations, the 'key' is used for encrypting the data to be transferred as depicted in Fig. 1 [1]. An important characteristic of this 'key' is that it should be undecipherable to anyone who is not a part of the entire process of communication.

Random Number Generators are an essential step in the security techniques for making the systems more secure and their usage in secure communication [2]. These hardware implemented crytographic devices are used for tackling various security related issues. Needless to say, they form the backbone of the modern day secure communication system. There is a wide usage of Pseudo-Random number generator (PRNG), but a deterministic algorithm can be written to identify the underlying repetition.

© The Author(s), under exclusive license to Springer Nature Switzerland AG 2022
A. P. Shah et al. (Eds.): VDAT 2022, CCIS 1687, pp. 345–357, 2022.
https://doi.org/10.1007/978-3-031-21514-8_29

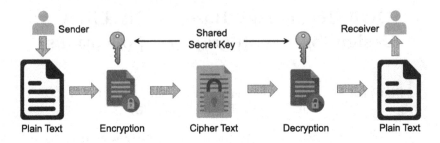

Fig. 1. Use of secure keys in data encryption

So, we intend to create a True Random Number Generator (TRNG) whose randomness is due to the underlying faults of the intrinsic material of the generator structure itself, which in turn gives random outputs every time. TRNG is a novel technology based on the concept of randomness associated with the physical nature of the quantum dots (qubits) [3–5]. To overcome the shortcomings faced due to continuous scaling down of the CMOS technology various alternative device technologies have been proposed. QCA is one of the most important among them [6]. QCA based designs offer low-energy and area-efficient solutions to the existing CMOS circuit designs [7]. In case of CMOS technology the voltage levels are used for dictating the logic levels whereas in the case of QCA technology the polarization of the individual cells are used for accomplishing the same. QCA is a computational paradigm that utilizes a zero current and transistorless framework which is then used for propagating information on the basis of electrostatic charge interaction due to the coulombic forces of interaction which operate between the cells [8]. This paper provides a comprehensive description of QCA preliminaries.

The rest of the paper is organized in the following sections: The introduction to security primitives are presented in Sect. 2. Section 3 provides a brief description of the QCA basics. Section 4 is about TRNG design and QCA based structure. The results and discussions of the paper are propounded in the Sect. 5. The conclusion and future work are presented in Sect. 6.

2   Security Primitives

2.1   TRNG and PUF

Security measures are of prime importance to prevent manipulation and leakage of transferred information by an attacker. Therefore the need for random and pseudorandom numbers arises in many cryptographic applications. Hardware based security primitives most prominently feature the Physical Unclonable Functions (PUFs) and the TRNGs. A PUF is based on the idea that even though the mask and manufacturing process is the same among different ICs, each IC is actually slightly different due to normal manufacturing variability. They are digital biometrics based on the uniqueness of their physical microstructure.

PUFs are basically an integrated circuit manufactured from semiconductors. During the process of manufacturing, uncontrollable and unpredictable random physical microstructures are introduced which makes it virtually impossible to duplicate or clone the structure. When a physical stimulus is applied to the structure, it reacts in an unpredictable way due the complex interactions between the random physical microstructures [9].

The applied stimulus is called the challenge and the reaction of the structure to the applied stimulus is called the response and together they form the challenge-response pair (CRP). A black-box challenge-response system can be modelled for each PUF. In other words, when a PUF is given an input challenge c, it responds with r = f(c), where f(.) specifies the PUF's input/output relations. Because the internal parameters of f(.) indicate the internal manufacturing variability that the PUF uses to build a unique challenge-response set, the blackbox model is suitable here. In contrast to a PUF, the RNG is a computational construct or a hardware design that is considered to produce arbitrary sets of numbers which are an encoded form of the input data in a way that the encryption can not be determined from the output sequence [10]. Pseudo Random Number Generators (PRNGs) and TRNGs are the two forms of RNGs. The main difference between these types is that the numbers that are generated from the PRNGs are software generated and hence are comparatively easier to predict. TRNGs on the other hand, produce numbers leveraging hardwares and entropies. A TRNG takes advantage of the environmental entropy sources or the seed values or a combination of both to produce a sequence of random numbers.

For studying about the topic and gettting a clearer picture on the works done previously on the TRNG and the QCA based structures in general, a lot of research papers were studied to understand the insights behind good and interesting designs. A lot of information was gathered about the variety of digital circuits that the QCA technique may be used to create. The majority voters and inverter gates are an important part of the QCA-based designs, and many TRNGs are made using those concepts.

In this paper, the quantum phenomenon is employed for the purpose of generating random sequences. Even though the internal structure of the TRNG can be known to the attacker, the output sequence cannot be replicated owing to the non-deterministic and unpredictable nature of the quantum environment. Therefore, a hardware-based cryptographically secure RNG has a broader perspective as compared to the PRNG and is a preferred choice.

3   QCA Basics

3.1   Quantum Cellular Automata

To overcome the shortcomings faced due to continuous scaling down of the CMOS technology various alternative device technologies have been proposed. These device technologies can solve the scaling limitations in the current prevalent CMOS technology. The search for these technologies lead to the development of various other device technologies such as QCA.

Among all these evolving technologies, QCA is the most promising. QCA based designs offer low energy and area efficient solutions to the existing CMOS circuit designs. In QCA based technology, the logic states are dictated by the polarizations of the individual electrons as compared to the voltage levels which do the same in the CMOS based technology. QCA is a computational paradigm in which information is transferred from one cell to another on the basis of electrostatic charge on the basis of coulombic interaction. The fundamental unit of the QCA technology is the quantum cell that basically consists of four quantum dots and each dot can hold one electron.

These quantum dots are placed along the four vertices of a square cell. This cell contains two mobile electrons that can tunnel between the dots [11]. These two electrons cannot tunnel from one cell to another because of the potential barrier between the two cells. Therefore, the two electrons confined in a single cell orient themselves in such a way so that the electrostatic repulsion between the two electrons is the minimum and as a result a stable system is obtained. For the cell to achieve this stable state, only two configurations of the electrons in the cell are possible. Both of these configurations are achieved when the two electrons are placed along the diagonally opposite ends. These possible sites are called the antipodal sites. These stable states that the electrons assume are called the polarizations of the quantum cell. These polarizations are energetically equal and can be interpreted as equivalent to the binary '0' and '1' [11]. The polarizations shown in Fig. 2 [12] can be interpreted in the following way: Polarisation, P = 1 implies logic 1; Polarisation, P = -1 implies logic 0. Polarisation of the cell can be calculated from the equation given below [13]:

$$P = \frac{(\rho_1 + \rho_3) - (\rho_2 + \rho_4)}{(\rho_1 + \rho_2 + \rho_3 + \rho_4)}$$

For the ground state eigen function, ρ_i is the expected value of the number operator on site (dot).

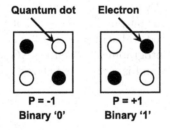

Fig. 2. Different polarization of the QCA cell [12].

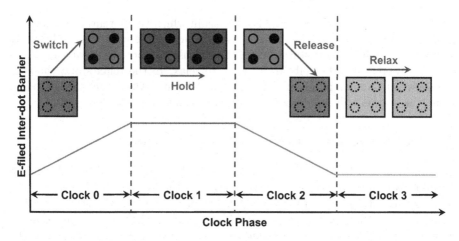

Fig. 3. Clocking zones of a QCA cell [12]

3.2   QCA Clocking

CMOS technology uses clocks to control the timing and the flow of data in most of the sequential circuits. However, that is not the case with the QCA technology. The switching and power gain are provided using the clocks in the QCA based circuits. The clock signal that is supplied to each and every QCA cell performs the task of lowering or raising the quantum tunnel barriers which help in regulating the transportation of electrons in and out of the cells. The electrons transport from one cell to another via quantum tunnelling. The clock signals are generated from the wires that are buried under the QCA surface using Carbon Nanotubes (CNTs) [14].

These generated electric fields are perpendicular to the plane of QCA surface. QCA circuits generally consist of a 4 phase clocking sequence that is used to control the flow of information across cells as shown in Fig. 3 [12]. The clock signals or zones consist of 4 phases namely switch, hold, release and relax. The frequency of each of the clock signals is the same with variations in the phase of the input signal. One of the clock signals are assumed to be at the zero phase shift and then the other signals are delayed by corresponding integral multiple of the time period, for instance considering the first phase to be at zero phase angle the remaining signals are delayed by one (phase $= \pi/2$) two (phase $= \pi$) and three (phase $= 3\pi/2$) quarters of the time period. In the switching phase the state of the cell is determined by the neighbouring cells and gets locked into a state that is independent from the neighbouring states. During the switching phase there is a surge in the potential barriers and it leads to the polarization of the cells as per the polarisation of the driver cells. It is during this clocking phase that the computation occurs. After the switching clock is complete the potential barriers of the cell are raised to suppress any kind of tunnelling. This causes the polarisation of the cell to be fixed.

The next clocking phase is the hold state in which the potential barriers are held high and in this way the cell acts as an input for the next stage. This state is followed by the release state. During this phase the potential barriers of the cell are lowered and the cells are allowed to relax. In the relax state, the cells are allowed to remain in an unpolarized, neutral state. After reaching the fourth state, the system will repolarize and revert to the first clock phase.

4   TRNG Design and QCA-based Structure

The purpose of TRNG is to generate incalculable, unpredictable and random outputs sequences. In this section, the design of the proposed TRNG structure is described with a concrete reasoning behind the choice of the structure. The objectives was that the structure should be energy efficient, judicial in terms of area and should have an innate randomness which would be showcased in the outputs. First, the basic 2-bit structure is described and then it is extrapolated into a full-fledged 8-bit TRNG.

4.1   Two-bit Structure

The two-bit basic layout of the proposed TRNG consists of 2 XOR gates, 1 AND gate, and a Random gate. The first bit comes out of a looped XOR and AND gate, while the other bit is generated by the "random" gate and XOR gate as shown in Fig. 4(a). The Random or Unknown gate is a vital novelty obtained by removing a cell from the QCA structure of an AND gate. This unknown gate's output is unpredictable because the nature of QCA cell interaction changes drastically due to the removal or addition of cells. These two cross-looped structures of XOR, AND as well as XOR and Unknown gate give the 2-bit output for the TRNG. The QCA implementation of 2-bit TRNG structure is shown in Fig. 4(b).

4.2   Eight-bit Proposed Structure

The Fig. 5 represents a novel structure of an eight-bit TRNG in QCA technology. This structure can be extended to any number of required bits. The structure

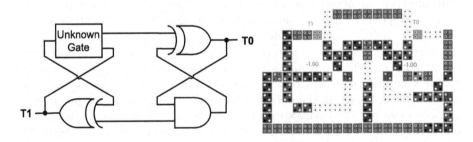

Fig. 4. (a) Logic diagram of basic 2-bit Structure (b) QCA implementation of the logic diagram.

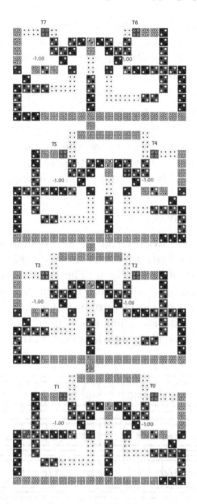

Fig. 5. Proposed structure of the eight-bit TRNG.

consists of a total of 416 QCA cells and it occupies an area of 0.38 μm^2 with a very nominal delay of a single clock pulse.

4.3   Seed Input

Seed Inputs in this context is the input given to the TRNG with the clock and is used to generate the random output from the TRNG. To get a more random and unpredictable output state a set of QCA cells are arranged in a particular way. The seed input can be thought of as the initial state of an algorithm that is used for generating random numbers. The initial state (consisting of initial set of vectors along with other fixed algorithm parameters) provides the direction for proceeding in a particular direction and any changes in the input state has a direct consequence on the series of random numbers that are generated by the algorithm. Seed input in hardware is also performing the same sort of function as the initial state in the random number generating algorithm. A random seed input will always increase the efficiency of the TRNG output because of the randomness of the input itself [15].

5   Results and Discussions

We conducted a performance analysis on the proposed TRNG design in this section. QCADesigner 2.0.3 [16] was used to perform the performance analysis run with the coherence and bistable approximation engines.

5.1   Performance Analysis

The simulation parameters have been left at their default settings. All the results of the proposed TRNG architecture were tested using the same clock signal, and the outputs are as shown in Fig. 6. The simulation works by taking the quantum interactions among the cells into account after calculating the sum of electrostatic energies in each clocked group of QCA cells for all possible logic states. Following each excitation, the cross-coupled loop circuit's contradicting input cells cause unexpected electrostatic effects on the cross-oriented cells [17].

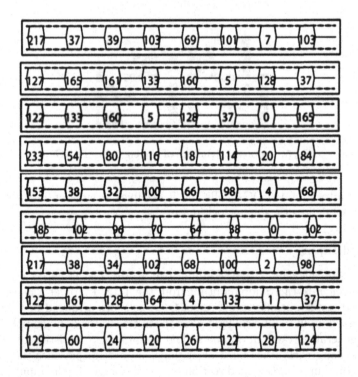

Fig. 6. Decimal Outputs of an 8-bit TRNG

Another factor that affects the randomness is the novel random or unknown gate whose indeterminate quantum outputs are important randomness generators. The whole architecture works together to generate the randomness in the output. An 8-bit digital system generates decimal values ranging from 0 to 255, therefore the proposed 8-bit TRNG is capable of generating any random number from 0 to 255.

5.2   Statistical Tests

A generated random sequence has to be fathomed for the amount of randomness. These tests aid in comparison of different sequences, which helps in making changes to improve the output of the random number generator. All the generated sequences are evaluated based on randomness and unpredictability. A truly random sequence of bits would mean that the probability of the next bit in the sequence is equal to 1/2 every time, almost like tossing an unbiased coin to decide the next bit. The generated sequence is going to be used for security purposes this mandates the need that the subsequent bits in the sequence cannot be determined by making the use of the previous bits in the sequence and, therefore, the sequence to be unpredictable. A statistical test is formulated to test a specific null hypothesis (H0) [18]. The null hypothesis for this paper is that the generated sequence under investigation is random. The alternative hypothesis (Ha) is associated with the null hypothesis, which in this case means that the sequence is not random. A decision or conclusion is derived for each applied test that accepts or rejects the null hypothesis, i.e., whether the generator is (or is not) producing random values based on the sequence that was generated [19].

A set of certified statistical tests on the proposed TRNG design have been performed in this section. Various industrial standard statistical test suites are available to assess randomnesses, such as NIST, Diehard, etc. The proposed TRNG's randomness was evaluated using the National Institute of Standards and Technology's (NIST) statistical test suite [20]. For each test of the proposed TRNG's randomness, 120 bit-streams of 10000 bits are prepared at a significance level of 0.05. According to the NIST statistical tests, the TRNG design will meet the industrial requirements if a specific test's passing value (P-value) is between 0.01 and 0.99. These tests have been performed on the proposed TRNG [21], and Table 1 displays the results of the NIST test on the proposed TRNG.

Table 1. Statistical performance of the proposed TRNG.

Test	Result
Frequency	0.134
Block frequency	0.2369
Longest run of Ones	0.419
Spectral DFT	0.297
Auto correlation function	−0.138

5.3 Power Analysis

While designing any VLSI circuit, power dissipation is one of the major concerns alongside area and delay. In this section, the proposed TRNG has been examined with low power dissipation as well as delay and area. Power dissipation has been calculated by a precise tool, QCAPro [22]. For the proposed TRNG, two significant energy dissipation sources in QCA, Leakage Energy and Switching Power, have been calculated.

The Switching Energy dissipation of the QCA cell is calculated throughout the switching period as per the specified input, whereas leakage energy is caused due to the clock transition. The proposed TRNG's power dissipation was calculated using three distinct energy ratios γ/E_k i.e. 0.5, 1 and 1.5. Table 2 shows the average leakage energy and switching energy dissipation of the proposed TRNG for all possible vector input. Figure 7 shows the QCAPro generated thermal layout of the proposed TRNG design at energy ratios γ/E_k 1.0.

We also compared the proposed TRNG design with earlier reported QCA TRNG designs [23–25]. Various TRNG have been presented and compared over

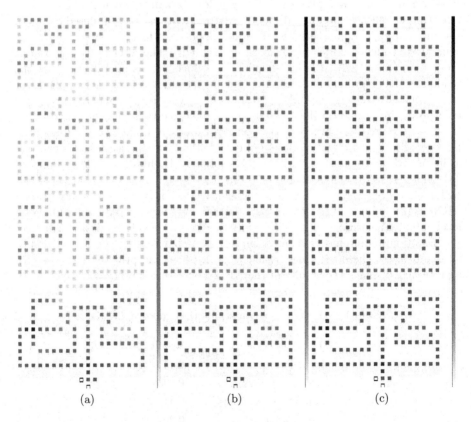

(a)   (b)   (c)

Fig. 7. Thermal Layout for average power dissipation of proposed 8-bit TRNG at (a) $0.5E_k$ (b) $1.0E_k$ and (c) $1.5E_k$

Table 2. Power dissipation data of the proposed TRNG.

Energy Ratio	$0.5E_k$	$1.0E_k$	$1.5E_k$
Avg. leakage energy dissipation (meV)	150.44	430.43	747.51
Avg. switching energy dissipation (meV)	104.68	88.80	74.50

Table 3. Parametric comparison of our proposed 8-bit TRNG w.r.t., reported TRNGs.

Parameter	[23]	[24]	[25]	Proposed TRNG
Complexity (No. of QCA cell)	498	463	388	416
Area (m^2)	0.52	0.46	0.36	0.38
Avg. Power/bit (meV)	62.35	57.74	57.06	64.9

different parameters like area, complexity and power dissipation. These parametric readings are derived from the simulation setup carried out using QCADesigner 2.0.3 and QCAPro, and are shown in Table 3. Results indicate that the proposed TRNG require less number of cells and less area as compared to the other considered TRNGs except reported in [25].

6 Conclusion

A novel structure of TRNG has been proposed in this paper based on QCA technology. The proposed TRNG is an efficient design in terms of area, delay, and energy, as demonstrated in the previous section. Improving the seed input can further boost the randomness and energy reduction. The proposed design is based on unpredictable polarisation in the QCA cells and a non-deterministic seed input. The major design theme was using a cross-looped 'AND' gate, 'XOR' gate, the irregular gate using QCA technology, to generate the random output. The proposed 8-bit TRNG is made up of 416 QCA cells and require $0.38\mu m^2$ area. We are aiming to improve the operating temperature of the QCA technology and trying to make it a more accessible technology that can exist and operate at more practical temperatures.

Acknowledgement. The authors would like to thank the SERB, Government of India for providing financial support under the Startup Research Grant Scheme with grant no. SRG/2021/001101.

References

1. Agrawal, V., Agrawal, S., Deshmukh, R.K.: Analysis and review of encryption and decryption for secure communication. Int. J. Sci. Eng. Res. **2**(2), 2347–3878 (2014)
2. Hedayatpour, S., Chuprat, S.: Random number generator based on transformed image data source. In: Advances in Computer, Communication, Control and Automation, pp. 457–464. Springer (2011). https://doi.org/10.1007/978-3-642-25541-0_58

3. Lim, D., Lee, J.W., Gassend, B., Suh, G.E., Van Dijk, M., Devadas, S.: Extracting secret keys from integrated circuits. IEEE Trans. Very Large Scale Integr. (VLSI) Syst. **13**(10), 1200–1205 (2005)

4. Holcomb, D.E., Burleson, W.P., Fu, K.: Power-up sram state as an identifying fingerprint and source of true random numbers. IEEE Trans. Comput. **58**(9), 1198–1210 (2008)

5. Laajimi, R., Ajimi, A., Touil, L., Bahar, A.N.: A novel design for xor gate used for quantum-dot cellular automata (QCA) to create a revolution in nanotechnology structure. Int. J. Adv. Comput. Sci. Appl. **8**(10), 279–287 (2017)

6. Lent, C.S., Tougaw, P.D., Porod, W., Bernstein, G.H.: Quantum cellular automata. Nanotechnology **4**(1), 49 (1993)

7. Blair, E.P., Yost, E., Lent, C.S.: Power dissipation in clocking wires for clocked molecular quantum-dot cellular automata. J. Comput. Electron. **9**(1), 49–55 (2010)

8. Sarkar, T.: Design of dflip-flip using nano-technology based quantum cellular automata. Int. J. Soft Computi. Eng. (IJSCE) **3**, 56 (2013)

9. Ennesser, F., Ganem, H.: Establishing security in machine-to-machine (m2m) communication devices and services. In: Machine-to-machine (M2M) Communications, pp. 227–248. Elsevier (2015)

10. Pain, P., Das, K., Sadhu, A., Kanjilal, M.R., De, D.: Novel true random number generator based hardware cryptographic architecture using quantum-dot cellular automata. Int. J. Theor. Phys. **58**(9), 3118–3137 (2019)

11. Tougaw, P.D., Lent, C.S.: Dynamic behavior of quantum cellular automata. J. Appl. Phys. **80**(8), 4722–4736 (1996)

12. Das, K., De, D., De, M.: Competent universal reversible logic gate design for quantum dot cellular automata. WSEAS Trans. Circ. Syst. **11**, 401–411 (2012)

13. Angizi, S., Sayedsalehi, S., Roohi, A., Bagherzadeh, N., Navi, K.: Design and verification of new n-bit quantum-dot synchronous counters using majority function-based JK flip-flops. J. Circ. Syst. Comput. **24**(10), 1550153 (2015)

14. Mehta, U., Dhare, V.: Quantum-dot cellular automata (QCA): A survey. arXiv preprint arXiv:1711.08153 (2017)

15. Sadhu, A., Das, K., De, D., Kanjilal, M.R.: MVTRNG: majority voter-based crossed loop quantum true random number generator in QCA nanotechnology. In: Maharatna, K., Kanjilal, M.R., Konar, S.C., Nandi, S., Das, K. (eds.) Computational Advancement in Communication Circuits and Systems. LNEE, vol. 575, pp. 241–253. Springer, Singapore (2020). https://doi.org/10.1007/978-981-13-8687-9_22

16. Walus, K., Dysart, T.J., Jullien, G.A., Budiman, R.A.: Qcadesigner: a rapid design and simulation tool for quantum-dot cellular automata. IEEE Trans. Nanotechnol. **3**(1), 26–31 (2004)

17. Welland, M.E., Gimzewski, J.K.: Ultimate Limits of Fabrication and Measurement, vol. 292. Springer Science & Business Media (2012)

18. Niu, X., Wang, Y., Wu, D.: A method to generate random number for cryptographic application. In: 2014 Tenth International Conference on Intelligent Information Hiding and Multimedia Signal Processing, pp. 235–238. IEEE (2014)

19. Smid, E.B., Leigh, S., Levenson, M., Vangel, M., DavidBanks, A., JamesDray, S.: A statistical test suite for random and pseudorandom number generators for cryptographic applications. Her research interest includes Computer security, secure operating systems, Access control, Distributed systems, Intrusion detection systems (2010)

20. Rukhin, A., Soto, J., Nechvatal, J., Smid, M., Barker, E.: A statistical test suite for random and pseudorandom number generators for cryptographic applications. Tech. rep, Booz-allen and hamilton inc mclean va (2001)
21. Kim, S.J., Umeno, K., Hasegawa, A.: Corrections of the Nist statistical test suite for randomness. arXiv preprint nlin/0401040 (2004)
22. Srivastava, S., Asthana, A., Bhanja, S., Sarkar, S.: Qcapro-an error-power estimation tool for QCA circuit design. In: 2011 IEEE International Symposium of Circuits and Systems (ISCAS), pp. 2377–2380. IEEE (2011)
23. Abutaleb, M.: A novel true random number generator based on QCA nanocomputing. Nano Commun. Netw. **17**, 14–20 (2018)
24. Pain, P., Das, K., Sadhu, A., Kanjilal, M.R., De, D.: Power analysis attack resistable hardware cryptographical circuit design using reversible logic gate in quantum cellular automata. Microsyst. Technol, 1–13 (2019)
25. Sadhu, A., Das, K., De, D., Kanjilal, M.R.: SSTRNG: self starved feedback SRAM based true random number generator using quantum cellular automata. Microsyst. Technol. **26**(7), 2203–2215 (2020)

Signal Integrity and Power Loss Analysis for Different Bump Structures in Cylindrical TSV

Shivangi Chandrakar[✉], Kunal Kranti Das, Deepika Gupta, and Manoj Kumar Majumder

International Institute of Information Technology, Naya Raipur 493661, Chhattisgarh, India
{shivangi,deepika,manojk}@iiitnr.edu.in

Abstract. The selection of a suitable bump shape is critical to the performance of a 3D packaging system. The most widely used bump shape (cylindrical) is facing significant reliability issues, including coefficient of thermal expansion (CTE) mismatch, stress and power loss. Bump with a tapered shape have procured a lot of attention recently because of their low volume fraction and coupling capacitance, which can significantly minimize stress and crosstalk related delay. In order to quantify the effective CTE and stress of different solder structures the bump/underfill composite assembly is quantitatively studied using 3D unit-cell technique, which takes evenly distributed bump in the underfill. The temperature-dependent effective CTE of the evenly distributed bump incorporating the volume fraction can be used for the analysis of the stress issues. Additionally, for the analysis of the power loss, the analytical π based impedance network is proposed. The model was successfully verified by EM simulation under the different frequency range. Furthermore, a distinctive electromagnetic (EM) based model is used to analyze the NEXT (Near end) and FEXT (Far end) crosstalk delay using coupled bump arrangement at 32 nm technology. Using Computer Simulation Microwave Studio (CST MWS) industry-standard EM simulations tool, the crosstalk induced delay is obtained upto 20 GHz operating frequencies for different bump architectures i.e. cylindrical, spherical and tapered. Considering a tapered bump, a substantial improvement in NEXT, FEXT, and CTE at 32 nm technology is observed as 3.39%, 4.02%, 7.03%, 8.08% 11.88%, and 40.18% respectively compared to the spherical and cylindrical bump.

Keywords: Near End Crosstalk · Far End Crosstalk · Coefficient of Thermal Expansion · Solder bump shape · 3D IC · Underfill · Z parameter · S parameter

1 Introduction

Solder bump model enables for the shortest interface with the utmost number of input outputs in three-dimensional (3D) IC packaging. A micro bump serves as a crucial joint between the vertical interconnect access in the microelectronics package [1]. While, in wake of recent trends, towards miniaturization, bump dimensions have shrunk dramatically, resulting in high current density, severe Joule heating, and high temperatures. As a result, high current stresses the solder joint structures, exacerbating electromigration in the bump assemblages [2]. Additionally, electromigration is well-known for being reliant on the shape of solder bumps, amount of solder volume and joint structure. Therefore, the appropriate selection of bump shape has piqued the interest in the research community. Furthermore, the advanced packaging technologies contains the solder bumps with the shape of spherical, cylindrical and tapered [3–5]. A cylindrical bump offers significant advantages over spherical and tapered structures because of its homogenous assembly, high breakdown voltage, and ease of production. However, the highly used cylindrical bump confronted electromigration, stress, and reliability issue due to its larger coefficient of thermal expansion (CTE) and solder volume [3]. In contrast to cylindrical shape, the spherical bumps are suitable for a structural stability and lower solder volume, resulting in higher package density. However, in case of the spherical bump, filling time of the flip-chip encapsulation process increases in the fabrication that causes inadvertent delay for the chip production [4]. Among all the other bump structure the tapered bump are suitable for a thermocompression bonding process with low temperature and load force, low cost material due to the sharp pointed tapering structure, high reliable, lower stress and better performance in terms of electromigration. Hence, the tapered shape bump recently received considerable interest from the research community [5].

The state-of-the-art research revealed in [6] are predominantly conferred about the conventional cylindrical shaped bump joint in the fabrication aspects. In order to produce cylindrical solder joints, Xu *et al.* [6] has been used a photolithographically defined photoresist patterns as stencils that provides comparatively higher-resolution and controllable size. However, because of the greater volume fraction and CTE, the cylindrical bump produces a high current density, Joule heating, and high temperature, resulting in significant electromigration failure. Later, using analytical, experimental, and computational methods, Ng *et al.* [7] published a thorough investigation of cylindrical and spherical bumps to evaluate the effect of solder bump shape on underfill flow during flip-chip encapsulation. Herein, the flip-chip underfill flow will be visualized using a particle image velocimetry (PIV) method. However, spherical bump possesses large neck diameter and low pad-to-neck ratio is realized to be a factor for a slower underfill flow that converts to a less efficient encapsulation and worsens the bump reliability and mechanical strength. In order to mitigate the problem associated with spherical bump, Motoyoshi *et al.* [8] investigated mechanical strength properties of a tapered shaped bump. Herein, the solid-state interdiffusion creates a bump junction, allowing for protrusion and oxidation-free bonding, as well as bump size scaling. The analysis carried in Ref. [8] reveals that the tapered shape bumps are appropriate for a low temperature bonding and resulting in a robust junction. However, the analysis carried in Ref. [8] puts an emphasis on fabrication aspects while neglecting to address reliability concerns. In recent, Depiver *et al.* [9] investigated Thermo-Mechanical Reliability of bump in microelectronics package. Herein, the author has used finite element (FE) model that includes Computer-aided design (CAD) connectivity, geometry pre-processing, meshing and materials support. However, the authors, on the other hand, focused solely on the bump with spherical shaped while neglecting the other shapes. Based on the aforementioned state-of-the-art study, it is apparent that a thorough investigation of various bump shape is required. Furthermore, a thorough analysis is necessary to apostrophize the reliability, stress and coupling analysis of different bump shapes.

In order to address the aforementioned research issues, this paper presents a comparative analysis of different bump shapes in terms of MTTF, stress, crosstalk delay and power losses for the first time. The current density and temperature distributions in solder bumps were computed using 3D electromagnetic (EM) simulations. Herein, the models of different types of bumps were created with the same height and radii. The present work also devoted to numerical characterization of effective CTE for the different bump structure. Herein, the stress characterization of bump is successfully evaluated by virtue of the effective complex CTE that is formulated by using volume fraction of bump shape. Additionally, in order to compute the CTE as a function of volume fraction, bump height, radii, and temperature, that can be used as an input. Furthermore, it is worth emphasizing that the sum of product (SOP) of individual bump and underfill is taken by the virtue of volume fraction that can be varied in the range of 0 to 1 for modelling larger-scale 3D packages. Additionally, for the validation of the model for the losses, the analytically obtained s parameters are compared with a simulation approach to benchmark the proposed model.

The manuscript is organized as follows: Sect. 1 addresses an overview of the current state-of-the-art research situation and summaries of the work carried out. The Sect. 2 shed light on the physical configuration of the cylindrical, spherical and tapered bump structures. Section 3 discourse the resistance-inductance- capacitance (RLC) and power loss model of the bump. Section 4 reveals a thorough insight of the reliability, stress, crosstalk and power loss analysis of different bump shapes. Finally, Sect. 5 summarizes the proposed work.

2   Physical Configuration of Bump

This section provides a comprehensive explanation of the bump structure as well as quantitative values for physical parameters and material attributes used in the elecro-thermal study of bumps. Figures 1(a)–(c) demonstrate the physical configurations of cylindrical, spherical, and tapered bumps, respectively. Herein, a BCB underfill layer is being used to separate the bumps in order to limit the cross-coupling and leakage issues. The bump, that incorporates Sn as a filler, connects the through silicon via (TSVs) to the system component of the 3D ICs. The implemented different micro bump shapes physical parameters are depicted in Table 1. There are three different bump packages being researched, each with a different shape of solder bump, such as spherical, cylindrical, and tapered.

Table 1 lists the geometrical specifications and schematic for these bump that are shown in Fig. 1. Herein, the physical parameters such as pitch and height of the bump were kept consistent across all of these bump geometries. This is due to the fact that the aforementioned characteristics have a direct influence on the underfill layer and were kept constant. The primary manipulating factor is the solder bump geometry, and that is the significant parameter of this research paper. Furthermore, the physical geometry of cylindrical bump three-dimensional structure is depicted in Fig. 1(a) that is comprised of two circular bases joined by a curved surface. Furthermore, the right cylinder structure is created by the center of the circular bases overlapping each other. Similarly, the spherical bump (as shown in Fig. 1(b)) is designed such that the integral surface of the following differential form $(xdx + ydy + zdz)$ is a sphere of any radius centered at zero. Additionally, tapered bump (demonstrated in Fig. 1(c)) on the contrary, is the piece of a solid (usually a cone) that is between one or two parallel planes that intersect them.

Table 1. Model symbol, parameters and its value [10].

Parameter	Symbol	Values
Bump pitch	P_{bump}	4 μm
Bump radius	r_{bump}	1.3–1.6 μm
Bump height	h_{bump}	2 μm
Tapered Bump Slope angle	θ	70°
Tapered bump upper radius	r_{b_bump}	1.3–1.6 μm
Tapered bump lower radius	r_{a_bump}	0.57–0.87 μm

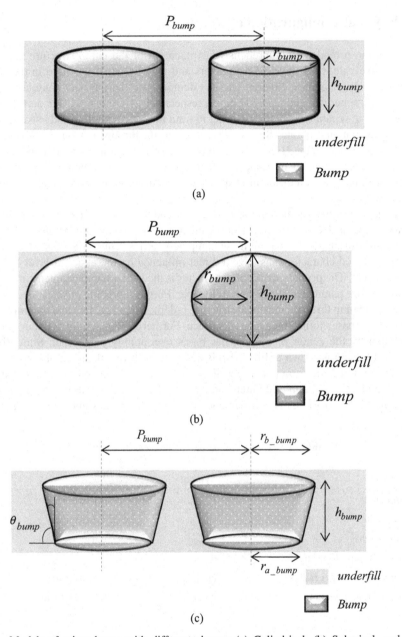

Fig. 1. Models of micro bump with different shapes: (a) Cylindrical, (b) Spherical, and (c) Tapered.

3 Power Loss Model of Bump

This section contains the electrical modeling of bump and its power loss. The Resistance-inductance-capacitance (RLC) model of the bump and underfill layer in Fig. 2 shows the total bump resistance (R_{total_bump}), inductance (L_{total_bump}) and the underfill capacitance ($C_{underfill}$) for the different shaped bump. The fundamental reason of bump resistance and inductance is due to the electron vibration and the generation of magnetic field owing to electron conduction. The aforementioned parasitics can be analyzed by integrating infinitesimally thin slice. Further, using the Biot-Savart law against magnetic flux density, the R_{total_bump}, L_{total_bump} can be obtained from [10–12]. Furthermore, the underfill capacitance ($C_{underfill}$) of the different bump shape can be investigated by integrating parallel capacitance and can be computed from [10, 13]. Additionally, for the power loss analysis, the bump and underfill layers are effectively arranged in terms of π-based RLC architecture. The model is primarily π-shaped network that can be effectively investigated by Z-parameters that are translated into S- parameters for the subsequent power i.e. insertion (S_{21}) and reflection (S_{11}) loss analysis. The S-parameters can be obtained using the below mentioned matrix as [14]

$$\begin{bmatrix} S_{11} & S_{12} \\ S_{21} & S_{22} \end{bmatrix} = \begin{bmatrix} \frac{(Z_{11}-Z_0)(Z_{22}+Z_0)-Z_{12}Z_{21}}{(Z_{11}+Z_0)(Z_{22}+Z_0)-Z_{12}Z_{21}} & \frac{2Z_{12}Z_0}{(Z_{11}+Z_0)(Z_{22}+Z_0)-Z_{12}Z_{21}} \\ \frac{2Z_{21}Z_0}{(Z_{11}+Z_0)(Z_{22}+Z_0)-Z_{12}Z_{21}} & \frac{(Z_{11}+Z_0)(Z_{22}-Z_0)-Z_{12}Z_{21}}{(Z_{11}+Z_0)(Z_{22}+Z_0)-Z_{12}Z_{21}} \end{bmatrix} \tag{1}$$

where the characteristic impedance $Z_0 = 50\Omega$; the open circuit input and transfer impedances (Z_{11}, Z_{21}) can be represented as

$$Z_{11} = \frac{\frac{2}{sC_{underfill}} \times \left(R_{total\_bump} + sL_{total\_bump} + \frac{2}{sC_{underfill}} \right)}{\frac{4}{sC_{underfill}} + R_{total\_bump} + sL_{total\_bump}} \tag{2}$$

$$Z_{21} = \frac{2/sC_{underfill}}{R_{total\_bump} + sL_{total\_bump} + \frac{2}{sC_{underfill}}} \tag{3}$$
$$\times \frac{\frac{2}{sC_{underfill}} \times \left(R_{total\_bump} + sL_{total\_bump} + \frac{2}{sC_{underfill}} \right)}{\frac{4}{sC_{underfill}} + R_{total\_bump} + sL_{total\_bump}}$$

The bump network depicted in Fig. 2 is the reciprocity in nature, that can be characterized as $Z_{11} = Z_{22}$ and $Z_{21} = Z_{12}$.

Using the electromagnetic expressions obtained from [10–13], the parasitics of the cylindrical, tapered and spherical bump are calculated. Table 2 illustrates the parasitic values for the different bump shapes considering a bump radius of 1.3μm. It is perceived that the tapered bump possesses a lower value of the equivalent R_{total_bump}, L_{total_bump} and $C_{underfill}$ compared to the other shapes counterparts. Additionally, using the Table 2 parasitic values, insertion and return losses obtained from model expressions (1) through (3) are computed analytically. Furthermore, for the validation of the analytical results, the EM simulation [15] is performed and discussed in the following section.

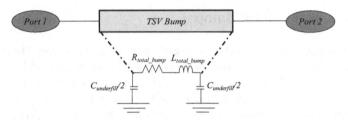

Fig. 2. Electrical model of TSV bump

Table 2. Parasitics of different bump structure for $r_{bump} = 1.3\ \mu m$.

Parasitic	Cylindrical	Spherical	Tapered
R_{total_bump} (kΩ)	20.5	5.13	2.2
L_{total_bump} (nH)	112.3	108.2	90.5
$C_{underfill}$ (pF)	74.0	60.1	48.8

4 Reliability, Crosstalk, Stress and Power Analysis

The closer vicinity of the micro bump creates massive movement of electrons, resulting in electromigration failure while driven by a high current. The electromigration-induced Mean Time To Failure (MTTF) is a vital characteristic to consider while evaluating the bump's lifespan. Because the EM lifespan of bump is reliant on the current density, the current analysis is employed to create the distribution map. Other EM driving mechanisms, such as heat gradients, have also been reported by researchers. Additionally, modeling of the gradual failure in a microbump is required for a thorough EM lifespan calculation that takes these current density and temperature gradients characteristics into account. Hence, the MTTF in terms of Black's equation [16] can be presented as

$$MTTF = A\frac{1}{j^{n}}\exp\frac{E_a}{KT} \tag{4}$$

where $A = 0.8$ represents the material property-dependent cross-sectional constant, $n = 1.82$ represents the current density model parameter, $E_a = 0.8$ eV/atom and K is the Activation energy and Boltzmann constant respectively. Whereas, the structural analysis can be used to obtain current density (j) and temperature (T) in the above-mentioned equation.

Table 3 summarizes a thorough investigation of MTTFs for spherical, cylindrical, and tapered shaped bumps. The tapered bump possesses 50.01% overall improvement in MTTF when compared to the cylindrical and spherical bumps, respectively. The reason behind this is that, MTTF is increased principally as a result of the reduced effect of lower solder volume, which results in less joule heating and higher reliability. As a result, in terms of better MTTF, a tapered shaped bump can be preferred for the 3D IC packaging. Additionally, Table 3 demonstrates relationship between the MTTF versus the various bump radii for the different bump shapes. In order to estimate the MTTF, current density and temperature are deciding factors. Moreover, in our study the current density obtained using structural simulations for all the bump radii and structure is constant with the value of 661.00 (A/m^2). The primary reason behind this is that, when the bump radius increases, area and the current rises at the same time, keeping the current density constant. Furthermore, it is observed that the temperature of the bump rises as the radius increases. This is due to the fact that the bump with larger volume can disperse the more Joule heat and increases its temperature. Hence, it is observed that among all the bump shapes with same radii and height, the bump volume decreased from cylindrical to tapered that intern reduces the temperature and may cause the longest MTTF.

Apart from MTTF, one of the factors that must be minimized for the micro bump is the equivalent tensile stress. High stress concentration reduces reliability that leads to an unanticipated fault. As a result, identifying the appropriate bump shape is critical for maintaining reliability. Equation (5), which is dependent on volume fraction, CTE of bump and underfill, is used to examine stress in terms of Coefficient of thermal expansion. As a result, the composite CTE and stress can be computed using the volume fraction of bump. Hence the expression of the composite CTE can be provides a

$$\alpha_{composite} = f\alpha_{bump} + (1 - f)\alpha_{underfill} \tag{5}$$

where f is the volume fraction of bump and $\alpha_{bump} = 21$, $\alpha_{underfill} = .5$ are the CTEs of bump and underfill, respectively [17, 18].

For cylindrical, spherical and tapered bump, the volume fraction f is represented as,

$$f_{cylindrical} = \frac{3.14 \times (r_{bump})^2}{(P_{bump})^2} \tag{6}$$

$$f_{spherical} = \frac{2.09 \times (r_{bump})^2}{(P_{bump})^2} \tag{7}$$

$$f_{tapered} = \frac{1.04 \times (r_{b\_bump}^2 + r_{a\_bump}^2 + r_{b\_bump} \times r_{a\_bump})}{(P_{bump})^2} \tag{8}$$

Using (5), it is perceived that the bump with smaller radii has enhanced immunity to sustain the CTE as compared to the larger bump as presented in Table 4. Furthermore, it is investigated that tapered bump is 26.03% more robust in resisting CTE as compared to spherical and cylindrical bump due to smaller solder volume. Additionally, Khor et al. [19] reported that by minimizing the solder bump volume fraction in the moulded package design, the stress on the IC induced during encapsulation could be minimized. Therefore, the lower volume fraction (f) in case of tapered bump can reduce the CTE that intern reduces the stress because of its direct dependency.

Apart from stress, the evolution of technology has a substantial impact on crosstalk-induced delay due to the smaller bump pitches and higher chip density. The region where a crosstalk signal is detected in bump is defined by near-end and far-end: near-end refers to the driver side of the victim connector, while far-end refers to the receiver side. As the signal travels, the crosstalk signal can be created from the aggressor bump into the victim bump, and the location of detection is determined by the coupling mechanism and signal swing direction (rising vs. falling trigger). Additionally, the crosstalk delay (Fig. 3) between the bump pair is being used to determine the influence of different bump shapes on IC performance. The substantial mismatch in CTE creates significant stress in the bump geometries when they are exposed to high temperatures during the fabrication process. Bump cracking or breaking, as well as interfacial delamination, are the most common consequences of this occurrence. The current leakage caused by the bump failure can be prevented by reducing the mutual coupling capacitance. Additionally, the lower mutual coupling of tapered bump and their smaller cross section enable them to achieve low capacitance and improved NEXT and FEXT.

Table 3. MTTF analysis of cylindrical, spherical and tapered bump structure.

Bump radius (μm)	Cylindrical bump		Spherical bump		Tapered bump	
	Temp (°C)	MTTF (h)	Temp (°C)	MTTF (h)	Temp (°C)	MTTF (h)
1.3	342	21.26	320	37.22	301	62.49
1.4	345	19.76	323	34.40	307	52.87
1.5	348	18.37	327	31.01	310	48.69
1.6	353	16.30	332	27.28	315	42.52

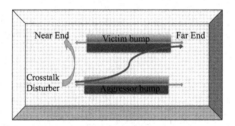

Fig. 3. Crosstalk disturber model of coupled bump.

Table 4. Composite CTE of cylindrical, tapered and spherical structure at different radii ranges.

Bump Radius (μm)	Cylindrical		Spherical		Tapered	
	CTE	Volume fraction	CTE	Volume Fraction	CTE	Volume Fraction
1.3	7.30	0.33	4.98	0.21	4.16	0.17
1.4	8.38	0.38	5.70	0.25	4.94	0.21
1.5	9.55	0.44	6.47	0.29	5.81	0.25
1.6	10.80	0.50	7.30	0.33	6.75	0.30

The Near End and Far End crosstalk delays of cylindrical, spherical, and tapered bump implemented at 32 nm technology are depicted in Fig. 4. It is perceived that the

NEXT, FEXT crosstalk delays of the tapered bump is much lower than the other shapes. It is due to the fact that the tapered bump has a lower volume fraction, resulting in a lower coupling capacitance. This fact can be validated using the capacitance expression $C = \oint_s D.ds \div \oint_l E.dl$, where D, E are the electric displacement and field respectively. Herein, it quantified that the mutually coupling capacitance are in direct relation with the closed surface integral, resulting in a lower crosstalk delay. Furthermore, it can be inferred that considering a tapered bump, the NEXT and FEXT under the range of 20 GHz frequency, are improved by 5.50%, 4.88%, 10.86%, and 11.25% compared to a spherical and cylindrical, respectively.

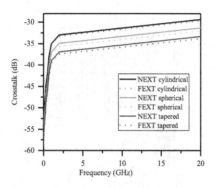

Fig. 4. NEXT, FEXT analysis of different bump architecture.

Additionally, Fig. 5 depicts the near-end and far-end crosstalk for the cylindrical, spherical and tapered bump shape of different radii and frequencies. It is observed that the overall reduction in crosstalk of spherical and cylindrical bumps for radius ranging from 1.3 μm to 1.6 μm is 3.70% and 7.55%, respectively compared to the tapered structure.

Additionally, it is also worth mentioning that the near-end crosstalk level is always higher than the far-end crosstalk level for different bump radii ranges. The reason for this is that, the magnetic and electric interaction are constructive at the close end but destructive at the distant end. Another observation from Fig. 5 is that the crosstalk induced delay increases significantly as the bump radii increases from a lower to a larger value. This is due to the fact that bumps with more radii have a higher volume fraction, and hence the mutual coupling increases the crosstalk induced delay. Furthermore, the smaller radii bumps have fewer capacitive parasitics, implying higher reactance. This results in less signal leakage from the bump to the underfill, and the reduced dielectric loss produced by the leakage improves the near and far end crosstalk.

Taking into account the overall crosstalk delay, Table 5 exhibits a comprehensive analysis of percentage improvement of NEXT, FEXT for tapered based bump in comparison to other shapes. It is perceived that, for a bump radius of 1.6 μm, the tapered bump outperformed by 2.41%, 4.77%, 2.04% and 3.11% in terms of NEXT and FEXT coupling as compared to cylindrical and spherical bump, respectively. The primary reason behind this reduced effect is that the tapered shape possesses relatively lower parasitic

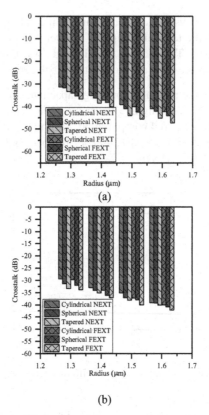

Fig. 5. Crosstalk analysis of different bump shapes *w.r.t.* various bump radii. (a) 10 GHz (b) 20 GHz.

as a result of the lesser surface area and volume, that can reduce the near and far end mutual coupling.

In order to examine the performance of a TSV bump, power loss is also a significant parameter. The primary concern of existing research industry is the lower power loss and the improved performance. As a result, the power dissipation in terms of insertion and reflection losses at 32 nm technology is explored in order to investigate a feasible bump topology. A comparative analysis of return and insertion loss is deliberated using the cylindrical, tapered and spherical bump. The power loss analysis is carried out analytically using the π based *RLC* architecture and structurally using the EM simulation. The reflected and the transmitted power (S_{11} and S_{21}) for the different shapes of bump in terms of the simulation results are depicted in Fig. 6 for the frequency range up to 20GHz. It is perceived that the reduced capacitance of the underfill layer between the two tapered bump, resulting in the increased impedance between the bump pair. As a result, the S_{11} and S_{21} losses in the underfill layer decreases due to the less leakage because of the higher underfill impedance in the tapered bump architecture. Additionally, as the frequency increases, the power loss through the bump is dominated by the leakage through the underfill layer. As a result, an increase of power losses at the higher

Table 5. Percentage improvement in crosstalk using tapered based bump for different bump radii.

Frequency	Bump radius (μm)	% Improvement in crosstalk for tapered bump in comparison to			
		NEXT		FEXT	
		Cylindrical	Spherical	Cylindrical	Spherical
20 GHz	1.3	11.85%	12.26%	6.00%	5.32%
	1.4	6.03%	8.35%	2.87%	2.66%
	1.5	7.81%	6.92%	2.65%	5.00%
	1.6	2.41%	4.77%	2.04%	3.11%
10 GHz	1.3	5.85%	4.95%	7.17%	3.62%
	1.4	8.92%	5.96%	7.45%	5.22%
	1.5	11.08%	7.07%	12.13%	6.81%
	1.6	9.10%	6.74%	10.58%	6.67%

frequency is due to the lower impedance along the leakage path to the underfill layer is demonstrated by the equation $Z = 1/j2\pi fC$.

Additionally, the power losses obtained using the *Pi* based *RLC* model are validated with the simulation results depicted in Fig. 6. Furthermore, Table 6 validates and illustrates that the calculated results for the S_{11} and S_{21} are found to be in good agreement with the simulated result with the average deviation of 0.86 dB and 0.03 dB, respectively.

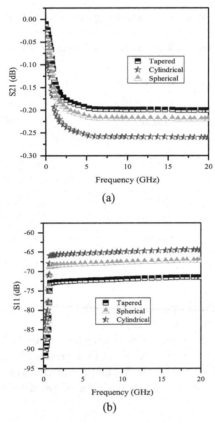

Fig. 6. Power loss analysis of different bump shapes *w.r.t.* various frequencies. (a) S_{21} (b) S_{11}.

Table 6. Validation of analytical and simulation result in terms of S_{11} and S_{21} parameter at 20 GHz frequency.

Bump Shape	S_{11} (in dB)			S_{21} (in dB)		
	Simulation	Analytical	Difference	Simulation	Analytical	Difference
Cylindrical	− 0.23	− 0.26	.03	− 63.67	− 64.48	0.81
Spherical	− 0.21	− 0.22	.01	− 66.28	− 67.23	0.95
Tapered	− 0.15	− 0.20	.05	− 70.66	− 71.48	0.82

5   Conclusion

The 3D EM procedure has been used to simulate the current density and temperature distributions in micro bump with different radii. It has been perceived that the tapered bump with an appropriated bump radius has a 36.87% and 63.13% longer MTTF than the spherical and cylindrical counterparts. This is primarily due to the reduced cross-section of tapered bumps that minimizes thermal distribution and hence, increases MTTF and electromigration reliability. Additionally, the effective CTE, used in 3D microelectronic packaging, has been studied using a three-dimensional unit cell. The mismatch in coefficient of thermal expansion (CTE) between the bump and the surrounding underfill generates an internal stress condition when the temperature of the bump and the surrounding underfill vary. The effective CTE increases approximately linearly with the volume fraction of bump when it is distributed uniformly. As a result, the tapered bump with reduced volume fraction improves CTE and, as a consequence, creates lesser stress and coupling effect. Furthermore, the power loss in terms of S parameter are investigated by using open circuit input and transfer impedances. The result reveals that the power loss is substantially lesser in case of tapered bump due to the lower impedance along the leakage path as compared to the other shapes counterparts.

References

1. Chang, N., Chung, C.K., Wang, Y.P., Lin, C.F., Su, P.J., Shih, T., Kao, N., Hung, J.: 3D micro bump interface enabling top die interconnect to true circuit through silicon via wafer. In: IEEE 70th Electronic Components and Technology Conference (ECTC), pp. 1888–1893. IEEE, Orlando, FL, USA (2020)
2. AbdelAziz, M., Xu, D.E., Wang, G., Mayer, M.: Electromigration in solder joints: A cross-sectioned model system for real-time observation. Microelectron. Reliab. **119**, 114068 (2021)
3. Chandrakar, S., Gupta, D., Majumder, M.K.: Role of through silicon via in 3D integration: Impact on delay and power. J. Circ. Syst. Comput. **30**(3), 2150051(2021)
4. Nashrudin, M.N., Gan, Z.L., Abas, A., Ishak, M.H.H., Ali, M.Y.T.: Effect of hourglass shape solder joints on underfill encapsulation process: numerical and experimental studies. Solder. Surf. Mount Technol. **32**(03), 147–156 (2020)
5. Imura, F., Watanabe, N., Nemoto, S., Feng, W., Kikuchi, K., Nakagawa, H., Aoyagi, M.: Development of micro bump joints fabrication process using cone shape Au bumps for 3D LSI chip stacking. In: IEEE 64th Electronic Components and Technology Conference (ECTC), pp. 1915–1920. IEEE, Orlando, FL, USA (2014)
6. Xu, P., Tong, F., Davis, V.A., Park, M., Hamilton, M.C.: Solution-based fabrication of carbon nanotube bumps for flip-chip interconnects. IEEE Trans. Nanotechnol. **13**(6), 1118–1126 (2014)
7. Ng, F.C., Abas, A., Abdullah, M.Z.: Effect of solder bump shapes on underfill flow in flip-chip encapsulation using analytical, numerical and PIV experimental approaches. Microelectron. Reliab. **81**, 41–63 (2018)
8. Motoyoshi, M., Yanagimura, K., Fushimi, T., Endo, S.: Stacked pixel sensor/detector technology using au micro-bump junction. In: International 3D Systems Integration Conference (3DIC), pp. 1–4. IEEE, Sendai, Japan (2019)
9. Depiver, J.A., Mallik, S., Amalu, E.H.: Effective solder for improved thermo-mechanical reliability of solder joints in a ball grid array (BGA) soldered on printed circuit board (PCB). J. Electron. Mater. **50**(1), 263–282 (2021)
10. Kim, J., et al.: High frequency scalable electrical model and analysis of a through silicon via (TSV). IEEE Trans. Comp. Pack. Manuf. Technol. **1**(2), 181–195 (2011)
11. Tong, J., Sato, Y., Panayappan, K., Sundaram, V., Peterson, A.F., Tummala, R.R.: Electrical modeling and analysis of tapered through-package via in glass interposers. IEEE Trans. Comp. Pack. Manuf. Technol. **6**(5), 775–783 (2016)
12. Liu, X., Zhu, Z., Yang, Y., Ding, R.: Parasitic inductance of non-uniform through-silicon vias (TSVs) for microwave applications. IEEE Microw. Wirel. Comp. Lett. **25**(7), 424–426 (2015)

13. Su, J., Wang, F., Zhang, W.: Capacitance expressions and electrical characterization of tapered through-silicon vias for 3-D ICs. IEEE Trans. Comp. Pack. Manuf. Technol. **5**(10), 1488–1496 (2015)
14. Sahu, C.C., Chandrakar, S. and Majumder, M.K.: Signal transmission and reflection losses of cylindrical and tapered shaped TSV in 3D integrated circuits. In: IEEE International Symposium on Smart Electronic Systems (iSES) (Formerly iNiS), pp. 44–47. IEEE, Chennai, India (2020)
15. CST Studio Suite, "CST Microwave Studio," 2008. http:// www.cst.com
16. Li, Y., Zhao, X.C., Liu, Y., Li, H.: Effect of bump shape on current density and temperature distributions in solder bump joints under electromigration. Adv. Mater. Res. **569**, 82–87 (2012)
17. Ladani, L.J.: Numerical analysis of thermo-mechanical reliability of through silicon vias (TSVs) and solder interconnects in 3-dimensional integrated circuits. Microelectron. Eng. **87**, 208–215 (2010)
18. Huang, C., Pan, L., Liu, R., Wang, Z.: Thermal and electrical properties of BCB-liner through-silicon vias. IEEE Trans. Comp. Pack. Manuf. Technol. **4**(12), 1936–1946 (2014)
19. Khor, C.Y., Abdullah, M.Z., Leong, W.C.: Fluid/structure interaction analysis of the effects of solder bump shapes and input/output counts on moulded packaging. IEEE Trans. Comp. Pack. Manuf. Technol. **2**(4), 604–616 (2012)

Reliability Aware Global Routing of Graphene Nanoribbon Based Interconnect

Subrata Das[1,2(✉)] ⓘ, Debesh Kumar Das[3] ⓘ, and Soumya Pandit[1]

[1] Institute of Radio Physics and Electronics, Calcutta University, Kolkata, India
dsubrata.mt@gmail.com sprpe@caluniv.ac.in
[2] Department of Computer Science and Engineering, Sister Nivedita University,
Kolkata, Newtown, India
[3] Department of Computer Science and Engineering, Jadavpur University,
Kolkata, India
debeshd@hotmail.com

Abstract. Graphene nanoribbon based interconnect has several advantageous properties over traditional interconnect like power dissipation, delay, and integration capability. But each wire segment of Graphene nanoribbon based interconnect has a chance of failure as each wire segment is associated with some survival probability. Hence reliability issues can play a major role in the routing of this type of interconnect. In this paper, we propose an algorithm for global routing of Graphene nanoribbon based interconnect considering reliability as an optimization function with minimum increase in cost. The cost due to routing of Graphene nanoribbon based interconnect depends on the interconnect length, angle of bending, and the number of bending, and this is known as the hybrid cost. The experiment is done on a random data set and the result shows the effectiveness of the method.

Keywords: Graphene nanoribbon · Survival probability · Routing reliability · Hybrid cost

1 Introduction

Graphene nanoribbon (GNR) based interconnect can be used as a potential alternative material over traditional interconnect due to its admirable electrical and thermal properties [1–3]. Usually, *Graphene nanoribbon* is of two types based on edge shape: zigzag and armchair. Zigzag *GNR* are always metallic whereas armchair *GNR* may be metallic or semiconducting based on the lattice structure [4]. Figure 1 shows the structure of armchair and zigzag graphene nanoribbon. In this paper, we use zigzag *GNR* as interconnect as it is always metallic. Due to the structure of *GNR*, it can be bent in some specific angles only. Bending in 30°, 90° and 150° angles converts an armchair (zigzag) *GNR* to zigzag (armchair). But zigzag (armchair) *GNR* remains zigzag (armchair) if the bending angles are

© The Author(s), under exclusive license to Springer Nature Switzerland AG 2022
A. P. Shah et al. (Eds.): VDAT 2022, CCIS 1687, pp. 373–386, 2022.
https://doi.org/10.1007/978-3-031-21514-8_31

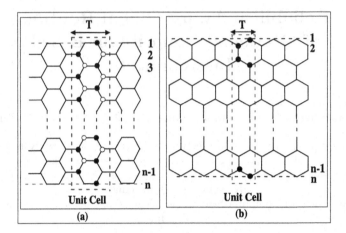

Fig. 1. Structure of a) Armchair b) Zigzag graphene nanoribbon

0°, 60°, and 120°. Hence for interconnect application only permissible bending angles are 0°, 60°, and 120° [5,6]. The purpose of global routing is to make rough connections of the signal net. The quality of this step has an enormous effect on the VLSI physical design.

Manufacturing reliability in VLSI designs is a vital issue in nanometer scale. In practice, some GNR wire segments have a connection defective rate. There may be connection failure in a few GNR wire segments during manufacturing [7]. In practice, each wire segment of *GNR* based interconnect has a survival probability and hence has a possibility of failure. As a result, the entire system may malfunction. This is the routing reliability problem.

For the routing of GNR based interconnect, the grid lines of routing grid are aligned in 0°, 60°, and 120° angles and such a routing grid is known as a triangular routing grid. In a triangular grid, single source and multiple sink terminals are given. To interconnect them with metallic GNR wire there may be a few extra interconnection points known as Steiner points. The construction of a routing tree for GNR based interconnect is a hexagonal Steiner tree [4,8] whereas for traditional copper-based interconnect the corresponding routing tree is a rectangular Steiner tree. For the routing of single source and multiple sink terminals using GNR based interconnect, the construction of hexagonal Steiner tree with different objective functions was discussed in different literatures [4,8–13]. It is not possible to construct a hexagonal Steiner tree using only a single wire segment. In our work we assume that a wire segment is of length 10 unit. Figure 2 shows the routing of a single source and 11 sink terminals. The routing path ST_1 can be established using four wire segments. To interconnect other sink terminals $(T_2, \ldots, T_{11})$ to the existing routing tree with different wire one or more wire segments are required. Now, as the number of wire segments increases the reliability decreases. In this paper, we focus on the global routing of *GNR* based interconnects considering the reliability issue.

The overview of our work is as follows. We are given a single source (S) and multiple (n) sink terminals $(T_1, T_2, \ldots T_n)$. First, we propose an algorithm to construct a hexagonal Steiner tree with minimum *cost*. This algorithm is a modified and improved version of the method as described in [8]. This is discussed later in the paper. Then the survival probability of all interconnects to each sink terminal is calculated. If the corresponding survival probability is below a certain limiting value (say 85%) then redundant paths are added to improve the survival probability.

Different reliability issues related to copper interconnect were discussed in [14]. Khang et al. [15] proposed reliability improvement for regular grid graphs with a uniform survival probability distribution. An interconnect reliability-driven routing technique for the avoidance of electromigration failure was discussed in [16] by the construction of the Steiner tree. In [14,15], and [16] the reliability issues and the improvement for traditional copper-based interconnect were discussed. As *GNR* based interconnect can be bent only in 0°, 60°, and 120° angles, the routing is different than that of traditional copper-based interconnect.

The maximization of survival probability by adding redundant wire segments in a graph with a given source-sink routing path is discussed in [17]. The work of [17] improves the survival probability for a pair of source and sink terminals. But our work improves the reliability when a single source drives multiple sink terminals.

The rest of the paper is organized as follows. The theoretical formulation of the paper is discussed in Sect. 2. The proposed methodology and algorithm for reliability-aware routing are discussed in Sect. 3. The experimental result is shown in Sect. 4. Finally, Sect. 5 discusses the future scope of the work and concludes the paper.

2 Theoretical Formulation of the Work

2.1 GNR Routing Problem

GNR routing problem can be described as the interconnection of a single source and multiple sink terminals in a triangular routing grid using GNR based interconnect with minimum cost. The cost due to routing is the function of interconnect length, the number of bending, and the angle of bending and is known as hybrid cost. Let the interconnect length is l, the number of 60° and 120° bending are respectively denoted by n_{60} and n_{120} and the cost due to unit length, 60° and 120° bending are respectively denoted by w_L, b_{60}, and b_{120}. Then the hybrid cost (HC) is given by the following equation

$$HC = l \times w_L + n_{60} \times b_{60} + n_{120} \times b_{120} \tag{1}$$

As reported in [5] and [6], $b_{120} = 3 \times b_{60}$. Consider the routing tree of Fig. 2 of a single source (S) and 11 sink terminals. The interconnect length (l), the number of 60° bending (n_{60}) and the number of 120° bending (n_{120}) are respectively 98, 11, and 0. Hence the *hybrid cost* for the routing tree of Fig. 2 is $98w_L + 11b_{60}$. As in [6] here also we assume $w_L=1$, $b_{60} = 11$. Hence total hybrid cost is 208.

2.2 Survival Probability and Reliability

Let a graph G(V, E) with each edge $e \in E$ has a survival probability P(e) and hence non-survival probability (probability of failure) is 1-P(e). The connection between two terminals (S) and (T) $(S, T \in V)$ contains a set of edges $\acute{e} \in E$. The probability that S and T are connected by the edges in $\acute{e}$ is the S-T connection survival probability [17].

To explain the survival probability we assume that a long interconnect is segmented at a length of 10 and the survival probability of a wire segment is 0.95. Consider the routing tree of Fig 2 of a single source (S) and 11 sink terminals. For the routing tree of Fig. 2 $l = 98$, $n_{60} = 11$, and $n_{120} = 0$, and hence the *hybrid cost* is 208. The routing path ST_1 is consisting of four edges and hence the survival probability of T_1 is $0.95^4 = 81.45\%$. The interconnection of a new sink terminal to the existing routing tree/graph can be treated as a new wire segment. Hence, the total number of wire segments for sink terminals T_2, T_3, and T_4 are respectively 4, 5 and 5. The survival probability of these three sink terminals are respectively $0.95^4 = 81.45\%$, $0.95^5 = 77.38\%$ and 77.38%. The second column of Table 1 shows the survival probability of all sink terminals of the routing tree in Fig. 2. The average survival probability is 83.11%. In this work, a sink terminal is defined to be reliable if the survival probability is at least 85%. Hence the number of reliable sinks for the routing tree of Fig. 2 is 5.

Figure 3 shows a different routing tree for the same source and sink terminals. For this routing tree, $l = 113$, $n_{60} = 11$ and $n_{120} = 0$ and hence *hybrid cost* is 223. The number of wire segments for each of the sink terminals T_5 and T_6, in this case, is 3. The corresponding routing reliability for each of these two sink terminals is 85.74%. Hence in this routing tree, the number of reliable sink terminals is 7. The average routing reliability is 85%. The modification of the routing tree in Fig. 3 in comparison to that of Fig. 2 increases the number of reliable sink terminals. But still, there are sink terminals below desired reliability.

The improvement of the survival probability of nodes can be increased by introducing redundant edges [15]. We take the same concept here as done in [15]. To reduce the failure probability of a node parallel edges are introduced.

In this paper, we assume that a single source drives many sink terminals. It is quite obvious that the survival probability of different sink terminals will be different. To maintain the routing reliability, the survival probability of any node must be above some limiting value. In this paper, we will allow redundant edges to those nodes whose survival probability is below 85%. Now consider the Fig. 4, here, a few redundant paths are added to the routing tree of Fig. 2. Here, redundant paths are added to each of the sink terminals T_1, T_2, T_3, T_4, T_5, and T_6 as the survival probability of each of these sink terminals is below 85%. The survival probabilities of these sink terminals are now increased to 95.08%, 95.09%, 95.08%, 95.08%, 95.56%, and 94.88% respectively due to the addition of redundant edges. The survival probabilities of T_1 and T_5 are calculated as $(1-(1-0.95^4)(1-0.95^5))$ and $(1-(1-0.95^4)(1-0.95^4))$. The fourth column of Table 1 shows the survival probability of each sink terminal of Figs. 4. Here, all the sink terminals are above desired reliability. The inclusion of parallel edges will

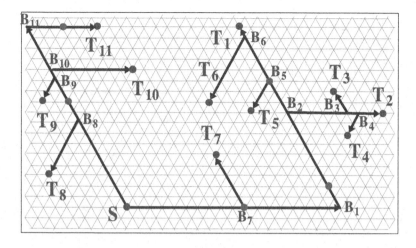

Fig. 2. Routing tree for single source and 11 sink terminals

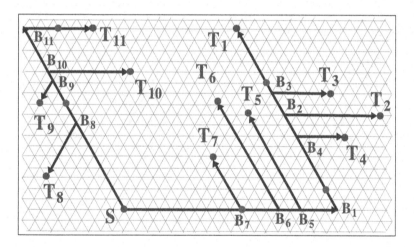

Fig. 3. A different routing tree of same source and sink terminals

increase the total *hybrid cost*. For the routing graph of Fig. 4 $l = 136$, $n_{60} = 18$ and $n_{120} = 0$ and hence *hybrid cost* $= 316$.

Figure 5 shows the routing graph corresponding to Fig. 3. Fifth column of Table 1 shows the routing reliability of the sink terminals of Fig. 5. Here, the total hybrid cost is 275 and all the sink terminals are above desired survival probability.

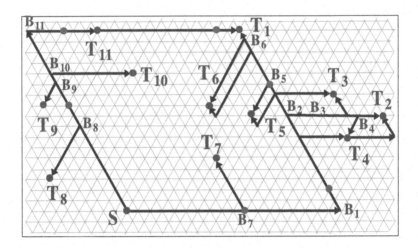

Fig. 4. Routing graph constructed from the routing tree of Fig. 2

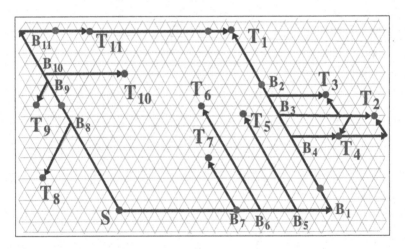

Fig. 5. Routing graph constructed from the routing tree of Fig. 3

3   Algorithm for Reliability Aware Global Routing of GNR Based Interconnect

Figure 6 shows the algorithms for reliability-aware routing of graphene nanoribbon based interconnect with a single source and multiple sinks. The specific steps of the algorithm are as follows.

i) First, for single source and multiple sink terminals a hexagonal Steiner tree is constructed so that the hybrid cost is minimum.

ii) The survival probability of each sink terminal is estimated.

Table 1. Reliability of sink terminals of Figs. 2, 3, 4 and 5

Sink	Routing reliability for routing tree/graph			
	Fig. 2	Fig. 3	Fig. 4	Fig. 5
T1	81.45%	81.45%	95.80%	95.80%
T2	81.45%	81.45%	95.09%	95.09%
T3	77.38%	81.45%	95.80%	95.80%
T4	77.38%	81.45%	95.80%	95.80%
T5	81.45%	90.25%	96.56%	85.74%
T6	77.38%	90.25%	94.88%	85.74%
T7	90.25%	90.25%	90.25%	90.25%
T8	90.25%	90.25%	90.25%	90.25%
T9	85.74%	85.74%	85.74%	85.74%
T10	85.74%	85.74%	85.74%	85.74%
T11	85.74%	85.74%	85.74%	85.74%

iii) If the survival probability of any sink terminal is less than some limiting value then additional paths are added to reach the desired survival probability.

Reliability Aware Routing of single source and multiple sink terminals

$Construction\_of\_Hexagonal\_Steiner\_Tree()$
for *each sink terminal* (T_i) *(i = 1, 2, ... n)* **do**
   if *the survival probability of* T_i < *limiting value* **then**
      $Path\_Augmenting\_for\_Reliability\_Trusted\_and\_Hybridcost\_$
      $Aware\_routing()$
   end
end

Fig. 6. Reliability aware routing of single source and multiple sink terminals

The detailed description of the algorithm is as follows. For the construction of a minimum hybrid cost hexagonal Steiner tree, a modified and improved algorithm than that of [8] is used here. In the absence of any congestion, for a pair of source and sink terminals with different y-coordinates, there are four routing paths each with one 60° bending and two routing paths each with one 120° bending [8]. First a routing path is established between the source and maximum distant sink terminal. The algorithm of [8] finds the maximum distant sink in the following way. To find the maximum distant sink first the distances of all sinks via all 60° bending points are calculated in [8]. For each pair of source and sink terminals, there are four such routing paths. Then the minimum of each of these four paths is selected and finally, the maximum value of these n-minimum values is selected to get the maximum distant sink. But here in this paper, to find the maximum distant sink, first, the linear distances from the source to all sink terminals are calculated. Then the maximum distance from these n-distances is calculated and the corresponding sink terminal is selected as the maximum distant sink terminal. Then for the maximum distance sink, the minimum hybrid cost is calculated. The number of sinks on both sides of the line joining the source and maximum distant sink is counted and the bending point of the side of the line is selected for which number of sinks is greater than other side. The remaining steps for the construction of the hexagonal Steiner tree is same as that of [8]. This modification reduces the time to find the maximum distant sink terminal. This is because for each of the sink terminals the algorithm as described in [8] calculates four distances via four bending points, whereas the algorithm proposed in this paper calculates only one such distance. Figure 7 shows the algorithm for the construction of minimum-hybrid cost hexagonal Steiner tree. Here, the coordinates of the source, i^{th} sink, and maximum distant sink terminal are respectively given by (x_s, y_s), (x_i, y_i), and (x_{max}, y_{max}). The function Calculate_Minimum_Hybrid Cost(x_s, y_s, x_t, y_t) is used to find the hybrid cost of any sink terminal. This function calculates the minimum hybrid cost for the maximum distant sink terminal to construct a hexagonal steiner tree.

Figure 8 shows the source $S(x_s, y_s)$ and i^{th} sink. Let the coordinates of source and i^{th} sink are respectively given by (x_s, y_s) and (x_i, y_i). If $x_s < (x_i - \frac{(y_i - y_s)}{\sqrt{3}})$ and $(y_i > y_s)$ then as shown in Fig. 8, B_1, B_2, B_3 and B_4 represent four $60°$ bending points and B_5 and B_6 represent two $120°$ bending points. Now $SP = x_i - x_s$, $PB_1 = \frac{(y_t - y_s)}{\sqrt{3}}$ and $B_1T_i = \frac{2}{\sqrt{3}}(y_i - y_s)$. Hence the total interconnect length in the path SB_1T is $\{((x_i - x_s) + \sqrt{3}(y_i - y_s)\}$ and hybrid cost in each of the routing path SB_1T_i or SB_2T_i is $HC_1 = \{((x_i - x_s) + \sqrt{3}(y_i - y_s)\}w_L + b_{60}$.

Now, $SB_5 = SB_3 = B_3B_5 = (x_i - x_s) - \frac{(y_i - y_s)}{\sqrt{3}}$, $B_5T_i = \frac{2}{\sqrt{3}}(y_i - y_s)$. Hence the hybrid cost in each of the routing paths SB_3T or SB_4T is $HC_2 =$

Construction_of_Hexagonal_Steiner_Tree()

---

for $i=1$ to n **do**
   | distance[i] $= \sqrt{(x_s - x_i)^2 + (y_s - y_i)^2}$
end
Max_distance=max(distance[i])
Calculate_Minimum_Hybrid Cost$(x_s, y_s, x_{max}, y_{max})$
Calculate the number of sinks on each side of line joining S and maximum distant sink.
Find the first bending in that side for which number of sink is maximum.
Remaining steps are same as described in [8]

Fig. 7. Construction of hexagonal steiner tree for single source and multiple sink terminals

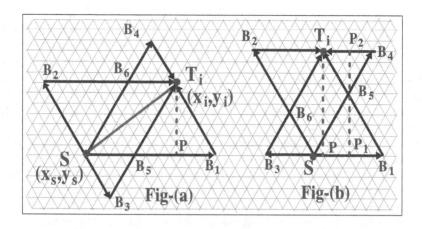

Fig. 8. Different routing paths between pair of source sink terminals

$2\{((x_t - x_s)\}w_L + b_{60}$. Similarly, the hybrid cost in each of the routing path SB_5T_i or SB_6T_i is $HC_3 = 2\{((x_t - x_s) + \frac{(y_i - y_s)}{\sqrt{3}}\}w_L + 3b_{60}$.

Similarly, if $x_s > (x_i - \frac{(y_i - y_s)}{\sqrt{3}})$ and $y_i > y_s$, then hybrid cost in the routing path SB_1T_i or SB_2T_i is $HC_1 = \{(x_t - x_s) + \sqrt{3}(y_t - y_s)\}w_L + b_{60}$. Hybrid cost in the routing path SB_3T_i or SB_4T_i is $HC_2 = \{\sqrt{3}(y_t - y_s) - (x_t - x_s)\}w_L + b_{60}$. The hybrid cost in either of the 120° routing path is $HC_3 = \{2\frac{(y_t - y_s)}{\sqrt{3}}\}w_L + 3b_{60}$.

Calculate_Minimum_Hybrid Cost(x_s, y_s, x_t, y_t)

---

if $(x_s < (x_i - \frac{(y_i - y_s)}{\sqrt{3}})$ *and* $(y_i > y_s))$ **then**

   $HC_1 = \{(x_t - x_s) + \sqrt{3}(y_t - y_s)\}w_L + b_{60}$
   $HC_2 = 2\{(x_t - x_s)\}w_L + b_{60}$
   $HC_3 = \{(x_t - x_s) + \frac{(y_t - y_s)}{\sqrt{3}}\}w_L + 3b_{60}$
   HC=minimum(HC_1, HC_2, HC_3)
end
if $(x_s > (x_i - \frac{(y_i - y_s)}{\sqrt{3}})$ *and* $(y_i > y_s))$ **then**

   $HC_1 = \{(x_t - x_s) + \sqrt{3}(y_t - y_s)\}w_L + b_{60}$
   $HC_2 = \{\sqrt{3}(y_t - y_s) - (x_t - x_s)\}w_L + b_{60}$
   $HC_3 = \{2\frac{(y_t - y_s)}{\sqrt{3}}\}w_L + 3b_{60}$
   HC=minimum(HC_1, HC_2, HC_3)
end

Fig. 9. Calculation of minimum hybrid cost for a sink

Figure 9 shows calculation of minimum hybrid cost for two cases only using the function $Calculate\_Minimum\_HybridCost()$. In a similar way for any other position of the source and sink minimum hybrid cost can be calculated.

The function $Path\_Augmenting\_for\_Reliability\_Trusted\_and\_Hybridcost\_$
$Aware\_routing(T)$ is used to enhance the survival probability of each terminal if it is less than some limiting value. For the maximum distant sink terminal the routing paths through other bending points are connected unless it reaches to desired reliability value. Now to interconnect the sink via other bending points it may happen that the new routing path may cross over other routing paths of different sink terminals. Consider Fig. 10, the routing of a single source (S) and three sink terminals T_1, T_2, and T_3. The survival probabilities of these sink terminals are respectively 81.45%, 81.45%, and 85.74%. Here it is assumed that the length of a wire segment is 8. Now suppose we want to increase the survival probability above 85%. If another path SB_4T_1 is connected to T_1 (as shown in Fig. 11) then the survival probability of T_1 is increased to 96.56%. Now the routing path SB_4T_1 crosses the routing paths SB_3T_3 and SB_2T_2. The survival probability of T_3 in the path $SB_4B_5T_3$ is 85.74%. Hence $SB_4B_5T_3$ path is considered and the previous routing path to T_3 is discarded. But the survival probability of T_2 in the routing path $SB_4B_6T_2$ is 81.45%. Hence to interconnect T_2 both the routing paths are considered and routing reliability is increased to 96.56%. The final routing graph for reliability-aware routing is shown in Fig. 12. For the sink other than the maximum distant sink terminal first, the routing reliability of the sink for the modified graph is calculated and if it is above the limiting value then that path is considered. But if it is less than the limiting value and for all possible routing paths to the sink are also less than the limiting value, the routing path with maximum routing reliability is considered. Then additional paths are added to sink to increase the reliability above the limit. It may happen that one path has reliability above the limiting value and then

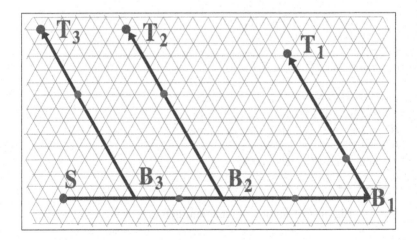

Fig. 10. Routing tree for single source and 3 sink terminals

that corresponding path is considered. There may exist more than one path with reliability greater than the limiting value. In that case the path with minimum hybrid cost is considered. Figure 13 shows the formal description of the function *Path_Augmenting_for_Reliability_Trusted_and_Hybridcost_Aware_routing(T)*.

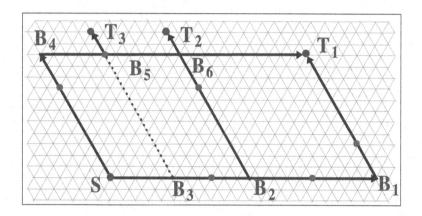

Fig. 11. Initial routing graph for single source and 3 sink terminals

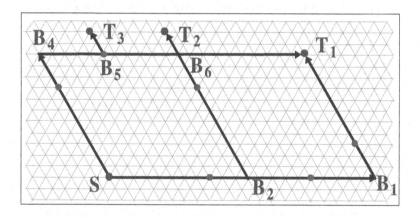

Fig. 12. Final routing graph for single source and 3 sink terminals

4   Experimental Results

Table 2 shows the experimental result. In this paper, the algorithm is tested on some random data sets. For each data set single source and multiple sink terminals are generated randomly. As in [4,6], in this paper also the cost due to unit interconnect length, due to 60° and 120° bending are respectively assumed to be 1, 10, and 30. First global routing is done to construct a hexagonal routing tree

---

Path_Augmenting_for_Reliability_Trusted_and
_Hybridcost_Aware_routing(T_i)

---

if T_i *is maximum distant sink from source* then
    while *the survival probability of the sink (T_i) < limiting value* do
        Add path from S to T_i trough other bending point
        if *the new path crosses other routing paths of any other sink T_j ($j \neq i$)* then
            if *the survival probability of the sink T_j ≥ limiting value considering only the new path* then
                Remove the previous path to T_j and consider the new path to T_j
            end
        else
            consider both the path to T_j
        end
        end
    end
end
else
    if *the survival probability of the sink T_i > limiting value* then
        Consider the path
    end
    else
        Find all possible path to T_i from the existing routing graph
        if *the survival probability of the sink T_i through all paths < Limiting value*
        then
            Find the path with maximum survival probability of sink T_i
            while *the survival probability of T_i < limiting value* do
                Add others path with minimum hybrid cost
            end
        end
        else
            Select the path with survival probability
            if *multiple paths with desired survival probability* then
                select the path with minimum hybrid cost
            end
        end
    end
end

Fig. 13. Reliability improvement of any sink above certain value

using the algorithm of [4] for the minimization of hybrid cost. Then the proposed algorithm of this paper is applied so that the reliability of each sink terminal is above the desired level. In each of these sets of source and sink terminals, three different wire segments of lengths 8, 10, and 12 are assumed to calculate routing reliability. We observed that in the routing tree constructed with the algorithm of [4] in all test cases few of the sink terminals are below desired survival probability. The number of sink terminals below desired reliability is also reduced with the increasing length of each wire segment. We observed that with

Table 2. Comparisons of hybrid cost and reliability

Test case	# sinks	Length of a wire segment	Method of [4]						Our proposed method						Improvement of reliability
			Total wire length	n_{60}	n_{120}	HC	% Sinks above desired reliability	Average % of survival probability	Total wire length	n_{60}	n_{120}	HC	% sinks above desired reliability	Average % of survival probability	
1	25	8	130	23	0	360	52	83.60	200	26	2	520	100	89.88	7.51
		10					64	85.20	195	27	1	495		89.05	4.52
		12					68	85.72	186	25	0	436		89.19	4.05
2	30	8	153	27	0	423	56.67	83.74	223	30	4	643	100	90.65	8.25
		10					60	84.47	234	32	2	614		89.73	6..23
		12					66.67	85.40	225	32	1	575		89.77	5.18
3	25	8	140	24	0	380	36	80.56	227	36	1	617	100	91.57	13.67
		10					40	81.05	219	33	1	579		90.06	11.12
		12					44	82.02	211	32	0	531		90.45	10.28

the algorithm of [4] the maximum number of sinks above desired reliability in these three test cases are respectively 68%, 66.67% and 44%. As in the routing tree with our proposed algorithm, a few redundant paths are added the hybrid cost in all cases are increased. Though the hybrid cost is increased in all cases survival probability of each sink terminal is now above the limiting value. In our proposed method if the length of the wire segment is increased then the hybrid cost is reduced. The average survival probability in the three test cases is improved by 7.51% to 8.25%, 13.67%. Though in our proposed method the improvement in the survival probability is small but all the sink terminals are above desired reliability. In test case 1, in our proposed method, though hybrid cost increases by 1.44, 1.38 and 1.21 times in comparison to that of [4] but the corresponding improvement in numbers of reliable sinks are 1.92, 1.56, and 1.47 times. Similarly, in test cases 2 and 3, the increase in hybrid cost are respectively (1.52, 1.45, and 1.36) times and (1.62, 1.52, and 1.40) times and the improvement of numbers of reliable sinks are respectively (1.76, 1.67, and 1.5) times and (2.78, 2.5, and 2.72) times. The improvement in the number of reliable sinks is much more significant than the increase in hybrid cost.

5 Conclusion

This paper discussed the routing for single source and multiple sink terminals of GNR-based interconnect considering reliability as the major objective. To increase the reliability additional paths may be added. As a consequence, the hexagonal tree is now converted into a graph and the total hybrid cost is also increased. But in the GNR based interconnect the power dissipation is much less than in the traditional interconnect. Hence the increase in reliability of GNR wire segment would be a good objective. In this paper, we attempt to achieve this objective. In our work, along with routing reliability, we also consider the hybrid cost. The work of this paper can be improved by considering electrical reliability such as crosstalk and other parameters such as interconnect delay and grid area.

References

1. Naeemi, A., Meindl, J.D.: Performance benchmarking for graphene nanoribbon, carbon nanotube, and cu interconnects. In: 2008 International Interconnect Technology Conference, pp. 183–185. IEEE (2008)
2. Shao, Q., Liu, G., Teweldebrhan, D., Balandin, A.: High-temperature quenching of electrical resistance in graphene interconnects. Appl. Phys. Lett. **92**(20), 202108 (2008)
3. Lemme, M.C., Echtermeyer, T.J., Baus, M., Kurz, H.: A graphene field-effect device. IEEE Electron Dev. Lett. **28**(4), 282–284 (2007)
4. Das, S., Das, D.K., Pandit, S.: A global routing method for graphene nanoribbons based circuits and interconnects. ACM J. Emerg. Technol. Comput. Syst. (JETC) **16**(3), 1–28 (2020)
5. Yan, T., Ma, Q., Chilstedt, S., Wong, M.D., Chen, D.: Routing with graphene nanoribbons. In: 16th Asia and South Pacific Design Automation Conference (ASP-DAC 2011), pp. 323–329. IEEE (2011)
6. Yan, T., Ma, Q., Chilstedt, S., Wong, M.D., Chen, D.: A routing algorithm for graphene nanoribbon circuit. ACM Trans. Des. Autom. Electron. Syst. (TODAES) **18**(4), 1–18 (2013)
7. Ritter, K.A., Lyding, J.W.: The influence of edge structure on the electronic properties of graphene quantum dots and nanoribbons. Nat. Mater. **8**(3), 235–242 (2009)
8. Das, S., Das, S., Majumder, A., Dasgupta, P., Das, D.K.: Delay estimates for graphene nanoribbons: a novel measure of fidelity and experiments with global routing trees. In: 2016 International Great Lakes Symposium on VLSI (GLSVLSI), pp. 263–268. IEEE (2016)
9. Das, S., Das, D.K.: A technique to construct global routing trees for graphene nanoribbon (GNR). In: 2017 18th International Symposium on Quality Electronic Design (ISQED), pp. 111–118. IEEE (2017)
10. Das, S., Das, D.K.: Steiner tree construction for graphene nanoribbon based circuits in presence of obstacles. In: 2018 International Symposium on Devices, Circuits and Systems (ISDCS), pp. 1–6. IEEE (2018)
11. Yan, J.T.: Single-layer GNR routing for minimization of bending delay. IEEE Trans. Comput. Aided Des. Integr. Circuits Syst. **38**(11), 2099–2112 (2018)
12. Yan, J.T.: Single-layer delay-driven GNR nontree routing under resource constraint for yield improvement. IEEE Trans. Very Large Scale Integr. (VLSI) Syst. **28**, 736–749 (2019)
13. Yan, J.T., Yen, C.H.: Construction of delay-driven GNR routing tree. In: 2019 17th IEEE International New Circuits and Systems Conference (NEWCAS), pp. 1–4. IEEE (2019)
14. Gupta, T.: Routing and reliability. In: Copper Interconnect Technology, pp. 347–403. Springer, New York (2009). https://doi.org/10.1007/978-1-4419-0076-0_8
15. Kahng, A.B., Liu, B., Mandoiu, I.I.: Nontree routing for reliability and yield improvement [IC layout]. IEEE Trans. Comput. Aided Des. Integr. Circuits Syst. **23**(1), 148–156 (2004)
16. Chen, X., Liao, C., Wei, T., Hu, S.: An interconnect reliability-driven routing technique for electromigration failure avoidance. IEEE Trans. Dependable Secur. Comput. **9**(5), 770–776 (2010)
17. Ma, Q., Xiao, Z., Wong, M.D.: Algorithmic study on the routing reliability problem. In: Thirteenth International Symposium on Quality Electronic Design (ISQED), pp. 483–488. IEEE (2012)

Low Cost Hardware Design of ECC Scalar Multiplication

Hariveer Inumarty and M. Mohamed Asan Basiri[⊠]

Indian Institute of Information Technology Design and Manufacturing,
Kurnool 518007, Andhra Pradesh, India
{edm17b002,asan}@iiitk.ac.in

Abstract. Elliptic curve cryptography (ECC) is one of the most popular asymmetric key cryptography techniques used in secured data communications. The scalar multiplication is the most expensive operation in the ECC. In this paper, we propose a low cost hardware for scalar multiplication in Affine coordinates based ECC. Here, we use a reconfigurable Galois field (GF) arithmetic circuit, which performs various GF arithmetic operations such as addition, multiplication, inverse, and fused multiply add (FMA) using a same set of hardware circuit. Instead of using a number of multipliers and adders in point addition/doubling, we have used only one reconfigurable GF arithmetic circuit. The existing and proposed designs are implemented in 45 nm CMOS technology using Cadence. The synthesis results show that the affine co-ordinate based proposed $GF(2^{163})$ scalar multiplier achieves 69% of reduction in the switching power dissipation as compared with the Lopez-Dahab projective co-ordinates based conventional design in 45 nm CMOS technology.

Keywords: Affine coordinates · Elliptic-curve cryptography ·
Lopez-Dahab coordinates · Point addition · Point doubling · Scalar
multiplication

1 Introduction

Cryptography [1] is the science of using mathematical theories and computation in order to encrypt and decrypt information. It treats prevention, detection of tampering the data, and other activity of which the digital data will suffer. ECC is an approach to public-key cryptography based on the elliptic curves over finite fields. It is a fast and efficient method for the creation of cryptographic keys. ECC allows smaller keys compared to other cryptographic techniques to provide equivalent security with minimum storage requirement. Scalar multiplication is the most essential and time consuming operation of the ECC. Lets assume a point P that lies on the elliptic curve, and k be some scalar, then $kP = P + P \ldots \ldots + P$ till k times. If kP and P are known, it is almost impossible to track down k. It behaves like a one-way function also known as trap door function. This is the

ⓒ The Author(s), under exclusive license to Springer Nature Switzerland AG 2022
A. P. Shah et al. (Eds.): VDAT 2022, CCIS 1687, pp. 387–396, 2022.
https://doi.org/10.1007/978-3-031-21514-8_32

reason why ECC is most preferred. Here, optimizing the cost of the hardware and improving the performance are the major factors to be considered. Many algorithms have been proposed to improve the efficiency of scalar multiplication during the past decade.

1.1   Related Works

This section elaborates the scalar multiplication in affine coordinates along with the literature of their hardware designs. In affine coordinates, an elliptic curve over $GF(2^m)$ is defined as the set of points (x, y), which satisfy (1).

$$y^2 + xy = x^3 + ax^2 + b, \tag{1}$$

Here, $a, b, x, y \in GF(2^m), b \neq 0$. Let $P = (x_1, y_1) \in E$ and $Q = (x_2, y_2) \in E$ (points on the Elliptic curve). The point addition and point doubling in affine coordinate based $GF(2^m)$ ECC are shown in (2) and (3) respectively.

$$R(x_3, y_3) = P(x_1, y_1) + Q(x_2, y_2) \in E,$$
$$x_3 = \lambda_1^2 + \lambda_1 + x_1 + x_2 + a,$$
$$y_3 = \lambda_1(x_1 + x_3) + y_1 + x_3, \tag{2}$$

$$R(x_3, y_3) = 2P(x_1, y_1) \in E,$$
$$x_3 = \lambda^2 + \lambda + a,$$
$$y_3 = x_1^2 + \lambda x_3 + x_3, \tag{3}$$

Here, $\lambda_1 = (y_2 + y_1)/(x_1 + x_2)$; $\lambda = x_1 + y_1/x_1$; where $R = 0$ when $x_1 = x_2$ and $y_1 \neq y_2$, or $x_1 = x_2 = 0$. As shown in Algorithm 1, elliptic curve scalar multiplication kP will be calculated using these equations.

Algorithm 1: Affine coordinates based right-to-left scalar multiplication
Inputs : Point P, Integer $k = (k_{l-1}....k_1 k_0)_2$
Outputs : Point $Q = kP$
1. $Q = 0$;
2. **for** $i = 0$ to $l - 1$ **do**
3.   **if** $k_i = 1$ then $Q = Q + P$;
4. $P = 2P$;
5. **end for**

The following research works are found in the architectures of ECC scalar multiplications. The conventional affine and Lopez-Dahab projective co-ordinates [2] based $GF(2^m)$ scalar multiplications are shown in [3] and [6] respectively. Here, the drawback is the requirement of a number of multipliers, but the number of cycles to complete the operation here is very less. Digit serial multiplier based $GF(2^m)$ scalar multiplications are shown in [4] and [7] respectively.

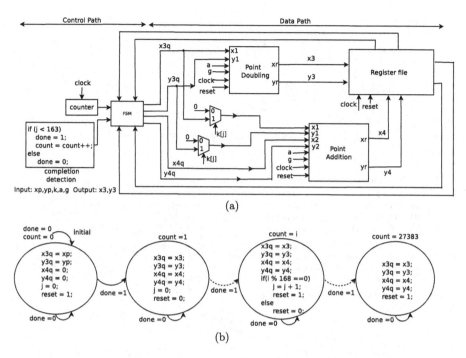

Fig. 1. (a) The proposed architecture of affine coordinate based $GF(2^{163})$ scalar multiplication and (b) FSM used in Fig. 1(a)

Here, the drawback is the requirement of a number of cycles, but the hardware units to complete the operation here is less than the conventional designs. In [5], the multiplication is performed during the idle cycles of $GF(2^m)$ inverse. In [8], bit parallel Montgomery algorithm based multiply-accumulate circuit is used in the projective co-ordinate based ECC, where the $GF(2^m)$ multiplication followed by an addition can be done in a same circuit. In [9], the add-shift unit based $GF(2^{163})$ multipliers are used in the projective co-ordinates based ECC scalar multiplication. In all the aforementioned existing techniques, the $GF(2^{163})$ multipliers, adders, and/or multiplicative inverses are explicitly used. Due to these number of arithmetic units, the hardware cost (area and power) of these designs is very great. This gives the motivation to our proposed design, where the configurable $GF(2^{163})$ arithmetic unit [12] can be used as $GF(2^{163})$ multipliers, adders, and/or multiplicative inverses. Due to the involvement of the configurable $GF(2^{163})$ arithmetic unit, our proposed scalar multiplier needs less hardware cost.

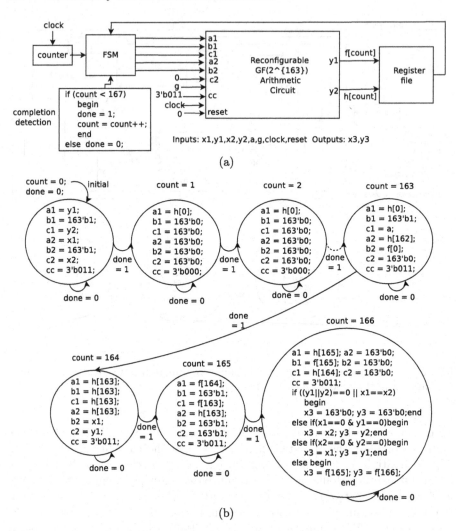

Fig. 2. (a) The proposed point addition architecture used in Fig. 1(a) and (b) FSM used in Fig. 2(a)

1.2   Contribution of This Paper

This paper proposes hardware for scalar multiplication in Affine coordinates with less hardware cost. The conventional design of scalar multiplication needs a number of adders, multipliers [10], and multiplicative inverse [11] in point addition/doubling of the scalar multiplication. A reconfigurable GF arithmetic circuit [12] is used repeatedly to do the various GF arithmetic operations in point addition/doubling. The existing and proposed hardwares for scalar multiplication in Affine coordinates are implemented using 45nm CMOS technology with Cadence.

The rest of the paper is organized as follows: Sect. 2 describes the proposed hardware implementation of Scalar Multiplication in Affine coordinates. Design, Modelling, Implementation, and Results are shown in Sect. 3, followed by a conclusion in Sect. 4.

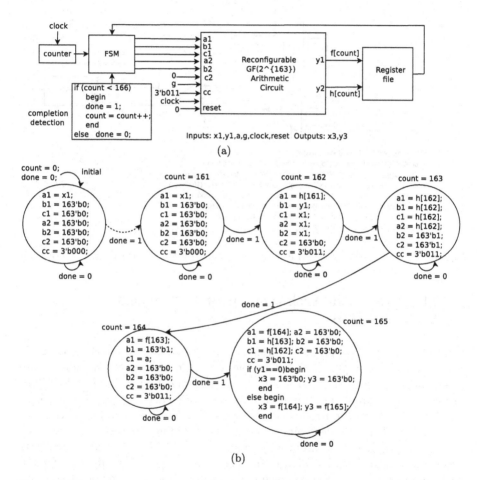

Fig. 3. (a) The proposed point doubling architecture used in Fig. 1(a) and (b) FSM used in Fig. 3(a)

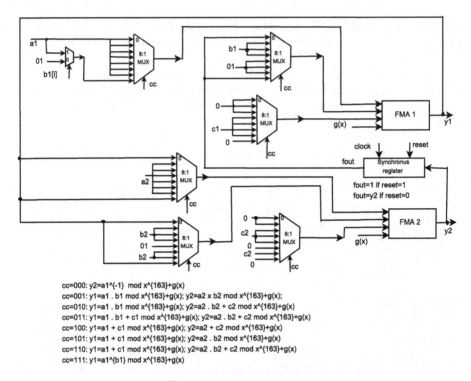

cc=000: y2=a1^{-1} mod x^{163}+g(x)
cc=001: y1=a1 . b1 mod x^{163}+g(x); y2=a2 x b2 mod x^{163}+g(x);
cc=010: y1=a1 . b1 mod x^{163}+g(x); y2=a2 . b2 + c2 mod x^{163}+g(x)
cc=011: y1=a1 . b1 + c1 mod x^{163}+g(x); y2=a2 . b2 + c2 mod x^{163}+g(x)
cc=100: y1=a1 + c1 mod x^{163}+g(x); y2=a2 + c2 mod x^{163}+g(x)
cc=101: y1=a1 + c1 mod x^{163}+g(x); y2=a2 . b2 mod x^{163}+g(x)
cc=110: y1=a1 + c1 mod x^{163}+g(x); y2=a2 . b2 + c2 mod x^{163}+g(x)
cc=111: y1=a1^{b1} mod x^{163}+g(x)

Fig. 4. Reconfigurable $GF(2^{163})$ arithmetic circuit [12] to perform various operations

2   The Proposed Architecture of ECC Scalar Multiplication

Figure 1(a) shows the proposed design of Affine coordinates based $GF(2^{163})$ scalar multiplication [3], which follows the Algorithm 1. The corresponding finite state machine (FSM) of the proposed scalar multiplication is shown in Fig. 1(b). In Fig. 1(a), the inputs are the point on the Elliptic curve (x_p, y_p), the scalar k, the constant a, and the irreducible polynomial g. The proposed architecture as shown in Fig. 1(a) includes point addition and doubling circuits.

Figure 2(a) shows the proposed architecture for the point addition and its FSM is shown in Fig. 2(b). Figure 3(a) shows the proposed architecture for the point doubling and its FSM is shown in Fig. 3(b). In the proposed point addition and doubling architectures, only one reconfigurable $GF(2^{163})$ arithmetic circuit is used. In the reconfigurable $GF(2^{163})$ arithmetic circuit, two additions or multiplications or fused multiply adds (FMAs) [13] can be performed in parallel for every cycle. Based on the Algorithm 1, the respective inputs will be fed into the reconfigurable $GF(2^{163})$ arithmetic circuit and the respective outputs from the reconfigurable $GF(2^{163})$ arithmetic circuit will be stored temporarily in the register file. According to (2), the reconfigurable $GF(2^{163})$ arithmetic circuit based point addition takes 167 cycles to produce the output. According to (3), the reconfigurable $GF(2^{163})$ arithmetic circuit based point doubling takes 166 cycles to produce its output. Therefore, $GF(2^{163})$ scalar multiplication in affine coordinates takes $163 \times 168 = 27,384$ cycles to produce the output with respect to the Algorithm 1. The critical path of our proposed design is $T_{MUX} + T_{FMA}$, where T_{MUX} and T_{FMA} represent the critical path depths of the multiplexer and $GF(2^{163})$ FMA respectively.

Figure 4 shows the reconfigurable $GF(2^{163})$ arithmetic circuit [12] to perform addition, multiplication, fused multiply addition, inverse, and exponentiation with respect to the control line cc. Here, the fused multiply addition is nothing but the multiplication followed by an addition (AB+C). In Fig. 4, the $GF(2^{163})$ inputs are a1, b1, c1, a2, b2, and c2. The $GF(2^{163})$ irreducible polynomial is $x^{163} + g(x)$, where the $g(x)$ is of 163-bits wide. The outputs of Fig. 4 are y1 and y2. Figure 4 includes two LSB first $GF(2^{163})$ FMAs as shown in [12].

3 Design Modelling, Implementation, and Results

The existing and proposed architectures of $GF(2^{163})$ scalar multiplication are modelled/verified using Verilog HDL and synthesized using 45nm CMOS technology using Cadence ASIC Design Tool, where the operating voltage is 0.9 V. Also, Cadence Simvision and Conformal tools are used for the simulation and formal verification of these designs. The actual implementations (CMOS library or FPGA device) used in the reference papers for all the existing techniques are different. Due to the unavailability of those CMOS libraries and FPGA devices, the existing techniques are implemented in this manuscript as per the reference papers using one particular 45 nm library. Therefore, the comparisons of the existing designs with proposed techniques are valid. In all our implementations, *Ip_asserted_probability* and *Ip_asserted_toggle_count* are taken as 0.5 and 0.02 respectively. *Ip_asserted_probability* is the probability for the net to be one (high). For example, the tool considers all nets in the design to be at logic level 1 for total of 50% of the simulation time, then the probability is 0.5. *Ip_asserted_toggle_count* is the toggle count per toggle rate unit. For example, considering a signal toggling 2 times in 100 ns, then the toggle rate is 2/100 = 0.02.

The synthesis results are shown in Table 1, where the details of proposed designs are mentioned in bold letters. Since the conventional affine and Lopez-Dahab projective co-ordinates based $GF(2^{163})$ scalar multiplications are used in [3] and [6] need a number of multipliers, the number of LUTs, and slice registers are greater than the proposed designs. Here the trade-off is the number of cycles to complete the operation. Since the digit serial multiplier based $GF(2^{163})$ scalar multiplications are used in [4] and [7], the number of cycles required to complete the operations of these existing technique is greater than the conventional designs. In the digit serial $GF(2^{163})$ multiplier, the inputs are given as a series of words. So, a number of cycles are required to complete a multiplication using this digit serial multiplier. The proposed design uses the reconfigurable $GF(2^{163})$ arithmetic circuit, where the parallel LSB first multiplication can be

Table 1. Synthesis results of various $GF(2^{163})$ scalar multipliers using 45 nm CMOS technology

Parameters	Scalar multiplication in affine coordinates			Proposed (affine coordinate)
	Conventional [3]	[4]^a	[5]	
No. of cycles	26569	28102	16981	**27384**
Critical path delay (ps)	2542.2	1942.5	3182.9	**2143.5**
No of standard cells	63088	49966	65901	**30857**
Area (μm^2)	357989.4	304789.0	387902.3	**189857.2**
Switching power (nw)	43908.3	36890.2	52689.0	**27334.3**
Leakage power (nw)	6317.6	5265.5	8768.1	**3607.4**
Required H/W resources	2 adders, 2 multipliers, 1 inverse, Register file	Memory, 1 square, 2 multipliers, counter, shifter, 1 adder, Register file	5 multipliers, 1 inverse, Register file	4 FMAs, 2 counters, Register file
Parameters	Scalar multiplication in Lopez-Dahab coordinates			
	Conventional [6]	[7]^a	[8]	[9]
No. of cycles	2323	3753	2877	7698
Critical path delay (ps)	2843.7	3244.5	1783.7	1578.9
No of standard cells	95716	83718	71890	53987
Area (μm^2)	567893.4	478900.1	390087.2	237894.3
Switching power (nw)	87902.1	81345.8	72097.3	61980.3
Leakage power (nw)	11890.2	12589.3	10290.4	9807.2
Required H/W resources	5 square, 9 multipliers, 2 adders, 1 inverse Register file	2 adders, 2 squares, 2 multipliers, 1 inverse Register file	1 FMA, 1 square, 1 inverse, ROM, Register file	1 adder, 1 square 1 multiplier, 2 inverses, Register file

^{a}The digit serial $GF(2^m)$ multiplier with $\lceil m/w \rceil = 4$, where $m = 163$ and $w = 41$.

done in a cycle. The synthesis results show that the affine co-ordinate based proposed $GF(2^{163})$ scalar multiplier achieves 69% of reduction in the switching power dissipation as compared with the Lopez-Dahab projective co-ordinates based conventional design while the trade-off in number of cycles using the $45nm$ CMOS technology.

4   Conclusion

In this paper, a new hardware design for scalar multiplication in affine coordinates based ECC is proposed. Here, we use a reconfigurable GF arithmetic circuit only once in point addition/doubling to perform the scalar multiplication. Hence the separate GF adders, multipliers, and multiplicative inverses are eliminated. The existing and proposed designs are implemented in 45nm CMOS technology using Cadence. The synthesis results show that the affine co-ordinate based proposed $GF(2^{163})$ scalar multiplier achieves 69% of reduction in the switching power dissipation as compared with the Lopez-Dahab projective co-ordinates based conventional design in $45nm$ CMOS technology.

Acknowledgements. This work is a part of sponsored project (IHUB-NTIHAC/ 2021/01/1) of C3I Center, IIT Kanpur. Also, this work is fully supported and funded by the same. We thank IHUB-NTIHAC, C3I Center of IIT Kanpur for the given support.

References

1. Mohamed Asan Basiri, M., Shukla, S.K.: Hardware optimization for crypto implementation. In: IEEE International Symposium on VLSI Design and Test, pp. 1–6 (2016). https://doi.org/10.1109/ISVDAT.2016.8064877a
2. López, J., Dahab, R.: Fast multiplication on elliptic curves over $GF(2^m)$ without precomputation. In: Koç, Ç.K., Paar, C. (eds.) CHES 1999. LNCS, vol. 1717, pp. 316–327. Springer, Heidelberg (1999). https://doi.org/10.1007/3-540-48059-5_27
3. Hong, J., Wu, W.: The design of high performance elliptic curve cryptographic. In: 52nd IEEE International Midwest Symposium on Circuits and Systems, pp. 527–530 (2009). https://doi.org/10.1109/MWSCAS.2009.5236038
4. Ansari, B., Wu, H.: Efficient finite field processor for $GF(2^{163})$ and its VLSI implementation. In: Fourth IEEE International Conference on Information Technology, pp. 1–6 (2007). https://doi.org/10.1109/ITNG.2007.83
5. Venugopal, E., Hailu, T.: FPGA based architecture of elliptic curve scalar multiplication for IOT. In: IEEE International Conference on Emerging Devices and Smart Systems, pp. 178–182 (2018). https://doi.org/10.1109/ICEDSS.2018.8544305
6. Ansari, B., Hasan, M.A.: High performance architecture of elliptic curve scalar multiplication. IEEE Trans. Comput. **57**(11), 1443–1453 (2008)
7. Zhang, Y., Chen, D., Choi, Y., Chen, L., Ko, S.: A high performance pseudo-multicore ECC processor over $GF(2^{163})$. In: IEEE International Symposium on Circuits and Systems, pp. 701–704 (2010). https://doi.org/10.1109/ISCAS.2010.5537486
8. Li, L., Li, S.: High-performance pipelined architecture of elliptic curve scalar multiplication over $GF(2^m)$. IEEE Trans. Very Large Scale Integr. (VLSI) Syst. **24**(4), 1223–1232 (2016)
9. Rashid, M., Hazzazi, M.M., Khan, S.Z., Alharbi, A.R., Sajid, A., Aljaedi, A.: A novel low-area point multiplication architecture for elliptic-curve cryptography. Electronics **10**(2698), 1–16 (2021)
10. Song, L., Parhi, K.K.: Low-energy digit-serial/parallel finite field multipliers. J. VLSI Signal Process. Syst. Signal Image Video Technol. **19**, 149–166 (1998). https://doi.org/10.1023/A:1008013818413

11. Lin, C.-C., Chang, F.-K., Chang, H.-C., Lee, C.-Y.: An universal VLSI architecture for bit-parallel computation in $GF(2^m)$. In: IEEE Asia-Pacific Conference on Circuits and Systems, pp. 125–128 (2004). https://doi.org/10.1109/APCCAS.2004.1412708

12. Inumary, H., Mohamed Asan Basiri, M.: Reconfigurable hardware design for polynomial Galois field arithmetic operations. In: IEEE International Symposium on VLSI Design and Test, pp. 1–5 (2020). https://doi.org/10.1109/VDAT50263.2020.9190485

13. Mohamed Asan Basiri, M., Shukla, S.K.: Flexible VLSI architectures for Galois field multipliers. Integr. VLSI J. **50**, 109–124 (2017)

Scalable Construction of Formal Error Guaranteed LUT-Based Approximate Multipliers with Analytical Worst-Case Error Bound

Anishetti Venkatesh[1]([⊠]) [ID], Chandan Kumar Jha[2] [ID], G. U. Vinod[3] [ID], Masahiro Fujita[4] [ID], and Virendra Singh[1]

[1] Indian Institute of Technology Bombay, Mumbai, India
venkateshknpl@gmail.com, singhv@iitb.ac.in
[2] German Research Center for Artificial Intelligence,Bremen, Germany
chandan.jha@dfki.de
[3] Qualcomm,Chennai, India
[4] University of Tokyo, Tokyo, Japan
fujita@ee.t.u-tokyo.ac.jp

Abstract. In approximate circuits, the functionality of the circuit is modified to improve non-functional parameters such as area, power, and delay. These circuits are targeted for error-resilient applications like image processing, neural networks, etc. These applications can achieve acceptable output results even after the introduction of approximation in computations. Error computation becomes crucial in these applications and can be done either using simulation or formal approaches. Both these methods of error computation are not scalable for circuits with inputs larger than 32 bits. In this work, we used scalable construction of large array multipliers using smaller formally worst-case error guaranteed array multipliers obtained using an LUT-SAT based approach and guaranteed overall worst-case error bounds analytically. Our 8×8 approximate multipliers based on the LUT-SAT approach have 0.59% less area as compared to the state-of-the-art EvoApprox library-based multipliers. We compared the 16×16 multipliers constructed using four 8×8 LUT-SAT-based multipliers with 16×16 multipliers constructed using four 8×8 Evo multipliers. We have performed the area and various error metric comparisons.

Keywords: Scalable · LUT · SAT · Formal error · EvoApproxLib

1 Introduction

Approximate circuits are used in error-tolerant applications such as signal processing, image processing, machine learning, etc. These applications can produce acceptable quality outputs even after the introduction of approximation in computations [5]. In the case of neural network applications, billions of multiply and

C. K. Jha—The work was carried out when Chandan Kumar Jha was at CADSL, IIT Bombay.

accumulate (MAC) operations are performed in the convolutional layers. It has been shown in prior work that introducing approximations into these large numbers of multiplications can still give an acceptable quality of output [3]. After approximation, the error computations can be done either through a simulation approach or through formal methods. Both these methods do not scale well with the increase in the number of bits in the design. When the number of input bits is greater than 32, the simulation-based approach becomes impractical. Exhaustive simulation of 20 bit adders, for example, can take more than 19 years to complete [5]. When the circuit structure is complex, formal methods based on SAT will take exponential time and memory size will grow exponentially for reduced ordered binary decision diagrams (ROBDDs) [5].

In this work, our goal is to propose a scalable approach to approximation to give a formal error guarantee for the worst case error of the approximate multipliers. To this end, we constructed large array multipliers using small array multipliers for both signed and unsigned multipliers [1]. We used the LUT-SAT based approach proposed in [2] to design 8×8 multipliers having a formally worst-case error guarantee. We compared these 8×8 approximate multipliers obtained using the LUT-SAT approach with multipliers from the Evo approximate library having the same worst-case normalized error [4]. These approximate multipliers were then used in the scalable construction of 16×16 multipliers. Since the worst case error for the 8×8 multiplier is formally bound, the worst case error for the 16×16 multipliers can also be analytically bound. In order to see how closely the analytical error bound is estimated with respect to the actual error value, we also performed a simulation of 16×16 approximate multipliers and obtained worst-case error values and the time required for simulation. Since, depending on the application, different error metrics become important, we have also shown other important error metrics comparisons. We used exhaustive simulation to compare other error metrics like mean absolute error and mean square error of 16×16 approximate multipliers. While higher bits approximate multipliers like 32×32 and 64×64, they can be designed using similar construction. The remaining part of the paper is organized as follows: Sect. 2 discusses related works as well as the Cartesian genetic programming technique, which is the state-of-the art technique for designing approximate circuits with the greatest area savings. In Sect. 3, we explain the methodology of the design of approximate multipliers. In Sect. 4, we discuss the experimental setup used for the evaluation of the designs. In Sect. 5, we perform a comparison with the state-of-the-art multipliers. In Sect. 6, we conclude the paper.

2   Related Work

2.1   Error Metrics

Different error metrics are used to calculate the error between exact and approximate outputs. In this work, we have used the following error metrics: The worst case error (WCE) is defined as

$$WCE(f, \hat{f}) = \max_{\forall x \in \mathbb{B}^n} |\text{value}(f(x)) - \text{value}(\hat{f}(x))|$$

The worst case normalized error (WCNE) in percentage is defined as

$$WCNE(\%) = \frac{1}{((2^m - 1) * (2^m - 1))} * WCE(f, \hat{f}) * 100$$

here m is each input size.

The average case absolute error (MAE) is defined as

$$e_{mae}(f, \hat{f}) = \frac{1}{2^n} \sum_{\forall x \in \mathbb{B}^n} |\text{val}(f(x)) - \text{val}(\hat{f}(x))|$$

The mean square error (MSE) is defined as

$$e_{mse}(f, \hat{f}) = \frac{1}{2^n} \sum_{\forall x \in \mathbb{B}^n} \left(\text{val}(f(x)) - \text{val}(\hat{f}(x))\right)^2$$

here n is the total inputs bits f(x) is exact value, $\hat{f}(x)$ is approximate value of the function respectively. In [8], a systematic logic synthesis of approximate circuits (SALSA) that transforms the approximate logic synthesis problem into traditional logic synthesis problem is proposed. Symbolic computer algebra (SCA) based approximate circuit [9] suffers for polynomial explosion even for 8×8 approximate multipliers. Approximate logic synthesis using boolean factorization (BLASYS) [7] uses matrix based approximation. BLASYS performs better in terms of area savings when synthesized in synopsys design compiler using 65 nm technology library as compared to SALSA for all benchmarks considered in [7]. In truncated array multipliers [1], few least significant input bits are made to zero. In broken array multiplier [1] during partial product accumulation phase creates a horizontal and vertical break and make those cells to zero. Since both the truncated and broken array multipliers are regular structure, analytical model is used in [1] to get the worst case error (WCE) bound value. In [4], a library of approximate adders and multipliers called Evo approx library is proposed which is based on Cartesian Genetic Programming (CGP). CGP based approximation considers the genetic theory i.e., the fittest one exist. In their work the authors consider the approximate circuit [6] with least area should exist in case error-oriented design, and least error one should exist in case of resource-oriented design. In case of multi-objective the goal is to reduce the area as well as error. It takes the exact circuit gate-level netlist as input and converts it into an integer list. List contains a collection of nodes, each node contains 3 entries, first 2 entries are inputs of the gate and the third entry is type of gate. While doing approximation type of the gate is modified randomly from a set of predefined gate lists. Since integer-based lists are easy and faster to manipulate in software. CGP uses simulation for less number of inputs and uses SAT based approaches for complex circuits [3]. The designs obtained using CGP give more area savings for a given error metric with error threshold. For example 8×8 approximate multiplier for average case relative error threshold of 5%, 4.42%, BLASYS and Evo methods area saving are 28.8%, 44.25% respectively [4,7].

This is the state-of-the-art in the literature for the design of approximate multipliers. Hence in this work we have compared our proposed multipliers based on LUT-SAT against the Evoapprox multipliers. In the next section we discuss the methodology for the design of approximate multipliers based on LUT-SAT.

3   Methodology

3.1   Scalable Approximate Multiplier Construction

In Fig. 1, we show that any 2N × 2N multiplier can be constructed using 4 N × N multipliers of the same or different architectures. Building exact bigger multipliers using smaller multipliers will lead to extra hardware in terms of full adders since each N × N multiplier needs partial product accumulation and 2N bit adder in final addition separately. This will lead to more area, delay and power consumption. However, in the case of approximate multipliers, this is not true. Replacing exact N × N multiplier blocks with approximate multipliers reduce area and power consumption. The worst case error (WCE) for the N × N can be calculated using the formal method while the WCE for the 2N × 2N multiplier can be obtained analytically by the equation given below.

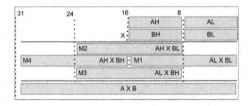

Fig. 1. Example construction of 16 × 16 integer multiplier using 4 8 × 8 multipliers.

$$\text{WCE}_M = 2^{2N}\text{WCE}_{M4} + 2^N\text{WCE}_{M3} + 2^N\text{WCE}_{M2} + \text{WCE}_{M1}$$

Depending upon the approximation introduced in the multipliers the error calculation for the worst case can be done. From Fig. 1 we can see that an approximate multiplier can be used for $A_L B_L$, $A_L B_H$, $A_H B_L$, and $A_H B_H$. However approximating most significant bits (MSBs) will leads to large errors. Also if the MSB blocks are approximated, they will dominate the approximation in the LSB blocks we will not get any area savings compared to applying approximation in $A_L B_L$ block alone. In [1], the authors trying to use the methodology described in Fig. 1 to construct large array multipliers using smaller blocks based on truncated array multipliers (TAM) and broken array multipliers (BAM). Both TAM, BAM multipliers are regular structure hence have error bound formulae analytically. The area savings of 8 × 8 approximate multipliers for TAM, BAM were not better as compared to Evo approxlib when synthesized in synopsys design compiler using 45 nm technology library [1], [4].

In this work we are using LUT-SAT based approximate multipliers instead of truncated and broken array multipliers to construct 16 × 16 approximate multipliers. We have implemented both 16 × 16 signed(assuming signed magnitude representation) and unsigned approximate multipliers using the construction technique shown in Fig. 1. The LUT-SAT based approach was used to design the 8 × 8 multiplier. LUT-SAT based approximation is a automatic approach [2] unlike TAM, BAM and the formal error is guaranteed using SAT miters. We compared the LUT-SAT based designs obtained after constructing the 16 × 16 multiplier compared by keeping approximate multipliers which are based on EvoApprox [4]

3.2   LUT-SAT Based Approximate Multiplier

LUT-SAT [2] methodology first considers the gate level net list of the exact circuit. This is an automatic method and does not assume anything about circuit structure. Even though this technique is can be applied to any arithmetic circuit, it was used for designing approximate adders in [2].

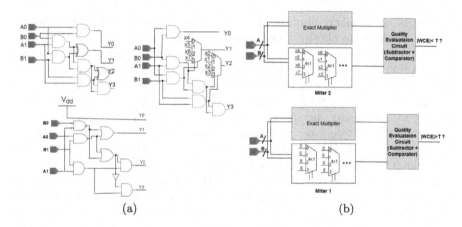

Fig. 2. (a) 2-bit Multiplier (b) Miters for LUT solution

In this work we are using the same for approximate multipliers. After a gate level netlist is selected, we identify the nets starting from least significant output side as shown in Fig. 2a. Once the output bit is chosen, few gates in its fan-in cone side are selected randomly and converted into look up tables (LUTs) for obtaining solution. In next iteration, this circuit is appended to the gates in the next significant output bits in its fan-in cone. This process is continued for some finite iterations. For example in Fig. 2a two XOR gates are replaced by two 2−input LUTs. After replacing gates by LUTs, basically there are two miters required in order to obtain a solution to the LUT. We need to find the solution to LUT input assignment under approximate worst case error threshold value. Consider miter2 Fig. 2b, in this will take exact multiplier and approximate multiplier (here initially the approximate multiplier is same as exact multiplier with LUTs inserted). Now in order to compute worst case error difference between two primary outputs, a subtractor is used. The comparator is used to check if the difference is lesser than the worst case error threshold value. From miter2 as shown in Fig. 2b, LUT inputs are unknown, i.e. x[7 : 0] variables. The solution is obtained by formulating it as a SAT problem by miter. If the worst case error is less than the given threshold value, x[7 : 0] solution is required. To obtain this some initial input i.e., in terms of primary inputs A,B is given to miter2.

$$\exists x \, |exact \, (assignment1) - approx \, (asignment1, x)| < WCE_\tau$$

x value is obtained by a SAT solver by finding a satisfying assignment in terms of x variable. But the obtained x solution may not be satisfying for all other primary inputs. So for that again one more miter is needed let say miter1 as shown in Fig. 2b. In this miter1, the obtained x solution in previous iteration is substituted and now will formulate the below condition and give to SAT solver.

$$\exists (A, B) \, |exact \, (A, B) - approx \, (A, B, x_{candidate})| > WCE_\tau$$

If there is no primary input (A, B), with x for which the error threshold is crossed, a solution is obtained. Otherwise, the circuit obtained is not the correct solution. Hence, we ignore the solution and use miter2 to give a new x solution through SAT formulation by replicating the miter2 twice. The x solution should satisfy for all possible primary inputs until then the miter2 is replicated and solved. Since this is a SAT-based solution, it cannot handle larger circuits as the circuit complexity increases. To handle this, we limit replication to some finite number of iterations. If it cannot be solved, then that gate is kept as the original gate itself without approximating and other gates are selected for approximating. If there is a solution within the mentioned iterations, then the area of the solution is checked in terms of the estimated number of transistors assuming CMOS technology using YOSYS (synthesis and formal verification tool) [10]. The few iterations are tried again with the SAT solver to obtain a lower transistor count solution by adding the previous x solution as a clause, i.e., telling the SAT solver to give other than this solution if it exists. After approximation of all possible gates, the area is checked in terms of the estimated number of transistors for an approximate 8 × 8 multiplier against the exact multiplier using the YOSYS tool [10] assuming CMOS technology. Figure 2a shows an example of the approximate multiplier obtained for the worst case error value =1. Since the SAT solvers are not scalable for multipliers. So these 8 × 8 multipliers are used in the scalable construction technique in $A_L B_L$ alone and in $A_L B_L$ and $A_L B_H$, $A_H B_L$ with different worst case arithmetic error values and synthesized the overall verilog gate level netlist using YOSYS and obtained area savings with respect to the original circuit. Compared with the same error EvoApprox libraries kept in smaller multiplier blocks in a similar way, and achieved better results interms of estimated number transistor savings compared to EvoApprox.

4   Experimental Setup

The experiments were carried out on an Ubuntu 20.04 machine having an Intel Core i7-7700 CPU at 3.60 GHz with 8 GB RAM. The open source synthesis and formal verification tool YOSYS [10] is used to compute the area in terms of the estimated number of transistors assuming CMOS technology.

5   Results

5.1   LUT Design Space Exploration

The LUT-SAT based approximate 8 × 8 multipliers are obtained and plotted against their area savings for a wide range of worst-case absolute error percentages as shown in Fig. 3. The area savings increase as the worst-case absolute error percentages increase. This happens because the design can be approximated more with the relaxing of the error constraints. Here, the LUT count means how many LUTs can be replaced by gates and solved by a SAT solver simultaneously. We have obtained for LUT4, LUT8, and LUT12, respectively.

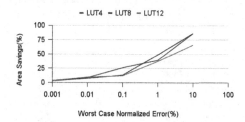

Fig. 3. %WCNE vs % area savings for 8 × 8 LUT-approximate multiplier

5.2   Unsigned Approximate Multipliers Designs

LUT vs. EvoApprox Area Comparision: 8 × 8 approximate multipliers obtained from the LUT-SAT based approach have 0.2%, 0.59% lesser area as compared to the EvoApprox library for the Worst Case Normalized Error values of 8.27% (EvoApprox1), 27% (EvoApprox2) respectively as shown Fig. 4. The area percentages are calculated with reference to the exact estimated transistor count, i.e., an 8 × 8 exact multiplier has 2688 transistors when estimated using the YOSYS tool. 8 × 8 multipliers obtained from the LUT-SAT based approach have 88.9%, 99.1% lesser area as compared to the exact 8 × 8 multiplier for Worst Case Normalized Error values of 8.27% (LUTApprox1), 27% (LUTApprox2), respectively.

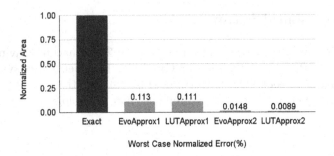

Fig. 4. Normalized area vs. % WCNE for 8 × 8 multiplier

Unsigned 16 × 16 Approximate Multipliers with Only $A_L B_L$ Approximated: In Fig. 5, the 16 × 16 multipliers are constructed using scalable method and only 8 × 8 lower block $(A_L B_L)$ being approximated to 8.27% and 27% WCNE. We see that we have slightly lesser area as compared to Evo approximate library. We see area savings of 17% and 18.8% for 1.2E−4% (corresponds to 8.27% in $A_L B_L$) and 4.1E−4% (corresponds to 27% in $A_L B_L$) WCNE respectively, with respect to exact 16 × 16 multiplier. Estimated transistor count for 16 × 16 exact multiplier = 11966 using YOSYS tool.

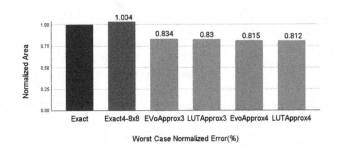

Fig. 5. Normalized area vs. % WCNE for 16 × 16 unsigned multiplier

EvoApprox3, LUTApprox3 are 16 × 16 approximate multipliers with overall WCNE bound of 1.2E−4%, when 8 × 8 $A_L B_L$ multiplier block is having 8.27% WCNE. Similarly EvoApprox4, LUTApprox4 are 16 × 16 approximate multipliers with overall WCNE bound 4.1E−4%, when 8 × 8 $A_L B_L$ multiplier block is having 27% WCNE.

Unsigned 16 × 16 Approximate Multipliers, Different blocks Approximated: While we have approximated $A_L B_L$ and shown the savings, we performed an analysis to show the reason behind not approximating the higher order blocks. We applied 5% WCNE in $A_L B_L$ block and 0.01% WCNE in $A_L B_H$, $A_H B_L$ then overall WCNE bound calculated using Fig. 1 is same as putting 10%

WCNE in $A_L B_L$ block alone. We see that the area savings in the one where only $A_L B_L$ is approximated is 17.7%, while for the design where $A_L B_L$, $A_L B_H$, and $A_H B_L$ is approximated is only 4.5% for same WCNE as shown in Fig. 6. By doing this analysis, we showed that allowing low error in middle blocks ($A_L B_H$, $A_H B_L$) does not give much area savings. Hence, the lower block should be approximated the most. Also, the middle blocks can be approximated when the lower block is fully approximated.

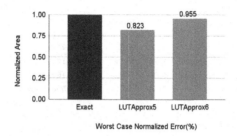

Fig. 6. Normalized area vs. % WCNE for 16×16 multiplier

LUTApprox5 is 16×16 approximate multiplier with 8×8 $A_L B_L$ having WCNE 10% alone. LUTApprox6 is 16×16 approximate multiplier, when 8×8 approximate multiplier blocks having $A_L B_L$ (WCNE 5%), $A_L B_H$ (WCNE 0.01%), $A_H B_L$ (WCNE 0.01%).

5.3 Signed Approximate Multipliers Designs

Signed approximate multipliers are constructed assuming the inputs are in signed magnitude, then instead of implementing 16×16 we can implement 15×15 i.e., the 4 blocks are $A_L B_L{=}8x8$, $A_H B_L{=}7x8$, $A_L B_H{=}8x7$, $A_H B_H{=}7x7$, and MSB bits decides the sign bit using xor operation and guarantee the worst case absolute normalized error (WCNE) using the same formula. In this case, we also have area savings similar to unsinged multipliers with respect to exact as well as Evo approximate library as shown in Fig. 7.

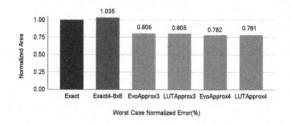

Fig. 7. Normalized area vs. % WCNE for 16×16 signed multiplier

5.4 Validating with Simulation Results

In order to cross check the 16×16 approximate multiplier results synthesized using scalable approach, the following table shows the analytical worst case error bound against to the actual simulated error values along with simulation times as shown in Table 1

Table 1. Worst case error metrics for 16×16 multipliers

	16×16 approximate multiplier with error in $A_L B_L$ block			
	8×8 EvoApprox		8×8 LUT-SAT	
	8.27%	27.45%	8.27%	27%
Theoretical worst case error bound	5380	17853	5380	17557
Simulated worst case error value	5380	17853	5234	16383
Time to simulate (in hours)	5.73	5.34	5.54	5.4

Since Evo approximate multipliers also use simulation for lower input sizes, typically in the case of 8-bit, the error magnitudes are the same when simulated also. The total simulation time for 16×16 approximate multipliers is >5 h for the considered designs using the resources mentioned in Sect. 4.

5.5 Computing Other Error Metrics via Simulation

In this we computed other error metrics, namely mean absolute error (MAE) and mean square error (MSE), along with the worst case normalized error (WCNE) using exhaustive simulation. These were done for 16×16 approximate multipliers built using 4–8×8 approximate multiplier blocks and in that lower 8×8 $A_L B_L$ block is replaced by 8.27% and 27% worst case normalized error percentages for LUT-SAT based and Evo based Approx multipliers as shown in Table 2

Table 2. Error metrics for 16×16 multipliers

	16×16 approximate multiplier with error in $A_L B_L$ Block			
	8×8 EvoApprox		8×8 LUT-SAT	
Error Metrics	8.27%	27.45%	8.27%	27%
Worst case normalized error (x10^{-4})%	1.25	4.16	1.22	3.81
Mean Absolute Error(%)	41.64	48.88	58.41	13.77
Mean square error (%)	99.22	75	75	75

6 Conclusion

We proposed the design of 16×16 approximate signed and unsigned multipliers using four 8×8 exact and approximate multipliers. We were able to achieve significant area savings as compared to exact multipliers. We had comparable area as compared (0.59% lesser) to Evo approximate multipliers, but ours is a formal method of introducing approximation and can be extended to other circuits, unlike Evo approximate multipliers. We also showed that approximating lower blocks more rather than approximating the middle blocks gives better area savings. We also compared other error metrics using exhaustive simulation. While we have limited ourselves to 16×16 multipliers in this work, the same can be extended to 32×32 multipliers.

References

1. Mrazek, V., Vasicek, Z., Sekanina, L., Jiang, H., Han, J.: Scalable construction of approximate multipliers with formally guaranteed worst case error. IEEE Trans. Very Large Scale Integr. (VLSI) Syst. **26**(11), 2572–2576 (2018). https://doi.org/10.1109/TVLSI.2018.2856362
2. Vinod, G.U., Vineesh, V.S., Tudu, J.T., Fujita, M., Singh, V.: LUT-based circuit approximation with targeted error guarantees. In: 2020 IEEE 29th Asian Test Symposium (ATS), pp. 1–6 (2020). https://doi.org/10.1109/ATS49688.2020.9301574
3. Mrazek, V., Sekanina, L., Vasicek, Z.: Using libraries of approximate circuits in design of hardware accelerators of deep neural networks. In: 2020 2nd IEEE International Conference on Artificial Intelligence Circuits and Systems (AICAS), pp. 243–247 (2020). https://doi.org/10.1109/AICAS48895.2020.9073837
4. Evo Approximate library. https://ehw.fit.vutbr.cz/evoapproxlib
5. Vasicek, Z.: Formal methods for exact analysis of approximate circuits. IEEE Access **7**, 177309–177331 (2019). https://doi.org/10.1109/ACCESS.2019.2958605
6. Češka, M., Matyaš, J., Mrazek, V., Sekanina, L., Vasicek, Z., Vojnar, T.: Approximating complex arithmetic circuits with formal error guarantees: 32-bit multipliers accomplished. In: 2017 IEEE/ACM International Conference on Computer-Aided Design (ICCAD), pp. 416–423 (2017). https://doi.org/10.1109/ICCAD.2017.8203807
7. Hashemi, S., Tann, H., Reda, S.: BLASYS: approximate logic synthesis using boolean matrix factorization. In: 2018 55th ACM/ESDA/IEEE Design Automation Conference (DAC), pp. 1–6 (2018). https://doi.org/10.1109/DAC.2018.8465702
8. Venkataramani, S., Sabne, A., Kozhikkottu, V., Roy, K., Raghunathan, A.: SALSA: systematic logic synthesis of approximate circuits. In: DAC Design Automation Conference 2012, pp. 796–801 (2012). https://doi.org/10.1145/2228360.2228504
9. Fröhlich, S., Große, D., Drechsler, R.: Approximate hardware generation using symbolic computer algebra employing grobner basis. In: Design, Automation & Test in Europe Conference & Exhibition (DATE) 2018, pp. 889–892 (2018)
10. YOSYS tool. http://www.clifford.at/yosys/

Design of a Programmable Delay Line with On-Chip Calibration to Achieve Immunity Against Process Variations

Kanika Monga, Eesha Karnawat, Nitin Chaturvedi[(⊠)], and S. Gurunarayanan

Birla Institute of Technology and Science, Pilani, India
{p20170027,f20190153,nitin80,sguru}@pilani.bits-pilani.ac.in

Abstract. In recent times, CMOS Delay Lines (DL) are rapidly gaining interest due to increased demand for high precision delay in VLSI systems. Delay lines serve as a fundamental block for a wide range of applications including Delay Locked Loops (DLL), Phase Locked Loop (PLL), ring oscillators, clock synchronizers, etc. providing precise time delays. However, one of the major challenges faced by the CMOS delay line is the deviation in delays due to process, voltage and temperature (PVT) variations. Addressing this challenge, in this work, we aim to mitigate the impact of one of these variations on the delay line. Therefore, we propose to design a programmable delay line (DL) based on a voltage-controlled buffer which is insensitive to the process variation. To achieve immunity against process variations and obtain a high precision delay value, a novel calibration technique is proposed which dynamically tunes the biasing voltage of the buffer resulting in a constant delay under all process corners. Our simulation results for the proposed DL demonstrate a total delay of 559 psec with a delay error of less than 2%.

Keywords: Digital Circuit · CMOS Delay Lines · Delay step · Voltage-Controlled Buffer and process variations

1 Introduction

Delay Lines (DL) are basic building blocks of many digital sub-systems. It is most commonly used to provide a constant delay to digital signals. It also finds application in clock synchronization and clock distribution network of high-speed and high-performance systems to provide a precise clock signal that minimizes the skew [1]. Furthermore, it forms a substantial part of delay-locked loops (DLL) and phase-locked loops (PLL) circuits providing high-resolution delay and good linearity [2, 3]. One of the simplest delay line structures is tapped delay line which is constructed by cascading the multiple delay elements in a linear sequence, as shown in Fig. 1 [4]. The conventional delay element consists of either a CMOS buffer or CMOS logic gate. Due to the advancement of CMOS technology, the performance of the delay elements and delay lines has improved over the years. The scaling of transistor dimensions has resulted in a lower delay, reduced power consumption, and a smaller on-chip area of delay lines [5]. However, it suffers

© The Author(s), under exclusive license to Springer Nature Switzerland AG 2022
A. P. Shah et al. (Eds.): VDAT 2022, CCIS 1687, pp. 408–419, 2022.
https://doi.org/10.1007/978-3-031-21514-8_34

from large deviation in the delay values, also defined as jitter due significant impact of process, voltage and temperature (PVT) variations at lower technology nodes [6]. Therefore, novel techniques are required to minimize the.

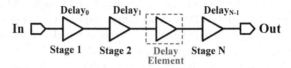

Fig. 1. Conventional Tapped Delay Line Structure.

Therefore, novel techniques are required to minimize the impact of variations on the delay. Therefore, in this work, we aim to address one of the challenges that significantly impact the delay i.e., process variations. We propose to design a programmable delay line which can be calibrated to achieve precise delay step under various process corners.

The major contributions of the work are:

- We design a programmable delay line based on voltage-controlled delay buffer which can be tuned to generate a precise delay.
- We propose a novel calibration technique that auto-adjust the controlling voltage of the delay buffer to maintain the same time delay under various process corners.
- We also compare the proposed delay line with the non-programmable CMOS buffer-based delay line in terms of delay error introduced due to variations.

The rest of the paper is organized as follows: Sect. 2 provides the background for CMOS delay lines along with various performance metrics used to characterize a delay line. Section 3 presents the architecture and operation of proposed delay line based on voltage-controlled buffer. Section 4 presents the simulation methodology and results. It also compares the proposed delay line with the conventional non-programmable delay line. Finally, in Section 5, conclusion is drawn.

2   Background

In this section, we briefly discuss the various types and operating principles of existing delay lines. We also present various performance metrics which are most commonly used to characterize a delay line.

2.1   Related Literature

The delay lines can be broadly categorized into optical delay lines and CMOS delay lines [4]. The optical delay lines are based on optical fiber and it is used to provide delays in the optical communication systems and phased array antennas. The optical delay line offers the advantage of an extremely small delay in the range of sub-picoseconds with high linearity. One of the most commonly used methods to obtain delay in an optical line is to adjust the free space gap between the input and transceiver. The larger the gap the longer the delay by the optical line. Using this approach, an optical line can produce a delay step in the range of sub-pico-seconds to hundreds of picoseconds. For larger delays, multiple optical lines are cascaded. Since it utilizes optical fiber in the delay structure, the cost of the overall architecture increases significantly [7]. Moreover, cascading multiple optical lines make the system bulky and complex. On the other hand, CMOS based delay line offers a large delay range, reduced cost, and complexity. The CMOS-based delay line can further be categorized based on delay tuning strategies as a digitally controlled delay line or analog controlled delay line. In the analog controlled delay line, the effective resistance or the capacitor of the delay elements is altered either by adding capacitive load or changing the biasing voltages to effectively change the RC constant [8–12]. On the other hand, in the digitally controlled delay element, a binary input is utilized to vary the delay.

2.2 Performance Metrics

The parameters used to evaluate the performance of a DL includes resolution or delay step, range, and delay error.

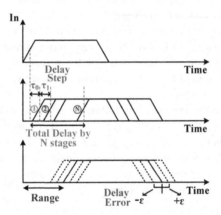

Fig. 2. Performance metrics of a delay line (a) Input signal applied to a delay line (b) Delay step (c) Range and Delay Error.

2.2.1 Resolution/Delay Step

The resolution or delay step is defined as the minimum incremental time step that a delay line can produce [13, 14]. For an ideal DL with a constant resolution, each stage provides a delay equivalent to a single delay step, defined as τ_i., as shown in Fig. 2(b).

2.2.2 Range

It is defined as the maximum time period by which an input signal can be delayed, as shown in Fig. 2(c) [13, 14]. The range of a DL is evaluated by summing the delay step of each stage, as presented by (1) where τ_i is the delay step of each stage.

$$R = \left(\sum_{i=0}^{N} \tau_i \right) \qquad (1)$$

2.2.3 Delay Error

The delay error ε is defined as the maximum deviation from the delay value evaluated at nominal conditions [13, 14]. The delay error can be negative or positive, as illustrated in Fig. 2(c). In Fig. 2(c), the solid line represents the output under nominal conditions whereas the variations in the delay are presented by the dotted lines.

3 Proposed Programmable Delay Line Architecture

The proposed delay line consists of N identical serially connected voltage-controlled buffer, as shown in Fig. 3. The delay controlling voltage (Vcontrol) is applied to every buffer to obtain a similar delay between the stages ($\text{Delay}_0 = \text{Delay}_1 = \text{Delay}_{N-1}$). The smallest delay achieved (i.e. delay step) is limited to the propagation delay of the voltage-controlled buffer utilized in the delay line. The major advantage of using a voltage-controlled buffer element is that the value of biasing voltage (Vcontrol) can be changed to obtain a wide range of delay values. In this work, we design a programmable delay line with N = 4 stages, achieving 559 psec of total delay. Further, we propose a novel calibration circuit that adjust the basing voltage to compensate process variations within the range of + 10%. The following sub-section describes the delay buffer and calibration unit in details.

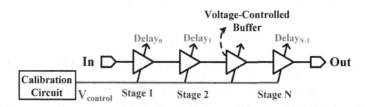

Fig. 3. Proposed programmable Delay Line based on voltage-controlled buffers

3.1 Voltage-Controlled Delay Buffer (VC-DB)

A high-resolution voltage-controlled delay buffer presented in Fig. 4, forms the basic building block of the proposed delay line. As shown in Fig. 4, the delay buffer consists of two inverters (M1-M2 & M3-M4) connected in series. The charging and discharging current of the input inverter (M1-M2) is controlled by: 1) a PMOS transistor (M5) connected in between transistor M1 of the input inverter and the power supply and 2) a NMOS transistor (M6) connected in between transistor M3 of the input inverter and ground. Using the transistors M5 and M6, both the rise time and fall time of the input signal can be controlled. A biasing voltage Vcontrol is applied at the gate of the M6 transistor altering the fall time of the input signal. On the other hand, transistors M7 and M8 form a current mirror that supplies biasing voltage to the gate of transistor M5, thereby controlling the rise time of the input signal. The second stage inverter or the output inverter (M3-M4) is then utilized to improve the rise and fall time of the output signal.

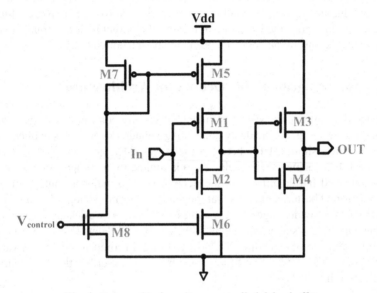

Fig. 4. Schematic of a voltage-controlled delay buffer

3.2   Proposed Calibration Circuit for Generation of Vcontrol for VC-DB

We propose a novel calibration circuit that detects various corner conditions of the IC and dynamically tunes the voltage supplied to delay buffers to maintain the same delay under variations. The proposed calibration circuit presented in Fig. 5 consists of a delay chain (Delay chain 0) whose delay is monitored to determine the different process corner. In the proposed approach, we compare the delay of the delay chain 0, presented by pulse_dt with the reference pulse_ref. The reference pulse (pulse_ref) is applied externally which corresponds to a delay value obtained under nominal conditions. Ideally, both the pulses should have same delay with respect to input pulse (applied at the input of delay chain 0). However, due to process variations the delay of the pulse_dt changes. By sampling pulse_dt with respect to pulse_ref, we can determine whether the pulse_dt has a greater or smaller delay than the reference pulse_ref. The sampling results are stored in the set of D Flip-Flops, as shown in Fig. 5. The output of flip-flops are then utilized to generate control signals using a control signal generator. The control signals are applied to the set of PMOS and NMOS transistors. By turning ON either the PMOS or NMOS transistor, the voltage (Vcontrol) can be modulated as follows: If a PMOS transistor is turned ON, the voltage increases which reduces the delay of the buffer element. On the other hand, if a NMOS transistor is turned ON, the voltage lowers increasing the delay of the buffer element. Hence, controlling voltage (Vcontrol) is able to reach a balanced value which provides the same delay as the reference pulse.

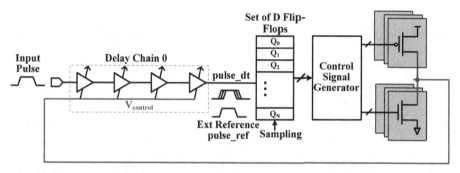

Fig. 5. Architecture of proposed calibration circuit.

4   Simulation Methodology and Results

In this section, we implement the proposed delay line with the calibration circuit using 180 nm CMOS technology. Further, using spice simulations, we demonstrate that the proposed delay line is insensitive to the process variation achieving a total delay of approx. 559 psec under all TT, SS and FF corners with a very small delay error.

We first present the simulation results for the voltage-controlled delay buffer element. Table 1 tabulates the delay of the voltage-controlled buffer under different biasing voltages. With decreases in the basing voltage, the current through the inverter decreases resulting in larger delays and vice-versa. Moreover, delays at different process corners are also tabulated in Table 1.

Table 1. Delay of Voltage-Controlled Buffer under different Vcontrol.

Vcontrol	Delay (ps)		
	FF	TT	SS
1.8 V	65.8	79.2	96.7
1.6 V	67.5	81.6	99.7
1.4 V	70.5	85.8	105
1.2 V	76.5	94.8	118
0.9 V	106	143	198

Next, we simulate the delay line consisting of 4 serially connected voltage-controlled buffer element. Table 2 tabulates the delay of complete delay line at a constant basing voltage (Vcontrol) of 0.9 V. Without the calibration circuit, the delay line suffers from process variations. We simulate the delay line under various process conditions considering TT, SS and FF process corners however maintaining the temperature and voltage supply constant at 25 °C and 1.8 V. The variations in the delay in terms of delay error values are also presented in Table 2.

Table 2. Delay of proposed delay line (without calibartion) under various process conditions

Process Corners	Resolution / Delay Step (ps)	Delay (ps)	Delay Error (ps)	% error
FF	106	411	−148	−26.4%
TT	143	559	0	0
SS	123	766	+207	+37.03%

To address the fluctuation in the delay due to process variation, we integrate the proposed calibration circuit with the aforementioned voltage-controlled buffer-based delay line, as illustrated in Fig. 6. From Fig. 6, we observe that the test set-up utilizes two D Flip-flop for sampling and generates two control signals a0 and a1 using a simple buffer logic. The control signal a0 is applied to the gate of a PMOS (M1) whereas control signal a1 is applied at the gate of NMOS (M2). The Input Pulse and the pulse_ref are the external reference signals used for calibration. The proposed calibration circuit remain same even for the N-stage voltage-controlled buffer-based delay line. Hence, the overhead due to additional calibrated can be compensated if the number of stages in a delay line is large.

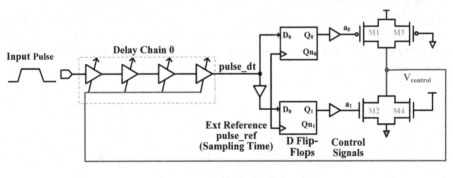

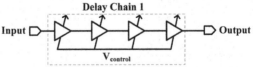

Fig. 6. Schematic of the test circuit for the proposed delay line.

Figure 7 plots the simulation waveform for the proposed circuit at TT corner. The simulations are performed in two phases: 1) Calibration Phase and 2) Evaluation Phase. During the calibration phase, we first reset the flip-flops to logic '0' (Q0 = 0, Q1 = 0). With Q0 = 0 and Q1 = 0, both the control signals a0 and a1 are pulled to gnd which set the initial value of Vcontrol to 1.28 V (M1-ON; M2-OFF). Next, we apply external input signal (Input Pulse) to the delay chain (delay chain 0). The output of the delay chain is represented by the pulse_dt waveform in the Fig. 7. The pulse_dt is compared with the reference signal represented by pulse_ref and the outputs are sampled in the two flip-flops. The output of flip-flops are then used to indicate various process corners, as tabulated in the Table 3.

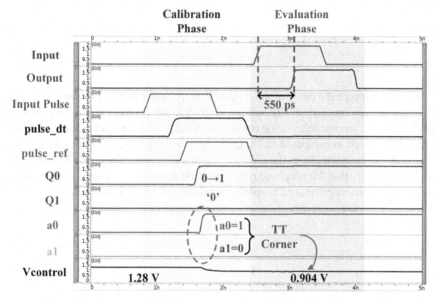

Fig. 7. Simulation waveform of proposed delay line at TT corner.

Table 3. Status of D flip-flops and control signals for various process corners

Process Corners	Q0	Q1	a0	a1	Status of M1 and M2 transistors
FF	1	1	1	1	NMOS is turned ON; PMOS is turned OFF
TT	1	0	1	0	Both NMOS and PMOS are turned OFF
SS	0	0	0	0	NMOS is turned OFF; PMOS is turned ON

From Fig. 7, we can observe that Q0 = 1 and Q0 = 0 which indicates TT corner. The control signals a0 and a1 are logic '1' and logic '0' respectively which turns both the NMOS and PMOS transistors OFF. Consequently, the Vcontrol falls to 0.904 V providing a total delay of 551 psec during evaluation phase. Similarly, Fig. 8 plots the simulation waveform at SS and FF corners. Summarizing the simulation results, we tabulate the delay of the proposed delay at different corner in Table 4.

Table 4. Delay of proposed delay line (with calibration) under various process conditions

Process corners	Vcontrol (After calibration)	Delay (ps)
FF	0.774	559
TT	0.904	551
SS	1.28	549

We also compare the delay of the proposed delay line with non-programmable delay line based on conventional CMOS buffer and tabulate the results in Table 5. It is observed that to obtain the similar delay in the conventional delay line 10 stages of identical CMOS buffer are required as compared to 4 stages of voltage-controlled buffer in the proposed delay line. Furthermore, from the tabulated results of delay error under TT, SS and FF corners, we verify that the proposed programmable delay lines perform better under the process variations as compared to conventional CMOS buffer-based delay line.

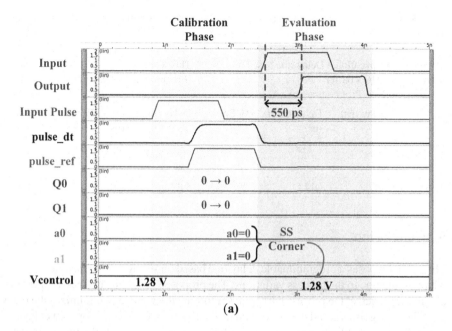

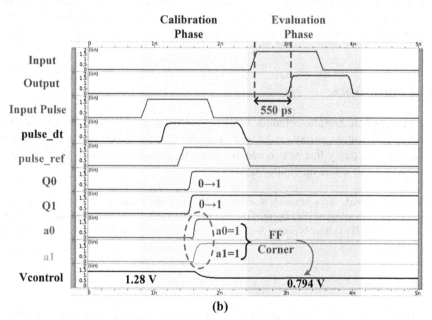

Fig. 8. (a) Simulation Waveform at SS corner (b) Simulation Waveform at FF corner.

Table 5. Comparison of Delay of proposed delay line and CMOS-buffer based conventional delay line

Process Corners	Conventional Delay line based on CMOS buffer (Non-Programmable)			This work (Programmable delay line)		
	Delay (ps)	Delay Error (ps)	% Error	Delay (ps)	Delay Error (ps)	% Error
FF	441	−118	−21.1%	559	0	0
TT	557	−2	−0.35%	551	−8	−1.4%
SS	722	+143	29.15%	549	+10	+1.78%

5 Conclusion

This work proposes a programmable delay line based on voltage-controlled delay buffer which is immune to the process variations. The proposed delay line utilizes a calibration circuit which detect the process corner and auto-tune the voltage to minimizes the delay error. Using rigorous simulation, we validate the functionality of the proposed delay line under TT, SS and FF process corners. With the calibration circuit, the proposed delay line is able to achieve a constant delay of 559 psec with delay error less than 2% as compared to conventional CMOS buffer-based delay line which present a delay error of 30%.

6 Future Work

The proposed calibration technique can be extended to provide immunity against temperature and voltage variations as well. Therefore, in the future, we plan to design a programmable delay line which can be tuned to provide a constant delay under all process, voltage and temperature variations.

Acknowledgement. This research was funded by the Department of Science Department of Science and Technology (DST) in collaboration with the Ministry of Electronics and Information Technology (MeITy) under National Supercomputing Mission and R&D to Exascale computing.

References

1. Geannopoulos, G., Dai, X.: An adaptive digital deskewing circuit for clock distribution networks. In: 1998 IEEE International Solid-State Circuits Conference. Digest of Technical Papers, ISSCC. First Edition (Cat. No.98CH36156), pp. 400–401 (1998)
2. Melloni, A., et al.: Tunable delay lines in silicon photonics: Coupled resonators and photonic crystals, a comparison. IEEE Photon. J. **2**, 181–194 (2010)
3. Chen, C., Liu, S.: An infinite phase shift delay-locked loop with voltage-controlled sawtooth delay line. IEEE J. Solid-State Circ. **43**, 2413–2421 (2008)

4. Bult, K., Wallinga, H.: A CMOS analog continuous-time delay line with adaptive delay-time control. IEEE J. Solid-State Circ. **23**, 759–766 (1988)
5. Rehman, S., Khafaji, M., Carta, C., Ellinger, F.: A comparison of broadband and tunable delay-line structures in 45-nm CMOS. In: 2018 International Workshop on Integrated Nonlinear Microwave and Millimetre-wave Circuits (INMMIC) (2018)
6. Morales, J., Chierchie, F., Mandolesi, P., Paolini, E.: Design and evaluation of an all-digital programmable delay line in 130-nm CMOS. In: 2019 XVIII Workshop on Information Processing and Control (RPIC) (2019)
7. Hashimoto, K., Kano, S., Wada, A.: Optical delay line for high time resolution measurement: W-type delay line. Rev. Sci. Instrum. **79**, 083108 (2008)
8. Bal, A., Tiwari, J., Narayan Tripathi, J., Achar, R.: A novel programmable delay line for VLSI systems. In: 2019 IEEE 23rd Workshop on Signal and Power Integrity (SPI) (2019)
9. Moreno, A., Cortadella, J.: Synthesis of all-digital delay lines. In: 2017 23rd IEEE International Symposium on Asynchronous Circuits and Systems (ASYNC) (2017)
10. Garakoui, S., Klumperink, E., Nauta, B., van Vliet, F.: Compact Cascadable g m -C all-pass true time delay cell with reduced delay variation over frequency. IEEE J. Solid-State Circ. **50**, 693–703 (2015)
11. Chou, P., Wang, J.: An all-digital on-chip peak-to-peak jitter measurement circuit with automatic resolution calibration for high PVT-variation resilience. IEEE Trans. Circ. SystI: Regular Papers. **66**, 2508–2518 (2019)
12. Park, H., Sim, J., Choi, Y., Choi, J., Kwon, Y., Park, S., Park, G., Chung, J., Kim, K., Jung, H., Kim, H., Chun, J., Kim, C.: A 1.3–4-GHz quadrature-phase digital DLL using sequential delay control and reconfigurable delay line. IEEE J. Solid-State Circ. **56**, 1886–1896 (2021)
13. G. Kim, M.-K. Kim, B.-Soo Chang, Wonchan Kim: A low-voltage, low-power CMOS delay element. IEEE J. Solid-State Circ. **31**, 966–971 (1996)

High Performance Ternary Full Adder in CNFET-Memristor Logic Technology

Panasa Srikanth[iD] and B. Srinivasu[✉][iD]

Indian Institute of Technology Mandi, Mandi, India
srinivasu@iitmandi.ac.in

Abstract. This paper presents ternary unary operators and multiplexer circuits in carbon nanotube field effect transistor and memristor technology. The designed circuits can be used in designing ternary arithmetic circuits, a ternary full adder is proposed in this paper using ternary unary operators and multiplexers. The proposed circuits are simulated in Cadence Virtuoso using MOSFET-like CNFET and VTEAM memristor model. The proposed ternary full adder is having a savings of 17% in the power delay product to the best existing designs. Noise margin analysis was carried out on the proposed circuits and proposed ternary full adder is having a good noise margin.

Keywords: Adders · Ternary logic · CNFET · Memristor · Unary operators · Multiplexer · Emerging technologies

1 Introduction

In past few years, the research in the beyond binary arithmetic has grown rapidly mainly in the base-3 (ternary logic) [1]. The research in ternary has grown from designing ternary arithmetic circuits [2] to designing ternary SRAM cells [3]. Ternary arithmetic circuits such as ternary adders [4] and multipliers [5] are studied. Ternary circuits can be implemented with devices, which support multi-threshold voltages. A CMOS-based ternary multiplier is presented in [6]. With the limitations in Silicon based devices, the emergence of device technologies other than Silicon has emerged in recent years such as Carbon Nanotube FET (CNFET) [4], Quantum Dot Gate FET (QDGFET) [7].

As an alternative to the contemporary "Von-Neumann" architectures, the in-memory computing using memristors has been explored in recent years from digital circuits [8] to multi level memory design [9]. The two level logic can be implemented using memristor as high resistance and low resistance of the memristor respectively. The memristor based logic has various implementations such as memory aided logic (MAGIC) [10] and material implication (IMPLY) logic [11]. Various designs of full adders and multi-bit adders are presented in

This work has been supported by the DST, Start up Research Grant - SRG/2021/001255.

these topologies. As an extension to the binary arithmetic, authors in [12] proposed ternary NAND, NOR gate and decoder in CMOS-Memristor technology. A ternary half adder is presented in CNFET-Memristor technology [13].

Ternary circuits can be designed in two approaches as reported in literature. Firstly, using a ternary decoder to decode a ternary signal into three two valued binary signals and deriving the circuits using binary logic gates [4]. Second approach is to use the ternary unary operators [14] and designing using ternary logic gates [15]. A ternary 3×1 multiplexer-based ternary full adder is presented in [15]. Another ternary full adder using 2×1 multiplexer is presented in [16].

Authors in [12] presented a CMOS-memristor based ternary NOR gate and ternary decoder. CNFET-Memristor based inverter is proposed in [13] while [17] reports a ternary half adder and one-digit ternary multiplier. In [12], authors have presented circuits for ternary standard inverter and a ternary decoder, the threshold voltage of the CMOS can be set by different biasing voltages. While threshold voltage of the CNFET can be varied by changing the geometry of the carbon nanotube.

This paper presents a ternary full adder in the CNFET-Memristor technology. As a part of ternary full adder design, we propose a circuits for ternary unary operators and ternary multiplexers. The proposed circuits are compared with the existing designs and comparisons are provided with simulations performed on the same technology. All the simulations were performed using MOSFET-like CNFET [18] and VTEAM model of the memristor [8]. The threshold voltage of the CNFET is directly proportional to the diameter of the CNT and the chirality of the $(10, 0)$ and $(19, 0)$ will results in a threshold voltage of 0.53 V and 0.29 V respectively [4].

The main contributions from the proposed designs in CNFET-Memristor technology are as follows.

- We propose circuits for ternary unary operators such as cycle operators and other operators used in carry computation of a ternary full adder.
- The proposed ternary multiplexers using unary operators takes only 40% of the energy consumed by decoder based design using the decoder presented in [12].
- The proposed full adder saves 17% of energy compared to the best existing design in [16].
- The proposed full adder is having a good noise margin in comparable with existing designs.

The paper is organized as follows. Section 2 presents the ternary unary operators and their implementation in the CNFET-Memristor technology. Section 3 presents the ternary multiplexer design. Ternary full adder is proposed in Sect. 4, Simulations and comparisons are presented in Sect. 5. Section 6 concludes the paper.

2 Ternary Unary Circuits in CNFET-Memristor Technology

Ternary unary operators such as *cycle operators, inverters* and *decisive operators* are mostly used in designing the data path circuits of an ALU such as adders and multipliers. Ternary supports three types of inverters as reported in [14], such as *positive ternary inverter (PTI, A_P), negative ternary inverter (NTI, A_N)* and *standard ternary inverter (STI, $\overline{A}$)*. The operation of these ternary inverters are explained via truth table in Table 1. Next important unary operators are the *cycle operators* defined as A^1 and A^2. These cycle operators have the inherent addition property and can be calculated as $A + i$ for cycle operator A^i, here 'i' equals to 1, 2 for ternary. The outputs of the cycle operators A^1 and A^2 are explained in Table 1. Lastly, the *decisive operators* as defined in Table 1 has three variations for each logic '0', '1' and '2' as A_0, A_1 and A_2 respectively.

Table 1. Truth table for unary operators [14]: A^1, A^2 are the cycle operators; A_P, A_N and $\overline{A}$ are the positive, negative and standard ternary inverters respectively; A_0, A_1 and A_2 are decisive operators

Input	Cycle Operator		Inverters			Decisive operators		
A	A^1	A^2	A_P	A_N	$\overline{A}$	A_0	A_1	A_2
0	1	2	2	2	2	2	0	0
1	2	0	2	0	1	0	2	0
2	0	1	0	0	0	0	0	2

Figure 1 presents the CNFET-Memristor based implementation for the cycle operators (A^1 and A^2). The operation of the cycle operator A^1 as shown in Fig. 1(a) is as follows. Consider the ternary input to the cycle operator is A. The threshold voltage of the transistors are as follows. For transistor N_1 with chirality C19, threshold voltage is 0.29 V, less than $\frac{V_{DD}}{2}$ for $V_{DD} = 0.9$ V. While transistors N_2 and N_3 with chirality C10 are having a threshold voltage of 0.53 V which is greater than $\frac{V_{DD}}{2}$. Now, considering 'A' as logic '0' results A_N (negative ternary inverter output) equal to logic '2'. The gate input of CNFET connected with A_N will be ON and the CNFETs gate inputs connected with A are OFF. In the circuit shown in Fig. 1(a), CNFET N_1 is ON while the transistors N_2 and N_3 are OFF. This results a path from V_{DD} to Gnd through memristors M_1, M_2 and CNFET N_1. The two memristors M_1 and M_2 act like a resistive divider network and generates a voltage $\frac{V_{DD}}{2}$ at the output, which is equivalent to logic '1'. When input 'A' is equal to logic '1', the negative ternary inverter output A_N is equal to logic '0'. This results three CNFETs N_1, N_2 and N_3 are OFF, results the output of the circuit is connected to V_{DD}, which is equivalent to logic '2'. Consider the input 'A' is equal to logic '2', equivalent to a voltage of V_{DD}. This leads the CNFETs N_2 and N_3 are turning ON while transistor N_1 is OFF.

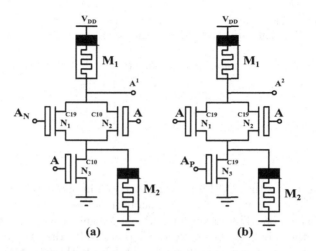

Fig. 1. Proposed CNFET-Memristor based cycle operators circuits: (a) A^1 and (b)A^2

The output of the circuit is now having a path to *Gnd*, results the output of the circuit equivalent to logic '0'. The simulation of the proposed cycle operator circuits are shown in Fig. 2.

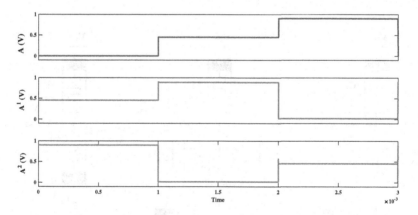

Fig. 2. Simulations of ternary cycle operators A^1 and A^2

The unary operators can be derived from decisive operators (A_0, A_1 and A_2) and ternary inverters (A_P, A_N) such as $1 \cdot \overline{A_P}$, $1 \cdot \overline{A_N}$ and $1 + \overline{A_P}$ as shown in Table 2. Here, the operators '·' and '+' are the ternary *min* and *max* operators as defined in [14]. These are mostly used in designing arithmetic circuits, mainly in the carry output (presented in Sect. 4).

Table 2. Truth table for unary operators [14]: $1 \cdot \overline{A_P}$, $1 \cdot \overline{A_N}$ and $1 + \overline{A_P}$ are operators obtained via $\cdot$ (denoting *min*) and $+$ (denoting *max*)

Input	Unary operator		
A	$1 \cdot \overline{A_P}$	$1 \cdot \overline{A_N}$	$1 + \overline{A_P}$
0	0	0	1
1	0	1	1
2	1	1	2

Figure 3 presents the CNFET-Memristor based implementation of the unary operators $1 \cdot \overline{A_P}$, $1 \cdot \overline{A_N}$ and $1 + \overline{A_P}$. The operation of the circuit $1 \cdot \overline{A_N}$ as shown in Fig. 3 (b) is as follows. The circuit for $1 \cdot \overline{A_N}$ is designed using A_N and the input A. Consider the input 'A' being logic '0', this results the output of negative ternary inverter (A_N) equals to logic '2'. This leads the CNFETs N_2 and N_3 turning ON and CNFET N_1 being tuned OFF. Since the output is connected to Gnd through CNFETs N_2 and N_3 leads the output equals to logic '0'. Along the same lines, considering the input 'A' as logic '1' (or '2'), A_N results logic '0'. These signals lead the CNFETs N_2 and N_3 are tuning OFF while N_1 being turned ON. The memristors M_1 and M_2 leads a voltage divider configuration leads the output as logic '1'. The simulations of these unary operators are shown in Fig. 4.

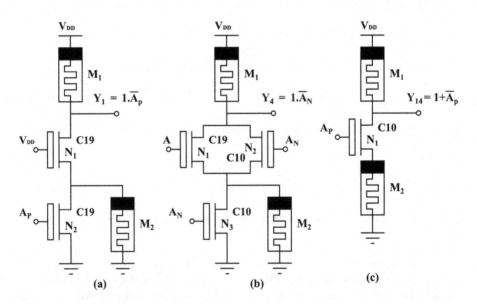

Fig. 3. Proposed CNFET-Memristor based unary operators circuits (a) $Y_1 = 1 \cdot \overline{A_P}$, (b) $Y_4 = 1 \cdot \overline{A_N}$ and (c) $Y_{14} = 1 + \overline{A_P}$

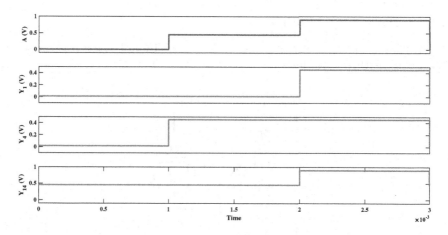

Fig. 4. Simulation of CNFET-Memristor based unary operators: (a) $Y_1 = 1 \cdot \overline{A_P}$, (b) $Y_4 = 1 \cdot \overline{A_N}$ and (c) $Y_{14} = 1 + \overline{A_P}$

Next section discusses on designing of ternary multiplexer (TMUX) using the unary operators.

Table 3. Ternary 3×1 multiplexer

Select line (S)	Output (Y)
0	D_0
1	D_1
2	D_2

3   CNFET-Memristor Based Ternary Multiplexers

Multiplexer is a data selection circuit which can be used as an universal logic gate in designing arithmetic circuits such as adders and multipliers. This section proposes a ternary multiplexer in the CNFET-Memristor based technology. There exists two type of ternary multiplexers in literature, one is a ternary 3×1 multiplexer in [5] with three data inputs, one select line and one output line, Second is a ternary 2×1 multiplexer with two data lines, one select signal and output line as reported in [16]. Ternary multiplexers can be designed using decoders [4]. A ternary decoder, which decodes the a ternary signal into three binary signals using decisive operator. Now, we propose CNFET-Memristor based circuits for the ternary 3×1 multiplexers using unary operators, which are further used in designing adders.

3.1   Ternary 3 × 1 Multiplexer

The truth table of a 3×1 multiplexer is defined in Table 3. Here, S is the select line while the three data lines are named as D_0, D_1 and D_2.

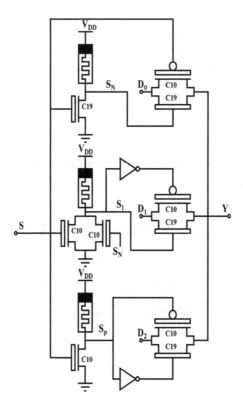

Fig. 5. Proposed CNFET-Memristor based ternary 3×1 multiplexer, S is the select line while D_0, D_1 and D_2 are the three data lines

Figure 5 presents CNFET-Memristor based implementation of a ternary 3×1 multiplexer using positive, negative ternary inverters (A_P, A_N) and decisive operator (A_1). A transmission gate is used to transmit the data $(D_0, D_1$ and $D_2)$ to output (Y). The transmission gate is controlled using unary operators.

Next, we present a ternary 3×1 multiplexer design using ternary 2×1 multiplexers.

3.2   Ternary 2 × 1 Multiplexer

A ternary 3×1 MUX can be designed using the positive and negative ternary inverters alone. A 3×1 MUX is designed using two 2×1 multiplexers as defined in Table 4 [16]. Here, one multiplexer controlled using positive ternary inverter

Table 4. Ternary 2×1 multiplexer

Select line	Output (F)	
S	PTI-MUX	NTI-MUX
0	D_2	D_2
1	D_2	D_0
2	D_0	D_0

is known as PTI-MUX and the MUX controlled using negative ternary multiplexer is termed as NTI-MUX. A CNFET-Memristor based $2 times 1$ PTI and NTI-multiplexers are shown in Fig. 6. A 3×1 multiplexer designed using these multiplexers is also shown in Fig. 6.

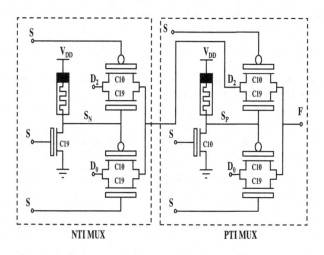

Fig. 6. Proposed CNFET-Memristor based ternary 3×1 multiplexer

The simulation plots for the proposed ternary 3×1 multiplexer are shown in Fig. 7. The proposed CNFET-Memristor based ternary 3×1 MUX comparisons with respect to number of CNFETs and number of memristors is given in Table 5. The comparison is given with unary operator based MUX and decoder-based MUX using decoder in [12].

4 Proposed Ternary Full Adder in CNFET-Memristor Logic Technology

A ternary full adder (TFA) is an one-digit ternary addition circuit with three inputs and two outputs such as *sum* and *carry*. The truth table of the ternary full adder is defined in terms of unary operators as depicted in Table 6. The full

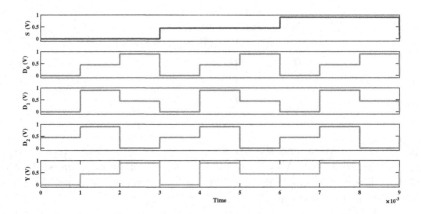

Fig. 7. CNFET-Memristor based simulations of 3×1 multiplexer

Table 5. Area comparison for various ternary multiplexer designs; decoder based MUX is designed using the decoder from [12]

Device type	Ternary 3×1 multiplexer		
	3×1 MUX	2×1 MUX	Decoder-based MUX
Memristors	3	2	3
CNFET	10	10	12

Table 6. Truth table for ternary full adder; A, B and C are ternary inputs while SUM and $CARRY$ are outputs of the full adder

C	B	A	$Carry$	Sum
0	0	A	0	A
0	1	A	$1 \cdot \overline{A_P}$	A^1
0	2	A	$1 \cdot \overline{A_N}$	A^2
1	0	A	$1 \cdot \overline{A_P}$	A^1
1	1	A	$1 \cdot \overline{A_N}$	A^2
1	2	A	1	A
2	0	A	$1 \cdot \overline{A_N}$	A^2
2	1	A	1	A
2	2	A	$1 + \overline{A_P}$	A^1

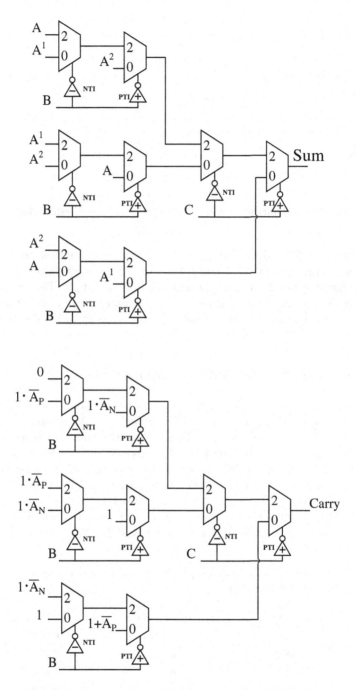

Fig. 8. Proposed ternary full adder using 2×1 multiplexer

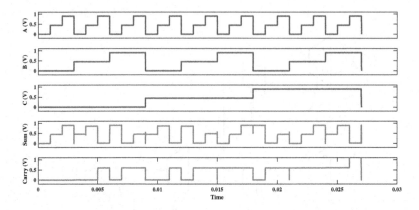

Fig. 9. CMOS-Memristor based simulations of proposed ternary full adder

adder defined in Table 6 can be designed using ternary multiplexers. This can be designed using ternary 3×1 multiplexer or a 2×1 multiplexer. Ternary full adder designed using 2×1 multiplexers is shown in Fig. 8. The propsoed full adder requires sixteen 2×1 multiplexers with required unary operators derived from input 'A'. The simulations of the proposed ternary full adder is shown in Fig. 9.

5   Simulation Studies and Comparisons

The simulations of the proposed ternary full adder circuits performed using Cadence Virtuoso using stanford CNFET model [18]. Memristor VTEAM [8] model is used in proposed circuits. To simulate the transient response of the ternary full adder transient time is set to 2 ns and voltage levels set to 0.9 V (V_{DD}), 0.45 V $(\frac{V_{DD}}{2})$, 0 V (GND). Performance metrics such as worst case delay and average power consumption were considered to estimate the efficiency of the proposed circuits. Worst case delay is the delay between transitions such as "$0 \to 1$", "$1 \to 2$", "$2 \to 1$" "$1 \to 0$", "$0 \to 2$" and "$2 \to 0$". The maximum delay of these transitions was considered as the worst case delay. While the average power

Table 7. Worst case delay and average power consumption of ternary unary operators in CNFET-Memristor technology

Unary operator	Worst case delay (ps)	Average power (μW)	PDP ($\times 10^{-18}$ J)
A^1	42.6	0.023	0.979
A^2	56.2	0.052	2.76
$1 \cdot \overline{A_P}$	47.6	0.018	0.856
$1 \cdot \overline{A_N}$	45.8	0.031	1.419
$1 + \overline{A_p}$	39.6	0.019	0.752

over all transitions was considered. The product of worst-case delay and average power is used to estimate the power delay product (PDP).

5.1   Comparison of Performance Metrics

Performance metrics of proposed unary operators is given in Table 7. Table 8 gives the worst-case delay, power and power delay product of the proposed CNFET-Memristor based ternary multiplexers and full adder. The comparisons are given with the simulations of the designs in the CNFET-Memristor technology. The proposed circuits for ternary multiplexer presented in Fig. 6 takes only 40% of the energy consumed by design using the decoder presented in [12]. The ternary full adder presented in Fig. 8 saves 17% of the energy consumed compared to the design in [16]. Figure 10 gives the comparison of the proposed ternary full adders in terms of power, delay, number of CNFETs and number of memristors required to compute the output.

Table 8. Comparison of ternary multiplexers (TMUX) and ternary full adder (TFA) in CNFET-Memristor Technology; Decoder based design results are reproduced using decoder from [12]

Design	Worst case delay (ps)	Avg power (μW)	PDP ($\times 10^{-18}$ J)
Ternary multiplexer			
Decoder based TMUX	86.31	0.632	54.55
TMUX in Fig. 5	78.89	0.568	44.81
TMUX in Fig. 6	67.46	0.39	22.13
Ternary full adder			
TFA using 3 × 1 MUX [15]	160.3	1.92	307.77
TFA using 2 × 1 MUX [16]	120.8	1.18	142.54
TFA using decoder based 3 × 1 MUX	157.5	3.89	612.65
Proposed design	120.6	0.98	118.18

5.2   Noise Margin Analysis

Digital circuits are more immune to noise, the multi valued logic with three logic levels with very slight voltage difference in the output might lead to change the output logic. Moreover, the implementation of the ternary logic using emerging technologies needs analysis of the noise to justify the reliability of the circuits. Ternary logic has categorized the noise margin as NM_0, NM_2 for logic '0' and '2' while logic '1' has two noise margins defined as NM_1^- and NM_1^+. These noise margin values can be calculated using the relations in Eq. (1) [15].

$$NM_1^- = V_{O1}^- - V_{I1}^-$$
$$NM_1^+ = V_{I1}^+ - V_{O1}^+$$
$$NM_2 = V_{O2} - V_{I2}$$
$$NM_0 = V_{I0} - V_{00} \tag{1}$$

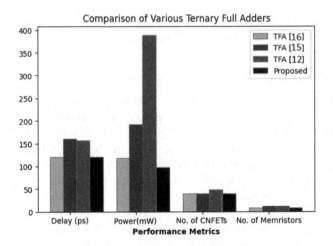

Fig. 10. Comparison of various ternary full adders in CNFET-Memristor Technology

Noise margin analysis was performed using DC analysis in *Cadence virtuoso* tool. The noise margin of the unary operators can be calculated by doing the DC analysis by varying the input from 0 to V_{DD}. The voltages used in Eq. (1) can be calculated from the DC simulation. The noise margin for the ternary unary operators such as cycle operators is shown in Fig. 11.

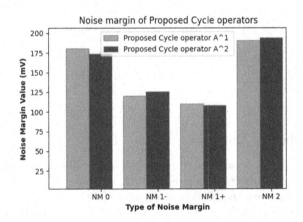

Fig. 11. Static noise margin of ternary cycle operators A^1 and A^2

The noise margin for ternary full adder was performed by varying one of the input from 0 to V_{DD} and maintaining the other inputs at either of the voltages 0, $\frac{V_{DD}}{2}$ or V_{DD}. A comparison of the noise margin for ternary full adders is presented in Fig. 12. The proposed ternary full adder circuits are having a good noise margin.

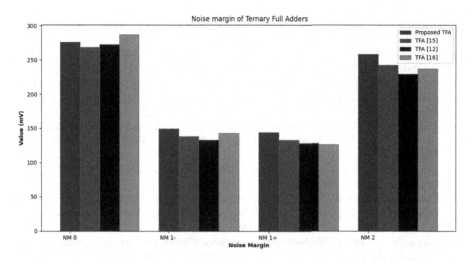

Fig. 12. Noise margin of ternary full adders in CNFET-Memristor logic technology

6 Conclusions

This paper presents the study of ternary unary operators and full adder designs in Carbon Nanotube Field Effect Transistor and Memristor based hybrid technology. The geometry dependent threshold voltage of the CNFET is used in designing multi valued logic circuits. The memristive network is used as resistive divider network. As part of the full adder design, this paper proposes a ternary multiplexer. The performance of these circuits are studied using worst case delay, average power and noise margin. The proposed unary operators in this paper leads the ternary multiplexer to save 60% of the energy consumed by recent design. The proposed ternary full adder saves 17% of the energy consumed by recent design. The noise margin analysis shows the proposed cycle operators and ternary full adder are having a good noise margin.

References

1. Smith, K.C.: The prospects for multivalued logic: a technology and applications view. IEEE Trans. Comput. **C–30**(9), 619–634 (1981)
2. Raychowdhury, A., Roy, K.: Carbon-nanotube-based voltage-mode multiple-valued logic design. IEEE Trans. Nanotechnol. **4**(2), 168–179 (2005)
3. Lin, S., Kim, Y.-B., Lombardi, F.: Design of a ternary memory cell using CNT-FETs. IEEE Trans. Nanotechnol. **11**(5), 1019–1025 (2012)
4. Lin, S., Kim, Y.-B., Lombardi, F.: CNTFET-based design of ternary logic gates and arithmetic circuits. IEEE Trans. Nanotechnol. **10**(2), 217–225 (2011)
5. Srinivasu, B., Sridharan, K.: Low-complexity multiternary digit multiplier design in CNTFET technology. IEEE Trans. Circuits Syst. II Express Briefs **63**(8), 753–757 (2016)

6. Hurst, S.L.: Multiple-valued logic? Its status and its future. IEEE Trans. Comput. **33**(12), 1160–1179 (1984)
7. Karmakar, S., Jain, F.C.: Ternary static random access memory using quantum dot gate field-effect transistor. Micro Nano Lett. **10**(11), 621–624 (2015)
8. Kvatinsky, S., Ramadan, M., Friedman, E.G., Kolodny, A.: VTEAM: a general model for voltage-controlled memristors. IEEE Trans. Circuits Syst. II Express Briefs **62**(8), 786–790 (2015)
9. Zangeneh, M., Joshi, A.: Design and optimization of nonvolatile multibit 1T1R resistive RAM. IEEE Trans. Very Large Scale Integr. (VLSI) Syst. **22**(8), 1815–1828 (2013)
10. Kvatinsky, S., Belousov, D., et al.: MAGIC-memristor-aided logic. IEEE Trans. Circuits Syst. II Express Briefs **61**(11), 895–899 (2014)
11. Kvatinsky, S., Satat, G., et al.: Memristor-based material implication (IMPLY) logic: design principles and methodologies. IEEE Trans. Very Large Scale Integr. (VLSI) Syst. **22**(10), 2054–2066 (2013)
12. Wang, X.-Y., et al.: High-density memristor-CMOS ternary logic family. IEEE Trans. Circuits Syst. I Regul. Pap. **68**(1), 264–274 (2020)
13. Mohammed, M.U., Vijjapuram, R., Chowdhury, M.H.: Novel CNTFET and memristor based unbalanced ternary logic gate. In: 2018 IEEE 61st International Midwest Symposium on Circuits and Systems (MWSCAS), pp. 1106–1109 (2018)
14. Miller, D.M., Thornton, M.A.: Multiple valued logic: concepts and representations. Synth. Lect. Digit. Circuits Syst. **2**(1), 1–127 (2007)
15. Srinivasu, B., Sridharan, K.: A synthesis methodology for ternary logic circuits in emerging device technologies. IEEE Trans. Circuits Syst. I Regul. Pap. **64**(8), 2146–2159 (2017)
16. Vudadha, C., Surya, A., Agrawal, S., Srinivas, M.: Synthesis of ternary logic circuits using 2: 1 multiplexers. IEEE Trans. Circuits Syst. I Regul. Pap. **65**(12), 4313–4325 (2018)
17. Zahoor, F., Zulkifli, T.Z.A., Khanday, F.A., Zainol Murad, S.A.: Carbon nanotube and resistive random access memory based unbalanced ternary logic gates and basic arithmetic circuits. IEEE Access **8**, 104 701–104 717 (2020)
18. Stanford University CNTFET model. Stanford University, Stanford, CA (2008). http://nano.stanford.edu/model_stan_cnt.htm

Synthesis of LUT Based Approximating Adder Circuits with Formal Error Guarantees

Pooja Choudhary[1,2]([✉]) [iD], Lava Bhargava[1] [iD], Masahiro Fujita[3] [iD],
and Virendra Singh[4] [iD]

[1] Department of Electronics and Communication Engineering,
Malaviya National Institute of Technology, Jaipur 302017, India
{2018rec9049,lavab}@mnit.ac.in
[2] Department of Electronics and Communication Engineering,
Swami Keshvanand Institute of Technology Management and Gramothan, Jaipur 302017, India
[3] Design and Education Center, VLSI, University of Tokyo, Bunkyo City, Japan
fujita@ee.t.u-tokyo.ac.jp
[4] Department of Electrical Engineering & Department of Computer Science and Engineering,
Indian Institute of Technology, Bombay 400076, India
viren@ee.iitb.ac.in

Abstract. Approximate computing relaxes accuracy, enhance efficiency, and benefit in terms of area. It is widely popular in emerging applications like mining, search, vision, recognition where inaccuracies are tolerable. This tolerance towards errors is exploited to design circuits. The most crucial stage is to strike the proper balance between error and output quality. A systematic framework is used for generating approximate circuits with a specific error guarantee. The key idea is to use the property checking technique based on SAT to compute the worst-case error. In this design method Look-up Table (LUT) is used to acquire approximation with worst-case error metric as a constraint. A novel technique is proposed to select nodes for insertion of LUTs is discussed. The method evolved around toggle count and observability of nodes in the circuit. The number of transistors used, and errors is examined for analysis. This analysis will help in evaluating the output of the adder circuit obtained through approximation. This method was implemented using Yosys and evaluated adder circuit. The aim of this paper is to adopt formal methods such as satiability solvers for analysis of approximate adder circuits. When the worst-case absolute error and area are taken into account for 64 bit, 32 bit and 16 bit our solution will provide a superior trade-off.

Keywords: SAT · Approximation · LUT · Adder circuits · Approximate computing

1 Introduction

In recent years, approximate computing approaches, which utilizes applications' inherent error-resilient nature, have grown in prominence. Precision of the related computations can be traded-off for better efficiency, chip area and performance because many essential applications are inherently error tolerant [1]. Approximate computing has been promoted as a novel way to save space and power while boosting performance with a minimal compromise in accuracy. In recent years, a number of techniques based on this principle have been developed and presented under the banner of "approximate computing" [2]. The approximation design flow adds a new optimization parameter as "error", which extends the concept of logic synthesis.

Approximation computing techniques have emerged at many layers of computing, i.e., circuit, architecture and software. Considering circuit approximation techniques it is divided into two approaches. In first, circuit is operated at over-scaled timings/voltages conditions due to which timing-induced error appears known as Frequency/voltage over-scaling. Second approach is functional approximation where approximate circuit is designed which differs from golden circuit but many parameters are enhanced like area, power efficiency. However, in this approach approximate circuits exhibits few errors [3]. We will focus on functional approach in this paper.

The rest of the paper is organized in the following way. Section 2 shows literature review of adders and techniques used for approximation of circuits. Section 3 introduces the approximate logic synthesis for LUT based adders Sect. 4 will focus on proposed methodology for node selection to replace LUTs. Implementation is presented in Sect. 5. At last conclusion and experimental results are drawn in Sects. 6 & 7 respectively.

2 Previous Work

Various adders are used in arithmetic circuits which are mostly used in applications like image processing, video processing, neural network etc. which are inherently error tolerant. So we focus on approximation of adder circuits so that area can be reduced and efficiency can be enhanced.

Various schemes and techniques have been proposed to reduce delay, area and hardware complexity. Four categories [4] are used to design these approximate adders namely a) Speculative adders, b) Segmented adders, c) Carry Select adders, and d) Approximate full adders. Segmented adders are further divided into: i) the equal segmentation adder (ESA), ii) the error-tolerant adder type II (ETA II), iii) accuracy-configurable approximate adder, and iv) the dithering adder. Carry select adders are divided into: i) The speculative carry select adder (SCSA), ii) the carry skip adder (CSA), iii) the gracefully-degrading accuracy-configurable adder (GDA), iv) the consistent carry approximate adder, and v) the generate signals exploited carry speculation adder (GCSA). At last the approximate full adders are divided into: i) the lower-part-OR adder (LOA), ii) Approximate Mirror Adders (AMAs), and iii) Approximate Full adders using Pass Transistors [18].

At various levels of approximation many techniques for designing have been proposed. Initially, the circuits were approximated manually. Kulkarni et al. [2] cites that, they designed a 2 bit approximate multiplier, MSB was removed to achieve the approximation. To replace manual approximation systematic methods came into existence which will improve the productivity, quality and complexity of circuits. In approximate computing for modeling and analysis of circuits MACACO [5] is proposed. It assists a designer in systematically evaluating the impact of approximate circuits. Errors are analyzed using Boolean approximation techniques that are SAT solver and Monte Carlo Simulation. ABACUS [6] is automated synthesis method for creating approximate circuits from behavioral description. It generates abstract synthesis tree (AST) for identification of inexact design. Pareto frontier trade-off between accuracy and power consumption is obtained from optimal design. Automated methodology for Sequential Logic Approximation ASLAN [8] generates an approximate circuit which consumes less energy. It constructs SQCC and employ formal verification techniques to meet the quality constraints. In [9] logic complexity is reduced at transistor level. An imprecise adder is proposed and due to reduced complexity switching capacitances gets reduced which shortens the critical path. The proposed arithmetic unit is used in video and image processing architecture to see the impact on efficiency. Methodology such as SALSA [10]/SASIMI [11] employs various heuristics for identification of appropriate part of circuit for approximation. In [12] Verifiability-driven search and Cartesian Genetic Programming was proposed. Automated design with formal error guarantees proves a stepping stone for energy efficient systems. The above strategy was further improved in [13] ADAC. It represents additional error metrics combining simulation and BDD-based methods to obtain diverse designs. With all the advancement and research a novel approach came into picture to add LUT into circuits [14] to improve debugging and rectification in post-silicon/in-field. So this method of using LUT is utilized in [15] to present a general framework to achieve approximated circuits. We utilized this framework and further improved it to obtain approximation. In this framework arithmetic adder circuit are approximated. Among all the adder circuits carry lookahead adder (CLA) circuit is used. As we know that CLA uses generate and propagate signals for generation of carry due to which delay in circuit is of logarithmic in nature. However CLA requires larger area and higher power dissipation. For large number of bits CLA generator becomes very complex. So to reduce the complexity and power dissipation CLA is opted as Golden circuit in this work. The few gates from golden circuit are replaced by LUT. Miters are constructed to obtain input values for LUT, so that they can be replaced with simplified logic gates to obtain approximate circuit. In this paper, two methods are used for selection of nodes to replace LUT in circuit i.e. random selection and toggle count and observability based selection method.

3 Approximate Logic Synthesis for LUT Based Adders

3.1 Problem Formulation

The design problem is composed to optimized the design by reducing number of components used and/or another criterion so that error of solution is within a predefined level. Let us represent a golden circuit $G(x, y)$ and LUT based circuit $L(x, y, a)$, here a denotes input vector for LUT and threshold error for approximate circuit as e.

Problem Formulation for the Golden circuit $G(x, y)$ with threshold error e, the aim is to find out approximate circuit $L(x, y, a)$ with minimal size such that error WCR (G, L) $\leq$ e. The circuit is based on LUT insertion using both the selection methods. SAT formulation [15] will be done as follows:

$$\exists a |G(assign) - L(assign, a)| \leq e \qquad (1)$$

assign is an input assignment specified as x, y = constant e.g., x = 0, y = 0, $a_{candidate}$ vector which maybe a solution for LUT configuration. This is substituted in the following SAT query:

$$\exists(x, y)|G(x.y) - L(x, y, a_{candidate})| > e \tag{2}$$

If the above equation satisfies then $a_{candidate}$ is the solution of LUT. Here x, y are input assignments for golden circuit as well as LUT based Miter circuit. Otherwise the solution x_{sol}, y_{sol} for the current $a_{candidate}$ are appended to the first condition as follows:

$$\exists a\{(|G(assign) - L(assign, a)e \wedge (|G(x_{Sol}, y_{Sol}, a)| \leq e)\}) \tag{3}$$

3.2 Worst Case Error (WCE)

The error magnitude is difference between golden circuit fG and approximate circuit fL

$$E_{wc}(f_G, f_L) = \max_{x \in \{0,1\}^n} |int(f_G(x)) - int(f_L(x))|$$

3.3 Overall Methodology

To generate Approximate circuit, overall methodology is shown in Fig. 1. It is divided into following steps:

1. A golden circuit that needs to be approximated.
2. Selection of nodes for insertion of LUTs.
3. Construction of Miter that incorporates LUTs.
4. Solving SAT to obtain good solutions for LUT configuration.
5. Analysis for area, approximate function and error tolerance.

Iterative approach is used in this methodology. It passes through two loops, i.e., internal and external. Internal loop to discover the best LUT solution, and external loop for top iterations to get the best possible approximate circuit within the limits of threshold and constraints. Obtained approximate circuit has area less than that of circuits obtained in previous iterations.

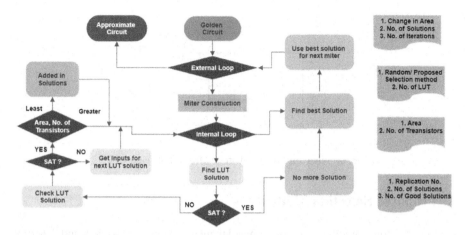

Fig. 1. Overall flow of methodology for circuit approximation

LUTs are incorporated in golden circuit replacing nodes, then LUT based miter circuit is obtained. After solving SAT and achieving good solution for LUTs final approximate circuit is achieved shown through Fig. 2, Fig. 3 Fig. 4.

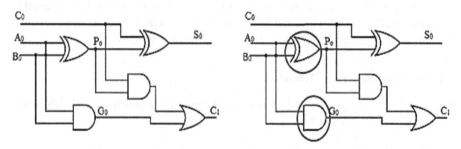

Fig. 2. Insertion of LUT (a) Golden Circuit (b) Nodes selected for LUT insertion

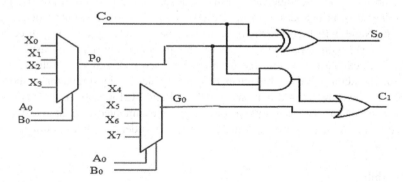

Fig. 3. LUT based Miter Circuit

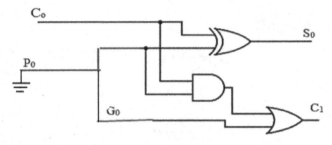

Fig. 4. Final approximate Circuit after simplifying LUTs

4 Proposed Selection Method

For the selection of nodes to be approximated there are two ways: Random and Selection Method.

4.1 Random Method

In this method nets are selected randomly without any constraints. After the first iteration for finding approximation, it is repeated with new set of nets to find another approximate circuit. This method of replacing nets with LUTs is very easy and can be done quickly. However quality of circuit may not be the best one. So to find out exact nets we follow a novel selection method based on activity and observability of nets.

4.2 Proposed Selection Method

The proposed selection method does not consider random selection of nodes. The nodes are decided on two parameters:

Activity or Toggle Count (TC)
The number of times the logic value at that node has changed as a result of changes in logic values at the prior node due to input test vectors defines toggle count for that specific node [16]. Nodes with highest activity are more sensitive and they are mostly affected by changes. Nodes with lowest activity have low toggle count value and are least sensitive. These nodes can easily be removed from circuit. Each wire activity is retrieved from SAIF file (Switching Activity Interchange Format) generated by simulation as shown in Fig. 5. This file provides information about T0, T1 and TC for each wire. TC is used to rank nodes based on their activity. The circuit must be simulated with input test vectors that are reflective of the circuit's actual behaviour in order to obtain accurate activity estimation.

Observability
The difficulty of viewing the state of a logic signal is characterized as observability [17] for a digital circuit. With the goal of providing a quantitative assessment of the difficulty of observing the logical values of nodes. Goldstein introduced SCOAP measures. In

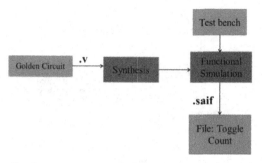

Fig. 5. Generating saif file by simulating the circuit

this paper combinational circuit is considered. The gate level circuit is considered and computes values for each node are Combinational zero controllability (CC0), Combinational one controllability (CC1), Combinational Observability (CO). For 2-input OR gate, x and y are inputs and f is output. The combinational observabilities for OR gate are formulated as:

CO (x) = CO (f) + CC0(y) + 1.
CO (y) = CO (f) + CC0(x) + 1.

OR Gate

For replacing the nodes with LUT the node must be hardest to observe. Therefore nodes which are hardest to observe are preferred to be removed from the circuit. Figure 6 shows circuit with calculated observability for each node. Values written in red color are assessment for observability and black color values represents controllability assessment. Figure 7 shows the complete flow for node selection and obtaining equivalent circuit.

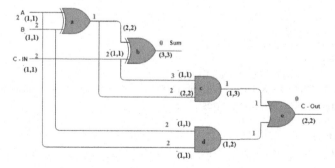

Fig. 6. Observability and controllability for each node in circuit

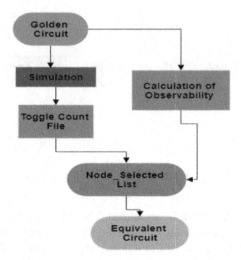

Fig. 7. Flowchart to find equivalent circuit

4.3   Steps to Choose a Node

Following are the steps to choose a node:

1. Choose the nodes (n) which are hardest to observe.

$$Y1 = max (CO(n)).$$

2. Check for Node having Lowest Toggle count.

$$Y2 = min (TC(Y1)).$$

3. Nodes which satisfies both the above conditions will be replaced with LUT.

4.4   Algorithm

Input: SAIF file, CO
Output : node_selectedList (Ns_{list})
While (n) do
For each node (n) read CO from file do
        find the nodes (n) with highest CO   -- condition 1
      check for node having lowest TC,
      if n (TC) lowest then   -- condition 2
      return Ns;
      end
end
Repeat for i iterations until all nodes with highest CO are observed and lowest TC;
end

5   Implementation

With the proposed design choices in miter creation the approximate adder circuit is obtained.

5.1   Design Choices in Miter Creation

Following parameters must be taken into consideration while introducing LUTs in circuit.

1) Selection Method: As mentioned in Sect. 2 we can choose random selection method and proposed selection method for LUTs.
2) LUT Size: LUTs are available in many sizes 2:1, 4:1 and 8:1. In this methodology, 4:1 and mix of 2:1 and 4:1 is used to obtain results. 8:1 is used rarely.
3) Number of LUTs: Area decreases faster as number of LUTs increases. However increasing number of LUTs in circuit increases inputs whose solution to be obtained and it will take time. So by increasing LUTs time taken to obtain the results increases and process goes slow.

5.2   Internal Loop and Best Solution

As shown in overall methodology in Fig. 1, there are two loops: internal and external. Internal loop specifies configuration of LUT. The solutions of LUTs are obtained through this loop. If internal loop iterations are large then after finding good solution loop keep on iterating unless limit is reached. Figure 8 shows that graph between error v/s replication

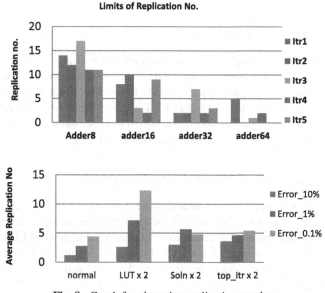

Fig. 8. Graph for observing replication number

no and Replication no v/s adders. Observation is made that lesser number of iteration is required to obtain solution. So there is need to put constraint on number of replication. In the Fig. 8 normal indicates that 10 LUTs are inserted randomly. LUTx2 depicts number of LUT insertion is doubled. Solx2 meaning good solutions obtained are doubled and top_itrx2 means outer loop iteration is also doubled. This figure indicates that good solutions are obtained at smaller number of iterations. This observation tells us to put constraints on replication number.

Best solution depends on least area with maximum error, i.e., worst case error. The best solution obtained is substituted against LUTs and solved in form of gates as shown in Fig. 4. The simplified circuit can be the approximate circuit obtained from the flow of methodology.

5.3 Outer Loop

The top iteration gives the best solution based on threshold and constraints.

6 Results

The overall methodology for creating approximate circuits using both the selection methods i.e. random and proposed is evaluated. We have used Yosys as SAT solver, area analyzer and synthesizer. Python code is used as user interface and golden circuit code written in Verilog acts as input. To generate approximate circuits for 8 bit, 16 bit, 32 bit and 64 bit using random and proposed selection approach are shown in Fig. 9(a) &(b). Rand 10, 20, 30 indicate random selection of nodes with number of LUTs inserted are 10, 20, 30. Sel method represents proposed selection method. The final approximate circuit obtained as output is the LUTs are replaced by simplified logic gates.

6.1 Normalized Area v/s Top Iteration

Area is normalized with respect to golden circuit and it is analyzed with outer loop iteration (top iteration) to achieve approximate circuit for 64 bit adder. Figure 10 shows gradual decrement in area and then saturates. As the number of LUTs increases the area drops at faster rate because the number of LUT is proportional to circuit coverage. The area is reduced and approximate circuit is achieved in lesser number of iterations which does not indicate that time required to achieve result is lesser.

6.2 Random Approach v/s Proposed Selection Method

The results on 8 bit, 16 bit, 32 bit, 64 bit adders are shown in Fig. 9. The graphs are plotted between normalized area v/s error percentage and total time taken v/s error percentage to obtain result. Each bar with different color indicates the number of LUTs in random approach and last bar represents the selection method. The graphs show that selection method based approximate adder circuit require less area and time as compared with random approach circuit.

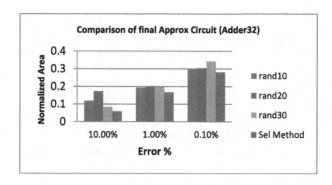

(a) Adder 32 : Area v/s Error

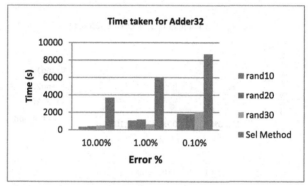

(b) Adder 32 : Time (s) v/s Error

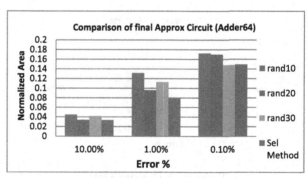

(c) Adder 64 : Area v/s Error

Fig. 9. Graph between Area v/s error and Time v/s error to compare both node selection approach

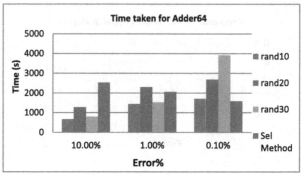

(d) Adder 64 : Time (s) v/s Error

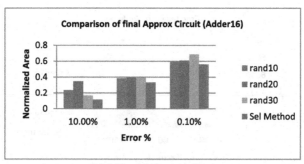

(e) Adder 16: Area v/s Error

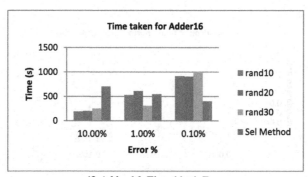

(f) Adder 16: Time (s) v/s Error

Fig. 9. (*continued*)

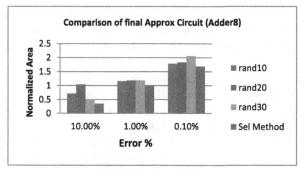

(g) Adder 8: Area v/s Error

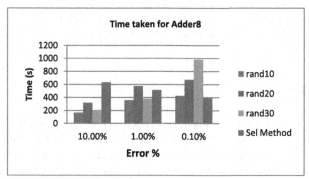

(h) Adder 8: Time (s) v/s Error

Fig. 9. (*continued*)

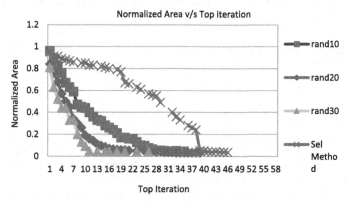

Fig. 10. Graph between Normalized area and iteration

The observations are as follows:

- The proposed selection method using toggle count and observability provides approximate circuit with least area. Selection method will give the precise and known location to insert LUT with a valid reason to remove the node, however in random approach the nodes are removed randomly so sometimes it does not give best solution and fails while iterating. The proposed selection method always gives best solution, does not fail.

- As seen in graphs selection method always provide the approximate circuit with least area. This holds good for adders as well as for error percentages.
- As the number of LUTs increases the area drops faster however this not indication of time taken to achieve good solution is lesser.
- Fig. 9(b) shows that time taken by 32 bit proposed selection method is large because to see the variation when there is no constraints are used. The output variables have a lot of freedom it will keep iterating thus reaching maximum solutions without change in area. On the contrary in Fig (d) we can see that time taken by 64 bit adder using selection method is less because no constraints were taken into account.
- For 0.1% error the normalized area for 16 bit adder circuit is 0.7, 32 bit is 0.28 and for 64 bit is 0.19.

7 Conclusion

Approximate circuit can provide the trade-off between accuracy and power dissipation. Researchers are focusing on approximating circuit with minimum degradation in performance. In this work we proposed a novel selection method to accurately define the nodes which can be replaced rather than randomly choosing them. The results were observed and analyzed. The effect of constraints on parameters is also clearly seen. Our selection method shows scalability and constructs a way to design more complex circuits. In future, we intend to design approximate circuits with relative error metrics based on novel selection method and add few more parameters like delay and power consumption for calculations.

Acknowledgment. This work is supported by Visvesvaraya Ph.D. Scheme, Meity, Govt. of India. MEITY-PHD-2950.

References

1. Chippa, V.K., Chakradhar, S.T., Roy, K., Raghunathan, A.: Analysis and characterization of inherent application resilience for approximate computing. In: Proceedings of the 50th Annual Design Automation Conference, pp. 1–9 (2013)
2. Kulkarni, P., Gupta, P., Ercegovac, M.D.: Trading accuracy for power in a multiplier architecture. J. Low Power Electron. **7**(4), 490–501 (2011)
3. May, D., Stechele, W.:Voltage over-scaling in sequential circuits for approximate computing. In: 2016 International Conference on Design and Technology of Integrated Systems in Nanoscale Era (DTIS), pp. 1–6. IEEE (2016)
4. Venkataramani, S., Chakradhar, S.T., Roy, K., Raghunathan, A.: Computing approximately, and efficiently. In: 2015 Design, Automation & Test in Europe Conference & Exhibition (DATE), pp. 748–751. IEEE (2015)

5. Venkatesan, R., Agarwal, A., Roy, K., Raghunathan, A.: MACACO: modeling and analysis of circuits for approximate computing. In: IEEE/ACM International Conference on Computer-Aided Design (IC- CAD), San Jose, CA, pp. 667–673 (2011)
6. Nepal, K., Li, Y., Bahar, R.I., Reda, S.: ABACUS: a technique for automated behavioral synthesis of approximate computing circuits, InL Design, Automation and Test in Europe Conference & Exhibition (DATE), Dresden, pp. 1–6 (2014)
7. Ceška, M., Matyáš, J., Mrazek, V., Sekanina, L., Vasicek, Z., Vojnar, T.: ADAC: automated design of approximate circuits. In: CAV. LNCS, vol. 10981, pp. 612–620. Springer, Cham (2018)
8. Ranjan, A., Raha, A., Venkataramani, S., Roy, K., Raghunathan, A.: ASLAN: synthesis of approximate sequential circuits. In: Design, Automation Test in Europe Conference & Exhibition (DATE), Dresden, pp. 1–6 (2014)
9. Gupta, V., et al.: Low-power digital signal processing using approximate adders. IEEE Trans. Comput.-Aided Des. Integr. Circuits Syst. $32(1)$, 124–137 (2012)
10. Venkataramani, S., Sabne, A., Kozhikkottu, V., Roy, K., Raghunathan, A.: SALSA: systematic logic synthesis of approximate circuits. In: DAC Design Automation Conference, pp. 796–801 (2012)
11. Venkataramani, S., Roy, K., Raghunathan, A.: Substitute-and-simplify: a unified design paradigm for approximate and quality configurable circuits. In: 2013 Design, Automation & Test in Europe Conference & Exhibition (DATE), pp. 1367–1372. IEEE (2013)
12. Češka, M., Matyáš, J., Mrazek, V., Sekanina, L., Vasicek, Z., Vojnar, T.: Approximating complex arithmetic circuits with formal error guarantees: 32-bit multipliers accomplished. In: 2017 IEEE/ACM International Conference on Computer-Aided Design (ICCAD), pp. 416–423. IEEE (2017)
13. Češka, M., Matyáš, J., Mrazek, V., Sekanina, L., Vasicek, Z., Vojnar, T.: ADAC: automated design of approximate circuits. In: International Conference on Computer Aided Verification, pp. 612–620. Springer, Cham (2018)
14. Jo, S., Matsumoto, T., Fujita, M.: SAT-based automatic rectification and debugging of combinational circuits with LUT insertions. IPSJ Trans. Syst. LSI Design Methodol. 7, 46–55 (2014)
15. Vinod, G. U., V. S. Vineesh, Jaynarayan T. Tudu, Masahiro Fujita, and Virendra Singh.: LUT-based Circuit Approximation with Targeted Error Guarantees. In 2020 IEEE 29th Asian Test Symposium (ATS), IEEE, pp. 1–6, (2020)
16. Lingamneni, A., Enz, C., Nagel, J.-L., Palem, K., Piguet, C.: Energy parsimonious circuit design through probabilistic pruning. In: 2011 Design, Automation & Test in Europe, IEEE, pp. 1–6 (2011)
17. Mirzaie, N., Seyyed Mahdavi, S.J., Mohammadi, K.: Evolving more testable digital combinational circuits. In: CDES, pp. 40–45 (2010)
18. Jiang, H., Han, J., Lombardi, F.: A comparative review and evaluation of approximate adders. In: Proceedings of the 25th Edition on Great Lakes Symposium on VLSI, pp. 343–348 (2015)

Emerging Technologies and Memory

CAR: Community Aware Graph Reordering for Efficient Cache Utilization in Graph Analytics

Shubham Singhania[1] , Neelam Sharma[1](✉) , Varun Venkitaraman[1] ,
and Chandan Kumar Jha[2]

[1] Indian Institute of Technology Bombay, Mumbai, India
singhania@ee.iitb.ac.in, neelam09.iitb@gmail.com, varunvbel@gmail.com
[2] German Research Center for Artificial Intelligence, DFKI, Bremen, Germany
chandan.jha@dfki.de

Abstract. Graph workloads exhibit highly irregular memory access patterns, resulting in poor cache utilization. By modifying the layout of the stored graph prior to processing, cache utilization can be enhanced. Two factors need to be considered for modifying the layout of the graph. First, the nature of computation in vertex-centric algorithms suggests that vertex neighbours are visited in succession throughout processing. Second, the degree distribution of vertices in real-world networks exhibits *power-law* distribution, implying that a few vertices are responsible for the majority of the connections. As a result, such nodes can be clustered together to improve temporal and spatial locality. In this paper, we propose *Community Aware Graph Reordering* (CAR), which leverages both these aspects to enhance the performance of graph applications when compared to existing reordering strategies. While previous state-of-the-art reordering techniques with comparable reordering overheads, such as *Hub Cluster*, *DBG*, and *Sorder*, deliver speedup of 9%, 11%, and 17%, respectively, *CAR* provides a speedup of 20%.

Keywords: Graph analytics · Lightweight graph reordering · Caches

1 Introduction

Graph analytics has become highly significant in the modern era because of its applicability in different areas such as social networks, distribution chains, artificial intelligence, IoT, and many others [1]. Various techniques have already been explored to accelerate graphs applications. Some of the methods include i) utilizing an approximation version of an algorithm for a task, ii) using knowledge of the graph structure and, iii) applying parallelization techniques to reduce the run time of graph applications [2–4]. While these approaches speed up graph

---

S. Singhania and N. Sharma—Both authors have contributed equally

C. K. Jha—The work was carried out when Chandan Kumar Jha was at CADSL, IIT Bombay.

A. P. Shah et al. (Eds.): VDAT 2022, CCIS 1687, pp. 453–467, 2022.
https://doi.org/10.1007/978-3-031-21514-8_37

processing significantly, they do not address the issues related to irregular memory accesses, resulting in sub-optimal performance. In this work we minimize cache misses due to irregular access in graph applications with improved data layout.

Vertex-centric graph applications need data from their in/out neighbours to perform computations. As a result, putting a vertex's neighbours within the same cache line or in the neighbouring cache lines can improve cache utilization. Furthermore, most real-world datasets have a *power-law* distribution [5–8], which means that a small fraction of vertices (hot vertices) are responsible for the majority of the connections in a graph. Therefore, grouping such nodes can further aid in enhancing cache's performance. These hot vertices can be placed together by rearranging the nodes.

Although graph reordering is an NP-hard problem [7], various approaches have been developed, ranging from sophisticated techniques such as *Gorder* [7] to lightweight reordering algorithms [5,6,9] based on the *power-law* characteristics of real-world graph datasets. *Gorder* develops a scoring function to be maximized that measures the number of connections between vertices. This method aids in keeping vertices that are accessed in conjunction together. The number of calculations necessary to identify the optimal reordering is quite large, resulting in significant pre-processing overhead. Thus, reordering takes a long time which may not be feasible for all applications.

To reduce the cost of reordering, *Hub Cluster* [5], a lightweight reordering solution, arranges high-degree and low-degree nodes at the two ends of the memory space, preserving the original relative order among the vertices. A degree-based reordering has a shorter reordering time and provides speedup owing to the segregation of vertices into high and low-degree vertices, as it can be parallelized. *Hub Cluster* assumes an existing community structure in graphs while maintaining relative order among vertices. In addition, even though hot-vertices represent a small percentage of all vertices in *Hub Cluster*, owing to the large size of graphs even the hot nodes are still too large to accommodate in the cache.

Degree-based Grouping (DBG) [6] is an upgrade over *Hub Cluster* because it prioritizes hottest vertices over hotter vertices by coarsely binning them over specified degree ranges. It is also a lightweight reordering and outperforms *Gorder* in terms of reordering time. While it reduces the size of the hot vertices, *DBG*, like *Hub Cluster*, expects a community structure in input graphs. *Sorder*, a recent work, attempts to balance reordering time with detecting community structure in graphs. It arranges vertices within a certain hop radius, which aids in determining community structure, divides them into hot and cold vertices. However the cache footprint of hot vertices is still quite large.

To overcome the limitations of prior approaches, we propose *Community Aware Reordering (CAR)*, a lightweight ordering scheme, in which we do not presume any underlying community structure and instead explore it through breadth-first traversal. To summarise, contributions of our work are:

1. Unlike previous works which assume a community structure, to learn about the existing communities, we utilized breadth-first traversal. Binding the vertices with other vertices of a similar degree allows us to take advantage of both temporal and spatial locality.

2. When compared to *Sorder*, the state-of-the-art lightweight reordering scheme, the speedup achieved using proposed community aware reordering *(CAR)* is up to 2.26×. *CAR* also has 4× faster reordering time as compared to *Sorder*.
3. We also demonstrated that *CAR* outperforms all lightweight reordering methods - *Hub Cluster*, *DBG* and *Sorder* to varying degrees across graph applications.

The remainder of the paper is organised as follows: Sect. 2 describes the background and motivation for this work, Sect. 3 presents our proposed *Community Aware Reordering (CAR)* scheme, Sect. 4 describes the experimental setup used, Sect. 5 provides results and analysis, and Sect. 6 concludes the paper with related work.

2   Background and Motivation

2.1   Graph Datasets

Power-Law Graphs. Many of the real-world graph datasets follow a *power-law* degree distribution of vertices. Here only a few fraction of vertices contribute to the majority of the edges in the graph [5–7]. We refer to the richly connected vertices, which comprise a small fraction of the overall footprint as hot vertices. Whereas the rest of the vertices which comprise a large fraction of the overall footprint are referred to as cold vertices.

Structured & Unstructured Datasets. A *community* is a set of highly connected vertices that are relatively independent of the rest of the graph. Such community structure is frequently represented by vertex ordering inside a graph dataset by grouping vertices from the same community in memory. *Structured datasets* are graphs in which the community structure is retained. *Unstructured datasets* are graphs with random vertex ordering. Figure 1 depicts the distinction between *structured* and *unstructured* graph datasets.

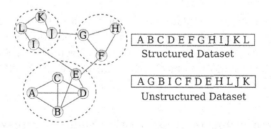

Fig. 1. Graph with three communities, indicated by dashed lines

2.2 Overview of Graph Applications

Processing a Graph. Typical Graph processing kernel is shown in Algorithm 1 involves visiting all the vertices in the graph and iterating over the neighbours of each vertices [5]. These applications process the kernel iteratively, covering either fraction of vertices in applications such as *Single Source Shortest Path (SSSP)*, or all the vertices like the *Page Rank* application.

Algorithm 1: Graph Processing Kernel

---

1 **for** *v in G* **do**
2   **for** *u in Neigh(v)* **do**
3   process(...,Property[u],...)

Push-Pull Computation. In push based, a vertex pushes (writes) its property data to its out-neighbour. In pull based computation, a vertex pulls (reads) property data of it in-neighbours and updates its own state.

2.3 Data Layout Using Hilbert Space Filling Curve

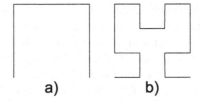

Fig. 2. Hilbert curve a) first-order b) second-order

Hilbert is a space-filling curve that closely passes close to every point in a multidimensional space, preserving the locality of the points. Its recursive nature aids in the preservation of locality. It has recently been used [10] to reorder data in order to improve memory subsystem performance. Figure 2 depicts *Hilbert curves* of 1-D and 2-D order.

2.4 Graph Reordering to Improve the Memory Subsystem Performance

Graph applications execute a small amount of computation per vertex or edge. Data access patterns in graph applications are highly irregular, and real-world graph datasets cannot fit entirely into caches. Because of these irregular accesses, main memory requests are frequent, making the memory subsystem critical for boosting performance.

Graph reordering is necessary to assist caches and prefetchers in utilizing the temporal and spatial locality they were designed for. Although graph reordering is an NP-hard problem [7], it may be simplified by an understanding the skewed nature of real-world graphs and the access patterns of vertices in graph applications. Because graph reordering does not need any hardware changes, it is a more lightweight option than existing hardware-based solutions [11–14]. In this research, we focus on reordering algorithms that improve memory subsystem efficiency by combining structural properties of the graph with information of the sequence of vertex accesses.

2.5 Limitation of Existing Lightweight Reordering

Existing skew-aware lightweight reordering approaches are based on the *power-law* nature of real-world graphs, which does not retain the community structure-based processing of graph applications. They attempt to achieve a comparable speed up with more complex approaches such as *Gorder* while keeping the reordering time to a minimum. However, doing so either destroys the community structure or presupposes that the raw datasets already have a community structure in place for coarse-grained reordering.

We employed a recent state-of-the-art lightweight reordering approach, *DBG* [6], to demonstrate that these lightweight reordering schemes when applied over random reordered graphs (no community structure) slows down the system performance when compared with a DBG reordered graph (without pre-processing) where there is existing community structure within the original ordering. The consequence of slowdowns in the performance of *DBG* when a random reordered dataset is supplied as input is shown in Fig. 3. We examined two datasets, *lj* (structured) and *pld* (unstructured). *DBG* suffers a slowdown of up to 16.3% for the *lj* dataset. However, the *pld* dataset suffers a maximum slowdown of 9.4% because it is already unstructured. The slowdowns can be attributed to an increase in the MPKI (Misses Per Kilo Instructions) at all cache levels.

DBG-like reordering schemes perform poorly when there is no existing community structure in the original ordering because lightweight reordering schemes assume an inherent community structure present in the input graphs. While we investigate such community structure using breadth-first traversal, we will outperform these reordering schemes. It has also been reported in previous work [6] that even hot-vertices (vertices with degrees greater than or equal to avg degree) cannot fit inside modern-processor caches. As a result, vertices must be binned and similar degree vertices must be grouped together to improve temporal locality and reduce cache footprint of hot-vertices. Building on these two motivations, we proposed our *Community Aware Reordering (CAR)* technique, in which neighbouring vertices are stored together in memory and vertices of similar degree are binned together.

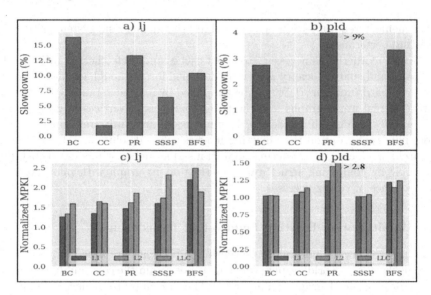

Fig. 3. a) & b) Slowdown c) & d) increase in MPKI when DBG is applied to a randomly ordered real-world graph

3   Community Aware Reordering (CAR)

To address the limitation of existing lightweight reordering techniques, which fail to preserve the main purpose of graph reordering - community structure preservation and reduce the reordering cost instead. We propose *Community Aware Reordering (CAR)*, which finds the community structure using breadth-first traversal and takes advantage of the *power-law* nature exhibited by real-world graphs by coarsely binning them into different groups to preserve the explored graph structure.

Basic Design. First step in Algorithm 2, creates bins of exclusive degree ranges that follow a *power-law* distribution similar to *DBG*. Assignment of a vertex to a given bin is decided s.t. $D[v] \in [P_k, Q_k)$. It is done to keep the hottest vertices of a graph together and reduce their cache footprint. In the fourth step, we greedily choose a vertex *start* with the maximum degree $(max(D[]))$ in a graph to start a breadth-first traversal. *CAR* places each of the traversed vertices to an assigned bin. When placing the vertices in one of the bins, we keep track of the relative order of traversal by stacking the vertices in a bin. To start the traversal for the next connected component of a graph, we use the next unvisited vertex.

Improvement. Figure 4, gives a pictorial representation of vertices at a given level with a different colour placed in a bin. One way of numbering vertices is to give them consecutive ids in a given bin in the order they are stacked in a bin, i.e., from bottom to top. We see that vertices present in the first bin at the bottom are closer to those at the bottom of the second bin because the vertices present at the bottom are from the same traversal level. Similarly, vertices present at the

---

Algorithm 2: Proposed Reordering Algorithm

Input: Graph **G(V, E)** has $|V|$ vertices and $|E|$ edges. Degree Distribution $D[]$, where $D[v]$ is the degree of vertex v.

Output: Mapping $M[]$, where $M[v]$ is the new ID of vertex v using **K** bins

1   Assign continuous range $[P_k, Q_k]$ to every $Group_k$ such that, $Q_1 > max(D[])$ & $P_K \leq min(D[])$ & $Q_{k+1} = P_k < Q_k$ for every k < **K**   // Generating bin ranges

2   **for** $v \in V$ **do**

3     $visited[v] \leftarrow$ false

4   $start \leftarrow v_i$ where $deg(v_i) = max(D[])$

5   Append $start$ to the $Group_k$ for which $D[start] \in [P_k, Q_k]$

6   $Queue\ q$

7   $visited[start] \leftarrow$ true; $q.enqueue(start)$

8   **while** $q \neq \phi$ **do**

9     $u \leftarrow dequeue(q)$

10   **for** vertex v adjacent to u **do**

11   **if** $!visited[v]$ **then**

12         $visited[v] \leftarrow$ true

13   Append v to the $Group_k$ for which $D[v] \in [P_k, Q_k]$ /* Placing vertices in respective bins   */

14         $q.enqueue(v)$

15   **for** $v_i \in V$ and $!visited[v_i]$ **do**

16     $visited[v_i] \leftarrow$ true; $q.enqueue(v_i)$;   **go to** 8

17   $id = 0$

18   **for** i in 1 to **K** **do**

19   **if** i mod $2 == 1$ **then**

20   **for** $v \in Group_i$ **do**

21         $M[v] := id++$ // top-down traversal

22   **else**

23   **for** $v \in Group_i$ **do**

24         $M[v] := id++$ // bottom-up traversal

---

top of the second bin are closer to those at the top of the third bin and so on. The first order *Hilbert curve* [10] is used in the algorithm to keep spatial locality among the vertices at the initial and final levels of traversal of a neighbouring bin, where the vertices of the odd-numbered bin are assigned consecutive ids in a top-down direction and the even-numbered bin in a bottom-up direction of stacking. The first-level vertices of a bin will now share cache lines with the same level of vertices in the next bin, as motivated by the *Hilbert curve*. Figure 5 shows an example graph along with the order in which vertices are traversed while reordering with k as the seed vertex. Bins are created using *power-law* with the average degree of the graph as two - $[0, 1), [1, 2), [2, 4)$ and $[4, 8)$. The vertices are stacked into their respective bin in the order which they were traversed and

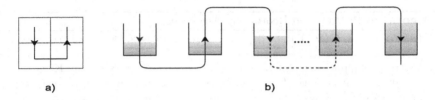

a)   b)

Fig. 4. a) First-order Hilbert curve b) Vertex assignment to the bucket vertices following Hilbert curve

then reordered with the first-order *Hilbert curve* i.e., top-to-bottom (right-to-left in Fig. 6) for bin 1, bottom-to-top (left-to-right in Fig. 6) for bin 2 and so on. Assuming a single cache line can accommodate three vertices, Fig. 6 shows that the hot vertices of bin 1, 2 can now be placed in five cache lines, whereas they were previously spread across seven cache lines. We can see that after *Hilbert curve* reordering step when vertex e is tries to access its neighbours a, x they will be within the same cache line after reordering. Similarly, after reordering, vertices m, p will be placed within the same cache line.

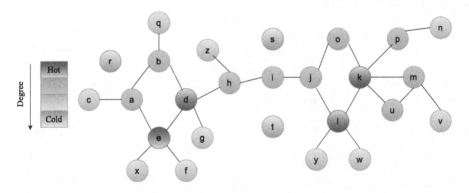

Traversal: k, l, m, p, o, u, j, w, y, v, n, i, h, d, z, b, e, g, a, q, f, x, c, r, s, t

Fig. 5. Example graph with original ordering

Breadth-first traversal helps learn about community relationships among the vertices, and coarse partition achieves the temporal locality for hot vertices. Binning the vertices into degree-based groups reduce the cache footprint of hot vertices. To preserve sibling relationships when moving from one group to the next, findings of the *Hilbert curve* explains that closely spaced vertices can be future neighbours or siblings, which can help achieve a better locality of reference.

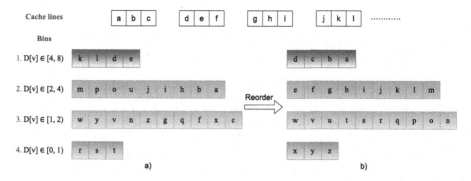

Fig. 6. Bin formation of the traversed vertices. a) Before reordering b) After reordering

4   Experimental Setup

In this Section we expand on the simulation infrastructure and the applications used. The evaluation is done on a dual-socket server with one Broadwell based Intel Xeon CPU E5-2620 with eight cores in one socket clocked at 2.10 GHz and having 32 GB memory. In addition, the L1D, L1I, L2, and L3 cache size of the machine are 32 KB, 32 KB, 256 KB, and 20 MB, respectively. For fair evaluations thread pinning is enabled to avoid performance variations due to OS scheduling. The dynamic voltage and frequency scaling (DVFS) feature is disabled to reduce sources of performance variation and the transparent huge pages is kept on to reduce the TLB overhead, i.e., TLB misses [6]. The cache replacement policies are orthogonal to the graph reordering algorithms [15]. Cache replacement policies focus on identification of best eviction candidate whereas graph reordering algorithms emphasize on data mapping in the memory. Better data mapping in memory enables cache replacement policies to further enhance system's performance. Thus, we do not analyse impact of different cache replacement policies on our graph reordering scheme.

We evaluate each reordering technique on all graph datasets for applications shown in Table 1. The datasets used are shown in Table 2. For single-source kernels such as BFS, SSSP and BC, since there is a substantial natural variation in execution time, we execute 64 trials from different source vertices. For the whole-graph kernels (PR and CC), we execute 16 trials. We record the average runtime, excluding the first executions timing to allow the caches to warm up. The reordering time is not included in the performance indicators acquired during the evaluation as it needs to be done once and the cost can be amortized across multiple runs.

5   Results and Analysis

In this Section we compare *CAR* against the existing state-of-the-art reordering techniques.

Table 1. Applications

Graph kernel	Compute type	Degree used	Trials	Output per trial
BFS	Pull-Push	in	64 trials from 64 sources	$\|V\|$-sized array of 32-bit integer
PR	Pull Only	out	16 trials	$\|V\|$-sized array of 32-bit floating point integers
CC	Pull-Push	in	16 trials	$\|V\|$-sized array of 32-bit integer
SSSP	Push only	in	64 trials from 64 sources	$\|V\|$-sized array of 32-bit integer
BC	Push only	in	16 trials from 4 sources	$\|V\|$-sized array of 32-bit floating point integers

Table 2. Properties of Evaluated Datasets

Dataset	# vertices	# edges	Avg degree	Type	Structured/unstructured	Size
Twitter (tw)	62M	1468M	23	Real	Unstructured	25 GB
PLD (pld)	43M	623M	14	Real	Unstructured	10.9 GB
LiveJournal (lj)	5M	68M	14	Real	Structured	1.1 GB
Pokec (pok)	2M	31M	18	Real	Structured	0.5 GB
Kron	4M	67M	15	Synthetic	Unstructured	1.2 GB
Urand	4M	64M	15	Synthetic	Unstructured	1.5 GB

5.1   Speedup Comparison

The reduction in execution times of several applications is depicted in Fig. 7. The speedup obtained is normalized to that of unordered graphs. *CAR* gives a 20% speedup (average across all applications), whereas the existing lightweight reordering techniques provide the following speedups: *Hub Cluster* (9%), *DBG* (11%), and *Sorder* (17%). While *Gorder* the overall performance by 25%, it has a relatively long reordering time (Ref. Table 3).

Gorder v/s *CAR:* Overall *Gorder* achieves a speed-up of 27%, 2%, 42%, 33% and 26% whereas *CAR* achieves 22%, 1%, 42%, 25% and 14% for *BC, CC, PR, SSSP* and *BFS* applications respectively. Significant speed ups in *SSSP* applications is from the use of vertex connectivity information used in *Gorder* where *CAR* utilizes traversal and degree-based information. *BFS* application uses both a push and pull type computation where *CAR* uses either of in/out degree (or edges) for reordering where *Gorder's* structural analysis of a graph helps in achieving a better speed up. *Gorder*, on the other hand, is not a lightweight reordering technique, but we included it for completeness.

Sorder v/s *CAR:* For *structured* datasets, *Sorder* gives an average speedup of 8% (vs. 7% for *CAR*) for *unstructured* datasets and a speedup of 22% (vs. 27% for *CAR*) for *structured datasets*. *Sorder* beat *CAR* and even *Gorder* for *SSSP* applications due to the best speed in the *kron* and *pokec* datasets, where *Gorder* fails to determine the optimal ordering due to the dataset's low clustering co-efficient, indicating a difficult-to-identify community structure for *CAR* as well.

We observed that reordering approaches do not result in a substantial speed increase for the *CC* application. This is attributed to the reason that it already has a low execution time.

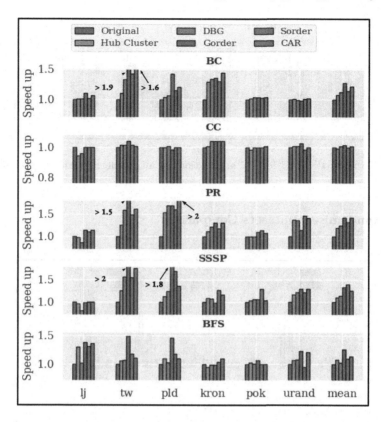

Fig. 7. Normalized speedup w.r.t unordered graphs

5.2 MPKI Comparison

We used the *VTune* profiler [16] to capture cache performance information, such as cache misses at L1, L2, and L3, and instructions performed inside region-of-interests (ROI), to evaluate the speedup results achieved by various graph reordering schemes.

Normalized MPKIs for all reordering strategies for *BC* application are shown in Fig. 8. *Sorder* was the best among the lightweight reordering algorithms (in prior works). However, *CAR* surpasses *Sorder*, as demonstrated in Sect. 5.1. This is due to the decrease in MPKIs for *CAR* compared to *Sorder*, as seen in Fig. 8. In the *urand* dataset, for example, *Sorder* reduces L1, L2, and L3 MPKIs by 0.6%, 0.3%, and 13.7%, respectively, whereas *CAR* reduces L1, L2, and L3 MPKIs by 2.8%, 4.8%, and 9.7%, respectively. Overall, MPKI is reduced by 7.3%, 13.7%, 30.7%, 18%, and 26% using *Hub Cluster*, *DBG*, *Gorder*, *Sorder*, and *CAR* respectively. *Gorder*, as predicted, provides the best reduction in the MPKIs, but it has a very high reordering time; it is thus unsuitable, as discussed in Sect. 5.5.

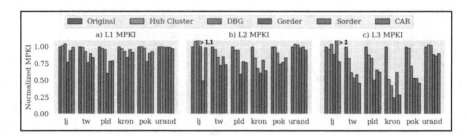

Fig. 8. Normalized MPKI for BC application for all reordering schemes over original ordering

5.3 Randomised Datasets Comparison

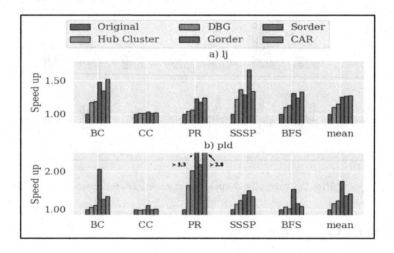

Fig. 9. Speedup comparison of randomized datasets

In this subsection, we examine the performance of two real-world datasets, *lj* (structured) and *pld* (unstructured), following randomization of the respective datasets. We randomized the datasets to eliminate any temporal and spatial locality that may have existed in the original vertex ID assignment. Lightweight and skew-aware reordering approaches will fail to capture the community structure in randomized reordered datasets.

As seen in Fig. 9, none of the skew-aware lightweight reorderings schemes - *Hub Cluster* and *DBG* - provide the comparable speedup (with respect to *Gorder*, *Sorder* and *CAR*). *Gorder*, *Sorder*, and *CAR* can provide considerable speedups because they do not presume that real-world datasets contain inherent community structure. The overall geometric means of speedup for the *lj* dataset obtained by *Sorder* and *CAR* are 27% and 28%, respectively. Similarly, the speedups for the *pld* dataset are 37% and 42%, respectively.

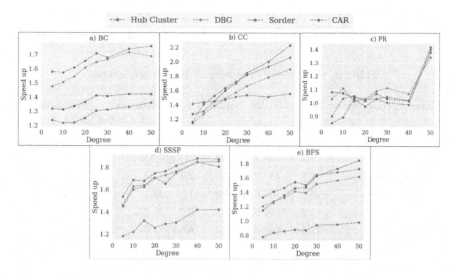

Fig. 10. *kron* sensitivity analysis

5.4 Scalability Analysis

We intended to demonstrate that *CAR* is a scalable reordering algorithm, which means that the advantages do not diminish for large degree graphs. We omitted *Gorder* since the time necessary for reordering is too long. We generated graphs with the Kronecker function and a vertex count of 16 million for degrees - 5, 10, 15, 20, 25, 30, 40 and 50 [4]. In Fig. 10, we can observe that *CAR* provides the best speedup for *BC*, *SSSP*, and *BFS*, whereas *Hub Cluster* provides comparable performance for *CC* application. *Sorder* does not segregate the hot vertices from the hottest vertices in a graph, hence it does not provide equivalent speed gain for higher degree graphs.

5.5 Reordering Time

The execution time for various reordering tasks is displayed in Table 3. We can observe that the reordering time for *Gorder* may be up to 31× longer than that of *CAR*. Because reordering is done just once, the cost of reordering may be amortized over several application runs. *Gorder* necessitates up to 10,000 application runs for cost amortization, which is quite costly. *CAR* provides up to 4× quicker reordering than *Sorder* (best among all the lightweight reordering methods).

The reordering times for *Hub Cluster* and *DBG* are pretty short. This is because these algorithms can be parallelized, and we have published the results of their multi-threaded implementation. While *CAR* may be made multi-threaded, we used a single-threaded version for this study. In any scenario, we have observed that the *Hub Cluster* and *DBG* algorithms provide the least performance improvement compared to any reordering approach through the application runs. As a result, even though they have a short reordering time, the diminished advantages make them unsuitable for usage in graph applications.

Table 3. Comparison of reordering time (Unit: seconds)

Dataset	Hub cluster	DBG	Gorder	Sorder	CAR	Speed up w.r.t. Gorder	Speed up w.r.t. Sorder
lj	0.8	1.2	84.8	22.7	5.8	3.8X	4X
pokec	0.4	0.4	20.2	5.4	2.2	3.8X	2.5X
kron	0.8	1.3	240.2	29.3	12.1	8.2X	2.5X
urand	0.8	0.8	105.6	4.6	11	23X	0.5X
pld	6.1	5.4	5766.6	216.1	72.9	26.7X	3X
Twitter	22.6	27.6	9865.3	318.3	182.3	31X	1.8X

6 Related Work

While graph reordering is a software solution, researchers have worked hard to develop hardware-based solutions to improve memory subsystem performance in irregular workloads such as graph processing. Cache policies such as SHiP [17] and Hawkeye [18] were created to handle a wide range of irregular workloads. However, these techniques were domain-agnostic, so domain-specific cache policies such as GRASP [12] and P-OPT [14] were designed to improve performance even further. Similarly, a generic prefetcher like IMP [11] prefetched data by detecting irregular patterns in memory accesses that lacked graph knowledge, and DROPLET [13] overcame this limitation by making the prefetcher data-aware. Because they are orthogonal to graph reordering, these hardware solutions are compatible with the proposed solution to improve performance.

7 Conclusion

Without assuming any community structure in the input graph, we proposed a *Community Aware Reordering (CAR)* that places fairly similar degree vertices in the neighbourhood to offer improved spatial and temporal locality in caches. *CAR* performs the reordering using breadth-first search and the *Hilbert curve*. *CAR* outperforms all lightweight reordering techniques, with a speedup of 20% compared to the 17% performance boost provided by *Sorder*, with up to 4× reduction in reordering time.

References

1. Cuzzocrea, A., et al.: Big graph analytics: the state of the art and future research agenda. In: Proceedings of the 17th International Workshop on Data Warehousing and OLAP, pp. 99–101 (2014)

2. Beamer, S., et al.: Direction-optimizing breadth-first search. In: SC 2012: Proceedings of the International Conference on High Performance Computing, Networking, Storage and Analysis, pp. 1–10. IEEE (2012)

3. Shiloach, Y., et al.: An O(logn) parallel connectivity algorithm. J. Algorithms **3**(1), 57–67 (1982)

4. Beamer, S., et al.: The gap benchmark suite. arXiv preprint arXiv:1508.03619 (2015)

5. Balaji, V., et al.: When is graph reordering an optimization? Studying the effect of lightweight graph reordering across applications and input graphs. In: 2018 IEEE International Symposium on Workload Characterization (IISWC), pp. 203–214. IEEE (2018)

6. Faldu, P., et al.: A closer look at lightweight graph reordering. In: 2019 IEEE International Symposium on Workload Characterization (IISWC), pp. 1–13. IEEE (2019)

7. Wei, H., et al.: Speedup graph processing by graph ordering. In: Proceedings of the 2016 International Conference on Management of Data, pp. 1813–1828 (2016)

8. Leskovec, J., et al.: SNAP Datasets: Stanford large network dataset collection, June 2014. http://snap.stanford.edu/data

9. Huang, B., et al.: Structure preserved graph reordering for fast graph processing without the pain. In: 2020 IEEE 22nd International Conference on High Performance Computing and Communications; IEEE 18th International Conference on Smart City; IEEE 6th International Conference on Data Science and Systems (HPCC/SmartCity/DSS), pp. 44–51. IEEE (2020)

10. Mellor-Crummey, J., et al.: Improving memory hierarchy performance for irregular applications using data and computation reorderings. Int. J. Parallel Programm. **29**(3), 217–247 (2001)

11. Yu, X. et al.: IMP: indirect memory prefetcher. In: Proceedings of the 48th International Symposium on Microarchitecture, pp. 178–190 (2015)

12. Faldu, P., et al.: Domain-specialized cache management for graph analytics. In: 2020 IEEE International Symposium on High Performance Computer Architecture (HPCA), pp. 234–248. IEEE (2020)

13. Basak, A., et al.: Analysis and optimization of the memory hierarchy for graph processing workloads. In: 2019 IEEE International Symposium on High Performance Computer Architecture (HPCA), pp. 373–386. IEEE (2019)

14. Balaji, V., et al.: P-OPT: practical optimal cache replacement for graph analytics. In: 2021 IEEE International Symposium on High-Performance Computer Architecture (HPCA), pp. 668–681. IEEE (2021)

15. Sharma, N., et al.: Data-aware cache management for graph analytics. In: 2022 Design, Automation and Test in Europe Conference and Exhibition (DATE), pp. 843–848. IEEE (2022)

16. Intel VTune Profiler (2021). https://software.intel.com/content/www/us/en/develop/tools/oneapi/components/vtune-profiler.html#gs.34axdf

17. Wu, C.-J., et al.: SHiP: signature-based hit predictor for high performance caching. In: Proceedings of the 44th Annual IEEE/ACM International Symposium on Microarchitecture, pp. 430–441 (2011)

18. Jain, A., et al.: Back to the future: leveraging Belady's algorithm for improved cache replacement. In: 2016 ACM/IEEE 43rd Annual International Symposium on Computer Architecture (ISCA), pp. 78–89. IEEE (2016)

Indigenous Fab-Lab Hybrid Device Integration for Phase Change Memory for In-Memory Computing

Wasi Uddin[1]([✉]), Ankit Bende[1], Avinash Singh[2], Tarun Malviya[2], Rohit Ranjan[2], Kumar Priyadarshi[1]([✉]), and Udayan Ganguly[1]

[1] Indian Institute of Technology, Bombay, India
{wasi89,kumar.priyadarshi}@iitb.ac.in
[2] Semiconductor Laboratory (SCL), Chandigarh, India

Abstract. Finding novel materials in an established semiconductor foundry is difficult. As a result, most foundries use a contract research model in which an academic or dedicated research lab investigates material for them. Due to a shortage of cutting-edge lithography equipment, many research facilities are forced to limit their study to scaled devices. For the first time in India, we offer a hybrid paradigm for material discovery in which IIT Bombay's research lab does post processing on a semi-processed wafer from an Indian foundry (SCL Chandigarh). BEOL integration of a phase change material (PCM) (GST-225) in a 180 nm CMOS line with device sizes ranging from 100F to 1F (where F is the minimum feature size that can be resolved by lithography and etching, in our case it is 260 nm) has been successfully demonstrated. With SET and RESET timings of 500 and 50 ns, these MIM-like devices demonstrate stable memory operation. The devices were put through 1000 endurance cycles and found stable. When the devices were annealed at 85 °C for 2 h, the SET and RESET state resistances showed no change. To test if these PCM devices are suitable for in-memory computing, we performed AND & OR logic operations on them.

Keywords: Phase Change Memory · PCM · In-memory computing · 180 nm CMOS · Lab-Fab Hybrid Model

1 Introduction

The traditional computer system (CPUs, GPUs, and FPGAs) uses von- Neumann architecture, which separates the processor unit from the memory [1]. The dataflow between memory and processing units limits the performance of such architectures [2]. Large amounts of data must be computed for artificial intelligence (AI) applications, which necessitates data transport back and forth between memory and processor unit [3]. The amount of energy required to access memory is significantly larger than that required for arithmetic and logic operations [4]. As a result, novel computing architectures with better memory and processing unit correlations should be investigated for more efficient AI hardware. Researchers have been investigating a unique computing technology in

A. P. Shah et al. (Eds.): VDAT 2022, CCIS 1687, pp. 468–477, 2022.
https://doi.org/10.1007/978-3-031-21514-8_38

which some computing operations can be conducted within the memory throughout the previous decade. This is accomplished by utilizing the physical data storing mechanism in developing class memory [5, 6]. With collocated design, the memory element can not only store data but also conduct computational activities. In-memory computing (IMC) of this type allows for faster operations and lower temporal complexity [7] (Fig. 1).

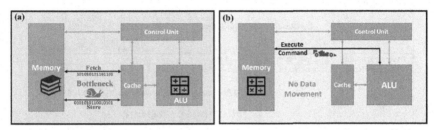

Fig. 1. The "Memory Wall" bottleneck is resolved by computing in memory: (a) Conventional von-Neumann architecture for computing, showing physical separated memory and computational unit. (b) In-memory computational architecture exploiting physical properties of memory to compute by eliminating the data movement requirement.

Digital storage capability, analogue storage capability, accumulative behavior, and linear mapping capability in a crossbar architecture are all required for IMC capabilities [8]. Several memristive devices [9, 10] can provide a precondition for in memory computing. For IMC, various memory has been considered. Because SRAM/DRAM is volatile, it requires standby power. Flash provides non-volatility but has high write/read requirements and a longer access time. RRAM has a smaller memory window, device variability, and resistance drift, but it has faster access times and is non-volatile. On the other hand, PCM gives you the best of both worlds. It allows for analogue programming, accumulative behavior, shorter access times, and minimal device variability [11, 12]. Table 1 compares the various memory technologies based on IMC-relevant factors.

As India develops its manufacturing innovation ecosystem, scaled memories showing with repeatability is a big challenge. Manufacturing labs provide process control but no materials flexibility, whereas university nano labs (e.g. IITB Nanofabs) have process control but no materials flexibility. These are game changers in terms of materials and process innovation to advance domestic scaled memory engineering. To overcome the issue of memory innovation in the Indian ecosystem, a Fab-Lab Hybrid model (used in other R&D Centres like IMEC) must be used. The hybrid model ecosystem is represented in Fig. 2. SCL has previously adopted one-time programmable memory technology [20] but integrating new materials into a CMOS fab process is difficult.

For the first time in India, a fab-lab hybrid model for building scaled test structures for new material integration is exhibited. To begin, test structure wafers are manufactured on a 180 nm CMOS production platform at India's most advanced manufacturing facility. New materials cannot be introduced into these fabs without significant feasibility and performance data because to strict materials/contamination limits. So, in a university nanofab "lab" where materials flexibility is accessible, we devise a method to post process

Table 1. Comparison of memory technologies

Parameter	SRAM	NAND Flash	RRAM	PCM
Non-Volatility	Volatile	Non-volatile	Non-volatile	Non-volatile
Standby Power	Required	Not required	Not required	Not required
Analog programmability	No	Yes [13]	Yes [14]	Yes [15]
Access time	Very Fast	Slow	Fast	Fast
	~1ns (Read)	~10µs (Read)	<10ns (Read)	<10ns (Read)
	~1ns (Write)	~1ms (Write)	<10ns (Write)	~50ns (Write)
Device Variability	Very low	Low	High	Low
Maturity level	In manufacturing [16]	In manufacturing	In Manufacturing	In Manufacturing
		2D Embedded	Panasonic	Intel-Micron 3D Xpoint [19]
		3D NAND [17]	Fujitsu [18]	

the wafer. Based on this, we show scaled PCM technology for advanced memories employing an indigenous fab-lab hybrid mode for the first time.

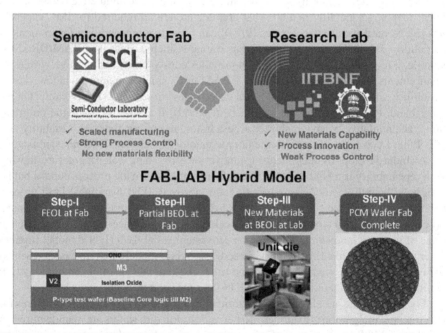

Fig. 2. An attractive FAB-LAB Hybrid model that exploits scaled manufacturing and strong process control of semiconductor Fabs, and new materials and process innovation capabilities of research labs. Wafers are initially processed at tighter node fabs for scaled manufacturing and later transferred to research lab for new materials enablement.

A device's resistance (or conductance) state can be utilized to store data, for example, a low resistance state (LRS) and a high resistance state (HRS) can be coded as 'logic 0' and 'logic 1', respectively [21]. For memristive behavior, many physical mechanisms such as ionic drift [22], magnetoresistance [23], and phase change [24] are investigated in depth. The main difficulties with ionic drift and magnetoresistance type memory are resistance drift, drift in time, read disturb, and the effect of radiation on the stored data [25]. On the other hand, memories based on phase change are substantially more resilient, with less drift, minimal read disturb, and are naturally radiation resistant [26–28].

The chalcogenide glass, which may exist in both an amorphous and crystalline state, is the basis for phase change memory (PCM). The phase transition happens at the crystallization temperature (T_{cryst}), and it results in the amorphous phase if the material is heated to its melting point (T_{melt}) then quenched rapidly. This phase transition can be repeated indefinitely. When a phase transition material is in a crystalline condition, its electrical resistance is LRS, and when it is in an amorphous form, it is HRS [29]. The phase change material is sandwiched between two metals in PCMs, which are similar to MIMs. Depending on the applied electrical pulse, joule heating inside the phase change material causes the temperature to rise to Tcryst or Tmelt [30]. There have been several phase change materials developed, each with its own set of advantages and disadvantages [31], but $Ge_2Sb_2Te_5$ (GST-225) is the most frequently utilized for commercial purposes [32]. PCM is highly suited for CMOS integration due to its basic MIM-like structure, which provides a low-cost solution without requiring significant changes to the production line [33].

We have demonstrated a GST-225-based non-volatile memory that is compatible with 180 nm CMOS. On a short loop wafer, the GST-225 was integrated at the BEOL of a 180 nm line. The device sizes available are 100F, 30F, 10F, 3F, 2F, and 1F. The existing programming needs scale linearly with device size. The LRS and HRS states are stable and have been tested for 1000 endurance cycles. They also hold their state for up to 6 h at 85 °C. These PCM-based devices have im-memory computing qualities, in that logic operations like AND and OR may be performed on them, opening the door to scalable, low-cost, CMOS-integrable, and ultrafast in-memory computation capabilities.

2 Experimental Section

2.1 Active Layer Process Development (GST-225 Deposition)

The properties of the active layer (GST-225) were thoroughly investigated before beginning device construction. GST-225 films were deposited via RF magnetron sputtering, with a stoichiometric target utilised to assure compositional uniformity. The chamber's base pressure was 1x10–7 mTorr, whereas the sputtering pressure was 3 mTorr. A deposition rate of 4.8 nm/min has been calculated. For all of the trials, the GST layer thickness was 50 nm. AFM imaging of a 2 μm2 scan area with RMS roughness of 0.75 nm for as deposited films and 0.95 nm for films annealed at 250 °C validated the film homogeneity. The AFM surface scans of the as deposited and 250 °C annealed films are shown in Fig. 3(a) and (b).

As can be seen from the XRD spectra in Fig. 3(c), the as deposited films are in an amorphous phase. No GST-225 associated peaks were found in the as deposited films.

However, for films annealed at 150 and 200 °C, the fcc (200) and fcc (220) peaks are dominant, whereas the hcp (005) and hcp (027) peaks are dominant for films annealed at 250 and 300 °C, as shown in Fig. 3(d). This supports the presence of two different crystalline phases in GST-225, which is supported by temperature-dependent resistivity studies on blanket films. Sheet resistance of GST-225 films annealed at different temperatures from 25 to 300 °C with a step of 25 °C is shown in Fig. 3 (e). At 120 and 220 °C, two sharp transitions were observed: the first is from the amorphous phase to the fcc phase, with a 3-order change in sheet resistance, and the second is from fcc to hcp, with a further 1 order decrease in sheet resistance. These transition temperatures are similar to those previously reported [34, 35]. This proves that deposited films can exist in three different states. Furthermore, the fcc and hcp phases have distinct polycrystalline sizes, which allows for tunable conductance of films, which is a critical prerequisite for in memory computing [36].

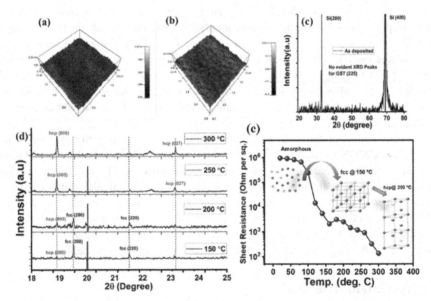

Fig. 3. 3 Phase change results in change in the electrical resistance of the films: (a) AFM surface scan of as-deposited GST films (b) 250 °C annealed films on bare silicon wafer, the scan area is 5 μm2 with RMS roughness of ~ 0.75 nm and ~ 0.95 nm respectively. (c) XRD spectra of as deposited GST-225 films, Si (200) and (400) peaks are form the substrate whereas no evident XRD peaks for GST-225 were observed (d) XRD spectra of the annealed films at 150, 200, 250 and 300 °C, at 150 °C fcc (200) and fcc (220) peaks are dominant while we have evident peak of hcp (005). It is observed that fcc peaks are diminishing and hcp peaks are becoming more dominant with increasing annealing temperature from 200 to 300 °C. (e) Effect of annealing temperature on sheet resistance of the film, two phase transitions are observed at ~120 and 220 °C.

2.2 Device Fabrication

The PCM devices were fabricated on a 180 nm industrial wafer without disrupting the backend core circuitry. For bottom electrode (BE) (M3) access, contact openings ranging from 1 F to 100 F were opened in the oxide-nitride-oxide (ONO) layer. Photolithography was used to define the device, followed by GST-225 and tungsten deposition in situ (50 nm each). After lift-off, device construction was finished; Fig. 4 (a) depicts the post-processing flow at the IIT Bombay research lab. Figure 4 (b) depicts constructed die with 100F BE access; Fig. 4 (c) depicts an enlarged optical view of a typical 10F device (c). A schematic of the cross-sectional configuration of the PCM cell is shown in Fig. 4. (d).

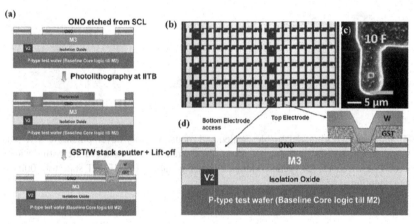

Fig. 4. Post processing at research lab on an industrial wafer: (a) Process flow for post processing (b) Fabricated die showing device sizes from 100 F to 1 F with a 100 F size bottom electrode access via. (c) Enlarged image of a 10 F device (d) Cross sectional schematic of the device showing BEOL integration of the PCM devices.

3 Results and Discussions

3.1 Memory Characteristics and Data Retention

A SET pulse of 2.5 V and 500 ns is applied when the devices are in HRS, which warms up the active layer until T_{cryst} and a specific volume crystalizes (called the programmed volume). This results in a 2-order reduction in device resistance and a SET state. A 4V, 50 ns pulse is required to RESET the device; this high amplitude, ultra-short duration pulse melts a portion of the programmed volume, and quick quenching prevents recrystallization, resulting in an amorphous phase, or RESET state [37]. The SET and RESET pulses is shown in Fig. 5(a). We utilized two WGFMU to apply the pulses. As illustrated in Fig. 5(b), FEOL processing in the fab under a fab-lab hybrid model allows device scalability from 100 F to 1F, reducing phase change current requirements. We tested cyclic endurance using a 0.5 V read pulse; this low read voltage has no effect on the device's condition during read operation. The cyclic with stable SET and RESET states up to 1000 cycles is shown in Fig. 5(c). High-speed operations and low RESET energy are ensured by rapid SET and ultra-quick RESET pulses. Several devices were examined, and there is very little variation amongst them. The SET and RESET states are stable under temperature stress; we evaluated the devices' SET/RESET resistance after heating them at 85 °C for 2 h. At 85 °C, the devices' retention properties are as shown in Fig. 5(d).

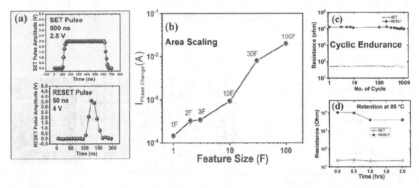

Fig. 5. Fab-Lab hybrid model enables scaled and robust memory development: (a SET pulse of 2.5 V and 500 ns RESET pulse of 4V 50 ns. (b) Current requirement scaling with device sizes from 100 F down to 1F. (c) cyclic endurance showing stable SET/RESET state for 1000 cycles, (d) data retention at 85 °C.

3.2   In-Memory AND & OR Logic Implementation

Three PCM cells are chosen to conduct AND & OR logic, one of which is employed as a select S and the other two as inputs A and B. The common bottom electrode serves as a bit line (BL), and the switch matrix is used to choose A, B, and S. As shown in Fig. 6(a), total bit line current is fed to one of the inputs of the sense amplifier (SA), with I_{ref} as the second input to the SA. Bit line current (I_{BL}) is the total of three PCM cells' individual currents; Fig. 6(b) and (c) show measured I_{BL} for various bit combinations, where '0' indicates HRS and '1' indicates LRS. The SA output (Y) will be '1' when $I_{BL} > I_{ref}$ and '0' when $I_{BL} > I_{ref}$ when a reference current of 3 mA is used. Figure 6 depicts the truth table that represents the AND & OR logic (d).

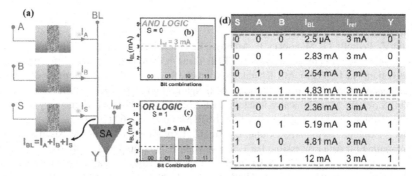

Fig. 6. In-memory computing demonstration on PCM memory cells: (a) Circuit diagram for in-memory AND & OR Logic implementation, three PCM devices of 30F size were selected out of which one is assigned as select (S) and other two are inputs A and B, input current to the sense amplifier (SA) is the bit line current (I_{BL}) is the sum of individual device currents of select S, input A and B, I_{ref} of SA is set to 3 mA. (b) AND logic implementation by selecting S = 0 (RESET state). (c) OR logic implementation by selecting S = 1 (SET state). (d) Truth table representing the implemented AND & OR logic, the SA output (Y) will be '1' when $I_{BL} > I_{ref}$ and '0' when $I_{BL} < I_{ref}$.

4   Conclusions

The constraining structure of fabs with stringent requirements hinders the development of manufacturable emerging class memory based on new materials. Exotic materials can be discovered at a research centre, but process control and scalability are lacking. As a result, a hybrid development strategy is required, in which the FEOL process is performed in a fab and BEOL integration and post processing is performed in a research lab, resulting in scalable and reliable memory. In an academic research lab, we successfully implemented PCM-based non-volatile memory integration on an industrial wafer. Both in terms of high-speed memory operation and its application in in-memory computation, the results seem encouraging. This is a practical and appealing methodology for exploring materials for upcoming technology.

References

1. Šilc, J., Silc, J., Robic, B., Ungerer, T.: Processor Architecture: From Dataflow to Superscalar and Beyond; with 34 Tables. Springer, New York (1999)
2. Jouppi, N. P., Young, C., Patil, N., Patterson, D., Agrawal, G., Bajwa, R., Bates, S., Bhatia, S., Boden, N., Borchers, A.: In: Proceedings of the 44th Annual International Symposium on Computer Architecture (2017)
3. Patterson, D. A.: Future of computer architecture. In: Berkeley EECS Annual Research Symposium (BEARS), College of Engineering, UC Berkeley, US (2006)
4. Chen, Y.-H.: Emer, J., Sze, V.: Using dataflow to optimize energy efficiency of deep neural network accelerators. IEEE Micro. **37**, 12–21 (2017)
5. Mehonic, A., Sebastian, A., Rajendran, B., Simeone, O., Vasilaki, E., Kenyon, A.J.: Memristors—from in-memory computing, deep learning acceleration, and spiking neural networks to the future of neuromorphic and bio-inspired computing. Adv. Intell. Syst. **2**, 2000085 (2020)

6. Ielmini, D., Wong, H.-S.P.: In-memory computing with resistive switching devices. Nature electronics **1**, 333–343 (2018)
7. Sun, Z., Pedretti, G., Mannocci, P., Ambrosi, E., Bricalli, A., Ielmini, D.: Time complexity of in-memory solution of linear systems. IEEE Trans. Electron Device. **67**, 2945–2951 (2020)
8. Sebastian, A., Le Gallo, M., Khaddam-Aljameh, R., Eleftheriou, E.: Memory devices and applications for in-memory computing. Nat. Nanotechnol. **15**, 529–544 (2020)
9. Yin, S., et al.: Monolithically integrated RRAM-and CMOS-based in-memory computing optimizations for efficient deep learning. IEEE Micro **39**, 54–63 (2019)
10. He, Z., Zhang, Y., Angizi, S., Gong, B., Fan, D.: Exploring a SOT-MRAM based in-memory computing for data processing. IEEE Trans. Multi-Scale Comput. Syst. **4**, 676–685 (2018)
11. Chakraborty, I., Jaiswal, A., Saha, A.K., Gupta, S.K., Roy, K.: Pathways to efficient neuromorphic computing with non-volatile memory technologies. Appl. Phys. Rev. **7**, 021308 (2020)
12. Rajendran, B., Alibart, F.: Neuromorphic computing based on emerging memory technologies. IEEE J. Emerg. Select. Top. Circ. Syst. **6**, 198–211 (2016)
13. Bayat, F. M., Guo, X., Klachko, M., Do, N., Likharev, K., Strukov, D.: Model-based high-precision tuning of NOR flash memory cells for analog computing applications. In 2016 74th Annual Device Research Conference (DRC) (2016)
14. Yu, S., Shim, W., Peng, X., Luo, Y.: RRAM for compute-in-memory: From inference to training. In IEEE Transactions on Circuits and Systems I: Regular Papers (2021)
15. Ambrogio, S., Narayanan, P., Tsai, H., Mackin, C., Spoon, K., Chen, A., Fasoli, A., Friz A., Burr, G. W.: Inference of deep neural networks with analog memory devices. In: 2020 International Symposium on VLSI Technology, Systems and Applications (VLSI-TSA) (2020)
16. Kumar, H., Tomar, V.K.: A review on performance evaluation of different low power SRAM cells in nano-scale era. Wirel. Pers. Commun. **117**, 1959–1984 (2021)
17. Bennett, S., Sullivan, J.: NAND flash memory and its place in IoT. In: 2021 32nd Irish Signals and Systems Conference (ISSC) (2021)
18. Petryk, D., et al.: sensitivity of HfO_2-based RRAM cells to laser irradiation. Microproc. Microsyst. **87**, 104376 (2021)
19. Choe, J.: Memory technology 2021: trends and challenges. In: 2021 International Conference on Simulation of Semiconductor Processes and Devices (SISPAD) (2021)
20. Malviya, P., Sadana, S., Lele, A., Priyadarshi, K., Sharma, A., Naik, A., Bandhu, L., Bende, A., Tsundus, S., Kumar, S.: A differential OTP memory based highly unique and reliable PUF at 180 nm technology node. Solid-State Electron. **188**, 108207 (2022)
21. Chua, L.: Resistance switching memories are memristors. In Handbook of Memristor Networks, pp. 197–230. Springer, New York (2019)
22. Waser, R., Aono, M.: Nanoionics-based resistive switching memories. In Nanoscience and Technology: A Collection of Reviews from Nature Journals, pp. 158–165. World Scientific, Singapore (2010)
23. Khvalkovskiy, A. V., Apalkov, D., Watts, S., Chepulskii, R., Beach, R. S., Ong, A., Tang, X., Driskill-Smith, A., Butler, W. H., Visscher, P. B.: Basic principles of STT-MRAM cell operation in memory arrays. J. Phys. D: Appl. Phys. **46**, 074001 (2013)
24. Wong, H.-S.P., et al.: Phase change memory. Proc. IEEE **98**, 2201–2227 (2010)
25. Krestinskaya, O., Dolzhikova, I., James, A.P.: Hierarchical temporal memory using memristor networks: A survey. IEEE Trans. Emerg. Top. Comput. Intell. **2**, 380–395 (2018)
26. Li, C., et al.: Understanding phase-change materials with unexpectedly low resistance drift for phase-change memories. J. Mater. Chem. C. **6**, 3387–3394 (2018)
27. Pirovano, A., et al.: Reliability study of phase-change nonvolatile memories. IEEE Trans. Device Mater. Reliab. **4**, 422–427 (2004)

28. Ferreira, A. P., Childers, B., Melhem, R., Mossé D., Yousif, M.: Using PCM in next-generation embedded space applications. In 2010 16th IEEE Real-Time and Embedded Technology and Applications Symposium (2010)
29. Burr, G. W., Breitwisch, M. J., Franceschini, M., Garetto, D., Gopalakrishnan, K., Jackson, B., Kurdi, B., Lam, C., Lastras, L. A., Padilla A.: Phase change memory technology. J. Vac. Sci. Technol. B Nanotechnol. Microelectron. Mater. Proces. Measur. Phen. **28**, 223–262 (2010)
30. Lankhorst, M.H.R., Ketelaars, B.W.S.M.M., Wolters, R.A.M.: Low-cost and nanoscale non-volatile memory concept for future silicon chips. Nat. Mater. **4**, 347–352 (2005)
31. Raoux, S., Wełnic, W., Ielmini, D.: Phase change materials and their application to nonvolatile memories. Chem. Rev. **110**, 240–267 (2010)
32. Walko, J.: Ovshinsky's memories. IEE Rev. **51**, 42–45 (2005)
33. Servalli, G.: A 45nm generation phase change memory technology. In 2009 IEEE International Electron Devices Meeting (IEDM) (2009)
34. Friedrich, I., Weidenhof, V., Njoroge, W., Franz, P., Wuttig, M.: Structural transformations of $Ge_2Sb_2Te_5$ films studied by electrical resistance measurements. J. Appl. Phys. **87**, 4130–4134 (2000)
35. Chen, K.-N., Cabral, C., Jr., Krusin-Elbaum, L.: Thermal stress effects of $Ge_2Sb_2Te_5$ phase change material: Irreversible modification with Ti adhesion layers and segregation of Te. Microelectron. Eng. **85**, 2346–2349 (2008)
36. Sarwat, S.G., Kersting, B., Moraitis, T., Jonnalagadda, V.P., Sebastian, A.: Phase-change memtransistive synapses for mixed-plasticity neural computations. Nat. Nanotechnol. **17**, 507–503 (2022)
37. Papandreou, N., Pozidis, H., Pantazi, A., Sebastian, A., Breitwisch, M., Lam C., Eleftheriou, E.: Programming algorithms for multilevel phase-change memory. In 2011 IEEE International Symposium of Circuits and Systems (ISCAS) (2011)

Resistive Switching Behavior of TiO$_2$/(PVP:MoS$_2$) Nanocomposite Bilayer Hybrid RRAM

Shalu Saini, Anil Lodhi⊙, Anurag Dwivedi, Arpit Khandelwal,
and Shree Prakash Tiwari$^{(\boxtimes)}$ ⊙

Flexible Large Area Microelectronics (FLAME) Research Group, Department of Electrical
Engineering, Indian Institute of Technology Jodhpur, Jodhpur, India
sptiwari@iitj.ac.in

Abstract. Resistive switching behavior of TiO$_2$ and (PVP:MoS$_2$) nanocomposite (NC) bilayer in resistive random-access memory (RRAM) devices fabricated on indium tin oxide (ITO) coated glass with ITO acting as bottom electrode and Ag as top electrode was explored. These RRAM devices exhibited excellent resistive switching with very low SET and RESET voltages of 1.04 V and − 1.18 V respectively. A good repeatability up to 100 cycles was demonstrated with high on/off current ratios of more than 10^3 at read voltage of 0.2 V. These results indicate that NC bilayer of PVP and MoS$_2$ can be a promising candidate for exploration of high performance RRAM devices.

Keywords: Resistive Switching · Hybrid Memory · RRAM

1 Introduction

In the recent trend of digitalization of the world, there is always an increasing need for reliable memory to store the data. Resistive random-access memory (RRAM) is one of the excellent emerging choices for non-volatile memory (NVM) due to its fast-switching speed, simple structure and low power consumption properties [1, 2]. RRAM can store one or multi bit data in the form of low resistance state (LRS) and high resistance state (HRS) [3]. To demonstrate high performance RRAM devices, various dielectric materials including inorganic materials such as titanium dioxide (TiO$_x$), aluminum oxide (AlO$_x$), hafnium oxide (HfO$_x$) and tantalum pentoxide (Ta$_2$O$_5$) [4–7], organic polymers like polyvinylcarbazole (PVK), polyvinylpyrrolidone, polyvinyl alcohol (PVA) [8–10], and 2D materials like graphene oxide (GO), molybdenum disulfide (MoS$_2$), tungsten disulfide (WS$_2$) and molybdenum diselenide (MoSe$_2$) [11–14], are investigated for resistive switching. On the basis of filament formation between electrodes, RRAM device can be classified as a conducting bridge RRAM and metal oxide RRAM. In conducting bridge RRAM, switching occurs due to the diffusion of active metal ions typically from copper (Cu), and silver (Ag). Filament occurs in metal oxide RRAM due to the trap sites [2]. Metal oxide TiO$_2$ has high reversible capacity with higher structural stability in RRAM

© The Author(s), under exclusive license to Springer Nature Switzerland AG 2022
A. P. Shah et al. (Eds.): VDAT 2022, CCIS 1687, pp. 478–485, 2022.
https://doi.org/10.1007/978-3-031-21514-8_39

devices [15]. Moreover, MoS_2 is a widely explored transition metal chalcogenide (TMD) 2D material in RRAM devices to enhance the switching behavior [16]. Composition of MoS_2 with polymers such as PVP and PVA has shown improvement in the RRAM device performance including improved switching window and low SET/RESET voltages [9, 12]. Though there are reports with use of nanocomposite (NC) of polymers in RRAM devices to improve the performance [17], this area is still underexplored.

In this paper, a bilayer of high-k dielectric TiO_2 with NC of $PVP:MoS_2$ is explored for its resistive switching behavior. For the same, $Ag/(PVP:MoS_2)NC/TiO_2/ITO$ hybrid RRAM devices are fabricated and studied for the switching performance. The devices show bipolar resistive switching behavior with SET and RESET voltages (V_{SET} and V_{RESET}) of ~ 1 V. The retention time up to 2000 s and DC endurance of 100 cycle confirm the decent NVM behavior of devices.

2   Experimentation

RRAM devices were fabricated on ITO coated glass substrate. Figure 1(a) represents the schematic structure of the fabricated device. Substrates were firstly cleaned by bath ultrasonication method for around 15 min in isopropyl alcohol (IPA) and then rinsed in DI water. Subsequently, these substrates were further cleaned in acetone and methanol for 10 min each, followed by drying with nitrogen. A 10-nm thick TiO_2 was deposited over the ITO bottom electrode (BE) using the Savannah (S200) thermal atomic layer deposition (ALD) technique using Tetrakis(dimethylamido)titanium(IV) and H_2O as precursors at 150 °C. Molybdenum(IV) sulfide (MoS_2) (Mw: 160.07 g/mol) and poly(4-vinylphenol) (PVP) (Mw ~ 25000) were procured from Sigma Aldrich and mixed in 1:4 ratio with ethanol solvent. $MoS_2:PVP$ NC was prepared by liquid exfoliation technique [18].

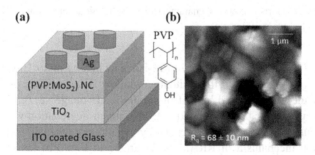

Fig. 1. (a) Schematic structure of Ag /(PVP:MoS₂)NC/TiO₂/ITO coated glass (b) AFM image of (PVP:MoS₂) NC layer. Chemical structure of polymer (PVP) is shown between both the figures.

The composite solution was prepared by ice water bath sonication up to 12 h and then kept properly to settle down for three days. The solution was then deposited over oxide layer with the help of a spin coater at 4000 rpm for around 45 s. To improve the film uniformity and for removing the residual solvent, samples were annealed at 60 °C for 1 h. At final fabrication step, top Ag electrodes were thermally evaporated through shadow mask under the high vacuum of 1.2×10^{-6} torr. Keithley 4200 SCS was used to perform the electrical characterization of the devices.

3 Results and Discussion

Figure 1(b) shows the surface morphology of PVP:MoS$_2$ film showing the average roughness (R_q) of 68 ± 10 nm. Resistive switching behavior of the devices is shown in Fig. 2. Initially, all the fabricated devices were in HRS state and the filament formation process was required to SET the device or to shift from HRS to LRS. The continuous voltage sweep pulse was carefully applied from $0 \rightarrow V_{max} \rightarrow 0 \rightarrow -V_{max} \rightarrow 0$ across bottom electrode (BE) and top electrode (TE) and the corresponding formation resistive switching behavior is plotted in Fig. 2(a). The device is switched from HRS to LRS after increase in value of current at V_{SET} (1.04 V). The filament rupture occurs, when applied a reverse sweep V_{RESET} of $- 1.18$ V, resulted in abrupt decrease of current and the device reaches to HRS. As it can be seen from these results, an excellent memory window with distinct SET and RESET were observed.

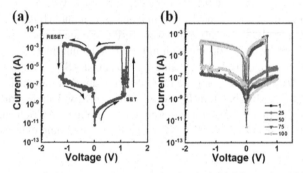

Fig. 2. Device characteristics. (a) I-V characteristics for the initial formation of filament, and (b) Repeatability of I-V up to 100 cycles.

Figure 2(b) shows the repeatability of resistive switching up to 100 cycles without any remarkable degradation in the switching window. The retention plot is shown in Fig. 3(a). For the same, a fixed bias of minimum read voltage i.e. 0.2 V was applied across the electrodes for both HRS and LRS. No major degradation was observed for 2000 s from this measurement and a decent on/off ratio more than 10^3 was maintained. The conduction mechanism of RRAM is illustrated in Fig. 3(b) (as in SET), which has a slope value of ~ 1 in ohmic region of the device. This slope indicates an ohmic conduction due to partially filled trap sites and thermally genrated charge carriers. The electric field increases, when the voltage across the electrodes increases, as shown in Fig. 3(b). The slope of the ln(V) versus. ln(I) graph reaches a maximum of 1.5. Inside the dielectric layer, all trap-sites are entirely filled, and a sharp spike in current indicates that the device has reached the SET state. The steep current switching follows the space charge limited conduction (SCLC), which is governed by the Child's law:

$$J_{SCLC} = q\varepsilon_m\mu\theta V^2/8d^3 \tag{1}$$

where, ε_m indicates the dielectric constant of the material, θ is the ratio between free and total carrier density, μ identifies the mobility of charge carriers, V is the applied voltage, and d is the separation between two electrodes [18]. Similarly, after the RESET state current voltage (I-V) characteristic follows the Child's Law in the higher voltages and ohmic conduction under the low voltages as shown in Fig. 3(c). These results confirm excellent switching behavior of duly engineered (PVP:MoS$_2$)NC/TiO$_2$ layer facilitating conductive bridge resistive switching by Ag electrodes (Fig. 4).

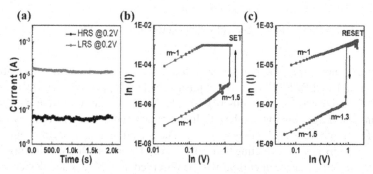

Fig. 3. (a) Retention time plot up to 2000 seconds at 0.2 V read voltage. Conduction mechanism for (b) SET and (c) RESET is demonstrated by taking double log I-V plot with 1 mA compliance current

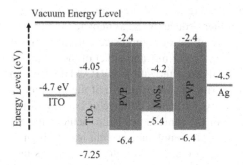

Fig. 4. Schematic energy band diagram

This switching behavior depends on energy levels of various materials and electrodes. The energy band diagram of proposed Ag/(PVP:MoS$_2$)/TiO$_2$/ITO RRAM device without biasing is depicted in Fig. 4. The work function of ITO (BE) and Ag (TE) are -4.7 eV and 4.5 eV respectively. The highest occupied molecule orbital (HOMO) and lowest unoccupied molecular orbital (LUMO) of PVP are -6.4 eV and -2.4 eV respectively [5]. The energy levels and work function differences provide first hand idea of the required voltage levels. Moreover, the low thickness of inorganic TiO$_2$ layer can facilitate both thermionic transport as well as tunneling through the layer. Though it is not shown here, the corresponding bending in energy bands will occur upon application of voltages leading to charge conduction and formation of filament.

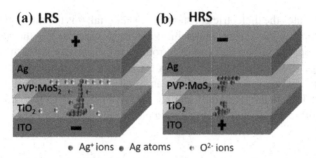

Fig. 5. Schematic diagram of switching mechanism (a) SET (b) RESET

Figure 5 shows the schematic of switching mechanism of filament formation and rupture in SET and RESET state. When positive voltage applied across the TE and BE, Ag electrode oxidizes to Ag^+ ions ($Ag \rightarrow Ag^+ + e^-$) and due to the electric field, these ions start migrating toward the BE. In the same manner, the electrons start moving toward TE from BE and Ag^+ will become Ag. The accumulation of electrochemically Ag atoms helps to form the conducting filament [11, 12]. Upon complete conducting filament formation, a sharp change in current will be observed at the V_{SET} and device will shift from HRS to LRS as depicted in Fig. 5(a). The data will be stored in the memory until the negative supply (V_{RESET}) is applied across the TE and BE. This behavior indicates the non-volatile property of RRAM. Upon application of negative voltage to TE, a high current running starts flowing in opposite direction through conductive filament. This results towards a Joule heating-assisted breakdown causing Ag^+ ions to move towards the TE. These ions will then reduce to Ag, as depicted in Fig. 5(b).

Finally, to explore the effect of compliance current in our devices, the same was varied 100 μA to reducing from 1 mA and effect of the same was studied on current in the SET side. For electrical characterization of RRAM device, compliance current plays a very crucial role. The primary role of it is to lit the maximum current flowing in the devices which prevents any permanent damage or burning of the devices. Moreover, a suitable sufficient value of the same is needed to achieve the SET state operation. On the other hand, having a high compliance current lead to high power dissipation from the devices during switching operations. Figure 6(a) shows the I-V characteristics of proposed RRAM device under compliance current variation. Though the variation in the HRS current is negligible, the increase in compliance current helps in decreasing the SET voltage. The LRS and HRS current at 0.2 V with varying compliance current from 100 μA to 1mA are plotted as shown in Fig. 6(b). As it can be seen from this plot, both the HRS and LRS current values are increasing with increase, however, the current on/off ratio is fairly constant with variation in compliance current. Our results indicate that these devices offer possibility for compliance current reduction which will eventually lead to low power dissipation.

Table 1 compares the performances of few recently reported RRAM devices based on PVP as an active material on rigid glass substrates. As it can be seen, Ag/(PVP:MoS$_2$)/TiO$_2$/ITO RRAM device compares very well in terms of performance compared to other similar reports. The SET and RESET voltages for this device are on

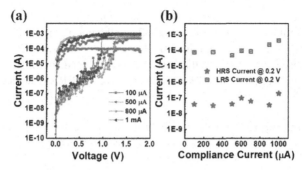

Fig. 6. (a) I-V curve with varying compliance current. (b) Variation of LRS current and HRS current at 0.2 V with different compliance current from 100 μA to 1 mA.

lower sides compared to other devices. Moreover, the current on/off ratio is on higher side. The endurence need to be improved. The reported retention time for all these cases are in the range of 10^3 - 10^4. The device had the capability of being evaluate for higher retention time.

Table 1. Summary of performance parameters of some recently reported RRAM devices with PVP as an active material component on rigid glass substrates

Switching Layer	Substrate	V_{SET} (V)	V_{RESET} (V)	Memory Window	Endurance Cycles	Retention Time (s)	Ref
PVP-PBD	ITO/Glass	− 1.4	3.55	10^4	300	10^4	[19]
PVP-DDQ	ITO/Glass	3	− 1.3	10^6	20	10^3	[20]
N-doped MoS$_2$-PVP	ITO/Glass	0.75	− 0.5	–	200	3×10^3	[21]
PVP/HfOx	ITO/Glass	1.03	− 0.68	80	2000	7×10^3	[22]
PVP:GO/TiO$_x$	FTO/Glass	1	− 2	10^3	128	7×10^3	[5]
PVP:MOS$_2$ NC/ TiO$_2$	ITO/Glass	~ 1	− 1.1	~ 10^4	100	2×10^3	This work

In overall, the perfomance of the reported device was impressive considering comparing with other rigid RRAM devices with PVP as a material component in switching layer. Our results indicate that (PVP:MoS$_2$)/TiO$_2$ can be a good choice for exploration for high performance RRAM devices. Moreover, these bilayers consisting NC of polymer and 2D materials can also be excellent candidate for exploration in emerging technologies such as large area and flexible electronics due to capability of solution processing.

4 Conclusion

RRAM devices with Ag/(PVP:MoS$_2$)NC/TiO$_2$/ITO structure have shown reliable resistive switching with low values of V_{SET} (1.0 V) and V_{RESET} (−1.2 V). NVM behavior with excellent retention up to 2000 s and decent on/off current ratio more than 10^3 was achieved. The endurance up to 100 cycles indicate the good repeatability of the device. ln(V) versus ln(I) graph shows dominating ohmic conduction and SCLC mechanism in the devices. These results indicate that these bilayers with NC of 2D material and polymers can be excellent alternatives for switching layer in RRAM devices for polymer electronics.

Acknowledgment. Support from the Sir Visvesvaraya Young Faculty Research Fellowship (YFRF), Ministry of Electronics and Information Technology (MeitY), Govt. of India is gratefully acknowledged.

References

1. Lanza, M., et al.: Recommended methods to study resistive switching devices. Adv. Electron. Mater. **5**, 1800143 (2019)
2. Wong, H.S.P., et al.: Metal-oxide RRAM. Proc. IEEE **100**(6), 1951–1970 (2012)
3. Zahoor, F., Azni Zulkifli, T.Z., Khanday, F.A.: Resistive Random Access Memory (RRAM): an Overview of Materials, Switching Mechanism, Performance, Multilevel Cell (mlc) Storage, Modeling, and Applications. Nanoscale Res. Lett. **15**(1), 1–26 (2020). https://doi.org/10. 1186/s11671-020-03299-9
4. Trapatseli, M., et al.: Engineering the switching dynamics of TiOx-based RRAM with Al doping. J. Appl. Phys. **120**, 2x (2016)
5. Lodhi, A., et al.: Bipolar resistive switching properties of TiO x/graphene oxide doped PVP based bilayer ReRAM. J. Micromech. Microeng. **32**, 4 (2022)
6. Jin, S., Kwon, J.D., Kim, Y.: Statistical analysis of uniform switching characteristics of Ta_2O_5-based memristors by embedding in-situ grown 2D-MoS_2 buffer layers. Materials (Basel) **14**, 21 (2021)
7. Shen, Z., et al.: Effect of annealing temperature for Ni/AlOx/Pt RRAM devices fabricated with solution-based dielectric. Micromachines **10**, 7 (2019)
8. Li, J.C., Zhang, C., Shao, S.J.: Effect of bottom electrode materials on resistive switching of flexible poly(N-vinylcarbazole) film embedded with TiO_2 nanoparticles. Thin Solid Films **664**, 136–142 (2018)
9. Rehman, M.M., et al.: Resistive switching in all-printed, flexible and hybrid MoS_2-PVA nanocomposite based memristive device fabricated by reverse offset. Sci. Rep. **6**, 36195 (2016)
10. Zhang, H., et al.: Bistable non-volatile resistive memory devices based on ZnO nanoparticles embedded in polyvinylpyrrolidone. RSC Adv. **10**(25), 14662–14669 (2020)
11. Varun, I., et al.: High-performance flexible resistive RAM with PVP:GO composite and ultrathin HfO_x hybrid bilayer. IEEE Trans. Electron Devic. **67**(3), 949–954 (2020)
12. Varun, I., et al.: Ultralow current switching in flexible hybrid PVP:MoS_2/HfO_x bilayer devices. IEEE Trans. Electron Devic. **67**(8), 3472–3477 (2020)
13. Jian, J., et al.: Low-operating-voltage resistive switching memory based on the interlayer-spacing regulation of $MoSe_2$. Adv. Electron. Mater. **8**, 3 (2022)
14. Lee, J.H., et al.: Highly flexible and stable resistive switching devices based on WS2 nanosheets:poly(methylmethacrylate) nanocomposites. Sci. Rep. **9**, 1 (2019)
15. Pham, K.N., et al.: TiO_2 thin film based transparent flexible resistive switching random access memory. Adv. Nat. Sci. Nanosci. Nanotechnol. **7**, 1 (2016)

16. Wang, X.F., et al.: Interface engineering with MoS$_2$–Pd nanoparticles hybrid structure for a low voltage resistive switching memory. Small **14**, 2 (2018)

17. Zhang, P., et al.: Structural phase transition effect on resistive switching behavior of MoS$_2$-polyvinylpyrrolidone nanocomposites films for flexible memory devices. Small **12**(15), 2077–2084 (2016)

18. Wright, G.T.: Mechanisms of space-charge-limited current in solids. Solid State Electron. **2**(2–3), 165–189 (1961)

19. Sun, Y., et al.: Resistive switching memory devices based on electrical conductance tuning in poly(4-vinyl phenol)-oxadiazole composites. Phys. Chem. Chem. Phys. **17**(44), 29978–29984 (2015)

20. Vyas, G., Dagar, P., Sahu, S.: A complementary switching mechanism for organic memory devices to regulate the conductance of binary states. Appl. Phys. Lett. **108**, 23 (2016)

21. Wu, Z., et al.: Resistive switching effect of N-doped MoS2-PVP nanocomposites films for nonvolatile memory devices. AIP Adv. **7**, 12 (2017)

22. Varun, I., et al.: Investigation of resistive switching in PVP and ultra-thin HfOx based bilayer hybrid RRAM. Solid State Ion. **325**, 196–200 (2018)

RTQCC-14T: Radiation Tolerant Quadruple Cross Coupled Robust SRAM Design for Radiation Prone Environments

Pramod Kumar Bharti[✉][iD] and Joycee Mekie[iD]

Department of Electrical Engineering, IIT Gandhinagar, Gandhinagar, India
{pramod.bharti,joycee}@iitgn.ac.in

Abstract. The state-of-the-art DICE SRAM is immune to Single Node Upset (SNU) in the radiation environment; however, it consumes significant leakage power. The leakage power is reduced in the state-of-the-art Quatro-10T SRAM, but Quatro-10T is not entirely immune to SNU and suffers from it in high radiation environment. In this work, we propose a Radiation Tolerant Quadruple Cross Coupled-14T (RTQCC-14T) SRAM with improved SNU tolerance with the least leakage power among existing techniques. The proposed design also shows better results in other SRAM parameters such as write access time, read access time, read static noise margin, word line write trip voltage and critical charge than most existing techniques. It exhibits better figure of merit among all the state-of-the-art methods. As compared to Quatro-10T, the proposed design has 1.48× shorter write access time, 1.42× less leakage power, 3.99× higher word line write trip voltage, and 1.94× higher critical charge respectively @ VDD = 0.9 V at 28 nm CMOS technology.

Keywords: SNU · DNU · SEMNU · Soft error · Quatro · DICE · Radiation hardening SRAM

1 Introduction

Electronic circuits used in space are highly susceptible to radiation [1]. It is mainly affected by Alpha particles generated by packaging material and Cosmic Rays produced by intergalactic rays [2]. These particles ionize the silicon where extra created charges are accumulated on sensitive nodes forming a Single Event Transient (SET) [3]. A sequential circuit such as SRAM is more susceptible to radiation as a SET can cause the storage node flips its value through a cross-coupled inverter. Flipping of a node due to SET is called SNU. Due to the scaling of the technology node, the area of SRAM cell and its node capacitance is decreasing over the years. As SRAM is becoming highly dense over the years, the vulnerability of sensitive nodes of SRAM due to radiation also increases [2,4]. A single particle strike may also affect multi nodes due to charge sharing called Single Event Multiple Node Upset (SEMNU) [5].

A. P. Shah et al. (Eds.): VDAT 2022, CCIS 1687, pp. 486–498, 2022.
https://doi.org/10.1007/978-3-031-21514-8_40

To mitigate the issue of SNU and SEMNU, various radiation hard-ened/tolerant SRAMs have been proposed [2,4,6–13]. DICE [4] SRAM is immune to SNU; however, the design suffers from large area requirement and leakage power. The Quatro-10T [2] SRAM requires less leakage power and area. How-ever, the design is not entirely immune to SNU and suffers from write failure at the lower voltage. The issue is circumvented in WE-Quatro-12T [10] by using two extra access transistors, but bit-line leakage increases through two additional access transistors. The internal node storing '1' of both Quatro-10T and WE-Quatro-12T are most sensitive to SNU due to the least effective critical charge (Q_C). The design proposed in RHD-12T [6] immune to SNU at internal node storing '1'; however, the storage node '0' is still sensitive to radiation. RHM-12T SRAM proposed in [7] is immune to SNU; however, due to the use of nMOS transistor in the pull-up path, the storage node is not entirely '1'. Weak '1' con-nected to pull down transistor reduces its strength and hence the design suffers from high read disturb. Also, large bit line leakage incurs in the cell through access transistor (as V_{DS} of access transistor is >0). Similarly, SEA-14T [14] and RHBD-14T [15] suffers from large leakage and read disturb due to weak '1' and weak '0' nodes, respectively. To summarize, the existing designs either have a significant leakage power or are not highly tolerant to SNU, especially at storage node '0'.

In this work, we propose a Radiation Tolerant Quadruple Cross Coupled-14T (RTQCC-14T) SRAM, which alleviates the above issue. The design consumes the least leakage power among surveyed state-of-the-art existing techniques. Also, the proposed design is highly tolerant to radiation at storing node '0'. The major contributions of our proposed design are as follows:

- The proposed design has better SNU tolerance and can recover from SNU at all the sensitive nodes.
- It shows least leakage power than existing techniques.
- The proposed RTQCC-14T SRAM shows adequate Read Static Noise Margin (RSNM) and Wordline Write Trip Voltage (WWTV)
- The read delay and write delay of the proposed design are shorter than various existing techniques.

The rest of the paper is organized as follows:

Section 2 explains the working of the proposed RTQCC-14T cell. The com-parison results with existing techniques are discussed in Sect. 3. Finally, Sect. 4 concludes the paper.

2   Proposed RTQCC-14T SRAM Cell

The schematic of the proposed Radiation Tolerant Quadruple Cross Coupled-14T (RTQCC-14T) SRAM cell is shown in Fig. 1. The proposed SRAM has two storage nodes A, B and two internal nodes C, D. It consists of 14 transistors. All the transistors are kept minimum sized except N3, N4, N5 and N6. The sizes (W/L) of pull down transistors (N3, N4, N5, and N6) are increased by 3.3 times as compared to minimum sized transistor for proper read operation. Figure 1 shows the scenario when the RTQCC-14T cell stores 1, that is, $A = D = 1$ and $B = C = 0$. The read/write operations are performed through the access transistors N7 and N8. The simulation results of normal read/write/hold of proposed RTQCC-14T SRAM (frequency $= 200$ MHz, VDD $= 0.9$ V) are illustrated in the Fig. 2.

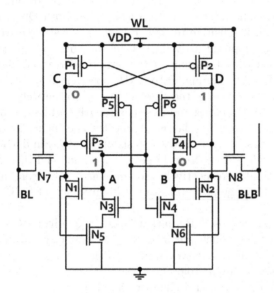

Fig. 1. Proposed RTQCC-14T SRAM.

2.1   Write Operation

We have considered the case of writing-0. To write 0, BL is made '0' while BLB is made '1'. When WL is changed from $0 \rightarrow 1$, A goes from $1 \rightarrow 0$, turning off transistor N4, so B goes from $0 \rightarrow \sim1$[1] through transistor N8. $B = \sim1$ turns ON transistor N2, making $D = 0$. Since $D = 0$, C goes from $0 \rightarrow 1$ through transistor P1. Node B is restored to 1 through P6 and P4. In conclusion, all the nodes are updated for write-0 ($A = D = 0$, $B = C = 1$).

2.2   Hold Operation

During hold operation, WL remains low as no read/write operation occurs. The SRAM retains its stored data through negative feedbacks. Assuming the data stored in the SRAM is 1 ($A = D = 1$ and $B = C = 0$). The transistors N1, N4, N6, P2, P3 and P5 are ON, whereas N2, N3, N5, P1, P4 and P6 are OFF, which hold the data stored in the SRAM.

---

[1] ~1-approximate 1, ~0-approximate 0.

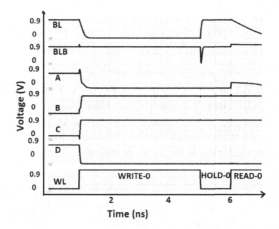

Fig. 2. Simulation results of normal write/read operation of proposed RTQCC-14T SRAM, frequency = 200 MHz, VDD = 0.9 V.

2.3 Read Operation

We have considered the case of reading-0 (A = D = 0 and B = C = 1). BL and BLB (BLB) are first pre-charged to 1 and kept floating. Afterward, WL is made high. Since transistors N3, N5, and N7 are ON, the voltage of BL decreases while the voltage of BLB does not change. The sense amplifier senses the difference between BL and BLB voltage after a specified voltage difference (50 mV) and provides the output. It is clearly seen from the Fig. 2 that the proposed SRAM successfully performs read/write/hold operation. Since proposed SRAM is symmetrical in nature so only one of the operation (read-0, write-0 and hold-0) are illustrated. Read-1, write-1 and hold-1 operation are performed in a similar way by choosing the respective conditions for read-1/write-1/hold-1.

2.4 Self Recovery from SNU

The fault-tolerance principles of the proposed RTQCC-14T cell are described in this subsection. Here, we still consider the case where the cell stores 1 (A = D = 1 and B = C = 0). The proposed design can recover from both SNU and DNU cases illustrated below. First, we discuss the SNU self-recovery principle of the proposed RTQCC-14T cell.

SET at Node C: When SET occurs at node C, C changes from 0 to 1. Transistor P2 gets turned OFF. Since A remains at 1, hence it turns ON transistor N1 and node C gets restored from 1 to 0 through it. The node C self recovers from SNU of any radiation is shown in Fig. 3 (a).

SET at Node D: When SET occurs at node D, D changes from 1 to 0. Transistor P1 gets turned ON, which tries to make C goes from 0 to 1. Since A remains at 1, it turns ON N1, and as transistor N1 is stronger than P1 (N1 > P1), makes C remains at $\sim$0. C = $\sim$0[2] makes D goes from 0 to 1 (P2 = ON). The recovery of node D from SNU of any radiation is being shown in Fig. 3 (b).

SET at Node A: When SET occurs at node A, A changes from 1 to 0. Transistor P6 becomes ON, and N1, N4 become OFF. The nodes B and C do not change due to SET at A. Since voltage of nodes B and C do not change, A is recovered through P3 (C = 0) and P5 (B = 0) transistors. The recovery of node A from SNU of any radiation is being shown in Fig. 3 (c).

SET at Node B: When SET occurs at node B, B changes from 0 to 1. Transistors N2 and N3 get turned ON, whereas transistor P5 remains OFF. As P5 (A = 1) is OFF, node A remains at 1, keeping C = 0. A very high radiation on node B make D goes from 1 to 0 forcing C goes from 0 to 1. Node B also flips node A. The node B self recovers from SNU up-to a very high critical charge of 33 fC.

In conclusion, the proposed RTQCC-14T cell can self-recover from SNUs. It also recovers from DNU at node C and node D.

2.5   Self Recovery from DNU

SET at Node C and Node D: When radiation affects nodes C and D, node C changes from 0 to 1, whereas node D changes from 1 to 0. D = 0 turns ON transistor P1 whereas C = 1 turns OFF the transistor P2. Since A = 1, it turns ON transistor N1, and as N1 > P1, so C goes from 1 to 0. Node C recovers node D through transistor P2 (C = 0) as N2 is OFF (B = 0). In conclusion, all the nodes can self recover after SET on C and D as shown in Fig. 3 (d).[3]

Hence our proposed design can recover from SNUs and DNU (at node C and D). As compared to existing techniques including Quatro-10T and WE-Quatro-12T, where storage node '0' (node B) is directly connected to storage node '1' (node A), an SET on storage node '0' (node B) promptly flips the storage node '1' (node A). Since pull down path of storage node '1' (node A) of our proposed design is disconnected from node B, SNU tolerance of storage node '0' (node B) has been improved. Also as compared to Quatro-10T and WE-Quatro-12T, the critical internal node '1' (node D) has been made radiation immune in our proposed design.

3   Simulation Results and Discussion

This section describes the simulation results of different parameters compared with existing techniques. The proposed SRAM is compared with other existing designs in terms of Read Static Noise Margin (RSNM), Read Access Time

---

[2] $\sim$1-approximate 1, $\sim$0-approximate 0.

[3] $\sim$1-approximate 1, $\sim$0-approximate 0.

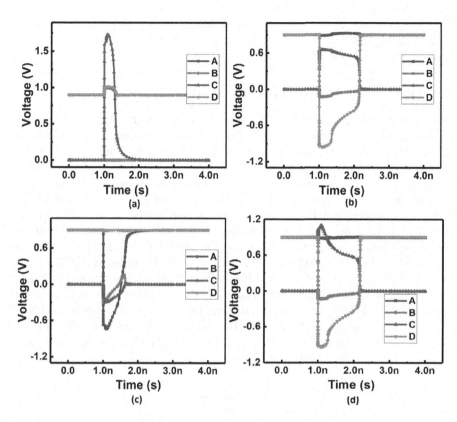

Fig. 3. SNU recovery when (a) SET occurs node C (b) SET occurs at D (c) SET occurs at node A (d) SET occurs at nodes C and D @ VDD = 0.9 V, Technology = 28 nm.

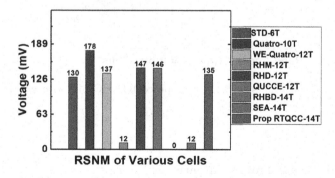

Fig. 4. Comparison results of RSNM of proposed RTQCC-14T SRAM with existing techniques, VDD = 0.9 V, Technology = 28 nm.

(RAT), Wordline Write Trip Voltage (WWTV), Write Access Time (WAT), and leakage power. Schematics of 256 × 64 SRAM array are designed for both proposed and existing techniques and aforementioned parameters are calculated at UMC 28 nm technology, VDD = 0.9 V.

3.1   Read Static Noise Margin Comparisons:

Read Static Noise Margin (RSNM) quantitatively measures the stability of the cell during read operation. The RSNM of various existing and proposed SRAMs are estimated and compared as shown in Fig. 4. RHM-12T and SEA-14T have the negligible RSNMs as logic '1' is not entirely stored. The feedback provided by the logic '1' in the latch-up path is weak, leading to an easy rise up of logic '0' node during the read operation leading to read disturb. The RSNM of RHBD-14T is also negligible since the logic '0' is not completely latched, which makes the connected pull-up transistor in the feedback path weaker, leading to an easy flip of node voltage during the read operation. The QUCCE-12T [16] (Cell Ratio, CR = 2.2) has better RSNM due to higher CR value. Proposed RTQCC-14T has less RSNM than Quatro-10T and WE-Quatro-12T due to the stacked pull-down path which is intentionally used to increase the radiation tolerance. It has an adequate RSNM of 135 mV which is sufficient for proper read operation. RSNM of proposed design outperforms over RHM-12T, Standard-6T (STD-6T), and SEA-14T cells. It has 11.25×, 1.03×, and 11.25× higher RSNM than RHM-12T, STD-6T, and SEA-14T cells respectively.

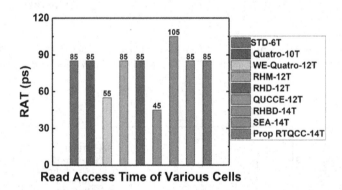

Read Access Time of Various Cells

Fig. 5. Comparison results of RAT of proposed RTQCC-14T with existing works at VDD = 0.9 V, Technology = 28 nm.

3.2   Read Access Time Comparisons

Read Access Time (RAT) is a critical parameter for deciding the speed of operation of SRAM. It is illustrated as the time difference between WL crosses 50% of its full swing and the time required to achieve a 50 mV difference between

BL and BLB [14]. The voltage difference is developed between the bit lines due to the discharge of BL/BLB through access transistor and pull-down transistor; hence, the SRAM cell having a high CR value has less RAT. SRAM arrays of 256 × 64 are designed for both proposed and existing techniques, and RATs are calculated. To have a high fan-out, external capacitances each of 50fF are also added to the BL and BLB respectively. The estimated read access times of various SRAMs are shown in Fig. 5. The RHBD-14T has the highest RAT due to its minimum CR (CR = 1) value. The RAT of RHM-12T (CR = 2.2) and SEA-14T (CR = 2.2) are the same as Quatro-10T (CR = 1.5) despite having a larger CR (CR = 2.2) values. It is because since both RHM-12T and SEA-14T do not entirely restore logic '1', it weakens the pull down transistor connected to it and hence has less read discharge current. WE-Quatro-12T (CR = 1.5) has less RAT than Quatro-10T as it has two additional access transistors for the bit line to discharge. Although nMOS transistors are being stacked in the pull-down path, due to large sized nMOS transistors, the proposed design has similar read discharge current than Quatro-10T cell and hence has similar read access time than Quatro-10T cell. It also has similar RAT than RHM-12T, and RHD-12T respectively. The proposed SRAM has 1.24× shorter read access time than RHBD-14T SRAM and same read access time than STD-6T, Quatro-10T, RHM-12T, and RHD-12T respectively.

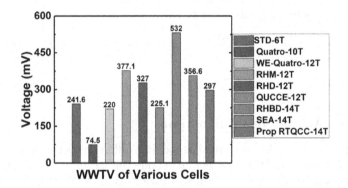

Fig. 6. Comparison results of WWTV of proposed RTQCC-14T SRAM with existing techniques, VDD = 0.9 V, Technology = 28 nm.

3.3   Wordline Write Trip Voltage Comparisons

Wordline Write Trip Voltage (WWTV) quantitatively measures the ease of writing into the SRAM. It is illustrated as the voltage difference between VDD and ramped WL signal at the intersection of node A and node B. WL is slowly ramped from 0 to VDD during write operation. The voltage at which storage node A and B crosses are calculated and subtracted from VDD to calculate the WWTV. The WWTV of various existing and proposed SRAMs are estimated and compared as shown in Fig. 6. RHBD-14T SRAM has the highest WWTV due to weak '0' storage node, which easily flips the node voltage during write operation. Similarly, RHM-12T and SEA-14T have very high WWTV due to the weak '1' storage node. RHD-12T has better WWTV as storage nodes are directly connected to the pull-down path, which helps in writing, unlike the proposed design. The pull-down path of the proposed design is intentionally modified so that the design is more radiation tolerant for storage node B (logic - '0') where node A and B are not directly connected in the proposed design. The proposed RTQCC-14T SRAM has 3.99×, 1.32×, 1.23×, and 1.35× higher WWTV than Quatro-10T, QUCCE-12T, STD-6T, and WE-Quatro-12T respectively.

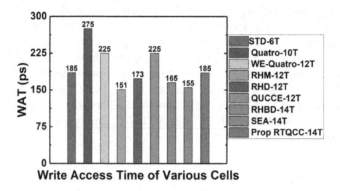

Fig. 7. Comparison results of WAT of proposed RTQCC-14T with existing works at 0.9 V, Technology = 28 nm.

3.4   Write Access Time Comparisons

Write Access Time (WAT) is defined as the time difference between the WL rising 50% of its full swing and the intersection of node voltages A and B. Figure 7 shows the comparison results of WAT values of various cells. WAT mainly depends on three factors: 1. cell ratio (CR), 2. pull-up ratio, and 3. the time required for the feedback path to flip the data. To have less WAT, the pull-up ratio should be large; however, the cell ratio should be small. RHM-12T has the least WAT as node voltage is not fully restored and hence it takes less time to flip the internal nodes of RHM-12T. Also, as three pMOS transistors are stacked in the pull-up path, the internal node voltage of RHM-12T SRAM can be easily disturbed. SEA-14T and RHBD-14T also have less WAT as node voltages are not fully restored and can be easily flipped. Quatro-10T has the highest WAT due to delayed feedback path to flip the storage nodes A and B. WE-Quatro-12T has two additional access transistors, which help write the cell faster and thus has less WAT than Quatro-10T. Proposed SRAM has stacked pMOS transistors (P3, P5) in the pull-up path and stacked nMOS transistors (N3, N5) in the pull down path. Due to the stacking of pMOS transistors (P3, P5) in the pull path, effective resistance of the pull-up path of proposed SRAM increases which favors the write operation and takes less time to perform the write. Hence WAT of the proposed design is less than Quatro-10T, WE-Quatro-12T and QUCCE-12T SRAM cells. Though stacking of nMOS is also done in the pull down path of the proposed cell, it does not contribute much to WAT as nMOS transistors are large sized for proper read operation. The proposed RTQCC-14T SRAM has $1.21\times$, $1.21\times$, and $1.48\times$ shorter write access time than QUCCE-12T, WE-Quatro-12T, and Quatro-10T respectively.

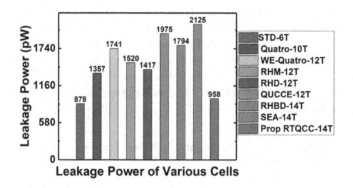

Fig. 8. Comparison results of leakage power per cell of proposed RTQCC-14T with existing works at 0.9 V, Technology $= 28$ nm.

3.5 Leakage Power Comparisons

This section describes the leakage power consumption with existing techniques. Leakage mainly occurs due to bit-line leakage through precharge circuitry and cell leakage into the SRAM. The simulation results are shown in Fig. 8. STD-6T SRAM has less leakage power due to only two VDD to ground paths for cell leakage. Leakage power increases in Quatro-10T due to four VDD to ground paths as compared to STD-6T SRAM. The leakage power of the WE-Quatro-12T cell is even higher than Quatro-10T because of the high bit line leakage through 4 access transistors. SEA-14T has very high leakage. As the nodes are not fully restored, there is huge bit-line leakage through access transistors. The QUCCE-12T has four different pull-up paths to the ground and four access transistors, and hence leakage power is very high due to high cell leakage and bit line leakage. Our proposed design has less cell leakage due to the stacking of both pMOS transistors (P4, P6) and nMOS transistors (N4, N6) in the VDD to ground path and has less bit line leakage through only two access transistors (N8) and stacked pull-down (N4, N6) path. Hence it outperforms existing techniques and has overall the least leakage power (cell leakage + bit line leakage). The proposed cell consumes $1.42\times$, $1.82\times$, $1.59\times$, $1.48\times$, $2.06\times$, $1.87\times$, and $2.22\times$ less leakage power than Quatro-10T, WE-Quatro-12T, RHM-12T, RHD-12T, QUCCE-12T, RHBD-14T, and SEA-14T respectively.

3.6 Soft Error Robustness Analyses and Comparisons

To validate the soft error resilience, a double exponential current pulse is used to analyze the effect of SEU. The double exponential current is represented as follows:

$$I(t) = \frac{Q}{\tau_\alpha - \tau_\beta}(exp(-t/\tau_\alpha) - exp(-t/\tau_\beta)) \tag{1}$$

where Q is the total deposited charge, τ_α represents the collection time constant of the MOSFET junction, and τ_β stands for the time constant for initial ion track establishment [14]. We have considered τ_α and τ_β as 200 ps and 50 ps, respectively [14]. The minimum charge that can flip the node of SRAM is called critical charge (Q_C) of the node. The least Q_C found among the different nodes of SRAM is called effective Q_C. The robustness of the SRAM is measured in terms of effective Q_C. The effective Q_C of existing and proposed SRAM are tabulated in Table 1.

Table 1. Effective critical charge and relative Figure of Merit comparisons, VDD = 0.9 V, Technology = 28 nm.

	Effective Q_C	Relative Figure of Merit
STD-6T	16	0.41
Quatro-10T	17	0.08
WE-Quatro-12T	17	0.27
RHD-12T	28	0.74
QUCCE-12T	35	0.66
Prop RTQCC-14T	33	1

It is clear from the table that our proposed design has better effective Q_C than other existing techniques. RHM-12T and SEA-14T designs have high critical charge values; however, since the RSNM of both the designs are negligible, the designs are not practically feasible. Similarly RHBD-14T ($Q_C = 10$) has very less RSNM (~0), and hence the design is also not practically possible. The effective Q_C of our proposed SRAM is 2.06×, 1.94×, 1.94×, 1.17×, and 3.3× higher than STD-6T, Quatro-10T, WE-Quatro-12T, RHD-12T, and RHBD-14T respectively.

3.7 New Figure of Merit Metric for SRAM

We have compared our proposed design with respect to other existing techniques in terms of various parameters such as RSNM, RAT, WAT, WWTV, and leakage power (LPWR). However, it is less likely to have a design that outperforms all the parameters. Improving one parameter might give trade off in others parameters. For example, since read and write operations of 6T SRAM are conflicting in nature, improving WWTV might deteriorate RSNM. Hence there is a requirement for a new metric that mimics the behavior of all the other parameters. Our design uses the new Figure of Merit metric (FoM), which is defined as:

$$FoM = \frac{Q_C \times WWTV \times RSNM}{LPWR \times WAT \times RAT} \tag{2}$$

The new Figure of Merit (FoM) illustrates the overall performance of the SRAM cell in terms of various parameters. Parameters of SRAM such as Q_C, WWTV, and RSNM should be high, whereas parameters such as LPWR, WAT, and RAT should be low. Hence the FoM of the SRAM should be high. The relative FoMs $\left(\frac{FOM_{Existing\_SRAM}}{FOM_{Proposed\_SRAM}}\right)$ of various SRAMs are reported in the Table 1. It is clearly seen from the Table that our proposed RTQCC-14T SRAM has better relative FoM than other existing techniques.

4 Conclusions

This paper proposed a Radiation Tolerant Quadruple Cross Coupled 14T SRAM for radiation environments. The proposed design has least leakage power than the existing SRAM. It has an adequately high read static noise margin and write noise margin. Also, the proposed design has lower read access time and write access time than most existing techniques. The proposed RTQCC-14T SRAM can recover all the possible SNU making it suitable for space applications.

Acknowledgements. This work is supported through grants received from Science and Engineering Research Board (SERB), Government of India, under CRG/2018/005013, MTR/2019/001605, and SPR/2020/000450.

References

1. Baumann, R.C.: Soft errors in advanced semiconductor devices-Part I: the three radiation sources. IEEE Trans. Dev. Mater. Reliab. **1**(1), 17–22 (2001)
2. Jahinuzzaman, S.M., Rennie, D.J., Sachdev, M.: A soft error tolerant 10T SRAM bit-cell with differential read capability. IEEE Trans. Nucl. Sci. **56**(6), 3768–3773 (2009)
3. Velazco, R., et al.: SEU-hardened storage cell validation using a pulsed laser. IEEE Trans. Nucl. Sci. **43**(6), 2843–2848 (1996)
4. Calin, T., Nicolaidis, M., Velazco, R.: Upset hardened memory design for submicron CMOS technology. IEEE Trans. Nucl. Sci. **43**(6), 2874–2878 (1996)
5. Amusan, O.A., et al.: Single event upsets in deep-submicrometer technologies due to charge sharing. IEEE Trans. Dev. Mater. Reliab. **8**(3), 582–589 (2008)
6. Qi, C., Xiao, L., Wang, T., Li, J., Li, L.: A highly reliable memory cell design combined with layout-level approach to tolerant single-event upsets. IEEE Trans. Dev. Mater. Reliab. **16**(3), 388–395 (2016)
7. Guo, J., Xiao, L., Mao, Z.: Novel low-power and highly reliable radiation hardened memory cell for 65 nm CMOS technology. IEEE Trans. Circuits Syst. I Regul. Pap. **61**(7), 1994–2001 (2014)

8. Jung, I.-S., Kim, Y.-B., Lombardi, F.: A novel sort error hardened 10T SRAM cells for low voltage operation. In: 2012 IEEE 55th International Midwest Symposium on Circuits and Systems (MWSCAS), pp. 714–717. IEEE (2012)

9. Peng, C., et al.: Radiation-hardened 14T SRAM bitcell with speed and power optimized for space application. IEEE Trans. Very Large Scale Integr. (VLSI) Syst. **27**(2), 407–415 (2018)

10. Kim, J.S., Chang, I.J., et al.: We-Quatro: radiation-hardened SRAM cell with parametric process variation tolerance. IEEE Trans. Nucl. Sci. **64**(9), 2489–2496 (2017)

11. Chen, J., Chen, S., Liang, B., Liu, B.: Simulation study of the layout technique for P-hit single-event transient mitigation via the source isolation. IEEE Trans. Dev. Mater. Reliab. **12**(2), 501–509 (2012)

12. Li, H., Xiao, L., Qi, C., Li, J.: Design of high-reliability memory cell to mitigate single event multiple node upsets. IEEE Trans. Circuits Syst. I Regul. Pap. **68**(10), 4170–4181 (2021)

13. Han, Y., et al.: Radiation hardened 12T SRAM with crossbar-based peripheral circuit in 28 nm CMOS technology. IEEE Trans. Circuits Syst. I Regul. Pap. **68**(7), 2962–2975 (2021)

14. Pal, S., Mohapatra, S., Ki, W.-H., Islam, A.: Design of soft-error-aware SRAM with multi-node upset recovery for aerospace applications. IEEE Trans. Circuits Syst. I Regul. Pap. **68**(6), 2470–2480 (2021)

15. Prasad, G., Mandi, B.C., Ali, M.: Power optimized SRAM cell with high radiation hardened for aerospace applications. Microelectron. J. **103**, 104843 (2020)

16. Jiang, J., Yiran, X., Zhu, W., Xiao, J., Zou, S.: Quadruple cross-coupled latch-based 10T and 12T SRAM bit-cell designs for highly reliable terrestrial applications. IEEE Trans. Circuits Syst. I Regul. Pap. **66**(3), 967–977 (2018)

Disrupting Low-Write-Energy vs. Fast-Read Dilemma in RRAM to Enable L1 Instruction Cache

Ashwin Lele[1], Srivatsava Jandhyala[2], Saurabh Gangurde[1],
Virendra Singh[1], Sreenivas Subramoney[2], and Udayan Ganguly[1]

[1] Indian Institute of Technology Bombay, Mumbai, India
udayan@ee.iitb.ac.in
[2] Processor Architecture Research Lab, Intel Labs, Bangalore, India

Abstract. RRAM has emerged as a non-volatile and denser alternative to SRAM memory. Various RRAMs show a range of write energies related to write currents. The write current magnitude is proportional to the read current magnitude, which is inversely related to the read latency. Hence, lower write energy leads to higher read latency - producing a fundamental trade-off. This trade-off leads to a fast-read vs. low write power dilemma, hindering the application of RRAM to lower level cache. In this work, we propose a modified bitcell design to overcome this and analyze its impact on L1 instruction cache replacement. We propose a modification in conventional one selection transistor (1T) and RRAM (1R) based 1T1R cell by adding another transistor (i.e. 2T1R cell) to drive high current for fast read irrespective of the RRAM current magnitude. We demonstrate that the read latency vs. write energy trade-off is mitigated using circuit simulations. The impact of the 2T1R bit cell for a fast read and slow write is compared with SRAM and 1T1R scheme for L1 cache replacement. We report an energy-delay product (EDP) reduction of 82% for high performance and 53% for embedded architecture with SRAM comparable throughput. Thus, the fast read capability establishes the potential of RRAM as a lower-level cache substitute for both high performance and embedded applications.

Keywords: Memristors · Crossbar array · Instruction cache · Level-1 Cache · Non-volatile Memory (NVM)

RRAM memory systems have been demonstrated to have low switching power [23], and higher density [29] compared to regular 6T-SRAM cells. Fabrication of large arrays [7,8,19] along with integration in CMOS process flow affirm its potential at industry scale [14,26]. RRAMs also show an additional power advantage with their non-volatility, where the crossbar array can be isolated from the power source when not in use, thus saving power [24]. However, the application of RRAMs as cache substitutes as an alternative to SRAM has been restricted because of the high latencies [17]. RRAM shows long write times (10–100 ns)

© The Author(s), under exclusive license to Springer Nature Switzerland AG 2022
A. P. Shah et al. (Eds.): VDAT 2022, CCIS 1687, pp. 499–512, 2022.
https://doi.org/10.1007/978-3-031-21514-8_41

limiting their performance in programs requiring frequent and fast write operations [11,16]. Additionally, fabricated large arrays have shown high read latencies [7,8,19].

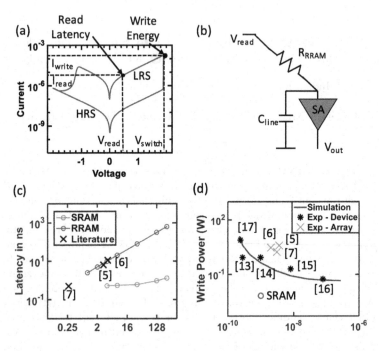

Fig. 1. (a) RRAM IV curve generated using model [9] (b) Circuit configuration in reading requires charging of line capacitance through RRAM (c) Size dependence of read latency of SRAM and RRAM with increasing array size. RRAM can be seen to have significantly higher latency compared to SRAM. SRAM latencies are extracted using CACTI while, for RRAM, capacitance charge time is calculated as a function of the array size (d) write energy vs. read latency trade-off for different RRAM resistance values. The simulation curve assumes write latency of 10 ns

The prior exploration for using RRAM for memory application can be seen to leverage its key density advantages [2]. Specifically, RRAM is attractive for L2-L4 cache from an area and energy perspective for a small penalty in performance. Thus, RRAMs have mostly been used as last-level caches [6,20,30] and main memory [18] due to their greater tolerance for higher latencies. However, L1 cache read latency requirements are more stringent. Reducing latency becomes an important requirement for the application of RRAMs in lower level caches. L1 instruction cache has a fast read requirement but has fewer write operations - which is an excellent application to benchmark fast reading in RRAM to the conventional SRAM.

Typical RRAM characteristics (Fig. 1(a)) show that read and write currents are of similar magnitude. The reduction in write current to reduce write energy produces a reduction in read current. The lower read current needs a longer timescale to charge up the line capacitance (C_{line}) to enable the sense amplifier to read (Fig. 1(b)). Naturally, the larger arrays have a larger read latency as C_{line} increases with array size, which is consistent with literature [8,19]. The read latency with the scaling of array size is shown in Fig. 1(c) for both SRAM and RRAM, where RRAM can be seen to have significantly higher read latency. Thus, write energy vs. read latency trade-off is observed in RRAMs based on literature [10,22,23,25,28]. Usage of low resistance device for quick reading might seem attractive with resistance values reported for RRAMs in the literature varying 3 orders of magnitude ($10k\Omega$-$10M\Omega$) [10,22,23,25,28]. However, these high current devices increase the energy consumption in the array proportional to the current values, which makes competition with SRAM difficult (Fig. 1(d). Thus, attractive RRAM with low write energy and low read latency is forbidden by the write energy vs. read latency trade-off.

In this paper, we present a bitcell design to mitigate the write energy vs. read latency trade-off and evaluate its impact on instruction cache level performance. First, we present a modified 2T1R bitcell by adding 1 NMOS transistor to the conventional select transistor (1T) and RRAM (1R) based 1T1R bitcell to produce a high read-current. Second, we show that our proposal 'breaks' the write energy vs. read latency trade-off at the cost of the increased bitcell area. Third, we analyze the effect at the architectural level for instruction cache replacement by comparing our proposal with conventional 1T1R bitcell and SRAM in terms of improved energy-delay-product (EDP) for both high performance and embedded processor configuration.

1   Proposal

1.1   Fast Read Solution

Figure 2(a–c) shows bitcells for SRAM and RRAM schemes. An NMOS (1T) is used to select an RRAM (1R) for reading/writing to define the conventional 1T1R bitcell [15]. The read-write scheme is taken from [29]. We propose that the voltage ($V_{read-select}$) between 1T and 1R devices on the 1T1R is applied on the gate of an NMOS transistor to form the 2T1R bitcell as shown in Fig. 2(c). The drain and source of read transistor are connected to another bit and word line. This modification makes the read transistor supply the read current that charges the line capacitance to the sense amplifier instead of the RRAM current. Thus, the read transistor can be independently designed for a fast read, while the resistance of the RRAM can be increased for low energy to disable the write energy vs. read latency trade-off.

Array level schematics of these bitcells are shown in Fig. 2(d–f). The conventional 1T1R scheme has one bitcell at the intersection of a cross-bars with two wordlines and a bitline. One complimentary pass transistor switch performs as a row selector (RS) to apply different voltages for reading and writing. A select line turns the select transistors on when a row is to be read or written. The bitline connects the bitcell to the sense amplifier through a column selector

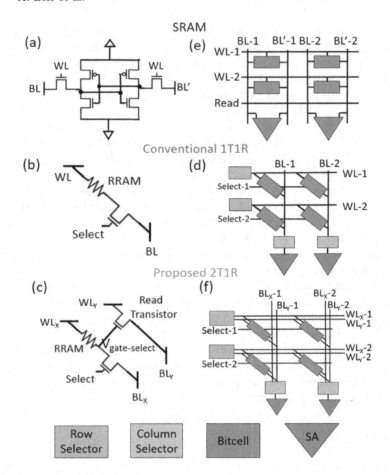

Fig. 2. Bitcells for (a) SRAM (b) conventional 1T1R and (c) proposed 2T1R scheme. (d–f) Array level schematics for these schemes. (g) Schematic for architecture level evaluation where smaller RRAM bitcell area accommodates more memory

(CS) while reading. The proposed scheme requires one pair of additional word-line and bitline connecting the source and drain of the read transistor as shown in Fig. 2(f).

1.2 Targeted Application

Fast reading achieved by the proposed scheme is tested for L1 instruction cache replacement as it requires infrequent writing and frequent reading instances. This produces an aggressive read latency requirement but is tolerant to slow writing. We exploit the area advantage offered by RRAM to accommodate higher memory size in the same area. Thus, we intend to compensate for the high write latency of RRAM using a higher memory size (Fig. 3) - so that the larger cache enables less data miss in L1 to cause a data fetch from L2 and thereby reduce the frequency

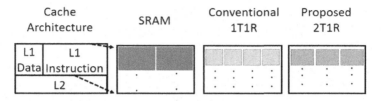

Fig. 3. Cache memory schematic with RRAM accommodating more memory in the same area compared to SRAM. This area advantage along with fast read capability is to be examined for potential of RRAM as L1 instruction cache substitute

of write operations. We study the performance of the proposed scheme (2T1R) for both high-performance and embedded architectures.

2 New Read Scheme

2.1 Circuit Schematic

Figure 4 shows circuit schematics for both RRAM schemes in the reading configuration. For the conventional 1T1R scheme, V_{read} is applied through the RS switch at wordline and CS is grounded as shown. The voltage gets divided across the RRAM and R_{CS} and is sensed by the sense amplifier (SA) [27]. C_{line} denotes the line capacitance to be charged by RRAM read current. This sets the charge-up time. The proposed scheme has similar reading configurations with RS and CS driving two word and bitlines to voltages shown. The select transistor is biased at $V_{read-select}$, which acts as a resistive voltage divider to produce a voltage ($V_{gate-select}$), which drives the read transistor. Read transistor allows high current flow charging the line capacitance (C_{line}) and SA_{in} terminal. A diode-connected transistor in CS (drain shorted to the gate) acts as a current to voltage converter to drive the SA.

In this scheme, the RRAM resistance charges primarily the 'small' gate capacitance of the read transistor, while the read transistor charges the substantial line capacitance. The approximate time constants of charging show the 1T1R scheme charging the line capacitance ($\sim$10 fF) while the proposed scheme charging the small gate capacitance ($\sim$0.1 fF) resulting in faster reading (Fig. 5).

2.2 Maximizing Sense Margin

Choosing the $V_{read-select}$ determines the gate voltage for read transistor. We use Verilog-A RRAM model [9] and 45nm CMOS technology [31] for HSPICE simulations of circuits. From the vast range of resistances reported in the literature, we consider the case of a high resistance RRAM with a low resistance state (LRS) = 1 MΩ and high resistance state (HRS) = 10 MΩ as described in Fig. 6. We fix the R_{RRAM} and vary $V_{read-select}$. The task is to create a maximum voltage difference at the input of the SA for the given LRS and HRS. For this choice

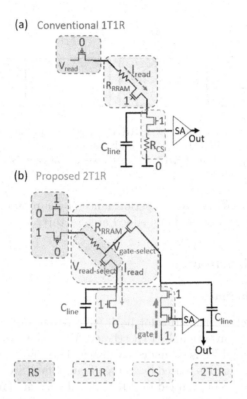

Fig. 4. Circuit schematic in reading for the (a) conventional 1T1R and (b) proposed 2T1R schemes. Additional read transistor in 2T1R scheme provides high current path for read current demonstrating quick reading

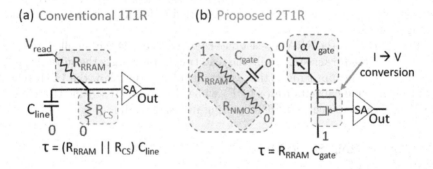

Fig. 5. Equivalent circuits for (a) conventional 1T1R and (b) proposed 2T1R schemes. The decrease in time constant is because of reduction in load capacitance to be charged

of RRAM resistances, $V_{read-select}$ of 280 mV turns on for LRS and remains off for HRS (Fig. 6(b)). The read current, therefore, shows the maximum difference (Fig. 6(c)) for the two resistances. The read current is converted to voltage and applied to the input of SA shown in Fig. 6(d) to give the maximum sense margin.

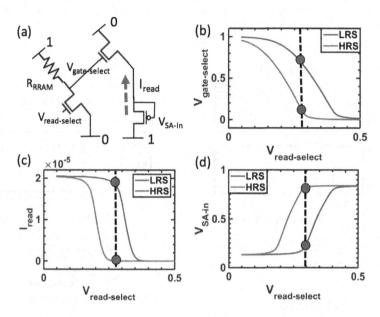

Fig. 6. Dependence of (a) $V_{gate-select}$ (b) I_{read} (c) V_{SA-in} on $V_{read-select}$. $V_{read-select} = 0.28$ is selected to maximize the swing at the input of the SA

2.3 Breaking the Trade-off

Figure 7(a) shows the timing diagrams for reading in both the 1T1R and 2T1R schemes for the device. The RRAM switching voltage of 0.8 V is assumed, given a range of switching voltages (0.2–4 V) reported in the literature [10,22,23,25,28]. The array size of 256 × 64 is taken for calculating the line capacitance. The line capacitance of 15.07 fF is calculated using the 45 nm interconnect technology manual [21].

The voltage at the input terminal of the SA is shown for both schemes along with the output of the SA in Fig. 7(a). The conventional scheme requires more than 2 ns for the SA_{in} to charge up and the SA output to respond. On the other hand, the proposed scheme charges the SA input terminal quickly in less than a nanosecond response time. Figure 7(b) shows the response time of SA output increases with device LRS resistance with a fixed LRS/HRS ratio. The read time drastically increases with an increase in device resistance for the 1T1R scheme. In comparison, the proposed bitcell does not show degradation of latency with

R_{LRS} to enable fast read (<1 ns) even with high resistance devices. However, for very large resistance (100 MΩ) the performance of the proposed scheme degrades because the extreme low RRAM currents take a long time to charge the gate capacitance of the read transistor. Figure 7(c) shows the reduced read latency with the proposed scheme for various RRAM resistances. The circuit consumes comparable write energy as the previous scheme with much lower read latencies thus, breaking the trade-off (Fig. 7(d)).

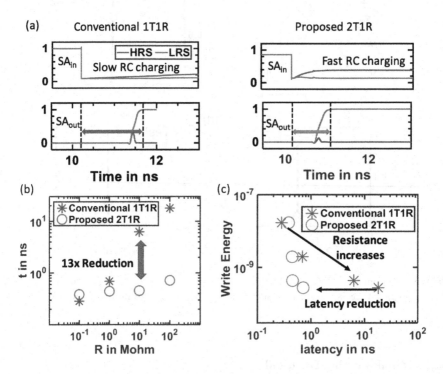

Fig. 7. (a) Faster RC charging in the proposed scheme improves the response time (b) Read latency increases with the LRS resistance keeping HRS/LRS constant. The read latency degradation is mitigated by the proposed 2T1R scheme. (c) Isolating the RRAM from the critical read path decouples the read and write current paths breaking the write energy vs read latency trade-off

3   Architecture Level Performance Estimation

Figure 8 shows the bank schematics for SRAM and RRAM memory banks. The components are briefly divided into 4 categories which are colour coded as shown. Same CMOS peripheral components are used in both cases. The components specific to one of the schemes are shown in blue colour. SRAM bank of 16 × 8 size is simulated using NCSU SRAM compiler [13] in 45 nm technology [31].

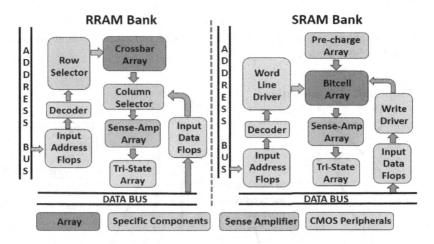

Fig. 8. Memory banks for SRAM and RRAM with components colour coded (Color figure online)

RRAM bank of the same size is also simulated in HSPICE. The energies are calculated and scaled for the array size of 256×64. The comparison of area and energy between the conventional and proposed schemes is explained next.

3.1 Energy

Both RRAM and SRAM arrays are simulated in HSPICE and instantaneous power is recorded for each component. The total energy consumed in the writing or reading cycle is calculated. For the RRAM array, the devices are made to switch from LRS to HRS for the calculation of write energy while energy spent in reading a device in LRS is taken as read energy. The write latency is assumed to be 10 ns and read latency is taken to be 1 ns. The standby (SB) energy is calculated by turning the RS and CS off and isolating the array from the power source. For SRAM, all bits are programmed in state 0 and are made to flip in extracting write energy consumption. These energy per cycle values are used in architectural simulations to calculate the total energy consumed. Component-wise write, read and standby energies consumed by SRAM and RRAM banks are shown in Fig. 9(a).

RRAM consumes significantly more energy than SRAM during write mode because of long times scales. This makes the reduction in write energy important by the usage of highly resistive devices. Read energy consumed in RRAM and SRAM is comparable. However, in both reading and writing, the proposed scheme consumes higher energy due to additional transistors present. RRAM specific components (i.e. row/column selectors) consume the major fraction of power in writing, while SA consumes a major fraction of power in reading for RRAMs. In standby mode, SRAM consumes static power, while the RRAM array is disconnected from peripherals by turning off the RS and CS passgate switches. This causes power saving. This results in 20× energy reduction in SB mode. These energy values are used in the cache replacement simulation presented in the next section.

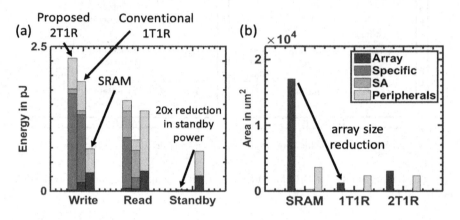

Fig. 9. (a) Energy in SRAM and RRAM banks in different regimes of operation (b) Component wise area consumption in the memory banks

3.2 Area

Figure 9(b) shows area reduction achieved by using RRAM in place of SRAM in the bitcell array. SRAM bitcell area is reported to be $146F^2$ [29] while RRAM 1T1R structure consumes $> 8F^2$ [5]. We assume a conservative estimate of $10F^2$ for 1T1R and $25F^2$ for the 2T1R scheme. Therefore, the area advantage is 14.6× and 5.84× respectively for conventional and proposed schemes. A part of this is taken by the RRAM-specific blocks shown in Fig. 8 like new sense amplifiers and drivers. Thus 1T1R and 2T1R schemes can conservatively pack 8× and 4× more memory compared to SRAM. A more rigorous area estimation can be carried out in the future.

3.3 Cache Replacement

Table I shows the simulation parameters used. We use both high performance (x86) [3] and embedded (ARM) [4] processor architectures to analyze the applicability of this scheme (Fig. 10). We use 10 programs from MiBench benchmark suite [12] for embedded and 10 programs from SPECS benchmark suite [1] for high-performance architecture. 2 kB (256 × 64) memory banks are used as shown in Fig. 10. We choose the L1 instruction cache in HP and L0 instruction cache in embedded processors for replacement with RRAM in gem5 simulations [5].

(a) High Performance (x86)
Intel Haswell

Parameter	Value
L1 Data	32 kB
L1 Instruction	**32 kB**
L2	256 kB
L3	8 MB
Frequency	1 GHz

(b)   Embedded (ARM)
Qualcomm Krait

Parameter	Value
L0 Data	4 kB
L0 Instruction	**4 kB**
L1 Data	16 kB
L1 Instruction	16 kB
L2	1 MB
Frequency	1 GHz

(c)

Parameter	SRAM	Conventional 1T1R	Proposed 2T1R
Size	1×	8×	4×
Write Latency	1 ns	10 ns	10 ns
Read Latency	1 ns	10 ns	1 ns

Fig. 10. Processor configuration in (a) high performance and (b) embedded architectures. (c) Memory specifications for the instruction cache

Throughput. Throughput (instructions per cycle - IPC) for each of the case is extracted from gem5 [5] simulations. Figure 11(a) shows that the conventional 1T1R scheme causes huge degradation in the IPC while the proposed scheme makes it comparable to SRAM with only 0.1% degradation for HP and 1.6% degradation in embedded architecture. This is because the proposed scheme along with faster reading provides a larger memory size which reduces the miss rate, which is defined as the need to request data from the L2 cache to store in the L1 cache. The resultant reduction in high latency write instances due to larger memory size enables improved performance.

Energy. The energy per read/write/SB cycle extracted from Fig. 11(b) is used to calculate the total energy consumption for different benchmark programs. The number of read/write accesses is extracted from the simulations to get the energy spent in reading and writing. During the remaining cycles, the memory consumes standby energy. The normalized energy plot in Fig. 11(b) shows a reduction in energy in both of the RRAM schemes. Mean energy reduction of 81% is observed in HP and 53% for embedded programs. Energy-saving occurs in RRAMs due to a large number of cycles in standby mode as RRAMs have very low SB energy consumption compared to SRAMs.

Energy-Delay Product (EDP). The energy calculated above is used to compare the performance of RRAM and SRAM using EDP defined only for the instruction cache. The delay is defined as the duration for which the cache is active for writing or reading. Mathematically,

$$L1_{delay} = L1_{read\ latency} + L1_{miss\ rate} \times (L1_{write\ latency} + L2_{access\ latency})$$

$$L2_{access\ latency} = L2_{read\ latency} + L2_{miss\ rate} \times (L2_{write\ latency} + L3_{access\ latency})$$

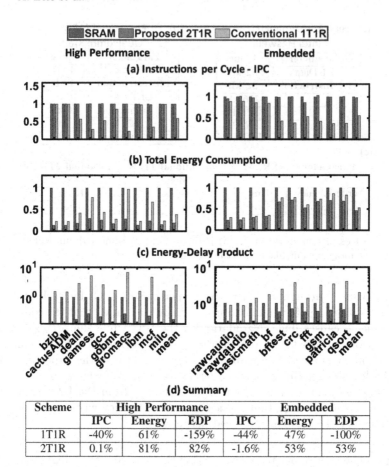

Fig. 11. Comparison of performance parameters for conventional and proposed scheme by normalization with SRAM for high performance x86 architecture (a) Marginal degradation in the mean throughput can be observed compared to baseline SRAM throughput which is attributed to larger memory size with read latency same as that of SRAM (b) RRAM is seen to consume lesser energy for both proposed and conventional schemes (c) Mean energy-delay product reduces by 82% compared to SRAM

Normalized EDP (Fig. 11(c)) reduces by 82% for HP and 53% for embedded processing for the proposed scheme. Table II summarizes the cache replacement results.

4   Conclusion

We proposed a circuit modification in the conventional 1T1R RRAM bitcell to boost the read speed for high resistance devices. This resolves the fast-read vs. low energy dilemma. We analyzed the performance of this fast read based RRAM memory for SRAM replacement at the instruction cache level. EDP reduction of 82% and 53% was observed for x86 and ARM architectures respectively showing the potential of RRAM in lower level caches as a substitute for SRAM. Extensive circuit-level exploration of the variability and reliability of the scheme may be taken up in the near future.

References

1. Benchmarks, s. p. e. c.: Standard performance evaluation corporation (2000)
2. https://web.stanford.edu/bartolo/assets/nvm-cache.pdf
3. https://www.7-cpu.com/cpu/haswell.html
4. https://www.7-cpu.com/cpu/krait.html
5. Binkert, N., et al.: The gem5 simulator. ACM SIGARCH Comput. Archit. News **39**(2), 1–7 (2011)
6. Catanzaro, M., Kudithipudi, D.: Reconfigurable RRAM for LUT logic mapping: a case study for reliability enhancement. In: 2012 IEEE International SOC Conference, pp. 94–99. IEEE (2012)
7. Chang, M.F., et al.: 17.5 a 3T1R nonvolatile TCAM using MLC RaRAM with sub-1ns search time. In: 2015 IEEE International Solid-State Circuits Conference-(ISSCC) Digest of Technical Papers, pp. 1–3. IEEE (2015)
8. Chang, M.F., et al.: 19.4 embedded 1mb ReRAM in 28nm CMOS with 0.27-to-1v read using swing-sample-and-couple sense amplifier and self-boost-write-termination scheme. In: 2014 IEEE International Solid-State Circuits Conference Digest of Technical Papers (ISSCC), pp. 332–333. IEEE (2014)
9. Chen, P.Y., Yu, S.: Compact modeling of RRAM devices and its applications in 1T1R and 1S1R array design. IEEE Trans. Electron Devices **62**(12), 4022–4028 (2015)
10. Cheng, C.H., Chin, A., Yeh, F.: Ultralow switching energy nigeoxhfontan RRAM. IEEE Electron Device Lett. **32**(3), 366–368 (2011)
11. Govoreanu, B., et al.: 10× 10nm 2 Hf/HfO x crossbar resistive RAM with excellent performance, reliability and low-energy operation. In: 2011 International Electron Devices Meeting, pp. 31–6. IEEE (2011)
12. Guthaus, M.R., Ringenberg, J.S., Ernst, D., Austin, T.M., Mudge, T., Brown, R.B.: MiBench: a free, commercially representative embedded benchmark suite. In: Proceedings of the fourth annual IEEE international workshop on workload characterization. WWC-4 (Cat. No. 01EX538). pp. 3–14. IEEE (2001)
13. Guthaus, M.R., Stine, J.E., Ataei, S., Chen, B., Wu, B., Sarwar, M.: OpenRAM: an open-source memory compiler. In: 2016 IEEE/ACM International Conference on Computer-Aided Design (ICCAD), pp. 1–6. IEEE (2016)
14. Hsieh, M.C., et al.: Ultra high density 3D via RRAM in pure 28nm CMOS process. In: 2013 IEEE International Electron Devices Meeting, pp. 10–3. IEEE (2013)
15. Huang, J.J., Tseng, Y.M., Luo, W.C., Hsu, C.W., Hou, T.H.: One selector-one resistor (1S1R) crossbar array for high-density flexible memory applications. In: 2011 International Electron Devices Meeting, pp. 31–7. IEEE (2011)
16. Ielmini, D.: Resistive switching memories based on metal oxides: mechanisms, reliability and scaling. Semicond. Sci. Technol. **31**(6), 063002 (2016)
17. Jokar, M.R., Arjomand, M., Sarbazi-Azad, H.: Sequoia: a high-endurance NVM-based cache architecture. IEEE Trans. Very Large Scale Integr. (VLSI) Syst. **24**(3), 954–967 (2015)

18. Jung, M., Shalf, J., Kandemir, M.: Design of a large-scale storage-class RRAM system. In: Proceedings of the 27th International ACM Conference on International Conference on Supercomputing, pp. 103–114 (2013)

19. Kawahara, A., et al.: An 8 mb multi-layered cross-point ReRAM macro with 443 mb/s write throughput. IEEE J. Solid-State Circuits **48**(1), 178–185 (2012)

20. Kotra, J.B., Arjomand, M., Guttman, D., Kandemir, M.T., Das, C.R.: Re-NUCA: a practical NUCA architecture for ReRAM based last-level caches. In: 2016 IEEE International Parallel and Distributed Processing Symposium (IPDPS), pp. 576–585. IEEE (2016)

21. Kuhn, K., et al.: Managing process variation in Intel's 45nm CMOS technology. Intel Technol. J. **12**(2) (2008)

22. Lashkare, S., Chouhan, S., Chavan, T., Bhat, A., Kumbhare, P., Ganguly, U.: PCMO RRAM for integrate-and-fire neuron in spiking neural networks. IEEE Electron Device Lett. **39**(4), 484–487 (2018)

23. Lee, H., et al.: Low power and high speed bipolar switching with a thin reactive TI buffer layer in robust HfO2 based RRAM. In: 2008 IEEE International Electron Devices Meeting, pp. 1–4. IEEE (2008)

24. Sheu, S.S., et al.: A 5ns fast write multi-level non-volatile 1 k bits RRAM memory with advance write scheme. In: 2009 Symposium on VLSI Circuits, pp. 82–83. IEEE (2009)

25. Shih, C.C., et al.: Ultra-low switching voltage induced by inserting SIO 2 layer in indium-tin-oxide-based resistance random access memory. IEEE Electron Device Lett. **37**(10), 1276–1279 (2016)

26. Wang, C.H., et al.: Three-dimensional 4f 2 ReRAM cell with CMOS logic compatible process. In: 2010 International Electron Devices Meeting, pp. 29–6. IEEE (2010)

27. Wang, Y.T., Razavi, B.: An 8-bit 150-MHz CMOS A/D converter. IEEE J. Solid-State Circuits **35**(3), 308–317 (2000)

28. Wu, Y., Lee, B., Wong, H.S.P.: Ultra-low power al 2 o 3-based RRAM with 1μa reset current. In: Proceedings of 2010 International Symposium on VLSI Technology, System and Application, pp. 136–137. IEEE (2010)

29. Xu, C., Dong, X., Jouppi, N.P., Xie, Y.: Design implications of memristor-based RRAM cross-point structures. In: 2011 Design, Automation and Test in Europe, pp. 1–6. IEEE (2011)

30. Zhang, J., Donofrio, D., Shalf, J., Jung, M.: Integrating 3D resistive memory cache into GPGPU for energy-efficient data processing. In: 2015 International Conference on Parallel Architecture and Compilation (PACT), pp. 496–497. IEEE (2015)

31. Zhao, W., Cao, Y.: New generation of predictive technology model for sub-45 nm early design exploration. IEEE Trans. Electron Devices **53**(11), 2816–2823 (2006)

System Design

Implementation and Analysis of Convolution Image Filtering with RISC-V Based Architecture

M. K. Aparna Nair(✉) ⓘ, Vishwas Vasuki Gautam, Abhishek Revinipati, and J. Soumya

Department of EEE, BITS Pilani-Hyderabad Campus, Hyderabad 500078, India
aparnanairmullachery@gmail.com, soumyaj@hyderabad.bits-pilani.ac.in

Abstract. Convolution image filtering technique has been extensively used in image processing applications for sharpening the image, detecting the edges, blurring the image, noise removal etc. Optimization of the convolution algorithm for execution speed has become crucial as the size of the image increases. Loop unrolling is an optimization technique that is adopted for reducing the execution time of the algorithm by reducing the overheads caused by the loops in the algorithm implementation. RISC-V ISA based processing elements being open source are widely used in academia and industry. Hence, in this paper, we have attempted to implement convolution algorithm sequentially and with loop unrolling technique on a custom-developed RISC-V soft core processor. Further, to enhance the speed of operation, a multiprocessor framework has also been developed with Network-on-Chip based inter-core communication platform. The implemented algorithms are tested with RARS tool at assembly level and with Vivado tool at the architectural level. The architecture is also synthesized and implemented on Kintex FPGA evaluation platform.

Keywords: Image convolution · RISC-V · Multi-core computing · Parallel processing

1 Introduction

Image processing techniques have been widely used in several fields like medical technology, social media, traffic sensing technology, image restoration, etc. Regardless of the fields in which the image processing techniques have been applied, they have shown various benefits like images could be improved for better human interpretation (for example, while interpreting medical/satellite images), images could be stored and retrieved easily, information from the images could be extracted for processing by the machines and many more. Convolution is an image filtering operation that is one of the most used image processing techniques [1]. Various applications of convolution filtering include removal of noise from the image, highlighting the borders of the image, blurring, edge detection,

© The Author(s), under exclusive license to Springer Nature Switzerland AG 2022
A. P. Shah et al. (Eds.): VDAT 2022, CCIS 1687, pp. 515–526, 2022.
https://doi.org/10.1007/978-3-031-21514-8_42

etc. Convolution involves the multiplication and addition of the image pixel values with the coefficients of a filter kernel. Various optimization techniques are applied to the convolution algorithm. Loop unrolling is one of the techniques employed to enhance the execution speed of the convolution algorithm [2,3]. A critical decision has to be made while choosing an Instruction Set Architecture (ISA) for implementing the image processing applications with System-on-Chips (SoCs) [4]. Reduced Instruction Set Computer (RISC)-V is an open-source ISA based on RISC principles and supports several extensions [5]. Choosing RISC-V based ISA over other ISAs is based on the fact that RISC-V allows for the implementation of only the core functionalities while keeping compliance with the standard [6]. Hence the users are free to use their custom modules for implementing the required functionality. The requirement of large loops of multiplications and additions in the implementation of convolution algorithms increases the computational intensity. With the technology scaling, multiple cores could be integrated onto a chip resulting in parallel processing and thereby making efficient computations [7]. In this paper, we have implemented and analyzed the convolution image filtering algorithm in three different ways on a custom RISC-V based processor architecture. Section 2 briefs the prior works in the literature on the implementation of convolution algorithms. Section 3 explains the design considerations and methodology adopted in our work. Experimental procedure/setup and results are detailed in Sect. 4 and Sect. 5 concludes the paper.

2   Literature Review

Several works are published in the literature regarding convolution image filtering. In [8], the authors proposed the design of an FPGA-based 2D convolver as a coprocessor for the TMS320C40 DSP microprocessor. The performance and architectural tradeoffs involved in the design are explored in the paper. The authors in [9] have studied the effect of loop unrolling on the FPGA area, clock speed, and throughput within the architecture. Their results show that inner loop unrolling makes the controllers more complicated compared with the outer loops. Parallel processing of images has gained importance with the increasing image size and also with the video processing applications. The advent of multi-core processors has paved the way for achieving this. In [10], performance evaluations of parallel image convolution have been done. The study has been made on a multi-core computer with Java thread utilities. Real-time image processing using multithreading is studied in [11]. A comparison between the multithread approach and the single thread approach is done by testing the techniques on images of various sizes. A survey of image analysis using a multithread approach is made by the authors in [12]. Authors in [13] proposed a multithread algorithm using the standard OpenMP threading library for parallel processing the image processing computations. In their work, the authors used two Intel multi-core processors. Different implementations of convolution algorithm with single as well as multiple processors are found in the literature. A comparative study on the performance of the algorithm with single/multiple cores is studied. With this background study of optimization of image convolution algorithm for speedup and with the open-source RISC-V ISA based processors, the implementation of the algorithm on RISC-V cores is made as the problem to be studied in our work.

3 Methodology and Design Framework

The methodology adopted in implementing the convolution techniques on RISC-V based cores is explained in this section.

3.1 Convolution

Image convolution is the process in which each pixel of the image is added with its local neighbors weighted by the kernel. Convolution algorithm has been extensively used in image processing for extracting certain characteristics of the image. A pictorial representation of the basic convolution algorithm is depicted in Fig. 1.

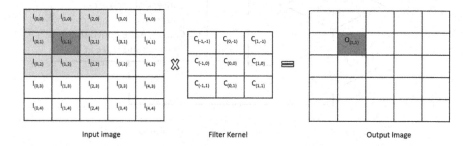

Fig. 1. Basic convolution process for an image filtering

The equation governing the algorithm is

$$O(x,y) = \sum_{i=-\infty}^{\infty} \sum_{j=-\infty}^{\infty} I(x-i, y-j).H(i,j) \tag{1}$$

'O' represents output image, 'I', the input image and 'H' the kernel. The weights of kernel matrix determines the filtering characteristics. Convolution is done on the images by sliding the kernel matrix over the image, multiplying the corresponding elements and adding them. The flowchart given in Fig. 2 shows the convolution for image filtering operation.

It is visible from the flowchart as well as from the convolution equation that there are loops involved in the convolution process. Testing the conditions for loop execution and incrementing the variables every iteration has an overhead. Hence, to optimize the convolution algorithm in terms of execution time, the loop unrolling technique has been adopted. Loop unrolling technique reduces the frequency of branches and loop maintenance instructions.

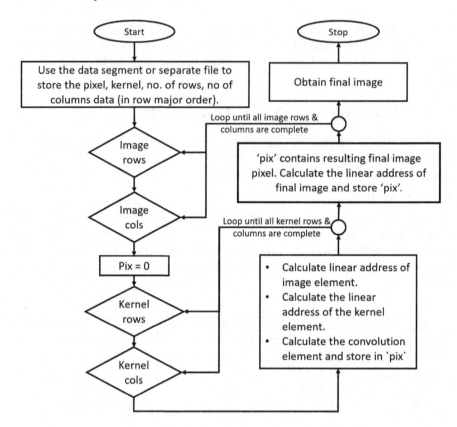

Fig. 2. Flowchart depicting sequential convolution algorithm

3.2   RISC-V Based Processing Element

To validate the algorithm, we have developed a 32-bit RISC-V based soft-core processor as processing element. The implemented RISC-V based core has a five-stage pipelined architecture and supports integer instruction set and multiplication extension. The core has an Arithmetic and Logic Unit (ALU) and a multiplication/division unit which are used for the execution of the convolution algorithm. A separate data and instruction memory are used along with the core.

3.3   Parallel Processing

The execution time of convolution image filtering can be further improved with a parallel processing approach. Figure 3 shows the block diagram representation of the convolution approach in multiprocessor environment.

Since each pixel in an image is treated individually, the input image can be divided into sub-images and each sub-image is processed separately by multiple processors. This approach enables processing of multiple pixels simultaneously.

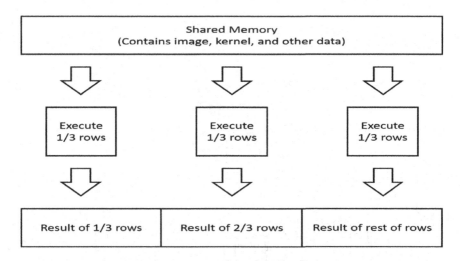

Fig. 3. Convolution approach in multiprocessor environment

The images are divided into three parts horizontally in our methodology. Each part is then sent to the RISC-V core for parallel computation of the convolution algorithm on them and the convolved image pixels are collected back at the shared memory to retrieve the final result.

3.4   Network-on-Chip Router

As the number of processing elements/cores increase on the chip, the performance of bus-based communication system has started degrading. A router-based communication paradigm, Network-on-Chip/NoC [14] has been introduced as a solution for efficient communication in a multiprocessor environment. The router used in our design has five links for connecting with the adjacent routers (global links) and the processing elements (local links). Four virtual channels are used in the router design and follow Y-X algorithm for routing the data from source to destination. Virtual Channel Allocator and Switch Allocator at the output link help in outputting data from the current router to the downstream router. We have used the router architecture from [15] in our work. A Network Interface (NI) interfaces the RISC-V core with the NoC router. The data conversion between the core and router and synchronization is taken care of by the NI. Figure 4 shows a 2×2 mesh NoC with RISC-V cores and NI developed for our studies.

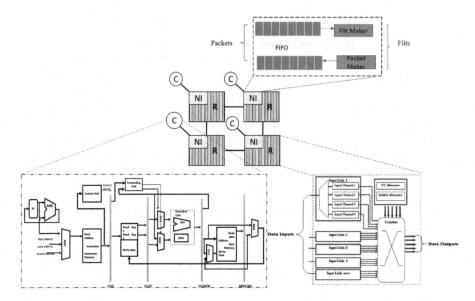

Fig. 4. A complete architectural framework of RISC-V-NoC to run convolution algorithm

4   Experimental Setup and Results

The procedure for implementing the convolution algorithm, the software tools/hardware, and the experimental results are discussed in this section.

4.1   Experimental Setup/Procedure

The initial phase in the experimental procedure is to develop RISC-V ISA based assembly code for the convolution algorithm i) sequentially ii) with loop unrolling and iii) parallel programming. RISC-V Assembler and Runtime Simulator (RARS) [16] is used in the assembling and running of the developed codes. In the second phase, hardware implementation of RISC-V framework with NoC-based inter-core communication is developed for the validation of the algorithm on FPGA. 32-bit RISC-V core, NI, and NoC router are developed in Verilog Hardware Description Language (HDL) [17] and a 2×2 mesh topology is implemented for the multiprocessor environment. Xilinx Vivado 2016.2 [18] is the simulator used for verifying the convolution algorithm on the framework. A single core is used for the initial verification of sequential and loop unrolled algorithms for convolution. Further, the design is synthesized on Kintex [19] FPGA evaluation platform.

Procedure

– Both black and white image and RGB colored image are considered for the testing purpose.

- The image features like size of the image and pixel values are extracted from the input image using Python script. The script also does the zero padding to all the edge pixels to avoid loss of information after convolution.
- The extracted contents are written to the data segment of the RISC-V assembly code by the script. Kernel size is also written to the data memory.
- The assembly code written is then run with RARS - RISC-V Assembler and Runtime Simulator and the results of the convolution are stored in the data segment and converted to a text file using Python to get back the resulting image.
- The instruction codes obtained from the RARS are then stored in the instruction memory of the RISC-V architecture developed in Verilog Hardware Description Language (HDL) [17] to validate on FPGA.

4.2 Results and Discussion

The assembly code written in RISC-V assembly is assembled in the RARS [16] simulator to verify the algorithm. A test input and kernel function are taken for the verification of the algorithm as shown below. 'x' operator represents the convolution operation here.

$$
\begin{bmatrix}
0 & 0 & 0 & 0 & 0 \\
0 & 12 & 2 & 19 & 0 \\
0 & 7 & 10 & 11 & 0 \\
0 & 45 & 68 & 21 & 0 \\
0 & 0 & 0 & 0 & 0
\end{bmatrix}
\times
\begin{bmatrix}
0 & -1 & 0 \\
-1 & 5 & -1 \\
0 & -1 & 0
\end{bmatrix}
=
\begin{bmatrix}
51 & 0 & 82 \\
0 & 0 & 5 \\
150 & 255 & 26
\end{bmatrix}
$$

Figure 5 shows a part of the convolution code and the above-provided results verified with the RARS tool. Both the sequential convolution algorithm (Fig. 5(a)) and the convolution with loop unrolled technique (Fig. 5(b)) are depicted in Fig. 5. The text segment seen in the figure represents the segment where the assembly code is written. The instruction code corresponding to each assembly instruction is also shown in the text segment. The data segment represents the data memory where the input values of image pixels/test inputs are stored. After the convolution process, each pixel value/test input is updated and stored

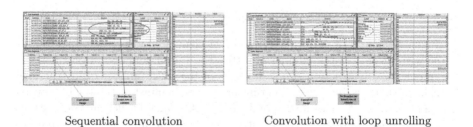

Sequential convolution   Convolution with loop unrolling

Fig. 5. Assembly code and simulated results for convolution with RARS tool

linearly in the data segment address locations. The status of various registers used in the program is also seen next to the text segment. The updated memory locations and the changes in the code for implementing loop unrolled technique compared with the sequential technique are highlighted in Fig. 6. Both sequential convolution and loop unrolled techniques provide the same result. However, the advantages of the loop unrolled technique over convolution are discussed later in this section.

Lena image is given as a test input to the developed assembly code to further verify the algorithm. The experimental results show that the algorithm works well with both black and white image as well as RGB image. Figure 6 and Fig. 7 show the results of the sharpening filter operation done on Lena image in black and white as well as RGB.

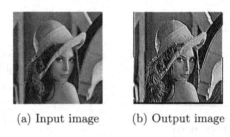

(a) Input image   (b) Output image

Fig. 6. Application of sharpening filter on black and white Lena image

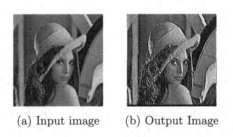

(a) Input image   (b) Output Image

Fig. 7. Application of sharpening filter on RGB Lena image

Figure 8 shows the performance of the implemented algorithms that is evaluated with respect to the number of instructions used, and execution time. The parameters like instruction count in terms of the total number of instructions, branch instructions, and execution time are plotted against increasing bandwidth size. The total number of instructions and particularly branch instructions are lesser when convolution is implemented with loop unrolling. Since the number of branch instructions is reduced, an improvement in the overhead due to loops could be obtained.

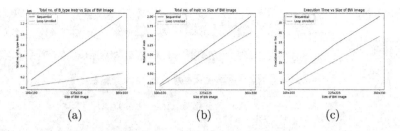

(a)   (b)   (c)

Fig. 8. Performance evaluation of the convolution algorithm in terms of number of instructions and execution time (a) Total number of branch instructions vs Size (b) Total number of instructions vs Size (c) Execution time vs size

A comparison is made between the performance parameters of the convolution algorithm implemented sequentially, with loop unrolled technique, and with multiple cores. The results of the comparison are updated in Table 1.

Table 1. Performance parameters of convolution algorithm implemented in three different ways with an input image of size 300×300

Performance parameters	Sequential convolution	With loop unrolling	Parallel processing
Total instruction count	28859399	24653831	8082688
Execution time (seconds)	51	43	14
Branch instructions	1665003	613611	201084

It can be seen from the table that the number of branch instructions has reduced drastically with the loop unrolling optimization technique. This has caused a reduction in execution time. Also, there is a speedup of 3x times with parallel processing compared to the single sequential convolution approach. Since we have used three processors for parallel processing there is an improvement of 3x in the execution speed. However, if further improvement on execution time is required, the number of processors can be increased provided area and power requirements are met in the design.

Figure 9 shows the simulation results for the convolution algorithm implemented on the developed Verilog HDL based RISC-V core with single core architecture. However, we have implemented the algorithm on multicore architecture as well on a 2×2 mesh NoC platform. Three cores are taken for parallel processing of the image input and a fourth processing element is connected to the NoC router as memory element to collect the processed image pixels. The simulation results show the instruction codes which were stored in the instruction memory obtained from the RARS [16] tool, and also the memory locations. To compare the results with the results obtained from RARS [16] tool, the same input values are stored in the data memory of the RISC-V architecture. It is observed from the simulation results that after the execution of the instruction codes, memory values are updated. The updated memory values are exactly same as the

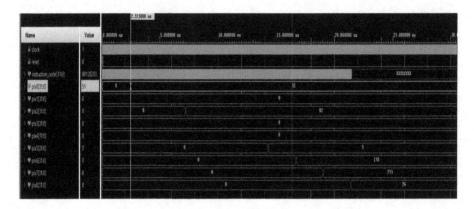

Fig. 9. Behavioural simulation of sequential convolution algorithm implemented on single core RISC-V architecture

results with RARS [16] tool as with which we could verify the functionality of the implemented RISC-V core. After the behavioral simulations are done, the developed architecture is synthesized and implemented on Kintex-7 KC705 Evaluation Platform (xc7k325tffq900-2) [19] and the resource utilization and power consumption are reported. The reported values are tabulated in Table 2. As the number of cores increase more resources are utilized. However, parallel processing is advisable for improving the execution speed of the algorithm provided the design constraints in terms of area or power are met.

Table 2. Performance parameters of single core and multi-core implementation in terms of resource utilization and on-chip power

Performance parameters		Single-core	Multi-core
Resource utilization (%)	LUT	7.66	28.92
	LUTRAM	0.04	2.15
	FF	1.41	4.42
	DSP	1.43	4.29
	IO	0.40	0.40
	BUFG	18.75	50.00
	MMCM	10.00	10.00
On-chip power (W)		0.426	0.618

5   Conclusion

This paper studies the implementation of the convolution algorithm on a RISC-V ISA based processing element. Three different implementations of convolution algorithm for image filtering applications have been studied; sequential implementation followed by employing loop unrolling method and parallel programming for optimizing the execution speed of the algorithm. RISC-V assembly code for all the methods is developed, verified with the RARS tool, and synthesized on FPGA with a RISC-V softcore developed in Verilog HDL. NoC is used as the inter-core communication system. The performance of the algorithm has been evaluated in terms of the number of instructions and execution speed. Also, the developed architecture is analyzed for area in terms of resource utilization and on-chip power. Future works include introducing new techniques for further optimization of convolution algorithm for RISC-V based designs. Also, partitioning the image for multiprocessing and assigning it to the cores is another area to be explored.

References

1. Capobianco, G., et al.: Image convolution: a linear programming approach for filters design. Soft Comput. **25**(14), 8941–8956 (2021). https://doi.org/10.1007/s00500-021-05783-5
2. Toolchain Primer. Power and Performance in Enterprise Systems, pp. 207–239 (2015)
3. Loop unrolling - Wikipedia. https://en.wikipedia.org/wiki/Loop_unrolling
4. Getting started with RISC-V and its Architecture - Softnautics. https://www.softnautics.com/getting-started-with-risc-v-and-its-architecture/
5. Waterman, A., Asanovi'c, K. (eds.): The RISC-V Instruction Set Manual, Volume I: User-Level ISA, Document Version 2.2, RISC-V Foundation (2017). https://riscv.org/wp-content/uploads/2017/05/riscv-spec-v2.2.pdf. Accessed 07 Nov 2021
6. Garcia-Ramirez, R., et al.: Siwa: a RISC-V RV32I based micro-controller for implantable medical applications. In: 2020 IEEE 11th Latin American Symposium on Circuits and Systems, LASCAS 2020, February 2020
7. Bilbao-Castro, J.R., Martínez, J.A., Baldó, J.I.A.: Multicore computing. In: Dubitzky, W., Wolkenhauer, O., Cho, K.H., Yokota, H. (eds.) Encyclopedia of Systems Biology, pp. 1461–1463. Springer, New York (2013). https://doi.org/10.1007/978-1-4419-9863-7_1000
8. Bosi, B., Bois, G., Savaria, Y.: Reconfigurable pipelined 2-D convolvers for fast digital signal processing. IEEE Trans. Very Large Scale Integr. (VLSI) Syst. **7**(3), 299–308 (1999)
9. Yazhuo, D., Jie, Z., Yong, D., Lin, D., Jinjing, Z.: Impact of loop unrolling on area, throughput and clock frequency for window operations based on a data schedule method. In: Proceedings - 1st International Congress on Image and Signal Processing, CISP 2008, vol. 1, pp. 641–645 (2008)
10. Akgün, D.: Performance evaluations for parallel image filter on multi - core computer using Java threads. Int. J. Comput. Appl. **74**(11), 13–19 (2013)
11. Samyan, Q.W., Sahar, W., Talha, W., Aslam, M., Martinez-Enriquez, A.M.: Real time digital image processing using point operations in multithreaded systems. Proceedings - 14th Mexican International Conference on Artificial Intelligence: Advances in Artificial Intelligence, MICAI 2015, pp. 52–57, March 2016
12. Pour, E.S.H.: A survey of multithreading image analysis, June 2015. http://arxiv.org/abs/1506.04472

13. Zekri, A.S.: Multi-threaded computation of the Sobel image gradient on intel multi-core processors using OpenMP library. Int. J. Comput. Sci. Inf. Technol. **8**(2), 87–100 (2016)
14. Micheli, G.D., Benini, L.: Networks on Chips. Morgan Kaufmann, San Fransisco (2006)
15. Kundu, S., Soumya, J., Chattopadhyay, S.: Design and evaluation of mesh-of-tree based network-on-chip using virtual channel router. Microprocess. Microsyst. **36**(6), 471–488 (2012)
16. RARS RISC-V Simulator [ECEN 323]. http://ecen323wiki.groups.et.byu.net/dokuwiki/doku.php?id=labs:riscv_rars
17. Palnitker, S.: Verilog HDL. Prentice Hall Press, Upper Saddle River (2003)
18. UG973 (v2016.2): Vivado Design Suite User Guide, Xilinx, June 2016
19. Xilinx and Inc.: KC705 Evaluation Board for the Kintex-7 FPGA User Guide. www.xilinx.com

Development of Distributed Controller for Electronic Beam Steering Using Indigenous Rad-Hard ASIC

Ramesh Kumar, Ajay Kumar Singh$^{(\boxtimes)}$, Chiragkumar Patel, S. Vinay Kumar, Himanshu N. Patel, and B. Saravana Kumar

Space Applications Centre, Indian Space Research Organisation, Ahmedabad, India
{rameshkumar,ajaysingh,chiragkumar,vinay,hnpatel,
saravana}@sac.isro.gov.in

Abstract. This paper describes design and development of OBC-2.3 ASIC based Transmit/Receive controller (TRC) Hardware. This digital hardware is used to control T/R Modules (TRM) of Phased Array Antenna for electronic beam steering in RISAT-1A Synthetic Aperture RADAR. TRC is mainly responsible for Phase computation, Temperature compensation, Temperature data linearization, Beam data loading on transmit /receive event at PRF rate, Tele command etc. The beam information is transmitted by payload controller (PLC) to TRC through Tile Control Unit (TCU) using serial interface. Radiation Hardened Indigenous On Board Controller (OBC-2.3) Application Specific Integrated Circuit (ASIC) is the brain of TRC. The mixed signal OBC-2.3 ASIC is based on 8-bit micro-controller soft IP core. It has inbuilt 32-bit IEEE 754 compliant Floating Point Co-processor (FPC), UART, Event Programmable Serial/Parallel Interface (EPSPI), Transmit/Receive module switch control (TRMSW), RS422 and RS485, ADC etc. modules which are required to control T/R modules and its associated circuitry for different imaging operations. TRC operates at 6 MHz clock and consume less than 1 W power. It has been characterized for -15 °C to $+75$ °C operating environment. This paper also includes the development of Bed of nails test fixture for automatic testing and verification of TRC hardware.

Keywords: Transmit Receive controllers (TRC) · ASIC · Synthetic Aperture Radar (SAR) · Electronic beam steering · Floating Point Coprocessor

1 Introduction

Synthetic Aperture Radar (SAR) payload of Radar Imaging Satellite is based on active phased array antenna. It is widely used as imaging satellite due to its capability of electronics beam steering, multi-beam operations, large bandwidth and high efficiency. Electronic beam steering requires real time loading of digital amplitude and phase values to the array of Transmit/Receive Modules (TRMs) on transmit and receive events at PRF rate [1]. There are multiple number of TR modules in the active phased array antenna and each module is controlled by one TRC. The main function of TRC is to load the amplitude

© The Author(s), under exclusive license to Springer Nature Switzerland AG 2022
A. P. Shah et al. (Eds.): VDAT 2022, CCIS 1687, pp. 527–539, 2022.
https://doi.org/10.1007/978-3-031-21514-8_43

and the phase information to the TR-RF modules which are temperature compensated for all the modes of SAR operation. Transmit and the receive parameters are loaded to the TR module at every PRF. The TRC will select between transmit and receive switch as per the requirement and ensures protection to the sensitive parts of the RF modules. The TRC also controls the power supplies of the Transmit and Receive amplifiers.

This paper also describes design & development of indigenous On-Board Controller (OBC-2.3) ASIC to meet the requirements of the control sub-systems of SAR. OBC-2.3 is mixed signal ASIC with 8051 core and floating point co-processor. OBC-2.3 ASIC is the indigenous design of Space Applications Centre (SAC), Ahmedabad and Semi-Conductor Laboratory (SCL), Chandigarh. It has been fabricated at SCL's 180 nm CMOS process. OBC-2.3 ASIC is System on Chip (SoC) implementation optimized for T/R Control (TRC) application.

Section 2 of this paper describes distributed controller hierarchy of SAR payload. Section 3 describes T/R Controller, Section 4 describes OBC-2.3 ASIC and Section 5 describes implementation results and Automation testing by bed of nails test fixture.

2 Distributed Controller Hierarchy

For imaging satellite digital control hierarchy is mission specific and depends upon different factors such as phase array antenna size, power requirement etc. For RISAT-1A SAR, three-level control hierarchy has used to control TR modules as shown in Fig. 1. Payload Controller (PLC) is the central beam controller. PLC controls 12 Tile Control Units (TCU) which is at 2nd level.

Each TCU further controls 24 Transmit/Receive Controller (TRC) which is at 3rd level. Thus, the phased array active antenna has total 288 (12 × 24) TRCs. Communication among distributed controllers is done through RS-422 serial link for better noise immunity. Timing signals used for synchronization and controlling is centrally generated by PLC and routed in parallel from PLC to TRC through TCU along with serial Tele-command line over RS422. Multipoint RS485 bus has been used for health monitoring. TRC has been designed to control TR Modules for H and V polarization.

3 T/R Controller (TRC)

The functional block diagram of T/R Controller is shown in Fig. 2. The main functionality of TRC is to control, coordination and status monitoring of TRiM (T/R integrated Module). TRC has RS-422 interface with TCU for serial command & RS485 for telemetry. TRC also receives timing signal reference from TCU over RS-422 interface. TRC gets analog signal from thermistor of TRiM for temperature compensation. During SAR mode configuration, each TRC receives the beam-forming information from PLC through TCU. TRC loads temperature compensated attenuation and phase values to the TRM during transmit and receive cycles for all the modes of SAR operation. TRC also generates switch control signals for TRM and PCPU.

Techniques used in the software development for TRC as described below-

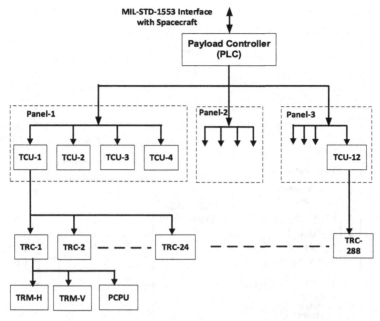

Fig. 1. Distributed Controller hierarchy of RISAT-1A

3.1   Real Time Phase Computation

6-bit digital phase control for TRM is computed using Eq. 1.

$$\text{Phase} = \frac{2\pi}{\lambda} \times K_{el} \times SIN(\theta_{el}) \tag{1}$$

where, K_{el} is elevation position of TRiM based on mounting on phased array antenna and will be stored in EEPROM as a constant. The value of the elevation pointing angle (θ_{el}) is received from PLC through TCU in the range of $-25°$ to $+25°$. Wavelength (λ) is a constant and its value depends upon center frequency which is 5.4 GHz in RISAT-1A. To develop time efficient code, SINE value of pointing angle in elevation direction, received from PLC for each beam is computed by Floating point co-processor instead of standard mathematical library. Taylor series shown in Eq. 2 is used to compute $SIN(\theta_{el})$.

$$SIN(\theta_{el}) = \theta_{el} - \frac{\theta_{el}^3}{3!} + \frac{\theta_{el}^5}{5!} - \ldots \tag{2}$$

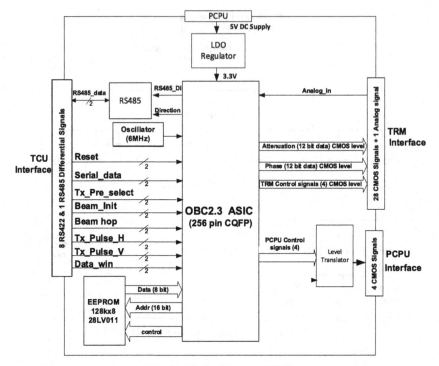

Fig. 2. Block diagram of TRC

3.2 Temperature Linearization

The analog temperature sensed from the thermistor is digitized by inbuilt 8-bit Sigma-Delta ADC of OBC-2.3 ASIC. Third order polynomial Eq. 3 is used to convert 8-bit ADC data into real time temperature.

$$f(x) = ax^3 + bx^2 + cx + d \qquad (3)$$

where a = −0.00026474, b = 0.041108, c = −3.0043 d = 96.8296 and x = ADC count. Coefficients value for polynomial equations are computed using best-fitted curve method using MATLAB tool.

Figure 3 shows actual Temperature Vs ADC reading and best-fitted curve.

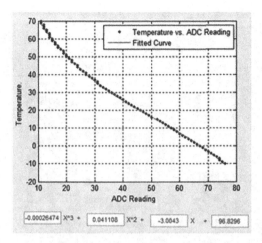

Fig. 3. Curve fitting for temperature linearization

Measurement for characterization has been done in the step of 1 °C for temperature range from −10 °C to +65 °C. Validation of the theoretical best-fit curve equation is also carried out for the same temperature range. Computation time for Eq. 3 using Floating point co-processor is ~180 μs. Temperature compensation is applied when the temperature difference is more than ± 2.5 °C, therefore steps size is 5 °C.

3.3 Temperature Compensation

Real time temperature is used to generate LUT pointer. Equation 4 is used to calculate pointer value for attenuation and phase control of each TRM.

$$\text{Pointer} = \text{Base Add.} + \left[8 * ((\text{Temperature}/\text{Step Size}) + 2)\right] \qquad (4)$$

Pointer is used to access offset values for attenuation and phase controls of each TR Modules. These offset values are added to commanded values for temperature compensation.

3.4 Attenuation and Phase Control Loading for TRM

EPSPI module of OBC2.3 ASIC is utilized for event-based loading of temperature compensated phase and attenuation values for Transmit and Receive events. The transmit and receive control signals for generation of pulsed drain supply of TR module are generated by TRMSW module based on mode of operation. Transmit/Receive (T/R) switches of TR Module is also configured through TRMSW module as per mode of operation.

Fig. 4. RISAT-1A TRC FM photograph

OBC-2.3 ASIC has been mounted on RISAT-1A TRC flight model PCB board as shown in Fig. 4, which is 8-layer PCB having dimensions of 136.2 mm × 98.8 mm × 2 mm. TRC PCB board have 100 Ω impedance lines for the RS422 and RS485 interface and 50 Ω impedance lines for clock signal. RF feeder lines through cutouts from TRM (RF) to TRC and digital interface of TRC in single board makes it mixed signal PCB layout design. Signal and power integrity was carried out to avoid any discontinuity in the flow of signals and power of the design.

The TRC and TR modules (RF) are integrated within a single package in a back-to-back fashion. Cut outs are made in TRC PCB at appropriate places to establish physical connection between the TR modules and the TRC through jumper wires.

4   OBC-2.3 ASIC

Architecture of OBC-2.3 ASIC is shown in Fig. 5. OBC-2.3 ASIC is based on 8 bit DW8051 micro-controller soft core along with 32 bit IEEE STD 754 compliant Floating Point Coprocessor (FPC). Peripherals and FPC are interfaced to DW8051 as a memory mapped I/O and controlled using SFR (Special Function Register). Specifications of OBC-2.3 ASIC is shown in Table 1.

4.1   Digital Modules

The RTL design of OBC-2.3 ASIC has been developed in VHDL. Each module has been verified at module level and then integrated at top level. DW8051 Microcontroller

Table 1. Specifications of OBC-2.3 ASIC

Parameters	Specifications
ASIC Type	Mixed Signal
Process	180 nm CMOS
Foundry	Semi-Conductor Laboratory
Clock Frequency	24 MHz
Supply Voltages	3.3V (1.8V for core is generated by on chip LVR)
Micro-Processor	DW8051
Co-processor	32-bit Floating Point Co-Pprocessor as per IEEE 754
On Chip Memory	1024 × 8 bits SRAM
No of TRM ports	Up to 8 TRM ports (configurable parallel/serial)
UARTs	Total 6 UARTs (1-RS422, 3-CMOS, 2-RS485)
I/Os	178 functional I/Os
Radiation Hardness	Rad Hard by Design (RHBD)
Package	CQFP-256
Power Dissipation	500 mW @ 24 MHz

is 8-bit micro-controller core is complaint to intel MCS-51 instruction set with 4 clocks instruction cycle. Clock & Reset Module generates internal reset which is asserted asynchronously and de-asserted synchronously. Clock divider module divides on chip oscillator clock based on selection on external pins. Watch Dog Timer generates reset/NMI (Non Makeable Interrupt) whenever the software fails to access it within specific time interval. 8 ports of Event Programmable Serial Parallel Interface (EPSPI) module implements 8-bit parallel I/O and in serial mode each port implements 3 wire (clock, strobe, data) SPI interface. TRM Switch Control Module (TRMSW) module generates switch and pulse control signals for TRM (T/R Module) & Power supply sub-systems. Floating Point Coprocessor (FPC) module implements 32-bit floating point (IEEE 754 standard) arithmetic functions like addition, subtraction, multiplication, division, compare etc. [2, 3]. Timing Signal Re-Generator (TSRG) is generic timing signal generator, which can generate up to 8 programmable pulses with ON and OFF programmable duration. There will be total 6 UARTs in OBC-2.3 ASIC, out of which 2 are DW8051 internal UARTs and 4 UARTs are implemented external to DW8051 with feature of noise removal filter for input serial data [4]. Bus Arbitrator module implements bus-arbitration logic to access external program & data memory.

Monitor ROM is used for debug and "in-circuit programming" of EEPROM through UART serial interface when set to high at reset.

4.2 Analog Modules

Standard RS422 and RS485 IP are part of the ASIC for better noise immunity in communications. Power on Reset Generator module will generate low level pulse of 40 us at

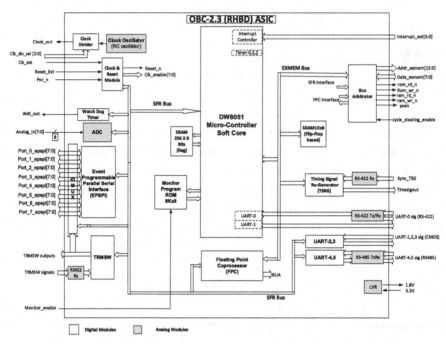

Fig. 5. OBC-2.3 ASIC block diagram

power on to bring the digital module to a known state. A sigma delta type 24-bit ADC having sampling rate of 160 kHz with 8 channel analog mux is used to digitize analog signals. A Linear Voltage Regulator IP is used to generate 1.8V core supply voltage from 3.3 V. It can supply up to 150 mA current. The OBC-2.3 die has been packaged in standard CQFP 256 pin package (Fig. 6).

Fig. 6. Photograph of OBC-2.3 ASIC package & die

5 Testing and Verification

5.1 OBC 2.3 ASIC Functional Verification

Functional verification of OBC-2.3 design has been carried out with DW8051 as a central processor. Individual test benches are developed for all the modules of OBC-2.3 ASIC. Figure 7 shows the block diagram of functional verification environment of OBC-2.3 ASIC.

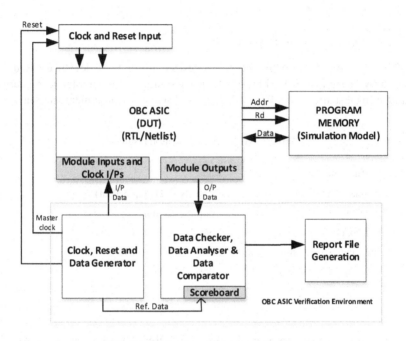

Fig. 7. Top level verification environment

OBC-2.3 ASIC digital core is verified by an automated test bench. The test strategy covers verification of each SFR or Memory Mapped modules of OBC-2.3 ASIC for all the modes of operation independently. A separate Data Checker unit is developed which accept the input from DUT as well as the test benches. Data Checker unit compares both the inputs and generates report file to indicate the pass/fail of test case. The test cases at the top-level consist of assembly/C code as well as the VHDL test procedures. Assembly/C code is required for 8051-core programming and VHDL test procedures are required to generate test-vectors for the modular interfaces as well as data checker. Program memory is initialized with a test case program. Once reset is removed from OBC-2.3 ASIC, it fetches the instruction from a Program Memory. Functional verification has been carried out at different design stages; RTL Level, Synthesized Netlist Level, Pre-Layout Netlist and Post Layout Netlist Level. Timing Simulation has also been carried out on Post Layout Netlist. Table 2 shows functional verification results of the ASIC.

Table 2. Functional verification results

Parameters	Values
Total no of module level test cases	950
Total no of top level test cases	300
Code coverage	>97%
Total simulation run time	7–8 s

5.2 ASIC Implementation Results

OBC-2.3 ASIC digital core has been synthesized using SCL developed Radiation Hardened by Design (RHBD) library. Digital design contains internal scan chain for manufacturing test after wafer fabrication. Table 3 shows major implementation results.

Table 3. ASIC implementation results

Parameter	Value
Gate Count	458 K (NAND2 equivalent)
Die Size	15 mm × 15 mm
Max clock frequency	24 MHz
Scan Chain length	Chain-1: 16670, Chain-2: 726
ATPG test coverage	>95%
ESD Sensitivity	2 kV HBM

Customized test board has been developed for OBC-2.3 ASIC package for testing. Figure 8 shows photograph of OBC 2.3 ASIC functionality test Setup. RS232 protocol is used for communication in between computer and UART of OBC 2.3 ASIC. A windows based software is developed to facilitate the functional testing of OBC 2.3 ASIC. This software provides a user friendly Graphical User Interface (GUI). More than 150 test cases have been built into the software to ensure the complete functional testing of the ASIC. The software will display detailed test results on the console window and also generates the user friendly reports of the test results. Heavy ion Single Event Effect (SEE) radiation testing of OBC2.3 ASIC was carried out at three different heavy ion beams with LET of 22 meV-cm^2/mg (^{48}Ti^{11+}), 30meV-cm^2/mg (^{58}Ni^{9+}), 50 meV-cm^2/mg (^{107}Ag^{9+}). No upsets and no latch-up were observed in the device. During irradiation nominal supply current around 122 mA @ 3.3V was observed.

5.3 TRC Digital Card Test Methodology

Figure 9 shows the block diagram of Ground Checkout Unit and its interface with TRC through test fixture. The output signals of the Ground Checkout Unit are connected to

Fig. 8. OBC-2.3 ASIC test setup

the input connector K1 of TRC through test fixture and CMOS signals are received from DUT. Figure 10 shows photograph of the test setup and bed of nails test fixture module. Simulator card receives the signal from test fixture and shows the pass/fail report on GUI.

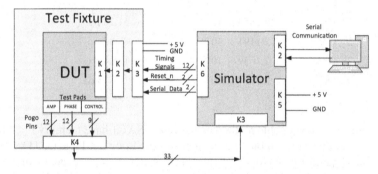

Fig. 9. Ground checkout unit interface diagram for auto testing

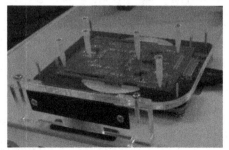

Fig. 10. Test setup of TRiM - digital card with bed of nails

5.4 TRC Software Testing

Static analysis (quality check) of TRC microcontroller code was performed using MAT-LAB's Polyspace tool. Dynamic analysis was also performed using the possible test vectors. Timing analysis of ISR routines and critical function such as phase computation etc. was also performed using the hardware simulator and test bench.

5.5 SINE Value Computations

Table 4 shows comparison of maximum absolute error and computation time for $SIN(\theta_{el})$ computation using Taylor series. Trade-off between accuracy and computation time shows that accuracy of 5th order polynomial equation is quite enough to compute phase with error of less than half LSB. Figure 11 shows simulation of SINE computation results using Taylor series equation.

Table 4. $SIN(\theta_{el})$ Computation time and error using Taylor series

Order (Up to)	Maximum Absolute Error	Computation Time
1st Order	0.0236	–
3rd Order	3.2853×10^{-4}	51.28 μs
5th Order	2.1191×10^{-6}	88.47 μs
7th Order	2.1639×10^{-8}	125.42 μs
9th Order	2.9797×10^{-9}	162.15 μs

Traditional Look Up Table method as used in RISAT-1 have memory fetch time of 64.14 μs. It requires large amount of memory to store Look Up Table (LUT). LUT size depends upon number of factors such as a beam viewing angle range, resolutions etc. Computation method used in RISAT-1A has a computation time of 133.27 μs. This time is double than traditional method but it removes memory requirement limitations and it computes phase value for any beam angle.

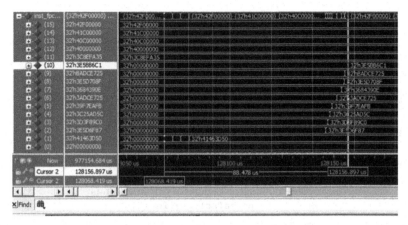

Fig. 11. Simulation result of computation SINE

6 Conclusion

On Board Controller (OBC-2.3) ASIC has been described which was developed indigenously for use in T/R controller (TRC) of Synthetic Aperture Radar (SAR) payload of RISAT-1A satellite. OBC 2.3 ASIC testing has been carried out using various test methodology at different stages of realization. The design of TRC digital card using OBC 2.3 offers real time phase computation, thermal compensation using Floating point co-processor which reduce memory requirement and results into higher accuracy in beam computing. In addition to that, inbuilt RS422, RS485, LVR etc. reduce external component requirement, which help to reduce size of PCB. Using EPSPI & TRMSW module, control data and signals are loaded within a clock period. Automated testing of TRC using bed of nails test fixture reduces probability of human error, which is highly desirable for space mission. Total 350 TRC flight modules are developed and out of that, 288 TRC used in onboard for RISAT-1A.

References

1. Waldron, T.P., Chin, S.K., Naster, R.J.: Distributed beam steering control of phased array radars. Microwave J., 133–146 (September 1996)
2. Patel, H., Raman, B.S., Desai, N.M.: Floating point coprocessor for distributed array controller. In: IEEE International Conference on Advances in Computing, Communications and Informatics (ICACCI-2014), New Delhi
3. Karlstrom, P., Ehliar, A., Liu, D.: High-performance, low-latency field-programmable gate array-based floating-point adder and multiplier units in a Virtex 4. IET Comput. Tech. 2(4), 305–313 (2008)
4. Patel, H., Trivedi, S.M., Neelkanthan, R., Gujraty, V.R.: A robust UART architecture based on recursive running sum filter for better noise performance. In: IEEE International Conference on VLSI design – 2007, Bangalore

Tile Serial Protocol (TSP) ASIC for Distributed Controllers of Space-Borne RADAR

Chiragkumar B. Patel[1]([✉]), Ganesh A. Mulay[1], Himanshu N. Patel[1], and Pooja Dhankher[2]

[1] Space Applications Centre, Indian Space Research Organisation, Gujarat, India
{chiragkumar,ganesh,hnpatel}@sac.isro.gov.in
[2] Semi-Conductor Laboratory, Punjab, India
pooja@scl.gov.in

Abstract. This paper describes novel serial protocol for transmission of data and timing events for distributed controllers of Space-borne Radar systems. This paper also describes implementation of this protocol as Radiation Hardened (RH) Application Specific Integrated Circuit (ASIC) based on 180 nm CMOS process. Traditionally, serial data and timing signals are transmitted as separate inter-connect lines from central controller to distributed controllers. Phased array radar systems consists of hundreds of such distributed controllers, which results in huge inter-connect harness cables. In the proposed protocol, a single differential line is used to transmit tele-command data and timing events from central controller to all distributed controllers as well as to receive the telemetry data. Serial data is transmitted in the form of frames of 20 bits each. A unique sync frame is transmitted from central controller to distributed controllers periodically which serves as a reference for all timing signals. There are different types of frames for transmission of tele-command, telemetry and timing signal parameters. Advantage of this protocol is significant reduction in harness, which leads to reduced payload weight and size. It provides higher reliability due to inbuilt dual redundant channels. This IP has been designed using VHDL and is implemented on 180 nm CMOS process as a mixed signal ASIC. The TSP ASIC contains digital modules like frame encoder & decoder, sync pulse generator, timing sampler & re-generator, channel selector, wave encoder & decoder, fail safe module and analog modules like LVR, RS485. The ASIC can operate up to 60 MHz and consumes 0.21 W power. The TSP ASIC has been packaged in 256 pins CQFP package and has been electrically characterized. The ASIC has been radiation tested for heavy ions single event effect and it has successfully cleared 70 MeV $-$ cm^2/mg LET and 185 Mev beam energy levels.

Keywords: Application specific integrated circuit · ASIC · Space-borne synthetic aperture radar · SAR · RS-485 transceiver · Radiation hardening · Distributed controller · Multi-drop serial communication · Timing signals re-generation · Central controller

© The Author(s), under exclusive license to Springer Nature Switzerland AG 2022
A. P. Shah et al. (Eds.): VDAT 2022, CCIS 1687, pp. 540–550, 2022.
https://doi.org/10.1007/978-3-031-21514-8_44

1   Introduction

A typical active phased array based system requires distributed controllers to load amplitude and phase data to each RF element which is connected to a group of antenna patches [5]. The volume and weight of harness used to connect subsystems in spacecraft is increasing day by day due to diversified on-board mission systems. Also manual assembly of cables has resulted in to long lead times. For communication between central controller and distributed controller, industry standard data protocols such as SPI, RS422, RS485, MIL-STD-1533B, Space wire, CAN Bus, UART etc. are used. In addition to that, one or more timing signals are used for synchronization and control. These signals are routed using differential pairs to provide better noise immunity. Also redundant channels are used to provide higher reliability. The harness contributes up to 15% to the dry mass in satellite and leads to additional launch cost [1].

The Harness requirement is mission specific and depends upon number of factor such as redundancy, numbers of subsystems, control hierarchy levels etc. In weather monitoring radar [4], 4 differential lines and 9 single ended lines are used for beam steering control. Angelo et al. has used total 6 signals such Serial Data, Data Clock, Next Angle Ready, Reset, Enable, Clock for beam forming operation in SAR [2]. The architecture [3] describe by N. Pallavi et al. Chip enable, Clock, Data, Strob and Telemetry lines are used for TR module control. Vishakh has used Start of Burst (SOBu), Blanking signal, Normal/Cal control, Range clock and Pre-trigger etc. signal from Embedded Central Unit to TR modules for Active Phased Array Radar [6].

The proposed protocol is a single chip solution to control distributed system using central unit. It requires only single RS485 bus for overall communication. It supports tele-command, telemetry and timing signal communication in synchronous mode. A master-slave system has one master node that issues commands to each of the slave nodes and processes responses. Slave nodes do not typically transmit data without a request from the master node and do not communicate with each other. Each slave has a unique address so that it can be addressed independently of other nodes.

2   Proposed Protocol

The proposed protocol is a custom protocol used for distributed control subsystems of phased array radar. This protocol will be useful for communication of tele-command/telemetry data as well as sharing of information related to timing signals from master to slave. The protocol is controlled by microcontroller/microprocessor using memory bus interface. Instead of transmitting actual timing signal, master node serially transfers parameters of timing signals with reference to sync pulse. Each timing signal is described by OFFSET (16 bits), ON (16 bits), POLARITY (1 bit), TYPE (2 bits). The slave re-generates original timing signal from this timing parameter data. Figure 1 shows timing signal sampling at master terminal and its re-generation at slave terminal.

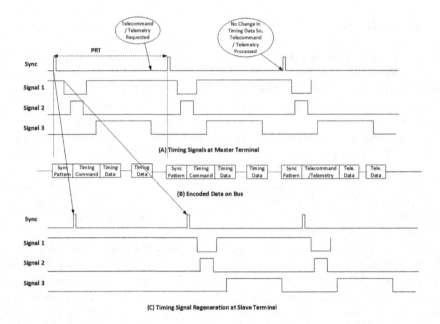

Fig. 1. Transmission and re-generation of timing signals

POLARITY of a signal is level of timing signal at the rising edge of sync pulse. A signal can be of four types that are, DC, Step, Pulse or Toggle (only valid for fixed duty cycle during Pulse Repetition Interval (PRI). Type of a signal is defined using signal edge transition within sync period (e.g. DC signal has no transition, Step Signal has 1 transition, Pulse signal has two transitions and Toggle signal contain more than 2 transitions). Duration between sync pulse falling edge to timing signal's 1st transition is called as OFFSET whereas, duration between signal's 1st transition period to timing signal's 2nd transition period is called as ON period. The OFFSET and ON counter value are described by Eq. 1.

$$Counter = [Period_{offset} \times Clk_{freq}] - 1 \qquad (1)$$

The protocol supports 8 timing signal information. For achieving higher Pulse Repetition Frequency (PRF) and reduced bus load, unused timing can be disabled thereby resulting in reduced data transfer. At each sync pulse, received timing data is verified against any change. Otherwise, Tele-command or Telemetry activity will be performed. The re-generated timing signal will have a latency of two sync periods due to sampling of timing signals and transmission of timing information. This Latency is across all distributed modules and has a synchronization with common sync pattern transmitted by master. Lower limit Pulse Repetition Interval (PRI) of sync pulse is descried by Eq. 2.

$$PRI_{sync} \geq [2^{(n+1)} + 1] \times T_{Frame} \qquad (2)$$

where, n = number of timing signal is enabled and T_{Frame} is one frame transmission time.

2.1   Frame Structure

Two distinct word types are used by the protocol: Command Word and Data word. Each word type has a unique format even within a common structure. Each word is twenty bits in length. The first three bits are used as a synchronization field, thereby allowing the decode clock to re-sync at the beginning of each new word. The next sixteen bits are the information field. The last bit is the odd parity bit. The use of this distinct pattern allows the decoder to re-sync at the beginning of each word and maintains the overall stability of the communication. Figure 2 shows command word and data word frame structure.

Bit	19 18 17	16 15 14 13 12	11	10 9 8 7 6	5 4 3 2 1	0
Command Word	Frame Id	Terminal Address	T/R	Sub Address	Word Count	P
Data Word	Frame Id	Data				P

Fig. 2. Type of word format

Command Word. Command word specifies which operation is going to be performed and number of data words followed by a particular command word. Only the master terminal transmits command word. Slave terminal generates the sync pulse in response to SP (Sync Pattern) command which synchronizes the timing signals. Timing Signal (TS) command is used to update timing signal parameters. Timing signal data will be transmitted by master followed by TS command. Tele-command (TC) contains information related to data transmission from master to salve such as number of words, receiver address and memory location where received data will be stored in slave. Telemetry (TM) command asks intended slave to send the data to master. It contains information related to data transmission from slave to master such as number of words, slave address and memory location from where data will be sent to master. Frame ID is used to identify whether received frame is data frame or command frame. For command word, Frame Id is $(100)_B$. The five bits Terminal Address (TA) field states to which remote terminal(s) are intended for particular command. Protocol support unicast and broadcast mode for communication. Terminal Address $(11111)_B$ is reserved as a broadcast address. The Sync pattern (SP) command always works in broadcasting mode whereas telemetry can be taken in unicast mode only. The maximum number of terminals the data bus can support is 32 out of which 1 is master and rest 31 are slaves. Each terminal has a unique address which is referred as a device address. Terminal address $(11111)_B$ is fixed for master terminal. Device address will be written in each slave by host controller during initialization. The Transmit/Receive (T/R) bit denotes the direction of information flow with respect to slave. A transmit command (logic 1) indicates the slave terminal to transmit data, while a receive command (logic 0) denotes data reception by slave. The Sub Address (SA) field is fixed for sync pattern and timing command whereas for tele-command and telemetry, it indicates memory segment location. The Word Count (WC) defines the number of data words to be received or transmitted after particular command word. Word Count is fixed for sync pattern command as no data frame needs to be transmitted after sync pattern. Odd parity is used for this protocol.

2.2   Data Word

The Data Word (DW) contains the actual information that is being transferred within a message. Data words can be transmitted by either master or slave. At the slave end, words are received or transmitted depending on the T/R bit of command word. The first 3 bits of a data word contains a Frame Id. The next sixteen bits of information is the data in big endian format. The last bit is the odd parity bit.

3   Architectural Overview and ASIC Development

The Tile Serial Protocol (TSP) is designed to control and synchronize distributed T/R controllers from a central controller. Along with tele-command, timing events data and health monitoring telemetry is provided on the same bus. Block diagram of Tile Serial Protocol ASIC architecture is shown in Fig. 3. The device has master and slave device functionalities available on the same chip and can be selected by *MasterSlaveIn* pin. Also slave devices can be configured using five bits device address register.

The sync pulse generator module generates sync pulse at Pulse Repetition Interval (PRI). Here master device sends unique sync pattern once sync pulse rising edge is detected. The slave device re-generates sync pulse when sync pattern is received. Sync pulse is a reference signal for timing signal sampler and re-generator module. Timing signal sampler module samples the timing signals with one clock resolution and generates signal parameters which are stored in special function registers. Upon next sync detection, master device sends signal parameters to all the slave devices. All the slave devices store received signal parameters in the buffer and update timing signals on forthcoming sync pulse. The device supports up to 8 timing signals sampling and re-generation. The data transfer takes place depending on the priority wherein sync pulse has the highest priority and will be followed by timing signal, tele-command and telemetry operations. Wave encoder module converts parallel data frame into serial data for data transmission over physical layer. Transmission time for sending one frame is calculated using Eq. 3.

$$T_{frame} = (\frac{Bits}{Frame}) \times Rate_{oversampling} \tag{3}$$

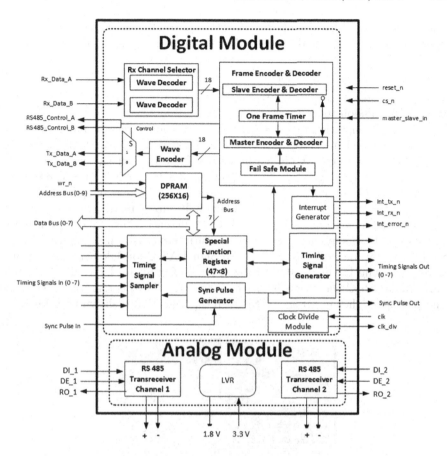

Fig. 3. Architecture of Tile Serial Protocol (TSP)

where, bus over sampling rate is 12.

The protocol takes 256 clock cycles to transmit one frame of 20 bits with 16 clock gap band between two frames. It has an inbuilt channel redundancy in which master selects serial data transmission channel. At the receiving end, slave unit samples bus activity using wave decoder and locks the channel on which command frame has been received. Wave decoder receives serial data over bus and stores it in a buffer/memory. 256×16 Dual Port RAM (DPRAM) is used for data storage during tele-command and telemetry operation. DPRAM is divided virtually in 16 segments of 16 data words each. First 8 segments are used for tele-command and rest are used for telemetry operation. Timing signal sampling and re-generation is carried out by the protocol independently. For tele-command and telemetry operations, controls are performed by user using memory mapped Special Function Registers (SFR) such as control, segment, frame length etc. Master device is responsible for the bus control. For the telemetry operation, Bus access is provided to a particular slave after telemetry command frame transmission. Fail Safe Module handover bus control to master device if telemetry operation is not completed during fail safe time period which is calculated using Eq. 4.

$$T_{failsafe} = (n + 1) \times T_{frame} \tag{4}$$

where, n = No. of telemetry data frame requested by master and T_{frame} is one frame transmission time.

Interrupt generation module generates active low interrupt pulse once tele-command and telemetry operation is completed successfully. It also generates active low error interrupt pulse when fail safe occurs during telemetry operation. Low Voltage Regulator (LVR) converts 3.3 V supply to 1.8 V used as a core voltage. Two standard RS485 transceivers are also part of the architecture. RS485 transceivers are selected as it offers half duplex multi point communication and better noise immunity over single differential line. Analog and digital modules I/O are kept separate hence use of internal as well as external RS485 transceiver can be explored. The Mixed Signal ASIC for Tile Serial Protocol is developed using 180 nm CMOS Process at Semi-Conductor Laboratory, Chandigarh, India. ASIC Die Size is 9057 μm× 9057 μm. The photograph of ASIC die and package is shown in Fig. 4. TSP ASIC specification is shown in Table 1.

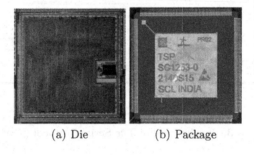

(a) Die   (b) Package

Fig. 4. Photograph of TSP ASIC die and package

4   Testing and Validation

4.1   Test Board Development

DW8051 controller based On Board Controller (OBC) 2.3 ASIC is interfaced with TSP ASIC through memory mapped interface. Test board can test TSP ASIC in standalone as well as master-slave configuration. Test code is written in C language and uses EEPROM as a code memory. Microprocessor supervisory circuit (Watchdog Timer) is used to provide power on reset. The overall operation is controlled using RS232 communication using computer through MAX232 IC. For master slave communication, jumper selectable internal/external RS485 transceiver are part of test board. TSP ASIC input clock frequency is 48 MHz. TSP ASIC test board photograph is shown in Fig. 5.

Table 1. ASIC specification

Parameter	Specifications
ASIC type	Mixed Signal ASIC
Process	180 nm CMOS
Foundry	SCL, Chandigarh
Clock frequency	48 MHz (can work up to 60 MHz)
Power Supply	3.3 V
On chip Memory	DPRAM: 256 X 16 bits (Using RH Flip-flops)
Types of I/O	3.3 V CMOS I/Os, RS-485
Number of I/O	63
Area	Die size: 9.057 mm × 9.057 mm
Testability Features	SCAN and ATPG with Fault Coverage of 100%
Power Dissipation	<1 W at 48 MHz

Fig. 5. Tile serial protocol ASIC test board

4.2 Test Cases

Automated GUI software control the TSP ASIC functionality over a RS232 channel through OBC 2.3 ASIC during test. Total number of errors and error address location(s) with read back data and expected data are sent to computer for display by OBC 2.3 ASIC. DPRAM is tested using chess board pattern and ramp pattern through port A & Port B. Tele-command and telemetry operations are performed with different data frame counts and memory segment combinations. For fail safe analysis, telemetry operation is performed with invalid slave address. Above mentioned operations are performed with both Channel A and Channel B. Cumulatively, 310 test cases are generated and tested with different combinations to check TSP ASIC functionality.

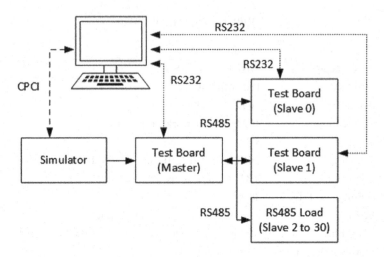

Fig. 6. Functional test set up block diagram

4.3   Functional and Thermal Test Setup

Figure 6 shows block diagram of TSP ASIC functionality test setup. Total 3 test boards are used in the test setup. One Device Under Test (DUT) is configured as master device and rest two devices are configured as slave. In addition to that, RS485 load of remaining slaves are connected on bus. RS232 protocol is used for communication between computer and UART of OBC 2.3 ASIC. MATLAB based user friendly GUI is developed where detailed test results are displayed on console window. cPCI based FPGA card has been used for simulating input timing signals to TSP ASIC. GUI has been developed to interface to communicate with FPGA board over cPCI interface and supports 8 timing signals and sync generation.

4.4   Functional Test Results

TSP ASIC has been tested successfully with 310 test cases. Synchronization between sync pulse generated by slaves and master has been found out to be within one clock cycle. One frame transmission takes 4.9324 µs. Time required to transit tele-command with 15 data frames (maximum) 86.023 µs whereas to receive telemetry of 15 data frames (maximum) is 86.770 µs. Bus handover time during telemetry operation is 622 ns.

4.5   Thermal Test Results

ASIC device has been tested over a temperature range of −20 °C to 85 °C in step of 10 °C. It has successfully cleared all 310 test cases over various temperatures. Supply current deviation over temperature is measured as ±3 mA.

5   Radiation Test

The intense heavy ion environment encountered in space applications can cause a variety of transient and destructive effects in devices, including Single Event Latch-up (SEL), Single Event Upset (SEU) and Single Event Burnout (SEB). These effects can lead to system-level failures including disruption and permanent damage. For reliable space system operation, these components have to be specifically designed and fabricated for Radiation hardness, followed by SEE testing to validate the design. This testing was performed to determine the single event effect (SEE) sensitivity of Tile Serial Protocol (TSP) ASIC.

5.1   Test Setup

Radiation test has been performed using General Purpose Scattering Chamber (GPSC) beam line of the pelletron facility. As shown in Fig. 7, TSP ASIC test board in master configuration without lid (die exposed) was subjected to irradiation. The TSP ASIC test board in slave configuration as shown in Fig. 7 was kept outside the chamber. Both test boards (Master & Slave) are controlled using GUI through RS232 interface. ASIC functionality, current consumption and signal characteristics were monitored continuously when DUT was being irradiated. Read/write operations of the memory locations and functionality verification was performed. Total number of errors were recorded during the SEE test for each memory & functionality test. A provision to check Address, read data, expected data was provided in the event of error occurrence.

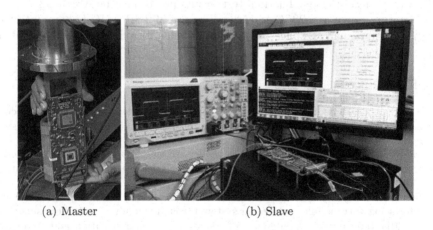

(a) Master   (b) Slave

Fig. 7. SEE test setup

5.2   Results

Nominal current drawn by TSP ASIC is 46 mA. It was tested at three different heavy ion beams with LET of 30 MeV $-$ cm^2/mg (Nickel), 50 MeV $-$ cm^2/mg

(Silver) and 70 MeV $-$ cm^2/mg. Detail of test results are given in Table 2. No upsets and no latch-up were observed in the device. During irradiation maximum supply current deviation of $3mA$ has been observed.

Table 2. SEE test results

Beam type	LET	Beam energy (Mev)	Test cycles	Test duration	Current
Gold	70	185	20	23 min	47 mA
Silver	50	180	40	42 min	49 mA
Nickel	30	150	50	54 min	48 mA

6   Conclusions

A TSP protocol described in this paper is used for communication between master & slave terminals and to send timing data from master to slave terminals over a signal differential line. Timing signals re-generated at slave terminals have accuracy of one clock period with reference to the master device. Measured latency for timing signal sampling at master and its re-generation at slave terminal is $2 \times PRI_{Sync}$ by design. Independent slave units have timing signals synchronization within one clock period. 3 Mbps data rate is achieved at 48 MHz operational frequency. The ASIC has been tested for a frequency ranging between 6 MHz to 60 MHz and performance of ASIC has been satisfactory. No upsets or latch-ups were observed in the ASIC during SEE testing using Gold, Silver and Nickel Beams. Thermal test results prove that the ASIC can work in temperature range of $-20\,°C$ to $85\,°C$. The use of TSP ASIC reduces interface harness requirement in space project which helps to reduce payload weight by 10% or higher.

References

1. Amini, R., Aalbers, G., Hamann, R., Jongkind, W.: Newgenerations of spacecraft data handling systems: Less harness, more reliability. In: 57th International Astronautical Congress (2006)
2. Manco, A., Ugo, V.: Beam steering controller architectures for an active electrically scanned array antenna: comparison and a cost effective implementation. Int. J. Comput. Appl. **179**, 1–8 (2018)
3. Pallavi, N., Anjaneyulu, P., Natarajan, P.B., Mahendra, V., Karthik, R.: Design and interfacing of tr modules with radar system through tr module controller using fpga. In: 2017 International Conference of Electronics, Communication and Aerospace Technology (ICECA), vol. 2, pp. 231–233 (2017)
4. Rafael: Beam steering control system for low cost phased array weather radar: Design and calibration techniques. In: University of Massachusetts Amherst (2014)
5. Dai, P.C., Phong, L.D., Van Tuan, L., Nguyen, N.H., Linh, D.N.: Novel fpga based t/r module controller for active phased array radar. In: 2019 IEEE International Symposium on Phased Array System Technology, pp. 1–5 (2019)
6. Vishakh: Fpga based embedded central unit for active phased primary radar. Int. J. Eng. Res. Technol. **4**, 729–733 (2015)

A Deep Dive into CORDIC Architectures to Implement Trigonometric Functions

Narnindi Ramani[1] and Saroj Mondal[2]

[1] BITS Pilani, Hyderabad Campus, Hyderabad, Telangana, India
h20181230203h@alumni.bits-pilani.ac.in
[2] IIT Dharwad, WALMI Campus, Dharwad, Karnataka, India
saroj@iitdh.ac.in

Abstract. Coordinate Rotation Digital Computer (CORDIC) Algorithms provide an area efficient way to implement complex mathematical functions. This algorithm remains relevant to this day where trigonometric functions are used repetitively. CORDIC algorithms are used in various stages of signal processing applications and robotics. A deep dive into the concept and implementation of three types of the algorithm are presented in this paper. A comparison of three versions of the CORDIC Algorithm, viz. rotation mode-Basic CORDIC, Scale Free CORDIC, and Redundant CORDIC, is made in terms of power, area, and speed. The three algorithms are modeled in Verilog HDL and then implemented with Xilinx Vivado. The performance metrics are compared using Synopsys Design Vision tool.

Keywords: CORDIC Algorithm · Range of convergence · Redundant arithmetic

1 Introduction

CORDIC Algorithm was introduced by Volder in 1959 [1], to evaluate trigonometric, hyperbolic, logarithmic, exponential functions using rotation based mathematics, since many functions can be obtained from rotation of a vector. The fundamental equations for rotation of a vector from $(x_0,\ y_0)$ to $(x_f,\ y_f)$ through an angle θ are given as,

$$x_f = x_0 \cos\theta - y_0 \sin\theta \qquad (1) \qquad\qquad y_f = y_0 \cos\theta + x_0 \sin\theta \qquad (2)$$

CORDIC algorithm implements the above equations using simple architectures comprising of shifters, adders, and other basic hardware elements. Multipliers are avoided as they occupy more area. Two modes of CORDIC Algorithm are defined based on the unknown entity i.e. rotation mode if the final coordinates are unknown and vectoring mode if the angle is unknown. In rotation mode, if the initial coordinates (x_0, y_0) are taken as $(1, 0)$, then the outputs will be $(\cos\theta, \sin\theta)$, the cosine and sine values of the given angle.

A. P. Shah et al. (Eds.): VDAT 2022, CCIS 1687, pp. 551–561, 2022.
https://doi.org/10.1007/978-3-031-21514-8_45

Different versions of the CORDIC algorithm are proposed in the literature to bring some form of improvement over the original [1] in terms of computation speed, area, and/or overall hardware complexity. This paper reviews the original CORDIC algorithm and two enhanced versions of the algorithm, viz. scale-free CORDIC and redundant CORDIC which provide an enhancement in area usage and computational speed, respectively. The unique contributions of the paper are (1) a comprehensive comparison of the features of the basic, scale-free, and redundant CORDIC algorithms; (2) a thorough look at redundant number system and implementing the RBSD adder used in redundant CORDIC algorithm; and (3) an in depth explanation of the techniques used in extension of range of convergence in scale- free CORDIC.

2   Basic CORDIC Algorithm

The basic CORDIC algorithm uses two concepts to implement the aforementioned equations using only shifters and adders. The first concept is the use of pseudo rotations which results in either an increment or decrement of the vector length based on the direction of rotation in contrast to a pure rotation where the vector length remains constant. The second concept is to avoid multiplications and utilize a set of micro angles to attain the total angle of rotation. These micro angles are chosen in such a way that $\theta_i = \arctan\left(2^{-i}\right)$ and their summation gives the net angle $\sum \theta_i = \theta$.

$$x_{i+1} = x_i - y_i \tan \theta_i \qquad (3) \qquad\qquad y_{i+1} = y_i + x_i \tan \theta_i \qquad (4)$$

$$K = \prod_{i=0}^{n} cos\theta_i \qquad (5)$$

The Eqs. (3) and (4) are obtained by taking cos θ term common in the original vector rotation Eqs. (1) and (2).

It is to be noted that multiplication with $\cos \theta_i$ term is being avoided at every iteration. This must be compensated later on by multiplying a scaling factor to the final output. For 'n' number of iterations, the scaling factor K is given by Eq. (5).

As 'n' approaches infinity, the scale factor converges to a constant value. Therefore, instead of multiplying with $\cos \theta_i$ term at every turn, a constant value is multiplied to the final output. Before this constant multiplication, for a given input angle, a series of rotations take place either in clockwise or anti-clockwise directions instead of a single rotation, until the vector converges to the required angle. Figure 1 illustrates the process of rotation in the basic CORDIC algorithm. $R_{initial}$ represents the initial position of the vector. The vector undergoes a pseudo rotation of θ_1, which is the first micro angle. As this exceeds the required angle, the vector undergoes another pseudo rotation of θ_2 in the opposite direction. As this is lower than the required angle, the vector undergoes an anticlockwise rotation through a micro angle of θ_3. This process continues until the vector converges to the required position (R_{final}). It is to be noted that the vector length keeps changing for every rotation.

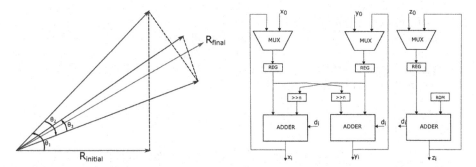

Fig. 1. Rotation mechanism in the basic CORDIC algorithm

Fig. 2. Basic CORDIC architecture [1]

The equations to represent this iterative process where θ_i is substituted with arctan (2^{-i}) in the Eqs. (3) and (4) and the coefficient d_i represents the direction of rotation are as follows [1]:

$$x_{i+1} = x_i - d_i y_i 2^{-i} \qquad (6) \qquad y_{i+1} = y_i + d_i x_i 2^{-i} \qquad (7)$$

$$z_{i+1} = z_i + d_i \arctan(2^{-i}) \qquad (8)$$

where z_i represents the sum of the angles through which the vector rotates. It is evident that the above three equations can be realized using shifters and adders. If the initial coordinates are taken as $(1, 0)$ and an angle is given as input, the outputs will be the sine and cosine of the given input angle. The micro angles, $\theta_i = \arctan(2^{-i})$ are stored in a ROM and the direction of rotation is chosen based on the sign of z_{i+1}. The drawback in the basic CORDIC is that the use of pseudo rotations leads to change in vector length resulting in a scaling factor (K). This scaling factor will be a constant value provided number of iterations is fixed. As mentioned in the Eq. (5), the scaling factor is given by,

$$K = \prod_{i=0}^{n} cos\theta_i = \prod_{i=0}^{n} \frac{1}{\sqrt{1 + 2^{-2i}}} \qquad (9)$$

Therefore, ultimately the outputs obtained have to be multiplied with a scaling factor K, which implies that the basic CORDIC algorithm cannot be implemented using only shifters and adders and thereby an additional constant multiplication module is needed to realize the architecture. Figure 2 shows the basic CORDIC architecture. In this implementation, the number of iterations is equal to the number of bits. The scale factor will also be constant for a constant number of iterations. This constant scale factor must be multiplied with the final x_{i+1}, y_{i+1} values to get the actual values.

3   Scale Free CORDIC Algorithm

The scale-free CORDIC algorithm [2] overcomes the drawback of having a scaling factor K in the basic CORDIC algorithm. The basic CORDIC equations in matrix form are in Eq. (10).

Here the microangles (θ_i) are chosen small enough so that the following approximation becomes valid if $\sin\theta_i = \theta_i = 2^{-i}$. By using Taylor's series expansion for $\sin\theta_i$ and $\cos\theta_i$, we can write $\sin\theta_i = 2^{-i}$, $\cos\theta_i = 1 - 2^{-(2i+1)}$, and the final expression can be written as Eq. (11).

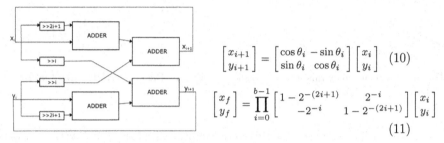

$$\begin{bmatrix} x_{i+1} \\ y_{i+1} \end{bmatrix} = \begin{bmatrix} \cos\theta_i & -\sin\theta_i \\ \sin\theta_i & \cos\theta_i \end{bmatrix} \begin{bmatrix} x_i \\ y_i \end{bmatrix} \quad (10)$$

$$\begin{bmatrix} x_f \\ y_f \end{bmatrix} = \prod_{i=0}^{b-1} \begin{bmatrix} 1 - 2^{-(2i+1)} & 2^{-i} \\ -2^{-i} & 1 - 2^{-(2i+1)} \end{bmatrix} \begin{bmatrix} x_i \\ y_i \end{bmatrix} \quad (11)$$

Fig. 3. Scale-Free CORDIC x_{i+1}, y_{i+1} Computation Architecture [2]

The lower and upper limits for the multiplication are obtained from the Taylor series approximation and the total bit length, respectively. If b is the number of bits then the max value of the upper limit is (b-1) because for a left shift of b-bits the output will become machine zero [2]. The lower limit is set by the Taylor series approximation because we choose $\sin\alpha_i$ and $\cos\alpha_i$ to be 2^{-i} and $1 - 2^{-(2i+1)}$, where i must be greater than a particular value for this approximation to be possible depending on the input length. For instance, a 16-bit input iteration range is from i = 4 to 15. Figure 3 shows a part of the implemented scale-free CORDIC architecture specifically the x_{i+1}, y_{i+1} computation according to Eq. (11).

The limitation in scale-free CORDIC is the reduction of the range of convergence. Even though the scaling factor is eliminated by taking $\sin\theta_i = \theta_i$ as the micro angle, this will reduce the maximum angle that can be computed. For 16-bit scale-free CORDIC the maximum angle can be calculated is, $\sum_{i=0}^{15} 2^{-i} = 0.1249$ rad $= 7.16\,^\circ$. Two techniques are used to extend this range, domain folding [3] and repetition of iteration steps [2].

3.1   Domain Folding

Each quadrant of the coordinate space is divided into 4 parts i.e. the first quadrant is divided into $(0, \frac{\Pi}{8})$, $(\frac{\Pi}{8}, \frac{\Pi}{4})$, $(\frac{\Pi}{4}, \frac{3\Pi}{8})$ and $(\frac{3\Pi}{8}, \frac{\Pi}{2})$. So the entire coordinate space is divided into 16 parts. When the input angle θ falls within these 4 domains, the angle β is chosen in such a way that $\theta = \beta$ in domain 1, $\frac{\Pi}{4} - \beta$

in domain 2, $\frac{\Pi}{4} + \beta$ in domain 3, and $\frac{\Pi}{2} - \beta$ in domain 4. So the angle β always lies in the range $(0, \frac{\Pi}{8})$. Substituting these in the original equations of the scale-free CORDIC algorithm, the trigonometric functions can be evaluated for any angle in the coordinate space. If (x_+, y_+) denote clockwise and (x_-, y_-) denote anticlockwise rotation vectors in domain 1, then substituting $\theta = \beta$ in Eq. (11) will give (12), (13).

$$\begin{bmatrix} x_- \\ y_- \end{bmatrix} = \begin{bmatrix} \cos\beta & -\sin\beta \\ \sin\beta & \cos\beta \end{bmatrix} \begin{bmatrix} x_i \\ y_i \end{bmatrix} \quad (12) \qquad \begin{bmatrix} x_+ \\ y_+ \end{bmatrix} = \begin{bmatrix} \cos\beta & \sin\beta \\ -\sin\beta & \cos\beta \end{bmatrix} \begin{bmatrix} x_i \\ y_i \end{bmatrix} \quad (13)$$

Similarly, the equations for other domains can be obtained by substituting appropriate θ in Eq. (11). The final expressions for all four domains can be obtained in terms of the equations in the first domain as follows [2]: in domain 1 $[x_f \ y_f] = [x_- y_-]$, in domain 2 $[x_f \ y_f] = [\frac{1}{\sqrt{2}}(x_+ + y_+) \ \frac{1}{\sqrt{2}}(-x_+ + y_+)]$, in domain 3 $[x_f \ y_f] = [\frac{1}{\sqrt{2}}(x_- + y_-) \ \frac{1}{\sqrt{2}}(-x_- + y_-)]$, and in domain 4 $[x_f \ y_f] = [y_+ - x_+]$. But there is still a gap between the two ranges of convergence. Using domain folding, the new range is $(0, \frac{\Pi}{8})$ i.e. for any angle, the above substitutions are done to make sure the input angle to a scale-free CORDIC equations lies in the range $(0, \frac{\Pi}{8})$. This range still has angles greater than 7.16 deg, which is the maximum angle evaluated using scale-free CORDIC for 16-bit input length. To eliminate this discrepancy, another technique is used where certain iteration steps are repeated.

3.2   Repetition of Iteration Steps

Some iteration needs to be repeated in order to extend the range of convergence in scale-free CORDIC [2]. As mentioned in the previous section, domain folding makes sure that the angle input to the scale-free CORDIC equations lies in the range $(0, \frac{\Pi}{8})$. But the maximum angle that can be computed by summing all the microangles in the case of 16-bit scale-free CORDIC algorithm is 7.16°. So, when the angle lies in the range $(0, \frac{\Pi}{8})$ after domain folding, but is greater than 7.16°, repetition of iteration steps is done.

In this technique, some of the microangles are used repeatedly which is different from the general case where a new microangle is used in every iteration. For instance, in the basic CORDIC implementation, in each iteration a new microangle is either added or subtracted to the previous summation by default. There is no need of repeating an iteration since the microangles ($\theta_i = \arctan(2^{-i})$) used in the basic CORDIC algorithm are high enough to converge to the required angle. But in the case of scale-free CORDIC, the microangles ($\theta_i = 2^{-i}$) are relatively less, convergence is not guaranteed and repetition is needed. Therefore, the process of repetition is done as follows: at the beginning of an iteration, check if using the same microangle again i.e. repeating the previous iteration step will surpass the required angle. If yes, then proceed to the next microangle and do not repeat the iteration with the same microangle, else repeat the step.

A proof is mentioned in [2] stating that it is enough to follow this process for the highest microangle to ensure convergence. This technique will become

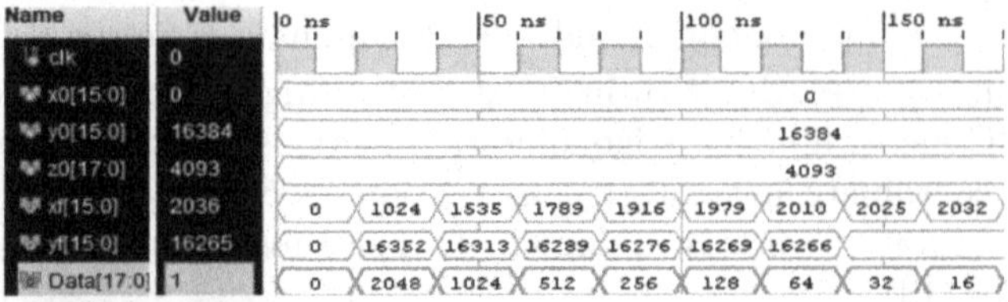

Case 1: Angle=7.16 deg: Every iteration happens once

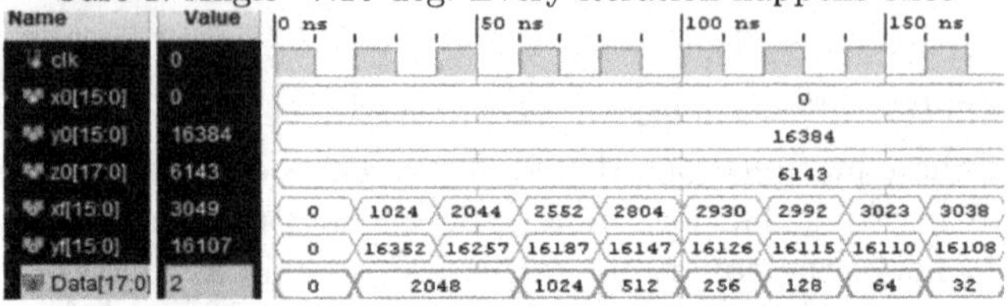

Case 2: Angle=10.74 deg: First iteration repeats twice

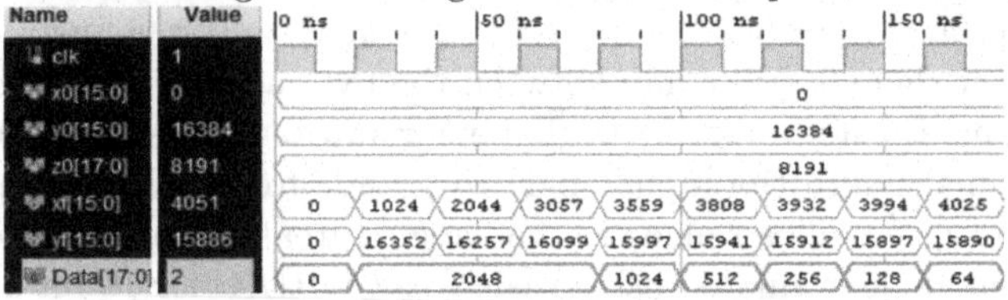

Case 3: Angle=14.322 deg: First iteration repeats thrice

Fig. 4. Simulated result of 16-bit Scale-Free CORDIC

clear by observing the behavioral simulation waveforms of the 16-bit scale-free CORDIC implementation having this repetition functionality shown in Fig. 4. The set of microangles scaled and in radians is 2048,1024,512.... In Case 1, the required angle is 7.16° whose scaled value in radians is 4093. Repeating the first iteration i.e. using the same microangle will exceed the required angle (2048+2048 >4093). Hence, the iteration is not repeated. But in Case 2, the required angle is 10.74 degrees whose scaled value is 6143, and here using the same microangle will not exceed the required angle (2048+2048<6143), therefore the iteration is repeated. Similarly in Case 3, the first iteration repeats thrice.

4   Redundant CORDIC Algorithm

The ripple carry adders which are used in conventional CORDIC architectures require high computation time as the bit size of the inputs increases [4]. In order to overcome this, adders are replaced by redundant adders and the computations are performed using redundant arithmetic [5–7]. The additions/subtractions do not require carry propagation which reduces the computation time significantly.

4.1   Redundant Arithmetic

The number of digits in a redundant signed digit number system are higher than the conventional system. For a radix r, a conventional number system will have digits from $\{0, .., (r-1)\}$, whereas the maximum range a redundant system can have is $\{-(r-1), .., (r-1)\}$. The consequence of having more digits than the conventional range is that a number can have more than one representation, hence the name redundant, because representation is not unique. For example, in radix 2, conventional 4-bit representation of '1' is 0001. The redundant system representations for '1' are 0001, $001\bar{1}$ and $1\bar{1}\bar{1}\bar{1}$ ($\bar{1}$ represents -1). The value represented by the redundant system is obtained by using the equation given in [8],

$$Integer\ value\ of\ redundant\ number = \sum_{i=0}^{n-1} r^i d_i \qquad (14)$$

where r is the radix, d_i is the interpreted value of the redundant digit, and n is the number of bits. For example, the integer value of a radix 2, four-bit redundant number is given by, $\sum_{i=0}^{3} 2^i d_i$. Hence, the integer value of $001\bar{1}$ is given by, $0(2^3) + 0(2^2) + 1(2^1) + (-1)(2^0) = 1$.

Computation of addition/subtraction of redundant numbers of any radix (r) happens in 2 stages. In the first stage, interim sum (s_i) and carry bits (c_i) are generated for all the input bits (x_i, y_i) at a time such that following relation is satisfied,

$$x_i + y_i = rc_i + s_i \qquad (15)$$

In the second stage, the interim sum and carry are added to generate the final sum (z_i).

For example, consider a signed digit set $\{-6, -5....6\}$ with radix $= 10$ [9]. The integer values of the two redundant numbers to be added $(24\bar{3}5\bar{1}, 11\bar{6}16)$ are $(23749, 10416)$. Redundant addition is done in two stages. The computations in the first stage are as follows,

$$x_4 + y_4 = rc_4 + s_4 : 2 + 1 = 10(0) + 3$$
$$x_3 + y_3 = rc_3 + s_3 : 4 + 1 = 10(0) + 5$$
$$x_2 + y_2 = rc_2 + s_2 : \bar{3} + \bar{6} = 10(\bar{1}) + 1$$
$$x_1 + y_1 = rc_1 + s_1 : 5 + 1 = 10(1) + \bar{4}$$
$$x_0 + y_0 = rc_0 + s_0 : \bar{1} + 6 = 10(0) + 5$$

In the second stage, the final sum is obtained by adding the interim sum and carry. Therefore, the interim sum, interim carry, and the final sum are, $s_i : 351\bar{4}5$; $c_i : 0\bar{1}100$; $z_i : 342\bar{4}5$

Here, the integer value of the obtained sum is 34165. From the aforementioned example, the main observation to be made is that the interim sum bits and the carry bits are chosen in such a way that no carry is generated during summation in the second stage. For instance, during the second LSB summation $(5 + 1)$, the relation $(10(1) + \bar{4})$ is chosen instead of $(10(0) + 6)$ because if the latter relation is chosen, in case the interim carry bit at that position is 1, then during the second stage when the interim carry and interim sum are added $(1 + 6)$, a carry will be generated. Hence the first relation is chosen. Table 1 described in [9] gives the appropriate relation i.e., the appropriate interim sum and carry values to be chosen for every possible combination of inputs. The same principle is used for RBSD addition in redundant CORDIC algorithm.

4.2 RBSD Addition

In the Redundant CORDIC algorithm, the inputs are of radix 2, the following table gives the values of interim carry (c_i) and sum (s_i) for all combinations of input augend (x_i) and addend (y_i) in radix-2 Redundant Binary Signed Digit (RBSD) number system for the first stage. In order to avoid carry generation in the second stage, c_i, s_i must be chosen appropriately. Table 1 describes the process of choosing c_i, s_i by observing the lower order bits x_{i-1}, y_{i-1}.

1. If (x_i, y_i) is (1, 1) or (0, 0) or (1, $\bar{1}$) or ($\bar{1}$, 1) or ($\bar{1}$, $\bar{1}$), then no need to check lower order bits (x_{i-1}, y_{i-1}). (c_i, s_i) will be (1, 0), (0, 0), (0, 0), (0, 0), ($\bar{1}$,0), respectively for the five cases, when both augend and addend are 1, and ($\bar{1}$, 0) when both of them are $\bar{1}$.
2. If (x_i, y_i) is either (1, 0) or (0, 1) then the lower order bits (x_{i-1}, y_{i-1}) are checked. If (x_{i-1}, y_{i-1}) are non negative then (c_i, s_i) will be (1, $\bar{1}$), else, (c_i, s_i) will be (0, 1).
3. Similarly, if (x_i, y_i) is either (0, $\bar{1}$) or ($\bar{1}$, 0), lower order bits are checked and assigned (c_i, s_i) accordingly.

Table 1. RBSD addition [10]

Augend (x_i)	Addend (y_i)	x_{i-1}, y_{i-1}	Interim carry (c_i)	Interim sum (s_i)
1	1	-	1	0
1	0	x_{i-1}, y_{i-1} not negative	1	$\bar{1}$
0	1	Remaining cases	0	1
0	0	–	0	0
1	$\bar{1}$	–	0	0
$\bar{1}$	1	–	0	0
0	$\bar{1}$	x_{i-1}, y_{i-1} not negative	0	$\bar{1}$
$\bar{1}$	0	Remaining cases	$\bar{1}$	1
$\bar{1}$	$\bar{1}$	–	$\bar{1}$	0

In second stage, the interim sum and carry are added to get the final sum. For example, consider (x_i, y_i) = (87,101)

$$x_i : 10\bar{1}0\bar{1}00\bar{1}; y_i : 1\bar{1}100111; s_i : 0100\bar{1}\bar{1}10; c_i : 1\bar{1}0001010; z_i : 1\bar{1}1000\bar{1}00$$

The obtained output z_i is the RBSD representation of the sum of (87,101). We can clearly observe that the carry propagation is completely avoided in RBSD addition. As the number of bits increases, the RBSD adder will be much more efficient than a ripple carry adder. The tradeoff in RBSD representation is that unlike conventional binary system where a single bit is enough to represent 2 digits { (0, 1) : (0, 1) }, RBSD needs 2 bits { (−1, 0, 1) : (10, 00, 01) }. This is called (n, p) encoding [8].

4.3   Conversion of Binary to RBSD and Vice-Versa

All the computations in the Redundant CORDIC algorithm are in terms of redundant arithmetic, so the inputs have to be in RBSD form and final output in RBSD form must be converted to binary. Conversion of Binary to RBSD can be done by WMA (Weight Minimization Algorithm) [11] as follows

1. Traverse the binary number from LSB to MSB to find a string which has 0 followed by a series of 1's
2. Replace the 0 with 1, the least significant 1 with $\bar{1}$ and the remaining 1's in between with 0's
3. Repeat previous two steps until there are no sequences of 0 followed by 1's

For example, to represent 93 in RBSD: 01**011101**; 01**100**$\bar{1}$01; **01100**$\bar{1}$01; **10**$\bar{1}$00$\bar{1}$01; no more sequences of 0's followed by 1's we can stop. Conversion of RBSD to binary can be done using the following algorithm [8].

1. Traverse the length of RBSD number from LSB to MSB to find $\bar{1}$
2. Replace $\bar{1}$ with 1 and generate a borrow of 1
3. Repeat the previous two steps until there are no $\bar{1}$'s in the number

For example, to represent 10$\bar{1}$00$\bar{1}$01 in binary: 10$\bar{1}$00$\bar{1}$01; 10$\bar{1}$00101; **01011101**

4.4   Redundant CORDIC Using Double Rotation Technique

The design of the Redundant CORDIC unit is based on double rotation logic. The normal version of the Redundant CORDIC algorithm without double rotation technique will use the same equations as the basic CORDIC algorithm, but now, x_i, y_i, θ_i will be in RBSD form and d_i can take the values $(+1, 0, -1)$. This means whenever d_i takes the value '0', there is no rotation, so some iterations will have rotations and some iterations won't have rotations unlike the basic CORDIC algorithm where every iteration has either a clockwise or anti-clockwise rotation. The consequence of some iterations not having rotations is that the scale factor becomes variable. Additional logic must be designed to compute the scale factor. To avoid this in the Redundant CORDIC algorithm, a double rotation technique is used [12].

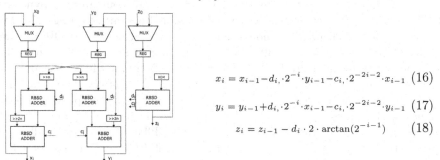

$$x_i = x_{i-1} - d_i \cdot 2^{-i} \cdot y_{i-1} - c_i \cdot 2^{-2i-2} \cdot x_{i-1} \quad (16)$$

$$y_i = y_{i-1} + d_i \cdot 2^{-i} \cdot x_{i-1} - c_i \cdot 2^{-2i-2} \cdot y_{i-1} \quad (17)$$

$$z_i = z_{i-1} - d_i \cdot 2 \cdot \arctan(2^{-i-1}) \quad (18)$$

Fig. 5. Redundant CORDIC architecture

Table 2. Comparison of CORDIC algorithms

	Basic [1]	Scale free [2]	Redundant [12]
Scale factor	Constant	None	Constant
Scale factor compensation	Needed	Not needed	Needed
Additional units	None	Units for:	RBSD:
		(1) domain folding &	(1) adders &
		(2) steps repetition	(2) converters
Rotations per iteration	Single rotation	clockwise & anticlockwise rotations	Two sub-rotations
Advantage	Area efficient	No multiplication needed	Less computation time

In double rotation technique, a negative rotation is performed as 2 negative sub rotations, a positive rotation is performed as 2 positive sub rotations and no rotation is a combination of a positive sub rotation and negative sub rotation. Therefore always 2 rotations take place so, the scale factor is constant. The redundant CORDIC equations for double rotation method are given in [12] as Eqs. (16), (17), (18) where d_i, c_i are taken as $\{(\bar{1}, 1), (1, 1), (0, \bar{1})\}$ based on the required sub rotations. Figure 5 shows the architecture of Redundant CORDIC with double rotation technique. d_i, c_i which determine the direction of sub rotations are chosen for every iteration so that the vector converges to the required position.

5   Results and Discussion

Two versions, Basic and Scale Free CORDIC algorithms in rotation mode and an RBSD adder which utilized in Redundant CORDIC are implemented in Xilinx Vivado 2014. For Basic CORDIC, Slice LUTs: 198 out of 53200, Slice Registers: 108 out of 106400 where as for Scale Free, Slice LUTs: 375 out of 53200, Slice Registers: 96 out of 106400. This Basic CORDIC algorithm implementation does not incorporate scale factor multiplication and hence the outputs obtained are not the exact trigonometric values. The RBSD adders needed for Redundant CORDIC require additional area to implement the logic for RBSD addition, but the computation time is reduced greatly.

The performance metrics of the 3 algorithms are compared in Synopsys Design Vision using 90 nm technology with a global operating voltage of 1.2 V. Total cell area (90 nm tech node) for Basic and Scale Free CORDIC are 17293.824108 and 28587.110439 and the total powers are 1.3244e+3 uW and 1.4383e+3 uW respectively. Scale factor multiplication unit which must be used in Basic CORDIC will consume large area and drain resources. The Scale Free CORDIC implementation might consume some area for the compensation techniques used to increase the range of convergence, but as scale factor compensation is not needed, this is more efficient. The different features in all three architectures, viz. basic, scale-free, and redundant CORDIC are compared in Table 2.

6   Conclusion

From Table 2, we can conclude that for less computation time, the Redundant CORDIC algorithm is preferred over the other two algorithms. But, there is a tradeoff between area and computation time as RBSD adders consume more area. There are other ways to implement the RBSD adder with lesser area so that area consumption is still moderate for the Redundant CORDIC implementation. This is done by obtaining reduced logical expressions for RBSD interim sum and carry evaluation. If there is an extreme area constraint, then Scale Free CORDIC is preferred as scale factor multiplication consumes more area. Depending on the requirement, an appropriate version of the Basic CORDIC algorithm can be used. If there is a time constraint then the version of the algorithm where a variable number of iterations are done based on the input angle is used, this will result in a variable scale factor and a scale factor evaluation unit must be added. The implemented version of the Basic CORDIC algorithm is used when there is no time constraint and a constant scale factor is preferred to avoid adding the variable scale factor evaluation unit. Overall, the Redundant CORDIC algorithm has the best attributes among the three algorithms.

References

1. Volder, J. The CORDIC trigonometric computing technique. IRE Trans. Electron. Comput. **EC-8**, 330–334 (1959)
2. Maharatna, K., Banerjee, S., Grass, E., Krstic, M., Troya, A.: Modified virtually scaling-free adaptive CORDIC rotator algorithm and architecture. IEEE Trans. Circuits Syst. Video Technol. **15**, 1463–1474 (2005)
3. Hu, X., Harber, R., Bass, S.: Expanding the range of convergence of the CORDIC algorithm. IEEE Trans. Comput. **40**, 13–21 (1991)
4. Noll, T.: Carry-save arithmetic for high-speed digital signal processing. In: IEEE International Symposium on Circuits and Systems
5. Avizienis, A.: Signed-digit numbe representations for fast parallel arithmetic. IEEE Trans. Electron. Comput. **EC-10**, 389–400 (1961)
6. Atkins, D.: Introduction to the Role of Redundancy in Computer Arithmetic. Computer **8**, 74–77 (1975)
7. Parhami, B.: Generalized signed-digit number systems: a unifying framework for redundant number representations. IEEE Trans. Comput. **39**, 89–98 (1990)
8. Parhami, B.: Carry-free addition of recoded binary signed-digit numbers. IEEE Trans. Comput. **37**, 1470–1476 (1988)
9. Sacks-Davis, R.: Applications of redundant number representations to decimal arithmetic. Comput. J. **25**, 471–477 (1982)
10. Kuninobu, S., Nishiyama, T., Edamatsu, H., Taniguchi, T., Takagi, N.: Design of high speed MOS multiplier and divider using redundant binary representation. In: 1987 IEEE 8th Symposium On Computer Arithmetic (ARITH) (1987)
11. Jedwab, J., Mitchell, C.: Minimum weight modified signed-digit representations and fast exponentiation. Electron. Lett. **25**, 1171 (1989)
12. Takagi, N., Asada, T., Yajima, S.: Redundant CORDIC methods with a constant scale factor for sine and cosine computation. IEEE Trans. Comput. **40**, 989–995 (1991)

Impact of Operand Ordering in Approximate Multiplication in Neural Network and Image Processing Applications

Kailash Prasad$^{(\boxtimes)}$ ⓘ, Jinay Dagli ⓘ, Neel Shah ⓘ, Mallikarjun Pidagannavar ⓘ, and Joycee Mekie ⓘ

Department of Electrical Engineering, Indian Institute of Technology Gandhinagar, Gandhinagar, India
{kailash.prasad,jinay.dagli,shah.neel,p_mallikarjun,joycee}@iitgn.ac.in

Abstract. Approximate arithmetic circuits are designed to improve energy efficiency and performance in error-tolerant applications. The approximate arithmetic circuits behave differently for different applications. Also, the approximation may violate basic algebraic properties like commutativity, associativity, identity, etc. The violation of algebraic properties makes the output of the approximate circuits dependent on the order of the inputs. The existing work [1] has been on approximate adders and their application to image addition. This paper investigates the impact of approximation and commutativity in the 12 compressor-based multipliers for image processing applications and CNNs. The first observation is that the accuracy of the neural network drops drastically if the multiplication of zero is approximated. Second, the outcomes of neural networks and error-resilient image processing applications tend to differ depending on the order of the inputs. For instance, when the Yang2 [2] design is implemented on ResNet18, we observe an accuracy of 58.07% for $a \times b$ and 69.4% for $b \times a$. Based on our findings, we propose that prior knowledge can be used to organize input data to increase output quality for these applications.

Keywords: Error-resilience · Approximate computing · Compressors · Image processing

1 Introduction

Approximate computing uses accuracy loss to improve an application's power, energy, area, and performance. Image and video processing, AI and ML, data analytics, and speech recognition applications are all examples of error-resilient applications [3–5]. The approximate arithmetic circuits being used in these applications violate the algebraic properties such as commutativity, associativity, identity, etc. This means that the output depends on the inputs making the

J. Dagli and N. Shah—Contributed equally to this work.

© The Author(s), under exclusive license to Springer Nature Switzerland AG 2022
A. P. Shah et al. (Eds.): VDAT 2022, CCIS 1687, pp. 562–572, 2022.
https://doi.org/10.1007/978-3-031-21514-8_46

circuit data-dependent. The existing work [1] analyses the commutative property of approximate adders and is limited to image processing applications.

This paper analyses the violation of commutative properties of approximate multipliers. We have used twelve approximate multiplier designs using approximate 4:2 compressors for our study. We have carried out a detailed analysis to show the effect of input data ordering on the output quality in image processing applications and the accuracy of neural networks. This exhaustive analysis also shows that the output quality and accuracy depend on input order. The contributions of the paper are as follows:

- We show the impact of approximation and commutativity on Neural Networks and Image processing applications.
- We have evaluated twelve compressor-based multiplier designs on Neural Network and Image processing applications for the analysis.
- We show that the accuracy of Neural Network and PSNR/SSIM of Image processing application [6] drops drastically if the multiplication of zeroes is approximated.
- We also show the violation of the commutative law for approximate circuits and propose to appropriately use this property of different outputs in different operand sequences for better results.

2 Background

2.1 Approximate Compressors

Several studies [7,8] have concentrated on approximate multipliers with high performance. In most cases, multipliers are implemented in three steps: 1) generation of partial products; 2) array compression of partial products; and 3) addition. As a result, approximate multiplier techniques can be divided into 1) approximation of generation of partial product, 2) approximation of partial product compression, and 3) approximation of addition. We concentrated on the second technique during our endeavor. Following the partial products' matrix formation, the resultant array is usually compressed into two rows and then added to get the final result. The partial product accumulation frequently uses approximate compressors with reduced complexity as a bottleneck in the multiplication (Fig. 1).

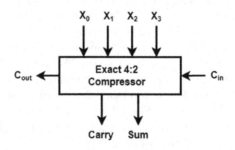

Fig. 1. 4-2 exact compressor [7]

An exact 4-2 compressor has five inputs of equal weight (denoted as X_0, X_1, X_2, X_3, C_{in}) and three outputs, Sum, Carry and C_{out}. The Sum output has the same weight as the inputs, while Carry and C_{out} have a double weight. The compressor is designed such that C_{out} is independent of C_{in} (Fig. 2).

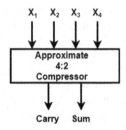

Fig. 2. 4-2 approximate compressor [9]

The C_{in} and C_{out} pins are not used in most of the 4-2 compressors in order to simplify both circuit implementation and wiring. So the designs for approximate compressors were proposed, which did not contain C_{in} and C_{out} pins. The maximum value that can be encoded using only Sum and Carry outputs is three. Having four inputs X_1, X_2, X_3, X_4, it is obvious that at least one error (when all inputs are '1') is unavoidable.

Various approximate compressor designs have been proposed throughout the years. In this work, we explore and implement 12 such designs. The twelve designs are displayed in Fig. 4. C and S represent the carry and sum outputs of the compressors, while E represents the difference between the obtained value and the expected value. The truth table of these designs has been presented in Table 1.

2.2 Types of Approximate Compressors

High-Accuracy Approximate Compressors. High-precision compressors are essential in high-precision multipliers. It has been observed that compressors with less than four errors can give greater multiplier accuracy. The approximate 4-2 compressor commonly omits the "c_{in}" and "c_{out}" pins as compared to the exact 4-2 compressor, which includes c_{out}, carry, and sum as outputs and x_1, x_2, x_3, x_4, and c_{in} as inputs. This type of omission disrupts carry propagation between compressors, causing the products to accumulate faster. The "Yang" compressors proposed in [2] only introduce four errors at most, with the most accurate, "Yang1," introducing only one error. The 4-2 compressor proposed in [10], referred to as "Lin," has two errors and a shorter critical path than "Yang". Lin has an XOR, an inverter, and a MUX-2 on the critical path, as shown in Fig. 4(f). The study [7] proposes "Strollo" compressor designs using the "stacking circuit." Strollo compressors' front-end circuit complexity grows with accuracy, as can be seen in Fig. 4(h)–(i). Both these architectures have a common compound gate "full adder," as shown in Fig. 4(h)–(i). The truth tables for strollo1 and strollo2 are shown in Table 1.

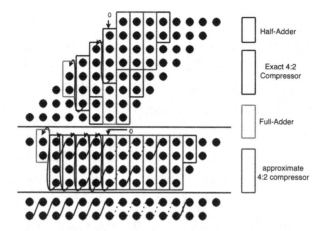

Fig. 3. Partial product reduction [7]

Low-Accuracy Approximate Compressors. The approximate 4–2 compressors with more than four errors are low-accuracy compressors. These low-
accuracy compressors have considerable performance advantages due to simpler architectures shown in Fig. 4, and their behavior is documented in Table 1.
"Momeni", "Sabetz", "Venka", "Akbari", etc., are some of the low-accuracy compressors that are hardware efficient. The approximate 4–2 compressor "Momeni"
described in [9] is displayed in Fig. 4(d). To achieve a simpler logic implementation, the circuit of "Momeni" inserts four errors in the truth table. [11] proposes a simple approximate compressor circuit named "Sabetz." It is depicted
in Fig. 4(e). Sabetz is a majority gate compressor that ignores the x_2 input and
assumes that S output is constant and equal to "1". The compressor "Ahma",
proposed in [12], is also very hardware efficient as it uses only three NOR gates
and a NAND gate, as shown in Fig. 4(g).

3 Commutative Property in Approximate Circuits

It has been observed that approximate circuits (approximate adders and multipliers) do not necessarily follow commutative properties. In other words, X.Y
$\neq$ Y.X. This also makes the output dependent on the operand order or the
operand sequence in which the multiplication is carried out. Sometimes this violation might lead to an increase in the output quality. Therefore, appropriately
ordering the operands for different compressors might lead to better quality and
output accuracy.

4 Experimental Setup

We have implemented 12 8 × 8 multiplier designs using the 12 compressors discussed above in this work. The design for reducing the partial product matrix

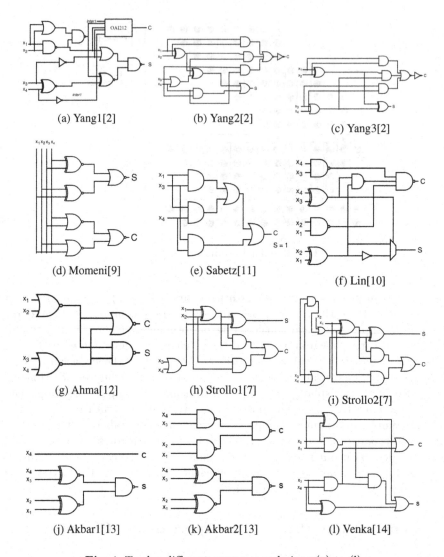

Fig. 4. Twelve different compressor designs (a) to (l)

(PPM) is developed using a method similar to the Dadda multiplier [15], reducing the maximum height of the PPM to two rows by employing numerous stages of compressors. To achieve the needed reduction in PPM, full and half adders were utilized along with compressors. The reduction technique for unsigned 8 × 8 approximate integer multiplier is shown in Fig. 3 as an example [7]. Dotted lines connect the Carry and Sum outputs of approximate 4-2 compressors, while solid lines connect the outputs of exact 4-2 compressors and full adders in this diagram. The approximate multiplier is implemented in CN configuration [7], wherein approximate compressors are used in the lesser significant eight

Table 1. Truth Table for compressor designs (a)–(l) [7]

x4....x1	Momeni [9]		Sabetz [11]		Yang2 [2]		Strollo1 [7]		Strollo2 [7]		Lin [10]		Ahma [12]		Yang1 [2]		Yang3 [2]		Akbar1 [13]		Akbar2 [13]		Venka [14]	
	CS	E	CS	E	CS	E	CS	E	CS	E	CS	E	CS	E	CS	E	CS	E	CS	E	CS	E	CS	E
0000	01	+1	01	+1	00		00		00		00		00		00		00		00		00		00	
0001	01		01		01		01		01		01		01		01		01		01		01		01	
0010	01		01		01		01		01		01		01		01		01		01		01		01	
0011	01	-1	01	-1	10		10		10		10		01	-1	10		10		00	-2	10		10	
0100	01		01		01		01		01		01		01		01		01		01		01		01	
0101	10		11	+1	10		10		10		10		11	+1	10		10		01	-1	01	-1	01	-1
0110	10		01	-1	10		10		10		10		11	+1	10		10		01	-1	01	-1	01	-1
0111	11		11		11		11		10	-1	11		11		11		11		01	-2	11		11	
1000	01		01		01		01		01		01		01		01		01		11	+2	01		01	
1001	10		11	+1	10		10		10		10		11	+1	10		10		11	+1	01	-1	01	-1
1010	10		01	-1	10		10		10		10		11	+1	10		10		11	+1	01	-1	01	-1
1011	11		11		11		11		11		11		11		11		11		11		11		11	
1100	01	-1	11	+1	11	+1	01	-1	10		10		01	-1	10		11	+1	10		10		10	
1101	11		11		11		10	-1	11		11		11		11		10	-1	11		11		11	
1110	11		11		11		10	-1	11		11		11		11		10	-1	11		11		11	
1111	11	-1	11	-1	11	-1	11	-1	11	-1	10	-2	11	-1	11	-1	11	-1	11	-1	10	-2	11	-1

Table 2. Accuracy for LeNet5 and ResNet18 Networks for both operand sequences

Model	LeNet5		ResNet18	
	$a \times b$	$b \times a$	$a \times b$	$b \times a$
Yang1 [2]	98.57%	98.56%	59.68%	59.92%
Yang2 [2]	98.48%	98.46%	58.07%	69.4%
Yang3 [2]	98.3%	98.36%	55.86%	67.98%
Lin [10]	98.56%	98.59%	58.65%	58.68%
Strollo1 [7]	98.36%	98.32%	55.18%	38.08%
Strollo2 [7]	98.58%	98.57%	59.37%	59.74%
Momeni [9]	13.84%	14.04%	10%	10%
Venka [14]	98.47%	98.27%	48.23%	49.74%
Akbar1 [13]	94.96%	92.12%	22.46%	12.3%
Akbar2 [13]	98.42%	98.36%	61.09%	60.7%
Sabetz [11]	9.61%	9.82%	10%	10%
Ahma [12]	98.46%	98.42%	55.24%	43.73%

columns, and exact compressors are used in the higher significant eight columns, as shown in Fig. 3.

The twelve multiplier designs are evaluated on Neural Network and Image processing applications. The approximation was incorporated into the neural networks, and the accuracies and outputs were obtained for both the operand sequences ($a \times b$ and $b \times a$). During the convolution operation of CNNs, the compressor-based approximate multiplication was used to multiply the normalized weights. The approximation and violation of commutative property were checked for two neural networks: LeNet5 and ResNet18. The results are reported in Table 2. The base accuracies for the LeNet5 and ResNet18 networks for integer multiplication (98.55 % for LeNet and 53.18% for ResNet18).

Table 3. Image processing results

Design	Image smoothening				Image sharpening				JPEG compression			
	PSNR		SSIM		PSNR		SSIM		PSNR		SSIM	
	$a \times b$	$b \times a$	$a \times b$	$b \times a$	$a \times b$	$b \times a$	$a \times b$	$b \times a$	$a \times b$	$b \times a$	$a \times b$	$b \times a$
Yang1 [2]	72.59	62.64	1	0.9998	inf	inf	1	1	57.04	57.7	0.9997	0.9998
Yang2 [2]	57.52	43.64	0.9995	0.998	51.66	33.9	0.9996	0.9929	50	52.06	0.9985	0.999
Yang3 [2]	56.13	46.82	0.9994	0.9986	46.84	35.11	0.9995	0.9949	49.16	50.48	0.9982	0.9986
Lin [10]	69.62	59.07	1	0.9997	inf	inf	1	1	54.35	54.88	0.9995	0.9995
Strollo1 [7]	54.37	44.12	0.9993	0.9987	46.5	32.83	0.9994	0.991	49.22	50.57	0.9982	0.9986
Strollo2 [7]	51.91	55.37	0.9989	0.9993	35.64	40.5	0.9938	0.9971	51.18	50.66	0.9988	0.9986
Momeni [9]	35.81	33.2	0.9917	0.9912	17.09	16.59	0.8509	0.8352	38.44	38.43	0.993	0.993
Venka [14]	37.91	39.09	0.9955	0.9957	27.45	29.11	0.9735	0.9812	45.9	45.63	0.9961	0.9958
Akbar1 [13]	34.76	33.01	0.9921	0.9921	27.55	24.31	0.9747	0.9533	44.24	41	0.9942	0.9904
Akbar2 [13]	37.9	39.03	0.9954	0.9956	27.44	29.11	0.9735	0.9812	45.86	45.58	0.996	0.9957
Sabetz [11]	28.03	25.52	0.9851	0.9803	13.71	12.73	0.7397	0.692	36.07	36.01	0.9909	0.9904
Ahma [12]	42.85	43.01	0.9957	0.9954	32.09	31.8	0.9889	0.9884	45.23	45.34	0.9954	0.9955

Table 3 shows the results obtained when 12 multipliers designs were incorporated into image processing. The image data is represented by a, and b represents the kernel data. The three image processing applications are Image Smoothening, Image Sharpening, and JPEG Compression. JPEG compression is implemented by approximating the Discrete Cosine Transfer (DCT) section and using exact Inverse Discrete Cosine Transfer (IDCT). Normalization and Denormalization are also implemented as exact functions. PSNR and SSIM are calculated by comparing each output image with the reference image generated by implementing exact DCT and IDCT.

For image smoothening, b is a 3×3 kernel data given by

$$\begin{bmatrix} 3 & 21 & 3 \\ 21 & 158 & 21 \\ 3 & 21 & 3 \end{bmatrix}$$

For image sharpening, b is a 5×5 kernel data given by

$$\begin{bmatrix} 1 & 4 & 7 & 4 & 1 \\ 4 & 16 & 26 & 16 & 4 \\ 7 & 26 & 41 & 26 & 7 \\ 4 & 16 & 26 & 16 & 4 \\ 1 & 4 & 7 & 4 & 1 \end{bmatrix}$$

For JPEG compression, the quantization matrix used is as given below

$$\begin{bmatrix} 16 & 11 & 10 & 16 & 24 & 40 & 51 & 61 \\ 12 & 12 & 14 & 19 & 26 & 58 & 60 & 55 \\ 14 & 13 & 16 & 24 & 40 & 57 & 69 & 56 \\ 14 & 17 & 22 & 29 & 51 & 87 & 80 & 62 \\ 18 & 22 & 37 & 56 & 68 & 109 & 103 & 77 \\ 24 & 35 & 55 & 64 & 81 & 104 & 113 & 92 \\ 49 & 64 & 78 & 87 & 103 & 121 & 120 & 101 \\ 72 & 92 & 95 & 98 & 112 & 100 & 103 & 99 \end{bmatrix}$$

The image processing results have been reported after averaging the results obtained on a total of ten images.

5   Discussion

This section discusses the impact of approximation and commutativity (input order) on Accuracy and PSNR/SSIM of Neural networks and Image processing applications, respectively.

5.1   Impact of Approximation

The weights in a neural network are very small (nearly equal to zero). Therefore, during the partial product reduction step of the multiplier (used during the convolution of the neural network), the value zero is encountered at many stages. Compressor designs, Momeni [9] and Sabetz [11], introduce error (that is, $S = 1$) when all inputs are zero. This leads to non-zero outputs when the inputs are zero, which induces errors at every later stage of multiplication of zero or very small weights. We can see from Table 2 that Sabetz [11] and Momeni [9] give very low accuracies (less than 15%) for both the networks, Lenet5 and Resnet18. So, the approximation has a great impact on the accuracy when Sabetz [11] and Momeni [9] designs are used in the multiplier. The Akbar1 [13] design for the LeNet5 network has poorer accuracy (about 93%) than the Akbar2 [13] design (around 98%) (see Table 2) as Akbar2 [13] introduces fewer errors than Akbar1 [13] and does not have any errors for the most recurring pattern in these networks' PPM. Akbar1 [13]'s accuracy reduces to approximately 20% when the network grows larger (that is, for ResNet18), whereas Akbar2 [13]'s accuracy goes to around 60%. Because the ResNet18 network is quite larger than the LeNet5 network, the accuracy drop (in terms of base accuracy) is substantially worse for the Akbar1 [13] design due to the approximation.

The Yang [2] compressor designs are high precision compressors because they approximate at most four input patterns, as shown in Table 1. The most accurate design among Yang compressors is Yang1 [2], which introduces approximation at only one place in the truth table. Yang2 [2] also has a high level of accuracy, whereas Yang3 [2] has the lowest level of accuracy due to four errors in its truth table. This is typically true for both the applications that we are looking at in this study. However, in some circumstances, such as for the ResNet18 network when the operand sequence is $b \times a$, there is a lesser impact of approximation on Yang2 [2] and Yang3 [2] designs as compared to Yang1 [2]. Thus, we can say that the impact of approximation for Yang [2] designs depends on the application and the operand sequence. From Table 2, we observe that the Strollo [7] designs give good accuracy in most cases. Moreover, the Strollo2 [7] design performs better than the Strollo1 [7] design in both the networks and provides an accuracy higher than the base accuracy. On the other hand, the drop in accuracy in Strollo1 [7] is because of the four errors that it introduces for the high inputs. One of the very efficient designs is the Lin [10] compressor design, which, as observed from Table 2, gives an accuracy higher than the base accuracy in both the networks. This is due to Lin [10] introducing just a single approximation when all the inputs are high, and since we have to deal with weights in neural networks' application, we rarely encounter this case. Venka [14] and Ahma [12] introduce a total of five errors, and hence, they are low-accuracy compressors. When we observe them for smaller neural networks, such as LeNet5, we see that they give a significant accuracy, and this is because the approximation is generally made when both of its most significant bits are non-zero. Since that type of input does not frequently occur in partial product matrices, these designs give sufficient accuracy for smaller networks.

A very low PSNR/SSIM is retained while using Momeni [9] and Sabetz [11] designs in image sharpening. So the results of the image processing applications are consistent with the fact that the approximation in Momeni [9] and Sabetz [11] designs has the highest impact on the performance of the multiplier. Similarly, Akbar2 [13] has a greater SSIM and PSNR than Akbar1 [13] for image smoothening, sharpening, and JPEG compression applications, which is also consistent with the above observations from neural networks' application. As seen above, Yang1 [2] is better than Yang2 [2] and Yang3 [2] in image processing applications as well. Yang3 [2] occasionally outperforms Yang2 [2] in terms of smoothening, sharpening or JPEG compression PSNR or SSIM. The approximation techniques in the integer multiplier cause these exceptions. The Lin [10] compressor design is very accurate, as can be observed from the results of image processing as well, where Lin [10] gives a high smoothening, sharpening, and JPEG compression PSNR or SSIM. Again the image processing results verify that the Venka [14] and Ahma [12] compressors are low-accuracy compressors, as observed in neural networks' application. Strollo1 [7] and Strollo2 [7] designs give consistent results across applications, that is, Strollo1 [7] gives a lesser SSIM/PSNR as its truth table introduces four errors.

5.2   Impact of Commutativity

Approximate circuits and multipliers do not follow the commutative law. This can be observed from the results of $a \times b$ and $b \times a$ multiplication in Tables 2 and 3. For Yang designs, we observe that the Yang1 design generally performs better than Yang2 and Yang3. In some circumstances, such as the ResNet18 network, Yang2 [2] and Yang3 [2] designs are superior to Yang1 [2] when the operand sequence is $b \times a$. Also, a change of around ten % in the accuracy is observed when the operand sequence is changed from $a \times b$ to $b \times a$, except for the LeNet5 network, where a smaller change takes place (Table 2). Similarly, the Strollo2 [7] design performs better than the Strollo1 [12] design in both the networks. An interesting point to note here is the significant drop in Strollo1 [7] for the ResNet18 network when the operand sequence is interchanged. The reason for this is the approximation technique that leads to the drop in the accuracy of the Strollo1 [7] design. The drop is also evident in the LeNet5 network, but it is not significant. It is expected that as we move on to even larger networks, this drop in the accuracy of Strollo1 [7] would increase on changing the operand sequence. Strollo1 performs better for $a \times b$, while Strollo2 performs better for $b \times a$. For the Lin [10] compressor, we observe that there is no significant drop in the accuracy for both the networks when the order of operands is changed.

For the Akbar [13] compressors (both Akbar1 and Akbar2), accuracies obtained are very less since both are low-accuracy compressors, and we see that both perform better for $a \times b$ operand sequence. Sabetz [11] and Momeni [9], as could be observed, provide very less accuracy in comparison to other compressor designs. From Table 2, we observe a very slight variation in the accuracy of Sabetz [11] and Momeni [9] when the operand sequence is changed in the neural networks. Venka can be classified as a compressor that performs better for $b \times a$ operand sequence (as observed for a relatively larger network, such as ResNet18). On the other hand, Ahma [12] performs better for the $a \times b$ operand sequence.

A similar observation can be drawn from Table 3 for image processing results. Few designs work best for $a \times b$ operand order, while few work best for $b \times a$ order. For example, if for a design, (*larger number* $\times$ *smaller number*) works better, then if it is a brighter image, $a \times b$ works better. If it is a darker shade image, then $b \times a$ works better. Momeni [9], Yang1 [2], Yang2 [2], Yang3 [2], Lin [10], Akbar1 [13], Strollo1 [7], and Sabetz [11] give better PSNR and SSIM in image smoothening and sharpening for $a \times b$, and better PSNR and SSIM in JPEG compression for $b \times a$. On the other hand, Strollo2 [7], Akbar2 [13] and Venka [14] give better PSNR and SSIM in image smoothening and sharpening for $b \times a$, and better PSNR and SSIM in JPEG compression for $a \times b$. While Ahma [12] somewhat lies in a gray zone. We observe that the PSNR and SSIM results for image sharpening and smoothening are very consistent with the results obtained in neural networks.

6 Conclusions

This paper shows the impact of approximation and commutativity on Neural networks and Image processing applications. We have evaluated twelve compressor-based multiplier designs on Neural Network and Image processing applications for the analysis. We show that the accuracy of Neural Network and PSNR/SSIM of Image processing application drops drastically if the multiplication of zeroes is approximated. We also show the violation of the commutative law for approximate circuits and propose to appropriately use this property of different outputs in different operand sequences for better results.

Acknowledgement. This work is supported through grants received from Prime Minister Research Fellowship, Intel India Research Fellowship, Science and Engineering Research Board (SERB), Government of India, under CRG/2018/005013, MTR/2019/001605, SPR/2020/000450, and Semiconductor Research Corporation (SRC) through contract 2020-IR-2980.

References

1. Nandi, A., Jha, C.K., Mekie, J.: Should we code differently when using approximate circuits? In: 2019 IEEE Asia Pacific Conference on Circuits and Systems (APCCAS) (2019)
2. Yang, Z., Han, J., Lombardi, F.: Approximate compressors for error-resilient multiplier design. In: 2015 IEEE International Symposium on Defect and Fault Tolerance in VLSI and Nanotechnology Systems (DFTS) (2015)
3. Jha, C.K., Prasad, K., Tomar, A., et al.: SEDAAF: FPGA based single exact dual approximate adders for approximate processors. In: IEEE Xplore (2020)
4. Jha, C.K., Prasad, K., Srivastava, V., et al.: FPAD: a multistage approximation methodology for designing floating point approximate dividers. In: 2020 IEEE International Symposium on Circuits and Systems (ISCAS) (2020)
5. Jiang, H., Liu, L., Lombardi, F., Han, J.: Approximate arithmetic circuits: design and evaluation. In: Reda, S., Shafique, M. (eds.) Approximate Circuits, pp. 67–98. Springer, Cham (2019). https://doi.org/10.1007/978-3-319-99322-5_4
6. Hore, A., Ziou, D.: Image quality metrics: PSNR vs. SSIM. In: 2010 20th International Conference on Pattern Recognition (2010)
7. Strollo, A.G., Napoli, E., De Caro, D., et al.: Comparison and extension of approximate 4–2 compressors for low-power approximate multipliers. IEEE Trans. Circuits Syst. I: Regular Papers **67**(9), 3021–3034 (2020)
8. Kong, T., Li, S.: Design and analysis of approximate 4–2 compressors for high-accuracy multipliers. IEEE Trans. Very Large Scale Integr. (VLSI) Syst. **29**(10), 1771–1781 (2021)
9. Momeni, A., Han, J., Montuschi, P., et al.: Design and analysis of approximate compressors for multiplication. IEEE Trans. Comput. **64**(4), 984–994 (2015)
10. Lin, C.-H., Lin, I.-C.: High accuracy approximate multiplier with error correction. In: 2013 IEEE 31st International Conference on Computer Design (ICCD) (2013)
11. Sabetzadeh, F., Moaiyeri, M.H., Ahmadinejad, M.: A majority-based imprecise multiplier for ultra-efficient approximate image multiplication. IEEE Trans. Circuits Syst. I: Regular Papers **66**(11), 4200–4208 (2019)
12. Ahmadinejad, M., Moaiyeri, M.H., Sabetzadeh, F.: Energy and area efficient imprecise compressors for approximate multiplication at nanoscale. AEU Int. J. Electron. Commun. **110**, 152859 (2019)
13. Akbari, O., Kamal, M., Afzali-Kusha, A., et al.: Dual-quality 4:2 compressors for utilizing in dynamic accuracy configurable multipliers. IEEE Trans. Very Large Scale Integr. (VLSI) Syst. **25**(4), 1352–1361 (2017)
14. Venkatachalam, S., Ko, S.-B.: Design of power and area efficient approximate multipliers. IEEE Trans. Very Large Scale Integr. (VLSI) Syst. **25**(5), 1782–1786 (2017)
15. Ramkumar, B., Sradeep, V., Kittur, H.: A design technique for delay and power efficient dadda-multiplier. In: IEEE Xplore (2021)

An Overlap-and-Add Based Time Domain Acceleration of CNNs on FPGA-CPU Systems

Rudresh Pratap Singh[1]([✉]) [iD], Shreyam Kumar[1], and Jai Gopal Pandey[2] [iD]

[1] Birla Institute of Technology and Science, Hyderabad 500078, India
[2] CSIR - Central Electronics Engineering Research Institute, Pilani 333031, India
jai@ceeri.res.in

Abstract. Convolutional neural networks (CNNs) have become widespread in the area of image recognition and are widely implemented in modern facial recognition systems. With the increasing use of CNNs, their run-time speed becomes critical for faster real-world systems. Traditional FPGA-based acceleration requires either large on-chip memory or high bandwidth and memory access time. We present an algorithm and subsequent hardware design for computing CNN using an overlap-and-add-based technique in the time domain. In the proposed algorithm, the input image is broken into tiles which can be processed independently without involving the overheads of computing in the frequency domain. This also allows efficient concurrency of the convolution process which results in higher throughput and lower power consumption. At the same time, we maintain the low on-chip memory requirements necessary for the fabrication of faster and cheaper processor designs. We implement CNN VGG16 and AlexNet models with our design on the Xilinx Virtex 7 and Zynq boards. Performance analysis of our design provides a 0.48× better throughput than the state-of-the-art AlexNet and uses 0.15× lesser multipliers and other resources than the state-of-the-art VGG16.

Keywords: Convolution neural networks (CNNs) · Hardware architectures · Performance analysis · FPGA-CPU Accelerators

1 Introduction

Convolutional neural network (CNN) is a class of neural network that is predominantly used in the fields of image and video processing [1–3]. CNN's are composed of multiple stages (layers) that are broadly classified as 'convolution', 'fully connected' (FC), and 'pooling and non-linear' layers [4]. Each layer of the CNN has its computational complexity and needs to be handled appropriately while designing a system for the same. The convolution layer is compute-intensive while the fully connected layer is bandwidth-intensive. In the AlexNet network, the convolution/FC layers account for 93/7% of total computation. They have 5/95% of the total weight [5]. According to [6], on average, FC layers only represent around 0.11% of the total execution time of the CNN. As such, efforts to accelerate the convolutional process of neural networks can be shown to have a greater impact on the overall performance of the CNN architecture [7].

With the increasing size of images emerging into use, the neural network itself needs a large number of variables to process images with any form of accuracy. For example, an AlexNet is composed of 61 Million(M) parameters and around 600M connections. Storing these as 32-bit floating-point numbers requires approximately 250 MB of storage space on a device [7]. This far exceeds the available memory on field-programmable gate array (FPGA) on-chip storage. This presents a challenge that needs to be overcome during accelerator design. Data can be stored on an off-chip memory for execution. However, the large energy and performance overhead encountered in shifting data makes this approach undesirable [4].

In the proposed work, we put forward a streaming algorithm that vastly reduces the amount of data that needs to be stored on the chip at any particular time. In addition, we make a comparison between the various state-of-the-art convolvers using their delay multiplier products (a composite performance metric used in signal processing). The proposed work is then evaluated by implementing VGG16 and AlexNet on Xilinx Virtex 7 and Zynq FPGA-based platforms for practical benchmarks. The results show a 0.48× increase in throughput along with a 0.49× lesser power consumption.

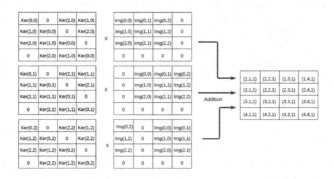

Fig. 1. Rotate, multiply and accumulate operations.

2 Background and Related Work

2.1 Convolution Neural Network

A CNN is comprised of multiple layers that work together to achieve the core functionality. Approximately all CNNs can be divided into three groups of layers, Convolution (CONV), pooling, and fully connected layers. The details of these layers are as follows:

(1) Convolution (CONV) layer

(2) Pooling and non-linear layers
(3) fully-connected layers

While all CNNs have these three layers, the pooling function, activation functions, and a number of neurons change with different CNN architectures. Only the convolution layer remains common, with the size of the kernel changing based on the requirements. In addition to this, the convolution layer is also the most computation-intensive when processing or training a given image [8]. Due to these reasons, it is more efficient and flexible to design a hardware architecture for a CONV layer while implementing other layers on a general purpose processor [9–11].

2.2   Overlap-and-Add

Overlap-and-add (OaA) allows independent operation on each tile and hence the entire input feature map can be handled simultaneously or in a streaming fashion, depending on resource constraints. Furthermore, each tile is generally computed using Fast Fourier Transform (FFT) in frequency domain [12,13]. In this paper, we propose an algorithm to compute in the time domain while maintaining the tile operation of OaA, to avoid the frequency domain overheads.

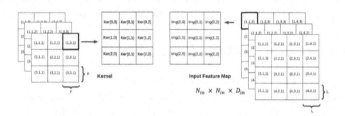

Fig. 2. Tiling of input feature map and kernel.

2.3   Related Work

In [13], convolution has been performed in the frequency domain using OaA. Subsequently, the input tiles are Fourier transformed, used in further computation, and then undergo an inverse Fourier transform. However, computing the Fourier transform results in zero-padding that slows the performance unless dealt with by the design architecture itself. Moreover, as observed in [14], a new algorithm has been required to handle these zero values in the Fourier transform result. Here, we propose an architecture that performs OaA convolution in the time domain, which reduces the effect of the resulting zero-padding through the use of sparse matrix multiplication during computation. This eliminates the need for separate methods to handle padding values while also maintaining the accelerator performance requirements. Additionally, in the frequency domain OaA,

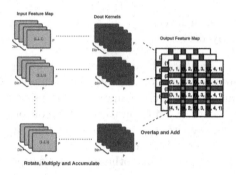

Fig. 3. Time domain overlap-and-add.

the multiply-accumulate (MAC) unit must support complex numbers. A canonical complex number multiplier contains 3 floating-point multipliers [15], which further add to the resources needed by the design. Our proposed architecture in the time domain entirely eliminates the need for complex number multiplication. Prior work [16] has incorporated parallelism in the computation by unrolling the 2D convolution with matrix multiplication. However, parallelism by unrolling encounters a bottleneck with the limited on-chip memory of FPGAs. To address this bottleneck, the proposed architecture uses OaA method time domain matrix multiplication, to provide an algorithm suited for streaming data on FPGAs.

3   Time Domain 2D Overlap-and-Add

The overlap-and-add method is mostly used in digital signal processing to perform convolution on a running stream of data. The ability to operate on streaming data prevents storing the entire feature map on on-chip memory, reducing the memory fetch latency in the architecture. OaA based convolution is most efficient when the size of the filter is small compared to the input data. Most CNN architectures have kernel sizes of 1×1, 3×3, 5×5 and 7×7, making OaA an ideal tool for such convolutions. The inputs are $N \times N \times D$ in feature map and *Dout* kernels, each of size $F \times F \times Din$. Figure 2 Steps for time domain 2D overlap-and-add are as follows:

(i) Divide the input feature map into tiles of size $L \times L$. Where, L is an arbitrary constant chosen for division of image into independent tiles. L can be tuned for optimal performance Fig. 2, Table 1.

(ii) Pad both $L \times L$ image tile and $F \times F$ kernel feature map tiles with zeroes to make it $P \times P$ where $P = L + F - 1$. After padding, transpose the image feature tile. (Number of multipliers utilized at a given time is directly proportional to P. Depending on the availability of resources we can reduce the computation time of convolution by choosing a higher value of P).

(iii) Select each transformed kernel row and convert it into a $P \times P$ sized matrix. Each row is a rotated version of the previous row. The result of this operation is F non-zero matrices of size $P \times P$ as shown in Fig. 1.

(iv) As shown in Fig. 1, matrix multiplication of these F matrices are performed independently with F versions of input feature tile where each version is obtained by a single right rotation of the columns of the previous version.

(v) All output tiles from the above operations are added to obtain a single tile of size $P \times P$.

(vi) Transpose the previous output tile and overlap-and-add it with the adjacent tiles as per the scheme shown in Fig. 3. This gives us the final convolution result for one tile. After performing the transpose operation on the output tile, it can be sent back to the CPU releasing the on-chip memory. This makes the proposed architecture memory-efficient, as at any given point a very limited number of memory units is being used.

(vii) Repeat steps 2 to 7 for all the tiles of the input feature map and for all *Dout* kernels. Add the results to obtain the convolved output feature map.

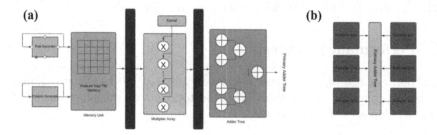

Fig. 4. Hardware resources (a) multiplier (b) convolver.

4   Overlap-and-Add Based 2D Convolver

The aim of this design is to bring data-level parallelism to the convolution process by using multiple smaller modules. To this effect, the modules are organized in a hierarchical fashion as shown in Fig. 4, with every complete convolver composed of M subunits joined by an adder tree. Each unit takes a $P \times P$ transformed input, and the transformed kernel, both are stored in a shared local memory space. The output of each outer unit is generated from the primary adder tree which combines its individual subunit results into a single integer. The MAC units used in the design do not need to support complex arithmetic operations, which saves computational power and greatly simplifies the arithmetic compared to the frequency domain-based overlap-and-add operation.

An observation drawn from the algorithm in the previous section; all elements are accessed from memory in a row cyclic or column cyclic fashion. This cyclic property can be replicated in hardware with the use of shifters for both rows as well as columns. Moreover, by constraining the shifting to only nonzero elements, we can further optimize the sparse matrix multiplication process. Including these optimizations, we put forward an efficient data pipeline keeping in line with the original concept of the overlap-and-add algorithm. The proposed unit and subunit are shown in Fig. 4 and Fig. 5. Every subunit of the architecture are composed of i) Onchip memory which stores the matrix that will be used in convolution. ii) Multiplier array which receives input from the on-chip memory and forwards the output to the local adder tree. iii) Adder tree, which is two in number. The first adder tree (henceforth called the local adder tree) computes the result of the sparse matrix multiplication of the transformed kernel and tile. The second adder tree (henceforth called the primary adder tree) computes the sum of the results of the individual sparse matrix multiplications performed by the subunits. This tree provides the final result of the unit.

5   Performance Analysis

The performance of a convolver could be evaluated by the delay required to process a complete convolution layer, the total power consumption, and the total on-chip area of the convolver.

5.1   Performance Metric

On-chip area and power consumption of the convolver are directly proportional to the number of multipliers and on-chip memory size. One of the main reasons to design a convolver using overlap and add algorithms is to bring down the on-chip memory considerably. Delay multiplier (DM) product is defined as the delay (no. of clocks) to run the complete convolution process times the total number of multipliers used per clock cycle.

5.2   OaA Time Domain Convolver

The number of floating point multipliers (Mul-ker) needed to perform the multiplication operation on one column of the extracted feature tile is:

$$Mul_k = (P - 2F + 1)F + (F - 1) + (F - 2) + \ldots + (F - r) + (F - r) + \ldots (to\ P\ terms) \tag{1}$$

where,

P = Size of padded tile; F = Size of kernel; L = Total number of nonzero columns in each feature tile; r = Number of nonzero entries in a column $(P - L)$

$$Mul_k = \frac{F \times (2P - 3F + 3)}{2} \tag{2}$$

(i) Total number of nonzero columns in each feature tile (L)
(ii) Total number of matrix multiplications for each kernel (F)
(iii) Number of tiles for each layer of input feature map $((N/L)^2)$
(iv) Number of layers in input feature map (Din)
(v) Number of filters $(Dout)$

The final number of multiplications for each column is given by (2). Extending this to all columns during operation, the delay multiplier product for OaA based time domain convolver can be shown as:

$$DM = L \times F \times \frac{N^2}{L^2} \times Din \times Dout \times Eq.(2) \tag{3}$$

5.3 Space Convolver

The number of multiplications required to calculate one output tile is $F \times F$. Here, for ease of calculation and comparison unit stride has been considered. Now, the number of clock cycles to perform the entire convolution is:

$$Nclk = (N + F - 1)^2 \times Din \times Dout \tag{4}$$

The delay multiplier product as $DMspace = (4) \times F^2$.

5.4 Performance Comparison

To compare the performance of the time-division OaA with the space convolver, we define:

$$DMratio = \frac{DMspace}{DMtdOaA} \tag{5}$$

Substituting $L = P - F + 1$ and simplifying we get:

$$DMratio = \frac{(N + F - 1)^2 \times 2 \times (P - F + 1) \times F}{N^2 \times (2P - 3F + 3)} \tag{6}$$

Considering $N >> F$,

$$DMratio = \frac{2P - 2F + 2}{2P - 3F + 3} \tag{7}$$

Table 1. Space-time domain OaA convolver DM ratio for various kernel size and feature map tile size.

Kernal Size	3	3	5	5	5	7	7	7	9	9	11	11
L	4	6	8	10	12	9	11	13	11	13	13	15
DM Ratio	1.5	1.2	**1.33**	1.25	1.2	**1.5**	1.375	1.3	**1.57**	1.44	**1.625**	1.5

Table 2. Execution time for VGG16 and AlexNet.

Layer (Group)	VGG16 execution time (in ms)				AlexNet Execution Time (in ms)		
	FPGA(Theoretical)	FPGA (Actual)	CPU	Sequential	FPGA (Actual)	CPU	Sequential
CONV1	48.73	49.57	7.42	56.99	8.34	1.32	9.66
CONV2	73.38	75.33	5.23	80.56	11.42	0.13	11.55
CONV3	57.84	60.24	3.49	63.73	4.21	0.18	4.39
CONV4	57.84	59.19	1.28	60.47	5.98	0.23	6.21
CONV5	10.21	12.32	0.33	12.65	4.21	0.16	4.37
Total	248	256.65	17.75	274.4	34.16	2.02	36.18

Table 3. Performance comparison with the other CNN implementations on FPGA.

	[8]	[17]	This Work	This Work
Platform	Virtex7 VX485t	Zynq XC7Z045	Virtex7	Zynq-700
Clock (MHz)	100	150	100	150
Data precision	32-bit float	16-bit fixed	32-bit float	32-bit float
Bandwidth (GB/s)	12.8	4.2	5.0	5.0
CNN Model	AlexNet	VGG16-SVD	AlexNet	VGG16-SVD
BRAM	4.5 MB	2.13 MB	3.03 MB	3.03 MB
DSP, Multipliers	2240,747	780,780	243,243	243,243
Throughput (GOP/s)	61.62	187.80	91.3	135.48
Delay (CONV) (ms)	21.61	163.42	45.64	270.21
Power (FPGA) (W)	18.61	9.63	9.353	9.353
Delay × Multipliers	16142	127647	**11090**	65610
Resource efficiency	0.082	0.241	0.135	0.200
Power efficiency	3.31	19.50	9.76	14.48
Classification accuracy	Lossless	Lossy	Lossless	Lossless
Flexibility	Any CNN	Limited	Any CNN	Any CNN

5.5 Computational Complexity

The number of floating point multiplications can be brought down considerably by a time domain OaA convolver, as compared to a space convolver as per the Table 1. For GoogleNet, a time domain OaA convolver can reduce the number of floating point operations by 47.64%. For AlexNet, this value increases to 49.16%. For VGG16, we get the maximum theoretical improvement of 50% reduction over the number of operations.

6 Experimental Setup, Results and Analysis

The FPGA-based accelerator has been designed in Xilinx Vivado v.2019.1 using Verilog. Here, the CPU-based portions have been implemented using thread-based parallelism in Python. We first elaborate upon the implementation of FPGA-based architecture and then move toward the CPU and its integration

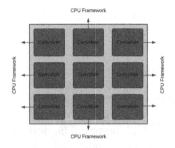

Fig. 5. Time based OaA convolver.

with the FPGA. The implementation has been performed on a Xilinx FPGA Virtex7 485t, having a 37 Mb on-chip BRAM used for storing image and kernel data. We have used a working frequency of 100 MHz. A shared memory has been used to transfer data to the CPU platform for the overlap stage of the protocol.

The CPU platform used for implementation has been a 10 Core Intel Xeon E5-2600 v2 processor. The CPU and FPGA have been configured to be used in the sequential execution mode. In sequential execution, the CPU performs the final Overlap and ReLU step after completion of the FPGA based steps. In this section, we will provide the results of the experiments performed on the Virtex 7 FPGA. We then move towards comparison of the results with existing FPGA accelerators for CNNs.

6.1   Resource Utilization

The utilization of resources for the design on the Xilinx Virtex 7 485t and Zynq-700 FPGAs are given in Table 3. Here, 18.36% LUTs are used with a power consumption of 9.35 W. The amount of on-chip memory used for the design is 3.03 MB. It includes the double-buffered cache as well as the BRAM units used for storing the image, kernel, and temporary data. The total multipliers used in the design on each FPGA equals 243 and contribute to the bulk of FPGA-based consumption by the design.

6.2   Comparison

The performance of the design on AlexNet and VGG16 is shown in Table 3. Here, a breakup of each layer of the CNN design is also given. It can be seen that the actual performance of the model with VGG16 is similar to the calculated theoretical performance. The slight mismatch in the values can be attributed to slight delays in data transfer occurring through the pipelines in the model. As shown in Table 3, in AlexNet, our design provides 0.32 × improvement over the memory used along with a 0.48 × better throughput and a 0.49 × lesser power consumption over the state-of-the-art CNN implemented in [8]. For VGG16, on a Zynq board, our implementation needs 0.15 × lesser multipliers and gives a comparable performance in power estimation as [11], without sacrificing accuracy in classification.

6.3 Fully Connected Layer

Our fully connected layer has been executed and benchmarked on a CPU. This provides greater flexibility and allows for making the design more generalized compared to a traditional FPGA design. The performance in sequential execution is given in Table 2. The power consumed and the time taken by the CPU will not change drastically for minor changes in model [13].

7 Conclusion

In this paper, an overlap-and-add algorithm for reducing the computational complexity of the convolution layer has been given. A hardware architecture has been proposed to accelerate the CNN on the FPGA using time-domain computations. It eliminates the overheads of traditional frequency domain operations. The fully connected layers have been implemented on the CPU to provide additional flexibility to the overall design, allowing the execution of any CNN with only minor changes to the hardware. Finally, two state-of-the-art CNN models, AlexNet and VGG16, have been tested on the proposed design with considerable improvements in power and memory consumption and the number of multipliers used. Further improvements could be achieved, depending on the requirement, by exploiting the sparsity of the feature map by employing more efficient *SpVM* and *SpMM* algorithms and gathering the necessary information to design a framework for the automatic generation of an optimized design.

References

1. Simonyan, K., Zisserman, A.: Very deep convolutional networks for large-scale image recognition. arXiv preprint arXiv:1409.1556 (2014
2. Szegedy, C., et al.: Going deeper with convolutions. In Proceedings of the IEEE Conference on Computer Vision and Pattern Recognition, pp. 1–9 (2015)
3. Zeiler, Matthew D.., Fergus, Rob: Visualizing and understanding convolutional networks. In: Fleet, David, Pajdla, Tomas, Schiele, Bernt, Tuytelaars, Tinne (eds.) ECCV 2014. LNCS, vol. 8689, pp. 818–833. Springer, Cham (2014). https://doi.org/10.1007/978-3-319-10590-1_53
4. Mittal, S.: A survey of FPGA-based accelerators for convolutional neural networks. Neural Comput. Appl. **32**(4), 1109–1139 (2020)
5. Zhang, C., Sun, G., Fang, Z., Zhou, P., Pan, P., Cong, J.: Caffeine: toward uniformed representation and acceleration for deep convolutional neural networks. IEEE Trans. Comput. Aided Des. Integr. Circuits Syst. **38**(11), 2072–2085 (2018)
6. Motamedi, M., Gysel, P., Ghiasi, S.: Placid: a platform for FPGA-based accelerator creation for DCNNs. ACM Trans. Multimed. Comput. Commun. Appl. (TOMM) **13**(4), 1–21 (2017)

7. Suda, N., et al.: Throughput-optimized opencl-based fpga accelerator for large-scale convolutional neural networks. In: Proceedings of the 2016 ACM/SIGDA International Symposium on Field-Programmable Gate Arrays, pp. 16–25 (2016)
8. Zhang, C., Li, P., Sun, G., Guan, Y., Xiao, B., Cong, J.: Optimizing FPGA-based accelerator design for deep convolutional neural networks. In: Proceedings of the 2015 ACM/SIGDA International Symposium on Field-Programmable Gate Arrays, pp. 161–170 (2015)
9. DiCecco, R., Lacey, G., Vasiljevic, J., Chow, P., Taylor, G., Areibi, S.: Caffeinated FPGAs: FPGA framework for convolutional neural networks. In: 2016 International Conference on Field-Programmable Technology (FPT), pp. 265–268. IEEE (2016)
10. Meloni, P., Capotondi, A., Deriu, G., Brian, M., Conti, F., Rossi, D., Raffo, L., Benini, L.: Neuraghe: exploiting CPU-FPGA synergies for efficient and flexible CNN inference acceleration on Zynq SoCs. ACM Trans. Reconfigurable Technol. Syst. (TRETS) 11(3), 1–24 (2018)
11. Zhao, W., et al.: F-CNN: an FPGA-based framework for training convolutional neural networks. In: 2016 IEEE 27Th International Conference on Application-Specific Systems, Architectures and Processors (ASAP), pp. 107–114. IEEE (2016)
12. Highlander, T., Rodriguez, A.: Very efficient training of convolutional neural networks using Fast Fourier Transform and overlap-and-add. arXiv preprint arXiv:1601.06815 (2016)
13. Zhang, C., Prasanna, V.: Frequency domain acceleration of convolutional neural networks on cpu-fpga shared memory system. In: Proceedings of the 2017 ACM/SIGDA International Symposium on Field-Programmable Gate Arrays, pp. 35–44 (2017)
14. Zeng, H., Chen, R., Zhang, C., Prasanna, V.: A framework for generating high throughput CNN implementations on FPGAs. In: Proceedings of the 2018 ACM/SIGDA International Symposium on Field-Programmable Gate Arrays, pp. 117–126 (2018)
15. Hemnani, M., Palekar, S., Dixit, P., Joshi, P.: Hardware optimization of complex multiplication scheme for DSP application. In: 2015 International Conference on Computer, Communication and Control (IC4), pp. 1–4. IEEE (2015)
16. Qiao, Y., Shen, J., Xiao, T., Yang, Q., Wen, M., Zhang, C.: FPGA-accelerated deep convolutional neural networks for high throughput and energy efficiency. Concurrency Comput. Pract. Exp. 29(20), e3850 (2017)
17. Qiu, J., et al.: Going deeper with embedded FPGA platform for convolutional neural network. In: Proceedings of the 2016 ACM/SIGDA International Symposium on Field-Programmable Gate Arrays, pp. 26–35 (2016)

Low Cost Implementation of Deep Neural Network on Hardware

Gaurav Kumar[✉][ID], Anuj Kumar[ID], Satyadev Ahlawat[ID], and Yamuna Prasad[ID]

Indian Institute of Technology Jammu, Jammu, India
{gaurav.kumar,anuj,satyadev.ahlawat,yamuna.prasad}@iitjammu.ac.in

Abstract. Recently, deep learning framework gained extreme importance in various domains such as Computer Vision, Natural Language Processing, Bioinformatics, etc. The general architecture of deep learning framework is very complex that includes various tunable hyperparameters and millions/billions of learnable weight parameters. In many of these Deep Neural Network (DNN) models, a single forward pass requires billions of operations such as multiplication, addition, comparison and exponentiation. Thus, it requires large computation time and dissipates huge amount of power even at the inference/prediction phase. Due to the success of DNN models in many application domains, the area and power efficient hardware implementations of DNNs in resource constraint systems have recently become highly desirable. To ensure the programmable flexibility and shorten the development period, field-programmable gate array (FPGA) is suitable for implementing the DNN models. However, the limited bandwidth and low on-chip memory storage of FPGA are the bottlenecks for deploying DNN on these FPGAs for inferencing.

In this paper, Binary Particle Swarm Optimization (PSO) based approach is presented to reduce the hardware cost in terms of memory and power consumption. The number of weight parameters of the model and floating point units are reduced without any degradation in the generalization accuracy. It is observed that 85% of the weight parameters are reduced with 1% loss in accuracy.

Keywords: Deep neural network · FPGA · Optimization · PSO

1 Introduction

Deep learning techniques on hardware have gained popularity because of their good accuracy and use in wide range of applications. These techniques are used in many modern machine learning applications such as driver assistance systems, speech recognition, natural language processing, healthcare etc. DNNs are being used in various applications because of their self-adaptive features, non-linear characteristics and their ability to adapt versatile configurations [6,9,12]. Furthermore, DNNs learn the input data pattern layer by layer and then extract

© The Author(s), under exclusive license to Springer Nature Switzerland AG 2022
A. P. Shah et al. (Eds.): VDAT 2022, CCIS 1687, pp. 584–594, 2022.
https://doi.org/10.1007/978-3-031-21514-8_48

the features. Various problems such as face recognition, medical image segmentation and classification, action recognition/classification, autonomous vehicle driving and machine translations have been successfully solved using deep learning frameworks. The top leading industries such as Google, Microsoft, IBM and Amazon etc. are exploiting and enhancing these deep learning models for analyzing the massive data collected from various social media sources.

As the research moves toward success in terms of accuracy, there is a trade-off between computational time and model complexity. To reduce the computational time, research is facilitated towards the efficient implementation of these models on hardware. Since deep learning techniques need to extract a large number of features from raw data, it requires huge computational resources and hence complex hardware to perform operations such as addition and multiplication on large matrices. Thus, as the models get complex, it becomes difficult to implement these DNN applications in resource constraint embedded devices. Also, various parameters such as cost, efficiency, power consumption and accuracy will influence the hardware implementation of these deep neural networks, especially for resource constraint applications. In the learning phase, these DNNs learn millions/billions of parameters which are stored in the memory. On the other hand, inference is a compute-intensive task with a large number of floating-point operations. The limited on-chip memory is a considerable bottleneck in storing these millions/billions of parameters and the low power budget becomes a huddle in inference. In order to exploit the FPGAs in real-time inferencing, the following three approaches are popular in the literature [11,18,20]:

1. Reducing the precision of floating point units.
2. Parameter reduction and use of approximate computing architectures.
3. Partitioning of the problem to implement on multiple FPGAs.

In this work, a Particle Swarm Optimization (PSO) based approach is proposed to decrease the memory requirement and power consumption. The proposed mechanism reduces the hardware cost by reducing the weights of the model using a stochastic optimization technique. This results in alleviation of the precision of floating point units with insignificant loss in the accuracy. Our contributions in this study are as follows:

1. The memory used to store the model weights is reduced by parameter pruning. The parameters of trained DNN Models are pruned using evolutionary algorithms without much loss in generalization accuracy.
2. The power consumption in computation is reduced by low precision transformation on the pruned model parameters.
3. A generalized mechanism is created to reduce the number of weights of any heavy DNN models such as AlexNet, DenseNet, VGG16, etc.

2   Background

In the literature, evolutionary algorithm based approaches have been widely studied for multi objective optimizations and parameter tuning [7,19]. These approaches look for an approximate solution by choosing an initial population of candidate vectors with random values and refining the solution based on the multi-objective fitness criteria [19]. These approaches could be explored to reduce the number of parameters in the trained deep learning models.

2.1 Formulating the Optimization Problem

The heuristic algorithms such as Genetic Algorithms, Differential Evolution [16] and Particle Swarm Optimization (PSO) are widely used in non-convex and multi-objective optimization problems. These methods primarily require a fitness function whose value (fitness value) is calculated for a given set of decision variables. Before the beginning of the optimization procedure in the algorithm, a population is randomly generated. This population is termed as a collection of chromosomes/particles/agents/individuals in the framework of heuristic algorithms. As the iterations of the algorithm proceed, the members of the population are modified because of the evolutionary approach being followed. At the end of iterations, the particle or chromosome that gives the optimized value for the fitness function is selected. Depending upon the kind of optimization (maximization/minimization) being done, either highest value or lowest value is selected as the optimized value and thereby the particle or chromosome which gives the optimized value is taken as the solution.

To fit the problem of parameter estimation of the Deep Learning model into this framework, a fitness function and decision variables are required. The purpose of the fitness function is to indicate how good are the solutions given by the heuristic algorithm. Furthermore, the decision variables' values influence the fitness function's value. However, it might be possible that the best values require a large number of iterations. Thus, to reduce the time, the termination criteria for the algorithm is the number of iterations.

2.2 Deep Learning for Hardware

In recent years, various types of dedicated hardware have been developed that target deep learning techniques. For example, in order to perform multiple floating-point operations with quick processing and high precision, a 16-bit floating-point arithmetic is being used in Nvidia Tesla P100. Also, Big Basin is a Facebook deep neural network server that performs DNN processing efficiently [13].

Deep neural network models could be implemented on various hardware platforms such as FPGAs, ASICs and SOCs [10,14]. Although the DNN implementation on CPU is flexible as well as cost-efficient, it is performance constrained. On the other hand, DNN implementation on ASIC results in better performance than CPU. The DNN implementation on SOCs is also gaining popularity due to its ability to provide both hardware as well as software processing ability in a single device. Hardware could be used as an accelerator, whereas software is coded to perform a specific job/task.

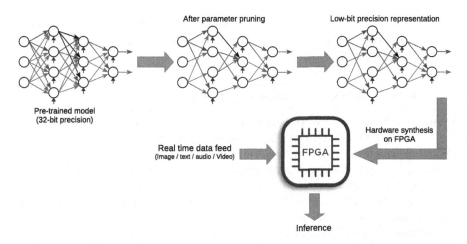

Fig. 1. The overall architecture of proposed approach.

3 Methodology

The proposed approach is shown in Fig. 1, which consists of basic DNN, an optimization algorithm to reduce the number of weights and FPGA implementation of the reduced model.

3.1 Deep Neural Network

To train the DNN model, MNIST [1] dataset has been taken as input, which is a hand digit recognition dataset. The DNN model represented as $F(X)$ have input X where, $X \in (x_1, x_2, x_3, ..., x_n)$, and output Y where, $Y \in (y_0, y_2, y_3, ..., y_m)$. The practical DNNs have hundreds or thousands of layers with thousands of neurons in each layer, making total parameters in millions or billions. These parameters need to be stored in the memory for inferencing phase.

There are many pre-trained models available in well known TensorFlow library[1]. A few of them are briefly explained below:

1. **AlexNet [8]:** Standard AlexNet consists of 8 layers, out of which 5 are convolution layers and 3 are fully connected layers. It is trained on the ImageNet dataset. AlexNet revolutionized the state-of-the-art in object recognition in the real time.
2. **DenseNet [5]:** This model is similar to a dense layer feed-forward network where each layer is fully connected with the successive layer. This model has been primarily used for object recognition tasks on ImageNet, CIFAR, SVHN and CIFAR100 datasets.
3. **VGG16 [15]:** This model has been used for ImageNet dataset classification and is also widely used as a transfer learning pre-trained model in low resource domains.

---

[1] https://keras.io/api/applications/.

In our experiments, AlexNet [8] is chosen to demonstrate the effectiveness of the proposed approach. The chosen model is a moderate-size DNN model suitable for the proof of the concept.

3.2 Particle Swarm Optimization (PSO)

To optimize the number of parameters, an existing optimization algorithm, i.e., Particle Swarm Optimization (PSO) algorithm [7] is used. This is a bio-inspired algorithm which does not require a convex objective function. This algorithm works for any non-convex, discrete and multi-objective function optimization scenario. In most cases, the objective function serves as part of the fitness function. The fitness of a particle/position/individual represents the goodness of the solutions. A few hyper-parameters are required for the PSO algorithm. The fitness function for the minimization is

$$f = \alpha \times (1 - accuracy) + (1 - \alpha) \times \frac{count_x(1)}{total\_features(x)} \tag{1}$$

Here, accuracy is the model accuracy after parameter pruning by particle swarm optimization (PSO) algorithm, and $count_x(1)$ is the remaining number of parameters after pruning. The proposed non-convex fitness function jointly minimizes the validation error and number of parameters. The parameter α controls the contribution of model validation error and the number of parameters in the joint optimization.

The PSO algorithm tries to minimize the fitness function so that it can increase the accuracy as well as decrease the number of parameters. It tries to get the best position for each particle by updating its local best (*pbest*) and then global best (*gbest*) position. In this work, the position vector is represented using a binary vector of '1s' and '0s'. The value '1' represents the inclusion/selection of the corresponding weight parameters, while the value '0' represents the rejection of the corresponding weight parameters in the model. Thus, an optimized position vector represents the optimized number of parameters. Initial velocities and positions are randomly generated for each particle and then updated according to the following equation:

$$v_{(i+1)} = w \times v_i + c_1 \times r_1 \times (pbest_i - x_i) + c_2 \times r_2 \times (gbest - x_i) \tag{2}$$

where v_i is the velocity of ith particle, x_i is the position of ith particle, $w \in (-1,1)$, $c1 + c2 \leq 4$, and $r_1, r_2 \in (0,1)$ which are randomly generated

$$x_{i+1} = \begin{cases} 1 & \text{if sigmoid}(v_{i+1}) \geq 0.5 \\ 0 & \text{else} \end{cases} \tag{3}$$

The PSO Algorithm 1 follows the following steps to find out the optimum solution:

1. In first step, random positions and random velocities for each particle are collected. Each particle has its own *pbest* position and each iteration has a *gbest* position.
2. In second step, the fitness function is calculated on the positions of all the particles and again choose the *pbest* and *gbest*.
3. In next step, the algorithm re-calculates the velocities of each particle with local best and global best positions.
4. Then, with the help of new velocities, it re-calculates the optimum positions, i.e., local best of each particle. Because of binary PSO, rather than simply adding the position vector with velocity, it uses another method explained in next step.
5. Finally, to update the position vector, sigmoid of velocities are taken and if they are greater than 0.5, then the position vector has a value of 1; else 0.
6. The above steps are repeated until a near-optimum solution is observed or some loop-breaking condition is met.

Complexity: The complexity of the Algorithm 1 is $\mathcal{O}(T.k.m.F)$; where T denotes the number of maximum iterations, k denotes the number of particles/individuals, m denotes the number of parameters and F denotes the complexity of fitness function.

Algorithm 1. Binary Particle Swarm Optimization

1: **Input:** Fitness Function, Initial Positions(x_i), Initial Velocities(v_i)
2: **Output:** Optimal Solution
3: **for** each particle (i) **do**
4:     Calculate fitness function (f_i)
5:     Update *pbest*$_i$ and *gbest*
6: **end for**
7: **while** iteration **do**
8:     **for** each particle (i) **do**
9:         Update velocities ($v_{(i+1)}$) and positions ($x_{(i+1)}$)
10:         Update *pbest*$_{(i+1)}$ and *gbest*
11:     **end for**
12: **end while**
13: **Return:** Optimal Solution

3.3 Low Bit Precision Representation

For the floating point representation of real numbers, the IEEE 754 standard is used. It has three components: sign, exponent and fraction. The sign is of 1 bit, exponent is of 8 bit and fraction is of 23 bit, which makes a word size of 32 bits. The reduction in the number of bits for floating point representation requires less complex hardware and hence reduces the power consumption. Floating point is a quantization of infinite precise real numbers. The standard floating point representation can exactly represent the real number in the range of 10^{-5} to 10^5. If the number is out of this range then, it is rounded off. However, most deep neural networks perform their calculations in a relatively small range, such as -10.0 to 10.0. Thus, by compressing the 32-bit weight matrix into 8 or 16 bits after parameter pruning, there is no significant loss in the accuracy. The experiments show that 1 bit for sign, 5 bit for exponent and 2 bit for fraction in case of 8 bit representation and 1 bit for sign, 11 bit for exponent and 4 bit for fraction in case of 16 bit representation produce best results.

4   Experiments

To evaluate the effectiveness of the proposed approach, extensive experiments are performed. The training of deep learning models involves various matrix operations such as multiplication (MACC), addition (ADD), comparison (COMP), division (DIV) and exponentiation. In many DNN models, billions of operations are required, as shown in Table 1. Thus it requires high power budget and computation time. The Graphics Processing Units (GPUs) were designed to exploit SIMD architecture. The GPUs provide more computational power with a fast connection to memory. The GPU architectures are widely used to train and inference large deep layered neural networks such as VGG16 [15], Inception V3 [17], ResNet-152 [4] and BERT [2] etc. The GPU devices are very power-hungry, which limits their usage for real-time applications using mobile devices, IoTs etc.

As shown in Table 1, AlexNet has 60.97 M parameters which are trained and stored in the memory for inferencing. Also, it has 17.86 M parameters in convolution layers. We use AlexNet for our experiments as it has significantly large number of parameters.

4.1   Results

The PSO algorithm optimizes the number of parameters without any significant loss in generalization accuracy. As can be observed from Fig. 2, the fitness func-

Table 1. Deep learning model details [3]

Model	MACC	COMP	ADD	DIV	Activations	Params
InceptionV4	12.27 G	21.87 M	53.42 M	15.09 M	72.56 M	42.71 M
InceptionV3	5.72 G	16.53 M	25.94 M	8.97 M	41.33 M	23.83 M
InceptionV2	13.18 G	31.57 M	38.81 M	25.06 M	117.8 M	55.97 M
ResNet-152	11.3 G	22.33 M	35.27 M	22.03 M	100.11 M	60.19 M
ResNet-50	3.87 G	10.89 M	16.21 M	10.59 M	46.72 M	25.56 M
AlexNet	7.27 G	17.69 M	4.78 M	9.55 M	20.81 M	60.97 M
GoogleNet	16.04 G	161.07 M	8.83 M	16.64 M	102.19 M	7 M
VGG16	154.7 G	196.85 M	10 K	10 K	288.03 M	138.36 M
BERT -12	–	–	–	–	–	110 M
BERT-24	–	–	–	–	–	345 M

Table 2. Parameter values for PSO

Name	Value of the parameter
Number of particles	10
Maximum iteration	100
alpha(α)	0.7
omega(w)	0.99
c_1	2.0
c_2	2.0

tion is minimized as the number of iterations increases. The inertia weight w and velocity vector are initialized with 1.0 and 0.1, respectively, in the experiments. After every iteration, w is multiplied by 0.99. Table 2 provides the details of other parameters. It should be noted that there are some rises and falls due to the local minima. As shown in Fig. 2, the fitness value saturates after 8th iteration. There is no further reduction which denotes the completion of the algorithm. Now, the reduced number of parameters is calculated using the *gbest* position vector. The parameters after parameter pruning are only 15% of the total parameters with 1% loss in accuracy (i.e., 98.20%, Table 3). It has also been observed that proposed optimization heuristic achieves 50% reduction in the number of parameters without any degradation in the validation accuracy (Table 3). Additionally, a comparison of the proposed PSO based approach with the Random Parameter selection method (RP) is provided in Table 3. The RP method achieves a 50% reduction in total parameters with 8% loss in accuracy.

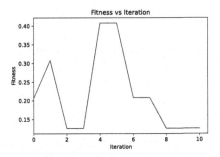

Fig. 2. Fitness vs Iteration

The parameters count after each iteration of the algorithm is shown in Fig. 3. It is evident from Figs. 2 and 3 that as the number of parameters increases, the fitness value also increases. The accuracy of the model after each iteration of parameter pruning by the PSO algorithm is shown in Fig. 4. The proposed approach achieves a similar set of accuracy with 85% reduction in the number of parameters.

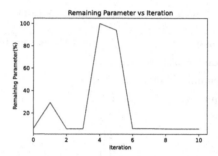

Fig. 3. Remaining Parameters vs Iteration

The original model and model after parameter pruning (proposed model) with different floating-point precision are compared in Table 4. It can be observed that the proposed model reduces the model size by 50% while producing a similar set of accuracy. It should be noted that the accuracy degrades when the floating point precision is reduced (Table 4).

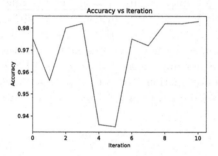

Fig. 4. Accuracy vs Iteration

4.2   Hardware Cost

By using PSO algorithm, 85% of the total parameters are reduced, which directly results in the reduction of total required memory. A further saving of the memory (by a factor of two) can be achieved using low bit representation for the remaining 15% parameters. Moreover, the reduction in the total parameters directly reduces the required power budget. This is because the energy required for the floating point multiplication reduces significantly. Instead of a floating point multiplication, now it becomes an integer multiplication with zero.

Table 3. Model validation accuracies for MNIST dataset

Method	#Parameters	Accuracy
Original Model (AlexNet)	17,866,752	99.40
Random parameter selection	9,930,946	91.65
Proposed Model (without any loss)	**8,933,370**	**99.40**
Proposed Model (with loss)	**2,680,012**	**98.20**

Table 4. Model Sizes with different floating point precision and accuracy

Name	64-bit float		32-bit float		16-bit float	
	Size (in MB)	ACC	Size (in MB)	ACC	Size (in MB)	ACC
Original model	142.934	99.40	71.467	98.20	35.733	97.50
Proposed model	69.467	98.20	33.733	97.80	17.733	96.80

5 Conclusion and Future Work

In this paper, a generalized mechanism to reduce the cost (in terms of area and power) of a hardware implementation of Deep Neural Network is proposed. It has been shown that 85% of parameters could be reduced with 1% loss of accuracy with parameter pruning. A further reduction in required memory space is achieved with low bit floating point representation for remaining parameters. Thus, making it suitable for resource constrained embedded devices. For future work, the more advanced and complex deep neural network will be implemented on hardware using this scheme.

Acknowledgements. This work has been partially supported by the SERB DST under project number SRG/2020/002551 and IHUB NTIHAC FOUNDATION under project numbers IHUB-NTIHAC/2021/01/14, IHUB-NTIHAC/2021/01/15.

References

1. Deng, L.: The MNIST database of handwritten digit images for machine learning research. IEEE Signal Process. Mag. **29**(6), 141–142 (2012)
2. Devlin, J., Chang, M.W., Lee, K., Toutanova, K.: Bert: Pre-training of deep bidirectional transformers for language understanding (2018). https://doi.org/10.48550/ARXIV.1810.04805
3. GitHub: Details of deep learning models. http://dgschwend.github.io/netscope/quickstart.html
4. He, K., Zhang, X., Ren, S., Sun, J.: Deep residual learning for image recognition (2015). https://doi.org/10.48550/ARXIV.1512.03385
5. Huang, G., Liu, Z., van der Maaten, L., Weinberger, K.Q.: Densely connected convolutional networks (2018)

6. Kamnitsas, K., et al.: Efficient multi-scale 3D CNN with fully connected crf for accurate brain lesion segmentation. Med. Image Anal. **36**, 61–78 (2017). https://doi.org/10.1016/j.media.2016.10.004

7. Kennedy, J., Eberhart, R.: Particle swarm optimization. In: Proceedings of ICNN'95 - International Conference on Neural Networks, vol. 4, pp. 1942–1948 (1995). https://doi.org/10.1109/ICNN.1995.488968

8. Krizhevsky, A., Sutskever, I., Hinton, G.E.: Imagenet classification with deep convolutional neural networks. In: Pereira, F., Burges, C., Bottou, L., Weinberger, K. (eds.) Advances in Neural Information Processing Systems, vol. 25. Curran Associates, Inc. (2012)

9. Litjens, G., et al.: A survey on deep learning in medical image analysis. Med. Image Anal. **42**, 60–88 (2017). https://doi.org/10.1016/j.media.2017.07.005

10. Lu, L., Liang, Y., Xiao, Q., Yan, S.: Evaluating fast algorithms for convolutional neural networks on FPGAs. In: 2017 IEEE 25th Annual International Symposium on Field-Programmable Custom Computing Machines (FCCM), pp. 101–108 (2017). https://doi.org/10.1109/FCCM.2017.64

11. Nakahara, H., Zhiqiang, Q., Jinguji, A., Luk, W.: R2CNN: recurrent residual convolutional neural network on FPGA. In: Proceedings of the 2020 ACM/SIGDA International Symposium on Field-Programmable Gate Arrays, FPGA 2020, p. 319. Association for Computing Machinery, New York (2020). https://doi.org/10.1145/3373087.3375367

12. Norouzi, A., Rahim, M., Altameem, A., Saba, T., Ehsani Rad, A., Rehman, A., Uddin, M.: Medical image segmentation methods, algorithms, and applications. IETE Techn. Rev. **31**, 199–213 (2014). https://doi.org/10.1080/02564602.2014.906861

13. NVIDIA Developer: Deep learning frameworks. https://developer.nvidia.com/deep-learning-frameworks

14. Shawahna, A., Sait, S.M., El-Maleh, A.: FPGA-based accelerators of deep learning networks for learning and classification: a review. IEEE Access **7**, 7823–7859 (2018)

15. Simonyan, K., Zisserman, A.: Very deep convolutional networks for large-scale image recognition (2014). https://doi.org/10.48550/ARXIV.1409.1556

16. Storn, R., Price, K.: Differential evolution - a simple and efficient heuristic for global optimization over continuous spaces (1997)

17. Szegedy, C., Vanhoucke, V., Ioffe, S., Shlens, J., Wojna, Z.: Rethinking the inception architecture for computer vision (2015). https://doi.org/10.48550/ARXIV.1512.00567

18. Wang, J., Cong, J.: Automated generation of high-performance large-scale matrix multiplication accelerator on fpga (2016)

19. Yamuna Prasad, Kanad K. Biswas, Â.K.J.: SVM classifier based feature selection using GA, ACO and PSO for siRNA design (2010)

20. Zeng, S., et al.: Enabling efficient and flexible FPGA virtualization for deep learning in the cloud (2020). https://doi.org/10.48550/ARXIV.2003.12101

Author Index

Printed in the United States
by Baker & Taylor Publisher Services